African American Literary Criticism, 1773 to 2000

African American Literary Criticism, 1773 to 2000

edited by

HAZEL ARNETT ERVIN

Twayne Publishers
New York

African American Literary Criticism, 1773 to 2000
Hazel Arnett Ervin

Twayne Publishers
1633 Broadway
New York, NY 10019

Library of Congress Cataloging-in-Publication Data

African American literary criticism, 1773 to 2000 / edited by Hazel
Arnett Ervin.
    p. cm.
   Includes bibliographical references and index.
   ISBN 0-8057-1683-1 (alk. paper)
   1. American literature—Afro-American authors—History and
criticism—Theory, etc. 2. American literature—Afro-American
authors—History and criticism. 3. Afro-Americans—Intellectual
life. 4. Afro-Americans in literature. 5. Criticism—United
States. I. Ervin, Hazel Arnett.
PS153.N5A33   1999
810.9′896073—dc21   99-29491

For
my mother, Gladys A. Arnett,
and
my father, the late Harrison M. Arnett Sr.,
and
the late Stephen E. Henderson, professor emeritus of
English and African American Literature

Contents

◆

1976–2000: AESTHETIC VALUES, RECONSTRUCTIONS OF
BLACKNESS AND BOUNDARIES, AND POSTMODERNISM

CULTURE-BASED STUDIES

PSYCHOANALYTIC

RHETORIC AND READER-RESPONSE

FILM

DETECTIVE NOVEL

SCIENCE FICTION

JAZZ, RAP, AND HIP-HOP

Preface

◆

This Reader may be used in several capacities. For some teachers, students, scholars, and critics, it is a textbook of African American literary theory and criticism. For others, in African American literature, American literature, women's studies, cultural studies, comparative studies, and African American studies, it is a companion text. Overall, this Reader is an essential source for scholars, critics, and others who are interested in ongoing discussions not only about the function of African American literary art, the role of the African American writer, and the artistic responsibility of the audience, but also about the epistemology, communications, aesthetics, and theoretical methodology within the African American literary tradition. Particularly, it attempts to fill a void in the annals of African American arts and letters, by addressing aesthetic sensibilities in African American literary art and by tracing the stages of development of philosophical thought on cultural blackness and of black speech and black music as poetic and theoretical references.

There are so many people whose comments over the years have helped me to get this book out. Foremost, I wish to express my debt to the late Dr. Stephen E. Henderson, professor emeritus of English and African American Literature at Howard University, for having engaged with me in conversations about the criticism of Alexander Pope, Sir Philip Sidney, Henry James, D. H. Lawrence, James Weldon Johnson, Larry Neal, James Baldwin, Ralph Ellison, Houston Baker, and Henry Louis Gates, especially on those days in the late 1980s and early 1990s while I was a graduate student and his research assistant. I am also thankful to Dr. Henderson for his vote of confidence in the fall of 1989 when I decided to go beyond an assignment in Dr. Sandra G. Shannon's criticism course at Howard, and, unlike the other students in the class, to produce an anthology of African American literary theory and criticism. Although the historical overview and select readings in that anthology (*African American Critics at Work*) have been expanded, *African American Critics at Work* remains the impetus for this Reader. Some of my later thoughts about a collection on literary criticism have been confirmed, in particular, by the following works: Abby Arthur Johnson and Ronald Maberry Johnson's *Propaganda and Aesthetics: The Literary Politics of African-American Magazines in the Twentieth Century,* Robert B. Stepto and Dexter Fisher's *Afro American Literature: The Reconstruction of Instruction,* Chester Fontenot and Joe Weixlmann's many edited volumes of *Studies in Black American Literature,* and Carolyn Fowler's (Carolyn F. Gerald's) *Black Arts and Black Aesthetics: A Bibliography.*

Next, a sincere debt of gratitude goes to Catherine Carter, my editor for *Ann Petry: A Bio-Bibliography* at G. K. Hall, for her continued interest in my work and for having forwarded my query of a reader in African American literary criticism to Anne Davidson at Twayne Publishers. Words alone cannot express my gratitude to Anne Davidson for recognizing the need for such a reader and for her energy and devotion to the end.

Finally, I feel very lucky to have had the support of librarian Robert Quarles at the Woodruff Library here at the Atlanta University Center in Atlanta. I have known or read about a distinguished list of librarians who personalized the research of their patrons and did not rest until you had all that you sought. Such a list includes, among others, Arna Bontemps, Dorothy Parker, Charles Blockson, Ann Shockley, Janet Wood Sims, and added to the list is Robert Quarles. I am also thankful for the assistance of those in the Archives and in the African American Reading Room at the Woodruff Library and of those in the Auburn Avenue Research Library of African American Culture and History in Atlanta.

It is good to have friends with whom you can freely share your ideas. I wish to say how grateful I am to those who read my manuscript: Ann Kelly and Jennifer Jordan at Howard University, Melvin Rahming at Morehouse College, and Sally Ann Ferguson at the University of North Carolina at Greensboro. And I want to thank others for listening and responding: Dolan Hubbard at Morgan State University, James A. Miller at George Washington University, Keith Clark at James Mason University, E. Ethelbert Miller at Howard University, Jerry Ward at Tougaloo College, Chester Fontenot Jr. at the University of Illinois, Alexs Pate at the University of Minnesota, William "Bill" Carroll and Annie Perkins at Norfolk State University, Sheikh Kamarah at Shaw University, Carol Marsh Lockett at Georgia State University, and, of course, Ann Kelly and Jennifer Jordan at Howard University, Melvin Rahming at Morehouse College, and Sally Ann Ferguson at the University of North Carolina at Greensboro, .

My research for this Reader was supported by a grant awarded to me by the office of Dr. Obie Clayton, vice president of research and grants at Morehouse College. Supported also were my research assistants Kewan Smith, Kevin Ervin, and Rod L. Hollimon. Thank you Carolyn Arnett and Antoinnette Kerr. Also thank you Dr. E. Delores Stephens, chair of the Department of English and Linguistics at Morehouse, and members of Academic Affairs at Morehouse, for your enthusiasm and support.

Acknowledgments

♦

The editor is grateful to the following who granted her permission to reprint:

Tuzyline Jita Allan. "Introduction" in *Womanist and Feminist Aesthetics, A Comparative Review,* by Tuzyline Jita Allan, 1995. Reprinted by permission of Ohio University Press/Swallow Press, Athens.

William L. Andrews. "The First Century of Afro-American Autobiography: Theory and Explication." First appeared in *Studies in Black American Literature Vol 1: Black American Prose* Theory. Joe Weixlmann and Chester Fontenot Jr., editors, 1984. Reprinted by permission of William L. Andrews.

Houston A. Baker Jr. "Toward a Critical Prospect for the Future," *The Journey Back,* 1980. Copyright © 1980 by The University of Chicago. Reprinted by permission of The University of Chicago Press and Houston A. Baker Jr.

James Baldwin. "The Creative Process" © 1962 by James Baldwin is excerpted from *Creative America,* published by Ridge Press. Collected in *The Price of the Ticket,* © 1985 by James Baldwin. Published by St. Martin's. Reprinted by arrangement with the James Baldwin Estate.

James Baldwin. Excerpt from "Everybody's Protest Novel," from *Notes of a Native Son.* © 1955, renewed 1983, by James Baldwin. Reprinted by permission of Beacon Press, Boston.

James Baldwin. Excerpt from "Many Thousand Gone," from *Notes of a Native Son.* © 1955, renewed 1983, by James Baldwin. Reprinted by permission of Beacon Press, Boston.

Toni Cade Bambara. "Salvation Is the Issue," from *Black Women Writers (1950–1980)* by Mari Evans. Copyright © 1984 by Mari Evans. Used by permission of Doubleday, a division of Random House, Inc.

Homi K. Bhabha. "Cultural Diversity and Cultural Differences" from *New Formations* 5, Summer 1988. Reprinted by permission of Lawrence & Wishart.

Lloyd W. Brown. "The Expatriate Consciousness in Black American Literature" from *Studies in Black Literature,* 3.2 (Summer 1972). Copyright © Raman K. Singh. Used by permission.

Sterling A. Brown. "Negro Characters as Seen by White Authors." *Journal of Negro Education,* 2 (1933), 179–203. Copyright © 1933 by Howard University. All rights reserved.

Sterling A. Brown. "Our Literary Audience." *Opportunity* 8 (1930). Reprinted by permission of the National Urban League.

Charles W. Chesnutt, journal entry 1880 May 29, in Richard Brodhead, ed. *The Journals of Charles W. Chesnutt,* pp. 139–140. Copyright 1993, Duke University Press. Reprinted with permission.

Ossie Davis. "The Significance of Lorraine Hansberry." *Freedomways* 5.3 (Summer 1965): 397–402. Reprinted by permission of *Freedomways* Magazine.

Thulani Davis. "Walter Mosley (An Interview)." Copyright © 1993 New Art Publications, Inc., New York, New York. Published by permission of Gordon and Breach Arts International.

Madhu Dubey. *Black Women Novelists and the Nationalist Aesthetic* by Madhu Dubey, 1994. Reprinted with permission from Indiana University Press.

W. E. B. DuBois. "Criteria of Negro Art." The author thanks the Crisis Publishing Co., Inc., the magazine of the National Association for the Advancement of Colored People, for authorizing the use of this work.

Cornelius Eady (Interviewed by E. Ethelbert Miller). "An Interview with Cornelius Eady." Copyright © 1995 Cornelius Eady. This interview first appeared in *Crab Orchard Review* Spring/Summer 1997 Vol 2, No. 2. Used with permission of Cornelius Eady.

Ralph Ellison. "The Art of Fiction" from *Shadow and Act* by Ralph Ellison. Copyright © 1953, 1964 and renewed 1981, 1992 by Ralph Ellison. Reprinted by permission of Random House, Inc.

Ralph Ellison. Excerpt from "The Little Man at Chehaw Station" from *Going to the Territory* by Ralph Ellison. Copyright © 1977 by Ralph Ellison. Reprinted by permission of Random House, Inc.

Duane Frank. " 'Soul Food' Director Isn't Holding His Breath." *Milwaukee Journal Sentinel,* October 11, 1997. © 1998 Journal Sentinel Inc., reproduced with permission.

Joan Fry, "An Interview with Octavia Butler." Reprinted by permission of the publisher, Poets & Writers, Inc., 72 Spring Street, New York, NY 10012.

Joanne V. Gabbin. Excerpt from *Sterling A. Brown: Building the Black Aesthetic Tradition,* 1994. Reprinted with permission of the University Press of Virginia.

Henry Louis Gates Jr. From *The Signifying Monkey: A Theory of African-American Literary Criticism* by Henry Louis Gates Jr., Copyright © 1988 by Henry Louis Gates Jr. Used by permission of Oxford University Press, Inc.

Carolyn F. Gerald. "The Black Writer and His Role." Copyright © 1969, Johnson Publishing Company, Inc. Reprinted by permission.

Farah Jasmine Griffin. "Introduction" from *"Who Set You Flowin'?" The African-American Migration Narrative* by Farah Jasmine Griffin. Copyright © 1995 by Farah Jasmine Griffin. Used by permission of Oxford University Press, Inc.

Joy Harjo. "An Interview with June Jordan." Reprinted by permission of Joy Harjo.

Trudier Harris. "Miss-Trained or Untrained? Jackleg Critics and African American Literature (Or, Some of My Adventures in Academia)." Copyright © 1995. Reprinted by permission of the author.

Stephen E. Henderson. From *Understanding the New Black Poetry* by Stephen E. Henderson. Copyright © 1972 by Stephen E. Henderson. Reprinted by permission of William Morrow and Company, Inc.

Joseph Henry. "A MELUS Interview: Ishmael Reed." Copyright © 1984 MELUS, The Society for the Study of the Multi-Ethnic Literature of the United States. Reprinted by permission.

Karla F. C. Holloway. *Moorings and Metaphors: Figures of Culture and Gender in Black Women's Literature.* Copyright © 1992 by Karla F. C. Holloway. Reprinted by permission of Rutgers University Press.

bell hooks. "Introduction" from *Black Looks: Race and Representation,* with permission from the publisher, South End Press, 116 Saint Botolph Street, Boston, MA 02115.

Dolan Hubbard. "Voices and Visions" reprinted from *The Sermon and the African American Literary Imagination* by Dolan Hubbard, by permission of the University of Missouri Press. Copyright © 1994 by the Curators of the University of Missouri.

Langston Hughes. "The Negro Artist and the Racial Mountain." Reprinted by permission of Harold Ober Associates Incorporated. Copyright © 1926 by Langston Hughes. Copyright renewed by 1980 by George Houston Bass.

Gale Jackson. "The Way We Do: A Preliminary Investigation of the African Roots of African American Performance." First appeared in *Black American Literature Forum* (Spring 1991). Reprinted by permission of the author.

Alain Locke. "Art or Propaganda?" from *The Critical Temper of Alain Locke: A Selection of His Essays on Art and Culture.* Reprinted by permission of Garland Publishing Inc. and Jeffrey C. Stewart, ed.

Tommy L. Lott. "A No-Theory Theory of Contemporary Black Cinema." First appeared in *African American Review,* 1992. Reprinted by permission of the author.

Victoria Earle Matthews. "The Value of Race Literature." Reprinted by permission of Moorland-Spingarn Research Center, Howard University.

Terry McMillan, "Introduction," copyright © 1990 by Terry McMillan, from *Breaking Ice* by Terry McMillan. Used by permission of Viking Penguin, a division of Penguin Books USA Inc.

Toni Morrison. "Rootedness: The Ancestor as Foundation," from *Black Women Writers (1950–1980)* by Mari Evans. Copyright © 1984 by Mari Evans. Used by permission of Doubleday, a division of Random House, Inc.

Larry Neal. "The Black Arts Movement," first appeared in *The Drama Review,* Vol 12, No 4 (T40) Summer 1968: 29–39. Reprinted by permission of Evelyn Neal and Avatar Larry Neal.

Charles I. Nero. "Toward a Black Gay Aesthetic: Signifying in Contemporary Black Gay Literature." Reprinted by permission of Charles I. Nero, Associate Professor of Rhetoric and Theater, Bates College.

Alexs Pate. "Making Home in the New Millennium: Reflections." Copyright © 1999 Alexs Pate. Reprinted by permission of author.

Ann Petry. "The Novel as Social Criticism." Reprinted by the permission of Russell & Volkening as agents for the author. Copyright © 1950 by Ann Petry, renewed in 1978 by Ann Petry.

Richard J. Powell. "The Blues Aesthetic: Black Culture and Modernism" in *The Blues Aesthetic: Black Culture and Modernism* (1989), pp. 19–35. Reprinted by permission of the author.

Max Roach. "Jazz." *Freedomways* 2.2 (Spring 1962): 173–176. Reprinted by permission of *Freedomways* Magazine.

Shauneille Perry Ryder. "Will the Real Black Theater Please Stand Up?" *Freedomways* 24.1 (First Quarter 1984): 23–27. Reprinted by permission of *Freedomways* Magazine.

Mtume ya Salaam. "The Aesthetics of Rap." First appeared in *African American Review,* 1995. Copyright © 1995 by Mtume ya Salaam. Reprinted by permission of the author.

Ropo Sekoni. "Features of Yoruba Trickster Tale Aesthetics" from *Folk Poetics: A Sociosemiotic Study of Yoruba Trickster Tales,* Ropo Sekoni. Copyright © 1994 by Ropo Sekoni. Reprinted with permission of Greenwood Publishing Group, Inc., Westport, CT.

Sandra G. Shannon. "Blues, History and Dramaturgy: An Interview with August Wilson." Reprinted with permission of the author.

Barbara Smith. "Toward a Black Feminist Criticism." Published with permission of the author.

Geneva Smitherman. Excerpt from *Black Talk.* Copyright © 1994 by Geneva Smitherman. Reprinted by permission of Houghton Mifflin Company. All rights reserved.

James A. Snead. "Repetition as a figure of black culture" from *Literature and Literary Theory,* edited by Henry Louis Gates Jr. Reprinted by permission of Methuen and Company.

Claudia Tate. From *Psychoanalysis and Black Novels, Desire and the Protocols of Race* by Claudia Tate. Copyright © 1998 by Claudia Tate. Used by permission of Oxford University Press, Inc.

Eleanor W. Traylor. "A Blues View of Life (Literature and the Blues Vision)" in *The Blues Aesthetic: Black Culture and Modernism* (1989), pp. 43–44. Reprinted by permission of the author.

Alice Walker. "Saving the Life that Is Your Own: The Importance of Models in the Artist's Life" from *In Search of Our Mothers' Gardens: Womanist Prose,* copyright © 1976 by Alice Walker, reprinted by permission of Harcourt Brace & Company.

Jerry W. Ward Jr. "Alvin Aubert: The Levee, the Blues, the Mighty Mississippi" copyright © 1989 by Jerry W. Ward, Jr. is reprinted by permission of the author.

Jerry W. Ward Jr. "Foreword" in *Black Southern Voices: An Anthology of Fiction, Poetry, Drama, Nonfiction, and Critical Essays.* Copyright © Jerry W. Ward, Jr., 1992; reprinted by permission of the author.

John Edgar Wideman. "Preface" by John Wideman, copyright © 1990 by John Edgar Wideman, from *Breaking Ice* by Terry McMillan. Used by permission of Viking Penguin, a division of Penguin Books USA Inc.

Sherley A. Williams. "The Blues Roots of Contemporary Afro-American Poetry" first appeared in *Chants of Saints: A Gathering of Afro-American Literature, Art, and Scholarship,* edited by Michael S. Harper and Robert B. Stepto, 123–135, 1979. Reprinted by permission of the author.

Richard Wright. "Blueprint for Negro Writing." Copyright © 1937 by Richard Wright. Reprinted by permission of John Hawkins & Associates, Inc.

Introduction

◆

Literature . . . is the verbal organization of experience into beautiful forms, but what is meant by "beautiful" and by "forms" is to a significant degree dependent upon a people's way of life, their needs, their aspirations, their history—in short, their culture.

Stephen E. Henderson
Understanding the New Black Poetry:
Black Music and Black Speech as Poetic References

[F]ull appreciation of the criticism of Afro-American literature will develop only when all readers perceive that a thorough knowledge and understanding of the Afro-American experience, culture, and literary history is a prerequisite for an individual who wishes to be a critic of that literature.

Darwin T. Turner
"Afro-American Literary Critics: An Introduction"

The need is rather for an . . . advanced volume . . . that presupposes an awareness of the literature and, from that posture, not only demonstrates the links between various critical approaches . . . , but also pursues this activity with considerable emphasis on what is literary (as opposed to sociological, ideological, etc.) in Afro American written art.

Robert B. Stepto
Introduction. *Afro-American Literature:*
The Reconstruction of Instruction

African American Literary Criticism, 1773 to 2000 is designed to deepen appreciation of the African American literary aesthetic and to broaden critical inquiries into the function of African American literary art, the role of the African American writer, and the artistic responsibility of the audience. Con-

1

stituting its makeup are creative artists and critics who, in their manifestoes, credos, prefaces, introductions, interviews, and critical essays (1) chronicle four stages of African American literary criticism, (2) posit a continuity of artistic and aesthetic positions with regard to literary form and judgment, (3) identify critical terms, and (4) present an impetus for ongoing discussions not only about artists, works, and audiences but also about aesthetics, communications, epistemology, and theoretical methodology (traditional and current) within an African American literary tradition.

History, culture, literary theory, philosophy, aesthetics, and linguistics inform the context of this Reader, and its composition reflects a continuity of historical-aesthetic legacies from West African civilizations (Yoruba, Mande, Dohomean, Kongo, and Ejagham) that have been—and are to be—passed on. The factors making up the vertical movement that characterizes African American literature, for example, are West African in provenance: syncopation (Mande), call and response (Ejagham), improvisation (Yoruba), circularity (Dohomean), multiplicity of meaning (Yoruba), and mysticism (Kongo).[1] In short, African American literature is fueled by the West African concept of artistic functionality—that is, by its relatedness to real life. Consequently, it reorders and rejuvenates African American life toward wholeness and is, therefore, cathartic. Then, as Bernard W. Bell notes in *The Afro-American Novel and Its Tradition,* African American literary art can also be described as "hybrid ... [,] derived basically from the sedimented indigenous roots of black American folklore and literary genres of the Western world" (1987, xii).

The context of this Reader also draws from a Black Poetics (i.e., the study of African folk sources and structural derivatives of those sources) and nonblack literary and cultural theory (i.e., critical approaches to African American literary art, such as semiotics and structuralism, psychoanalytic, rhetoric and reader-response, archetypal criticism, postcolonialism, and gender and cultural studies). Furthermore, the Reader's context is philosophical in that artists and critics speak in general about literary imagination, truth, beauty, the sublime, the ethical and moral purposes of literature, artistic freedom, and poetic license. Finally, the context of this Reader employs linguists who differentiate the use of the black vernacular from standard English, who underscore the African oral traditions of memory and Nommo (the layering of meaning through words), and who reassess the African American lexicon, beginning with West African cultures and extending to hip-hop culture in America.

Such diversity communicates complexity in African American culture and in African American literary art while also revealing continuity in practices and tradition, both of which point to and call for recognizing, understanding, and studying what Stephen Henderson in *Understanding the New Black Poetry* calls "a [black] people's way of life" (1973, 4) and what bell hooks calls "an aesthetic of blackness" (1990, 113).

Literary History: Form

One of the first book-length discussions of form or structure and style in African American literary art is to be found in the preface to the first edition of *The Book of American Negro Poetry,* edited by James Weldon Johnson. On several occasions in his preface, Johnson apologizes for having gone "far beyond" his purpose for compiling the anthology:

> It was my intention to gather together the best verses I could find by Negro poets and present them with a bare word of introduction. It was not my plan to make this collection inclusive nor to make the book in any sense a book of criticism. (1921, 40)

Yet in Johnson's preface, one of the earliest theoretical discussions of what the editor calls "gifts" and "touchstones" in African American culture—folk stories, spirituals, dance, and ragtime—occurs. Less discussed yet acknowledged just the same is dialect, the "musical folk speech as a medium of expression." According to Johnson, writers such as Thomas Nelson Page, Thomas Dixon, and even Joel Chandler Harris in the Uncle Remus stories did much, through their mutilation of English spelling and pronunciation and through the proliferation of stereotypical images, to limit the medium "to humor and pathos." Most discussed by Johnson are what he calls the "structural togetherness" or the "polyphonic" or intricate "rhythm(s)" and "repetition(s)" of spirituals and ragtime that made their way into the structure of African American poetry. Johnson wanted African American writers to deepen their understandings of the folk forms and styles and to employ them as had Langston Hughes and Sterling Brown in their dialect poetry. Johnson instructs them to

> [F]ind a *form* that [would] express the *racial spirit by symbols from within rather than by symbols from without,* such as the mere mutilation of English spelling and pronunciation . . . [,] *that* [would be] *freer and larger than dialect,* but which [would] *still hold the racial flavor* . . . [,] that [would] express the imagery, the idioms, the *peculiar* turns of thought, and the *distinctive* humor and pathos. (1921, 41–42; my emphasis)

For several decades, the Johnsonian viewpoint of creating and analyzing African American literature with its "symbols from within" and its "peculiar racial flavor" was merely echoed by other leading African American critics and creative writers in essays, prefaces, introductions, and interviews, but none attempted book-length theoretical criticism on the question of form until the late 1960s and early 1970s.

For instance, writing in the introduction to his bestseller *Native Son* ("How 'Bigger' Was Born"), Richard Wright admits that he followed the "principles of the novel" as learned by reading European novels, but Wright also admits that his intent was to express a "racial spirit" by way of "symbol[s] of all the larger things" (1940, xxi). "Larger" could be defined as cultural but Wright fails to be clear in his introduction.

In 1955, in "The Art of Fiction: An Interview," some three years after *Invisible Man,* Ralph Ellison appears to be in agreement with Johnson about the production of African American literary art. Although he advises the reader to disengage from discussions pleading the humanity of blacks, Ellison instructs the reader to pursue questions of aesthetics:

> Too many books by Negro writers are addressed to a white audience. By doing this authors run the risk of limiting themselves to the audience's presumptions of what a Negro is or should be; the tendency is to become involved in polemics, to plead the Negro's humanity. You know, many white people question that humanity but I don't think that Negroes can afford to indulge in such a false issue. For us the question should be, What are the specific *forms* of that humanity, and what in our background is worth preserving or abandoning? The clue to this can be found in [blues, folkways, and speech] folklore, which offers the first drawings of any group's character. (reprinted in this volume; Ellison's emphasis)

Ellison's interview is anthologized in *Shadow and Act,* his most popular collection of criticism, but, like his peers and predecessors, Ellison is less explicit and theoretical.

In 1959, the First Conference of Negro Writers was held in New York City. The theme for the conference was "The American Negro Writer and His Roots." One year later, under the same title, select papers from the conference were published by its sponsor, The American Society of African Culture. What the collection reveals about African American literary form is not a consensus, but polarity. At one end there were, for instance, Saunders Redding in "The Negro Writer and His Relationship to His Roots" and Arthur P. Davis in "Integration and Race Literature," both of whose views on the question of identity could be summarized in this manner: African American writers and their literary texts were a part of American culture. On another end there was John O. Killens in "Opportunities for Development of Negro Talent," who, along with Langston Hughes, Arna Bontemps, Loften Mitchell, Sarah E. Wright, Sarah Webster Fabio, and several black writers and critics from the South and abroad (Africa and France), viewed writers as descendents of an African oral tradition. Accordingly, Killens and others sought "explanations" of form and style from within the African American community. As suggested in the following, Killens sought a response mostly from the black southern writers and critics, but, in the final analysis, he sought an African American literary aesthetic that was explainable:

> The challenge to the Negro writer is to explore and create means of achieving deeper and broader dimensions of artistic reality in his interpretation of who he

is and where he comes from and where he is going. . . . The challenge . . . in the era of the new southern . . . Negro is to dig and dig for an artistic reality much bigger than the apparent truth, a reality which is sometimes ugly and at the same time contains a terrible beauty. . . . Is there a real community of cultural, social and economic experience in the United States which is historically known as "Negro life"? If the Negro writer were to listen, would he hear in this community a *rhythm of living which might suggest to him an esthetic way of life, differing in structure and in style from that portrayed by other American writers?* (1959, 67; my emphasis)

While Killens and others recognized that source and form of an African past were community oriented, he and others also recognized what was missing in the 1950s in the African American critical community—theoretical criticism that addressed explicitly the "esthetic ways of [Negro] life."

African American critics writing from the Left in the 1950s and 1960s must be included in this review, for like other critics and creative artists, writers such as C. Wilson Record in "The Negro as Creative Artist" (1965) and Doxey A. Wilkerson in "Negro Culture: Heritage and Weapon" (1949) maintained discussions, in Record's words, about "guideposts" from within African American culture for the creation, study, and evaluation of literary form and style in African American literature. While the leftist ideology of Record and Wilkerson calls attention to workers, American society, and the quality of life for black workers within that society, their political and ideological positions are, nonetheless, translatable into aesthetic ones. For instance, Record writes

I have argued that art is related to life and when the external aspects of life change, there follow invariably changes in the social and psychological qualities of life. . . . (1965, 158). If change provides new opportunities, it also engenders uncertainties. The more rapid, the greater are the difficulties in locating the *guide posts* whereby one seeks to steer a course. In the years ahead Negroes . . . making their way in a society in turmoil, will require, for the *attainment of minimal stability as a group and for a sense of individual well-being, all the sustenance that the cultural heritage can provide. But to draw upon it, they will need to search for and appreciate the elements in that heritage that are tough and durable. They will need a foundation on which to build. I am suggesting that the foundation is there; it has been there all along. But to build from it one needs to recognize it, to feel its massiveness, and to plant one's feet firmly upon it.* (1965, 193; my emphasis)

As Record concludes, the folkloric forms (folktales, spirituals, and ragtime— later called jazz) have become "guideposts" for critics and creative writers to recognize and draw upon. The leftist Wilkerson, echoing Record and others, adds to the discussion:

In the course of [their] development, Negro Americans have come to share a heightened group consciousness. . . . They experience common forms of oppression in Jim Crow America; they share common sentiments and aspirations; they organize and struggle—as Negroes—for those democratic rights which they, as a special group, have always been denied. The once diverse African peoples and their progeny, through centuries of common experience in America, have been welded into a distinct political entity, increasingly organized, characterized by greater unity than any other capable American minority, and with a strong sense of *"belongingness."* In short, there has been developed in America a new people, an oppressed people—the Negro people—with organizational forms and a *group consciousness peculiarly its own.* (1949, 7–8; my emphasis)

It was inevitable that this people, with its *special memories* and sentiments and aspirations, should develop its own body of *esthetic expression.* (1949, 8; my emphasis)

Again, like so many of their literary peers, who recognized there were "guideposts" in African American folk culture which designated "belongingness," "special memories," and organizational forms in literary art (folktales, spirituals, jazz), Record and Wilkerson left for subsequent critics the responsibility of translating this body of experiences into aesthetics, organizing principles, and evaluative criteria.

The same might be said of LeRoi Jones (Amiri Baraka) in "The Myth of a 'Negro Literature' " (1966). According to Jones

Only in music, and most notably in blues, jazz, and spirituals, i.e., "Negro Music," has there been a significantly profound contribution by American Negroes. (1966, 106)

Later in his essay, Jones points to writers who returned to "Negro Music" because of its "highly stylized and personal version of the Negro's life in America" (1966, 107), namely Jean Toomer, Richard Wright, Ralph Ellison, and James Baldwin. Jones does not, however, differentiate the blues, jazz, or spiritual context in the works of these writers.

In 1968, writing in the afterword ("An Afterword: And Shine Swam On") to *Black Fire: An Anthology of Afro-American Writing*—the anthology critics designate as having ushered in the Black Arts (literary) movement—coeditor Larry Neal responded to the question of form:

What of craft—the writer's craft? . . . [T]he poet must become a performer, the way James Brown is a performer—loud, gaudy, and racy. . . . He must learn *to embellish the context in which the work is executed; and where possible, link the work to all usable aspects of the music. For the context of the work is as important as the work itself. Poets must learn to sing, dance, and chant their works, tearing into the substance of their individual and collective experiences.* (1968, 655; my emphasis)

Worth repeating is that, like Johnson and other predecessors, Larry Neal recognized that this kind of "understanding" of form is central to transforming experience into aesthetic form. He recognized how "collective experiences" and "individual experiences" within an "[African American] context" could be "link[ed] . . . to all usable aspects of, [for instance], black music." One drawback in the magnificent *Black Fire,* especially for non–African Americans and African Americans who were less knowledgeable of black culture, was that the editors Neal and LeRoi Jones (Amiri Baraka) elected to illustrate rather than "explain" a black literary aesthetic. (Of course, Neal does attempt explanations in later works.)

In 1973, publishers at the William Morrow Company nominated Stephen E. Henderson, author of the seminal work *Understanding the New Black Poetry,* for the Pulitzer Prize. That year, Henderson did not become a recipient of the Pulitzer, but, as one book reviewer in *Black Creation* noted, *Understanding the New Black Poetry* became known "as one of the best books in the field . . . [for] helping [readers] understand, interpret as well as value Black poetry" (1973, 43). In his introduction, Henderson stated that he wanted to represent "the continuity and the wholeness of the Black Poetics tradition in the U.S." by providing a specific "critical framework, an organizing principle." As a Black Arts aesthetician, Henderson narrowed his views on who should judge black poetry—"black people." However, like James Weldon Johnson, Larry Neal, and others, Henderson recognized that any theoretical discussion or study of concrete forms in black poetry or other black literary art began with those elements in the black cultural heritage—be it music, folktales, or dialect (later called vernacular speech):

> Literature, accordingly, is the verbal organization of experience into beautiful forms, but what is meant by "beautiful" and by "forms" is to a significant degree dependent upon a people's way of life, their needs, their aspirations, their history—in short, their culture. (1973, 4)

In *Understanding the New Black Poetry* as well as in his essays, such as "Saturation: Progress Report on a Theory of Black Poetry" and "The Question of Form and Judgement [*sic*] in Contemporary Black Poetry," in speeches and even in one of his last papers, which was delivered at the criticism symposium sponsored by Houston Baker Jr. at the University of Pennsylvania in 1987, Henderson's focus remained consistent about a literary aesthetic that was explainable via the poetic references of black speech and black music:

> By Black speech I mean the speech of the majority of Black people. . . . and an understanding of the entire range of Black spoken language in America. This includes the *techniques* and *timbres* of the sermon and other forms of oratory, the dozens, the rap, the signifying, and the oral folktale.
>
> By Black music I mean essentially the vast fluid body of Black song—spirituals, shouts, jubilees, gospel songs, field cries, blues, pop songs by Blacks, and . . . jazz. (reprinted in this volume; my emphasis)

Henderson extended Johnson's views on an African American literary aesthetic and set some standards for analyzing and interpreting African American literary art. For instance, in his essay "The Heavy Blues of Sterling Brown: A Study of Craft and Tradition," Henderson used music (the blues) as a poetic reference and explained how form in classic blues allowed Brown to achieve similar form and style in his poetry:

> Of the varied forms of Black expressive culture, music is indisputably the most dramatic, moving, and pervasive, and of the many forms which the music takes, the most typical, the most potently charged is the blues. . . . The blues, then, are a music and a poetry of confrontation—with the self, with the family and loved ones, with the oppressive forces of society, with nature, and, on the heaviest level, with fate and the universe itself. And in the confrontation a man finds out who he is, a woman discovers her strengths, and if she is a Ma Rainey, she shares it with the community and in the process becomes immortal.
>
> The hallmark of Sterling Brown's poetry is its exploration of the bitter dimension of the blues (blues stanza, rhythm, movement, dramatic situations, mood, and imagery). (1980, 32)

Since the 1970s, creative writers and critics writing on form or structure and style in various African American art forms have returned to techniques and timbres in, for instance, the sermon, the dozens, the blues, oratory, pop songs, and jazz, and have sought to concretize further some organizing principles and evaluative criteria in African American literary criticism. In this Reader, under the critical approach Black Poetics (see the table of contents), critics return to several folk sources and read them in critical contexts. For instance, creative writer Gale Jackson looks at the use of folk rituals, customs, and performances in the art of storytelling. Ropo Sekoni returns to African oral traditions to study the roots of particular folk practices, beliefs, and expressions that are also identifiable in African and African American cultures and particularly in the trickster tales. Henry Louis Gates Jr. returns to the African American community to uncover practices in language that are traceable to Yoruba civilization. In Jerry Ward Jr.'s interview with Alvin Aubert, the South is discussed by both men as a folk source. Also under Black Poetics, there are critics who study and illustrate the influences of folk sources on form. For instance, Dolan Hubbard's focus is on the folk sermon and the African American literary imagination. Eleanor Traylor and Houston Baker Jr. study the influences of blues on African American literature and character. Ishmael Reed discusses his uses of folk rituals as art. While all of the critics who appear under Black Poetics go beyond Henderson in *Understanding the New Black Poetry* and Neal in his afterword to *Black Fire* to provide concrete ways of identifying touchstones of form in African American literary art, Johnson's preface in *The Book of American Negro Poetry* and Henderson's *Understanding the New Black Poetry*, indisputably, are the foundations upon which these critics build their ideas.

LITERARY HISTORY: JUDGMENT

1. What is African American literary art? Is it functional? Is it propaganda? Or is it art for art's sake?
2. What are the responsibilities of African American writers to their art forms? To themselves? To their audiences?
3. What are the responsibilities of audiences, particularly black audiences, white audiences, and others, to African American literary art?
4. How should African American literary art be approached? From the perspective of a black aesthetic? From the perspective of a new black aesthetic? From a black feminist or womanist perspective? From Western and current theoretical perspectives? Or from all of the above?

From 1773 to 2000, in essays (manifestoes, credos, and prescripts), in prefaces, in introductions, and in letters, journal entries, and interviews, critics and creative writers of African American literary art have posed such questions to themselves and to one another, either directly or indirectly. Responses from critics and creative writers on the aesthetics, communications, and epistemology of African American literary art and on the evaluation of writers and audiences have entailed, to borrow from Stephen Henderson in "The Question of Form and Judgement [*sic*] in Contemporary Black Poetry," "problems of contradiction, ideology and taste, resulting from differences in personal background and in political and cultural orientations" (1977, 24). Decades of discussion and debate, however, are translatable into an evolution of evaluative criteria in the following four stages:

1773–1894	Nurture vs. Nature
1895–1954	Art or Propaganda?
1955–1975	Cultural Autonomy and Understanding the Art of Black Poetry, Drama, Fiction, and Criticism
1976–2000	Aesthetic Values, Reconstructions of Blackness and Boundaries, and Postmodernism

Nurture vs. Nature

In 1773, Phillis Wheatley, a slave from Boston, published the first collection of African American poetry of international acclaim, *Poems on Various Subjects, Religious and Moral.* In the preface to *Poems,* there appeared "to the publick" an introduction by 18 of Boston's most honored men—a governor and several judges and ministers. What Wheatley's critics wrote is worth quoting, especially since their comments represent one of the earliest critiques of African American literature and the African American writer:

> We whose Names are under-written, do assure the World, that the POEMS specified in the following Page, were (as we verily believe) written by Phillis, a young Negro Girl, who was but a few Years since, brought an uncultivated Barbarian from *Africa,* and has ever since been, and now is, under the Disadvantage of serving as a Slave in a Family in this Town. She has been examined by some of the best Judges, and is thought qualified to write them. (1773, viii; emphasis in original)

When viewed in its historical context, the language of Wheatley's white critics reveals that Americans during the colonial period viewed Africa as barbarian and its people as incapable of reasoning—meaning that reasoning or natural ability for the darker people came by means of nurture rather than by nature. If in this implied chain of being, God is followed in descending rank by angels, humans, and then animals, where were African descendents ranked? Thought to be "uncultivated Barbarian(s)," African slaves and their descendents were ranked often alongside animals and, in some instances, below animals. While Wheatley's critics appear to rank her alongside humans, their categorization is precarious, for these men, like most Americans during this period, still see poet Wheatley as "under the Disadvantage of serving as a Slave." Thus, any attempts by Wheatley's critics to classify their introduction as literary criticism are undermined by words such as "Barbarian," "Disadvantage," and "Slave." Collectively, the words denote the eighteenth-century discourse of nurture versus nature. In other words, white Boston's best "believe" and "think" Wheatley is capable of having written her poems, but they devote little space to qualifying her poetic genius. Their criticism, which announces their amazement at Wheatley's production, leaves unanswered vital questions: What is African American literature? What is the responsibility of the writer to her art form? To her audience? Equally important, how should African American literature be evaluated?

Art or Propaganda?

During this stage (1895–1954), African American literary art, to quote W. E. B. DuBois, was expected to be indisputably "propagandistic." Most critics and creative writers elected to emphasize content over form or style in their literary art and criticism and to focus on the perceived similarities (in terms of aspirations, literary tastes, and experiences) between the rising black middle class and whites. Thus in 1895, while addressing the first Congress of Colored Women, Victoria Earle Matthews impressed upon her audience the need for African American writers to preserve in their literature "what [was] good, helpful and stimulating" in African American culture. According to Matthews, writers and critics were not to seek some loftier aesthetic practices. Instead, writers and critics should be responsible for "undermin[ing] and utterly driv[ing] out the traditional Negro in dialect—the subordinate, the servant as type representing the race" (1895, 131)—and for uplifting the race. W. E. B. DuBois, writing in "Criteria of Negro Art," was emphatically uninterested in any art that did not attempt to restore beauty, truth, and justice to the black community, for as DuBois concludes in his manifesto, art, justice, beauty, and truth were unseparated and inseparable.

However, while summarily advocating African American literature that promoted truth, beauty and justice, in the preface to *The Book of American Negro Poetry,* James Weldon Johnson signaled to African American writers that the highest function of literature was to exemplify the forms and the racial flavor of its African American folk practices. But like Matthews, DuBois, and others, Johnson must have privately expected literature to challenge the reality of race relations in America in the 1920s:

> The status of the Negro in the United States is more a question of national mental attitude toward the race than of actual condition. And nothing will do more to change that mental attitude and raise his status than a demonstration of intellectual parity by the Negro through the production of literature and art. (1921, 9)

In opposition to the ideological positions of those who saw literature and writers as functional were Alain Locke and Langston Hughes. Writing in "Art or Propaganda?" Locke condemned propaganda as a substitute for art, saying, "My chief objection to propaganda, apart from its besetting sin of monotony and disproportion, is that it perpetuates the position of group inferiority even in crying out against it" (reprinted in this volume). As a substitute, Locke called for "art of the people":

> It is the art of the people that needs to be cultivated, not the art of the coteries. Propaganda itself is preferable to shallow, truckling imitation. Negro things may reasonably be a fad for others; for us, they must be a religion. Beauty, however, is its best priest and psalms will be more effective than sermons. (reprinted in this volume)

In "The Negro Artist and the Racial Mountain," Hughes's response was based on his own experience:

> The Negro artist works against an undertow of sharp criticism and misunderstanding from his own group and unintentional bribes from the whites. "Oh, be respectable, write about nice people, show how good we are," say the Negroes. "Be stereotyped, don't go too far, don't shatter our illusions about you, don't amuse us too seriously. We will pay you," say the whites. . . . But in spite of the Nordicized Negro intelligentsia and the desires of some white editors we have an honest American Negro literature already with us. (reprinted in this volume)

Of course, Hughes and Locke had their own contradictions. Both Locke and Hughes advocated artistic freedom and self-expression for the writer, especially for the purpose of deepening the folk tradition. Only Hughes, however, insisted on using ordinary folk as subjects or models. Like DuBois and others, Locke expected the best models for subjects in literature to come from the black middle class.

Following the Harlem Renaissance, Richard Wright, writing in "Blueprint for Negro Writing" (1934), assesses the criticism and literature of that era. According to Wright, contradictions among Harlem's writers may have contributed to the lack of explicit evaluative criteria at the time:

> Negro writing in the past [had] been confined to humble novels, poems, and plays, prim and decorous ambassadors who went a-begging to white America. They entered the Court of American Public Opinion dressed in the knee-pants of servility, curtsying to show that the Negro was not inferior, that he was human, and that he had a life comparable to that of other people.
>
> Rarely was the best of this writing addressed to the Negro himself, his needs, his sufferings, his aspirations. Through misdirection, Negro writers [had] been far better to others than they [had] been to themselves. And the mere recognition of this places the whole question of Negro writing in a new light and raises a doubt as to the validity of its present direction. (reprinted in this volume)

In short, to quote Wright, if during this period some critics and writers had followed through and "continued and deepened [their understandings of] this folk tradition," the outcome for African American literary criticism during the Harlem Renaissance and at least during the next three decades might have been different (reprinted in this volume). Instead, with the few exceptions of critics and writers who recognized forms of folklore as "indigenous and complete expressions" and as guideposts for articulating both form and judgment in African American literary criticism, most of the leading critics and creative writers of the Harlem Renaissance, like white critics before them, failed to move beyond the debate of art versus propaganda.

Even during the Chicago Renaissance, a literary movement critics point to as an outgrowth of the Harlem Renaissance, the art versus propaganda debate is still evident. According to critic Robert Bone, in the lead article to a special issue of *Callaloo* (1986) dedicated to Richard Wright and the Chicago Renaissance (1935–1953),

> [T]he flowering of Negro letters that took place in Chicago from approximately 1935 to 1950 was in all respects comparable to the more familiar Harlem Renaissance. . . . (1986, 448) [A]s the writers of the Chicago School launched their careers[,] they wrote repeatedly of the Great Migration, and of the transformation that it wrought in the black community. They wrote of the pathology that was too often the price of adjustment to the urban scene. And they celebrated the common folk of Bronzeville as they accommodated to the conditions of urban life. Their basic outlook, reflecting the recent history of the black community, was integrationist. This orientation was reinforced by their contacts with the Chicago School of Sociology, which offered them a sophisticated theory of urbanization. (1986, 452)

Too, examinations of criticism by several major novelists and critics of the Chicago Renaissance (e.g., Richard Wright in "How 'Bigger' Was Born" in *Native Son,* Ann Petry's "The Novel as Social Criticism," many of Ralph Ellison's articles and interviews that appear in *Shadow and Act,* and even James Baldwin in "Many Thousand Gone" and "Everybody's Protest Novel") provide further evidence of the debate of art versus propaganda in African American literary criticism from 1935 to 1953.

Worth noting is that in the late 1930s in black periodicals, such as *Challenge* and *New Challenge,* edited at one time or another by Dorothy West and Richard Wright, the discussion of art versus propaganda was also significant. In the foreword to the first issue of *Challenge* (March 1934), guest writer James Weldon Johnson instructed "younger writers" that

[T]hey need not be propagandists; they need only be sincere artists, disdaining all cheap applause and remaining always true to themselves. (1934, 1)

Johnson wrote further,

It is one thing just to dabble in writing and another thing to be a writer. To those who really desire to become writers let me say: Writing is not only an art, it is also a trade, a trade that demands long, arduous and dogged effort for mastery. (1934, 1)

Johnson's voice would be echoed in forthcoming issues of *New Challenge.* Dorothy West, who was editor of *New Challenge,* often vowed her support in her "Dear Readers" editorials to young writers. She urged on "their sincere creation[s] of higher cultural values" (1937, 4).

Cultural Autonomy and Understanding the Art of Black Poetry, Drama, Fiction, and Criticism

In October 1966, the radically political Black Panther Party published its 10-point platform and program in (see Bobby Seale's *Seize the Time*). An excerpt of the platform read:

1. We want freedom. We want power to determine the destiny of our Black Community. . . .
5. We want education for our people that exposes the true nature of this decadent American society. We want education that teaches us our true history and our role in the present-day society. . . .
10. We want land, bread, housing, education, clothing, justice, and peace. And as our major political objective, a United Nations-supervised plebiscite to be held throughout the black colony in which only black colonial subjects will be allowed to participate, for the purpose of determining the will of black people as to their national destiny. (1970, 66–68)

In a cultural context, words such as "freedom," "destiny," and "power" spoken by a dispossessed group suggest self-determination. Phrases such as "our history," "our role," and "the will of black people" suggest a black nationhood. It is not surprising, then, that in 1968, writing in the manifesto "The Black Arts Movement," Larry Neal categorized the literary movement as "the aesthetic and spiritual sister of the Black Power concept," and, likewise, he specified the responsibilities of black writers as

> [S]peak[ing] directly to the needs and aspirations of Black America . . . confront[ing] the contradictions arising out of the Black man's experience in the racist west . . . [and] develop[ing] a "Black aesthetic." (reprinted in this volume)

In the foreword and afterword to their landmark contribution *Black Fire: An Anthology of Afro-American Writing*, Larry Neal and LeRoi Jones (Amiri Baraka) described black literature as collective and functional. As Baraka writes in the foreword to his (black) audience, "We are presenting. Your various selves." In this unconventional way, Baraka is speaking directly to the black masses in a familiar way of communicating. In the afterword, Neal instructed, "Black literature must become an integral part of the community's life style. . . . And . . . it must also be integral to the myths and experiences underlying the *total* history of black people" (1968, 653; Neal's emphasis). Both Baraka and Neal also specified that "the artist and the political activist [were] one" and that black poetry was to further the cause of political and social revolution.

If during the Harlem Renaissance critics and creative writers left more or less unanswered vital questions about aesthetics and form, leading critics, poets, and dramatists of the Black Arts movement responded. However, what the criticism of the 1960s and early 1970s reveals is that critics of the Black Arts movement could not render among themselves a consensus of evaluative criteria for judging their poetry and drama. Also, critics, poets, and dramatists could not agree, as specified in Neal's manifesto, on a definition of "Black aesthetics." According to Darwin Turner, writing in "Afro-American Literary Critics: An Introduction,"

> Black Aesthetic critics . . . are handicapped by the necessity of devising theory prior to the creation of works. [In comparison] Aristotle . . . examine[d] works he and other Greeks admired. He distinguished the elements these works shared. Then he stipulated that great literature must include such elements. Arnold, too, deduced his theories from literature already created. Many new black critics, however, are structuring theories while calling for writers to create the works that are needed to demonstrate the excellence of the theories. (1968, 95)

Turner was not alone in accusing creative writers and critics of this literary movement of devising theory prior to the creation of works. Jennifer Jordan in her sought-after essay "Cultural Nationalism in the 1960s: Politics and Poetry" observed:

> "Black Aesthetic," which should be a system by which to judge what good Black literature is [became] a term like "nationalism"—used and poorly defined. Part of the problem [was] that when the young cultural nationalists use the term they wanted to apply it only to the works of those who shared their ideology. (1986, 38)

Even Black Arts movement poet Carolyn Rodgers, writing in one of her signature pieces of criticism, "Un Nat'chal Thang—The Whole Truth—Us," observed:

> Many of the poets of the Sixties shouted, screamed and writhed on paper in pain. Others wrote pure desire to *off* the man and were often fantasy-oriented. There were gorried imagination and over-romantization [*sic*]of ourselves. . . . Black humanity was not as frequently found or appreciated. Seldom mentioned by some poets, except in terms of ridicule, put down and signification. (1971, 6–7; Rodgers's emphasis)

Like Turner, Jordan, and others, Rodgers ended her critical piece, instructing critics and creative writers, "We need feeling/forms/style" (1971, 9).

During the 1970s, not all leading Black Arts aestheticians were willing to rethink their ideological positions or the debate of craft versus politics. For instance, Addison Gayle Jr., editor of *The Black Aesthetic,* a collection of articles that categorized the cultural nationalistic concept, concedes in "A Blueprint for Black Criticism" that perhaps a critical framework for understanding, appreciating, and evaluating black literature was missing. Yet, in the same criticism, Gayle echoes Neal in "The Black Arts Movement" and in *Black Fire* on the function of black literature, the role of black writers, and the responsibilities of black audiences:

1. Black artists must refuse to accept the American definition of reality and propose a Black definition instead.
2. Black Art must offer alternatives to the stereotypes of Blacks created by white Americans and validated in the works and critical offerings of Black fellow travelers.
3. Black Art must emphasize those paradigms of the Black past that enabled Black people to survive the American nightmare.
4. Black Art must create images, symbols and metaphors of positive import from the Black experience.
5. Black Art must be written for, by and about Blacks and the Black American condition.
6. Black Art must redefine the definitions handed down from the Western world.

7. The objectives of Black Art must be to inculcate the values of communality between one Black person and another.
8. Black Art must be critical of any and all actions detrimental to the health and well-being of the Black community.
9. Black Art must divorce itself from the sociological attempts to explain the Black community in terms of pathology.
10. Black Art must be in continual revolt against the American attempt to dehumanize man. (1977, 43)

In many ways, what Gayle has begun to do is to summarize an aesthetic of blackness, or a black people's way of making things happen. Missing, nonetheless, are explanations of how he arrives at such summary. Which of his prescriptions are consistent with form derived from the community?

The debate of craft versus politics shifted in the early 1970s to the former when respected Black Aesthetic critics Larry Neal in various essays and Stephen Henderson in essays and in the introduction of *Understanding the New Black Poetry* called for continuity in theoretical and evaluative criteria, and demonstrated what it was they sought. Four years after his 1968 manifesto and the landmark work *Black Fire,* Larry Neal rethought the functions of African American literature and writers in, for instance, "The Black Contribution to American Letters: Part II, The Writer as Activist—1960 and After," writing:

> Unlike black music, [literature] has rarely been allowed to exist on its own terms, but rather been utilized as a means of public relations in that struggle for human rights. Literature can indeed make excellent propaganda, but through propaganda alone, the black writer can never perform the highest function of his art: that of revealing to man his most enduring human possibilities and limitations. (1976, 785)

Regarding evaluative criteria, in "A Survey: Black Writers' Views on Literary Lions and Values" Neal instructs other writers and critics that

> There is no need to establish a "black aesthetics." Rather, it is important to understand that one already exists. (1968, 35)

In agreement with Neal, Henderson in "The Forms of Things Unknown" addresses poets, dramatists, and others by saying that

> [T]he ultimate criteria for critical evaluation must be found in the sources of the creation, that is, in the Black Community itself. . . . What we are talking about then is the *depth* and *quality* of experience which a given work may evoke. We are also speaking about saturation. . . . By "saturation" in Black poetry, I mean . . . (a) the communication of Blackness in a given situation, and (b) a sense of fidelity to the observed and intuited truth of the Black Experience. (reprinted in this volume; my emphasis)

Henderson adds that "saturation" exists only in relationship to the entire work (form and style) and is employed merely to deal with an aspect of the poetry that warrants discussion and appreciation. For Henderson, appreciation comes from a black audience. In other words, "[O]ne must not consider the poem [or literary work] in isolation but in relationship to the reader/audience, and the reader to the wider context of the phenomenon which we call . . . the Black Experience" (reprinted in this volume)

Following the Black Arts movement, writers and critics moved beyond debating craft versus politics, or the existence of a black aesthetic. Even their use of "black" in "Black Aesthetic" goes from functioning as a noun to an adjective. As Houston Baker Jr. explains in the historical review "Generational Shifts and the Recent Criticism of Afro-American Literature," the 1970s brought forth a new group of critics and creative writers who sought "*sound* theoretical framework[s]" for the future study (analysis, classification, and evaluation) of an existing black aesthetic:

> [A] new and resplendent nation of Afro-Americans invested with Black Power . . . gave way in the late seventies to a new . . . group of intellectuals . . . [willing] . . . to separate the language of criticism from the vocabulary of political ideology. . . . Their proclaimed mission was to "reconstruct" the pedagogy and study of Afro-American literature so that it would reflect the most advanced thinking of a contemporary universe of literary-theoretical discourse. (1981, 80)

Aesthetic Values, Reconstructions of Blackness and Boundaries, and Postmodernism

Reconstructionists (those who are [or may not be] invested with Black Power but willing to separate the language of criticism from the vocabulary of political ideology and establish sound theory and aesthetic values) make up the present stage (1976–2000) of African American literary criticism. Titles of essays and books by critics since the late 1970s become somewhat self-explanatory of their focus and shifts. Sometimes discussions shift to pedagogy and canon revisions (e.g., Nick Aaron Ford, "Black Literature and the Problem of Evaluation"; Robert Stepto and Dexter Fisher, eds., *Afro-American Literature: The Reconstruction of Instruction;* Joyce Ann Joyce, "The Black Canon: Reconstructuring Black American Literary Criticism: New Literary History"; Cheryl Wall, ed., *Changing Our Own Words*). Sometimes discussions narrow to focus on gender (e.g., Claudia Tate, "ReShuffling the Deck: Or, (Re)Reading Race and Gender in Black Women's Writing"; Charles I. Nero, "Toward a Black Gay Aesthetic"; Barbara Smith, "Toward a Black Feminist Criticism"; Deborah McDowell, "New Directions for Black Feminist Criticism"; Gloria T. Hull, Patricia Bell Scott, and Barbara Smith, eds., *All the Women are White, All the Blacks Are Men, But Some of Us Are Brave*; or Michael

Awkward's *Inspiriting Influences: Tradition, Revision and Afro-American Women's Novels*). Often discussions return to literary history, individual authors, and individual works, only from new perspectives (e.g., George Kent, *Blackness and the Adventure of Western Culture*, Bernard W. Bell, *The Afro-American Novel and Its Tradition;* Abby Arthur Johnson and Ronald Maberry Johnson, *Propaganda and Aesthetics: The Literary Politics of African-American Magazines in the Twentieth Century*; Reginald Martin, *Ishmael Reed and the New Black Aesthetic;* Mary Helen Washington, foreword to *Their Eyes Were Watching God* by Zora Neale Hurston; Marjorie Pryse and Hortense Spillers, *Conjuring: Black Women, Fiction, and Literary Tradition;* and Jacqueline Coro, *The Blinking Eye: Ralph Ellison and His American, French, German and Italian Critics, 1952–1971);* or from critics who are not black and/or male (e.g., John Sekora [with Darwin Turner], *The Art of Slave Narratives: Original Essays in Criticism and Theory;* Eric J. Sundquist, *Cultural Context for Ralph Ellison's "Invisible Man";* William L. Andrews's numerous volumes on black autobiography; Robert Hemenway's and John Lowe's biographical works on Zora Neale Hurston; significant articles and books of traditional and current theory by Kimberly W. Benston, Susan Willis, and Barbara Johnson; and critical examinations of literature by black women writers by Keith Beyerman and Elliot Butler-Evans). Discussions also develop around popular interests (e.g., Gladstone Yearwood, "Towards a Theory of a Black Cinema Aesthetic"; Nikki Giovanni and Margaret Walker, "Content and Intent: Some Thoughts on Writing, Criticism and Film"; Mtume ya Salaam, "The Aesthetics of Rap"; Jeanne A. Taylor, "On Being Black and Writing for Television"; and Stuart Hall, "What Is This 'Black' in Black Popular Culture?"). Finally, discussions move toward the inclusion of Third World cultural identities (e.g., Tejumola Olaniyan, "African American Critical Discourse and the Invention of Cultural Identities"; Tommy L. Lott, "A No-Theory Theory of Contemporary Black Cinema"; Clyde Taylor, "Decolonizing the Image"; or Carol Boyce Davies, "From 'Post Coloniality' to Uprising Textualities"); or the question of who should teach, critique, or direct African American literary art, black or white people? (e.g., Shauneille Perry Ryder, "Will the Real Black Theater Please Stand Up?"; Trudier Harris, "Miss-Trained or Untrained? Jackleg Critics and African American Literature"; Nellie McKay, "Naming the Problem That Led to the Question 'Who Shall Teach African American Literature?'; or, Are We Ready to Disband the Wheatley Court?"; and Sandra G. Shannon, " 'In Their Respective Corners': A Post-Debate Interview with August Wilson").

In the late 1980s, black, suburban, mostly Ivy League graduates, many of whom went on to become, among other things, novelists, poets, screenwriters, critics, and curators, called for a "new black aesthetics" (NBA) that was more individualistic (but not in the mold of art for art's sake and not without social and political responsibility). At times the NBA was inclusive of traditions across boundaries of race and class. According to Trey Ellis in "The

New Black Aesthetic," icons for the NBA included "Ishmael Reed, Clarence Major, Toni Morrison, and John Edgar Wideman; George Clinton with his spaced-out funk band Parliament/Funkadelic; conceptual artist David Hammons who has hung empty Thunderbird bottles and spades from trees; Richard Pryor with his molten parodies of black life on his early albums and short-lived television show." At another point in his manifesto, Ellis describes the culturally eclectic NBA as "young blacks getting back into jazz and the blues; [or] the only ones you [saw] at punk concerts . . . [or] who admit liking both Jim and Toni Morrison . . . Eddie Murphy, Prince, and the Marsalis brothers". (1989, 234). In short, the black postmodernist intellectuals sought to communicate what Greg Tate in "Cult-Nats Meet Freaky Deke" called "the complexities of our culture" (1986, 5).

Many of the NBA writers appear in Terry McMillan's *Breaking Ice: An Anthology of Contemporary African-American Fiction.* In the preface to *Breaking Ice,* which might be considered one of the earliest in-depth focuses on literary judgment since Henderson's "saturation" in *Understanding the New Black Poetry,* John Edgar Wideman stipulates what makes contemporary African American literature contemporary:

> A long-tested view of history is incorporated in the art of African-American people, and our history can be derived from careful study of forms and influences that enter our cultural performances and rituals. In spite of and because of marginal status, a powerful, indigenous vernacular tradition has survived, not unbroken, but unbowed, a magnet, a focused energy, something with its own logic, rules, and integrity connecting current developments to the past. An articulate, syncretizing force our best artists have drawn upon, a force sustaining both individual talent and tradition.
>
> If what a writer wants is freedom of expression, then somehow that larger goal must be addressed implicitly/explicitly in our fictions. A story should somehow contain clues that align it with tradition and critique tradition, establish the new space it requires, demands, appropriates, hint at how it may bring forth other things like itself, where these others have, will, and are coming from. This does not mean defining criteria for admitting stories into some ideologically sound, privileged category, but seeking conditions, mining territory that maximizes the possibility of free, original expression. (reprinted in this volume)

Book-length studies on literary judgment—literary judgment explicitly—have yet to be written. As indicated by creative artists and critics appearing chronologically in this Reader (from Phillis Wheatley to James Baldwin to Ralph Ellison, Alice Walker, John Edgar Wideman, Trudier Harris, and Alexs Pate), discussions are ongoing. To borrow from Charles Johnson in the introduction to *Being and Race: Black Writing Since 1970,* conversations, however, can go "from loose casual talk about 'experiences' to esthetic and epistemological questions difficult to answer" (1987, 3).

In my brief introductions to the manifestoes, credos, prefaces, introductions, critical essays, interviews, letters, and journal entries that follow, I have tried to keep before readers (students, teachers, critics, creative writers, and others) those questions difficult to answer (the whats, hows, and whys) not only about African American literary texts, writers, and audiences but also about organizing principles of production, aesthetics, epistemology, communications, and theoretical methodology within the African American literary and critical tradition.

Notes

1.   See Robert Farris Thompson, *Flash of the Spirit, African and Afro-American Art and Philosophy* (New York: Vintage, 1984) and Joseph Holloway, *Africanisms in American Culture* (Bloomington, Ind.: Indiana University Press, 1990). These legacies are not unique to any one West African civilization. See also Robert Farris Thompson, *Black Gods and Kings*. Bloomington: Indiana University Press, 1976.

1773–1894:
NURTURE VS. NATURE

◆

PHILLIS WHEATLEY

On Imagination (1773)

Ordinarily, the neoclassical writer's use of Fancy involved ornamentation and imposed artificial rules and conventions from without. Through Imagination, the writer (beginning mostly with the Romantics) was free to transform what he/she perceived with freedom of expression and spontaneity. Wheatley uses Fancy and Imagination interchangeably; yet, like the Romantics, she anticipates temporary sterility of her creative powers ("Winter austere forbids me to aspire"). What else is being suggested in Wheatley's query about the writer? How does "Imagination" operate in the poem—as Neoclassical? As an appeal to the Muses? As African American? As protest? If Winter symbolizes slavery and oppression, is Wheatley, a slave, suggesting oppression has dampened "the rising fire" or her poetic and creative energies?

Thy various works, imperial queen, we see,
How bright their forms! how deck'd with pomp by thee!
Thy wond'rous acts in beauteous order stand,
And all attest how potent is thine hand.

From *Helicon's* refulgent heights attend,
Ye sacred choir, and my attempts befriend:
To tell her glories with a faithful tongue,
Ye blooming graces, triumph in my song.

Now here, now there, the roving *Fancy* flies,
Till some lov'd object strikes her wand'ring eyes,
Whose silken fetters all the senses bind,
And soft captivity involves the mind.

Imagination! who can sing thy force?
Or who describe the swiftness of thy course?
Soaring through air to find the bright abode,
Th' empyreal palace of the thund'ring God,
We on thy pinions can surpass the wind,
And leave the rolling universe behind:
From star to star the mental optics rove,
Measure the skies, and range the realms above.
There is one view we grasp the mighty whole,
Or with new worlds amaze th' unbounded soul.

Though *Winter* frowns to *Fancy's* raptur'd eyes
The fields may flourish, and gay scenes arise;
The frozen deeps may break their iron bands,
And bid their waters murmur o'er the sands.
Fair *Flora* may resume her fragrant reign,
And with her flow'ry riches deck the plain;
Sylvanus may diffuse his honours round,
And all the forest may with leaves be crown'd:
Show'rs may descend, and dews their gems disclose,
And nectar sparkle on the blooming rose.

Such is thy pow'r, nor are thine orders vain,
O thou the leader of the mental train:
In full perfection all thy works are wrought,
And thine the sceptre o'er the realms of thought.
Before thy throne the subject-passions bow,
Of subject-passions sov'reign ruler Thou,
At thy command joy rushes on the heart,
And through the glowing veins the spirits dart.

Fancy might now her silken pinions try
To rise from earth, and sweep th'expanse on high;
From *Tithon's* bed now might *Aurora* rise,
Her cheeks all glowing with celestial dies,
While a pure stream of light o'erflows the skies.
The monarch of the day I might behold,
And all the mountains tipt with radiant gold.
But I reluctant leave the pleasing views,
Which *Fancy* dresses to delight the *Muse*
Winter austere forbids me to aspire,
And northern tempests damp the rising fire;
They chill the tides of *Fancy's* flowing sea,
Cease then, my song, cease the unequal lay.

Suggested Readings with Similar Theme:

Rush, Benjamin. *An Address to the Inhabitants of the British Settlement in America, Upon Slave-Keeping*, 4. Philadelphia: John Dunlop, 1773.

Wheatley, Phillis. "An Hymn to the Morning." In *The Collected Works of Phillis Wheatley*. Reprint, edited with an essay by John C. Shields, New York: Oxford University Press, 1988.

Horton, George Moses. "George Moses Horton, Myself." In *Naked Genius*. Raleigh, N.C., 1865. Reprint, *Naked Genius: The Poetry of George Moses Horton*, edited by William Carroll. Chapel Hill: The University of North Carolina Press, 1977.

To Mæcenas (1773)

The poet wishes for the kind of poetic inspiration that Virgil received from the Muses so that she too might write scintillating verse. She laments that a lack of inspiration renders her unable to compose poetry worthy of her patron, John Wheatley. She questions if in the early history of the African American literary tradition, the Muses that inspired the African poet Terence could inspire her? In Wheatley's query about poetic inspiration, how has she as poet and as slave indirectly addressed the nature vs. nurture debate?

Mæcenas, you, beneath the myrtle shade,
Read o'er what poets sung, and shepherds play'd.
What felt those poets but you feel the same?
Does not your soul possess the sacred flame?
Their noble strains your equal genius shares
In softer language, and diviner airs.

While *Homer* paints lo! circumfus'd in air,
Celestial Gods in mortal forms appear;
Swift as they move hear each recess rebound,
Heav'n quakes, earth trembles, and the shores resound.
Great Sire of verse, before my mortal eyes,
The lightnings blaze across the vaulted skies,
And, as the thunder shakes the heav'nly plains,
A deep-felt horror thrills through all my veins.
When gentler strains demand thy graceful song,
The length'ning line moves languishing along.
When great *Patroclus* courts *Achilles'* aid,
The grateful tribute of my tears is paid;
Prone on the shore he feels the pangs of love,
And stern *Pelides* tend'rest passions move.

Great *Maro's* strain in heav'nly numbers flows,
The *Nine* inspire, and all the bosom glows.
O could I rival thine and *Virgil's* page,
Or claim the *Muses* with the *Mantuan* Sage:
Soon the same beauties should my mind adorn,
And the same ardors in my soul should burn:
Then should my song in bolder notes arise,

And all my numbers pleasingly surprize;
But here I sit, and mourn a grov'ling mind,
That fain would mount, and ride upon the wind.

Not you, my friend, these plaintive strains become,
Not you, whose bosom is the *Muses* home;
When they from tow'ring *Helicon* retire,
They fan in you the bright immortal fire,
But I less happy, cannot raise the song,
The fault'ring music dies upon my tongue.

The happier *Terence* all the choir inspir'd,
His soul replenish'd, and his bosom fir'd;
But say, ye *Muses*, why this partial grace,
To one alone of *Afric's* race;
From age to age transmitting thus his name
With the first glory in the rolls of fame?

Thy virtues, great *Mæcenas*! shall be sung
In praise of him, from whom those virtues sprung;
While blooming wreaths around thy temples spread,
I'll snatch a laurel from thine honour'd head,
While you indulgent smile upon the deed.

As long as *Thames* in streams majestic flows,
Or *Naiads* in their oozy beds repose,
While Poebus reigns above the starry train,
While bright *Aurora* purples o'er the main,
So long, great Sir, the muse thy praise shall sing,
So long thy praise shall make *Parnassus* ring:
Then grant, *Mæcenas*, thy paternal rays,
Hear me propitious, and defend my lays.

Suggested Readings with Similar Theme:

Rush, Benjamin. *A Vindication of the Address: To the Inhabitants of the British Settlements, On the Slavery of the Negroes in America, In Answer to a Pamphlet entitled "Slavery Not Forbidden by Scripture; Or, a Defense of the West Indian Planters from the Aspersions thrown against them by the author of the Address By a Pennsylvanian,* 3. Philadelphia: John Dunlop, 1773.
Horton, George Moses. "The Art of a Poet," "On the Poetic Muse," and "To the Muse." In *Naked Genius.* Raleigh, N.C., 1865. Reprint, *Naked Genius: The Poetry of George Moses Horton,* edited by William Carroll. Chapel Hill: The University of North Carolina Press, 1977.

IGNATIUS SANCHO

Letter LVII (1778)
in *Letters of the Late Ignatius Sancho* (1782)

Ignatius Sancho's letters reveal an African descendant of literary consciousness, and to many in the literary world, he is the first African American critic. In Letter LVII, Sancho comments about slave narratives and Phillis Wheatley's poetry. What are his findings? At what point in his letter does Sancho enter the debate of nurture vs. nature? What are his conclusions, particularly regarding slaveowners who associate "reasoning" and natural capabilities with race (or whites)?

To Mr. F_____.
Charles Street, January 27, 1778

Full heartily and moft cordially do I thank thee—good Mr. F_____, for your kindnefs in fending the books—that upon the unchriftian and moft dia- bolical ufage of my brother Negroes—the illegality—the horrid wickednefs of the traffic—the cruel carnage and depopulation of the human fpecies—is painted in fuch ftrong colours—that I fhould think would (if duly attended to) flafh conviction—and produce remorfe in every enlightened and candid reader.—The perufal affected me more than I can exprefs;—indeed I felt a double or mixt fenfation—for while my heart was torn for the fufferings— which, for aught I know—fome of my neareft kin might have undergone— my bofom, at the fame time, glowed with gratitude—and praife toward the humane—the Chriftian—the friendly and learned Author of that moft valu- able book.—Bleft be your fect!—and Heaven's peace be ever upon them!—I, who, thank God! am no bigot—but honour virtue—and the practice of the great moral duties—equally in the turban—or the lawn-fleeves—who think Heaven big enough for all the race of man—and hope to fee and mix amongft the whole family of Adam in blifs hereafter—I with thefe notions (which, perhaps, fome may ftyle abfurd) look upon the friendly Author—as a being far fuperior to any great name upon your continent.—I could with that every member of each houfe of parliament had one of thefe books.—And if his Majefty perufed one through before breakfaft—thought it might fpoil his appetite—yet the confcioufnefs of having it in his power facilitate the great work—would give an additional fweetnefs to his tea.—Phyllis's [*sic*] poems do credit to nature—and put art—merely as art—to the blufh.—It reflects nothing either to the glory or generofity of her mafter—if fhe is still his flave—except he glories in the low vanity of having in his wanton power a mind animated by Heaven—a genius fuperior to himfelf—the lift of fplendid—titled—learned names, in confirmation of her being the real authorefs.—alas! fhews how very poor the acquifition of wealth and knowledge are—without generofity—feeling—and humanity.—Thefe good great folks—all know—and perhaps admired—nay, praifed Genius in bondage— and then, like the priefts and the Levites in facred writ, paffed by—not one good Samaritan amongft them.—I fhall be ever glad to fee you—and am, with many thanks,

Your moft humble fervant,
IGNATIUS SANCHO.

Suggested Readings with Similar Theme:

Dunbar Nelson, Alice. "A Poet and His Song." *A.M.E. Church Review* (October 1914): 121–35.
Jefferson, Thomas. *Notes on the State of Virginia.* London: Stockdale, 1787, Book II, 196.
Kant, Immanuel. *Observations on the Feeling of the Beautiful and Sublime.* 1764. Tran. John T. Goldthwait. Berkeley: University of California, 1960, 111, 113.

CHARLOTTE FORTEN GRIMKÉ

Journal of Charlotte Forten (July 28, 1854)

How does Charlotte Forten {Grimké} enter philosophical discussions with Sancho about nurture vs. nature? What is her response to Wheatley's critics?

This morning Miss Creamer, a friend of our teacher, came into the school. She is a very learned lady; a Latin teacher in Troy Seminary, and an authoress. I certainly did feel some alarm, when I saw her entering the room. But she was so very kind and pleasant that I soon felt more at ease. . . . I do think reading one's compositions before strangers is a trying task. If I were to tell Mrs. R. this, I know she would ask how I could expect to become what I often say I should like to be—an Anti-Slavery lecturer. But I think that I should then trust to the inspiration of the subject.—This evening read "Poems of Phillis Wheatly [*sic*]," an African slave, who lived in Boston at the time of the Revolution. She was a wonderfully gifted woman, and many of her poems are very beautiful. Her character and genius afford a striking proof of the falseness of the assertion made by some that hers is an inferior race. . . .

Suggested Readings with Similar Theme:

Stevenson, Brenda. *The Journals of Charlotte Forten Grimké.* New York: Oxford University Press, 1988.

Braxton, Joanne. "A poet's Retreat: The Diaries of Charlotte Forten Grimké (1837–1914)." In *Wild Women in the Whirlwind: Afra-American Culture and the Contemporary Literary Renaissance,* edited by Joanne M. Braxton and Andree Nicola, 11–15. New Brunswick, N.J.: Rutgers University Press, 1989.

Fancy Etchings (April 24, 1873)

Jenny, the speaker, strives to join other notable African American poets of the nineteenth century, such as Paul Laurence Dunbar. According to Jenny, why during this time must there be poetry for the African American audience? Specifically, how does Jenny define her responsibility as a writer? How does Harper, nineteenth-century poet and novelist, bridge aesthetic and political arguments of the eighteenth and nineteenth centuries (the nurture vs. nature and the art or propaganda debates)?

"Ah, Aunty . . . one of my first thoughts after graduating was, how this will please Aunty. Aunty I want to be a poet, to earn and take my place among the poets of the nineteenth century; but with all the glowing enthusiasms that light up my life I cannot help thinking, that more valuable than the soarings of genius are the tender nestlings of love. Genius may charm the intellect, but love will refresh the spirit."

"I am glad, Jenny, that you feel so, for I think the intellect that will best help our race must be heart supplied: but do you think by being a poet you can best serve our people?"

"I think, Aunty, the best way to serve humanity, is by looking within ourselves, and becoming acquainted with our powers and capacities. The fact is we should all go to work and make the most of ourselves, and we cannot do that without helping others."

"And so having sounded the depths of your inner life, you have come to the conclusion that you have a talent or genius for poetry."

"Aunty, do you remember that poem I wrote some months since which you and others admired so? To me that poem was a revelation, I learned from it that I had power to create, and it gave me faith in myself, and I think faith in one's self is an element, of success. Perhaps you think this is egotism."

"Oh, no, I do not think that consciousness of one's ability to perform certain things, is egotism. If a woman is beautiful it is not vanity for her to know what the looking glass constantly reveals. A knowledge of powers and capacities should be an incentive to growth and not a stimulus for vain glory; but, Jenny, what do you expect to accomplish among our people of being a poet?"

"Aunty I want to learn myself and be able to teach others to strive to make the highest ideal, the most truly real of our lives[.]"

"But, Jenny, will not such an endeavor be love's labor lost? what time will our people have in their weary working every day life to listen to your songs?"

"It is just because our lives are apt to be so hard and dry, that I would scatter the flowers of poetry around our paths; and would if I could amid life's sad discords introduce the most entrancing strains of melody. I would teach men and women to love noble deeds by setting them to the music, of fitly spoken words. The first throb of interest that a person feels in the recital of a noble deed, a deed of high and holy worth, the first glow of admiration for suffering virtue, or thrill of joy in the triumph of goodness, forms a dividing line between the sensuous and material and the spiritual and progressive. I think poetry is one of the great agents of culture, civilization and refinement. What grander poetry can you find than among the ancient Hebrews; and to-day the Aryan race with all the splendor of its attainments and the magnificence of its culture; still lights the lamp of its devotion at Semitic altars. Ages have passed since the blind beggar of Chios was denied a pension, in his native place, but his poetry is still green in the world's memory."

Suggested Readings with Similar Theme:

Wilson, Harriet. Preface to *Our Nig; Or, Sketches from the Life of a Free Black. In a Two Story White House, North, Showing That Slavery's Shadows Fall Even There.* 1859. Reprint, New York: Vintage, 1983.

Carby, Hazel. Introduction to *Iola LeRoy*, by Frances Ellen Watkins Harper, ix–xxvi. Boston: Beacon, 1989.

Foster, Frances Smith. Introduction to *Iola LeRoy*, by Frances Ellen Watkins Harper, xxvii–xxxix. New York: Oxford University Press, 1988.

CHARLES W. CHESNUTT

Second Journal (May 29, 1880)

According to Chesnutt, how might one prepare to become a writer? Explain why Chesnutt sees literature useful in accomplishing a "moral revolution." How does Chesnutt anticipate the moral philosophical criticism of W. E. B DuBois?

I think I must write a book. I am almost afraid to undertake a book so early and with so little experience in composition. But it has been my cherished dream, and I feel an influence that I cannot resist calling me to the task. Besides, I do not know but I am as well prepared as some other successful writers. A fair knowledge of the classics, a speaking acquaintance with the modern languages, an intimate friendship with literature, etc.; seven years experience in the school room, two years of married life, and a habit of studying character have I think, left me not entirely unprepared to write even a book. Fifteen years of life in the South, in one of the most eventful eras of its history; among a people whose life is rich in the elements of romance; under conditions calculated to stir one's soul to the very depths;—I think there is here a fund of experience, a supply of material, which a skillful pers[on] could work up with tremendous effect. Besides, If I do write, I shall write for a purpose, a high, holy purpose, and this will inspire me to greater effort. The object of my writings would be not so much the elevation of the colored people as the elevation of the whites,—for I consider the unjust spirit of caste which is so insidious as to pervade a whole nation, and so powerful as to subject a whole race and all connected with it to scorn and social ostracism—I consider this a barrier to the moral progress of the American people; and I would be one of the first to head a determined, organized crusade against it. Not a fierce indiscriminate onslaught; not an appeal to force, for this is something that force can but slightly affect; but a moral revolution which must be brought about in a different manner. the Abolition[ist]s stirred up public opinion in behalf of justice and humanity which were only lying dormant in the northern heart. The iron hand of power set the slave free from personal bondage, and by admitting him to all the rights of citizenship—the ballot, education—is fast freeing him from the greater bondage of ignorance. But the subtle almost indefinable feeling of repulsion toward the negro, which is common to most Americans—and easily enough accounted for—, cannot be stormed and taken by assault; the garrison will not capitulate: so their position must be mined, and we will find ourselves in their midst before they think it.

This work is of a twofold character. The negro's part is to prepare himself for social recognition and equality; and it is the province of literature to open the way for him to get it—to accustom the public mind to the idea; and by while amusing them to familiarize lead them on imperceptibly, unconsciously step by step to the desired state of feeling. If I can do anything to further this work, and can see any likelihood of obtaining success in it, I would gladly devote my life to the work.

Suggested Readings with Similar Theme:

Lanusso, Armand. Introduction to *Les Cenelles: A Collection of Poems by Creole Writers of the Early Nineteenth Century.* New Orleans, 1845.

Hopkins, Pauline. Preface to *Contending Forces: A Romance Illustrative of Negro Life North and South.* Boston: The Colored Co-Operative Publishing Co., 1900. Reprint, New York: AMS, 1971.

Render, Sylvia Lyons. Introduction: Chestnutt—the Writer. In *The Short Fiction of Charles W. Chesnutt,* 11–15. Washington, D.C.: Howard University Press, 1981.

1895–1954:
ART OR PROPAGANDA?

◆

The Value of Race Literature:
An Address (1895)

How does Matthews anticipate Harlem Renaissance writers, such as Langston Hughes and Zora Neale Hurston, when she calls for race literature "built upon our own individuality"? How does Matthews anticipate NBA writers Terry McMillan, Trey Ellis, Alexs Pate—among others—when she predicts that eventually race literature will be built on "the simplicity of the story" and the "multiplicity of . . . dramatic situations"? Explain how Matthews's overall ideological position remains dubiously Art or Propaganda?

When the literature of our race is developed, it will of necessity be different in all essential points of greatness, true heroism and real Christianity from what we may at the present time, for convenience, call American Literature. When some master hand writes the stories as Dr. Dvorak has caught the melodies, when, amid the hearts of the people, there shall live a George Eliott [*sic*], moving this human world by the simple portrayal of the scenes of our ordinary existence; or when the pure, ennobling touch of a black Hannah More shall rightly interpret our unappreciated contribution to Christianity and make it into universal literature, such writers will attain and hold imperishable fame.

The novelists most read at the present time in this country find a remunerative source for their doubtful literary productions based upon the wrongly interpreted and too often grossly exaggerated frailties. This is patent to all intelligent people. The Negro need not envy such reputation, nor feel lost at not reveling in its ill-gotten wealth or repute. We are the only people most distinctive from those who have civilized and governed this country, who have become typical Americans, and we rank next to the Indians in originality of soil, and yet remain a distinct people.

In this connection, Joseph Wilson, in the "Black Phalanx," says: "The Negro race is the only race that has ever come in contact with the European race that has proved itself able to withstand its atrocities and oppression. All others like the Indians whom they could not make subservient to their use they have destroyed."

Prof. Sampson in his "Mixed Races" says, "The American Negro is a new race, and is not the direct descent of any people that has ever flourished."

On this supposition, and relying upon finely developed, native imaginative powers, and humane tendencies, I base my expectation that our Race Literature when developed will not only compare favorably with many, but will stand out preeminent, not only in the limited history of colored people, but in the broader field of universal literature.

Though Race Literature be founded upon the traditionary history of a people, yet its fullest and largest development ought not to be circumscribed by the narrow limits of race or creed, for the simple reason that literature in its loftiest development reaches out to the utmost limits of soul enlargement and outstrips all earthly limitations. Our history and individuality as a people, not only provides material for masterly treatment; but would seem to make a Race Literature a necessity as an outlet for the unnaturally suppressed inner lives which our people have been compelled to lead.

The literature of any people of varied nationality who have won a place in the literature of the world, presents certain cardinal points. French literature for instance, is said to be "not the wisest, not the weightiest, not certainly the purest and loftiest, but by odds the most brilliant and the most interesting literature in the world."

Ours, when brought out, and we must admit in reverence to truth that, as yet, we have done nothing distinctive, but may when we have built upon our own individuality, win a place by the simplicity of the story, thrown into strong relief by the multiplicity of its dramatic situations; the spirit of romance, and even tragedy, shadowy and as yet ill-defined, but from which our race on this continent can never be disassociated.

Suggested Reading with Similar Theme:

Mossell, N. F. (Mrs). "Life and Literature." *A.M.E. Church Review* 14 (January 1898): 318–26.

W. E. B. DuBois

Criteria of Negro Art (1926)

According to the sociologist, the ideal past for the African American is one of Truth, Beauty, and Justice. Furthermore, the writer has the responsibility of ensuring such a past. Why does DuBois regard beauty, truth, and justice, especially in America in 1926, to be unseparated and inseparable? Explain the critical past (Longinus, Horace, Sidney, and Pope) evoked by DuBois's charge that African American writers preserve beauty and truth with the "methods that men have used before" or with the "tools of the artists before {them}." For instance, Sidney places the responsibility of maintaining truth with artists rather than with historians and philosophers. DuBois charges artists with the same responsibility. Explain the critical past (of "Black and unknown bards") evoked by DuBois's charge to preserve beauty and truth as well. For DuBois, "the apostle of Beauty thus becomes the apostle of Truth and Right not by choice but by inner and outer compulsion." Is the role of the African American writer no longer optional? Compare and contrast DuBois's credo with Plato's "The Republic: Book X." Do the writings raise similar questions about the political and social status of literary art? Is DuBois, who is one of several architects of the Harlem Renaissance movement, implying formulaic or mimetic form and intent in African American literary texts? Could DuBois be defined as a moral critic who argues that "all art is propaganda"?

The question comes next as to the interpretation of these new stirrings, of this new spirit: Of what is the colored artist capable? We have had on the part of both colored and white people singular unanimity of judgment in the past. Colored people have said, "This work must be inferior because it comes from colored people." White people have said: "It is inferior because it is done by colored people." But today there is coming to both the realization that the work of the black man is not always inferior. Interesting stories come to us. A professor in the University of Chicago read to a class that had studied literature a passage of poetry and asked them to guess the author. They suggested a goodly company from Shelley and Robert Browning down to Tennyson and Masefield. The author was Countee Cullen. Or again the English critic John Drinkwater went down to a Southern seminary, one of the sort which finishes young white women of the South. The students sat with their wooden faces while he tried to get some response out of them. Finally he said, "Name me some of your Southern poets." They hesitated. He said finally, "I'll start out with your best: Paul Laurence Dunbar!"

With the growing recognition of Negro artists in spite of the severe handicaps, one comforting thing is occurring to both white and black. They are whispering, "Here is a way out. Here is the real solution of the color problem. The recognition accorded Cullen, Hughes, Fauset, White and others shows there is no real color line. Keep quiet! Don't complain! Work! All will be well!"

I will not say that already this chorus amounts to a conspiracy. Perhaps I am naturally too suspicious. But I will say that there are today a surprising number of white people who are getting great satisfaction out of these younger Negro writers because they think it is going to stop agitation of the Negro question. They say, "What is the use of your fighting and complaining; do the great thing and the reward is there." And many colored people are all too eager to follow this advice; especially those who weary of the eternal struggle along the color line, who are afraid to fight and to whom the money of philanthropists and the alluring publicity are subtle and deadly bribes. They say, "What is the use of fighting? Why not show simply what we deserve and let the reward come to us?"

And it is right here that the National Association for the Advancement of Colored People comes upon the field, comes with its great call to a new battle, a new fight and new things to fight before the old things are wholly won; and to say that the beauty of truth and freedom which shall some day be our heritage and the heritage of all civilized men is not in our hands yet and that we ourselves must not fail to realize.

There is in New York tonight a black woman molding clay by herself in a little bare room, because there is not a single school of sculpture in New York where she is welcome. Surely there are doors she might burst through, but when God makes a sculptor He does not always make the pushing sort of person who beats his way through doors thrust in his face. This girl is working her hands off to get out of this country so that she can get some sort of training.

There was Richard Brown. If he had been white he would have been alive today instead of dead of neglect. Many helped him when he asked but he was not the kind of boy that always asks. He was simply one who made colors sing.

There is a colored woman in Chicago who is a great musician. She thought she would like to study at Fontainebleau this summer where Walter Damrosch and a score of leaders of art have an American school of music. But the application blank of this school says: "I am a white American and I apply for admission to the school."

We can go on the stage; we can be just as funny as white Americans wish us to be; we can play all the sordid parts that America likes to assign to Negroes; but for anything else there is still small place for us.

And so I might go on. But let me sum up with this: Suppose the only Negro who survived some centuries hence was the Negro painted by white Americans in the novels and essays they have written. What would people in a hundred years say of black Americans? Now turn it around. Suppose you were to write a story and put in it the kind of people you know and like and imagine. You might get it published and you might not. And the "might not" is still far bigger than the "might." The white publishers catering to white folk would say, "It is not interesting"—to white folk, naturally not. They want Uncle Toms, Topsies, good "darkies" and clowns. I have in my office a story with all the earmarks of truth. A young man says that he started out to write and had his stories accepted. Then he began to write about the things he knew best about, that is, about his own people. He submitted a story to a magazine which said, "We are sorry, but we cannot take it." "I sat down and revised my story, changing the color of the characters and the locale and sent it under an assumed name with a change of address and it was accepted by the same magazine that had refused it, the editor promising to take anything else I might send in providing it was good enough."

We have, to be sure, a few recognized and successful Negro artists; but they are not all those fit to survive or even a good minority. They are but the remnants of that ability and genius among us whom the accidents of education and opportunity have raised on the tidal waves of chance. We black folk are not altogether peculiar in this. After all, in the world at large, it is only the accident, the remnant, that gets the chance to make the most of itself; but if this is true of the white world it is infinitely more true of the colored world. It is not simply the great clear tenor of Roland Hayes that opened the ears of America. We have had many voices of all kinds as fine as his and America was and is as deaf as she was for years to him. Then a foreign land heard Hayes and put its imprint on him and immediately America with all its imitative snobbery woke up. We approved Hayes because London, Paris, and Berlin approved him and not simply because he was a great singer.

Thus is it the bounden duty of black America to begin this great work of the creation of beauty, of the preservation of beauty, of the realization of beauty, and we must use in this work all the methods that men have used before. And what have been the tools of the artist in times gone by? First of all, he has used the truth—not for the sake of truth, not as a scientist seeking truth, but as one upon whom truth eternally thrusts itself as the highest handmaid of imagination, as the one great vehicle of universal understanding. Again artists have used goodness—goodness in all its aspects of justice, honor, and right—not for sake of an ethical sanction but as the one true method of gaining sympathy and human interest.

The apostle of beauty thus becomes the apostle of truth and right not by choice but by inner and outer compulsion. Free he is but his freedom is ever bounded by truth and justice; and slavery only dogs him when he is denied the right to tell the truth or recognize an ideal of justice.

Thus all art is propaganda and ever must be, despite the wailing of the purists. I stand in utter shamelessness and say that whatever art I have for writing has been used always for propaganda for gaining the right of black folk to love and enjoy. I do not care a damn for any art that is not used for propaganda. But I do care when propaganda is confined to one side while the other is stripped and silent.

In New York we have two plays: "White Cargo" and "Congo." In "White Cargo" there is a fallen woman. She is black. In "Congo" the fallen woman is white. In "White Cargo" the black woman goes down further and further and in "Congo" the white woman begins with degradation but in the end is one of the angels of the Lord.

You know the current magazine story: a young white man goes down to Central America and the most beautiful colored woman there falls in love with him. She crawls across the whole isthmus to get to him. The white man says nobly, "No." He goes back to his white sweetheart in New York.

In such cases, it is not the positive propaganda of people who believe white blood divine, infallible, and holy to which I object. It is the denial of a similar right to propaganda to those who believe black blood human, lovable, and inspired with new ideals for the world. White artists themselves suffer from this narrowing of their field. They cry for freedom in dealing with Negroes because they have so little freedom in dealing with whites. Du-Bose Heywood writes "Porgy" and writes beautifully of the black Charleston underworld. But why does he do this? Because he cannot do a similar thing for the white people of Charleston, or they would drum him out of town. The only chance he had to tell the truth of pitiful human degradation was to tell it of colored people. I should not be surprised if Octavius Roy Cohen had approached the Saturday Evening Post and asked permission to write about a different kind of colored folk than the monstrosities he has created; but if he has, the Post has replied, "No. You are getting paid to write about the kind of colored people you are writing about."

In other words, the white public today demands from its artists, literary and pictorial, racial pre-judgment which deliberately distorts truth and justice, as far as colored races are concerned and it will pay for no other.

On the other hand, the young and slowly growing black public still wants its prophets almost equally unfree. We are bound by all sorts of customs that have come down as second-hand soul clothes of white patrons. We are ashamed of sex and we lower our eyes when people will talk of it. Our religion holds us in superstition. Our worst side has been so shamelessly emphasized that we are denying we have or ever had a worst side. In all sorts of ways we are hemmed in and our new young artists have got to fight their way to freedom.

The ultimate judge has got to be you and you have got to build yourselves up into that wide judgment, that catholicity of temper which is going to enable the artist to have his widest chance for freedom. We can afford the truth. White folk today cannot. As it is now we are handing everything over to a white jury. If a colored man wants to publish a book, he has got to get a white publisher and a white newspaper to say it is great; and then you and I say so. We must come to the place where the work of art when it appears is reviewed and acclaimed by our own free and unfettered judgment. And we are going to have a real and valuable and eternal judgment only as we make ourselves free of mind, proud of body and just of soul to all men.

And then do you know what will be said? It is already saying. Just as soon as true art emerges; just as soon as the black artist appears, someone touches the race on the shoulder and says, "He, he was born here; he was trained here; he is not a Negro—what is a Negro anyhow? He is just human; it is the kind of thing you ought to expect."

I do not doubt that the ultimate art coming from black folk is going to be just as beautiful, and beautiful largely in the same ways, as the art that comes from white folk, or yellow, or red; but the point today is that until the art of the black folk compels recognition they will not be rated as human. And when through art they compel recognition then let the world discover if it will that their art is as new as it is old and as old as new.

I have a classmate once who did three beautiful things and died. One of them was a story of a folk who found fire and then went wandering in the gloom of night seeking again the stars they had once known and lost; suddenly out of blackness they looked up and there loomed the heavens; and what was it that they said? They raised a mighty cry: "It is the stars, it is the ancient stars, it is the young and everlasting stars!"

Suggested Readings with Similar Theme:

Matthews, Victoria Earle. "The Value of Race Literature: An Address Delivered at the First Congress of Colored Women of the United States." 1895. Reprint, Shirley Wilson Logan, ed. *With Pen and Voice, A Critical Anthology of Nineteenth-Century African American Women*. Carbondale: Southern Illinois University Press, 1995. Reprinted in this volume.

DuBois, W. E. B. "Of Our Spiritual Strivings." In *The Souls of Black Folk*. Chicago: A. C. McClurg, 1903.

Johnson, James Weldon. Preface to *The Book of American Negro Poetry Chosen and Edited with an Essay on the Negro's Creative Genius*. New York: Harcourt Brace & Company, 1921.

Chesnutt, Charles W. "Post-Bellum, Pre-Harlem." *Crisis* (June 1931): 193–94.

The Negro Artist and
the Racial Mountain (1926)

In 1926, critic George Schuyler published in the "Nation" what one critic called his "acerbic dismissal of an African American 'racial and literary heritage'." Almost immediately Schuyler drew a response from younger Harlem writers, especially Langston Hughes. Citing the folkways of African American people, particularly concerning language and music, Hughes defended an archive of African American cultural sources. How sound is Hughes's defense?

A large portion of Hughes's manifesto focuses on the responsibility of the African American writer. Using the metaphor "racial mountain," Hughes suggests there are social and cultural obstacles before the writer. According to Hughes, as a creative writer himself he feels responsible to the "low-down folk." What does he say is his responsibility to the "smug" black bourgeoisie? When Hughes writes, "an artist must be free to choose what he does, but he must also never be afraid to do what he might choose," is his ideological position on truth and beauty a compliment or a challenge to DuBois's? Is there an implication of art for art's sake in Hughes's desire for individual expression?

Discuss Hughes as the cultural nationalist who has written: "We younger Negro artists who create now intend to express our individual dark-skinned selves without fear or shame. If white people are pleased, we are glad. If they are not, it doesn't matter. We know we are beautiful. And ugly too. . . . We build our temples for tomorrow . . . free within ourselves." In this quotation, is Hughes anticipating the cultural nationalist of the 1960s? Are seeds planted for the Black Arts movement in the 1960s?

One of the most promising of the young Negro poets said to me once, "I want to be a poet—not a Negro poet," meaning, I believe, "I want to write like a white poet"; meaning subconsciously, "I would like to be a white poet"; meaning behind that, "I would like to be white." And I was sorry the young man said that, for no great poet has ever been afraid of being himself. And I doubted then that, with his desire to run away spiritually from his race, this boy would ever be a great poet. But this is the mountain standing in the way of any true Negro art in America—this urge within the race toward whiteness, the desire to pour racial individuality into the mold of American standardization, and to be as little Negro and as much American as possible.

But let us look at the immediate background of this young poet. His family is of what I suppose one would call the Negro middle class: people who are by no means rich yet never uncomfortable nor hungry—smug, contented, respectable folk, members of the Baptist church. The father goes to work every morning. He is a chief steward at a large white club. The mother sometimes does fancy sewing or supervises parties for the rich families of the town. The children go to a mixed school. In the home they read white papers and magazines. And the mother often says "Don't be like niggers" when the children are bad. A frequent phrase from the father is, "Look how well a white man does things." And so the word white comes to be unconsciously a symbol of all virtues. It holds for the children beauty, morality, and money. The whisper of "I want to be white" runs silently through their minds. This young poet's home is, I believe, a fairly typical home of the colored middle class. One sees immediately how difficult it would be for an artist born in such a home to interest himself in interpreting the beauty of his own people. He is never taught to see that beauty. He is taught rather not to see it, or if he does, to be ashamed of it when it is not according to Caucasian patterns.

For racial culture the home of a self-styled "high-class" Negro has nothing better to offer. Instead there will perhaps be more aping of things white than in a less cultured or less wealthy home. The father is perhaps a doctor, lawyer, landowner, or politician. The mother may be a social worker, or a teacher, or she may do nothing and have a maid. Father is often dark but he has usually married the lightest woman he could find. The family attend a fashionable church where few really colored faces are to be found. And they themselves draw a color line. In the North they go to white theatres and white movies. And in the South they have at least two cars and house "like white folks." Nordic manners, Nordic faces, Nordic hair, Nordic art (if any), and an Episcopal heaven. A very high mountain indeed for the would-be racial artist to climb in order to discover himself and his people.

But then there are the low-down folks, the so-called common element, and they are the majority—may the Lord be praised! The people who have their sip of gin on Saturday nights and are not too important to themselves or the community, or too well fed, or too learned to watch the lazy world go round. They live on Seventh Street in Washington or State Street in Chicago and they do not particularly care whether they are like white folks or anybody else. Their joy runs, bang! into ecstasy. Their religion soars to a shout. Work maybe a little today, rest a little tomorrow. Play awhile. Sing awhile. O, let's dance! These common people are not afraid of spirituals, as for a long time their more intellectual brethren were, and jazz is their child. They furnish a wealth of colorful, distinctive material for any artist because they still hold their own individuality in the face of American standardizations. And perhaps these common people will give to the world its truly great Negro artist, the one who is not afraid to be himself. Whereas the better-class Negro would tell the artist what to do, the people at least let him alone when he does appear. And they are not ashamed of him—if they know he exists at all. And they accept what beauty is their own without question.

Certainly there is, for the American Negro artist who can escape the restrictions the more advanced among his own group would put upon him, a great field of unused material ready for his art. Without going outside his race, and even among the better classes with their "white" culture and conscious American manners, but still Negro enough to be different, there is sufficient matter to furnish a black artist with a lifetime of creative work. And when he chooses to touch on the relations between Negroes and whites in this country with their innumerable overtones and undertones surely, and especially for literature and the drama, there is an inexhaustible supply of themes at hand. To these the Negro artist can give his racial individuality, his heritage of rhythm and warmth, and his incongruous humor that so often, as in the Blues, becomes ironic laughter mixed with tears. But let us look again at the mountain.

A prominent Negro clubwoman in Philadelphia paid eleven dollars to hear Raquel Meller sing Andalusian popular songs. But she told me a few weeks before she would not think of going to hear "that woman," Clara Smith, a great black artist, sing Negro folksongs. And many an upper-class Negro church, even now, would not dream of employing a spiritual in its services. The drab melodies in white folks' hymnbooks are much to be preferred. "We want to worship the Lord correctly and quietly. We don't believe in 'shouting.' Let's be dull like the Nordics," they say, in effect.

The road for the serious black artist, then, who would produce a racial art is most certainly rocky and the mountain is high. Until recently he received almost no encouragement for his work from either white or colored people. The fine novels of Chesnutt go out of print with neither race noticing their passing. The quaint charm and humor of Dunbar's dialect verse brought to him, in his day, largely the same kind of encouragement one would give a sideshow freak (A colored man writing poetry! How odd!) or a clown (How amusing!).

The present vogue in things Negro, although it may do as much harm as good for the budding colored artist, has at least done this: it has brought him forcibly to the attention of his own people among whom for so long, unless the other race had noticed him beforehand, he was a prophet with little honor. I understand that Charles Gilpin acted for years in Negro theatres without any special acclaim from his own, but when Broadway gave him eight curtain calls, Negroes, too, began to beat a tin pan in his honor. I know a young colored writer, a manual worker by day, who had been writing well for the colored magazines for some years, but it was not until he recently broke into the white publications and his first book was accepted by a prominent New York publisher that the "best" Negroes in his city took the trouble to discover that he lived there. Then almost immediately they decided to give a grand dinner for him. But the society ladies were careful to whisper to his mother that perhaps she'd better not come. They were not sure she would have an evening gown.

The Negro artist works against an undertow of sharp criticism and mis-understanding from his own group and unintentional bribes from the whites. "Oh, be respectable, write about nice people, show how good we are," say the Negroes. "Be stereotyped, don't go too far, don't shatter our illusions about you, don't amuse us too seriously. We will pay you," say the whites. Both would have told Jean Toomer not to write *Cane*. The colored people did not praise it. The white people did not buy it. Most of the colored people who did read *Cane* hate it. They are afraid of it. Although the critics gave it good reviews the public remained indifferent. Yet (excepting the work of DuBois) *Cane* contains the finest prose written by a Negro in America. And like the singing of Robeson, it is truly racial.

But in spite of the Nordicized Negro intelligentsia and the desires of some white editors we have an honest American Negro literature already with us. Now I await the rise of the Negro theatre. Our folk music, having achieved world-wide fame, offers itself to the genius of the great individual American composer who is to come. And within the next decade I expect to see the work of a growing school of colored artists who paint and model the beauty of dark faces and create with new technique the expressions of their own soul-world. And the Negro dancers who will dance like flame and the singers who will continue to carry our songs to all who listen—they will be with us in even greater numbers tomorrow.

Most of my own poems are racial in theme and treatment, derived from the life I know. In many of them I try to grasp and hold some of the meanings and rhythms of jazz. I am as sincere as I know how to be in these poems and yet after every reading I answer questions like these from my own people: Do you think Negroes should always write about Negroes? I wish you wouldn't read some of your poems to white folks. How do you find anything interest-ing in a place like a cabaret? Why do you write about black people? You aren't black. What makes you do so many jazz poems?

But jazz to me is one of the inherent expressions of Negro life in Amer-ica; the eternal tom-tom beating in the Negro soul—the tom-tom of revolt against weariness in a white world, a world of subway trains, and work, work, work; the tom-tom of joy and laughter, and pain swallowed in a smile. Yet the Philadelphia clubwoman is ashamed to say that her race created it and she does not like me to write about it. The old subconscious "white is best" runs through her mind. Years of study under white teachers, a lifetime of white books, pictures, and papers, and white manners, morals, and Puritan stan-dards made her dislike the spirituals. And now she turns up her nose at jazz and all its manifestations—likewise almost everything else distinctly racial. She doesn't care for the Winold Reiss portraits of Negroes because they are "too Negro." She does not want a true picture of herself from anybody. She wants the artist to flatter her, to make the white world believe that all Negroes are as smug and as near white in soul as she wants to be. But, to my mind, it is the duty of the younger Negro artist, if he accepts any duties at all from outsiders, to change through the force of his art that old whispering "I want to be white," hidden in the aspirations of his people, to "Why should I want to be white? I am a Negro—and beautiful!"

So I am ashamed for the black poet who says, "I want to be a poet, not a Negro poet," as though his own racial world were not as interesting as any other world. I am ashamed, too, for the colored artist who runs from the painting of Negro faces to the painting of sunsets after the manner of the academicians because he fears the strange un-whiteness of his own features. An artist must be free to choose what he does, certainly, but he must also never be afraid to do what he might choose.

Let the blare of Negro jazz bands and the bellowing voice of Bessie Smith singing Blues penetrate the closed ears of the colored near-intellectual until they listen and perhaps understand. Let Paul Robeson singing "Water Boy," and Rudolph Fisher writing about the streets of Harlem, and Jean Toomer holding the heart of Georgia in his hands, and Aaron Douglas drawing strange black fantasies cause the smug Negro middle class to turn from their white, respectable, ordinary books and papers to catch a glimmer of their own beauty. We younger Negro artists who create now intend to express our individual dark-skinned selves without fear or shame. If white people are pleased we are glad. If they are not, it doesn't matter. We know we are beautiful. And ugly too. The tom-tom cries and the tom-tom laughs. If colored people are pleased we are glad. If they are not, their displeasure doesn't matter either. We build our temples for tomorrow, strong as we know how, and we stand on top of the mountain, free within ourselves.

Suggested Readings with Similar Theme:

Schuyler, George S. "The Negro Art Hokum." *Nation* (1926): 662–63.

Chesnutt, Charles W. "The Negro in Art: How Shall He Be Portrayed?" *Crisis* 33, no. 1 (November 1926): 28–29.

Thurman, Wallace. "Negro Artists and the Negro." *New Republic* 52 (31 August 1927): 37–39.

Johnson, James Weldon. "The Dilemma of the Negro Author." *American Mercury* 15 (1928): 477–81.

Thurman, Wallace. "High, Low, Past and Present." *Harlem* 1, no. 1 (November 1928): 31–32, 35.

Hughes, Langston, and Arna Bontemps, eds. Introduction to *The Book of Negro Folklore*. New York: Dodd, Mead and Company, 1958.

Long, Richard A. "Renaissance Personality: An Interview with George Schuyler." *Black World* 25, no. 4 (February 1976): 68–78.

ALAIN LOCKE

Art or Propaganda? (1928)

Locke, who has a defining voice during the Harlem Renaissance, defines African American literary art when he states what it is not: "art for art's sake." Henry James once wrote that "Art is all life, all observation, all vision." Locke wrote that there should be "no mere idle acceptance of art for art's sake but deep realization of {its} fundamental purposes . . . as living art." What is specifically being stated about the function of American literature? About African American literature? As rhetor, Locke uses biblical and literary allusions and grammatical language, such as the repetition of the words "self," "prophets," and "spirit" to describe the artistic freedom required of African American artists. Translate the ideological positions of Locke and DuBois into aesthetic ones. Do the two men create different schools of philosophical thought in African American literary criticism during the 1920s?

Artistically it is the one fundamental question for us today.—Art or Propaganda. Which? Is this more the generation of the prophet or that of the poet; shall our intellectual and cultural leadership preach and exhort or sing? I believe we are at that interesting moment when the prophet becomes the poet and when prophecy becomes the expressive song, the chant of fulfillment. We have had too many Jeremiahs, major and minor;—and too much of the drab wilderness. My chief objection to propaganda, apart from its besetting sin of monotony and disproportion, is that it perpetuates the position of group inferiority even in crying out against it. For it lives and speaks under the shadow of a dominant majority whom it harangues, cajoles, threatens or supplicates. It is too extroverted for balance or poise or inner dignity and self-respect. Art in the best sense is rooted in self-expression and whether naive or sophisticated is self-contained. In our spiritual growth genius and talent must more and more choose the role of group expression, or even at times the role of free individualistic expression,—in a word must choose art and put aside propaganda.

The literature and art of the younger generation already reflects this shift of psychology, this regeneration of spirit. David should be its patron saint: it should confront the Philistines with its five smooth pebbles fearlessly. There is more strength in a confident camp than in a threatened enemy. The sense of inferiority must be innerly compensated, self-conviction must supplant self-justification, and in the dignity of this attitude a convinced minority must conform a condescending majority. Art cannot completely accomplish this, but I believe it can lead the way.

Our espousal of art thus becomes no mere idle acceptance of "art for art's sake," or cultivation of the last decadences of the over-civilized, but rather a deep realization of the fundamental purpose of art and of its function as a tap root of vigorous, flourishing living. Not all of our younger writers are deep enough in the sub-soil of their native materials—too many are pot-plants seeking a forced growth according to the exotic tastes of a pampered and decadent public. It is the art of the people that needs to be cultivated, not the art of the coteries. Propaganda itself is preferable to shallow, truckling imitation. Negro things may reasonably be a fad for others; for us they must be a religion. Beauty, however, is its best priest and psalms will be more effective than sermons.

To date we have had little sustained art unsubsidized by propaganda; we must admit this debt to these foster agencies. The three journals which have been vehicles of most of our artistic expressions have been the avowed organs of social movements and organized social programs. All our purely artistic publications have been sporadic. There is all the greater need then for a sustained vehicle of free and purely artistic expression. If HARLEM should happily fill this need, it will perform an honorable, and constructive service. I hope it may, but should it not, the need remains and the path toward it will at least be advanced a little.

We need, I suppose in addition to art some substitute for propaganda. What shall that be? Surely we must take some cognizance of the fact that we live at the centre of a social problem. Propaganda at least nurtured some form of serious social discussion, and social discussion was necessary, is still necessary. On this side: the difficulty and shortcoming of propaganda is its partisanship. It is one-sided and often prejudging. Should we not then have a journal of free discussion, open to all sides of the problem and to all camps of belief? Difficult, that,—but intriguing. Even if it has to begin on the note of dissent and criticism and assume Menckenian scepticism to escape the commonplaces of conformity. Yet, I hope we shall not remain at this negative pole. Can we not cultivate truly free and tolerant discussion, almost Socratically minded for the sake of truth? After Beauty, let Truth come into the Renaissance picture,—a later cue, but a welcome one. This may be premature, but one hopes not,—for eventually it must come and if we can accomplish that, instead of having to hang our prophets, we can silence them or change their lamentations to song with a Great Fulfillment.

Suggested Readings with Similar Theme:

Thurman, Wallace. "Art and Propaganda." *Messenger* 6 (April 1924): 111.

Johnson, James Weldon. Foreword to *Challenge* 1, no. 1 (March 1934): 1.

Hurston, Zora Neale. "Characteristics of Negro Expression." In *Mules and Men*. Philadelphia: Lippincott, 1935.

STERLING A. BROWN

From "Our Literary Audience" (1930)

In his discussion of the responsibilities of the African American audience, Brown reveals "certain fallacies." According to Brown, the African American audience has been stigmatized by images that were created by white writers, such as "brute," "comic," "exotic," etc. But what are the dangers when an audience attempts to prescribe standards for literary art in order to alter its negative images? How might such actions by the audience do great harm and perhaps render a "death warrant" to literature? Why does Brown address his audience as "We"? Define "a fit African American audience." How does Brown echo DuBois in his search for truth about African American culture and life? How does he echo Hughes in his call for artists to be free to create the beautiful and ugly too? Brown begins and ends his essay with a haunting warning: "Without great audiences we cannot have great literature." As affective rhetoric, what is the art of Brown's persuasion? Refer to Ralph Ellison's little man in the Chehaw Station elsewhere in this collection and compare his discussion of audience with Brown's.

I am holding no brief for any writer, or any coterie of writers, or any racial credo. I have as yet, no logs to roll, and no brickbats to heave. I have however a deep concern with the development of a literature worthy of our past, and of our destiny; without which literature certainly, we can never come to much. I have a deep concern with the development of an audience worthy of such a literature.

"Without great audiences we cannot have great poets." Whitman's trenchant commentary needs stressing today, universally. But particularly do we as a racial group need it? There is a great harm that we can do our incipient literature. With a few noteworthy exceptions, we are doing that harm, most effectually. It is hardly because of malice, it has its natural causes; but it is nonetheless destructive.

We are not a reading folk (present company of course forever excepted). There are reasons, of course, but even with those considered, it remains true that we do not read nearly so much as we should. I imagine our magazine editors and our authors if they chose, could bear this out. . . .

When we do condescend to read books about Negroes, we seem to read in order to confute. These are sample ejaculations: "But we're not all like that." "Why does he show such a level of society? We have better Negroes than that to write about." "What effect will this have on the opinions of white people." (Alas, for the ofay, forever ensconced in the lumber yard!) . . . "More dialect. Negroes don't use dialect anymore." Or, if that sin is too patent against the Holy Ghost of Truth—"Negroes of my class don't use dialect anyway" (which mought be so, and then again, which moughtn't).

Our criticism is vitiated therefore in many ways. Certain fallacies I have detected within at least the last six years are these:

> We look upon Negro books regardless of the author's intention, as representative of all Negroes, i.e. as sociological documents.
> We insist that Negro books must be idealistic, optimistic traces for race advertisement.
> We are afraid of truth telling, or satire.
> We criticize from the point of view of bourgeois America, or racial apologists.

In this division there are, of course, overlappings. Moreover all of these fallacies might be attributed to a single cause, such as an apologistic chip on the shoulder attitude, imposed by circumstance; an arising snobbishness; a delayed Victorianism; or a following of the wrong lead. Whatever may be the primary impulse, the fact remains that if these standards of criticism are perpetuated, and our authors are forced to heed them, we thereby dwarf their stature as interpreters. . . .

Books galore have been written, still are written with a definite inclusive thesis, purposing generally to discredit us. We have seen so much of the razor toting, gin guzzling, chicken stealing Negro; or the pompous walking dictionary spouting malapropisms; we have heard so much of "learned" tomes, establishing our characteristics, "appropriativeness," short memory for joys and griefs, imitativeness, and general inferiority. We are certainly fed up.

This has been so much our experience that by now it seems we should be able to distinguish between individual and race portraiture, i.e., between literature on the one hand and pseudoscience and propaganda on the other. These last we have with us always. From Dixon's melodramas down to Roark Bradford's funny stories, from Thomas Nelson Page's "Ole Virginny retainers" to Bowyer Campbell's Black Sadie the list is long and notorious. One doesn't wish to underestimate this prejudice. It is ubiquitous and dangerous. When it raises its head it is up to us to strike, and strike hard. But when it doesn't exist, there is no need of tilting at windmills.

In some cases the author's design to deal with the entire race is explicit, as in Vachel Lindsay's *The Congo* subtitled "A Study of the Negro Race"; in other cases, implicit. But an effort at understanding the work should enable us to detect whether his aim is to show one of ours, or all of us (in the latter case, whatever his freedom from bias, doomed to failure). We have had such practice that we should be rather able at this detection.

We have had so much practice that we are thin-skinned. Anybody would be. And it is natural that when pictures of us were almost entirely concerned with making us out to be either brutes or docile housedogs, i.e., infrahuman, we should have replied by making ourselves out superhuman. It is natural that we should insist that the pendulum be swung back to its other extreme. Life and letters follow the law of the pendulum. Yet, for the lover of the truth, neither extreme is desirable. And now, if we are coming of age, the truth should be our major concern.

This is not a disagreement with the apologistic belief in propaganda. Propaganda must be counter checked by propaganda. But let it be found where it should be found, in books explicitly propagandistic, in our newspapers, which perhaps must balance white playing up of crime with our own playing up of achievement; in the teaching of our youth that there is a great deal in our racial heritage of which we may be justly proud. Even so, it must be artistic, based on truth, not on exaggeration.

Propaganda, however legitimate, can speak no louder than the truth. Such a cause as ours needs no dressing up. The honest, unvarnished truth, presented as it is, is plea enough for us, in the unbiased courts of mankind. But such courts do not exist? Then what avails thumping the tub? Will that call them into being? Let the truth speak. There has never been a better persuader.

Since we need truthful delineation, let us not add every artist whose picture of us may not be flattering to our long list of traducers. We stand in no need today of such a defense mechanism. If a white audience today needs assurance that we are not all thievish or cowardly or vicious, it is composed of half wits, and can never be convinced anyway. Certainly we can never expect to justify ourselves by heated denials of charges which perhaps have not even been suggested in the work we are denouncing. . . .

The best rejoinder to the fuming criticism "But all Negroes aren't like that" should be "Well, what of it. Who said so?" or better, "Why bring that up?" . . . But if alas we must go out of our group for authority, let this be said, "All Frenchmen aren't like Emma Bovary but *Madame Bovary* is a great book; all Russians aren't like Vronsky, but *Anna Karenina* is a great book; all Norwegians aren't like Oswald but *Ghosts* is a great play." Books about us may not be true of all of us; but that has nothing to do with their worth. . . .

Each artist to his taste. Assuredly let a writer deal with that to which he can best give convincing embodiment and significant interpretation. To insist otherwise is to hamper the artist, and to add to the stereotyping which has unfortunately, been too apparent in books about us. To demand on the other hand that our books exclude treatment of any character other than the "successful" Negro is a death warrant to literature. . . .

To recapitulate. It is admitted that some books about us are definite propaganda; that in the books about us, the great diversity of our life has not been shown (which should not be surprising when we consider how recent is this movement toward realistic portraiture), that dramas about the Negro character are even yet few and far between. It is insisted that these books should be judged as works of literature; i.e., by their fidelity to the truth of their particular characters, not as representative pictures of all Negroes; that they should not be judged at all by the level of society shown, not at all as good or bad according to the "morality" of the characters; should not be judged as propaganda when there is no evidence, explicit or implicit, that propaganda was intended. Furthermore those who go to literature as an entertaining building up of dream worlds, purely for idle amusement, should not pass judgment at all on books which aim at fidelity to truth.

One doesn't wish to be pontifical about this matter of truth. "What is truth, asked Pontius Pilate, and would not stay for an answer." The answer would have been difficult. But it surely is not presumptuous for a Negro, in Twentieth Century America, to say that showing the world in idealistic rose colors is not fidelity to truth. We have got to look at our times and at ourselves searchingly and honestly; surely there is nothing of the farfetched in that injunction. . . .

Negro artists have enough to contend with in getting a hearing, in isolation, in the peculiar problems that beset all artists, in the mastery of form and in the understanding of life. It would be no less disastrous to demand of them that they shall evade truth, that they shall present us a Pollyanna philosophy of life, that, to suit our prejudices, they shall lie. It would mean that as self-respecting artists they could no longer exist.

The question might be asked, why should they exist? Such a question deserves no reply. It merely serves to bring us, alas, to the point at which I started.

Without great audiences we cannot have great literature.

Suggested Readings with Similar Theme:

Bontemps, Arna. "The Negro Renaissance: Jean Toomer and the Harlem Writers of the 1920s." In *Anger and Beyond: The Negro Writer in the United States,* edited by Herbert Hill, 20–36. New York: Harper and Row, 1966.

Hurston, Zora Neale. "My People! My People!" In *Dust Tracks on a Road: An Autobiography.* Edited and with an introduction by Robert E. Hemenway. Urbana: University of Illinios Press, 1984.

STERLING A. BROWN

Negro Characters as Seen by White Authors
(1933)

How does Brown justify the following statement: "{T}he sincere, sensitive artist, will-
ing to go beneath the cliches of popular belief to get at an underlying reality, will be
wary of confining a race's entire character to a half-dozen narrow grooves"? Explain
how Brown indicts American literature writers, particularly those of the plantation
literary era, for the perpetuation of the following stereotype characters: the contented
slave, the wretched freeman, the comic Negro, the brute Negro, the tragic mulatto, the
local color Negro, and the exotic primitive. Do such stereotype characters continue to
exist in contemporary media? Compare black dialect that was written by early white
writers with black dialect found in articles by Smitherman, Gates, and Henderson.
How does the mutilation of black southern and urban dialect by white writers substan-
tiate Brown's argument regarding true representation of black life? How does Trudier
Harris echo Brown regarding white critics writing about "the mythical Negro life"?
How does bell hooks echo Brown regarding the "colonial image" that is being perpetu-
ated by white and some black writers (in print and in film)? What, then, is the
responsibility of all writers (black and white) writing about African American life?

There are three types of Negroes, says Roark Bradford, in his sprightly manner: "the nigger, the 'colored person,' and the Negro—upper case N." In his
foreword to *Ol' Man Adam an' His Chillun,* the source from which Marc Connelly drew the *Green Pastures,* and a book causing the author to be considered,
in some circles, a valid interpreter of *the* Negro, Roark Bradford defines *the*
Negro's character and potentialities. The Negro, he says, is the race leader,
not too militant, concerned more with economic independence than with civil
equality. The colored person, "frequently of mixed blood, loathes the blacks
and despises the whites. . . . Generally he inherits the weaknesses of both
races and seldom inherits the strength of either. He has the black man's emotions and the white man's inhibitions." Together with the "poor white trash"
it is the "colored persons" who perpetuate racial hatreds and incite race riots
and lynchings. "The nigger" interests Mr. Bradford more than the rest. He is
indolent, entirely irresponsible, shiftless, the bugaboo of Anglo-Saxon ideals,
a poor fighter and a poor hater, primitively emotional and uproariously funny.
Such are the "original" contributions of Mr. Bradford, who states modestly
that, in spite of the Negro's penchant to lying:

I believe I know them pretty well. I was born on a plantation that was worked by them; I was nursed by one as an infant and I played with one when I was growing up. I have watched them at work in the fields, in the levee camps, and on the river. I have watched them at home, in church, at their picnics and their funerals.

All of this, he believes, gives him license to step forth as their interpreter and repeat stereotypes time-hallowed in the South. It doesn't. Mr. Bradford's stories remain highly amusing; his generalizations about *the* Negro remain a far better analysis of a white man than of *the* Negro. We see that, even in pontifical moments, one white Southerner cannot escape being influenced by current folk-beliefs.

Mr. Bradford's views have been restated at some length to show how obviously dangerous it is to rely upon literary artists when they advance themselves as sociologists and ethnologists. Mr. Bradford's easy pigeon-holing of an entire race into three small compartments is a familiar phenomenon in American literature, where the Indian, the Mexican, the Irishman, and the Jew have been similarly treated. Authors are too anxious to have it said, "Here is *the* Negro," rather than here are a few Negroes whom I have seen. If one wishes to learn of Negro individuals observed from very specialized points of view, American literature can help him out. Some books will shed a great deal of light upon Negro experience. But if one wishes to learn of *the* Negro, it would be best to study *the* Negro himself; a study that might result in the discovery that *the* Negro is more difficult to find than the countless human beings called Negroes.

The Negro has met with as great injustice in American literature as he has in American life. The majority of books about Negroes merely stereotype Negro character. It is the purpose of this paper to point out the prevalence and history of these stereotypes. Those considered important enough for separate classification, although overlappings *do* occur, are seven in number: (1) The Contented Slave, (2) The Wretched Freeman, (3) The Comic Negro, (4) The Brute Negro, (5) The Tragic Mulatto, (6) The Local Color Negro, and (7) The Exotic Primitive.

A detailed evaluation of each of these is impracticable because of limitations of space. It can be said, however, that all of these stereotypes are marked either by exaggeration or omissions; that they all agree in stressing the Negro's divergence from an Anglo-Saxon norm to the flattery of the latter; they could all be used, as they probably are, as justification of racial proscription; they all illustrate dangerous specious generalizing from a few particulars recorded by a single observer from a restricted point of view—which is itself generally dictated by the desire to perpetuate a stereotype. All of these stereotypes are abundantly to be found in American literature, and are generally accepted as contributions to true racial understanding. Thus one critic, setting out imposingly to discuss "the Negro character" in American literature, can still say, unabashedly, that *"The whole range of the Negro character is revealed thoroughly,"* in one twenty-six-line sketch by Joel Chandler Harris of Br'er Fox and Br'er Mud Turtle.

The writer of this essay does not consider everything a stereotype that shows up the weaknesses of Negro character; sometimes the stereotype makes the Negro appear too virtuous. Nor does he believe the stereotypes of contented slaves and buffoons are to be successfully balanced by pictures of Negroes who are unbelievably intellectual, noble, self-sacrificial, and faultless. Any stereotyping is fatal to great, or even to convincing literature. Furthermore, he believes that he has considered to be stereotypes only those patterns whose frequent and tedious recurrence can be demonstrably proved by even a cursory acquaintance with the literature of the subject.

THE CONTENTED SLAVE

"Massa make de darkies lub him 'Case he was so kind. . . ."

(Stephen Foster)

The first lukewarm stirrings of abolitionary sentiment in the South were chilled with Eli Whitney's invention of the cotton gin at the close of the 18th Century. Up until this time the *raison d'etre* of slavery had not been so powerful. But now there was a way open to quick wealth; Cotton was crowned King, and a huge army of black servitors was necessary to keep him upon the throne; considerations of abstract justice had to give way before economic expediency. A complete rationale of slavery was evolved.

One of the most influential of the authorities defending slavery was President Dew of William and Mary College, who stated, in 1832,

> . . . slavery had been the condition of all ancient culture, that Christianity approved servitude, and that the law of Moses had both assumed and positively established slavery. . . . It is the order of nature and of God that the being of superior faculties and knowledge, and therefore of superior power, should control and dispose of those who are inferior. It is as much in the order of nature that men should enslave each other as that other animals should prey upon each other.

The pamphlet of this young teacher was extensively circulated, and was substantiated by Chancellor Harper of the University of South Carolina in 1838:

> Man is born to subjection. . . . The proclivity of the natural man is to domineer or to be subservient. . . . If there are sordid, servile, and laborious offices to be performed, is it not better that there should be sordid, servile, and laborious beings to perform them?

The economic argument had frequent proponents; an ex-governor of Virginia showed that, although Virginia was denied the tremendous prosperity accruing from cotton raising, it was still granted the opportunity to profit from selling Negroes to the far South. Sociologists and anthropologists hastened forward with proof of the Negro's three-fold inferiority: physically (except for this adaptability to cotton fields and rice swamps), mentally, and morally. Theologists advanced the invulnerable arguments from the Bible; in one of the "Bible Defenses of Slavery" we read: "The curse of Noah upon *Ham,* had a *general* and *interminable* application to the whole Hamite race, in placing them under a *peculiar* liability of being enslaved by the races of the two other brothers."

The expressions of these dominant ideas in the fiction and poetry of the period did not lag far behind. In fact, one influential novel was among the leaders of the van, for in 1832, the year in which Professor Dew stated the argument that was to elevate him to the presidency of William and Mary College, John P. Kennedy published a work that was to make him one of the most widely read and praised authors of the Southland. His ideas of the character of the Negro and of slavery are in fundamental agreement with those of Dew and Harper. According to F. P. Gaines, in *The Southern Plantation,* Kennedy's *Swallow Barn* has the historical significance of starting the plantation tradition, a tradition hoary and mildewed in our own day, but by no means moribund.

Swallow Barn is an idyllic picture of slavery on a tidewater plantation. The narrator, imagined to be from the North (Kennedy himself was from Tidewater Maryland), comes to Virginia, expecting to see a drastic state of affairs. Instead, he finds a kindly patriarchy and grateful, happy slaves. After vignettes of the Negro's laziness, mirth, vanity, improvidence, done with some charm and, for a Southern audience, considerable persuasiveness, the "Northern" narrator concludes:

> I am quite sure they never could become a happier people than I find them here.... No tribe of people has ever passed from barbarism to civilization whose ... progress has been more secure from harm, more genial to their character, or better supplied with mild and beneficent guardianship, adapted to the actual state of their intellectual feebleness, than the Negroes of *Swallow Barn.* And, from what I can gather, it is pretty much the same on the other estates in this region.

Shortly after the publication of *Swallow Barn,* Edgar Allan Poe wrote:

> ... we must take into consideration the peculiar character (I may say the peculiar nature) of the Negro.... [Some believe that Negroes] are, like ourselves, the sons of Adam and must, therefore, have like passions and wants and feelings and tempers in all respects. This we deny and appeal to the knowledge of all who know.... We shall take leave to speak as of things *in esse,* in a degree of

loyal devotion on the part of the slave to which the white man's heart is a stranger, and of the master's reciprocal feeling of parental attachment to his humble dependent. . . . That these sentiments in the breast of the Negro and his master are stronger than they would be under like circumstances between individuals of the white race, we believe.

In *The Gold-Bug,* Poe shows this reciprocal relationship between Jupiter, a slave, and his master. Southern fiction of the thirties and forties supported the thesis of Kennedy and Poe without being so explicit. The mutual affection of the races, the slave's happiness with his status, and his refusal to accept freedom appear here and there, but the books were dedicated less to the defense of the peculiar institution than to entertainment. William Gilmore Simms, for instance, includes in *The Yemassee,* a novel published in the same year as *Swallow Barn,* the typical pro-slavery situation of a slave's refusing freedom: "I d—n to h—ll, maussa, ef I guine to be free!" roared the *adhesive* black, in a tone of unrestrainable determination. But the burden of this book is not pro-slavery; Hector earns his freedom by the unslavish qualities of physical prowess, foresight, and courage in battle.

In 1853, Simms, in joining forces with Dew and Harper in the *Pro-Slavery Argument,* writes: "Slavery has elevated the Negro from savagery. The black man's finer traits of fidelity and docility were encouraged in his servile position. . . ." Simms turned from cursory references to slavery to ardent pro-slavery defense, in company with other novelists of the South, for a perfectly definite reason. The abolitionary attacks made by men like Garrison had taken the form of pamphlets, and these had been answered in kind. The publication of *Uncle Tom's Cabin* in 1851, however, showed that the abolitionists had converted the novel into a powerful weapon. Pro-slavery authors were quick to take up this weapon, although their wielding of it was without the power of Harriet Beecher Stowe. *Swallow Barn* was reissued in 1851, and "besides the numerous controversial pamphlets and articles in periodicals there were no fewer than fourteen pro-slavery novels and one long poem published in the three years (1852–54) following the appearance of *Uncle Tom's Cabin.*"

These novels are all cut out of the same cloth. Like *Swallow Barn,* they omit the economic basis of slavery, and minimize "the sordid, servile and laborious offices" which Chancellor Harper had considered the due of "sordid, servile, and laborious beings." The pro-slavery authors use the first adjective only in considering free Negroes, or those who, by some quirk of nature, are disobedient; admit the second completely; and deny the third. Slavery to all of them is a beneficent guardianship, the natural and inevitable state for a childish people.

There is very little reference to Negroes working in the fields: even then they are assigned to easy tasks which they lazily perform to the tune of slave melodies. They are generally described as "leaving the fields." They are allowed to have, for additional provisions and huckstering, their own garden-plots, which they attend in their abundant leisure. Their holidays are described at full length: the corn huskings, barbecuing, Yuletide parties, and hunting the possum by the light of a kindly moon.

In *Life at the South, or Uncle Tom's Cabin as It Is* (1852), Uncle Tom, out of hurt vanity, but not for any more grievous cause, runs away. His wife, Aunt Dinah, although loving Tom, realizes that her greater loyalty is due to her master, and not to her errant spouse, and refuses to escape with him. Tom, after experiencing the harshness of the unfeeling North, begs to return to slavery. In *The Planter's Northern Bride,* the bride, having come to the slave South with misgivings, is quickly converted to an enthusiast for slavery, since it presents "an aspect so tender and affectionate." One fears that the bride is not unpartisan, however, since her appearance on the plantation elicited wild cries of worship, and her beloved husband is a great enthnologist, proving that the Negro's peculiar skull and skin were decreed by the divine fiat so that he could pick cotton. In *The Yankee Slave Dealer,* the meddling abolitionist cannot persuade any slaves to run off with him except a half-witted rogue. One slave recited to him *verbatim* a miniature *Bible Defence of Slavery,* citing the book of the Bible, the chapter, and the verse. In *The Hireling and The Slave,* William J. Grayson, "poet laureate" of South Carolina, contrasts the lot of the industrial worker of the North with that of the slave. Gems of this widely read poetical disquisition follow:

> And yet the life, so unassailed by care.
> So blessed with moderate work, with ample fare,
> With all the good the starving pauper needs,
> The happier slave on each plantation leads. . . . (p. 50)
> And Christian slaves may challenge as their own,
> The blessings claimed in fabled states alone. . . . (p. 50)

This pattern of the joyous contentment of the slave in a paradisiacal bondage persisted and was strongly reinforced in Reconstruction days. If it was no longer needed for the defense of a tottering institution, it was needed for reasons nearly as exigent. Ancestor worshippers, the sons of a fighting generation, remembering bitterly the deaths or sufferings of their fathers, became elegists of a lost cause and cast a golden glow over the plantation past; unreconstructed "fire-eaters," determined to resurrect slavery as far as they were able, needed as a cardinal principle the belief that Negroes were happy as slaves, and hopelessly unequipped for freedom. Both types were persuasive, the first because the romantic idealizing of the past will always be seductive to a certain large group of readers, and the second because the sincere unremitting harping upon one argument will finally make it seem plausible. We find, therefore, that whereas *Uncle Tom's Cabin* had triumphed in the antebellum controversy, the pro-slavery works of Page, Russell, and Harris swept the field in Reconstruction days. It is from these last skillful authors undeniably acquainted with Negro folk-like, and affectionate toward certain aspects of it, that the American reading public as a whole has accepted the delusion of the Negro as contented slave, entertaining child, and docile ward.

Mutual affection between the races is a dominant theme. Thus, Irwin Russell, the first American poet to treat Negro life in folk speech, has his exslave rhapsodizing about his "Mahsr John." "Washintum an' Franklum . . . wuzn't nar a one . . . come up to Mahsr John":

> Well times is changed. De war it come an' sot de niggers free
> An' now ol' Mahsr John ain't hardly wuf as much as me;
> He had to pay his debts, an' so his lan' is mos'ly gone—
> An' I declar' I's sorry for my pore ol' Mahsr John

The volume has many other references to the slave's docility toward, and worship of his master.

Irwin Russell implies throughout that the Southern white best understands how to treat the Negro. Perhaps this is one reason for Joel Chandler Harris' praise:

> But the most wonderful thing about the dialect poetry of Irwin Russell is his accurate conception of the negro character. . . . I do not know where could be found today a happier or a more perfect representation of negro character.

On reading Russell's few poems, one is struck by the limited gamut of characteristics allowed to Negroes. Inclined to the peccadilloes of cheating, lying easily; a good teller of comic stories, a child of mirth, his greatest hardship that of being kicked about by refractory mules, and his deepest emotion, compassion for his master's lost estate—surely this is hardly a "perfect" representation of even Negro folk character?

Thomas Nelson Page followed Russell's lead in poetry. In the poems of *Befo' De War,* Page puts into the mouths of his Negroes yearnings for the old days and expressions of the greatest love for old marster. One old slave welcomes death if it will replace him in old "Marster's service." Old Jack entrusts his life-earnings to his son to give to young "Marster," since the latter can't work and needs them more.

In most of Page's widely influential stories, there is the stock situation of the lifelong devotion of master and body-servant. In *Marse Chan,* old "Marse" is blinded in rescuing a slave from a burning barn. Sam accompanies his young Marse Chan to the war, his devotion overcoming "racial cowardice" to such a degree that he rides to the very cannon's mouth with him, and brings back his master's body. Of slavery, Sam speaks thus:

> Dem wuz good old times, marster—de bes, Sam ever see! Dey wuz, in fac'!
> Niggers didn't hed Nothin 't all to do—jes hed to 'ten to de feedin' an' cleanin'

de hosses, an' doin' what de marster tell 'em to do; an' when dey wuz sick, dey had things sont 'em out de house, an' de same doctor come to see 'em what ten' do de white folks when dey wuz po'ly. D'yar warn' no trouble nor nothin.

Over all his fiction there is the reminiscent melancholy of an exiled Adam, banished by a flaming sword—wielded not by Michael but by a Yankee devil, from what was truly an Eden. In *The Negro: The Southerner's Problem,* we read:

In fact, the ties of pride were such that it was often remarked that the affection of the slaves was stronger toward the whites than toward their own offspring.

And in the same book there is an apostrophe to the "mammy" that is a worthy forerunner of the bids so many orators make for interracial good-will, and of the many remunerative songs that emerge from Tin Pan Alley.

Joel Chandler Harris is better known for his valuable contribution to literature and folk-lore in recording the Uncle Remus stories than for his aid in perpetuation of the "plantation Negro" stereotype. Nevertheless, a merely cursory study of Uncle Remus' character would reveal his close relationship to the "Caesars," "Hectors," "Pompeys," et al. of the pro-slavery novel, and to Page's "Uncle Jack" and "Uncle Billy." In Uncle Remus philosophizing about the old days of slavery there is still the wistful nostalgia. Harris comments, "In Middle Georgia the relations between master and slave were as perfect as they could be under the circumstances." This might mean a great deal, or nothing, but it is obvious from other words of Harris that, fundamentally, slavery was to him a kindly institution, and the Negro was contented. Slavery was:

. . . in some of its aspects far more beautiful and inspiring than *any* of the relations between employers and the employed in this day.

George Washington Cable, although more liberal in his views upon the Negro than his Southern contemporaries, gives an example of the self-abnegating servant in *Posson Jone'.* This slave uses his wits to safeguard his master. A goodly proportion of the Negro servants are used to solve the complications of their "white-folks." They are in a long literary tradition—that of the faithful, clever servant—and they probably are just as true to Latin prototypes as to real Negroes. In the works of F. Hopkinson Smith, Harry Stilwell Edwards, and in Maurice Thompson's *Balance of Power,* we have this appearance of a black *deus ex machina.*

To deal adequately with the numerous books of elegiac reminiscence of days "befo' de war" would be beyond the scope and purpose of this essay. The tone of them all is to be found in such sad sentences as these:

Aunt Phebe, Uncle Tom, Black Mammy, Uncle Gus, Aunt Jonas, Uncle Isom, and all the rest—who shall speak all your virtues or enshrine your simple faith and fidelity? It is as impossible as it is to describe the affection showered upon you by those whom you called "Marster" and "Mistis."

Ambrose Gonzales grieves that "the old black folk are going fast" with the passing of the "strict but kindly discipline of slavery," yearning, in Tennysonian accents, "for the tender grace of a day that is dead."

Although the realism of today is successfully discounting the sentimentalizing of the Old South, there are still many contemporary manifestations of the tradition. Hergesheimer, arch-romanticist that he is, writes that he would be happy to pay with everything the wasted presence holds for the return of the pastoral civilization based on slavery.

Donald Davidson, a Tennessee poet, has written this:

> Black man, when you and I were young together,
> We knew each other's hearts. Though I am no longer
> A child, and you perhaps unfortunately
> Are no longer a child, we still understand
> Better maybe than others. There is the wall
> Between us, anciently erected. Once
> It might have been crossed, men say. But now I cannot
> Forget that I was master, and you can hardly
> Forget that you were slave. We did not build
> The ancient wall, but there it painfully is.
> Let us not bruise our foreheads on the wall.

Ol' Massa's People, by Orlanda Kay Armstrong, is one of the most recent of the books in which exslaves speak—as in Page apparently with their master's voice—their praise of slavery. The theme seems inexhaustible; in the February issue of the *Atlantic Monthly* it is restated in nearly the words that have already been quoted. Designed originally to defend slavery, it is now a convenient argument for those wishing to keep "the Negro in his place"—out of great love for him, naturally—believing that he will be happier so.

THE WRETCHED FREEMAN

"Go tell Marse Linkum, to tek his freedom back."

As a foil to the contented slave, pro-slavery authors set up another puppet— the wretched free Negro. He was necessary for the argument. Most of the pro-slavery novels paid a good deal of attention to his degradation. Either the novelist interpolated a long disquisition on the disadvantages of his state both to the country and to himself, or had his happy slaves fear contact with him as with a plague.

In *Life at the South, or Uncle Tom's Cabin as It Is,* Uncle Tom experiences harsh treatment from unfeeling Northern employers, sees Negroes frozen to death in snow storms, and all in all learns that the North and freedom is no stopping place for him. In *The Yankee Slave Dealer,* the slaves are insistent upon the poor lot of free Negroes. In *The Planter's Northern Bride,* Crissy runs away from freedom in order to be happy again in servitude. Grayson in *The Hireling and The Slave* prophesies thus:

> Such, too, the fate the Negro must deplore
> If slavery guards his subject race no more,
> If by weak friends or vicious counsels led
> To change his blessings for the hireling's bread. . . .
> There in the North in suburban dens and human sties,
> In foul excesses sung, the Negro lies;
> A moral pestilence to taint and stain.
> His life a curse, his death a social gain,
> Debased, despised, the Northern pariah knows
> He shares no good that liberty bestows;
> Spurned from his gifts, with each successive year,
> In drunken want his numbers disappear.

There was a carry-over of these ideas in the Reconstruction. Harris, in one of his most moving stories, *Free Joe,* showed the tragedy of a free Negro in a slave-holding South, where he was considered a bad model by slave-owners, an economic rival by poor whites, and something to be avoided by the slaves. The story might be considered as a condemnation of a system, but in all probability was taken to be another proof of the Negro's incapacity for freedom. Although Harris wrote generously of Negro advancement since emancipation, there is little doubt that the implications of many passages furthered the stereotype under consideration.

Page, a bourbon "fire-eater," for all of his yearnings for his old mammy, saw nothing of good for Negroes in emancipation:

> Universally, they [Southerners] will tell you that while the old-time Negroes were industrious, saving, and, when not misled, well-behaved, kindly, respectful, and self-respecting, and while the remnant of them who remain still retain generally these characteristics, the "new issue," for the most part, are lazy, thriftless, intemperate, insolent, dishonest, and without the most rudimentary elements of morality. . . . Universally, they report a general depravity and retrogression of the Negroes at large, in sections in which they are left to themselves, closely resembling a reversion to barbarism.

The notion of the Negro's being doomed to extinction was sounded by a chorus of pseudo-scientists, bringing forth a formidable (?) array of proofs. Lafcadio Hearn yielded to the lure of posing as a prophet:

As for the black man, he must disappear with the years. Dependent like the ivy, he needs some strong oak-like friend to cling to. His support has been cut from him, and his life must wither in its prostrate helplessness. Will he leave no trace of his past? . . . Ah, yes! . . . the weird and beautiful melodies born in the hearts of the poor, child-like people to whom freedom was destruction.

Many were the stories ringing changes on the theme: "Go tell Marse Linkum, to tek his freedom back." Thus, in *The Carolina Low Country,* Mr. Sass writes of Old Aleck, who, on being freed, spoke his little piece: "Miss, I don't want no wagis." "God bless you, old Aleck," sighs Mr. Sass.

Modern neo-confederates repeat the stereotype. Allen Tate, co-member with Donald Davidson of the Nashville saviors of the South, implies in *Jefferson Davis, His Rise and Fall,* that to educate a Negro beyond his station brings him unhappiness. One of the chief points of agreement in the Neo-Confederate *I'll Take My Stand* by Davidson, Tate and ten others is that freedom has proved to be a perilous state for the Negro. Joseph Hergesheimer agrees: "A free Negro is more often wretched than not." "Slavery was gone, the old serene days were gone. Negroes were bad because they were neither slave nor free." And finally, a modern illustration must suffice. Eleanor Mercein Kelly in an elegy for the vanishing South, called *Monkey Motions,* pities "the helplessness of a simple jungle folk, a bandar-log, set down in the life of cities and expected to be men."

It is, all in all, a sad picture that these savants give. What concerns us here, however, is its persistence, a thing inexpressibly more sad.

THE COMIC NEGRO

"That Reminds Me of a Story. There Were Once Two Ethiopians, Sambo and Rastus. . . ."

(1,001 After-Dinner Speakers.)

The stereotype of the "comic Negro" is about as ancient as the "contented slaves." Indeed, they might be considered complementary, since, if the Negro could be shown as perpetually mirthful, his state could not be so wretched. This is, of course, the familiar procedures when conquerors depict a subject people. English authors at the time of Ireland's greatest persecution built up the stereotype of the comic Irishman, who fascinated English audiences, and unfortunately, in a manner known to literary historians, influenced even Irish authors. Thus, we find, in a melodrama about Irish life, an English officer soliloquizing:

I swear, the Irish nature is beyond my comprehension. A strange people!— merry 'mid their misery—laughing through their tears, like the sun shining through the rain. Yet what simple philosophers they! They tread life's path as if 'twere strewn with roses devoid of thorns, and make the most of life with natures of sunshine and song.

Any American not reading the words "Irish nature" could be forgiven for taking the characterization to refer to American Negroes. Natures of sunshine and song, whose wretchedness becomes nothing since theirs in a simple philosophy of mirth! So runs the pattern.

In her excellent book, *American Humor*, Constance Rourke points out the Negro as one of the chief ingredients of the potpourri of American humor. She traces him as far back as the early '20's when Edwin Forrest made up as a Southern plantation Negro to excite the risibilities of Cincinnati. In *The Spy*, Cooper belabors the grotesqueness of Caesar's appearance, although Caesar is not purely and simply the buffoon:

> . . . . But it was in his legs that nature had indulged her most capricious humor. There was an abundance of material injudiciously used. The calves were neither before nor behind, but rather on the outer side of the limb, inclining forward . . . The leg was placed so near the center (of the foot) as to make it sometimes a matter of dispute whether he was not walking backward.

Kennedy in his *Swallow Barn* not only reveals the Negro as delighted by the master's benevolence, but also as delighting the master by his ludicrous departure from the Anglo-Saxon norm. Kennedy revels in such descriptions as the following:

> His face . . . was principally composed of a pair of protuberant lips, whose luxuriance seemed intended as an indemnity for a pair of crushed nostrils. . . . Two bony feet occupied shoes, each of the superficies and figure of a hoe. . . . Wrinkled, decrepit old men, with faces shortened as if with drawing strings, noses that seemed to have run all to nostril, and with feet of the configuration of a mattock. . . .

It was in the early '30's, however, that T. D. Rice first jumped "Jim Crow" in the theaters along the Ohio River and set upon the stage the "minstrel Negro." Apparently immortal, this stereotype was to involve in its perpetuation such famous actors as Joseph Jefferson and David Belasco, to make Amos 'n' Andy as essential to American domesticity as a car in every garage, and to mean affluence for a Jewish comedian of whom only one gesture was asked: that he sink upon one knee, extend his white-gloved hands, and cry out "Mammy."

In pro-slavery fiction the authors seemed to agree on the two aspects of the comic Negro—that he was ludicrous to others, and forever laughing himself. Grayson writes in *The Hireling and The Slave*:

> The long, loud laugh, that freemen seldom share,
> Heaven's boon to bosoms unapproached by care;
> And boisterous jest and humor unrefined. . . .

To introduce comic relief, perhaps in stories that might defeat their own purposes if confined only to the harrowing details of slavery, anti-slavery authors had their comic characters. Topsy is the classic example; it is noteworthy that in contemporary acting versions of "Uncle Tom's Cabin," Topsy and the minstrel show note, if not dominant, are at least of equal importance to the melodrama of Eliza and the bloodhounds.

Reconstruction literature developed the stereotype. Russell's Negroes give side-splitting versions of the Biblical story (foreshadowing Bradford's *Ol' Man Adam An' His Chillun*), or have a fatal fondness for propinquity to a mule's rear end. Page's Negroes punctuate their worship of "ole Marse" with "Kyah-kyahs," generally directed at themselves. The humor of Uncle Remus is nearer to genuine folk-humor, which—it might be said in passing—*is not* the same as the "comic Negro" humor. Negroes in general, in the Reconstruction stories, are seen as creatures of mirth—who wouldn't suffer from hardship, even if they had to undergo it. Thus a Negro, sentenced to the chaingang for stealing a pair of breeches, is made the theme of a comic poem. This is illustrative. There may be random jokes in Southern court rooms, but joking about the Negroes' experiences with Southern "justice" and with the chain-gang is rather ghastly—like laughter at the mouth of hell. Creatures of sunshine and of song!

The "comic Negro" came into his own in the present century, and brought his creators into theirs. Octavius Cohen, who looks upon the idea of Negro doctors and lawyers and society belles as the height of the ridiculous, served such clienteles as that of *The Saturday Evening Post* for a long time with the antics of Florian Slappey. His work is amusing at its best, but is pseudo-Negro. Instead of being a handicap, however, that seems a recommendation to his audience. Trusting to most moth-eaten devices of farce, and interlarding a Negro dialect never heard on land or sea—compounded more of Dogberry and Mrs. Malaprop than of Birmingham Negroes, he has proved to the whites that all along they have known the real Negro—"Isn't he funny, now!"—and has shown to Negroes what whites wanted them to resemble. Mrs. Octavius Roy Cohen follows in the wake of her illustrious husband in *Our Darktown Press,* a gleaning of "boners" from Aframerican newspapers. Editorial carelessness is sadly enough familiar in race journals; every item in the book is vouched for, but the total effect is the reinforcing of a stereotype that America loves to believe in.

Arthur E. Akers, with a following in another widely read magazine, is another farceur. He uses the situation of the domestic difficulty, as old as medieval fabliaux and farces—and places it in a Southern Negro community, and has his characters speak an approximation to Negro dialect—but too slick and "literary" for conviction. Irate shrews and "Milquetoast" husbands, with razors wielded at departing parts of the anatomy, are Akers' stock-in-trade. Hugh Wiley with his Wildcat, inseparable from his goat, Lady Luck, unsavory but a talisman, is another creator of the farce that Negro life is too generally believed to be. E. K. Means, with obvious knowledge of Southern Negro life, is concerned to show in the main its ludicrous side, and Irvin Cobb, with a reputation of after-dinner wit to uphold, is similarly confined.

The case of Roark Bradford is different. An undoubted humorist, in the great line of Twain and the tall tales of the Southwest, he gleans from a rich store of Negro speech and folkways undeniably amusing tales. But as his belief about the Negro (cf. Introduction) might attest, he has a definite attitude to the Negro to uphold. His stories of the easy loves of the levee (frequently found in *Collier's*) concentrate upon the comic aspect of Negro life, although another observer might well see the magic. In *Ol' Man Adam an' His Chillun* we have farce manufactured out of the Negro's religious beliefs. It seems to the writer that the weakest sections of *Green Pastures* stick closest to Bradford's stories, and that the majesty and reverence that can be found in the play must come from Marc Connelly. In *John Henry,* Bradford has definitely weakened his material by making over a folk-hero into a clown.

Although the situations in which the comic Negro finds himself range from the fantastic as in Cohen, to the possible as in "The Two Black Crows" and in "Amos 'n' Andy," his characteristics are fairly stable. The "comic Negro" is created for the delectation of a white audience, condescending and convinced that any departure from the Anglo-Saxon norm is amusing, and that any attempt to enter the special provinces of whites, such as wearing a dress suit, is doubly so. The "comic Negro" with certain physical attributes exaggerated—with his razor (generally harmless), his love for watermelon and gin, for craps, his haunting of chicken roosts, use of big words he doesn't understand, grandiloquent names and titles, "loud" clothes, bluster, hysterical cowardice, and manufactured word-play—has pranced his way by means of books, vaudeville skits, shows, radio programs, advertisements, and after-dinner speeches, into the folklore of the nation. As Guy B. Johnson urges there is a sort of—

> ... folk attitude of the white man toward the Negro. ... One cannot help noticing that the white man must have his fun out of the Negro, even when writing serious novels about him. This is partly conscious, indeed a necessity, if one is to portray Negro life as it is, for Negroes are human and behave like other human beings. Sometimes it is unconscious, rising out of our old habit of associating the Negro with the comical.

In pointing out the stereotype, one does not deny the rich comedy to be found in Negro life. One is insisting, however, that any picture concentrating upon this to the exclusion of all else is entirely inadequate, that many of the most popular creators of the "comic Negro," "doctor" their material, and are far from accurate in depicting even the small area of Negro experience they select, and that too often they exceed the prerogative of comedy by making copy out of persecution and injustice.

THE BRUTE NEGRO

"All Scientific Investigation of the Subject Proves the Negro to Be An Ape."
(Chas. Carroll, *The Negro a Beast.*)

Because the pro-slavery authors were anxious to prove that slavery had been a benefit to the Negro in removing him from savagery to Christianity, the stereotype of the "brute Negro" was relatively insignificant in antebellum days. There were references to vicious criminal Negroes in fiction (vicious and criminal being synonymous to discontented and refractory), but these were considered as exceptional cases of half-wits led astray by abolitionists. *The Bible Defense of Slavery,* however, in which the Rev. Priest in a most unclerical manner waxes wrathful at abolitionists, sets forth with a great array of theological argument and as much ridiculousness, proofs of the Negro's extreme lewdness. Sodom and Gomorrah were destroyed because these were strongholds of *Negro* vice The book of Leviticus proved that *Negroes*

outraged all order and decency of human society. Lewdness of the most hideous description was the crime of which they were guilty, blended with idolatry in their adoration of the gods, who were carved out of wood, painted and otherwise made, so as to represent the wild passions of lascivious desires. . . . The baleful fire of unchaste amour rages through the negro's blood more fiercely than in the blood of any other people . . . on which account they are a people who are suspected of being but little acquainted with the virtue of chastity, and of regarding very little the marriage oath. . . .

H. R. Helper, foe of slavery, was no friend of the Negro, writing, in 1867, *Nojoque,* a lurid condemnation of the Negro, setting up black and beastly as exact synonyms. Van Evrie's *White Supremacy and Negro Subordination, or Negroes A Subordinate Race, and (so-called) Slavery Its Normal Condition* gave "anthropological" support to the figment of the "beastly Negro," and *The Negro A Beast* (1900) gave theological support. The title page of this book runs:

The Reasoner of the Age, the Revelator of the Century! The Bible As It Is! The Negro and his Relation to the Human Family! The Negro a beast, but created with articulate speech, and hands, that he may be of service to his master—the White Man. . . . by Chas. Carroll, who has spent 15 years of his life and $20,000.00 in its compilation. . . .

Who could ask for anything more?

Authors stressing the mutual affection between the races looked upon the Negro as a docile mastiff. In the Reconstruction this mastiff turned into a mad dog. "Damyanks," carpetbaggers, scalawags, and New England school-marms affected him with the rabies. The works of Thomas Nelson Page are good examples of this metamorphosis. When his Negro characters are in their place, loyally serving and worshipping ole Marse, they are admirable creatures, but in freedom they are beasts, as his novel *Red Rock* attests. *The Negro: The Southerner's Problem* says that the state of the Negro since emancipation is one of minimum progress and maximum regress.

> [This] is borne out by the increase of crime among them, by the increase of superstition, with its black trail of unnamable immorality and vice; by the homicides and murders, and by the outbreak and growth of that brutal crime which has chiefly brought about the frightful crime of lynching which stains the *good name of the South* and has spread northward with the spread of the rav-isher. . . . The crime of rape. . . . is the fatal product of new conditions. . . . The Negro's passion, always his controlling force, is now, since the new teaching, for the white woman. [Lynching is justifiable] for it has its root deep in the basic passions of humanity; the determination to put an end to the *ravishing of their women by an inferior race,* or by any race, no matter what the conse-quence. . . . A crusade has been preached against lynching, even as far as En-gland; but none has been attempted against the ravishing and tearing to pieces of white women and children.

The best known author of Ku Klux Klan fiction after Page is Thomas Dixon. Such works as *The Clansman,* and *The Leopard's Spots,* because of their sensa-tionalism and chapter titles (e.g., "The Black Peril," "The Unspoken Terror," "A Thousand Legged Beast," "The Hunt for the Animal"), seemed just made for the mentality of Hollywood, where D. W. Griffith's in *The Birth of a Nation* made for Thomas Dixon a dubious sort of immortality, and finally fixed the stereotype in the mass-mind. The stock Negro in Dixon's books, unless the shuffling hat-in-hand servitor, is a gorilla-like imbecile, who "springs like a tiger" and has the "black claws of a beast." In both books there is a terrible rape, and a glorious ride of the Knights on a Holy Crusade to avenge Southern civilization. Dixon enables his white geniuses to discover that identity of the rapist by using "a microscope of sufficient power [to] reveal on the retina of the dead eyes the image of this devil as if etched there by fire." . . . The doctor sees "The bestial figure of a negro—his huge black hand plainly defined. . . . It was Gus." Will the wonders of science never cease? But, perhaps, after all, Negroes have been convicted on even flimsier evidence. Fortunately for the self-respect of American authors, this kind of writing is in abeyance today. Perhaps it fell because of the weight of its own absurdity. But it would be unwise to underestimate this stereotype. It is prob-ably of great potency in certain benighted sections where Dixon, if he could be read, would be applauded—and it certainly serves as a convenient self-justification for a mob about to uphold white supremacy by a lynching.

THE TRAGIC MULATTO

"The gods bestow on me
A life of hate,
The white man's gift to see
A nigger's fate."

("The Mulatto Addresses his Savior on Christmas Morning,"
Seymour Gordden Link.)

Stereotyping was by no means the monopoly of pro-slavery authors defending their type of commerce, or justifying their ancestors. Anti-slavery authors, too, fell into the easy habit, but with a striking difference. Where pro-slavery authors had predicated a different set of characteristics for the Negroes, a distinctive sub-human nature, and had stereotyped in accordance with such a comforting hypothesis, anti-slavery authors insisted that the Negro had a common humanity with the whites, that in given circumstances a typically human type of response was to be expected, unless certain other powerful influences were present. The stereotyping in abolitionary literature, therefore, is not stereotyping of *character,* but of *situation.* Since the novels were propagandistic, they concentrated upon abuses: floggings, the slave mart, the domestic slave trade, forced concubinage, runaways, slave hunts, and persecuted freeman—all of these were frequently repeated. Stereotyped or not, heightened if you will, the anti-slavery novel has been supported by the verdict of history—whether recorded by Southern or Northern historians. Facts, after all, are abolitionist. Especially the fact that the Colonel's lady and old Aunt Dinah are sisters under the skin.

Anti-slavery authors did at times help to perpetuate certain pro-slavery stereotypes. Probably the novelists knew that harping upon the gruesome, to the exclusion of all else, would repel readers, who—like their present-day descendants—yearn for happy endings and do not wish their quick consciences to be harrowed. At any rate, comic relief, kindly masters (in contrast to the many brutes), loyal and submissive slaves (to accentuate the wrongs inflicted upon them) were scattered throughout the books. Such tempering of the attacks was turned to pro-slavery uses. Thus, Harris writes:

It seems to me to be impossible for any unprejudiced person to read Mrs. Stowe's book and fail to see in it defence of American slavery as she found it in Kentucky. . . . The real moral that Mrs. Stowe's book teaches is that the possibilities of slavery . . . are shocking to the imagination, while the realities, under the best and happiest conditions, possess a romantic beauty and a tenderness all their own. . . .

Anti-slavery fiction did proffer one stereotype, doomed to unfortunate longevity. This is the tragic mulatto. Pro-slavery apologists had almost entirely omitted (with so many other omissions) mention of concubinage. If anti-slavery authors, in accordance with Victorian gentility, were wary of illustrating the practice, they made great use nevertheless of the offspring of illicit unions. Generally the heroes and heroines of their books are near-whites. These are the intransigent, the resentful, the mentally alert, the proofs of the Negro's possibilities. John Herbert Nelson says with some point:

> Abolitionists tried, by making many of their characters almost white, to work on racial feeling as well. This was a curious piece of inconsistency on their part, an indirect admission that a white man in chains was more pitiful to behold than the African similarly placed. Their most impassioned plea was in behalf of a person little resembling their swarthy proteges, the quadroon or octoroon.

Nelson himself, however, shows similar inconsistency, as he infers that the "true African—essentially gay, happy-go-lucky, rarely ambitious or idealistic, the eternal child of the present moment, able to leave trouble behind—is unsuited for such portrayal. . . . Only the mulattoes and others of mixed blood have, so far, furnished us with material for convincing tragedy."

The tragic mulatto appears in both of Mrs. Stowe's abolitionary novels. In *Uncle Tom's Cabin,* the fugitives Liza and George Harris and the rebellious Cassy are mulattoes. Uncle Tom, the pure black, remains the paragon of Christian submissiveness. In *Dred,* Harry Gordon and his wife are nearly white. Harry is an excellent manager, and a proud, unsubmissive type:

> Mr. Jekyl, that humbug don't go down with me! I'm no more of the race of Ham than you are! I'm Colonel Gordon's oldest son—as white as my brother, who you say owns me! Look at my eyes, and my hair, and say if any of the rules about Ham pertain to me.

The implication that there are "rules about Ham" that do pertain to blacks is to be found in other works. Richard Hildreth's *Archy Moore, or The White Slave,* has as its leading character a fearless, educated mulatto, indistinguishable from whites; Boucicault's *The Octoroon* sentimentalizes the hardships of a slave girl; both make the mixed blood the chief victim of slavery.

Cable, in the *Grandissimes,* shows a Creole mulatto educated beyond his means, and suffering ignominy, but he likewise shows in the character of Bras-Coupe that he does not consider intrepidity and vindictiveness the monopoly of mixed-bloods. In *Old Creole Days,* however, he discusses the beautiful octoroons, whose best fortune in life was to become the mistress of some New Orleans dandy. He shows the tragedy of their lives, but undoubtedly contributed to the modern stereotype that the greatest yearning of the girl of mixed life is for a white lover. Harriet Martineau, giving a contemporary portrait of old New Orleans, wrote:

> The quadroon girls. . . . are brought up by their mothers to be what they have been; the mistresses of white gentlemen. The boys are some of them sent to France; some placed on land in the back of the State. . . . The women of their own color object to them, *"ils sont si degoutants!"*

Lyle Saxon says that "the free men of color are always in the background; to use the Southern phrase, 'they know their place.' "

The Novelists have kept them in the background. Many recent novels show this: *White Girl, The No-Nation Girl, A Study in Bronze, Gulf Stream, Dark Lustre*—all of these show luridly the melodrama of the lovely octoroon girl. Indeed "octoroon" has come to be a feminine noun in popular usage.

The stereotype that demands attention, however, is the notion of mulatto character, whether shown in male or female. This character works itself out with mathematical symmetry. The older theses ran: First, the mulatto inherits the vices of both races and none of the virtues; second, any achievement of a Negro is to be attributed to the white blood in his veins. The logic runs that even inheriting the worst from whites is sufficient for achieving among Negroes. The present theses are based upon these: The mulatto is a victim of a divided inheritance; from his white blood come his intellectual strivings, his unwillingness to be a slave; from his Negro blood come his baser emotional urges, his indolence, his savagery.

Thus, in *The No-Nation Girl*, Evans Wall writes of his tragic heroine, Précieuse:

> Her dual nature had not developed its points of difference. The warring qualities, her double inheritance of Caucasian and black mingled in her blood, had not yet begun to disturb, and torture, and set her apart from either race. . . .
> [As a child,] Précieuse had learned to dance as soon as she could toddle about on her shapely little legs; half-savage little steps with strange movements of her body, exotic gestures and movements that had origination among the remote ancestors of her mother's people in some hot African jungle.
> . . . the wailing cry of the guitar was as primitive and disturbing as the beat of a tom-tom to dusky savages gathered for an orgy of dancing and passion in some moonflooded jungle. . . . Self-control reached its limit. The girl's half-heritage of savagery rose in a flood that washed away all trace of her father's people except the supersensitiveness imparted to her taut nerves. She must dance or scream to relieve the rising torrent of response to the wild, monotonous rhythm.

It is not long before the girl is unable to repress, what Wall calls, the lust inherited from her mother's people; the environment of debauchery, violence, and rapine is exchanged for concubinage with a white paragon, which ends, of course, in the inevitable tragedy. The girl "had no right to be born."

Dark Lustre, by Geoffrey Barnes, transfers the main essentials of the foregoing plot to Harlem. Aline, of the darkly lustrous body, thus analyzes herself in accordance with the old cliches: "The black half of me is ashamed of itself for being there, and every now and then crawls back into itself and tries to let the white go ahead and pass. . . ." Says the author: "There was too much of the nigger in her to let her follow a line of reasoning when the black cloud of her emotions settled over it." Half-white equals reason; half-black equals emotion. She too finds her ideal knight in a white man, and death comes again to the tragic octoroon who should never have been. *White Girl, Gulf Stream, A Study in Bronze* are in substance very similar to these.

Roark Bradford in *This Side of Jordan* gives an unconscious *reductio ad absurdum* of this stereotype.

> The blade of a razor flashed through the air. Scrap has concealed it in the folds of her dress. Her Negro blood sent it unerringly between two ribs. Her Indian blood sent it back for an unnecessary second and third slash.

It might be advanced that Esquimaux blood probably would have kept her from being chilled with horror. The strangest items are attributed to different racial strains: In *No-Nation Girl* a woman cries out in childbirth because of her Negro expressiveness; from the back of Précieuse's "ankles down to her heels, the flesh was slightly thicker"—due to her Negro blood; Lessie in Welbourn Kelley's *Inchin' Along* "strongly felt the urge to see people, to talk to people. . . . That was the white in her maybe. Or maybe it was the mixture of white and black."

This kind of writing should be discredited by its patent absurdity. It is generalizing of the wildest sort, without support from scientific authorities. And yet it has set these *idees fixes* in the mob mind: The Negro of unmixed blood is no theme for tragedy; rebellion and vindictiveness are to be expected only from the mulatto; the mulatto is victim of a divided inheritance and therefore miserable; he is a "man without a race" worshipping the whites and despised by them, despising and despised by Negroes, perplexed by his struggle to unite a white intellect with black sensuousness. The fate of the octoroon girl is intensified—the whole desire of her life is to find a white lover, and then go down, accompanied by slow music, to a tragic end. Her fate is so severe that in some works disclosure of "the single drop of midnight" in her veins makes her commit suicide.

The stereotype is very flattering to a race which, for all its self-assurance, seems to stand in great need of flattery. But merely looking at one of its particulars—that white blood means asceticism and Negro blood means unbridled lust—will reveal how flimsy the whole structure is. It is ingenious that mathematical computation of the amount of white blood in a mulatto's veins will explain his character. And it is a widely held belief. But it is nonsense, all the same.

THE LOCAL COLOR NEGRO

"The defects of local color inhere in the constitution of the cult itself, which, as its name suggests, thought. . . . first of the piquant surfaces and then—if at all—of the stubborn deeps of human life."

(Carl Van Doren, *Contemporary American Novelists.*)

Local color stresses the quaint, the odd, the picturesque, the different. It is an attempt to convey the peculiar quality of a locality. Good realistic practice would insist upon the localizing of speech, garb, and customs; great art upon the revelation of the universal beneath these local characteristics. Local color is now in disrepute because of its being contented with merely the peculiarity of dialect and manners. As B. A. Botkin, editor of *Folk-Say,* has stated: "In the past [local consciousness] has been narrowly sectional rather than broadly human, superficially picturesque rather than deeply interpretative, provincial without being indigenous."

The "local color Negro" is important in any study of the Negro character in American literature. But, since the local colorists of the Negro were more concerned with fidelity to speech and custom, with revelation of his difference in song and dance and story, than with revelation of Negro character, they accepted at face valuation the current moulds into which Negro character had been forced. Therefore, local colorists have been and will be considered under other heads. Page and Russell were local colorists in that they paid close attention to Negro speech, but the Negro they portrayed was the same old contented slave. Their study of Negro speech, however, was fruitful and needed—for pro-slavery authors had been as false in recording Negro speech as they were in picturing Negro experience. Kennedy, for instance, forces a confessedly wretched dialect into the mouths of poor Negroes, and W. L. G. Smith has his Shenandoah Negroes speak Gullah, because his master, Simms, had written of South Carolina Negroes.

Cable, one of the best of the local colorists in *The Grandissimes,* goes a step beyond the mere local color formula; *Old Creole Days* is local color, but, has been considered under the "Tragic Mulatto." The Negroes in Lyle Saxon's old and new New Orleans, E. Larocque Tinker's old New Orleans, R. Emmett Kennedy's Gretna Green, are in the main kinsfolk to the contented slave; in Evans Wall's Mississippi canebrakes are exotic primitives, or tragic mulattoes; on Roark Bradford's levees are primitives; and those on Julia Peterkin's Blue Brook plantation, in Heyward's Catfish Row, and in John Vandercook's Surinam, Liberia, and Haiti, usually surmount, in the writer's opinion, the deficiencies of local color. Stereotyped, or genuinely interpreted, however, they all agree in one respect: they show the peculiar differences of certain Negroes in well-defined localities.

John B. Sale in *The Tree Named John* records with Sympathy the dialect, superstitions, folk-ways of Mississippi Negroes. He is meticulous, perhaps to a fault, in his dialectal accuracy; the milieu is correspondingly convincing. His Negroes do carry on the pattern of mutual affection between the races—and yet they are far nearer flesh and blood than those of Page. Samuel Stoney and Gertrude Shelby, in *Black Genesis,* give the peculiarities of the Gullah Negro's cosmogony. Care is paid to fidelity in recording the dialect, but the authors' comments reveal a certain condescension toward quaintness which is the usual bane of local colorists. In *Po' Buckra* the authors reveal the localized tragedy of the "brass-ankle"—the Croatan-Negro-near-white caste. Much of the "tragic mulatto" theme is in this book, as well as the purely local color interest. Ambrose Gonzales in his Gullah renditions of Aesop, and in his tales of the "black border," reveals for the curious the intricacies of a little known Negro dialect, following the lead of Harris, and C. C. Jones, who recorded the Br'er Rabbit tales in the dialect of the Georgia coast.

Although most of these authors who dwell upon quaint and picturesque divergencies are discussed under other headings, it will not do to underestimate this local color Negro. The showing of Negro peculiarities in speech, superstitions, and customs has been popular for many years, and is likely to be for a long while yet. It undoubtedly has its artistic uses; but being an end in itself is surely not the chief of them.

THE EXOTIC PRIMITIVE

"Then I saw the Congo, cutting through the black. . . .

(Vachel Lindsay)

This stereotype grew up with America's post-war revolt against Puritanism and Babbittry. Literary critics urged a return to spontaneity, to unrestrained emotions; American literature had been too long conventional, drab, without music and color. Human nature had been viewed with too great a reticence. Sex, which the Victorians had considered unmentionable, was pronounced by the school of Freud to have an overwhelming importance in motivating our conduct. So the pendulum swung from the extreme of Victorian prudishness to that of modern expressiveness.

To authors searching "for life in the raw," Negro life and character seemed to beg for exploitation. There was the Negro's savage inheritance, as they conceived it: hot jungle nights, the tom-tom calling to esoteric orgies. There were the frankness and violence to be found in any underprivileged group, or on any frontier. There were the traditional beliefs of the Negro being a creature of his appetites, and although pro-slavery fiction had usually (because of Victorianism) limited these to his yearnings for hog meat and greens, 'possum and yams, and for whiskey on holidays, Reconstruction fiction had stressed his lustfulness. He seemed to be cut out for the hands of certain authors. They promptly rushed to Harlem for color. In Harlem dives and cabarets they found what they believed to be *the* Negro, *au naturel.*

The figure who emerges from their pages is a Negro synchronized to a savage rhythm, living a life of ecstasy, superinduced by jazz (repetition of the tom-tom, awakening vestigial memories of Africa) and gin, that lifted him over antebellum slavery, and contemporary economic slavery, and placed him in the comforting fastnesses of their "mother-land." A kinship exists between this stereotype and that of the contented slave; one is merely a "jazzed-up" version of the other, with cabarets supplanting cabins, and Harlemized "blues," instead of the spirituals and slave reels. Few were the observers who saw in the Negroes' abandon a release from the troubles of this world similar to that afforded in slavery by their singing. Many there were, however, who urged that the Harlem Negro's state was that of an inexhaustible *joie de vivre.* Carl Van Vechten was one of the pioneers of the hegira from downtown to Harlem; he was one of the early discoverers of the cabaret; and his novel *Nigger Heaven,* is to the exotic pattern what *Swallow Barn* was to the contented slave. All of the possibilities of the development of the type are inherent in the book. In the prologue, we have the portrait of the "creeper," Don Juan of Seventh Avenue, whose amatory prowess causes him to be sought by women unknown to him. We feel that this prologue sets the tone of the work: we are going to see the Harlem of gin mills and cabarets, of kept men and loose ladies, of all-day sleepers and all-night roisterers. Van Vechten, who was already famed as a sophisticated romantic novelist, writes graphically of this Harlem. His style invited emulation from young men desiring to be men-about-town first and then novelists, just as Kennedy invited emulation from young Southerners desiring to defend slavery first. Van Vechten's novel does more than present the local color of Harlem; there is as well the character study of a young Negro intellectual who cannot withstand the dissipations of the "greatest Negro city." But the Bohemian life in Harlem is the main thing, even in this youngster's life. According to the publisher's blurb, "Herein is caught the fascination and tortured ecstasies of Harlem . . . The author tells the story of modern Negro life." The blurb claims too much. There is another, there are many other Harlems. And *the* story of modern Negro life will never be found in one volume, or in a thousand.

Lasca Sartoris, exquisite, gorgeous, golden-brown Messaline of Seventh Avenue, is one of the chief characters of the book. On seeing her one of the characters comments: "Whew! She'll make a dent in Harlem." She does. She causes the young hero, Bryon, in a drunken rage, to empty his gun in the body of one of her lovers, although the man was already dead, and a policeman was approaching.

Van Vechten has a noted magazine editor comment pontifically on the possibilities of Negro literature:

> Nobody has yet written a good gambling story; nobody has gone into the curious subject of the divers tribes of the region. . . . There's the servant-girl, for instance. Nobody has ever done the Negro servant-girl, who refuses to "live in." Washing dishes in the day-time, she returns at night to her home in Harlem where she smacks her daddy in the jaw or else dances and makes love. On the whole I should say she has the best time of any domestic servant in the world. . . . The Negro fast set does everything the Long Island fast set does, plays bridge, keeps the bootlegger busy, drives around in Rolls-Royces and commits adultery, but it is vastly more amusing than the Long Island set for the simple reason that it is *amused*. . . . Why, Roy McKain visited Harlem just once and then brought me in a cabaret yarn about a Negro pimp. I don't suppose he even saw the fellow. Probably just made him up, imagined him, but his imagination was based on a background of observation. The milieu is correct. . . .

Although these are merely the off-hand comments of an editor, and not to be taken too seriously as final critical pronouncements on *the* Negro, still certain implications are obvious. The best Negro characters for literary purposes are suggested: gamblers, fast set, servant-girl-sweet-mamma, etc. All are similar in their great capacity for enjoyment—and it is that side that must be shown. The eternal playboys of the Western hemisphere! Why even one trip to Harlem will reveal the secret of their mystery. The connection of all of this to the contented slave, comic, local color Negro is patent. Another thing to be noticed is the statement issued by the literary market: Stereotypes wanted.

In *Black Sadie,* T. Bowyer Campbell, whose preference is for the stereotype of the contented slave of the South, ironically accounts for the Harlem fad by the desire of jaded sophisticates for a new thrill. But Campbell does agree in some degree with the Harlem stereotype: "Colored people demand nothing but easy happiness, good nature." Black Sadie, child of a man hanged for raping an old white woman, having become the toast of artistic New York, remaining a kleptomaniac—"it was in her blood"—even in affluence, causing a murder, returns—in the best tradition of minstrel songs—to happy Virginia. "Easy come, easy go, niggers," Campbell closes his book, philosophically.

Sherwood Anderson, in *Dark Laughter,* expresses a genuine Rousseauism. Hostile toward the routine of industrialism and Puritanism, Anderson sets up as a foil the happy-go-lucky sensuality of river-front Negroes, who laugh, with genial cynicism, at the self-lacerations of hypersensitive Nordics. His "dark laughter" lacks the sinister undertone of Llwellyn Powys' "black laughter" heard in Africa. Anderson's Negroes are too formalized a chorus, however, for conviction, and are more the dream-children of a romanticist than actual flesh-and-blood creations. Anderson has drawn some excellent Negro characters; in *Dark Laughter,* however, he characterizes the Negroes too straitly. That the chief response of the Negro to his experience is a series of deep rounds of laughter at white sex-tangles is difficult of credence.

William Seabrook in *Magic Island and Jungle Ways* writes sensational travel tales—according to some, in the tradition of Munchausen and Marco Polo. He exploits the exotic and primitive, recording voodoo rites, black magic, strange sexual practices, weird superstitions, and cannibalism. His work brings a sort of vicarious satisfaction to Main Street, and advances the stereotype. He traces back to original sources what downtown playboys come up to Harlem to see.

The stereotype of the exotic-primitive would require more than a dogmatic refutation. Not so patently a "wish-fulfillment," as the "contented slave" stereotype was, nor an expression of unreasoning hatred, as the "brute Negro," it is advanced by novelists realistic in technique and rather convincing, although demonstrably "romantic" in their choice of the sensational. But it would be pertinent to question the three basic assumptions—either insinuated or expressed—underlying the stereotype: that the "natural" Negro is to be found in Harlem cabarets; that the life and character depicted there are representative of Negro life in general; and that the Negro is "himself," and startlingly different in the sensational aspects of his life.

It is strange that the "natural" Negro should be looked for in the most sophisticated of environment. Even the names "Cotton Club," "Plantation Revue," the lavish, though inaccurate, cotton bolls decorating the walls, the choruses in silken overalls and bandanas do not disguise but rather enforce the fact that Negro entertainers, like entertainers everywhere, give the pubic what clever managers, generally Caucasian, believe the public wants. Unwise as it is to generalize about America, or New York State, or even Queens from the Great White Way, it is no less unwise to generalize about Negro life and character from Harlem. It is even unwise to generalize about Harlem, from *the* Harlem shown in books. Strange to say, there is a Harlem that can be observed by the cold glare of daylight.

The exotic primitives of Mississippi levees and cane-brakes, of Catfish Row and Blue Brook Plantation are more convincing, as examples of frontier communities, and of underprivileged groups who are known to live violent lives. It is surely not impossible, however, to believe that observers with an eye for environmental factors might see an entirely different picture from the one presented by searchers for exotic-primitive innate tendencies.

Harvey Wickham in *The Impuritans* writes:

> On Pacific Street, San Francisco, there used to be, and probably still is, a Negro dance hall called the So-Different Cafe. The name was deceptive. It was not so different from any other slum-hole. [A slum-hole] is tediously the same, whether it be in Harlem, lower Manhattan, London, Paris, Berlin, Rome, Athens, Pekin, or Timbuctoo. There is no possible variety in degradation. . . .

Such a comment surely deserves as careful attention as the stereotype of the exotic-primitive.

ATTEMPTS AT REALIZATION

"John Henry said to his captain, A man ain't nothin' but a man. . . ."
(Ballad of John Henry.)

It would be a mistake to believe that the works of all white authors bear out these stereotypes. Some of the best attacks upon stereotyping have come from white authors, and from Southerners, just as some of the strongest upholding of the stereotypes has come from Negroes. Moreover, the writer of this essay hopes that he will not be accused of calling everything a stereotype that does not flatter Negro character, or of insisting that the stereotypes have no basis in reality. Few of the most apologistic of "race" orators could deny the presence of contented slaves, of wretched freemen, in our past; nor of comic Negroes (even in the joke-book tradition), of self-pitying mulattoes, of brutes, of exotic primitives in our present. Negro life does have its local color, and a rich, glowing color it can be at times. What this essay has aimed to point out is the obvious unfairness of hardening racial character into fixed moulds. True in some particulars, each of these popular generalizations is dangerous when applied to the entire group. Furthermore, most of these generalizations spring from a desire to support what is considered social expediency rather than from a sincere attempt at interpretation, and are therefore bad art. . . .

It is likely that, in spite of the willingness of some Negro authors to accept at face value some of these stereotypes, the exploration of Negro life and character rather than its exploitation must come from Negro authors themselves. This, of course, runs counter to the American conviction that the Southern white man knows the Negro best, and can best interpret him. Nan Bagby Stephens states what other Southern authors have insinuated:

> Maybe it was because my slave-owning ancestors were fond of their darkies and treated them as individuals that I see them like that. It seems to me that no one, not even the negroes themselves, can get the perspective reached through generations of understanding such as we inherited.

This writer of this essay holds to the contrary opinion, agreeing with another Southerner, F. P. Gaines, that when a white man says that he knows the Negro he generally means that he knows the Negro of the joke-book tradition. Stephen Vincent Benet has written:

Oh blackskinned epic, epic with the black spear,
I cannot sing you, having too white a heart,
And yet, some day a poet will rise to sing you
And sing you with such truth and mellowness. . . .
That you will be a match for any song. . . .

But whether Negro life and character are to be best interpreted from without or within is an interesting by-path that we had better not enter here. One manifest truth, however, is this: the sincere, sensitive artist, willing to go beneath the cliches of popular belief to get at an underlying reality, will be wary of confining a race's entire character to a half-dozen narrow grooves. He will hardly have the temerity to say that his necessarily limited observation of a few Negroes in a restricted environment can be taken as the last word about some mythical *the* Negro. He will hesitate to do this, even though he had a Negro mammy, or spent a night in Harlem, or has been a Negro all his life. The writer submits that such an artist is the only one worth listening to, although the rest are legion.

Suggested Readings with Similar Theme:

Braithwaite, William Stanley. "The Negro in Literature." *Crisis* 28 (September 1924): 204–10.
Brown, Sterling A. *The Negro in American Fiction.* Washington, D.C.: Association in Negro Folk Education, 1937. Reprint, New York: Atheneum, 1969.
Thompson, Larry. "The Black Image in Early American Drama." *Black World* 24, no. 6 (April 1975): 54–69.

Blueprint for Negro Writing (1937)

According to Wright, what is the function of African American literature? What is the role of the African American writer? To whom does the African American writer speak? How does Wright echo James Weldon Johnson, Langston Hughes, Alain Locke, Ralph Ellison, and others about a Black Poetics that is pulled from African American folk culture? Are there contradictions in Wright's statement that "Writing has its professional autonomy; it should complement other professions," especially when applied to postwar novels? What are the other contradictions in Wright's manifesto when applied to "Native Son" or other post-war novels that protested segregation and promoted integration? Explain Wright's definition of nationalism.

1) THE ROLE OF NEGRO WRITING: TWO DEFINITIONS

Generally speaking, Negro writing in the past has been confined to humble novels, poems, and plays, prim and decorous ambassadors who went a-begging to white America. They entered the Court of American Public Opinion dressed in the knee-pants of servility, curtsying to show that the Negro was not inferior, that he was human, and that he had a life comparable to that of other people. For the most part these artistic ambassadors were received as though they were French poodles who do clever tricks.

White America never offered these Negro writers any serious criticism. The mere fact that a Negro could write was astonishing. Nor was there any deep concern on the part of white America with the role Negro writing should play in American culture; and the role it did play grew out of accident rather than intent or design. Either it crept in through the kitchen in the form of jokes; or it was the fruits of that foul soil which was the result of a liason [*sic*] between inferiority-complexed Negro "geniuses" and burnt-out white Bohemians with money.

On the other hand, these often technically brilliant performances by Negro writers were looked upon by the majority of literate Negroes as something to be proud of. At best, Negro writing has been something external to the lives of educated Negroes themselves. That the productions of their writers should have been something of a guide in their daily living is a matter which seems never to have been raised seriously.

Under these conditions Negro writing assumed two general aspects: 1) It became a sort of conspicuous ornamentation, the hallmark of "achievement." 2) It became the voice of the educated Negro pleading with white America for justice.

Rarely was the best of this writing addressed to the Negro himself, his needs, his sufferings, his aspirations. Through misdirection, Negro writers have been far better to others than they have been to themselves. And the mere recognition of this places the whole question of Negro writing in a new light and raises a doubt as to the validity of its present direction.

2) THE MINORITY OUTLOOK

Somewhere in his writings Lenin makes the observation that oppressed minorities often reflect the techniques of the bourgeoisie more brilliantly than some sections of the bourgeoisie themselves. The psychological importance of this becomes meaningful when it is recalled that oppressed minorities, and especially the petty bourgeois [sic] sections of oppressed minorities, strive to assimilate the virtues of the bourgeoisie in the assumption that by doing so they can lift themselves into a higher social sphere. But not only among the oppressed petty bourgeoisie does this occur. The workers of a minority people, chafing under exploitation, forge organizational forms of struggle to better their lot. Lacking the handicaps of false ambition and property, they have access to a wide social vision and a deep social consciousness. They display a greater freedom and initiative in pushing their claims upon civilization than even do the petty bourgeoisie. Their organizations show greater strength, adaptability, and efficiency than any other group or class in society.

That Negro workers, propelled by the harsh conditions of their lives, have demonstrated this consciousness and mobility for economic and political action there can be no doubt. But has this consciousness been reflected in the work of Negro writers to the same degree as it has in the Negro workers' struggle to free Herndon and the Scottsboro Boys, in the drive toward unionism, in the fight against lynching? Have they as creative writers taken advantage of their unique minority position?

The answer decidedly is *no*. Negro writers have lagged sadly, and as time passes the gap widens between them and their people.

How can this hiatus be bridged? How can the enervating effects of this long standing split be eliminated? . . .

3) A WHOLE CULTURE

There is, however, a culture of the Negro which is his and has been addressed to him; a culture which has, for good or ill, helped to clarify his consciousness and create emotional attitudes which are conducive to action. This culture has stemmed mainly from two sources: 1) the Negro church; 2) and the folklore of the Negro people.

It was through the portals of the church that the American Negro first entered the shrine of western culture. Living under slave conditions of life, bereft of his African heritage, the Negroes' struggle for religion on the plantations between 1820–60 assumed the form of a struggle for human rights. It remained a relatively revolutionary struggle until religion began to serve as an antidote for suffering and denial. But even today there are millions of American Negroes whose only sense of a whole universe, whose only relation to society and man, and whose only guide to personal dignity comes through the archaic morphology of Christian salvation.

It was, however, in a folklore moulded out of rigorous and inhuman conditions of life that the Negro achieved his most indigenous and complete expression. Blues, spirituals, and folk tales recounted from mouth to mouth; the whispered words of a black mother to her black daughter on the ways of men; the confidential wisdom of a black father to his black son; the swapping of sex experiences on street corners from boy to boy in the deepest vernacular; work songs sung under blazing suns—all these formed the channels through which the racial wisdom flowed.

One would have thought that Negro writers in the last century of striving at expression would have continued and deepened this folk tradition, would have tried to create a more intimate and yet a more profoundly social system of artistic communication between them and their people. But the illusion that they could escape through individual achievement the harsh lot of their race swung Negro writers away from any such path. Two separate cultures sprang up: one for the Negro masses, unwritten and unrecognized; and the other for the sons and daughters of a rising Negro bourgeoisie, parasitic and mannered.

Today the question is: Shall Negro writing be for the Negro masses, moulding the lives and consciousness of those masses toward new goals, or shall it continue begging the question of the Negroes' humanity?

4) The Problem of Nationalism in Negro Writing

In stressing the difference between the role Negro writing failed to play in the lives of the Negro pople [sic], and the role it should play in the future if it is to serve its historic function; in pointing out the fact that Negro writing has been addressed in the main to a small white audience rather than to a Negro one, it should be stated that no attempt is being made here to propagate a specious and blatant nationalism. Yet the nationalist character of the Negro people is unmistakable. Psychologically this nationalism is reflected in the whole of Negro culture, and especially in folklore.

In the absence of fixed and nourishing forms of culture, the Negro has a folklore which embodies the memories and hopes of his struggle for freedom. Not yet caught in paint or stone, and as yet but feebly depicted in the poem and novel, the Negroes' most powerful images of hope and despair still remain in the fluid state of daily speech. How many John Henrys have lived and died on the lips of these black people? How many mythical heroes in embryo have been allowed to perish for lack of husbanding by alert intelligence?

Negro folklore contains, in a measure that puts to shame more deliberate forms of Negro expression, the collective sense of Negro life in America. Let those who shy at the nationalist implications of Negro life look at this body of folklore, living and powerful, which rose out of a unified sense of a common life and a common fate. Here are those vital beginnings of a recognition of value in life as it is *lived,* a recognition that marks the emergence of a new culture in the shell of the old. And at the moment this process starts, at the moment when a people begin to realize a *meaning* in their suffering, the civilization that engenders that suffering is doomed.

The nationalist aspects of Negro life are as sharply manifest in the social institutions of Negro people as in folklore. There is a Negro church, a Negro press, a Negro social world, a Negro sporting world, a Negro business world, a Negro school system, Negro professions; in short, a Negro way of life in America. The Negro people did not ask for this, and deep down, though they express themselves through their institutions and adhere to this special way of life, they do not want it now. This special existence was forced upon them from without by lynch rope, bayonet and mob rule. They accepted these negative conditions with the inevitability of a tree which must live or perish in whatever soil it finds itself. . . .

5) The Basis and Meaning of Nationalism in Negro Writing

The social institutions of the Negro are imprisoned in the Jim Crow political system of the South, and this Jim Crow political system is in turn built upon a plantation-feudal economy. Hence, it can be seen that the emotional expression of group-feeling which puzzles so many whites and leads them to deplore what they call "black chauvinism" is not a morbidly inherent trait of the Negro, but rather the reflex expression of a life whose roots are imbedded deeply in Southern soil.

Negro writers must accept the nationalist implications of their lives, not in order to encourage them, but in order to change and transcend them. They must accept the concept of nationalism because, in order to transcend it, they must *possess* and *understand* it. And a nationalist spirit in Negro writing means a nationalism carrying the highest possible pitch of social consciousness. It means a nationalism that knows its origins, its limitations; that is aware of the dangers of its position; that knows its ultimate aims are unrealizable within the framework of capitalist America; a nationalism whose reason for being lies in the simple fact of self-possession and in the consciousness of the interdependence of people in modern society.

For purposes of creative expression it means that the Negro writer must realize within the area of his own personal experience those impulses which, when prefigured in terms of broad social movements, constitute the stuff of nationalism.

For Negro writers even more so than for Negro politicians, nationalism is a bewildering and vexing question, the full ramifications of which cannot be dealt with here. But among Negro workers and the Negro middle class the spirit of nationalism is rife in a hundred devious forms; and a simple literary realism which seeks to depict the lives of these people devoid of wider social connotations, devoid of the revolutionary significance of these nationalist tendencies, must of necessity do a rank injustice to the Negro people and alienate their possible allies in the struggle for freedom.

6) Social Consciousness and Responsibility

The Negro writer who seeks to function within his race as a purposeful agent has a serious responsibility. In order to do justice to his subject matter, in order to depict Negro life in all of its manifold and intricate relationships, a deep, informed, and complex consciousness is necessary; a consciousness which draws for its strength upon the fluid lore of a great people, and moulds this lore with the concepts that move and direct the forces of history today.

With the gradual decline of the moral authority of the Negro church, and with the increasing irresolution which is paralyzing Negro middle class leadership, a new role is developing upon the Negro writer. He is being called upon to do no less than create values by which his race is to struggle, live and die.

By his ability to fuse and make articulate the experiences of men, because his writing possesses the potential cunning to steal into the inmost recesses of the human heart, because he can create the myths and symbols that inspire a faith in life, he may expect either to be consigned to oblivion, or to be recognized for the valued agent he is.

This raises the question of the personality of the writer. It means that in the lives of Negro writers must be found those materials and experiences which will create a meaningful picture of the world today. Many young writers have grown to believe that a Marxist analysis of society presents such a picture. It creates a picture which, when placed before the eyes of the writer, should unify his personality, organize his emotions, buttress him with a tense and obdurate will to change the world.

And, in turn, this changed world will dialectically change the writer. Hence, it is through a Marxist conception of reality and society that the maximum degree of freedom in thought and feeling can be gained for the Negro writer. Further, this dramatic Marxist vision, when consciously grasped, endows the writer with a sense of dignity which no other vision can give. Ultimately, it restores to the writer his lost heritage, that is, his role as a creator of the world in which he lives, and as a creator of himself.

Yet, for the Negro writer, Marxism is but the starting point. No theory of life can take the place of life. After Marxism has laid bare the skeleton of society, there remains the task of the writer to plant flesh upon those bones out of his will to live. He may, with disgust and revulsion, say *no* and depict the horrors of capitalism encroaching upon the human being. Or he may, with hope and passion, say *yes* and depict the faint stirrings of a new and emerging life. But in whatever social voice he chooses to speak, whether positive or negative, there should always be heard or *over*-heard his faith, his necessity, his judgement [*sic*].

His vision need not be simple or rendered in primer-like terms; for the life of the Negro people is not simple. The presentation of their lives should be simple, yes; but all the complexity, the strangeness, the magic wonder of life that plays like a bright sheen over the most sordid existence, should be there. To borrow a phrase from the Russians, it should have a *complex simplicity*. Eliot, Stein, Joyce, Proust, Hemingway, and Anderson; Gorky, Barbusse, Nexo, and Jack London no less than the folklore of the Negro himself should form the heritage of the Negro writer. Every iota of gain in human thought and sensibility should be ready grist for his mill, no matter how far-fetched they may seem in their immediate implications.

7) The Problem of Perspective

What vision must Negro writers have before their eyes in order to feel the impelling necessity for an about face? What angle of vision can show them all the forces of modern society in process, all the lines of economic development converging toward a distant point of hope? Must they believe in some "ism"?

They may feel that only dupes believe in "isms"; they feel with some measure of justification that another commitment means only another disillusionment. But anyone destitute of a theory about the meaning, structure and direction of modern society is a lost victim in a world he cannot understand or control.

But even if Negro writers found themselves through some "ism," how would that influence their writing? Are they being called upon to "preach"? To be "salesmen"? To "prostitute" their writing? Must they "sully" themselves? Must they write "propaganda"?

No; it is a question of awareness, of consciousness; it is, above all, a question of perspective.

Perspective is that part of a poem, novel, or play which a writer never puts directly upon paper. It is that fixed point in intellectual space where a writer stands to view the struggles, hopes, and sufferings of his people. There are times when he may stand too close and the result is a blurred vision. Or he may stand too far away and the result is a neglect of important things.

Of all the problems faced by writers who as a whole have never allied themselves with world movements, perspective is the most difficult of achievement. At its best, perspective is a pre-conscious assumption, something which a writer takes for granted, something which he wins through his living.

A Spanish writer recently spoke of living in the heights of one's time. Surely, perspective means just *that*. It means that a Negro writer must learn to view the life of a Negro living in New York's Harlem or Chicago's South Side with the consciousness that one-sixth of the earth surface belongs to the working class. It means that a Negro writer must create in his readers' minds a relationship between a Negro woman hoeing cotton in the South and the men who loll in swivel chairs in Wall Street and take the fruits of her toil.

Perspective for Negro writers will come when they have looked and brooded so hard and long upon the harsh lot of their race and compared it with the hopes and struggles of minority peoples everywhere that the cold facts have begun to tell them something.

8) The Problem of Theme

This does not mean that a Negro writer's sole concern must be with rendering the social scene; but if his conception of the life of his people is broad and deep enough, if the sense of the *whole* life he is seeking is vivid and strong in him, then his writing will embrace all those social, political, and economic forms under which the life of his people is manifest.

In speaking of theme one must necessarily be general and abstract; the temperament of each writer moulds and colors the world he sees. Negro life may be approached from a thousand angles, with no limit to technical and stylistic freedom.

Negro writers spring from a family, a clan, a class, and a nation; and the social units in which they are bound have a story, a record. Sense of theme will emerge in Negro writing when Negro writers try to fix this story about some pole of meaning, remembering as they do so that in the creative process meaning proceeds *equally* as much from the contemplation of the subject matter as from the hopes and apprehensions that rage in the heart of the writer.

Reduced to its simplest and most general terms, theme for Negro writers will rise from understanding the meaning of their being transplanted from a "savage" to a "civilized" culture in all of its social, political, economic, and emotional implications. It means that Negro writers must have in their consciousness the foreshortened picture of the *whole,* nourishing culture from which they were torn in Africa, and of the long, complex (and for the most part, unconscious) struggle to regain in some form and under alien conditions of life a *whole* culture again.

It is not only this picture they must have, but also a knowledge of the social and emotional milieu that gives it tone and solidity of detail. Theme for Negro writers will emerge when they have begun to feel the meaning of the history of their race as though they in one life time had lived it themselves throughout all the long centuries.

9) Autonomy of Craft

For the Negro writer to depict this new reality requires a greater discipline and consciousness than was necessary for the so-called Harlem school of expression. Not only is the subject matter dealt with far more meaningful and complex, but the new role of the writer is qualitatively different. The Negro writers' new position demands a sharper definition of the status of his craft, and a sharper emphasis upon its functional autonomy.

Negro writers should seek through the medium of their craft to play as meaningful a role in the affairs of men as do other professionals. But if their writing is demanded to perform the social office of other professions, then the autonomy of craft is lost and writing detrimentally fused with other interests. The limitations of the craft constitute some of its greatest virtues. If the sensory vehicle of imaginative writing is required to carry too great a load of didactic material, the artistic sense is submerged.

The relationship between reality and the artistic image is not always direct and simple. The imaginative conception of a historical period will not be a carbon copy of reality. Image and emotion possess a logic of their own. A vulgarized simplicity constitutes the greatest danger in tracing the reciprocal interplay between the writer and his environment.

Writing has its professional autonomy; it should complement other professions, but it should not supplant them or be swamped by them.

10) The Necessity for Collective Work

It goes without saying that these things cannot be gained by Negro writers if their present mode of isolated writing and living continues. This isolation exists *among* Negro writers as well as *between* Negro and white writers. The

Negro writers' lack of thorough integration with the American scene, their lack of a clear realization among themselves of their possible role, have bred generation after generation of embittered and defeated literati.

Barred for decades from the theater and publishing houses, Negro writers have been *made* to feel a sense of difference. So deep has this white-hot iron of exclusion been burnt into their hearts that thousands have all but lost the desire to become identified with American civilization. The Negro writers' acceptance of this enforced isolation and their attempt to justify it is but a defense-reflex of the whole special way of life which has been rammed down their throats.

This problem, by its very nature, is one which must be approached contemporaneously from *two* points of view. The ideological unity of Negro writers and the alliance of that unity with all the progressive ideas of our day is the primary prerequisite for collective work. On the shoulders of white writers and Negro writers alike rest the responsibility of ending this mistrust and isolation.

By placing cultural health above narrow sectional prejudices, liberal writers of all races can help to break the stony soil of aggrandizement out of which the stunted plants of Negro nationalism grow. And, simultaneously, Negro writers can help to weed out these choking growths of reactionary nationalism and replace them with harder and sturdier types.

These tasks are imperative in light of the fact that we live in a time when the majority of the most basic assumptions of life can no longer be taken for granted. Tradition is no longer a guide. The world has grown huge and cold. Surely this is the moment to ask questions, to theorize, to speculate, to wonder out of what materials can a human world be built.

Each step along this unknown path should be taken with thought, care, self-consciousness, and deliberation. When Negro writers think they have arrived at something which smacks of truth, humanity, they should want to test it with others, feel it with a degree of passion and strength that will enable them to communicate it to millions who are groping like themselves.

Writers faced with such tasks can have no possible time for malice or jealousy. The conditions for the growth of each writer depend too much upon the good work of other writers. Every first rate novel, poem, or play lifts the level of consciousness higher.

Suggested Reading with Similar Theme:

Hurston, Zora Neale. "What White Publishers Won't Print." *Negro Digest* 8 (April 1950): 85–89.

JAMES BALDWIN

From "Everybody's Protest Novel" (1949)

Is Baldwin correct in his portrayal of Richard Wright's Bigger as "the brute Negro"? Review Sterling Brown's discussion of the stereotype. How does Baldwin enter discussions with Petry about the protest novel? Compare their concluding paragraphs. Do their ideological positions differ? According to Baldwin, what is the function of African American literature?

. . . [O]ne can hardly claim for the protest novels the lofty purpose they claim for themselves or share the present optimism concerning them. They emerge for what they are: a mirror of our confusion, dishonesty, panic, trapped and immobilized in the sunlit prison of the American dream. They are fantasies, connecting nowhere with reality, sentimental; in exactly the same sense that such movies as *The Best Years of Our Lives* or the works of Mr. James M. Cain are fantasies. Beneath the dazzling pyrotechnics of these current operas, one may still discern, as the controlling force, the intense theological preoccupations of Mrs. Stowe, the sick vacuities of *The Rover Boys*. Finally, the aim of the protest novel becomes something very closely resembling the zeal of those alabaster missionaries to Africa to cover the nakedness of the natives, to hurry them into the pallid arms of Jesus and thence into slavery. The aim has now become to reduce all Americans to the compulsive, bloodless dimensions of a guy named Joe.

It is the peculiar triumph of society—and its loss—that it is able to convince those people to whom it has given inferior status of the reality of this decree; it has the force and the weapons to translate its dictum into fact, so that the allegedly inferior are actually made so, insofar as the societal realities are concerned. This is a more hidden phenomenon now than it was in the days of serfdom, but it is no less implacable. Now, as then, we find ourselves bound, first without, then within, by the nature of our categorization. And escape is not effected through a bitter railing against this trap; it is as though this very striving were the only motion needed to spring the trap upon us. We take our shape, it is true, within and against that cage of reality bequeathed us at our birth; and yet it is precisely through our dependence on this reality that we are most endlessly betrayed. Society is held together by our need; we bind it together with legend, myth, coercion, fearing that without it we will be hurled into that void, within which, like the earth before the Word was spoken, the foundations of society are hidden. From this void—ourselves—it is the function of society to protect us; but it is only this void, our unknown selves, demanding, forever, a new act of creation, which can save us—"from the evil that is in the world." With the same motion, at the same time, it is this toward which we endlessly struggle and from which, endlessly, we struggle to escape.

It must be remembered that the oppressed and the oppressor are bound together within the same society; they accept the same criteria, they share the same beliefs, they both alike depend on the same reality. Within this cage it is romantic, more, meaningless, to speak of a "new" society as the desire of the oppressed, for that shivering dependence on the props of reality which he shares with the *Herrenvolk* makes a truly "new" society impossible to conceive. What is meant by a new society is one in which inequalities will disappear, in which vengeance will be exacted; either there will be no oppressed at all, or the oppressed and the oppressor will change places. But, finally, as it seems to me, what the rejected desire is, is an elevation of status, acceptance within the present community. Thus, the African, exile, pagan, hurried off the auction block and into the fields, fell on his knees before that God in Whom he must now believe; who had made him, but not in His image. This tableau, this impossibility, is the heritage of the Negro in America: *Wash me,* cried the slave to his Maker, *and I shall be whiter, whiter than snow*! For black is the color of evil; only the robes of the saved are white. It is this cry, implacable on the air and in the skull, that he must live with. Beneath the widely published catalogue of brutality—bringing to mind, somehow, an image, a memory of church-bells burdening the air—is this reality which, in the same nightmare notion, he both flees and rushes to embrace. In America, now, this country devoted to the death of the paradox—which may, therefore, be put to death by one—his lot is as ambiguous as a tableau by Kafka. To flee or not, to move or not, it is all the same; his doom is written on his forehead, it is carried in his heart. In *Native Son,* Bigger Thomas stands on a Chicago street corner watching airplanes flown by white men racing against the sun and "Goddamn" he says, the bitterness bubbling up like blood, remembering a million indignities, the terrible, rat-infested house, the humiliation of home-relief, the intense, aimless, ugly bickering, hating it; hatred smoulders through these pages like sulphur fire. All of Bigger's life is controlled, defined by his hatred and his fear. And later, his fear drives him to murder and his hatred to rape; he dies, having come, through this violence, we are told, for the first time, to a kind of life, having for the first time redeemed his manhood. Below the surface of this novel there lies, as it seems to me, a continuation, a complement of that monstrous legend it was written to destroy. Bigger is Uncle Tom's descendant, flesh of his flesh, so exactly opposite a portrait that, when the books are placed together, it seems that the contemporary Negro novelist and the dead New England woman are locked together in a deadly, timeless battle; the one uttering merciless exhortations, the other shouting curses.

And, indeed, within this web of lust and fury, black and white can only thrust and counter-thrust, long for each other's slow, exquisite death; death by torture, acid, knives and burning; the thrust, the counter-thrust, the longing making the heavier that cloud which blinds and suffocates them both, so that they go down into the pit together. Thus has the cage betrayed us all, this moment, our life, turned to nothing through our terrible attempts to insure it. For Bigger's tragedy is not that he is cold or black or hungry, not even that he is American, black; but that he has accepted a theology that denies him life, that he admits the possibility of his being sub-human and feels constrained, therefore, to battle for his humanity according to those brutal criteria bequeathed him at his birth. But our humanity is our burden, our life; we need not battle for it; we need only to do what is infinitely more difficult— that is, accept it. The failure of the protest novel lies in its rejection of life, the human being, the denial of his beauty, dread, power, in its insistence that it is his categorization alone which is real and which cannot be transcended.

Suggested Readings with Similar Theme:

Ellison, Ralph. "Richard Wright's Blues." *Antioch Review* 5 (Summer 1945): 198–211.
Baldwin, James. "Many Thousand Gone." *Partisan Review* 18 (November-December 1951): 665–68. Reprint, *Notes of a Native Son.* Boston: Beacon Press, 1955. Reprinted in this volume.

The Novel as Social Criticism (1950)

In defense of African American literary art of the 1940s, particularly protest which served moral and political ends, Petry once wrote, "The idea that a story should point a moral, convey a message, did not originate in the twentieth century." According to the author-critic, "modern novels with their messages are cut from the same bolt of cloth as the world's folk tales and fairy stories, the parables of the Bible, the old morality plays, the Greek tragedies, the Shakespearean tragedies." How is Petry defining the sociological novel? Explain how the author echoes DuBois and Ellison when she calls "all truly great art . . . propaganda." Of course, Petry cautions writers against forsaking the story and manipulating characters to serve the interests of some political and social theme. Has Petry contradicted herself? Has she contradicted DuBois or Ellison? Petry calls the socially conscious novelist "a man or woman with a conscience." What, then, is the role of the writer? Is the writer his or her brother's or sister's keeper? How is the writer to achieve balance between art and propaganda? Between ideology and aesthetics? How can one be certain that Petry does not expect writers to create in a vacuum? Or, that she does not expect their craft to reflect the political, economic, and social structures of the period in which they write?

After I had written a novel of social criticism (it was my first book, written for the most part without realizing that it belonged in a special category) I slowly became aware that such novels were regarded as a special and quite deplorable creation of American writers of the twentieth century. It took me quite awhile to realize that there were fashions in literary criticism and that they shifted and changed much like the fashions in women's hats.

Right now the latest style, in literary circles, is to say that the sociological novel reached its peak and its greatest glory in *The Grapes of Wrath,* and having served its purpose it now lies stone-cold dead in the market place. Perhaps it does. But the corpse is quick with life. Week after week it sits up and moves close to the top of the best-seller list.

It is my personal opinion that novels of this type will continue to be written until such time as man loses his ability to read and returns to the cave. Once there he will tell stories to his mate and to his children; and the stories will contain a message, make a comment on cave society; and he will, finally, work out a method of recording the stories, and having come full circle the novel of social criticism will be reborn.

Its rebirth in a cave or an underground mine seems inevitable because it is not easy to destroy an old art form. The idea that a story should point a moral, convey a message, did not originate in the twentieth century; it goes far back in the history of man. Modern novels with their "messages" are cut from the same bolt of cloth as the world's folk tales and fairy stories, the parables of the Bible, the old morality plays, the Greek tragedies, the Shakespearean tragedies. Even the basic theme of these novels is very old. It is derived from the best known murder study in literature. The cast and the setting vary, of course, but the message in *Knock on any Door, Gentleman's Agreement, Kingsblood Royal, Native Son, The Naked and the Dead, Strange Fruit, A Passage to India,* is essentially the same: And the Lord said unto Cain, Where is Abel thy brother: And he said, I know not: Am I my brother's keeper?

In one way or another, the novelist who criticizes some undesirable phase of the status quo is saying that man is his brother's keeper and that unless a social evil (war or racial prejudices or anti-Semitism or political corruption) is destroyed man cannot survive but will become what Cain feared he would become—a wanderer and a vagabond on the face of the earth.

The critical disapproval that I mentioned just above is largely based on an idea that had its origin in the latter part of the eighteenth century, the idea that art should exist for art's sake—l'art pour l'art, Poe's poem for the poem's sake. The argument runs something like this: the novel is an art form; art (any and all art) is prostituted, bastardized, when it is used to serve some moral or political end for it then becomes propaganda. This eighteenth century attitude is now as fashionable as Dior dresses. Hence, many a critic who keeps up with the literary Joneses reserves his most powerful ammunition for what he calls problem novels, thesis novels, propaganda novels.

Being a product of the twentieth century (Hitler, atomic energy, Hiroshima, Buchenwald, Mussolini, USSR) I find it difficult to subscribe to the idea that art exists for art's sake. It seems to me that all truly great art is propaganda, whether it be the Sistine Chapel, or *La Gioconda, Madame Bovary,* or *War and Peace.* The novel, like all other forms of art, will always reflect the political, economic, and social structure of the period in which it was created. I think I could make out a fairly good case for the idea that the finest novels are basically novels of social criticism, some obviously and intentionally, others less obviously, unintentionally, from *Crime and Punishment* to *Ulysses,* to *Remembrance of Things Past,* to *USA.* The moment the novelist begins to show how society affected the lives of his characters, how they were formed and shaped by the sprawling inchoate world in which they lived, he is writing a novel of social criticism whether he calls it that or not. The greatest novelists have been so sharply aware of the political and social aspects of their time that this awareness inevitably showed up in their major works. I think that this is as true of Dickens, Tolstoy, and Dostoevski as it is of Balzac, Hemingway, Dreiser, Faulkner. . . .

Naturalism and realism are terms that are used almost interchangeably. *Studs Lonigan* and *USA* are called naturalist novels. But *The Grapes of Wrath* is cited as an example of realism. So is *Tom Jones*. Time, that enemy of labels, makes this ridiculous. Dickens, George Sand, Mrs. Gaskell, George Elliot, Harriet Beecher Stowe, wrote books in which they advocated the rights of labor, condemned slums, slavery and anti-Semitism, roughly a hundred years ago. They are known as "the humanitarian novelists of the nineteenth century." Yet the novels produced in the thirties which made a similar comment on society are lumped together as proletarian literature and their origin contributed to the perfidious influence of Karl Marx. This particular label has been used so extensively in recent years that the ghost of Marx seems even livelier than that of Hamlet's father's ghost—or at least he, Marx, appears to have done his haunting over more of the world's surface.

I think it would make more sense if some of the fictional emphasis on social problems were attributed to the influence of the Old Testament idea that man is his brother's keeper. True it is an idea that has been corrupted in a thousand ways—sometimes it has been offered to the world as socialism, and then again as communism. It was used to justify the Inquisition of the Roman Church in Spain, the burning of witches in New England, the institution of slavery in the South. It seems plausible that so potent an idea should keep cropping up in fiction for it is a part of the cultural heritage of the West. If it is not recognized as such it is almost impossible to arrive at a satisfactory explanation for, let along classify, some of the novels that are derived from it. How should *Uncle Tom's Cabin, Germinal,* and *Mary Barton* be classified? As proletarian literature? If *Gentleman's Agreement* is a problem novel what is *Daniel Deronda*? Jack London may be a proletarian writer but his most famous book *The Call of the Wild* is an adventure story. George Sand has been called one of the founders of the "problem" novel but the bulk of her output dealt with those bourgeois emotions: love and passion.

I think one of the difficulties here is the refusal to recognize and admit the fact that not all of the concern about the shortcomings of society originated with Marx. Many a socially conscious novelist is merely a man or woman with a conscience. Though part of the cultural heritage of all of us derives from Marx, whether we subscribe to the Marxist theory or not, a larger portion of it stems from the Bible. . . .

No matter what these novels are called, the average reader seems to like them. Possibly the reading public, and here I include myself, is like the man who kept butting his head against a stone wall and when asked for an explanation said that he went in for this strange practice because it felt so good when he stopped. Perhaps there is a streak of masochism in all of us; or perhaps we all feel guilty because of the shortcomings of society and our sense of guilt is partially assuaged when we are accused, in the printed pages of a novel, of having done those things that we ought not to have done—and of having left undone those things we ought to have done.

The craftsmanship that goes into these novels is of a high order. It has to be. They differ from other novels only in the emphasis on the theme—but it is the theme which causes the most difficulty. All novelists attempt to record the slow struggle of man toward his long home, sometimes depicting only the beginning or the middle or the end of the journey, emphasizing the great emotional peaks of birth and marriage and death which occurs along the route. If it is a good job, the reader nods and says, Yes, that is how it must have been. Because the characters are as real as one's next-door-neighbor, predictable and yet unpredictable, lingering in the memory.

The sociological novelist sets out to do the same thing. But he is apt to become so obsessed by his theme, so entangled in it and fascinated by it, that his heroes resemble the early Christian martyrs; and his villains are showboat villains, first-class scoundrels with no redeeming features or virtues. If he is more pamphleteer than novelist, and something of a romanticist in the bargain, he will offer a solution to the social problem he has posed. He may be in love with a new world order, and try to sell it to his readers; or, and this happens more frequently, he has a trade union, usually the CIO, come to the rescue in the final scene, horse-opera fashion, and the curtain rings down on a happy ending as rosy as that of a western movie done in technicolor.

Characterization can be the greatest glory of the sociological novel. I offer as examples: Oliver Twist, child of the London slums, asking for more; Ma Joad, holding the family together in that long westward journey, somehow in her person epitomizing an earlier generation of women who traveled westward in search of a promised land; Bigger Thomas, who was both criminal and victim, fleeing for his life over the rooftops of Chicago; Jeeter Lester, clinging to his worn-out land in futile defiance of a mechanized world. They have an amazing vitality, much of which springs from the theme. People still discuss them, argue about them, as though they had had an actual existence.

Though characterization is the great strength of these novels, as it is of all novels, it can also be the great weakness. When society is given the role of fate, made the evil in the age-old battle between good and evil, the burden of responsibility for their actions is shifted away from the characters. This negates the Old Testament idea of evil as a thing of the spirit, with each individual carrying on his own personal battle against the evil within himself. In a book which is more political pamphlet or sermon than novel the characters do not battle with themselves to save their souls, so to speak. Their defeat or their victory is not their own—they are pawns in the hands of a deaf, blind, stupid, social system. Once the novelist begins to manipulate his characters to serve the interests of his theme they lose whatever vitality they had when their creator first thought about them. . . .

Why do people write these novels? . . .

I think the best answer to that question, on record, is to be found in Robert Van Gelder's *Writers and Writing*. He quotes Erich Remarque *(All Quiet on the Western Front, Three Comrades, Arch of Triumph)* as saying that people cannot count with their imaginations, that if five million die in a concentration camp it really does not equal one death in emotional impact and meaning—the death of someone you have known and loved: "If I say one died—a man I have made you know and understand—he lived so, this is what he thought, this is what he hoped, this was his faith, these were his difficulties, these his triumphs. . . ."

Suggested Readings with Similar Theme:

Wilkerson, Doxey A. "Negro Culture: Heritage and Weapon." *Masses and Mainstream* (1949): 3–24.

Baldwin, James. "Everybody's Protest Novel." *Partisan Review* 16 (June 1949): 578–723. Reprint, *Notes of a Native Son*. Boston: Beacon Press, 1955. Reprinted in this volume.

Hernton, Calvin. Foreword to *The Collected Stories of Chester Himes*, ix–xii. New York: Thunder's Mouth Press, 1996.

From "Many Thousand Gone" (1951)

Baldwin takes on the voice of white America in his analysis of African American images in protest fiction written by African American writers, especially by Richard Wright. But the voice of Black America also emerges. What images are disturbing to Baldwin? What is being suggested when he writes, "{T}he fact is not that the Negro has no tradition but that there has as yet arrived no sensibility sufficiently profound and tough to make this tradition articulate"? How does Baldwin define this tradition? As he sees it, what is the role of the African American writer?

Now the most powerful and celebrated statement we have yet had of what it means to be a Negro in America is unquestionably Richard Wright's *Native Son*. The feeling which prevailed at the time of its publication was that such a novel, bitter, uncompromising, shocking, gave proof, by its very existence, of what strides might be taken in a free democracy; and its indisputable success, proof that Americans were now able to look full in the face without flinching the dreadful facts. Americans, unhappily, have the most remarkable ability to alchemize all bitter truths into an innocuous but piquant confection and to transform their moral contradictions, or public discussion of such contradictions, into a proud decoration, such as are given for heroism on the field of battle. Such a book, we felt with pride, could never have been written before—which was true. Nor could it be written today. It bears already the aspect of a landmark; for Bigger and his brothers have undergone yet another metamorphosis; they have been accepted in baseball leagues and by colleges hitherto exclusive; and they have had a most favorable appearance on the national screen. We have yet to encounter, nevertheless, a report so indisputably authentic, or one that can begin to challenge this most significant novel.

It is, in a certain American tradition, the story of an unremarkable youth in battle with the force of circumstance; that force of circumstance which plays and which has played so important a part in the national fables of success or failure. In this case the force of circumstance is not poverty merely but color, a circumstance which cannot be overcome, against which the protagonist battles for his life and loses. It is, on the surface, remarkable that this book should have enjoyed among Americans the favor it did enjoy; no more remarkable, however, than that it should have been compared, exuberantly,

to Dostoevsky, though placed a shade below Dos Passos, Dreiser, and Stein-
beck; and when the book is examined, its impact does not seem remarkable
at all, but becomes, on the contrary, perfectly logical and inevitable.

We cannot, to begin with, divorce this book from the specific social climate of that time: it was one of the last of those angry productions, encountered in the late twenties and all through the thirties, dealing with the
inequities of the social structure of America. It was published one year before
our entry into the last world war—which is to say, very few years after the
dissolution of the WPA and the end of the New Deal and at a time when
bread lines and soup kitchens and bloody industrial battles were bright in
everyone's memory. The rigors of that unexpected time filled us not only with
a genuinely bewildered and despairing idealism—so that, because there at
least was something to fight for, young men went off to die in Spain—but
also with a genuinely bewildered self-consciousness. The Negro, who had
been during the magnificent twenties a passionate and delightful primitive,
now became, as one of the things we were most self-conscious about, our
most oppressed minority. In the thirties, swallowing Marx whole, we discovered the Worker and realized—I should think with some relief—that the
aims of the Worker and the aims of the Negro were one. This theorem—to
which we shall return—seems now to leave rather too much out of account; it
became, nevertheless, one of the slogans of the "class struggle" and the gospel
of the New Negro.

As for this New Negro, it was Wright who became his most eloquent
spokesman; and his work, from its beginning, is most clearly committed to
the social struggle. Leaving aside the considerable question of what relationship precisely the artist bears to the revolutionary, the reality of man as a
social being is not his only reality and that artist is strangled who is forced to
deal with human beings solely in social terms; and who has, moreover, as
Wright had, the necessity thrust on him of being the representative of some
thirteen million people. It is a false responsibility (since writers are not con-
gressmen) and impossible, by its nature, of fulfillment. The unlucky shepherd
soon finds that, so far from being able to feed the hungry sheep, he has lost
the wherewithal for his own nourishment: having not been allowed—so fearful was his burden, so present his audience!—to recreate his own experience.
Further, the militant men and women of the thirties were not, upon examination, significantly emancipated from their antecedents, however bitterly they
might consider themselves estranged or however gallantly they struggled to
build a better world. However they might extol Russia, their concept of a
better world was quite helplessly American and betrayal a certain thinness of
imagination, a suspect reliance on suspect and badly digested formula, and a
positively fretful romantic haste. Finally, the relationship of the Negro to the
Worker cannot be summed up, nor even greatly illuminated, by saying that
their aims are one. It is true only insofar as they both desire better working

conditions and useful only insofar as they unite their strengths as workers to achieve these ends. Further than this we cannot in honesty go.

In this climate Wright's voice first was heard and the struggle which promised for a time to shape his work and give it purpose also fixed it in an ever more unrewarding rage. Recording his days of anger he has also nevertheless recorded, as no Negro before him had ever done, that fantasy Americans hold in their minds when they speak of the Negro: that fantastic and fearful image which we have lived with since the first slave fell beneath the lash. This is the significance of *Native Son* and also, unhappily, its overwhelming limitation.

Native Son begins with the Brring! of an alarm clock in the squalid Chicago tenement where Bigger and his family live. Rats live there too, feeding off the garbage, and we first encounter Bigger in the act of killing one. One may consider that the entire book, from that harsh Brring! to Bigger's weak "Good-bye" as the lawyer, Max, leaves him in the death cell, is an extension, with the roles inverted, of this chilling metaphor. Bigger's situation and Bigger himself exert on the mind that same sort of fascination. The premise of the book is, as I take it, clearly conveyed in these first pages: we are confronting a monster created by the American republic and we are, through being made to share his experience, to receive illumination as regard the manner of this life and to feel both pity and horror at his awful and inevitable doom. This is an arresting and potentially rich idea and we would be discussing a very different novel if Wright's execution had been more perceptive and if he had not attempted to redeem a symbolic monster in social terms.

One may object that it was precisely Wright's intention to create in Bigger a social symbol, revelatory of social disease and prophetic of disaster. I think, however, that it is this assumption which we ought to examine more carefully. Bigger has no discernible relationship to himself, to his own life, to his own people, nor to any other people—in this respect, perhaps, his is most American—and his force comes, not from his significance as a social (or antisocial) unit, but from his significance as the incarnation of a myth. It is remarkable that, though we follow him step by step from the tenement room to the death cell, we know as little about him when this journey is ended as we did when it began; and, what is even more remarkable, we know almost as little about the social dynamic which we are to believe created him. Despite the details of slum life which we are given, I doubt that anyone who has thought about it, disengaging himself from sentimentality, can accept this most essential premise of the novel for a moment. Those Negroes who surround him, on the other hand, his hard-working mother, his ambitious sister, his poolroom cronies, Bessie, might be considered as far richer and far more subtle and accurate illustrations of the ways in which Negroes are controlled in our society and the complex techniques they have evolved for their survival. We are limited, however, to Bigger's view of them, part of a deliberate plan which might not have been disastrous if we were not also limited to Bigger's perceptions. What this means for the novel is that a necessary dimension has been cut away; this dimension being the relationship that Negroes bear to one another, the depth of involvement and unspoken recognition of shared experience which creates a way of life. What the novel reflects—and at no point interprets—is the isolation of the Negro within his own group and the resulting fury of impatient scorn. It is this which creates its climate of anarchy and unmotivated and unapprehended disaster; and it is this climate, common to most Negro protest novels, which has led us all to believe that in Negro life there exists no tradition, no field of manners, no possibility of ritual or intercourse, such as may, for example, sustain the Jew even after he has left his father's house. But the fact is not that the Negro has no tradition but that there has as yet arrived no sensibility sufficiently profound and tough to make this tradition articulate. For a tradition expresses, after all, nothing more than the long and painful experience of a people; it comes out of the battle waged to maintain their integrity or, to put it more simply, out of their struggle to survive. When we speak of the Jewish tradition we are speaking of centuries of exile and persecution, of the strength which endured and the sensibility which discovered in it the high possibility of the moral victory.

The sense of how Negroes live and how they have so long endured is hidden from us in part by the very speed of the Negro's public progress, a progress so heavy with complexity, so bewildering and kaleidoscopic, that he dare not pause to conjecture on the darkness which lies behind him; and by the nature of the American psychology which, in order to apprehend or be made able to accept it, must undergo a metamorphosis so profound as to be literally unthinkable and which there is no doubt we will resist until we are compelled to achieve our own identity by the rigors of a time that has yet to come. Bigger, in the meanwhile, and all his furious kin, serve only to whet the notorious national taste for the sensational and to reinforce all that we now find it necessary to believe. It is not Bigger whom we fear, since his appearance among us makes out victory certain. . . .

Suggested Readings with Similar Theme:

Ellison, Ralph. "Change the Joke and Slip the Yoke" and "The World and the Jug." In *Shadow and Act.* New York: Random House, 1964.
———. "A Dialogue with his Audience" *Barat Review* (1968): 51–53.

1955–1975:
CULTURAL AUTONOMY AND UNDERSTANDING THE ART OF BLACK POETRY, DRAMA, FICTION, AND CRITICISM

◆

RALPH ELLISON

From "The Art of Fiction:
An Interview" (1955)

Outline Ellison's discussion of the creative process. Based on his aesthetic positions, what are his philosophical conclusions about the protest novel? How does Ellison enter discussions with Baldwin, Petry, and Wright about literature of the 1940s and 1950s about African American sensibilities? According to to Ellison, what is the art of African American fiction?

Interviewers: Were you affected by the social realism of the period?
Ellison: I was seeking to learn and social realism was a highly regarded theory, though I didn't think too much of the so-called proletarian fiction even when I was most impressed by Marxism. I was intrigued by Malraux, who at that time was being claimed by the Communists. I noticed, however, that whenever the heroes of *Man's Fate* regarded their condition during moments of heightened self-consciousness, their thinking was something other than Marxist. Actually they were more profoundly intellectual than their real-life counterparts. Of course, Malraux was more of a humanist than most of the Marxist writers of that period—and also much more of an artist. He was the artist-revolutionary rather than a politician when he wrote *Man's Fate,* and the book lives not because of a political position embraced at the time, but because of its larger concern with the tragic struggle of humanity. Most of the social realists of the period were concerned less with tragedy than with injustice. I wasn't, and am not, primarily concerned with injustice, but with art.

Interviewers: Then you consider your novel a purely literary work as opposed to one in the tradition of social protest.
Ellison: Now mind! I recognize no dichotomy between art and protest. Dostoievsky's *Notes from Underground* is, among other things, a protest against the limitations of nineteenth-century rationalism; *Don Quixote, Man's Fate, Oedipus Rex, The Trial*—all these embody protest, even against the limitations of human life itself. If social protest is antithetical to art, what then shall we make of Goya, Dickens and Twain? One hears a lot of complaints about the so-called "protest" novel, especially when written by Negroes; but it seems to me that the critics could more accurately complain about their lack of craftsmanship and their provincialism.

Interviewers: But isn't it going to be difficult for the Negro writer to escape provincialism when his literature is concerned with a minority?

Ellison: All novels are about certain minorities: the individual is a minority. The universal in the novel—and isn't that what we're all clamoring for these days?—is reached only through the depiction of the specific circumstance.

Interviewers: But still, how is the Negro writer, in terms of what is expected of him by critics and readers, going to escape his particular need for social protest and reach the "universal" you speak of?

Ellison: If the Negro, or any other writer, is going to do what is expected of him, he's lost the battle before he takes the field. I suspect that all the agony that goes into writing is borne precisely because the writer longs for acceptance—but it must be acceptance on his own terms. Perhaps, though, this thing cuts both ways: the Negro novelist draws his blackness too tightly around him when he sits down to write—that's what the anti-protest critics believe—but perhaps the white reader draws his whiteness around himself when he sits down to read. He doesn't want to identify himself with Negro characters in terms of our immediate racial and social situation, though on the deeper human level, identification can become compelling when the situation is revealed artistically. The white reader doesn't want to get too close, not even in an imaginary re-creation of society. Negro writers have felt this and it has led to much of our failure.

Too many books by Negro writers are addressed to a white audience. By doing this the authors run the risk of limiting themselves to the audience's presumptions of what a Negro is or should be; the tendency is to become involved in polemics, to plead the Negro's humanity. You know, many white people question that humanity but I don't think that Negroes can afford to indulge in such a false issue. For us the question should be, What are the specific *forms* of that humanity, and what in our background is worth preserving or abandoning. The clue to this can be found in folklore, which offers the first drawings of any group's character. It preserves mainly those situations which have repeated themselves again and again in the history of any given group. It describes those rites, manners, customs, and so forth, which insure the good life, or destroy it; and it describes those boundaries of feeling, thought and action which that particular group has found to be the limitation of the human condition. It projects this wisdom in symbols which express the group's will to survive; it embodies those values by which the group lives and dies. These drawings may be crude but they are nonetheless profound in that they represent the group's attempt to humanize the world. It's no accident that great literature, the products of individual artists, is erected upon this humble base. The hero of Dostoievsky's *Notes from Underground* and the hero of Gogol's *The Overcoat* appear in their rudimentary forms far back in Russian folklore. French literature has never ceased exploring the nature of the Frenchman . . . Or take Picasso—

Interviewers: How does Picasso fit into all this?

Ellison: Why, he's the greatest wrestler with forms and techniques of them all. Just the same he's never abandoned the old symbolic forms of Spanish art: the guitar, the bull, daggers, women, shawls, veils, mirrors. Such symbols serve a dual function: they allow the artist to speak of complex experiences and to annihilate time with simple lines and curves; and they allow the viewer an orientation, both emotional and associative, which goes so deep that a total culture may resound in a simple rhythm, an image. It has been said that Escudero could recapitulate the history and spirit of the Spanish dance with a simple arabesque of his fingers.

Interviewers: But these are examples from homogeneous cultures. How representative of the American nation would you say Negro folklore is?

Ellison: The history of the American Negro is a most intimate part of American history. Through the very process of slavery came the building of the United States. Negro folklore, evolving within a larger culture which regarded it as inferior, was an especially courageous expression. It announced the Negro's willingness to trust his own experience, his own sensibilities as to the definition of reality, rather than allow his masters to define these crucial matters for him. His experience is that of America and the West, and is as rich a body of experience as one would find anywhere. We can view it narrowly as something exotic, folksy or "low-down," or we may identify ourselves with it and recognize it as an important segment of the larger American experience—not lying at the bottom of it, but intertwined, diffused in its very texture. I can't take this lightly or be impressed by those who cannot see its importance; it is important to *me.* One ironic witness to the beauty and the universality of this art is the fact that the descendants of the very men who enslaved us can now sing the spirituals and find in the singing an exultation of their own humanity. Just take a look at some of the slave songs, blues, folk ballads; their possibilities for the writer are infinitely suggestive. Some of them have named human situations so well that a whole corps of writers could not exhaust their universality. For instance, here's an old slave verse:

> *Ole Aunt Dinah, she's just like me*
> *She work so hard she want to be free*
> *But old Aunt Dinah's gittin' kinda ole*
> *She's afraid to go to Canada on account of the cold.*
>
> *Ole Uncle Jack, now he's a mighty "good nigger"*
> *You tell him that you want to be free for a fac'*
> *Next thin you know they done stripped the skin off your back.*
>
> *Now old Uncle Ned, he want to be free*
> *He found his way north by the moss on the tree*

He cross that river floating in a tub
The patateroller give him a mighty close rub.

It's crude, but in it you have three universal attitudes toward the problem of freedom. You can refine it and sketch in the psychological subtleties and historical and philosophical allusions, action and what not, but I don't think its basic definition can be exhausted. Perhaps some genius could do as much with it as Mann has done with the Joseph story.

Interviewers: Can you give us an example of the use of folklore in your own novel?

Ellison: Well, there are certain themes, symbols and images which are based on folk material. For example, there is the old saying amongst Negroes: if you're black, stay back; if you're brown, stick around; if you're white, you're right. And there is the joke Negroes tell on themselves about their being so black they can't be seen in the dark. In my book this sort of thing was merged with the meanings which blackness and light have long had in Western mythology: evil and goodness, ignorance and knowledge, and so on. In my novel the narrator's development is one through blackness to light; that is, from ignorance to enlightenment: invisibility. He leaves the South and goes North; this, as you will notice in reading Negro folktales, is always the road to freedom—the movement upward. You have the same thing again when he leaves his underground cave for the open.

It took me a long time to learn how to adapt such examples of myth into my work—also ritual. The use of ritual is equally a vital part of the creative process. I learned a few things from Eliot, Joyce and Hemingway, but not how to adapt them. When I started writing, I knew that in both *The Waste Land* and *Ulysses* ancient myth and ritual were used to give form and significance to the material; but it took me a few years to realize that the myths and rites which we find functioning in our everyday lives could be used in the same way. In my first attempt at a novel—which I was unable to complete—I began by trying to manipulate the simple structural unities of *beginning, middle* and *end,* but when I attempted to deal with the psychological strata—the images, symbols and emotional configurations—of the experience at hand, I discovered that the unities were simply cool points of stability on which one could suspend the narrative line—but beneath the surface of apparently rational human relationships there seethed a chaos before which I was helpless. People rationalize what they shun or are incapable of dealing with; these superstitions and their rationalizations become ritual as they govern behavior. The rituals become social forms, and it is one of the functions of the artist to recognize them and raise them to the level of art.

I don't know whether I'm getting this over or not. Let's put it this way: Take the "Battle Royal" passage in my novel, where the boys are blindfolded and forced to fight each other for the amusement of the white observers. This is a vital part of behavior pattern in the South, which both Negroes and whites thoughtlessly accept. It is a ritual in preservation of caste lines, a keeping of taboo to appease the gods and ward off bad luck. It is also the initiation ritual to which all greenhorns are subjected. This passage which states what Negroes will see I did not have to invent; the patterns were already there in society, so that all I had to do was present them in a broader context of meaning. In any society there are many rituals of situation which, for the most part, go unquestioned. They can be simple or elaborate, but they are the connective tissue between the work of art and the audience.

Interviewers: Do you think a reader unacquainted with this folklore can properly understand your work?
Ellison: Yes, I think so. It's like jazz; there's no inherent problem which prohibits understanding but the assumptions brought to it. We don't all dig Shakespeare uniformly, or even *Little Red Riding Hood.* The understanding of art depends finally upon one's willingness to extend one's humanity and one's knowledge of human life. I noticed, incidentally, that the Germans, having no special caste assumptions concerning American Negroes, dealt with my work simply as a novel. I think the Americans will come to view it that way in twenty years—if it's around that long.

Interviewers: Don't you think it will be?
Ellison: I doubt it. It's not an important novel. I failed of eloquence, and many of the immediate issues are rapidly fading away. If it does last, it will be simply because there are things going on in its depth that are of more permanent interest than on it surface. I hope so, anyway.

Interviewers: Have the critics given you any constructive help in your writing, or changed in any way your aims in fiction?
Ellison: No, except that I have a better idea of how the critics react, of what they see and fail to see, of how their sense of life differs with mine and mine with theirs. In some instances they were nice for the wrong reasons. In the United States—and I don't want this to sound like an apology for my own failures—some reviewers did not see what was before them because of this nonsense about protest.

Interviewers: Did the critics change your view of yourself as a writer?
Ellison: I can't say that they did. I've been seeing by my own candle too long for that. The critics did give me a sharper sense of a larger audience, yes; and some convinced me that they were willing to judge me in terms of my writing rather than in terms of my racial identity. But there is one widely syndicated critical bankrupt who made liberal noises during the thirties and has been frightened ever since. He attacked my book as a "literary race riot." By and large, the critics and readers gave me an affirmed sense of my identity as a

writer. You might know this within yourself, but to have it affirmed by others is of utmost importance. Writing is, after all, a form of communication.

Suggested Reading with Similar Theme:

Killens, John Oliver. "Opportunities for Development of Negro Talent." In *The American Negro Writer and His Roots*, 64–70. New York: The American Society of African Culture, 1959.

The Creative Process (1962)

First Phillis Wheatley and, now, Baldwin queries the muses: Is it Fancy or Imagination behind the creative process of literature? Does the writer create according to "rigorous rules" or is he or she free to use individual expressions? In responding to his own query, what does Baldwin conclude to be the responsibility of the writer? How does Baldwin echo the neoclassicists? Does Baldwin distinguish a specific race or gender for his writer? What are the implications when race or gender is left to be implied? How does Baldwin enter discussions about the creative process with Ralph Ellison? How does Baldwin anticipate contemporary critics such as McMillan and Pate?

Perhaps the primary distinction of the artist is that he must actively cultivate that state which most men, necessarily, must avoid: the state of being alone. That all men are, when the chips are down, alone, is a banality—a banality because it is very frequently stated, but very rarely, on the evidence believed. Most of us are not compelled to linger with the knowledge of our aloneness, for it is a knowledge that can paralyze all action in this world. There are, forever, swamps to be drained, cities to be created, mines to be exploited, children to be fed. None of these things can be done alone. But the conquest of the physical world is not man's only duty. He is also enjoined to conquer the great wilderness of himself. The precise role of the artist, then, is to illuminate that darkness, blaze roads through that vast forest, so that we will not, in all our doing, lose sight of its purpose, which is, after all, to make the world a more human dwelling place.

The state of being alone is not meant to bring to mind merely a rustic musing beside some silver lake. The aloneness of which I speak is much more like the aloneness of birth or death. It is like the fearful aloneness that one sees in the eyes of someone who is suffering, whom we cannot help. Or it is like the aloneness of love, the force and mystery that so many have extolled and so many have cursed, but which no one has ever understood or ever really been able to control. I put the matter this way, not out of any desire to create pity for the artist—God forbid!—but to suggest how nearly, after all, is his state the state of everyone, and in an attempt to make vivid his endeavor. The states of birth, suffering, love, and death are extreme states—extreme, universal, and inescapable. We all know this, but we would rather not know it.

The artist is present to correct the delusions to which we fall prey in our attempts to avoid this knowledge.

It is for this reason that all societies have battled with that incorrigible disturber of the peace—the artist. . . .

And a higher level of consciousness among the people is the only hope we have, now or in the future, of minimizing human damage. . . .

The artist is distinguished from all other responsible actors in society—the politicians, legislators, educators, and scientists—by the fact that he is his own test tube, his own laboratory, working according to very rigorous rules, however unstated these may be, and cannot allow any consideration to supersede his responsibility to reveal all that he can possibly discover concerning the mystery of the human being. A society must accept some things as real; but he must always know that visible reality hides a deeper one, and that all our action and achievement rest on things unseen. A society must assume that it is stable, but the artist must know, and he must let us know, that there is nothing stable under heaven. One cannot possibly build a school, teach a child, or drive a car without taking some things for granted. The artist cannot and must not take anything for granted, but must drive to the heart of every answer and expose the question the answer hides.

I seem to be making extremely grandiloquent claims for a breed of men and women historically despised while living and acclaimed when safely dead. But, in a way, the belated honor that all societies tender their artists proves the reality of the point I am trying to make. I am really trying to make clear the nature of the artist's responsibility to his society. The peculiar nature of this responsibility is that he must never cease warring with it, for its sake and for his own. . . .

Suggested Reading with Similar Theme:

Wright, Richard. "How 'Bigger' Was Born." In *Native Son*. New York: Harper and Row, 1940.

MAX ROACH

Jazz (1962)

Define jazz as a black poetic reference. Place jazz in historical-cultural contexts and explain how the art form becomes "the indigenous music of the indigent black man and woman." According to this jazz musician and essayist, how has the music been largely "misrepresented, misconstrued, and capitalized upon" by non-blacks?

A kind of music, generally improvised but sometimes arranged, achieving its effects by syncopation, heavily accented rhythms, dissonance, melodic variation, and particular tonal qualities of the saxophone, trumpet, clarinet, and other instruments. It was originated by New Orleans Negro musicians.

This interpretation, taken from the *Encyclopaedia Britannica Dictionary* is, at best, only a surface explanation of this many spectrumed terminology. "Jazz," has never, except in very vague terms, been answered, as to its meaning, intent and content by its creators. This phenomenon (its never being answered), for all its intrigue, however, will not be delved into at this time. I mean to deal only with what the music, in actuality, is.

"Jazz" is an extenuation of the African chants and songs. It is an extension of the pain and suffering of those long, and too often, destinationless trips across the Atlantic Ocean, deep in the holes of those dark, damp, filthy, human slave ships, endured by chained, innocent, black men, women and children. "Jazz" is an extension of the humiliations suffered by these same human beings while being sold as cattle or produce. It is an extension of the pain of the whip, the assaulter, the procurer, the "driva' man," the patrol wagons, the kidnapper, the sunup to sundown slave field and plantation. It is the extension of many, many lynchings, castrations, and other "improvisations" of genocide on these same black men, women and children. "Jazz" is an extension of the black man, "freed," who found himself still shackled to the same chain, all shined up, when he unwittingly ventured out into "their" free world of opportunity and wealth, only to be assaulted, whipped, murdered, and raped some more. The "Spiritual," "Race music," "Rhythm and Blues," "Dixieland," "Jazz," (and never, yet, any of the music named by its creators, but by the disdainful, master observer). "Jazz" is an extension of the black artist being relegated to practice his or her craft, even today, under these intolerable, too similar, conditions.

This is why I say the white musician has never made a contribution of any consequence, is not making a contribution of any consequence, and will never make a contribution of any consequence to what is known to this society as "Jazz." The white man named the music, is intrigued by the music, has made billions of dollars from the music, and now would claim to be its collaborator in the authoring of the music.

There are, however, those white musicians who have come to the music respectfully and sympathetically, and elaborate, within the bounds of their emotional ability to identify with their black brothers and humanity, on the music. To me, a contribution is a creation, and two mothers cannot give birth to the same child nor has it ever been so. "Jazz" is the indigenous music of the indigent black man and woman. The musical instruments and theories on harmony preceded the black man in this country, but it was, and is, the black man's hell on earth, which he sublimated, and is sublimating into beauty that makes for the esthetic contribution, "Jazz." The music, in its emotional intensity, brilliance and drive, and extended harmonic and rhythmic frontiers, is indicative of where the "Negro" came *from* and *to* and foretells where he might go one day.

Because the connotation of the word, "Jazz," has gained stature in the eyes of the society and the world, and its original spelling (jass), abandoned, it has not changed its original emotional and social content, just as to be born black has not changed in its punitive and despicable repercussions within the society that fosters repression. The music, consequently, is being misrepresented, distorted, misconstrued, and capitalized upon by others than its authors. (I, for one, do not feel called upon, nor obliged to let it pass so lightly.) Indeed, why should it be allowed to pass at all? For the sake of my children, and my children's children, I will not let it pass. Will we still be robbed and raped of our heritage? Is there to be no unclouded, "pure" legacy for mine? Can I have so little regard for all my years of "living," "learning," and *loving*? Has any man? All men are protective and jealous of the things they love, if they be "men."

The white musician, if he truly loves and respects the art form called "Jazz," will respectfully recognize its authors and bring whatever attitudes to the music he can, and will, honestly. The black musician is not so bigoted and insensitive as to shut out his white brother, as he (the black man) was and is still being shut out, as for example, in the "classical" concert stage, television, movies, "legitimate" theatre. (Though, in nearly all of these mediums, simulated "jazz" is being incorporated.) The shining crown of "Jazz" would be usurped.

To the white musicians who screams, "crow-jim," I ask him to justify this terminology, if indeed he can, by explaining how Dave Brubeck, Stan Kenton, Gerry Mulligan, Shelly Manne, Stan Getz, Gene Krupa, Anita O'Day, Al Hirt, Benny Goodman, Chet Baker, Peggy Lee, Buddy Rich, Gil Evans, Bill Evans, Pete Rugolo, Andre Previn, Jack Teagarden, June Christy, to name a few who make a very healthy living, and enjoy much fame, (state department tours to Africa, yet,) compared to our small black minority of an astronomical majority of very fine artists, who can boast of the kind of money the white artists are "privileged" to make. In what other society can an artist be so flagrantly plagiarized, ignored, and deprived and still be made the "heavy?" Would you see a man, finally allowed to produce, employ his proven rival, his dedicated rival, (in every walk of life) in preference to his brother and commiserator, who is not only in complete emotional sympathy with him, and therefore more suitable and adequate for the job to be done, but who would be left with no job at all, if not for the consideration, dependence and *finally* opportunity of the "employer" who is in essence, himself? Can a man be so charged for licking his own wounds?

"Jazz" is persevering, in the face of all obstacle and humiliation, to paint some musical, bitter sweet picture that comes out of the experience, suffering, and love of the black people of the United States. Until the white musician has been called upon to give and experience as much, and the same, he can not, in all honesty, claim the kind of affinity to the music he insists he has. Would you ask a man with heart trouble to describe a cancer? A man may die of both but one is infinitely more painful and less merciful than the other. Why not have two descriptions of sickness then? Heart trouble and cancer. Or would you be so ignorant of pain and so unsympathetic to its sufferer and humanity as to give a vague and untruthful diagnosis? Charlie Parker was a musical product of his experiences as a man. But he was a black man, first, last, and always. No intellectual analysis, or "understanding" of the man's experiences will work for a reproduction of the emotional tools of feeling he used. Each man must, by necessity, develop his or her artistic offering by use of the only emotional tools he has; his own . . . and his tools are shaped, and molded as an extension of his own unique emotional climate.

While the black man, lover and creator of his contribution, "Jazz," a product that grosses billions of dollars yearly on an international scale, has been so nicely raped of the glory (monetary benefits, although he is quite often a "poll winner") of his achievement, he (the militant) has been accused of practicing racism, of being weird (the "classical" musician, on the other hand, is called "sensitive") of being bitter, has been placed in insane asylums, penal institutions (rather than hospitals), pressured into leaving the country altogether, beaten for standing on a street corner, murdered on the highways, grave-robbed, preyed upon by socially outcast neurotic women and others. His plight can only be compared to the Harlem plebeian.

The royal family of "Jazz" is a joke. No other "Duke" (Ellington) has ever reigned so nobly and gotten such ill and paltry compensation. No other "Count" (Basie) has been so ignobly used. No other "Lady" (Holiday) has died so friendless and under such dire circumstances (and in jail, yet). No other "Pres" (Lester Young) has been so ill-abused or condemned to die so tortuously. No other "King" (Cole) has been so ignobly detested by sight.

Since our artistocracy is held in such low esteem, can the plebeian hope for God to save us?

Suggested Readings with Similar Theme:

Andrews, Dwight D. "From Black to Blues: Toward a Blues Aesthetic." In *The Blues Aesthetic: Black Culture and Modernism,* edited by Richard J. Powell, 37–39. Washington, D.C.: Washington Project for the Arts, 1989.

Cephas, John. "The Blues." In *The Blues Aesthetic: Black Culture and Modernism,* edited by Richard J. Powell, 15–17. Washington, D.C.: Washington Project for the Arts, 1989.

Long, Worth. "The Wisdom of the Blues—Defining Blues as the True Facts of Life: An Interview with Willie Dixon." *African American Review* 29, no. 2 (Summer 1995): 207–12.

OSSIE DAVIS

The Significance of Lorraine Hansberry (1965)

In remembering the playwright Lorraine Hansberry, actor and playwright Ossie Davis examines the "racial mountain" facing black playwrights in the 1950s: white audiences which refused to recognize truth, beauty, and justice in black art outside of public expectations of black art. According to Davis, one other obstacle was "that division of the art world—of common aesthetics and public taste—bounded all too often by what Broadway and Hollywood {thought could} be sold at a profit." What does Davis mean? Discuss Davis's conclusion about black art: "race will always be dragged into the judging of art" by white and black audiences. Define the following phrases: institutionalized response and pre-conscious judgment.

The central problem of every Negro artist, Lorraine Hansberry included, is not only that he is estranged from his culture, but also alienated from himself. For not only has Western culture in its racist orientation an ambivalence in its expectations from Negro art, it also forces the Negro artist to be ambivalent in his relations to himself. For—Franz Boas and the science of anthropology notwithstanding—Americans, to a large degree, but not entirely, still accept race as a determinant of value; as a measure of what is good and what is less good, what is beautiful and what is less perfect, and most of all what is worthy and what is trivial. To a large degree but not entirely. If three of our young men are struck dead in freedom's cause in Mississippi the shock of horror that shoots through the country is directly attributable to the fact that two of these sacrifices were of superior consequences to us, racially, than was the third. In our country, regardless of how they may have personally objected to it, a Mickey Schwerner and an Andy Goodman can confer status on a James Chaney merely by dying in his company. For they were white and he was black; and by sharing a death and a grave they raised him to the level of their importance—an importance he, because he was Negro, could never have achieved by dying for his freedom by himself. This realization that no matter what one does, or how well, race will always be dragged into the judging of it, will be decisive to a large degree but not entirely, must come one day sooner or later—like death—to every Negro artist.

He must then lay aside his life's work: all his tools, all his ideas and theories about the world and about himself—his artist's dreams and plannings ... and wrestle mightily within himself. He must fight the whole of Western

117

civilization within himself, trying to discover who and what he is in the light of a culture determined to avoid giving him a direct answer—that does not know whether to do with him, or to do without him—that has nowhere, just yet, to place him and his aspirations, but is afraid to leave him free to find a place for himself. And he must curse and rage and argue and fight and carry this muffled war within himself until he can, with whatever honor he has left, come to some sort of peace with the system, which he can only hope is short of total surrender. He must come to terms with the fact that in the light of Western culture he is different, maybe not permanently, but certainly as far as the human eye can see; that even in art he is a prisoner—to a large degree but not entirely—within the confines of his blackness. And that, though nobody expects him to remain in his cell forever—in fact the door is unlocked from time to time—still, nobody is prepared, or desirous, that he should come out of it . . . just yet.

Lorraine's particular prison, as is mine, was that division of the art world—of common aesthetics and public taste—bounded all too often by what Broadway and Hollywood think can be sold at a profit. . . . Where, to a large extent but not entirely, white is still right . . . a world which assumes almost without thinking that the good, the true, and the beautiful are eternally attributable to being white in the first place. And it is here, in this liberally persuaded, permissive, but yet reluctant, America, amidst these holier-than-thou, Anglo-Saxon assumptions mindlessly held; aristocratic intuitions of values felt at our expense; amidst these institutionalized responses, these pre-conscious judgments, subjective, privileged, and willful . . . about us, and against us: it is here that we black ones must live and love also—creating, out of our private anguish and eternal bafflement, the best art we know.

Our limits are handed down to us, like second-hand clothes, from the white man. But what else is there with which to clothe our nakedness? For not only does he set the standards by which all excellence is to be judged, he considers himself to a large degree but not entirely—to *be* that standard. That he, himself, is that *sweet perfection* which all legitimate aspiration, artistic and otherwise, must—in the very nature of things—move upward towards. And though we blacks rebel in full against this arrogant Categorical Imperative, this white world, against which we break our fists, our heads, and sometimes our hearts—is still the world that matters most to us. It is still a world of power, as opposed to our powerlessness; a world of life-or-death, which still, if it sees fit, confers status on Negro art and artists, raising a Lorraine Hansberry, a James Baldwin, a LeRoi Jones,—as James Chaney was raised—to a level of literary importance which none of them, being Negro, could have attained by himself. In practical terms the basic precepts of Western civilization—when Negro talent presents itself for judgment—keep shifting their grounds. And status, when finally conferred—in terms both of critical acclaim and public attention, seems almost tentative, as if something is being instinctively held back: like a white goddess trying dutifully to embrace a

Negro man without flinching. Yes, sometimes the lightning strikes and we succeed, but always we are uneasy in the terms of our success, for there is nothing so galling to the human spirit as to suspect that in your best effort you have succeeded—but for the wrong reasons. Take *A Raisin in the Sun.*

A Raisin in the Sun was a big success on Broadway, both critically and at the box office. It won the New York Drama Critics Circle award as the best play of the 1958–59 season, was subsequently made into a motion picture, and elevated Lorraine Hansberry to the first rank of American playwrights. The play deserved all this—the playwright deserved all this, and more. Without question! But I have a feeling that for all she got, Lorraine never got all she deserved in regards to *Raisin in the Sun*—that she got success, but that in her success she was cheated, both as a writer and as a Negro.

One of the biggest selling points about *Raisin*—filling the grapevine, riding the word-of-mouth, laying the foundation for its wide, wide acceptance—was how much the Younger family was just like any other American family. Some people were ecstatic to find that "it didn't really have to be about Negroes at all!" It was, rather, a walking, talking, living demonstration of our mythic conviction that, underneath, all of us Americans, *color-ain't-got-nothing-to-do-with-it,* are pretty much alike. People are just people, whoever they are; and all they want is a chance to be like other people. This uncritical assumption, sentimentally held by the audience, powerfully fixed in the character of the powerful mother with whom everybody could identify immediately and completely, made any other questions about the Youngers, and what living in the slums of Southside Chicago had done to them, not only irrelevant and impertinent, but also disloyal: *Raisin* was a great American play, and Lorraine was a great American playwright because everybody who walked into the theatre saw in Lena Younger—especially as she was portrayed by Claudia McNeil, his own great American Mama. And that was decisive.

It was good for the great American audience that all of the little guilt feelings and nagging reservations that are raised inevitably by the mere prospect of having to sit through a *Negro* play, could have been set so soon to rest by the simple expedient of seeing Lena Younger, and knowing she was in charge—that they could surrender themselves to her so completely, could find somebody they could trust absolutely up there on that stage—somebody so familiar to them—so comfortable. It was, I say, good for them—and certainly it was good for business. But was it—in the light of the author's real intention—good for the play? It was good that people of all color, strata, faiths and persuasions could identify so completely with Lena Younger, and her family, and their desire to better themselves in the American way. But that's not what the play was about!

The play was about Walter Lee, Lena's son, and what happened to him as a result of having his dream, his life's ambition, endlessly frustrated by poverty, and its attendant social and personal degradation. Walter Lee's dreams of "being somebody," of "making it," like everybody else, were not respectable to Mama, and not very important to us. He wanted a liquor store which would enable him to exploit the misery of his fellow slum dwellers like they were exploited by everybody else. Walter Lee is corrupted by the materialistic aspirations at the heart of Western civilization, and his corruption is bodied forth in his petty, little dream. But it was his dream, *and it was all he had*! And that made it a matter of life or death to him, revolutionary, dangerous in its implications. For it could explode if frustrated; it could destroy people, it could kill, if frustrated! That's what Lorraine was warning us about. But we would only listen to Mama, and Mama did not ever fully understand Walter Lee! Nor the millions of panicky young Americans just like him, caught up in the revolution of rising expectations, in the midst of an affluent society that insists on playing with fire as far as these distorted dreamers are concerned: dangling unspeakable wealth before their eyes every day, yet slapping down their every attempt to reach up and grab, like everybody else. Walter Lee's by the millions, most of them black, trapped in grinding poverty, hemmed in and pinned down in the ghetto, eating out their hearts waiting for the first cheap chance that comes along. But it never comes soon enough, and what is there left for the Walter Lee's to do, but to explode in violence and bloodshed? This is the Walter Lorraine was concerned about, Walter of the "Long, Hot Summers," Walter whose only way out is killing and being killed, blowing out his life in some filthy gutter! Or shooting dope into his veins!

Of course Lorraine seemed to let Walter escape from his fate into the suburbs, and by so doing to let us off the hook: we go out of the same door as Walter does. Whatever happens, Walter is still in Mama's hands, and things are just bound to work out all right. But will they? Has not Walter merely swapped one impossible dream for another? For surely Lorraine would be the last to suggest that life in the suburbs is the sufficient cure for life in the slums. For Walter belongs with the poor. Poverty is like an infectious plague and Walter Lee is a carrier, and will carry his spreading ghetto with him wherever he goes as long as he is poor.

Though *Raisin* made its name and its fame in terms of its surfaces which seem to reflect the fairy tale of success in "the American way" at all its points, Lorraine was not a Negro for nothing. She knew that the American dream held by Mama is as unworkable in this day and age as that held by Walter. She knew that Mama's old-fashioned morality was no solution to being poor and being black in America, even in the suburbs. It's all there, implicit, in Walter and in the play. But we were too busy smiling up at Mama, loving her, blessing her, needing her—to see it.

Lorraine, I am sure, wanted very much that we should understand Walter and his warning as much as we did Mama and her reassurance. But the people who sit in judgment made their choice: Walter's dream and the threat

it contained for our society ended for them when the curtain went down.*
But for Lorraine, and those of us who remember—the play's intent, was
expressed in those lines from Langston Hughes from which she chose her
title—

> *What happens to a dream deferred?*
> *Does it dry up*
> *Like a raisin in the sun?*
> *Or fester like a sore—*
> *And then run?*
> *Does it stink like rotten meat?*
> *Or crust and sugar over—*
> *Like a syrupy sweet?*
> *Maybe it just sags*
> *Like a heavy load.*
> *Or does it explode?*

Lorraine's play was meant to dramatize Langston's question, not to answer it.

But success and the great American audience decreed that Walter and
his dream was Mama's problem. And that as long as she was around to
straighten him out, nobody needed to worry. Lorraine accepted that success—and that verdict. What else could she do under the circumstances?

But she was to have another chance. To write another play, whose primary intent would not be short-circuited by having the audience kidnap a
character, as they had done Mama, and steal her away. Next time her intent
would be crystal clear, her approach absolutely straightforward. She would
insist the audience listen to—and the critic respect—what she had to say in
its sum and in its integrity. It was to be all or none. Take it whole, or leave it
entirely: don't tamper! That's the way she wrote it, and that's the way they
played it.

She called it: *The Sign in Sidney Brustein's Window.* Many of us thought it
her best. I'm glad she made them look at her again, before she died.

Suggested Readings with Similar Theme:

Neal, Larry. "Toward a Relevant Black Theatre." *Black Theatre* (1966): 14–15.
Salaam, Kalamu ya. "Lorraine Hansberry: Unhonored as a Prophet." *Black Collegian*
(March/April 1984): 45–46, 48.

---

*It is their God-given privilege to misread us whenever they want.

LARRY NEAL

The Black Arts Movement (1968)

*According to Neal, what specific concepts do artists of the 1960s adopt from the plat-
form of the Black Power movement? Why does the writer of the 1960s go from being
called "Negro" to "Black"? Specifically, how are black artists to reorder Western cultural aesthetics? According to Neal and others, in what ways is the black poet of the
1960s "a (black) man speaking to (black) men" in the "language of (black) men"?
How must artists maintain that "culture is the basis of all ideas, images, and
actions—i.e., a set of values given to you by your culture"? In what ways do the ideological positions of the creative writers of the 1960s challenge earlier ones by Locke,
Hughes, Petry, or Baldwin? Should writers combine ethical with aesthetic values some
of the time or none of the time?*

1.

The Black Arts Movement is radically opposed to any concept of the artist
that alienates him from his community. Black Art is the aesthetic and spiritual sister of the Black Power concept. As such, it envisions an art that speaks
directly to the needs and aspirations of Black America. In order to perform
this task, the Black Arts Movement proposes a radical reordering of the western cultural aesthetic. It proposes a separate symbolism, mythology, critique,
and iconology. The Black Arts and the Black Power concept both relate
broadly to the Afro-American's desire for self-determination and nationhood.
Both concepts are nationalistic. One is concerned with the relationship
between art and politics; the other with the art of politics.

Recently, these two movements have begun to merge: the political values inherent in the Black Power concept are now finding concrete expression
in the aesthetics of Afro-American dramatists, poets, choreographers, musicians, and novelists. A main tenet of Black Power is the necessity for Black
people to define the world in their own terms. The Black artist has made the
same point in the context of aesthetics. The two movements postulate that
there are in fact and in spirit two Americas—one black, one white. The Black
artist takes this to mean that his primary duty is to speak to the spiritual and
cultural needs of Black people. Therefore, the main thrust of this new breed
of contemporary writers is to confront the contradictions arising out of the
Black man's experience in the racist West. Currently, these writers are reeval-

uating western aesthetics, the traditional role of the writer, and the social function of art. Implicit in this reevaluation is the need to develop a "Black aesthetic." It is the opinion of many Black writers, I among them, that the Western aesthetic has run its course: it is impossible to construct anything meaningful within its decaying structure. We advocate a cultural revolution in art and ideas. The cultural values inherent in western history must either be radicalized or destroyed, and we will probably find that even radicalization is impossible. In fact, what is needed is a whole new system of ideas. Poet Don L. Lee (Haki Madhubuti) expresses it:

> ... We must destroy Faulkner, dick, jane, and other perpetuators of evil. It's time for DuBois, Nat Turner, and Kwame Nkrumah. As Frantz Fanon points out: destroy the culture and you destroy the people. This must not happen. Black artists are culture stabilizers; bringing back old values, and introducing new ones. Black Art will talk to the people and with the will of the people stop impending "protective custody."

The Black Arts Movement eschews "protest" literature. It speaks directly to Black people. Implicit in the concept of "protest" literature, as Brother Knight has made clear, is an appeal to white morality:

> Now any Black man who masters the technique of his particular art form, who adheres to the white aesthetic, and who directs his work toward a white audience is, in one sense, protesting. And implicit in the act of protest is the belief that a change will be forthcoming once the masters are aware of the protestor's "grievance" (the very word connotes begging, supplications to the gods). Only when that belief has faded and protestings end, will Black art begin.

Brother Knight also has some interesting statements about the development of a "Black aesthetic":

> Unless the Black artist establishes a "Black aesthetic" he will have no future at all. To accept the white aesthetic is to accept and validate a society that will not allow him to live. The Black artist must create new forms and new values, sing new songs (or purify old ones); and along with other Black authorities, he must create a new history, new symbols, myths and legends (and purify old ones by fire). And the Black artist, in creating his own aesthetic, must be accountable for it only to the Black people. Further, he must hasten his own dissolution of an individual (in the Western sense)—painful though the process may be, having been breast-fed the poison of "individual experience."

When we speak of a "Black aesthetic" several things are meant. First, we assume that there is already in existence the basis for such an aesthetic. Essentially, it consists of an African-American cultural tradition. But this aesthetic is finally, by implication, broader than that tradition. It encompasses most of the useable elements of Third World culture. The motive behind the Black aesthetic is the destruction of the white thing, the destruction of white ideas, and white ways of looking at the world. The new aesthetic is mostly predicated on an Ethics which asks the question: whose vision of the world is finally more meaningful, ours or the white oppressors? What is truth? Or more precisely, whose truth shall we express, that of the oppressed or of the oppressors? These are basic questions. Black intellectuals of previous decades failed to ask them. Further, national and international affairs demand that we appraise the world in terms of our own interests. It is clear that the question of human survival is at the core of contemporary experience. The Black artist must address himself to this reality in the strongest terms possible. In a context of world upheaval, ethics and aesthetics must interact positively and be consistent with the demands for a more spiritual world. Consequently, the Black Arts Movement is an ethical movement. Ethical, that is, from the viewpoint of the oppressed. And much of the oppression confronting the Third World and Black America is directly traceable to the Euro-American cultural sensibility. This sensibility, anti-human in nature, has, until recently, dominated the psyches of most Black artists and intellectuals; it must be destroyed before the Black creative artist can have a meaningful role in the transformation of society.

It is this natural reaction to an alien sensibility that informs the cultural attitudes of the Black Arts and the Black Power movement. It is a profound ethical sense that makes a Black artist question a society in which art is one thing and the actions of men another. The Black Arts Movement believes that your ethics and your aesthetics are one. That the contradictions between ethics and aesthetics in western society is symptomatic of a dying culture.

The term "Black Arts" is of ancient origin, but it was first used in a positive sense by LeRoi Jones (Amiri Baraka):

> We are unfair
> And unfair
> We are black magicians
> Black arts we make
> in black labs of the heart
> The fair are fair
> and deathly white
> The day will not save them
> And we own the night

There is also a section of the poem "Black Dada Nihilismus" that carries the same motif. But a fuller amplification of the nature of the new aesthetics appears in the poem "Black Art":

> Poems are bullshit unless they are
> teeth or trees or lemons piled

on a step. Or black ladies dying
of men leaving nickel hearts
beating them down. Fuck poems
and they are useful, would they shoot
come at you, love what you are,
breathe like wrestlers, or shudder
strangely after peeing. We want live
words of the hip world, live flesh &
coursing blood. Hearts and Brains
Souls splintering fire. We want poems
like fists beating niggers out of Jocks
or dagger poems in the slimy bellies
of the owner-jews . . .

Poetry is a concrete function, an action. No more abstractions. Poems are physical entities: fists, daggers, airplane poems, and poems that shoot guns. Poems are transformed from physical objects into personal forces:

. . . Put is on him poem. Strip him naked
to the world. Another bad poem cracking
steel knuckles in a jewlady's mouth
Poem scream poison gas on breasts in green berets . . .

Then the poem affirms the integral relationship between Black Art and Black people:

. . . Let Black people understand
that they are the lovers and the sons
of lovers and warriors and sons
of warriors Are poems & poets &
all the loveliness here in the world

It ends with the following lines, a central assertion in both the Black Arts Movement and the philosophy of Black Power:

We want a black poem. And a
Black World.
Let the world be a Black Poem
And let All Black People Speak This Poem
Silently
OR LOUD

The poem comes to stand for the collective conscious and unconscious of Black America—the real impulse in back of the Black Power movement, which is the will toward self-determination and nationhood, a radical reordering of the nature and function of both art and the artist.

2.

In the spring of 1964, LeRoi Jones, Charles Patterson, William Patterson, Clarence Reed, Johnny Moore, and a number of other Black artists opened the Black Arts Repertoire Theatre School. They produced a number of plays including Jones's *Experimental Death Unit # One, Black Mass, Jello* and *Dutchman*. They also initiated a series of poetry readings and concerts. These activities represented the most advanced tendencies in the movement and were of excellent artistic quality. The Black Arts School came under immediate attack by the New York power structure. The Establishment, fearing Black creativity, did exactly what it was expected to do—it attacked the theatre and all of its values. In the meantime, the school was granted funds by OEO through HARYOU-ACT. Lacking a cultural program itself, HARYOU turned to the only organization which addressed itself to the needs of the community. In keeping with its "revolutionary" cultural ideas, the Black Arts Theatre took its programs into the streets of Harlem. For three months, the theatre presented plays, concerts, and poetry readings to the people of the community. Plays that shattered the illusions of the American body politic, and awakened Black people to the meaning of their lives.

Then the hawks from the OEO moved in and chopped off the funds. Again, this should have been expected. The Black Arts Theatre stood in radical opposition to the feeble attitudes about culture of the "War on Poverty" bureaucrats. And later, because of internal problems, the theatre was forced to close. But the Black Arts group proved that the community could be served by a valid and dynamic art. It also proved that there was a definite need for a cultural revolution in the Black's community.

With the closing of the Black Arts Theatre, the implications of what Brother Jones and his colleagues were trying to do took on even more significance. Black Art groups sprang up on the West Coast and the idea spread to Detroit, Philadelphia, Jersey City, New Orleans, and Washington, D.C. Black Arts movements began on the campuses of San Francisco State College, Fisk University, Lincoln University, Hunter College in the Bronx, Columbia University, and Oberlin College. In Watts, after the rebellion, Maulana Karenga welded the Black Arts Movement into a cohesive cultural ideology which owed much to the work of LeRoi Jones. Karenga sees culture as the most important element in the struggle for self-determination.

Culture is the basis of all ideas, images and actions. To move is to move culturally, i.e. by a set of values given to you by your culture.

Without a culture Negroes are only a set of reactions to white people.

The seven criteria for culture are

1. Mythology
2. History
3. Social Organization

4. Political Organization
5. Economic Organization
6. Creative Motif
7. Ethos

In drama, LeRoi Jones represents the most advanced aspects of the movement. He is its prime mover and chief designer. In a poetic essay entitled "The Revolutionary Theatre," he outlines the iconology of the movement:

> The Revolutionary Theatre should force change: it should be change. (All their faces turned into the lights and you work on them black nigger magic, and cleanse them at having seen the ugliness. And if the beautiful see themselves, they will love themselves.) We are preaching virtue again, but by that to mean NOW, toward what seems the most constructive use of the word.

The theatre that Jones proposes is inextricably linked to the Afro-American political dynamic. And such a link is perfectly consistent with Black America's contemporary demands. For theatre is potentially the most social of all of the arts. It is an integral part of the socializing process. It exists in direct relationship to the audience it claims to serve. The decadence and inanity of the contemporary American theatre is an accurate reflection of the state of American society. Albee's *Who's Afraid of Virginia Woolf?* is very American: sick white lives in a homosexual hell hole. The theatre of white America is escapist, refusing to confront concrete reality. Into this cultural emptiness come the musicals, an up-tempo version of the same stale lives. And the use of Negroes in such plays as *Hello Dolly* and *Hallelujah Baby* does not alert their nature; it compounds the problem. These plays are simply hipper versions of the minstrel show. They present Negroes acting out the hang-ups of middle-class white America. Consequently, the American theatre is a palliative prescribed to bourgeois patients who refuse to see the world as it is. Or, more crucially, as the worlds sees them. It is no accident, therefore, that the most "important" plays come from Europe—Brecht, Weiss, and Ghelderode. And even these have begun to run dry.

The Black Arts theater, the theatre of LeRoi Jones, is a radical alternative to the sterility of the American theatre. It is primarily a theatre of the Spirit, confronting the Black man in his interaction with his brothers and with the white thing.

> Our theatre will show victims so that their brothers in the audience will be better able to understand that they are brothers of victims, and that they themselves are blood brothers. And what we show must cause the blood to rush, so that prerevolutionary temperaments will be bathed in this blood, and it will cause their deepest souls to move, and they will find themselves tensed and clenched, even ready to die, at what the soul has been taught. We will scream and cry, murder, run through the streets in agony, if it means some soul will be

moved, moved to actual life understanding of what the world is, and what it ought to be. We are preaching virtue and feeling, and a natural sense of the self in the world. All men live in the world, and the world ought to be a place for them to live. . . .

Suggested Readings with Similar Theme:

Wright, Richard. "Blueprint for Negro Writing," *New Challenge* (1937): 53–65. Reprinted in this volume.

Fuller, Hoyt. "Towards a Black Aesthetic." In *The Black Aesthetic,* edited by Addison Gayle Jr. Garden City, N.Y.: Doubleday, 1971.

Lee, Don L. (Haki Madhubuti). "Toward a Definition: Black Poetry of the Sixties (After LeRoi Jones)." In *The Black Aesthetic,* edited by Addison Gayle Jr. Garden City, N.Y.: Doubleday, 1971.

Thomas, Lorenza. "The Shadow World: New York's Umbra Workshop and Origins of the Black Arts Movement." *Callaloo* 1, no. 4 (October 1978): 53–72.

Giovanni, Nikki, and Margaret Walker. "Content and Intent: Some Thoughts on Writing, Criticism and Film." In *A Poetic Equation: Conversations between Nikki Giovanni and Margaret Walker.* Washington, D.C.: Howard University Press, 1983.

Smith, Lionel David. "The Black Arts Movement and Its Critics." *American Literary History* (Spring 1991): 93–110.

Reilly, Charlie. *Conversations with Amiri Baraka.* Jackson: University Press of Mississippi, 1994.

CAROLYN F. GERALD

The Black Writer and His Role (1969)

Why is image so central to one's self-identity? As Gerald concludes, "{T}he image we have of ourselves controls what we are capable of doing." Or, stated further, "Man projects his cultural and racial images upon the universe and he derives a sense of personal worth from the reflection he sees gazing back at him." Why must African American experience be represented not "by proxy and in someone else's image," but by familiar symbols, icons, and so on? Why must African Americans "define" for themselves their "peoplehood"? Is Gerald agreeing with Larry Neal? What is Gerald suggesting when she writes that the African American artist must become the "guardian of image" in his or her community and the "myth-maker of his {her} people"? Quoting Gerald, define "zero image," "real image," and "created image." Within historical and cultural contexts, how does Gerald echo earlier critics, such as DuBois and Locke, and anticipate contemporary critics, such as Barbara Smith, bell hooks, and Tommy Lott, regarding African American images and the responsibility of the African American writer?

> What is new (in black literature) is the deliberate desecration and smashing of idols, the turning inside-out of symbols . . . Bitterness is being replaced by wrath; a sense of frustration giving way before a sense of power.

Image is a term which we are using more and more in the black community because we are discovering that the image we have of ourselves controls what we are capable of doing. Image, in this sense, has the meaning of self-concept. We are giving cause and effect the same name. But the word image is properly speaking a concrete term meaning the projection or representation of an object; the image is the mirror of some aspect of reality.

At this point, we should draw a distinction between real and created images. Both are projections of reality, but the created image is projected by the imagination of man, and by the recall and associative power of his five senses. For instance, I can hold out a rose before you; the image of that rose is mirrored in your eye; it is a real image. Or I can describe a rose to you, and my words will create an image which you can visualize mentally. Perhaps you will even imagine the smell and the feel; the words I choose and the way I build them into the image will determine this. Usually a whole complex of

---

Carolyn F. Gerald is also Carolyn Fowler.

associations builds up around an image, secondary images are evoked, until well-defined patterns of associations based upon sensory perceptions pervade in a very vague way the whole area of a man's experience.

Why is image so central to a man's self-definition? Because all images, and especially created images, represent a certain way of focusing on the world outside, and therefore they represent a certain point of view. Now, if we hold a certain point of view, we have automatically emphasized some aspects of reality, blocked out others, and glossed over the rest, and the image which we project or which we perceive is not objective reality but our own—or someone else's—reshaping of reality. If it is someone else's reshaping of reality which we perceive, then we are within that other person's sphere of influence and can be led to believe whatever he wishes us to believe: that a rosebush is pleasant because it has a fragrant smell, or that it is unpleasant because it has thorns. If these two images of the rosebush are combined into a metaphor, we have created images which lead us to make an association between the reality of the rosebush and another level of reality, and we can be influenced, for instance, on a moral level: "Pleasant-smelling roses have unpleasant thorns; therefore, beware the sweet fragrance of pleasure for underneath it lie hidden the thorns of destruction." In this way, the association made in the mind of the hearer or reader is controlled. By guiding, by controlling our associations, the image-maker can, and usually does, shape our view of reality, because the images the words conjure up when they are put together artistically provoke an immediate emotional response in us, and dim out of our consciousness all the untold other points of view at our disposal.

Image-making is part of all human experience. However, we are speaking here of the image created by the magic of words. We are considering image not so much as life but as literary art. Art reshapes the raw materials of nature and of human interaction and, in so doing, interprets reality in a non-analytical, non-intellectual way. Art thus makes a direct appeal to the senses and calls forth a spontaneous emotional identification with other men and with the universe. Therefore, the effects of the literary image are most often intuitive, deep beyond the threshold of reason and common sense. When we spoke of the sweet fragrance of pleasure and the thorns of destruction, we made an appeal not to reason but to the emotional attractiveness of the images. In this way, we develop, quite aside from our rational perception, an intuitive view of nature and of the cosmos, and our own relation to it. The rose is an old, familiar example of how our attitude toward the surrounding environment takes form and grows. The body of imagery surrounding the rose is rooted historically deep in Western cultural patterns of looking at the world. The rose symbolizes beauty on the physical level, and purity and freshness on the moral level. Because this imagery is traditional and associations are unquestioned, and because they are unquestioned, they take on the quality of myth. In the case of the rose, the imagery may seem harmless but we will see in a moment how such myth-building images can be the very death of self-concept.

Notice too, in the case of the rose, that man has projected himself into his imagery. The purity, beauty and freshness of the rose are usually compared to an idealized womankind. This is because the natural impetus of man is to impart to the whole cosmos the qualities which he possesses. Man's imagery is thus anthropomorphic; he sees himself or his behavior in every projection he makes. Thus, a flower dances in the breeze; the thunder rushes angrily through the skies; the sun smiles down on the sleepy noontime village; Mother earth provides for us. It follows that man's self-concept must inevitably be tied to his view of the universe, since he sees his own reflection in it at every moment. And a reflection of ourselves cannot be neutral; it cannot be objective; it is either positive or negative. How we regard the phenomena of nature is an indication of what we think of ourselves. The howling wind, for example, is not the same image as the whining wind. If our literary tradition stresses the howling wind, then we feel emotively that a mysterious prowling creature stalks through our universe. If the whining wind is stressed, we feel the presence of a weak but persistent creature following us constantly around.

We've said that man projects his image upon the universe. But man does not exist in isolation. It is far more accurate to say that man projects his cultural and racial images upon the universe and he derives a sense of personal worth from the reflection he sees gazing back at him. For he defines himself and the world in terms of others like him. He discovers his identity within a group.

And now we come to the heart of the matter, for we cannot judge ourselves unless we see a continuity of ourselves in other people and in things and concepts. We question our very right to exist without other existences like our own. This is why image is so important to African Americans. We are black people living in a white world. When we consider that the black man sees white cultural and racial images projected upon the whole extent of his universe, we cannot help but realize that a very great deal of the time the black man sees a zero image of himself. The black child growing into adulthood through a series of week-end movies, seeing white protagonists constantly before him projecting the whole gamut of human experience, is, in extreme cases, persuaded that he too must be white, or (what is more likely), he experiences manhood by proxy and in someone else's image. He sees, in other words, a zero image of himself. If there are black people on the screen, they are subservient to, uncomfortably different from, or busy emulating the larger, all inclusive white culture. In that case, our young person sees a negative image of himself. Nor are the images which control personal worth always so direct or obvious. The very same image-myth process which we discovered through the example of the rose is present in the extensive body of color imagery in Western culture. Those associations with black and white have conditioned us to accept white as the symbol of goodness and purity; black as the symbol of evil and impurity.

This did not just happen. It is the result of white racial projection of its own best image upon the universe. Concomitant with that projection for several hundred years—ever since the black man has come within the sphere of influence of the white—the moral and aesthetic associations of black and white have been mixed up with race. Thus, the negative reflection of ourselves is, in the white man's system, the reverse side of his positive projection of himself. The white man has developed a myth of superiority based on images which compare him symbolically with the black man. The very fact of this interconnection is at once a holdover from previous bondage and the most effective means of perpetuating that bondage. We realize now that we are involved in a black-white war over the control of image. For to manipulate an image is to control a peoplehood. Zero image has for a long time meant the repression of our peoplehood.

Of course, the black American has not relied totally on the image projected by white culture. He has developed a literature, and that literature gives him a certain sense of self. We have, however, in spite of ourselves, not been successful in destroying zero image, for we have not been able to convince ourselves that our image is projected on any but a small and segregated strip of the universe. When a self-definition has proceeded spontaneously, the literature will reflect not only a group consciousness, shared points of view, common ancestry, common destiny and aspirations, but it reflects these in spiritual oneness with whatever natural and/or supernatural powers preside over and guide that destiny. For the black writer, the only possibility for spiritual oneness has been non-race or religious literature. But non-race or religious literature takes on insidiously the image projected by what is called the larger culture, and so takes on a white image. Black writers have also attempted to reflect spiritual oneness by writing within a totally black framework. But white images are implanted at the core of black life, the most obvious example being that of the Church, where God is white. Moreover, the black community is not self-sustaining, and a literature which would circumvent this essential feature of peoplehood cannot cope with the forces that shape us. For the most part though, black writers have avoided these two pitfalls, and our literature has been, as we have, slowly, painfully coming out of bondage and has been contributing to our growing sense of peoplehood. If black writers have historically concentrated on white-black animosity, it is because that animosity is an everyday fact of life and functional part of our universe.

The artist then, is the guardian of image; the writer is the myth-maker of his people. We still at times are not sure as to how much of our image is us; to what extent we are the sole authors of our myth, our peoplehood. There are those white people who would nullify any argument we advance on the basis that it is advanced in a white language. And it is true that languages project a specific cultural image. But I believe that we have arrived at a stage of self-awareness in our writing which sees this type of argument as irrelevant. Our very plain answer to this sophisticated argument is simply that we will not let white men define our peoplehood by telling us we're still using white tools to create it. Similarly, we must reject white attempts at portraying black reality. They are valid only in terms of the white man's projection of himself. They have no place in the definition of blackness, for they reveal the white writer's attempt to work through his own cultural guilt, fascination with blackness, or sense of spiritual emptiness. This includes all latterday Harriet Beecher Stowes. No one can hand us a peoplehood, complete with prefabricated images.

Even the word black is a translation from the Portuguese slave term negro, gone into the English language as Negro. But black is also the generalized term which we use to symbolize unity of origin, whether we are called Anglophone, Francophone, coloured, mulatto, West Indian or American Negro by the white, image-makers. Black is the highly imagistic term we use to do away with all such divisionary euphemisms. It is the term we use to destroy the myth based on the complex of images which polarize black and white. These images must be mythically torn down, ritually destroyed. We cannot bury our heads before the existing body of myth, nor before our own Europeanization. Therefore, we cannot return nostalgically to a past heritage and pretend that historical continuity exists in anything but fragmentary form. We cannot block out the black-white struggle for control of image and create a utopianized world of all-black reflections. Our work at this stage is clearly to destroy the zero and the negative image-myths of ourselves by turning them inside out. To do this, we reverse the symbolism, and we use that reverse symbolism as the tool for projecting our own image upon the universe.

Zero image, and the need to work through it, is not a new concept. Many black writers have understood the importance of image, and Ralph Ellison in the early fifties stated the same intent metaphorically in the title and outer structure of his novel, *Invisible Man*. What is new, I believe, is the deliberate desecration and smashing of idols, the turning inside-out of symbols, to which black writers are now proceeding with a vengeance. Bitterness, which runs through the whole of black literature, is being replaced by wrath; a sense of frustration is giving way before a sense of power. It is the sense of power which proceeds from a mythic consciousness based on a people's positive view of themselves and their destiny.

Perhaps we can best conclude with an illustration of the processes we've been discussing. The following poem attempts to desecrate the mythical and beautiful figure of the muse, entrenched in white culture since the time of its earliest flowering, Greco-Roman antiquity.

> Dress the muse in black . . .
> No!
> Kill her!

Make her jump
Burning bright white bitch
From the pitched peaks of our houses
Let her shriek
Pale old faded biddy . . .
Hear her?
Stomping her feet round
On our rooftops all these years?
And we, inside. Yassuh meek
Warming our hands by the fire (like sheep)
Phony 'fay!
Look at her!
Running past
Blond flames waving in the wind
Blow on her!
Grab a torch up in your hand and come outside
And watch her burn
And crackle
And topple
And lie
Fallen
Off our rooftops
Into the flame
Look up
And gather round
And shake your torch up at her!
Tease her like a yellow cat
Crouching on the roof
Make her jump
Make her howl
Make her yowl
Falling in the fire
Make it hot . . .
Make it hate.
Clap and stomp round the fire
And shout the spirit out of her.
And draw your circle close
For we'll kill us a devil tonight.
Come on away, now!
Now!
We'll find our own saint
(or another name for her)
No need for hell's fire now
The fire's weak
And burned out
The universe is black again.

LLOYD W. BROWN

The Expatriate Consciousness in Black American Literature (1972)

Brown urges an examination of the roots of "expatriate consciousness" in literature by black writers in exile (e.g., Wright, Himes, Baldwin, and Emanuel) and black litera- ture with expatriate themes (e.g., McKay, Cullen, and Bontemps). Via Brown's repeated phrases, such as "self-analysis," "self-critical enquiry," "uprooted quest for cul- tural roots," and "desire to establish a Black frame of reference," he directs readers to examine "the writer's image of himself." Is Brown proposing psychoanalytic and cul- tural readings of black expatriate writers? Does he encourage readers to move beyond expatriate writers' disillusionments with integration in the 1950s and 1960s? How does Carolyn Gerald's article speak to Brown's discussion of images? How does Brown's term "expatriate consciousness" allude to W. E. B. DuBois's term "double con- sciousness"?

Traditionally, the discussion of the Black American writer as an expatriate has centered primarily on those writers such as Wright, Baldwin, and Himes, who are in European exile from the United States. And, in turn, this attention has been mainly concerned with questions about the exile's realism or rele- vance vis-a-vis his American themes. But we also need some serious study of the phenomenon of the expatriate consciousness in the Black American writer in America—that is, the writer's image of himself, and other Black Ameri- cans like himself, as transplanted [*sic*] Africans, or at the very least, as rootless aliens in a hostile Western culture. And, simultaneously, this search for cul- tural roots in the African past is joined, or analogous with, the artist's attempt to rediscover the more immediate Black American roots, in the ghetto or rural South, from which his middleclass status has cut him off. The need for serious and careful study of such themes has become more urgent at this time with the insistent emphasis, in Black Nationalist literature, on some desirable alienation, and cultural separation, from the White West. And in this paper I shall attempt to demonstrate this general need by examining the expatriate themes of a specific group of writers—some of the major authors in the so-called Harlem Renaissance.

There has been a tradition among critics to dismiss certain Pan-African themes in earlier Afro-American literature as mere sentimental primitivism— with the so-called Renaissance writers bearing the main brunt of this oversimplification. Stephen H. Bronz, for example, attacks what he calls the "artificial tradition" of Africanist themes in Harlem Renaissance writing; according to Wayne Cooper, Black writers of the twenties merely perpetuated plantation images of the happy "primitive Negro"; Sterling Brown alleges that their idealization of Africa "was more poetic dreaming than understanding"; and Harold Isaacs sneers at what he calls "the poet-aesthetes of Harlem . . . trooping back to the Kraals and the jungle dens."[1]

These charges have important implications for the Black intellectual's relationship with whatever he chooses to call his cultural roots. How "artificial" or "real" are his images of the African heritage, the rural South, or the Northern ghetto? In using allegorical myths to project images of his African and Afro-American sources, does he confuse the mythic **symbol** with the geophysical or socio-economic **realities** of his subject? And if he does, has he simply reproduced the "noble savage," stereotype from Europe's eighteenth-century mythology? It is tempting, at first glance, to place the Black **bon vivants** of Claude McKay's fiction within this "noble savage" tradition, and to argue that McKay and the other "Renaissance" intellectuals sentimentalize their less fortunate brethren because of guilt about their own middleclass status—in much the same way that the guilt-ridden complexes of Rousseau's slave-trading Europe found expression in the original, eighteenth-century images of the noble savage. But I would suggest that in dealing with cultural images and Pan-Africanist symbols in "Renaissance" literature, we need to go beyond this "first glance," beyond the superficial impressions which for too long have substituted for careful analysis of these writers. Claude McKay's Black **bon vivants,** for example, exist in a far more complex and ambiguous relationship with the "noble savage" tradition than is usually assumed. In HOME TO HARLEM (1928) Jake does embody that "uninhibited vitalism" and "natural innocence" about which critics like Wayne Cooper and others have complained. And in this regard the novel's title implies that beyond the immediate "return" of Jake from Europe to his Harlem home, there is another return—the quest of the Black intellectual who has come home to Harlem in search of his cultural roots. But it is crucial that we grasp the full implications of this psychic return in the novel; for, granting that the return of the exile is fraught with sentimental expectations and romantic nostalgia, it does not follow that these are wholly sanctioned by the author himself.

Let us begin with Jake's own return to Harlem. It is noteworthy that the first, and most exaggerated, examples of Harlem as a Black Garden of Eden originate with Jake's expatriate consciousness, with his homesick longings, before he sails to New York from London. "It was two years since he had left Harlem. Fifth Avenue, Lenox Avenue, and One Hundred and Thirty-fifth Street, with their chocolate-brown and walnut-brown girls, were calling him . . ."

"Brown girls rouged and painted like dark pansies. Brown flesh draped in soft colorful clothes. Brown lips full and pouted for sweet kissing. Brown breasts throbbing with love."[2] But to assume that this nostalgic image totally defines Harlem throughout the novel is to ignore Jake's final judgement [*sic*] before he leaves New York at the end of the novel: he has discovered that Harlemites, including himself, are just as brutish as "those vile, vicious, villainous white men who, like hyenas and rattlers, had fought, murdered, and clawed the entrails out of black men over the common, commercial flesh of women" (*Home to Harlem*, p. 173). "Altogether, Jake's eventual disillusionment with Harlem represents a deliberate criticism of the earlier, sentimental view of the Black ghetto—a view which is as one-sidedly naive as that of White "slummers" to Harlem's cabarets: White visitors never "guessed that cautious reserve lurked" under the grin of the "jolly, compact manager." They see the grin only. Here are none of the well-patterned, well-made emotions of the respectable world. A laugh might finish in a sob. A moan end in hilarity" (p. 178).

In effect, Jake's evolving attitudes towards Harlem, from sentimental nostalgia to realistic ambivalence, is analogous to the perspectives which the novel brings to bear on Jake himself and on his environment. And, significantly, those perspectives are incarnated in the person of Raymond, the young Haitian emigre. It is not overly fanciful to see Raymond as McKay's fictional counterpart; they are both West Indian intellectuals trying to rediscover and give expression to their cultural roots in Black America. Hence, whatever romantic/sentimental images of Jake and Harlem appear in the novel are the product of McKay's (and Raymond's) expatriate consciousness—expatriate in a double sense: (1) as West Indians they sentimentalize Harlem because they are projecting their nostalgia and homesickness on it and (2) this nostalgia is integral to that broader and deeper longing, shared by Black middleclass intellectuals, for a world which now exists in a socio-economic and intellectual distance from them; and which, for that very reason, takes on all the proportions of an unspoiled Eden. Consequently, Raymond compares his happiness in Harlem's "rich blood-red color," and its laughter and rhythms with the "high-noon sunlight of his tropic island home." But, as in the case of Jake's attitudes towards Harlem, it would be an oversimplification to assume that Raymond is merely a nostalgic sentimentalist. For his vicarious identification with the excitement of Harlem is counterbalanced by revulsion at its less attractive side. He is aware, not only of its laughter, but also of its brutality, "gang rowdyism, promiscuous thickness" (p. 141). As for Jake, Raymond's personal fondness does not prevent him from comparing that "child of nature" with a "handsome hound, quick to snap up any tempting morsel of poisoned meat thrown carelessly on the pavement" (p. 121). And, even more incisively, Raymond's Black co-workers on the railroad repel him as animals: "These men claimed kinship with him. They were black like him. Man and nature had put them in the same race. He ought to love them and feel them (if they felt anything). He ought to if he had a shred of social morality in him. They were all chainganged together and he was counted as one link. Yet he loathed every soul in that great barrack-room, except Jake. Race . . . Why should he have and love a race?" (p. 81).

To sum up, Jake's relationship with Harlem, and Raymond's relationship with both Jake and Harlem dramatize the crucial implications of the search for cultural roots in McKay's novel. The sentimental images of a laughing Harlem are acknowledged, unequivocably, as projections of the expatriate consciousness, the creations of the Black man's nostalgia for a milieu from which he has been temporarily, or permanently, separated. And particularly in the case of the Black intellectual, these "artificial" images embody the very real psychological experiences of one who questions the White criteria of his intellectuality and his middleclass environment, but who is, simultaneously, cut off from the Black masses below him. In other words, and this is what separates a work like *Home to Harlem* from mere banality, McKay is not simply reproducing, or succumbing to, the sentimental traditions of the noble savage in the Black intellectual's imagination. He is examining its causes and tracing its effects, especially in a fictive personality (Raymond) whose status (middleclass, intellectual, and West Indian) is so similar to his own. In effect, this examination becomes a deliberate self-analysis of Black intellectuals like McKay himself. For McKay's (and Raymond's) West Indian identity is really symbolic of a psychological expatriation exile which, by definition, becomes the lot of that Black intellectual whose White frame of reference weakens or destroys immediate contact with the rest of the Black community. When Raymond admits his loathing for the bestial, and brutalizing, realities of Black poverty he is also acknowledging the real source of his idealistic images of that very environment: his assumptions about a Black Eden of noble, rhythmic savages are (1) a nostalgic reflex apropos of his expatriation from the West Indies (or of all Black middleclass intellectuals from their respective roots) and (2) a guilty attempt to compensate for his feeling of real incompatibility with that lost world. The fundamental issue in the novel is not Harlem as such, but the psychological process of coming "home" to the cultural origins which we associate with a Harlem, with an African Eden, or with a Caribbean paradise: McKay's object is to examine the expatriate/nostalgic consciousness of all uprooted Black people (symbolized by Jake as well as by Raymond) and, more incisively, of the Black intellectual (represented by Raymond). He is, admittedly, the victim of all the hang-ups, neuroses, and conflicts which are inherent in the search for cultural roots. But, even more important, he is, simultaneously, a critical analyst of all these things which comprise his expatriate consciousness.

So are poets like Countee Cullen and Arna Bontemps. Cullen's famous "Heritage" is not merely a reproduction of "unreal" concepts, or "poetic dreaming," about Africa. More precisely, is [*sic*] is also a self-critical enquiry into the nature and function of the African idyll in the Black American's consciousness:

> What is Africa to me:
> Copper sun or scarlet sea,
> Jungle star or jungle track.
> Strong bronzed men, or regal black
> Women from whose loins I sprang
> When the birds of Eden sang?[3]

The ambiguous tone of the opening line is the key to the psychological implications of the idyllic images which follow. For that initial statement suggests both contemptuous indifference/detachment and an earnest groping for Africa's meaning. But there is also a causal relationship between both moods: just as Raymond's loathing for the Black lumpenproletariat heightens his guilty idealization of it in McKay's novel, so are the "meanings"/images of Cullen's Africa-as-Eden attributable to a guilty recognition of that other, more negative response to Africa. Of course, the more obvious self-conflicts of Countee Cullen's themes are well known—the Black American's dual allegiance to a Black past and a White culture, the tension between Christian loyalties and "pagan" non-Christian longings. But once again, we need to go beyond the obvious to examine the symbolical texture of Cullen's statements. And as far as the quest for cultural roots (apropos of Africa) is concerned, Cullen appears to be (1) acknowledging the idyllic or "unreal" nature of the African image in his poem, and (2) attributing this sentimental unreality to the physical and psychological distance which makes Africa itself inaccessible. The crucial "meaning" of the poem does not lie with the actuality of Africa as such, but with the subjective emphasis of the opening query (What does Africa mean to me?), with the very nature of the poet's attempt to establish Africa's meaning. Like *Home to Harlem*, Cullen's poem is not so much about the noble savages or Black paradise that it purports to describe, but about the writer's/intellectual's personal relationship with his imagistic and mythic materials. What makes a work like "Heritage" so interesting in a psychological sense is that, like McKay's novel, it reproduces sentimental fantasies about cultural roots, but it does so with a self-critical awareness which acknowledges and analyses the mythic nature of his images.

This kind of dualism is evident in Arna Bontemps when he offers a comparable analysis of Africa's "meaning" in the anti-Christian themes of "Nocturne at Bethesda":

> And if there can be returning after death
> I shall come back. But it will not be here:
> if you want me you must search for me
> beneath the palms of Africa. Or if
> I am not there you may call to me
> across the shining dunes, perhaps I shall
> be following a desert caravan.[4]

"Palms," "shining dunes," "desert caravans"—these images are akin to the fanciful exotica which are usually manufactured in Hollywood. But the poet is aware that these are fantasies, for the images are placed in the highly suggestive context of deliberate wish fulfillment: "if there can be returning after death . . ." The poet's sentimental nostalgia is an acknowledged reflex of his disenchantment with the White Christian West and the resulting images of Africa represent a calculated symbolic analysis of the psychological needs that originate with this disenchantment.

This matter of need is paramount. For in writers like Bontemps, Cullen and McKay, the satiric analysis of the Black intellectual's expatriate consciousness goes hand in hand with the implication that "unrealistic" images of their roots and heritage reflect a very real psychological need, that these artificial symbols represent an existing desire to establish a Black frame of reference. In short, these writers are implying that the obvious issue, the "unreality" of the myths themselves, is not the crucial one. What is paramount are the psycho-existential needs which these myths project and which the writers themselves analyze in serious and highly self-conscious terms.

Notes

1. Stephen H. Bronz, *Roots of Negro Racial Consciousness* (New York, 1964), p. 15; Wayne Cooper, "Claude McKay and the New Negro of the 1920's" in *The Black American Writer Volume II: Poetry and Drama*, ed. C.W.E. Bigsby, Pelican ed (Baltimore, 1971), p. 61; Sterling Brown, *Negro Poetry and Drama*, Atheneum ed (New York, 1969), p. 75; Harold Isaacs, "Five Writers and their African Ancestors," *Phylon* XXI, iii (1960), 244. Cf Robert A. Bone, *The Negro Novel in America* (New Haven, 1958), pp. 58–61.

2. *Home to Harlem*, Pocket Cardinal ed (New York, 1965), p. 5.

3. *On These I Stand: An Anthology of the Best Poems of Countee Cullen* (New York, 1947), p. 24.

4. *Black Voices: An Anthology of Afro-American Literature*, ed. Abraham Chapman, Mentor ed (New York, 1968), p. 423.

(P.S. Professor Brown's paper was presented at the 1971 MLA Convention in Chicago)

Suggested Readings with Similar Theme:

Schatt, Stanley. "You Must Go Home Again: Today's Afro-American Expatriate Writers." *Negro American Literature Forum* 7, no. 3 (Fall 1973): 80–82.

Baker, Houston A. Jr. "On the Criticism of Black American Literature: One View of the Black Aesthetic." In *Reading Black: Essays in the Criticism of African, Caribbean and Black American Literature*, 48–58. Ithaca, N.Y.: Africana Studies and Research Center, Cornell University, Monograph Series, No. 4., 1976.

Fontenot, Chester Jr. "Alice Walker: Diary of an African Nun and DuBois Double-Consciousness." *Journal of Afro-American Issues* (1977). Reprint, Roseann P. Bell, et. al, eds. *Sturdy Black Bridges*, 150–56. New York: Doubleday, 1979.

Fabre, Michel, ed. *From Harlem to Paris: Black American Writers in France, 1840–1980*. Urbana: University of Illinois Press, 1991.

Gates, Henry Louis Jr. "The Welcome Table [James Baldwin]." In *Thirteen Ways of Looking at a Black Man*. New York: Vintage, 1997.

STEPHEN E. HENDERSON

From "The Forms of Things Unknown" in *Understanding the New Black Poetry:* *Black Speech and Black Music as Poetic References* (1973)

Henderson is interested in identifying "critical framework(s), organizing principles" for understanding black poetry. In a manner similar to Aristotle in Poetics, Henderson examines numerous significant works for their organizing principles, and he reveals specifically how folk sources such as black speech and black music have influenced the form and structure of black literature. Why are black speech and black music important in articulating the organizing principles—the theoretical principles—in black poetry? Returning to the section on saturation, explain Henderson's statement: "Literature . . . is the verbal organization of experience into forms. . . . What is meant by form is . . . dependent upon a people's way of life, their needs, their aspirations, their history—in short their culture." How clear is Henderson on criteria for evaluating black poetry? How do Roach and Henderson enter discussions about black music as a poetic reference? In readings to follow, identify and examine the extent of Henderson's theoretical influence on other critics. How does Henderson define the following terms and phrases: Blackness, mascon, Soul field, black speech as poetic reference, black music as poetic reference, theme, structure, and saturation?

Although it is an arbitrary scheme for the purpose of analysis, one may describe or discuss a "Black" poem in terms of the following broad critical categories: (1) Theme, (2) Structure, (3) Saturation.

(1) By theme I mean that which is being spoken of, whether the specific subject matter, the emotional response to it, or its intellectual formulation.

(2) By structure I mean chiefly some aspect of the poem such as diction, rhythm, figurative language, which goes into the total makeup. (At times, I use the word in an extended sense to include what is usually called genre.)

(3) By saturation I mean several things, chiefly the communication of "Blackness" and fidelity to the observed or intuited truth of the Black Experience in the United States. It follows that these categories should also be valid in any critical evaluation of the poem. . . .

[FROM "THEME"]

Historical surveys such as Brawley's *Early Negro American Writers,* Brown, Davis, and Lee's *The Negro Caravan,* and Robinson's *Early Black Poets* suggest that there are indeed thematic clusters in Black poetry around what could be called the idea of Liberation. And when we move to the present, we must consider certainly the essays by Richard Wright and the critical statements by the poets themselves in which they express their intent that, as a rule, follows the historical consciousness of the people. This is to say, that as Black people in the United States refine and clarify their conceptions of themselves the poetry reflects the process.

The early formal Black poetry reflected the concerns of those who were trained to read and to write. Thus, to follow Sterling Brown's account, there were those poets whose chief object was to demonstrate their ability to write as well as the whites, as in the case of Alberry Whitman and the "Mockingbird School of Poets." Other poets, like James Bell and Frances Ellen Harper, used their talents in the abolitionist cause. Another group wrote in dialect and took for their subject matter the lives of the common folk which they sometimes caricatured in the manner of white writers like Thomas Nelson Page. Others, like Paul Laurence Dunbar and James Edwin Campbell, while still influenced by white stereotypes and the expectations of white audiences, presented wholesome, if not altogether realistic, portraits of Black folk life. The period preceding the Harlem Renaissance not only produced the dialect poets but found many Black poets studiously avoiding overt racial considerations in a manner reminiscent of the late forties and the fifties. "Poetry was a romantic escape for many of them," states Brown, "not a perception of reality. . . ."

Although there were attempts at realistic depiction of Black life before they came on the scene, the writers of the Harlem Renaissance were the first to do this in a systematic manner, as even a cursory look at the period will reveal. One recalls Langston Hughes' famous declaration in "The Negro Artist and the Racial Mountain":

> These common people are not afraid of spirituals, as for a long time their more intellectual brethren were, and jazz is their child. They furnish a wealth of colorful, distinctive material for any artist because they still hold their own individuality in the face of American standardizations. And perhaps these common people will give to the world its truly great Negro artist, the one who is not afraid to be himself. Whereas the better-class Negro would tell the artist what to do, the people at least let him alone when he does appear. And they are not ashamed of him—if they know he exists at all. And they accept what beauty is their own without question.
>
> [*Black Expression,* pp. 259, 260.]

Notwithstanding the bravery of this kind of effort, Hughes and other realistic writers of his generation were sharply censured by middle-class members of their own race, including W. E. B. DuBois and Benjamin Brawley (*Negro Genius,* p. 248), for portraying the "seamy side" of Black life. Seen in retrospect, the poetry of this group, the poetry of the twenties, helped to balance the pieties of the abolitionist writers on the one hand and the bucolic idylls of the dialect school on the other. Alain Locke's essay entitled "The New Negro," which appeared in his larger "statement," the epoch-making volume of the same name, brought the issues into focus. Afro-Americans had come of age; they could look at themselves for what they were, without false piety and without shame, rejecting the "social nostrums and the panaceas," and realizing that although religion, freedom, and education were important to their cause, they alone were not sufficient. What was needed was group solidarity and collective effort.

> Each generation . . . will have its creed, and that of the present is the belief in the efficacy of collective effort, in race cooperation. This deep feeling of race is at present the mainspring of Negro life. It seems to be the outcome of the reaction to proscription and prejudice; an attempt, fairly successful on the whole, to convert a defensive into an offensive position, a handicap into an incentive. It is radical in tone, but not in purpose and only the most stupid forms of opposition, misunderstanding or persecution could make it otherwise. Of course, the thinking Negro has shifted a little toward the left with the worldtrend, and there is an increasing group who affiliate with radical and liberal movements. But fundamentally for the present the Negro is radical on race matters, conservative on others, in other words, a "forced radical," a social protestant rather than a genuine radical. Yet under further pressure and injustice, iconoclastic thought and motives will inevitably increase. Harlem's quixotic radicalisms call for their ounce of democracy to-day lest to-morrow they be beyond cure.
>
> [*New Negro,* p. 11.]

Locke's analysis was essentially correct. Unfortunately his warning was not heeded, and although the "stupid forms of opposition," the "misunderstanding," and the "persecution" which he warned against seemed to be abating during the Civil Rights Movement of the fifties and sixties, the failure of Dr. King's Northern Campaign which linked the anti-war and the Civil Rights issues, and his assassination in 1968 indicated that the country still intended to keep its Black citizens in subjection.

Disenchantment with the goals and strategies of the Civil Rights Movement led to the Black Power Movement and the subsequent widespread revival of nationalist and internationalist feeling and thought among Blacks. To the extent that Black artists today have influenced their community to view itself in the larger political and spiritual context of Blackness, they have moved beyond the Harlem Renaissance, though obviously influenced by it. The old theme of liberation took on new meaning. Thus the Black Arts Movement, though emerging before the Black Power Movement, is in some respects the cultural dimension of that phenomenon. Numerous eloquent spokesmen have appeared, among them Imamu Amiri Baraka (LeRoi Jones), Larry Neal, Ron Karenga, and Don L. Lee {Haki Madhubuti}.

In their statements, one can see the process of self-definition made clearer and sharper as the self-reliance and racial consciousness of an earlier period are revived and raised to the level of revolutionary thought.

The present movement is different from the Harlem Renaissance in the extent of its attempt to speak directly *to* Black people *about themselves* in order to move them toward self-knowledge and collective freedom. It is therefore not "protest" art but essentially an art of liberating vision. . . .

Sterling Brown's succinct statement is an indispensable point of departure. Speaking of the Renaissance poetry, he points out its five chief areas of interest:

> (1) a discovery of Africa as a source for race pride, (2) a use of Negro heroes and heroic episodes from American History, (3) propaganda of protest, (4) a treatment of the Negro masses frequently of the folk, less often of the workers with more understanding and less apology, and (5) franker and deeper self-revelation.
>
> [*Negro Poetry & Drama,* Atheneum ed., 1969, p. 61.]

Some of these concerns are also those of contemporary Black poetry, but with an important difference of emphasis. . . .

[FROM "STRUCTURE"]

Professor W. E. Farrison, one of the outstanding scholars in the field of Afro-American literature, is noticeably peeved, for example, in a review of *Today's Negro Voices: An Anthology by Young Negro Poets,* edited by Beatrice M. Murphy (Julian Messner, 1970). He questions the inclusion of certain poems for their deficiency "in the harmony of sound and clear sense which is essential to good poetry." Then he singles out the kind of typographical stylistics which were popularized by e. e. cummings. He tries to hold his peace, but finds it difficult.

> Now as is evidenced by the long history of the art of writing, if a writer can express himself well without the aid of capitals and punctuation, he can most probably express himself better with it; and if he cannot express himself well with their aid, it is doubtful that he can express himself better without it.
>
> [*CLA Journal* 14, no. 1 (1970): 96]

Although one could quarrel with the excessively stringent concept of poetry found in this review, it isn't difficult to sympathize with Farrison's impatience, because a good deal of modern poetry—white and Black—not only makes excessive demands on the reader's eyesight but tends too often to degenerate into artifice that however clever bears little real relationship to the oral aspect of the poem. Indeed, this emphasis on the visual has extensive and tenacious roots in Western poetry, not only in the cryptograms which Dryden satirized in Macflecknoe, but in the poetry of George Herbert, and long before him the Greek poems in the shape of altars, wings, and the like, which date from Simmias' poem in the shape of an egg in 300 B.C. (See *Art News Annual,* XXVIII, 1958, pp. 64–68, 178.) This tradition has also influenced modern Black poets, like Joe Goncalves in his "Now the Time is Ripe to Be" and "Sister Brother," both appearing in *Black Fire,* LeRoi Jones and Larry Neal, eds., and N. H. Pritchard's various "concrete" poems in *Dices or Black Bones,* Adam David Miller, ed.

Still if one is seriously interested in contemporary Black poetry, then one must examine some of the bases of this confusion. One must admit that typographically, at least, contemporary Black poets have been greatly influenced by white poets and frequently admit it, at least the older ones do. Imamu Amiri Baraka (LeRoi Jones) has said on several occasions that he owes a great technical debt to William Carlos Williams, and his early poetry embodies many of the attitudes and utilizes many of the techniques of the Beats who were also indebted to Williams. Much the same can be said of Bob Kaufman, who is considered by some to be the greatest innovator among the poets of that generation. But more fundamental than all of this is the fact that along with their immersion in Zen, the Beats themselves were enamored of jazz in particular and the Black life-style in general, and at times sought to communicate what has to be called a "Black feeling" in their work. Often their formal model was alleged to be jazz, so that accurately or not, Allen Ginsberg described Jack Kerouac's writing as a kind of "bop prosody." The words give us an important clue. They let us know that the Beats in their writing were striving to capture the rhythms and phrasings of Black music, to notate somehow those sounds on the printed page.

Of course, it was not all printed, and some of the poetry was read to the accompaniment of jazz combos. But the point needs to be made that this was a generation after Langston Hughes had done the same thing—and with greater success. So, in effect, the Beats were approaching through empathy with the Black Experience some of the very same considerations—technical and thematic—that the Harlem Renaissance, the Negritude Movement, and the present generation of Black poets have approached from the inside, so to speak.

In their insistence upon jazz as a model and inspiration for their poetry, these writers were and are confronted with enormous technical problems, some of which may be insoluble if they continue to write that poetry down.

For their model is dynamic, not static, and although one can suggest various vocal and musical effects with typography, an extensive use of these rather mechanical devices may be ultimately self-defeating. Thus Black poets are rediscovering the resources of their oral traditions and have occasionally been very successful with them. Some idea of that success may be obtained by listening to Imamu Amiri Baraka, Larry Neal, Don L. Lee, Nikki Giovanni, Ghylan Kain and the Original Last Poets. In the meantime, however, the question of typography is still quite formidable and still unresolved.

The central problem again is the printed page. Perhaps it will remain with us as a reminder of our compromise with a cold technology. Perhaps not. Though some of the poetry even on the page is highly effective, we still are confronted with Larry Neal's challenge of "the destruction of the text," in which the text of a poem is merely a "score," a single possible form of a poem. Much more theorizing and experimenting remain to be done.

Structurally speaking, however, whenever Black poetry is most distinctly and effectively Black, it derives its form from two basic sources, Black speech and Black music. It follows, then, if this is correct, that any serious appreciation of understanding of it must rest upon a deep and sympathetic knowledge of Black music and Black speech and—let us be plain—the Black people who make the music and who make the speech.

By Black speech I mean the speech of the majority of Black people in this country, and I do not exclude the speech of so-called educated people. By Black speech, I also imply a sensitivity to and an understanding of the entire range of Black spoken language in America. This includes the techniques and timbres of the sermon and other forms of oratory, the dozens, the rap, the signifying, and the oral folktale.

By Black music I mean essentially the vast fluid body of Black song—spirituals, shouts, jubilees, gospel songs, field cries, blues, pop songs by Blacks, and, in addition, jazz (by whatever name one calls it) and non-jazz music by Black composers who consciously or unconsciously draw upon the Black musical tradition.

These two "referents," as I shall call them, of Black poetry are themselves so closely related that it is quite naive, even foolish, to speak of the spirituals or the blues without considering their verbal components. And even in jazz the verbal component lurks somewhere in the rhythms, in the coloring, and in the phrasing, so that one hears talk, for example, of "speech inflected jazz"; one reads descriptions of the "scream" of Coltrane's horn. . . .

[FROM "BLACK SPEECH AS POETIC REFERENCE"]

Black linguistic elegance takes innumerable forms, many quite subtle, but some of the more obvious ones may be considered here. . . .

a. Virtuoso naming and enumerating. The roots of this technique might conceivably lie in the folk practice of riddling and similar kinds of wordplay. It may also be related to the kind of witty gesture involved in nicknaming. It is definitely related to the kind of product brand-name story that Roger Abrahams records in *Deep Down in the Jungle,* and which still flourishes in the Black Community.

Cavalier took a ride across the desert on a Camel, just 'cause he was in love with somebody called Fatima. Philip was blasting off to Morris. Now Raleigh decided since he had made a Lucky Strike he was going down to Chesterfield's. He had a whole pocket full of Old Gold. And so, last but not least, he decided to go on a Holiday.

[Kid, #100, p. 244.]

b. Jazzy rhythmic effects. Especially interesting to the listener is the fact that some of the rhythmic patterns of contemporary Black poetry go back to folk and street sources and are commonly known in the Black Community. Some of these occur in children's games and in the folk rhymes that were recorded by Talley in his *Negro Folk Rhymes.* Others are traceable to the rhythms of the dozens, and even to popular quasi-folk songs like the "Dirty Dozens" and to urban narratives and toasts like "Shine" and "The Signifying Monkey."

In Mari Evans' poem "Viva Noir!" the rhythms reflect the hipness of the folk tradition as it becomes urbanized.

> I'm tired
> of hand me downs
> shut me ups
> pin me ins
> keep me outs
> messing me over have
> just had it
> baby
> from
> you . . .

c. Virtuoso free-rhyming. This occurs both in speech and in poetry, and seems to be related to the impulse to lard speech and conversation with proverbs and aphoristic sayings, both sacred and secular, . . . For example, a Black man in his fifties recently said the following in an interview which I conducted on the meaning of "Soul"

> I don't want nothin' old but some gold;
> I don't want nothin' black but a Cadillac!

d. Hyperbolic imagery. The breathless virtuoso quality of free-rhyming comes from the utilization of single rhythm sound, the object being to get in as many rhymes as one can. Oratorically, this is balanced by a passage in which there is no rhyme at all, and the wit and the energy expend themselves in a series of hyperbolic wisecracks, rooted in the tradition of masculine boasting. Note,

> I'm the man who walked the water and tied the
> whale's tail in a knot
> Taught the little fishes how to swim
> Crossed the burning sands and shook the devil's hand
> Rode round the world on the back of a snail
> carrying a sack saying AIR MAIL

e. *Metaphysical imagery.* When hyperbolic imagery merges into the kind of figure in which precise intellectual statement is coupled with witty far-reaching comparison in a unified and passionate image. . . . A good example is this passage from Big Bill Broonzy's "Hollerin' the Blues":

> You'll never get to do me like you did my buddy Shine
> You'll never get to do me like you did my buddy Shine
> You worked him so hard on the levee—
> Till he went stone blind.
> I can hear my hamstring a-poppin', and my collar cryin'
> I can hear my hamstring a-poppin', and my collar cryin'.

f. *Understatement.* A supreme example would be these tragic blues lines:

> I'm gonna lay my head on some lonesome railroad line;
> I'm gonna wait on No. Nine, just to pacify my mind.

g. *Compressed and cryptic imagery.* Here is the street cleaner's rap to Ellison's hero.

> All it takes to get along in this here man's town
> is a little shit, grit and mother-wit. And man,
> I was bawn with all three. In fact, I'maseventh-
> sonofaseventhsonbawnwithacauloverbotheyesandraised-
> onblackcatboneshighjohntheconquerorandgreasygreens—
> [*Invisible Man,* Signet ed., p. 155.]

h. *Worrying the line.* This is the folk expression for the device of altering the pitch of a note in a given passage or for other kinds of ornamentation often associated with melismatic singing in the Black tradition. A verbal parallel exists in which a word or phrase is broken up to allow for affective or didactic comment. Here is an example from Rich Amerson's "Black Woman":

> Say, I feel superstitious, Mamma
> 'Bout my hoggin' bread, Lord help my hungry time,
> I feel superstitious, Baby, 'bout my hoggin' bread!

Ah-hmmm, Baby, I feel superstitious,
I say 'stitious, Black Woman!
Ah-hmmm, ah you hear me cryin'
About I done got hungry, oh Lordy!
Oh, Mamma, I feel superstitious
About my hog Lord God it's my bread.

BLACK MUSIC AS POETIC REFERENCE

Now let us formally, though briefly, consider this second referent—music—in further detail. Aside from mascon structures, there are other important ways in which music, Black music, lies at the basis of much of Black poetry, either consciously or covertly. I have been able to distinguish at least ten types of usage, but I am certain that there are others.

1. The casual, generalized reference
2. The careful allusion to song titles
3. The quotations from a song
4. The adaptation of song forms
5. The use of tonal memory as poetic structure
6. The use of precise musical notation in the text
7. The use of an assumed emotional response incorporated into the poem: the "subjective correlative"
8. The musician as subject/poem/history/myth
9. The use of language from the jazz life
10. The poem as "score" or "chart" . . .

SATURATION

By "saturation" in Black poetry, I mean several things, but chiefly (a) the communication of Blackness in a given situation, and (b) a sense of fidelity to the observed and intuited truth of the Black Experience. I postulate this concept as a third category for describing and evaluating Black poetry. As in the other two, theme and structure, this category exists only in relationship to the entire work and is employed merely to deal with an aspect of the poetry that warrants discussion and appreciation. In other words, just as it is misleading to speak of theme to the exclusion of structure and vice versa, it is difficult, if not impossible, to speak honestly about saturation without considering the poem in isolation but in relationship to the reader/audience, and the reader to the wider context of the phenomenon which we call, for the sake of convenience, the Black Experience.

We may first consider saturation as a perception by the reader that a given poem deals with the Black Experience even though there are no verbal or other clues to alert him. He simply knows that this is so. He may perceive this on varying levels, either sharply and precisely by gestalt, or obscurely upon reflection. Sometimes the awareness comes through as a kind of "tone," sometimes as "perspective," either that of the poet, or of the reader. Note these two examples from Mari Evans' collection, *I Am a Black Woman*

> I am not
> lazy . . . just
> . . . battered

Also (from "Where Have You Gone," p. 35):

> where have you gone
> with your confident
> walk your
> crooked smile the
> rent money
> in one pocket and
> my heart
> in another . . .

With Mari Evans the special despair that seeps through the jeweled diction, and sometimes the bitter wit itself, is somehow akin to the blues. In cases like these, the awareness is largely unverbalized and comes across as a "typical" situation, which we identify as true-to-life or part of the Black Experience. Perhaps there are minute linguistic or gestural clues, but these are highly ambiguous, as in the statement "I am not lazy." Anybody of any race could say that, of course, but what makes it special is the reaction to the implied historical stereotype of the lazy darky. Black people have a kind of hypersensitivity to those stereotypes even when their use is unintended or unperceived. Therefore, for one who is totally immersed, as it were, or saturated in the Black Experience the slightest formulation of the typical or true-to-life experience, whether positive or negative, is enough to bring on at least subliminal recognition.

Again, saturation may be viewed in terms of analogy, and one may use literature itself as a basis for comparison. There are, for example, passages in a poem that we may designate as very "English" or "American" without ever being able to explain ourselves more precisely than that. Or, even more basically, we may prefer an obviously flawed sonnet to one which is metrically perfect, and even consider it somehow to be a better poem or more poetic or meaningful. The same is true, more dramatically so, in more expansive forms like the epic or the novel, where some other consideration than mere structure causes us to prefer, for example, a Dreiser novel to one by Scott Fitzgerald, or Faulkner to Hemingway. The same kind of consideration enables Blacks to recognize *Native Son* as somehow truer to the Black Experience in America, somehow more typical than *Invisible Man,* even though, paradoxically, the latter deals with a wider range of that experience.

What we are talking about then is the depth and quality of experience which a given work may evoke. We are also speaking about saturation as a kind of condition. The kind of difference, for example, that exists between a Tin Pan Alley "blues" and a blues by Lightnin' Hopkins. Or if one protested because of the identifiable form of the blues, we could turn to the important phenomenon of Blacks taking over certain "white," i.e., general American cultural traits or features, and putting a decidedly Black stamp on them. One may think for example of Bessie Smith's rendition of a Tin Pan Alley song like "Muddy Water," which is much better by far than the song deserves. Was it pure commercial concern that motivated her? Didn't she understand the words? At any rate, anyone who has heard Mississippi bluesmen sing of catastrophic flooding in the Delta would perceive some commonality in the singing of Bessie Smith. More to the point is this: What is it, except some fundamental mechanism or set of values, that causes an Aretha Franklin to select for her special Black interpretation certain songs that were written and sometimes performed by whites. To speak of universal appeal, I think, is a cop-out, for the obvious rejoinder would be why is one particularly good song chosen and another rejected? Especially when the singer takes the trouble to give it a Black interpretation which is literally a reinvention. To speak purely in musical terms is, of course, a contradiction because of the virtual saturation of all Black music in the conditions which produced it. I would attribute the choice to an inner personal need or to cultural drive. Perhaps to a cultural imperative, to use Harold Cruse's phrase. At any rate, stylistic differences aside, the recognition on the part of the audience that the artist has made a selection based on a set of mutually shared experiences and/or values is another way of talking about saturation.

We may speak more directly of saturation with specific relationship to both theme and structure. In such cases, where style and subject matter are obviously Black, one may feel, for example, that a word, a phrase, a rhythm, is so right, so Black, that its employment illuminates the entire composition. An example would be Gwendolyn Brooks's observation of the Bronzeville man with the belted coat, or Sterling Brown's "Sister Lou," where the poem ends with the felicitous words, "Take your time, honey, take your *bressed* time" (my italics).

It is, in fact, in character drawing where questions of saturation become especially dramatic. Here one may feel that a given objectively described character, or self-revealed character, may be perfectly Black, i.e., that any additional touch would result in caricature or other distortion. The character is thus felt to be saturated in the Black Experience, and the poem itself a saturated one. This perception comes as a kind of gestalt in which the whole is more than the sum of the parts, the character more than his actions, his speech, or his thoughts, although they are in this case identifiably Black. Such characters abound in the poetry of the period from the twenties through the fifties. They may be inventions based on real life observations or they may be historical or legendary figures. . . . In brief, the Nat Turner of Robert Hayden and Margaret Walker are Black in ways that William Styron's Turner could not possibly be—or certainly is not. That is, I think, because the Black portrayal of Turner becomes almost a mascon image, as it were, a highly concentrated experienced reality that embodies somehow in a single man a major movement of the racial mind.

That, briefly, is what I mean by saturation as a descriptive category. How now does it function as a critical category, as a means of evaluation? In the first place, it lets us know that the recognition of Blackness in poetry is a value judgment which on certain levels and in certain instances, notably in matters of meaning that go beyond questions of structure and theme, must rest upon one's immersion in the totality of the Black Experience. It means that the ultimate criteria for critical evaluation must be found in the sources of the creation, that is, in the Black Community itself.

In the second place, it lets us know that judgments regarding fidelity to the Black Experience are both objective and subjective, and that although a Joel Chandler Harris may record Black folk tales, the inner truth of those tales must be decided by the people who told them and who listened. Here, of course, we are not speaking merely of realism as a literary phenomenon. Notwithstanding, in the history of Black literature generally, and Black poetry specifically, let us remember the circumstances in which the realists worked, and let us remember what they accomplished. Let us, then, assume the same attitudes in evaluating the realistic poetry of the sixties.

The concept of saturation as a critical category provides a clue to the philosophical meaning of phrases like "Black Is Beautiful," "Black People Are Poems," and so on. For Blacks the celebration of Blackness is an undertaking which makes value judgments, some of which certainly many American whites would reject. Nonetheless, if a Black celebratory poem is to be understood on the most elementary level it must be on these terms. There are none others that are valid. . . .

Suggested Reading with Similar Theme:

Henderson, Stephen E. "Saturation: Progress Report on a Theory of Black Poetry." *Black World* (June 1975): 4–17.

1976–2000:
AESTHETIC VALUES, RECONSTRUCTIONS OF BLACKNESS AND BOUNDARIES, AND POSTMODERNISM

◆

Alice Walker

Saving the Life That Is Your Own: The Importance of Models in the Artist's Life (1976)

How does Walker respond to Wheatley and Baldwin regarding the creative process and the role of the writer? How does Walker raise the consciousness of readers about the invisibility of models for black female writers and critical readers in the 1970s? Who are Walker's models? As advice for critics, how significant is Walker's essay on criticism?

There is a letter Vincent Van Gogh wrote to Emile Bernard that is very meaningful to me. A year before he wrote the letter, Van Gogh had had a fight with his domineering friend Gauguin, left his company, and cut off, in desperation and anguish, his own ear. The letter was written in Saint-Remy, in the South of France, from a mental institution to which Van Gogh had voluntarily committed himself.

I imagine Van Gogh sitting at a rough desk too small for him, looking out at the lovely Southern light, and occasionally glancing critically next to him at his own paintings of the landscape he loved so much. The date of the letter is December 1889. Van Gogh wrote:

> However hateful painting may be, and however cumbersome in the times we are living in, if anyone who has chosen this handicraft pursues it zealously, he is a man of duty, sound and faithful.
>
> Society makes our existence wretchedly difficult at times, hence our impotence and the imperfection of our work. . . . I myself am suffering under an absolute lack of models.
>
> But on the other hand, there are beautiful spots here. I have just done five size 30 canvasses, olive trees. And the reason I am staying on here is that my health is improving a great deal.
>
> What I am doing is hard, dry, but that is because I am trying to gather new strength by doing some rough work, and I'm afraid abstractions would make me soft.

Six months later, Van Gogh—whose health was "improving a great deal"—committed suicide. He had sold one painting during his lifetime. Three times was his work noticed in the press. But these are just details.

The real Vincent Van Gogh is the man who has "just done five size 30 canvasses, olive trees." To me, in context, one of the most moving and revealing descriptions of how a real artist thinks. And the knowledge that when he spoke of "suffering under an absolute lack of models" he spoke of that lack in terms of both the intensity of his commitment and the quality and singularity of his work, which was frequently ridiculed in his day.

The absence of models, in literature as in life, to say nothing of painting, is an occupational hazard for the artist, simply because models in art, in behavior, in growth of spirit and intellect—even if rejected—enrich and enlarge one's view of existence. Deadlier still, to the artist who lacks models, is the curse of ridicule, the bringing to bear on an artist's best work, especially his or her most original, most strikingly deviant, only a fund of ignorance and the presumption that, as an artist's critic, one's judgment is free of the restrictions imposed by prejudice, and is well informed, indeed, about all the art in the world that really matters.

What is always needed in the appreciation of art, or life, is the larger perspective. Connections made, or at least attempted, where none existed before, the straining to encompass in one's glance at the varied world the common thread, the unifying theme through immense diversity, a fearlessness of growth, of search, of looking, that enlarges the private and the public world. And yet, in our particular society, it is the narrowed and narrowing view of life that often wins.

Recently, I read at a college and was asked by one of the audience what I considered the major difference between the literature written by black and by white Americans. I had not spent a lot of time considering this question, since it is not the difference between them that interests me, but, rather, the way black writers and white writers seem to me to be writing one immense story—the same story, for the most part—with different parts of this immense story coming from a multitude of different perspectives. Until this is generally recognized, literature will always be broken into bits, black and white, and there will always be questions, wanting neat answers, such as this.

Still, I answered that I thought, for the most part, white American writers tended to end their books and their characters' lives as if there were no better existence for which to struggle. The gloom of defeat is thick.

By comparison, black writers seem always involved in a moral and/or physical struggle, the result of which is expected to be some kind of larger freedom. Perhaps this is because our literary tradition is based on the slave narrative, where escape for the body and freedom for the soul went together, or perhaps this is because black people have never felt themselves guilty of global, cosmic sins.

This comparison does not hold up in every case, of course, and perhaps does not really hold up at all. I am not a gatherer of statistics, only a curious reader, and this has been my impression from reading books by black and white writers.

There are, however, two books by American women that illustrate what I am talking about: *The Awakening,* by Kate Chopin, and *Their Eyes Were Watching God,* by Zora Neale Hurston.

The plight of Mme Pontellier is quite similar to that of Janie Crawford. Each woman is married to a dull, society-conscious husband and living in a dull, propriety-conscious community. Each woman desires a life of her own and a man who loves her and makes her feel alive. Each woman finds such a man.

Mme Pontellier, overcome by the strictures of society and the existence of her children (along with the cowardice of her lover), kills herself rather than defy the one and abandon the other. Janie Crawford, on the other hand, refuses to allow society to dictate behavior to her, enjoys the love of a much younger, freedom-loving man, and lives to tell others of her experience.

When I mentioned these two books to my audience, I was not surprised to learn that only one person, a young black poet in the first row, had ever heard of *Their Eyes Were Watching God* (*The Awakening* they had fortunately read in their "Women in Literature" class), primarily because it was written by a black woman, whose experience—in love and life—was apparently assumed to be unimportant to the students (and the teachers) of a predominantly white school.

Certainly, as a student, I was not directed toward this book, which would have urged me more toward freedom and experience than toward comfort and security, but was directed instead toward a plethora of books by mainly white male writers who thought most women worthless if they didn't enjoy bullfighting or hadn't volunteered for the trenches in World War I. Loving both these books, knowing each to be indispensable to my own growth, my own life, I choose the model, the example of Janie Crawford. And yet this book, as necessary to me and to other women as air and water, is again out of print. But I have distilled as much as I could of its wisdom in this poem about its heroine, Janie Crawford:

> I love the way Janie Crawford
> left her husbands
> the one who wanted to change her
> into a mule
> and the other who tried to interest her
> in being a queen.
> A woman, unless she submits,
> is neither mule
> nor a queen
> though like a mule she may suffer
> and like a queen pace the floor

It has been said that someone asked Toni Morrison why she writes the kind of books she writes, and that she replied: Because they are the kind of books I want to read.

This remains my favorite reply to that kind of question. As if anyone reading the magnificent, mysterious *Sula* or the grim, poetic *The Bluest Eye* would require more of a reason for their existence than for the brooding, haunting *Wuthering Heights,* for example, or the melancholy, triumphant *Jane Eyre.* (I am not speaking here of the most famous short line of that book, "Reader, I married him," as the triumph, but, rather, of the triumph of Jane Eyre's control over her own sense of morality and her own stout will, which are but reflections of her creator's Charlotte Bronte, who no doubt wished to write the sort of book *she* wished to read.)

Flannery O'Connor has written that more and more the serious novelist will write, not what other people want, and certainly not what other people expect, but whatever interests her or him. And that the direction taken, therefore, will be away from sociology, away from the "writing of explanation," of statistics, and further into mystery, into poetry, and into prophecy. I believe this is true, *fortunately true;* especially for "Third World Writers"; Morrison, Marquez, Ahmadi, Camara Laye make good examples. And not only do I believe it is true for serious writers in general, but I believe, as firmly as did O'Connor, that this is our only hope—in a culture so in love with flash, with trendiness, with superficiality, as ours—of acquiring a sense of essence, of timelessness, and of vision. Therefore, to write the books one wants to read is both to point the direction of vision and, at the same time, to follow it.

When Toni Morrison said she writes the kind of books she wants to read, she was acknowledging the fact that in a society in which "accepted literature" is so often sexist and racist and otherwise irrelevant or offensive to so many lives, she must do the work of two. She must be her own model as well as the artist attending, creating, learning from, realizing the model, which is to say, herself.

(It should be remembered that, as a black person, one cannot completely identify with a Jane Eyre, or with her creator, no matter how much one admires them. And certainly, if one allows history to impinge on one's reading pleasure, one must cringe at the thought of how Heathcliff, in the New World far from Wuthering Heights, amassed his Cathy-dazzling fortune.) I have often been asked why, in my own life and work, I have felt such a desperate need to know and assimilate the experiences of earlier black women writers, most of them unheard of by you and by me, until quite recently; why I felt a need to study them and to teach them.

I don't recall the exact moment I set out to explore the works of black women, mainly those in the past, and certainly, in the beginning, I had no desire to teach them. Teaching being for me, at that time, less rewarding than star-gazing on a frigid night. My discovery of them—most of them out of print, abandoned, discredited, maligned, nearly lost—came about, as many things of value do, almost by accident. As it turned out—and this should not have surprised me—I found I was in need of something that only one of them could provide.

Mindful that throughout my four years at a prestigious black and then a prestigious white college I had heard not one word about early black women writers, one of my first tasks was simply to determine whether they had existed. After this, I could breathe easier, with more assurance about the profession I myself had chosen.

But the incident that started my search began several years ago: I sat down at my desk one day, in a room of my own, with key and lock, and began preparations for a story about voodoo, a subject that had always fascinated me. . . .

I began reading all I could find on the subject of "The Negro and His Folkways and Superstitions." There were Botkin and Puckett and others, all white, most racist. How was I to believe anything they wrote, since at least one of them, Puckett, was capable of wondering, in his book, if "The Negro" had a large enough brain?

Well, I thought, where are the *black* collectors of folklore? Where is the *black* anthropologist? Where is the *black* person who took the time to travel the back roads of the South and collect the information I need: how to cure heart trouble, treat dropsy, hex somebody to death, lock bowels, cause joints to swell, eyes to fall out, and so on. Where was this black person?

And that is when I first saw, in a *footnote* to the white voices of authority, the name Zora Neale Hurston.

Folklorist, novelist, anthropologist, serious student of voodoo, also allaround black woman, with guts enough to take a slide rule and measure random black heads in Harlem; not to prove their inferiority, but to prove that whatever their size, shape, or present condition of servitude, those heads contained all the intelligence anyone could use to get through this world.

Zora Hurston, who went to Barnard to learn how to study what she really wanted to learn: the ways of her own people, and what ancient rituals, customs, and beliefs had made them unique.

Zora, of the sandy-colored hair and the daredevil eyes, a girl who escaped poverty and parental neglect by hard work and a sharp eye for the main chance.

Zora, who left the South only to return to look at it again. Who went to root doctors from Florida to Louisiana and said, "Here I am. I want to learn your trade."

Zora, who had collected all the black folklore I could ever use.
That Zora.

And having found *that Zora* (like a golden key to a storehouse of varied treasure), I was hooked.

What I had discovered, of course, was a model. A model, who, as it happened, provided more than voodoo for my story, more than one of the greatest novels America had produced—though, being America, it did not realize this. She had provided, as if she knew someday I would come along wandering in the wilderness, a nearly complete record of her life. And though her life sprouted an occasional wart, I am eternally grateful for that life, warts and all.

It is not irrelevant, nor is it bragging (except perhaps to gloat a little on the happy relatedness of Zora, my mother, and me), to mention here that the story I wrote, called "The Revenge of Hannah Kemhuff," based on my mother's experiences during the Depression, and on Zora Hurston's folklore collection of the 1920s, and on my own response to both out of a contemporary existence, was immediately published and was later selected, by a reputable collector of short stories, as one of the *Best Short Stories of 1974*.

I mention it because this story might never have been written, because the very bases of its structure, authentic black folklore, viewed from a black perspective, might have been lost. . . .

In that story I gathered up the historical and psychological threads of the life my ancestors lived, and in the writing of it I felt joy and strength and my own continuity. I had that wonderful feeling writers get sometimes, not very often, of being with a great many people, ancient spirits, all very happy to see me consulting and acknowledging them, and eager to let me know, through the joy of their presence, that, indeed, I am not alone.

To take Toni Morrison's statement further, if that is possible, in my own work I write not only what I want to read—understanding fully and indelibly that if I don't do it no one else is so vitally interested, or capable of doing it to my satisfaction—I write all the things *I should have been able to read*. Consulting, as belatedly discovered models, those writers—most of whom, not surprisingly, are women—who understood that their experience as ordinary human beings was also valuable, and in danger of being misrepresented, distorted, or lost:

Zora Hurston—novelist, essayist, anthropologist, autobiographer;
Jean Toomer—novelist, poet, philosopher, visionary, a man who cared what women felt;
Colette—whose crinkly hair enhances her French, part-black face; novelist, playwright, dancer, essayist, newspaperwoman, lover of women, men, small dogs; fortunate not to have been born in America;
Anais Nin—recorder of everything, no matter how minute;
Tillie Olson—a writer of such generosity and honesty, she literally saved lives;
Virginia Woolf—who has saved so many of us.

It is, in the end, the saving of lives that we writers are about. Whether we are "minority" writers or "majority." It is simply in our power to do this. We do it because we care. We care that Vincent Van Gogh mutilated his ear. We care that behind a pile of manure in the yard he destroyed his life. We care that Scott Joplin's music lives! We care because we know this: *the life we save is our own.*

Suggested Readings with Similar Theme:

Scarupa, Harriet Jackson. "E. Ethelbert Miller: Partisan of Literature." *New Directions* (July 1982): 24–29

Evans, Mari. "My Father's Passage." In *Black Women Writers (1950–1980): A Critical Evaluation.* Garden City, N.Y.: Anchor/Doubleday, 1984.

Sanchez, Sonia. "Ruminations/Reflections." In *Black Women Writers (1950–1980): A Critical Evaluation,* edited by Mari Evans. Garden City, N.Y.: Anchor/Doubleday, 1984.

Majors, Clarence. "Necessary Distance: Afterthoughts on Becoming a Writer." *African American Review* 28 (1994): 37–47.

BARBARA SMITH

Toward a Black Feminist Criticism (1977)

Smith calls for "consistent feminist analysis" of works by heterosexual and lesbian black women writers. What is the basis for Smith's request? Why is Smith calling for specific black feminist criteria? Explain the significance of Smith's quotations: "For books to be real and remembered they have to be talked about" and "For books to be understood they must be examined in such a way that the basic intentions of the writers are at least considered." How has Smith echoed Walker? How does Smith anticipate critic Karla Holloway, specifically Holloway's study of "women's ways of saying" in their created works? According to Smith, in African American literary history and literary criticism, there is mostly "silence" and "isolation" regarding lesbian black women writers. How might heterosexual and lesbian readers begin to "break" the silence and deal with the isolation of such writers?

FOR ALL MY SISTERS, ESPECIALLY BEVERLY AND DEMITA

I do not know where to begin. Long before I tried to write this I realized that I was attempting something unprecedented, something dangerous merely by writing about black women writers from a feminist perspective and about black lesbian writers from any perspective at all. These things have not been done. Not by white male critics, expectedly. Not by black male critics. Not by white women critics who think of themselves as feminists. And most crucially not by black women critics who, although they pay the most attention to black women writers as a group, seldom use a consistent feminist analysis or write about black lesbian literature. All segments of the literary world—whether establishment, progressive, black, female, or lesbian—do not know, or at least act as if they do not know, that black women writers and black lesbian writers exist.

For whites, this specialized lack of knowledge is inextricably connected to their not knowing in any concrete or politically transforming way that black women of any description dwell in this play. Black women's existence, experience and culture, and the brutally complex systems of oppression which shape these, are in the "real world" of white and/or male consciousness beneath consideration, invisible, unknown.

This invisibility, which goes beyond anything that either black men or white women experience and tell about in their writing, is one reason it is so difficult for me to know where to start. It seems overwhelming to break such a massive silence. Even more numbing, however, is the realization that so many of the women who will read this have not yet noticed us missing either from their reading matter, their politics or their lives. It is galling that ostensible feminists and acknowledged lesbians have been so blinded to the implications of any womanhood that is not white womanhood and that they have yet to struggle with the deep racism in themselves that is at the source of this blindness.

I think of the thousands and thousands of books, magazines and articles which have been devoted, by this time, to the subject of women's writing and I am filled with rage at the fraction of those pages that mention black and other Third World women. I finally do not know how to begin because in 1977 I want to be writing this for a black feminist publication, for black women who know and love these writers as I do and who, if they do not yet know their names, have at least profoundly felt the pain of their absence.

The conditions that coalesce into the impossibilities of this essay have as much to do with politics as with the practice of literature. Any discussion of Afro-American writers can rightfully begin with the fact that for most of the time we have been in this country we have been categorically denied not only literacy, but the most minimal possibility of a decent human life. In her landmark essay "In Search of Our Mothers' Gardens," Alice Walker discloses how the political, economic and social restrictions of slavery and racism have historically stunted the creative lives of black women.

At the present time I feel that the politics of feminism have a direct relationship to the state of black women's literature. A viable, autonomous black feminist movement in this country would open up the space needed for the exploration of black women's lives and the creation of consciously black woman-identified art. At the same time a redefinition of the goals and strategies of the white feminist movement would lead to much needed change in the focus and content of what is now generally accepted as women's culture.

I want to make in this essay some connections between the politics of black women's lives, what we write about and our situation as artists. In order to do this I will look at how black women have been viewed critically by outsiders, demonstrate the necessity for black feminist criticism, and try to understand what the existence or nonexistence of black lesbian writing reveals about the state of black women's culture and the intensity of all black women's oppression.

The role that criticism plays in making a body of literature recognizable and real hardly needs to be explained here. The necessity for nonhostile and perceptive analysis of works written by persons outside the mainstream of white/male cultural rule has been proven by the black cultural resurgence of the 1960s and 1970s and by the even more recent growth of feminist literary scholarship. For books to be real and remembered they have to be talked about. For books to be understood they must be examined in such a way that the basic intentions of the writers are at least considered. Because of racism, black literature has usually been viewed as a discrete subcategory of American literature and there have been black critics of black literature who did much to keep it alive long before it caught the attention of whites. Before the advent of specifically feminist criticism in this decade, books by white women, on the other hand, were not clearly perceived as the cultural manifestation of an oppressed people. It took the surfacing of the second wave of the North American feminist movement to expose the fact that these works contain a stunningly accurate record of the impact of patriarchal values and practice upon the lives of women and more significantly that literature by women provides essential insights into female experience.

In speaking about the current situation of black women writers, it is important to remember that the existence of a feminist movement was an essential precondition to the growth of feminist literature, criticism and women's studies, which focused at the beginning almost entirely upon investigations of literature. The fact that a parallel black feminist movement has been much slower in evolving cannot help but have impact upon the situation of black women writers and artists and explains in part why during this very same period we have been so ignored.

There is no political movement to give power or support to those who want to examine black women's experience through studying our history, literature and culture. There is no political presence that demands a minimal level of consciousness and respect from those who write or talk about our lives. Finally, there is not a developed body of black feminist political theory whose assumptions could be used in the study of black women's art. When black women's books are dealt with at all, it is usually in the context of black literature which largely ignores the implications of sexual politics. When white women look at black women's works they are of course ill-equipped to deal with the subtleties of racial politics. A black feminist approach to literature that embodies the realization that the politics of sex as well as the politics of race and class are crucially interlocking factors in the works of black women writers is an absolute necessity. Until a black feminist criticism exists we will not even know what these writers mean. The citations from a variety of critics which follow prove that without a black feminist critical perspective not only are books by black women misunderstood, they are destroyed in the process.

Jerry H. Bryant, the *Nation*'s white male reviewer of Alice Walker's *In Love and Trouble: Stories of Black Women,* wrote in 1973: "The subtitle of the collection, 'Stories of Black Women,' is probably an attempt by the publisher to exploit not only black subjects but feminine ones. There is nothing feminist about these stories, however." Blackness and feminism are to his mind mutually exclusive and peripheral to the act of writing fiction. Bryant of course does not consider that Walker might have titled the work herself, nor did he apparently read the book which unequivocally reveals the author's feminist consciousness.

In *The Negro Novel in America,* a book that black critics recognize as one of the worst examples of white racist pseudoscholarship, Robert Bone cavalierly dismisses Ann Petry's classic, *The Street.* He perceives it to be "a superficial social analysis" of how slums victimize their black inhabitants. He further objects that:

> It is an attempt to interpret slum life in terms of Negro experience, when a larger frame of reference is required. As Alain Locke has observed, *"Knock on Any Door* is superior to *The Street* because it designates class and environment, rather than mere race and environment, as its antagonist."

Neither Robert Bone nor Alain Locke, the black male critic he cites, can recognize that *The Street* is one of the best delineations in literature of how sex, race, and class interact to oppress black women.

In her review of Toni Morrison's *Sula* for the *New York Times Book Review* in 1973, putative feminist Sara Blackburn makes similarly racist comments. She writes:

> Toni Morrison is far too talented to remain only a marvelous recorder of the black side of provincial American life. If she is to maintain the large and serious audience she deserves, she is going to have to address a riskier contemporary reality than this beautiful but nevertheless distanced novel. *And if she does this, it seems to me that she might easily transcend that early and unintentionally limiting classification "black woman writer" and take her place among the most serious, important and talented American novelists now working.* [Smith's italics]

Recognizing Morrison's exquisite gift, Blackburn unashamedly asserts that Morrison is "too talented" to deal with mere black folk, particularly those double nonentities, black women. In order to be accepted as "serious," "important," "talented" and "American," she must obviously focus her efforts upon chronicling the doings of white men.

The mishandling of black women writers by whites is paralleled more often by their not being handled at all, particularly in feminist criticism. Although Elaine Showalter in her review essay on literary criticism for *Signs* states that: "The best work being produced today [in feminist criticism] is exacting and cosmopolitan," her essay is neither. If it were, she would not have failed to mention a single black or Third World woman writer, whether "major" or "minor," to cite her questionable categories. That she also does not even hint that lesbian writers of any color exist renders her purported overview virtually meaningless. Showalter obviously thinks that the identities of being black and female are mutually exclusive, as this statement illustrates: "Furthermore, there are other literary subcultures (black American novelists,

for example) whose history offers a precedent for feminist scholarship to use."
The idea of critics like Showalter using black literature is chilling, a case of
barely disguised cultural imperialism. The final insult is that she footnotes the
preceding remark by pointing readers to works on black literature by white
males Robert Bone and Roger Rosenblatt.

Two recent works by white women, Ellen Moers's *Literary Women: The
great writers* and Patricia Meyer Spacks's *The Female Imagination,* evidence the
same racist flaw. Moers includes the names of four black and one Puertor-
riquena writer in her seventy pages of bibliographical notes and does not deal
at all with Third World women in the body of her book. Spacks refers to a
comparison between Negroes and women in Many Ellman's *Thinking About
Women* under the index entry, "blacks, women and." "Black Boy (Wright)" is
the preceding entry. Nothing follows. Again there is absolutely no recognition that black and female identity ever coexist, specifically in a group of
black women writers. Perhaps one can assume that these women do not know
who black women writers are, that they have little opportunity like most
Americans to learn about them. Perhaps. Their ignorance seems suspiciously
selective, however, particularly in the light of the dozens of truly obscure
white women writers they are able to unearth. Spacks was herself employed
at Wellesley College at the same time Alice Walker was there teaching one of
the first courses on black women writers in the country.

I am not trying to encourage racist criticism by black women writers
like that of Sara Blackburn, to cite only one example. As a beginning I would
at least like to see in print white women's acknowledgment of the contradictions of who and what are being left out of their research and writing.

Black male critics can also act as if they do not know that black women
writers exist and are, of course, hampered by an inability to comprehend
black women's experience in sexual as well as racial terms. Unfortunately
there are also those who are as virulently sexist in their treatment of black
women as their white male counterparts. Darwin Turner's discussion of Zora
Neale Hurston in his *In a Minor Chord: Three Afro-American Writers and Their
Search for Identity* is a frightening example of the near assassination of a great
black woman writer. His descriptions of her and her work as "artful," "coy,"
"irrational," "superficial" and "shallow" bear no relationship to the actual
quality of her achievements. Turner is completely insensitive to the sexual
political dynamics of Hurston's life and writing.

In a recent interview, the notoriously misogynist writer, Ishmael Reed,
comments in this way upon the low sales of his newest novel:

> but the book only sold 8000 copies. I don't mind giving out the figure: 8000.
> Maybe if I was one of those young female Afro-American writers that are so
> hot now, I'd sell more. You know, fill my books with ghetto women who can do
> no wrong . . . But come on, I think I could have sold 8000 copies by myself.

The politics of the situation of black women are glaringly illuminated by this statement. Neither Reed nor his white male interviewer has the slightest compunction about attacking black women in print. They need not fear widespread public denunciation since Reed's statement is in perfect agreement with the values of a society that hates black people, women and black women. Finally the two of them feel free to base their actions on the premise that black women are powerless to alter either their political or their cultural oppression.

In her introduction to "A Bibliography of Works Written by American Black Women" Ora Williams quotes some of the reactions of her colleagues toward her efforts to do research on black women. She writes:

> Others have reacted negatively with such statements as, "I really don't think you are going to find very much written." "Have 'they' written anything that is any good?" and "I wouldn't go overboard with this woman's lib thing." When discussions touched on the possibility of teaching a course in which emphasis would be on the literature by black women, one response was, "Ha, ha. That will certainly be the most nothing course ever offered!"

A remark by Alice Walker capsulizes what all the preceding examples indicate about the position of black women writers and the reasons for the damaging criticism about them. In response to her interviewer's question "Why do you think that the black woman writer has been so ignored in America? Does she have even more difficulty than the black male writer, who perhaps has just begun to gain recognition?" Walker replies:

> There are two reasons why the black woman writer is not taken as seriously as the black male writer. One is that she's a woman. Critics seem usually ill-equipped to intelligently discuss and analyze the works of black women. Generally, they do not even make the attempt; they prefer, rather, to talk about the lives of black women writers, not about what they write. And, since black women writers are not—it would seem—very likable—until recently they were the least willing worshippers of male supremacy—comments about them tend to be cruel.

A convincing case for black feminist criticism can obviously be built solely upon the basis of the negativity of what already exists. It is far more gratifying, however, to demonstrate its necessity by showing how it can serve to reveal for the first time the profound subtleties of this particular body of literature.

Before suggesting how a black feminist approach might be used to examine a specific work I will outline some of the principles that I think a black feminist critic could use. Beginning with a primary commitment to exploring how both sexual and racial politics and black and female identity are inextricable elements in black women's writings, she would also work from the assumption that black women writers constitute an identifiable literary tradition. The breadth of her familiarity with these writers would have shown her that not only is theirs a verifiable historical tradition that parallels in time the tradition of black men and white women writing in this country, but that thematically, stylistically, aesthetically and conceptually black women writers manifest common approaches to the act of creating literature as a direct result of the specific political, social and economic experience they have been obliged to share. The way, for example, that Zora Neale Hurston, Margaret Walker, Toni Morrison and Alice Walker incorporate the traditional black female activities of rootworking, herbal medicine, conjure and midwifery into the fabric of their stories is not mere coincidence, nor is their use of specifically black female language to express their own and their characters' thoughts accidental. The use of black women's language and cultural experience in books by black women about black women results in a miraculously rich coalescing of form and content and also takes their writing far beyond the confines of white/male literary structures. The black feminist critic would find innumerable commonalities in works by black women.

Another principle which grows out of the concept of a tradition and which would also help to strengthen this tradition would be for the critic to look first for precedents and insights in interpretation within the works of other black women. In other words she would think and write out of her own identity and not try to graft the ideas or methodology of white/male literary thought upon the precious materials of black women's art. Black feminist criticism would by definition be highly innovative, embodying the daring spirit of the works themselves. The black feminist critic would be constantly aware of the political implications of her work and would assert the connections between it and the political situation of all black women. Logically developed, black feminist criticism would owe its existence to a black feminist movement while at the same time contributing ideas that women in the movement could use. . . .

In her interview in *Conditions: One* Adrienne Rich talks about unconsummated relationships and the need to reevaluate the meaning of intense yet supposedly nonerotic connections between women. She asserts: "We need a lot more documentation about what actually happened: I think we can also imagine it, because we know it happened—we know it out of our own lives." Black women are still in the position of having to "imagine," discover and verify black lesbian literature because so little has been written from an avowedly lesbian perspective. The near nonexistence of black lesbian literature which other black lesbians and I so deeply feel has everything to do with the politics of our lives, the total suppression of identity that all black women, lesbian or not, must face. This literary silence is again intensified by the unavailability of an autonomous black feminist movement through which we could fight our oppression and also begin to name ourselves.

In a speech, "The Autonomy of Black Lesbian Women," Wilmette Brown comments upon the connection between our political reality and the literature we must invent:

> Because the isolation of Black lesbian women, given that we are superfreaks, given that our lesbianism defies both the sexual identity that capital gives us and the racial identity that capital gives us, the isolation of Black lesbian women from heterosexual Black women is very profound. Very profound. I have searched throughout Black history, Black literature, whatever, looking for some women that I could see were somehow lesbian. Now I know that in a certain sense they were all lesbian. But that was a very painful search.

Heterosexual privilege is usually the only privilege that black women have. None of us have racial or sexual privilege, almost none of us have class privilege, maintaining "straightness" is our last resort. Being out, particularly out in print, is the final renunciation of any claim to the crumbs of tolerance that nonthreatening ladylike black women are sometimes fed. I am convinced that it is our lack of privilege and power in every other sphere that allows so few black women to make the leap that many white women, particularly writers, have been able to make in this decade, not merely because they are white or have economic leverage, but because they have had the strength and support of a movement behind them.

As black lesbians we must be out not only in white society, but in the black community as well, which is at least as homophobic. That the sanctions against black lesbians are extremely high is well illustrated in this comment by black male writer Ishmael Reed. Speaking about the inroads that whites make into black culture, he asserts:

> In Manhattan you find people actively trying to impede intellectual debate among Afro-Americans. The powerful "liberal/radical/existentialist" influences of the Manhattan literary and drama establishment speak through tokens, like for example that ancient notion of the one black ideologue (who's usually a Communist), the one black poetess (who's usually a feminist lesbian).

To Reed, "feminist" and "lesbian" are the most pejorative terms he can hurl at a black woman and totally invalidate anything she might say, regardless of her actual politics or sexual identity. Such accusations are quite effective for keeping black women writers who are writing with integrity and strength from any conceivable perspective in line, but especially ones who are actually feminist and lesbian. Unfortunately Reed's reactionary attitude is all too typical. A community which has not confronted sexism, because a widespread black feminist movement has not required it to, has likewise not been challenged to examine its heterosexism. Even at this moment I am not convinced that one can write explicitly as a black lesbian and live to tell about it.

Yet there are a handful of black writers who have risked everything for truth. Audre Lorde, Pat Parker and Ann Allen Shockley have at least broken ground in the vast wilderness of works that do not exist. Black feminist criticism will again have an essential role not only in creating a climate in which black lesbian writers can survive, but in undertaking the total reassessment of black literature and literary history needed to reveal the black woman-identified women that Wilmette Brown and so many of us are looking for.

Although I have concentrated here upon what does not exist and what needs to be done, a few black feminist critics have already begun this work. Gloria T. Hull at the University of Delaware has discovered in her research on black women poets of the Harlem Renaissance that many of the women who are considered minor writers of the period were in constant contact with each other and provided both intellectual stimulation and psychological support for each other's work. At least one of these writers, Angelina Weld Grimke, wrote many unpublished love poems to women. Lorraine Bethel, a recent graduate of Yale College, has done substantial work on black women writers, particularly in her senior essay, "This Infinity of Conscious Pain: Blues Lyricism and Hurston's Black Female Folk Aesthetic and Cultural Sensibility in *Their Eyes Were Watching God*," in which she brilliantly defines and uses the principles of black feminist criticism. Elaine Scott at the State University of New York at Old Westbury is also involved in highly creative and politically resonant research on Hurston and other writers.

The fact that these critics are young and, except for Hull, unpublished merely indicates the impediments we face. Undoubtedly there are other women working and writing whom I do not even know, simply because there is no place to read them. As Michele Wallace states in her article "A Black feminist's search for sisterhood":

> We exist as women who are Black who are feminists, each stranded for the moment, working independently because there is not yet an environment in this society remotely congenial to our struggle—[or our thoughts].

I only hope that this essay is one way of breaking our silences and our isolation, of helping us to know each other. . . .

Suggested Readings with Similar Theme:

Christian, Barbara. Introduction to *Black Women Novelists: The Development of a Tradition, 1892–1976*. Westport, Conn.: Greenwood Press, 1980.

Smith, Barbara, ed. Introduction to *Home Girls: A Black Feminist Anthology*. New York: Kitchen Table, 1983.

Lorde, Audre. "The Master's Tools Will Never Dismantle the Master's House." In *Sister Outsider.* New York: Crossing Press, 1984.

Washington, Mary Helen. "The Darkened Eye Restored: Notes Toward a Literary History of Black Women." In *Invented Lives: Narratives of Black Women 1860–1960.* Garden City, N.Y.: Doubleday, 1987.

McDowell, Deborah. "The Changing Same: Generational Connections and Black Women Novelists." *New Literary History* 18 (Winter 1987): 281–302.

Foster, Frances Smith. Introduction (II) to *A Brighter Coming Day: A Frances Ellen Watkins Harper Reader,* edited by Frances Smith Foster. New York: Feminist Press at the City University of New York, 1990.

The Little Man at Chehaw Station:
The American Artist and His Audience (1977)

Ellison said that he learned from experience something every artist should know about maintaining high standards for himself and his audience. Explain what Ellison observed: "{T} he man behind Chehaw's stove also serves a metaphor for those individuals we sometimes meet whose refinement of sensibility is inadequately explained by family background, formal education, or social status." Discuss other metaphors for the man behind Chehaw's stove. What are the risks when the artist applies class and economic restrictions to his audience? Compare Ellison's discussion of audience to Sterling Brown's, Baldwin's, and Petry's.

It was at Tuskegee Institute during the mid-1930s that I was made aware of the little man behind the stove. At the time I was a trumpeter majoring in music and had aspirations of becoming a classical composer. As such, shortly before the little man came to my attention, I had outraged the faculty members who judged my monthly student's recital by substituting a certain skill of lips and fingers for the intelligent and artistic structuring of emotion that was demanded in performing the music assigned to me. Afterward, still dressed in my hired tuxedo, my ears burning from the harsh negatives of their criticism, I had sought solace in the basement studio of Hazel Harrison, a highly respected concert pianist and teacher. Miss Harrison had been one of Ferruccio Busoni's prize pupils, had lived (until the rise of Hitler had driven her back to a U.S.A. that was not yet ready to recognize her talents) in Busoni's home in Berlin, and was a friend of such masters as Egon Petri, Percy Grainger, and Sergei Prokofiev. It was not the first time that I have appealed to Miss Harrison's generosity of spirit, but today her reaction to my rather adolescent complaint was less than sympathetic.

"But, baby," she said, "in this country you must always prepare yourself to play your very best wherever you are, and on all occasions."

"But everybody tells you that," I said.

"Yes," she said, "but there's more to it than you're usually told. Of course you've always been taught to do your best, look your best, be your best. You've been told such things all your life. But now you're becoming a musician, an artist, and when it comes to performing the classics in this country, there's something more involved."

Watching me closely, she paused.

"Are you ready to listen?"

"Yes, ma'am."

"All right," she said, "you must always play your best, even if it's only in the waiting room at Chehaw Station, because in this country there'll always be a little man hidden behind the stove."

"A what?"

She nodded. "That's right," she said. "There'll always be the little man whom you don't expect, and he'll know the music, and the tradition, and the standards of musicianship required for whatever you set out to perform."

Speechless, I stared at her. After the working-over I'd just received from the faculty, I was in no mood for joking. But no, Miss Harrison's face was quite serious. So what did she mean? Chehaw Station was a lonely whistle-stop where swift north- or southbound trains paused with haughty impatience to drop off or take on passengers; the point where, on homecoming weekends, special coaches crowded with festive visitors were cut loose, coupled to a waiting switch engine, and hauled to Tuskegee's railroad siding. I knew it well, and as I stood beside Miss Harrison's piano, visualizing the station, I told myself, She has GOT to be kidding!

For, in my view, the atmosphere of Chehaw's claustrophobic little waiting room was enough to discourage even a blind street musician from picking out blues on his guitar, no matter how tedious his wait for a train. Biased toward disaster by bruised feelings, my imagination pictured the vibrations set in motion by the winding of a trumpet within that drab, utilitarian structure: first shattering, then bringing its walls "a-tumbling down"—like Jericho's at the sounding of Joshua's priest-blown ram horns.

True, Tuskegee possessed a rich musical tradition, both classical and folk, and many music lovers and musicians lived or moved through its environs, but—and my regard for Miss Harrison notwithstanding—Chehaw Station was the last place in the area where I would expect to encounter a connoisseur lying in wait to pounce upon some rash, unsuspecting musician. Sure, a connoisseur might hear the haunting, blues-echoing, train-whistle rhapsodies blared by fast express trains as they thundered past—but the classics? Not a chance!

So as Miss Harrison watched to see the effect of her words, I said with a shrug, "Yes, ma'am."

She smiled, her prominent eyes a-twinkle.

"I hope so," she said. But if you don't just now, you will by the time you become an artist. So remember the little man behind the stove."

With that, seating herself at her piano, she began thumbing through a sheaf of scores—a signal that our discussion was ended. . . .

Thus, as I leaned into the curve of Miss Harrison's Steinway and listened to an interpretation of a Liszt rhapsody (during which she carried on an enthusiastic, stylistic analysis of passages that Busoni himself had marked for expressional subtlety), the little man of Chehaw Station fixed himself in my memory. And so vividly that today he not only continues to engage my mind, but often materializes when I least expect him.

As, for instance, when I'm brooding over some problem of literary criticism—like, say, the rhetoric of American fiction. Indeed, the little stove warmer has come to symbolize nothing less than the enigma of aesthetic communication in American democracy. I especially associate him with the metamorphic character of the general American audience, and with the unrecognized and unassimilated elements of its taste. For me he represents that unknown quality which renders the American audience far more than a receptive instrument that may be dominated through a skillful exercise of the sheerly "rhetorical" elements—the flash and filigree—of the artist's craft. While that audience is eager to be transported, astounded, thrilled, it counters the artist's manipulation of forms with an attitude of antagonistic cooperation; acting, for better of worse, as both collaborator and judge. Like a strange orchestra upon which a guest conductor would impose his artistic vision, it must be exhorted, persuaded—even wooed—as the price of its applause. It must be appealed to on the basis of what it assumes to be truth as a means of inducting it into new dimensions of artistic truth. By playing artfully upon the audience's sense of experience and form, the artist seeks to shape its emotions and perceptions to his vision; while it, in turn, simultaneously cooperates and resists, says yes and says no in an it-takes-two-to-tango binary response to his effort. As representative of the American audience writ small, the little man draws upon the uncodified Americanness of his experience—whether of life or of art—as he engages in a silent dialogue with the artist's exposition of forms, offering or rejecting the work of art on the basis of what he feels to be its affirmation or distortion of American experience.

Perhaps if they were fully aware of his incongruous existence, the little man's neighbors would reject him as a source of confusion, a threat to social order, and a reminder of the unfinished details of his powerful nation. But out of a stubborn individualism born of his democratic origins, he insists upon the cultural necessity of his role, and argues that if he didn't exist he would have to be invented. If he were not already manifest in the flesh, he would still exist and function as an idea and ideal because—like such character traits as individualism, restlessness, self-reliance, love of the new, and so on—he is a linguistic product of the American scene and language, and a manifestation of the idealistic action of the American Word as it goads its users toward a perfection of our revolutionary ideals.

For the artist, a lightning rod attracting unexpected insights and a warning against stale preconceptions, the man behind Chehaw's stove also serves as a metaphor for those individuals we sometimes meet whose refinement of sensibility is inadequately explained by family background, formal education, or social status. These individuals seem to have been sensitized by some obscure force that issues undetected from the chromatic scale of American social hierarchy: a force that throws off strange, ultrasonic ultrasemi-semitones that create within those attuned to its vibrations a mysterious enrichment of personality. In this, heredity doubtless plays an important role, but whatever that role may be, it would appear that, culturally and environmentally, such individuals are products of errant but sympathetic vibrations set up by the tension between America's social mobility, its universal education, and its relative freedom of cultural information. Characterized by a much broader "random accessibility" than class and economic restrictions would appear to allow, this cultural information includes many of the finest products of the arts and intellect—products that are so abundantly available in the form of books, graphics, recordings, and pictorial reproductions as to escape sustained attempts at critical evaluation. Just how these characteristics operate in concert involves the mysterious interaction between environment and personality, instinct and culture. But the frequency and wide dispersal of individuals who reveal the effects of this mysterious configuration of forces endows each American audience, whether of musician, poet, or plastic artist, with a special mystery of its own.

I say "mystery," but perhaps the phenomenon is simply a product of our neglect of serious cultural introspection, our failure to conceive of our fractured, vernacular-weighted culture as an intricate whole. And since there is no reliable sociology of the dispersal of ideas, styles, or tastes in this turbulent American society, it is possible that, personal origins aside, the cultural circumstances here described offer the intellectually adventurous individual what might be termed a broad "social mobility of intellect and taste"—plus an incalculable scale of possibilities for self-creation. While the force that seems to have sensitized those who share the little man of Chehaw Station's unaccountable knowingness—call it a climate of free-floating sensibility—appears to be a random effect generated by a society in which certain assertions of personality, formerly the prerogative of high social rank, have become the privilege of the anonymous and the lowly.

If this be true, the matter of the artist's ability to identify the mixed background and general character of his audience can be more problematical than might be assumed. In the field of literature it presents a problem of rhetoric, a question of how to fashion strategies of communication that will bridge the many divisions of background and taste which any representative American audience embodies. To the extent that American literature is both an art of discovery and an artistic agency for creating a consciousness of cultural identity, it is of such crucial importance as to demand of the artist not only an eclectic resourcefulness of skill, but an act of democratic faith. In this light, the American artist will do his best not only because of his dedication to his form, his craft, but because he realizes that, despite an inevitable unevenness of composition, the chances are that any American audience will conceal at least one individual whose knowledge and taste will complement, or surpass, his own. This (to paraphrase Miss Harrison) is because even the most homogeneous audiences are culturally mixed and embody, in their relative anonymity, the mystery of American cultural identity.

That identity—tentative, controversial, constantly changing—is confusing to artist and audience alike. To the audience because it is itself of mixed background, and seldom fully conscious of the cultural (or even political) implications of its own wise democratic range. To the artist, because in the broadest thrust of his effort he directs his finest effects to an abstract (and thus ideal) refinement of sensibility which, because it is not the exclusive property of a highly visible elite, is difficult to pinpoint. As one who operates within the historical frame of his given art, the artist may direct himself to those who are conscious of the most advanced state of his art: his artistic peers. But if his work has social impact, which is one gauge of its success as symbolic communication, it will reach in to unpredictable areas. Many of us, by the way, read our first Hemingway, Fitzgerald, Mann in barbershops, heard our first opera on phonographs. Thus, the ideal level of sensibility to which the American artist would address himself tends to transcend the lines of class, religion, region, and race—floating, as it were, free in the crowd. There, like the memory registers of certain computer systems, it is simultaneously accessible at any point in American society. Such are the circumstances that render the little man at Chehaw Station not only possible but inevitable.

But who, then is this little man of Miss Harrison's riddle? From behind what unlikely mask does he render his judgments? and by what magic of art can his most receptive attention, his grudging admiration, be excited? No idle questions these; like Shakespeare's Hamlet, the little man has his pride and complexity. He values his personal uniqueness, cherishes his privacy, and clings to that tricky democratic anonymity which makes locating him an unending challenge. . . .

Three years later, after having abandoned my hope of becoming a musician, I had just about forgotten Miss Harrison's mythical little man behind the stove. Then, in faraway New York, concrete evidence of his actual existence arose and blasted me like the heat from an internally combusted ton of coal.

As a member of the New York Writers' Project, I was spending a clammy, late fall afternoon of freedom circulating a petition in support of some now long-forgotten social issue that I regarded as indispensable to the public good. I found myself inside a tenement building in San Juan Hill, a Negro district that disappeared with the coming of Lincoln Center. Starting on the top floor of the building, I had collected an acceptable number of signatures and, having descended from the ground floor to the basement level, was moving along the dimly lit hallway toward a door through which I could hear loud voices. They were male Afro-American voices, raised in violent argument. The language was profane, the style of speech of southern idiomatic vernacular such as was spoken by formally uneducated Afro-American workingmen. Reaching the door, I paused, sounding out the lay of the land before knocking to present my petition.

But my delay led to indecision. Not, however, because of the loud, unmistakable anger sounding within; being myself, a slum dweller. I knew that voices in slums are often raised in anger, but that the rhetoric of anger, being in itself cathartic, is not necessarily a prelude to physical violence. Rather, it is frequently a form of symbolic action, a verbal equivalent of fisticuffs. No, I hesitated because I realized that behind the door a mystery was unfolding. A mystery so incongruous, outrageous, and surreal that it struck me as a threat to my sense of rational order. It was as though a bizarre practical joke had been staged and its perpetrators were waiting for me, its designated but unknowing scapegoat, to arrive; a joke designed to assault my knowledge of American culture and its hierarchical dispersal. At the very least, it appeared that my pride in my knowledge of my own people was under attack.

For the angry voices behind the door were proclaiming an intimate familiarity with a subject of which, by all the logic of their linguistically projected social status, they should have been oblivious. The subject of their contention confounded all my assumptions regarding the correlation between educational levels, class, race, and the possession of conscious culture. Impossible as it seemed, these foulmouthed black workingmen were locked in verbal combat over which of two celebrated Metropolitan Opera divas was the superior soprano!

I myself attended the opera only when I could raise the funds, and I knew full well that opera going was far from the usual cultural pursuit of men identified with the linguistic style of such voices. And yet, confounding such facile logic, they were voicing (and loudly) a familiarity with the Met far greater than my own. In their graphic, irreverent, and vehement criticism they were describing not only the sopranos' acting abilities but were ridiculing the gestures with which each gave animation to her roles, and they shouted strong opinions as to the ranges of the divas vocal equipment. Thus, with such a distortion of perspective being imposed upon me, I was challenged either to solve the mystery of their knowledge by entering into their midst or to leave the building with my sense of logic reduced forever to a level of college-trained absurdity. . . .

And then I blurted it out. "I'd like to ask you just one question." I said.

"Like what?" the standing one said.

"Like where on earth did you gentlemen learn so much about grand opera?"

For a moment he stared at me with parted lips; then, pounding the mantelpiece with his palm, he collapsed with a roar of laughter. As the laughter of the others erupted like a string of giant firecrackers I looked on with glowing feelings of embarrassment and insult, trying to grasp the handle to what appeared to be an unfriendly joke. Finally, wiping coal-dust-stained tears from his cheeks, he interrupted his laughter long enough to initiate me into the mystery.

"Hell, son," he laughed, "we learned it down at the Met, that's where . . ."

"You learned it where?"

"At the Metropolitan Opera, just like I told you. Strip us fellows down and give us some costumes and we make about the finest damn bunch of Egyptians you ever seen. Hell, we been down there wearing leopard skins and carrying spears or waving things like palm leafs and ostrich-tail fans for years!"

Now, purged by the revelation, and with Hazel Harrison's voice echoing in my ears, it was my turn to roar with laughter. With a shock of recognition I joined them in appreciation of the hilarious American joke that centered on the incongruities of race, economic status, and culture. My sense of order restored, my appreciation of the arcane ways of American cultural possibility was vastly extended. The men were products of both past and present; were both coal heavers and Met extras; were both workingmen and opera buffs. Seen in the clear, pluralistic, melting-pot light of American cultural possibility there was no contradiction. The joke, the apparent contradiction, sprang from my attempting to see them by the light of social concepts that cast less illumination than an inert lump of coal. I was delighted, because during a moment when I least expected to encounter the little man behind the stove (Miss Harrison's vernacular music critic, as it were), I had stumbled upon four such men. Not behind the stove, it is true, but even more wondrously, they had materialized at an even more unexpected location: at the depth of the American social hierarchy and, of all possible hiding places, behind a coal pile. Where there's a melting pot there's smoke, and where there's smoke it is not simply optimistic to expect fire, it's imperative to watch for the phoenix's vernacular, but transcendent.

Suggested Reading with Similar Theme:

Ellison, Ralph. *Shadow and Act.* New York: Random House, 1964.

SHERLEY A. WILLIAMS

The Blues Roots of Contemporary Afro-American Poetry (1979)

Williams examines the poetry of contemporary writers and illustrates how "classic blues forms are transformed, allowing poetry to function in much the same way as blues." Discuss the poetics of the blues forms. Might Tolstoy's term "infectiousness" of art— "feelings to be transmitted through the art"—be applied in Williams's demonstration of technique and transformation? How and when does Williams echo Stephen Henderson? Who are the critics to follow who are anticipated by Williams? Define the following terms and phrases: transformation, mascon images, worrying the line.

Ethnopoetics is for me the study of the new forms of poetry which develop as a result of the interfaces or confrontations between different cultures. The spirituals, play and work songs, cakewalks and hoe-downs, and the blues are the first recorded artifacts to grow out of the complex relationship between Africans and Europeans on the North American continent. Afro-American oral tradition, of which these lyric forms are a part, combines with white American literature whose traditions are rooted more in the literate cultures of the West than in the oral traditions, either indigenous or transplanted, of the New World. Afro-American literature is thus created within the framework of multiple relationships, and the tension between the white literary and the black oral traditions informs and influences the best contemporary Afro-American poetry at the level of structure as well as theme. The themes of the poetry are usually accessible to non-black audiences, but the poets' attempts to own the traditions to which they are heir create technical transformations which cannot be analyzed, much less evaluated, solely within the context of their European roots. Most critics pay lip service to the idea that Afro-American music, speech and life-styles influence the form and structure of Afro-American writing. Thus Stephen Henderson's discussion, in *Understanding the New Black Poetry* (1973), of some of the techniques of Afro-American speech and singing which have been carried over virtually unchanged into Afro-American poetry is rare in its concrete descriptions of these devices. This paper builds on his work, concentrating on the transformations which result when the blues of Afro-American oral tradition interfaces with the "poetry" of European literary tradition.

Blues is essentially an oral form meant to be heard rather than read; and the techniques and structures used to such powerful purpose in the songs cannot always be transferred directly to the literary traditions within which, by definition, Afro-American poets write. Blues is viewed here as a verbal—as distinct form musical—genre which developed out of the statement (or call) and response patterns of collective work groups. Blues culminated in a "classic" form (heard most consistently in the early blues recordings of Bessie Smith, Ma Rainey and the other "classic blues" singers) which embodies the distinctive features of Afro-American song forms in a standardized structure. In some contemporary Afro-American poetry, the devices and structures of the classic blues form are transformed, thus allowing the poetry to function in much the same way as blues forms once functioned within the black communities across the country.

I. FUNCTION

Afro-American music still functions to some extent as a reflector of a wide range of values in the national black community and often serves as a catalyst for discussions, reviews and revisions of these values. The immediacy of this process has been diminished by the advent of huge impersonal concerts, but records and local "soul" stations keep alive this supra-entertainment function of the music. The professional songwriter had modified what used to be a very close and personal relationship among singer, song, and the group tradition on which all depended for the act of creation and which the act of creation affirms and extends. In an age where almost everyone is singing someone else's song, performance has to some extent taken the place of authorship. Thus Otis Redding's version of "Respect," while very popular, was never made into the metaphor of Black Man/Black Woman or, just as importantly, Black/White relationships that Aretha Franklin's version became. Of course, Aretha was right on time, but there was also something about the way Aretha characterized respect as something given with force and great effort and cost. And when she even went so far as to spell the word "respect," we just knew that this sister wasn't playing around about getting Respect and keeping it. Early blues singers and their growing repertoire of songs probably helped to solidify community values and heighten community morale in the late nineteenth and early twentieth centuries. The singers provided welcome entertainment and a necessary reminder that there had to be more to the lives of audience than the struggle for material subsistence—if they were ever to achieve and enjoy the day the sun would shine in their back door. Michael S. Harper, in his liner notes to the album *John Coltrane*, alludes to the communal nature of the relationship between blues singer and blues audience when he speaks of the audience which assumes "we" even though the blues singer sings "I." Blues singers have also been aware of this function of their art, for as Henry Townsend said in an interview with Samuel B. Charters (*The Poetry of the Blues,* 1963):

> You know I'm going to put this a little blunt. I don't know if I should say it or not, because it might hurt the religious type of people, but when I sing the blues, I sing the truth. The religious type of people may not believe that it's good, because they think the blues is not the truth; but the blues, from a point of explaining yourself as facts, is the truth and I don't feel that the truth should be condemned. . . .

Unlike sacred music, the blues deals with a world where the inability to solve a problem does not necessarily mean that one can or ought to, transcend it. The internal strategy of the blues is action, rather than contemplation, for the song itself is the creation of reflection. And while not all blues actions achieve the desired result, the impulse to action is inherent in any blues which functions out of a collective purpose. But while the gospels, for example, are created for the purpose of preparing the congregation to receive the Holy Spirit and become possessed by it, the blues singer strives to create an atmosphere in which analysis can take place. This necessary analytic distance is achieved through the use of verbal and musical irony seldom found in the singing of the spirituals or the gospels. Thus Billie Holiday, in "Fine and Mellow," concludes the recital of the wrongs her man has done her with the mocking observation that

> Love is like a faucet
>   it turns off and on
> Sometimes when you think it's on, baby
>   it have turned off and gone.

The persona pointedly reminds her man that her patience with his trifling ways has its limits at the same time that she suggests that she might be in her present difficulties because she wasn't alert to the signs that her well was going dry. The self-mockery and irony of the blues pull one away from a total surrender to the emotions generated by the concreteness of the experiences and situations described in the song. Even where the verbal content of the songs is straightforward and taken at face value, the singer has musical techniques which create ironic effects.

The vocal techniques of Afro-American music—melisma, intentional stutters and hesitations, repetitions of words and phrases, and the interjection of exclamatory phrases and sounds—are used in the spirituals and gospels to facilitate emotional involvement. In blues singing, however, these same devices are often used in a deliberately random manner which emphasizes unimportant phrases or words as often as it does key ones. The devices themselves, especially melisma and changes in stress, have become standardized enough to have formed a substantial part of the artistry of Billie Holiday. At their worst, the devices become no more than meaningless vocal calisthenics, but at their best they disengage meaning from feeling. Put another way, the singer objectifies, almost symbolizes, the emotional content of the song through the use of melisma, stuttering and variations in stress, and, in so doing, places the situation in stark relief as an object for discussion. Thus, a member of the blues audience shouts "Tell it like it is" rather than "Amen" or "Yes, Jesus" as a response to a particularly pungent or witty truth, for the emphasis is on thinking, not tripping.

Charles Keil's analysis (*The Urban Blues,* 1966) of a Bobby Blue Bland performance illustrates how even the selection of songs in a blues performance underscores the relationship of singer and audience and the manner in which communal values are incorporated into the presentation of the blues performer's act. Many contemporary Afro-American poets consciously assume the role of people's voices—see, for example, Marvin X's second volume of poetry *The Son of Man*—and ask black people (rather than whites) to affirm their stance. That initial gesture may have grown out of the learned intellectual model provided by Marx and Herskovits; once having made it, however, it became real for many poets, at more than just the level of rhetoric and "kill the honkey" poems. We witness this realness in the increasing sureness with which Afro-American poets challenge the primacy of European forms.

II. STRUCTURE

A number of Afro-American poets have written poems based on the less structured blues forms; few, however, have attempted to utilize the deceptively simple classic blues structure. Langston Hughes is an exception. The sophistication of meaning and form which characterizes Hughes's poem "Young Gal's Blues" is, of course, characteristic of classic blues at its best and the literary sophistication is in fact made possible by the existence of such songs as "Backwater Blues" or the more contemporary variation on the classic form "Your Friends." "Young Gal's Blues," in which a young woman tries to fortify herself against the prospect of death (which can come at any time) and the loneliness of old age (which will certainly catch her if death don't do it first), is an example of an oral form moving unchanged into literary tradition:

> I'm gonna walk to the graveyard
> 'Hind ma friend, Miss Cora Lee
> Gonna walk to de graveyard
> 'Hind ma dear friend Cora Lee
> Cause when I'm dead some
> Body'll have to walk behind me.

Hughes worries the first line by dropping "I'm" in the repetition of the first half line and adding "dear" when he repeats the second half-line. Repetition in blues is seldom word for word and the definition of worrying the line includes changes in stress and pitch, the addition of exclamatory phrases, changes in word order, repetitions of phrases within the line itself, and the wordless blues cries which often punctuate the performance of the songs. The response to this opening statement repeats and broadens the idea of death even as it justifies and explains the blues persona's action. Ideally, each half line is a complete phrase or clause; but Hughes, even in breaking the line between "some" and "body" rather than after "dead" keeps within the convention of half lines on which the classic structure is based. The stanza is a closed unit without run-over lines or run-over thoughts; and the same pattern, response justifying the statement, is followed in the second stanza in which the persona tells of her determination to visit old Aunt Clew in "de po' house" because "When I'm old an' ugly / I'll want to see somebody, too." The "po' house" evokes the known social and political conditions rather than stating them directly.

In evoking rather than stating these conditions, Hughes makes the same assumption about his audience that a blues singer makes: both poet (singer) and audience share the same reality. The lives of the audience are bound by the same grim social reality in which one faces an old age characterized by the same grinding poverty which destroys youth before it can flower and makes the fact that while work is still necessary, one is no longer capable of doing it—this being the only distinction between middle and old age. The particularized, individual experience rooted in a common reality is the primary thematic characteristic of all blues songs no matter what their structure. The classic song form itself internalizes and echoes, through the statement/response pattern, the thematic relationship between individual and group experience which is implied in these evocations of social and political reality.

> De po' house is lonely
> an' de grave is cold.
> O, de po' house is lonely
> De grave is cold.
> But I'd rather be dead than to
> be ugly and old

The statement in this stanza is more general than the statement in either of the first two stanzas and while the stanza is self-contained, it places the personal reflection of the preceding stanza within a larger context. The response returns to the first person, the subjective testimony, as the persona says quite frankly that she would rather die than be ugly. It is also Hughes's definition of what it is to be young; to care more for the quality of one's life than the fact of life itself. Thus the response in this stanza makes explicit the persona's choices in life. But neither choice, death at an early age or an old age endured in poverty and loneliness, is particularly happy and the persona, recognizing that love is one of the few things which make any life bearable, concludes the fourth stanza and the poem with the plea "Keep on a-lovin me, daddy / Cause I don't want to be blue."

The response can also be the antithesis of the statement as in the opening stanza of "Billie's Blues,"

> I love my man
> I'm a lie if I say I don't
> But I'll quit my man
> I'm a lie if I say I won't

where the paradox also provides the frame for the distinctions which the persona later makes between being a slave, which she is quite prepared to be for her man, and a "dog" which she refuses to become, between mere good looks typified by white features ("I ain't good looking and my hair ain't curled") and the confidence, the affirmation of self necessary to get one through the world.

The change in focus from individual to communal reality may be done as in the Hughes poem or through simply worrying the line as in the blues standard "The Things I Used to Do": "The things I used to do / I won't do no more. / Lawd the things I used to I'm tryna tell yo' all / I won't do no more," where the singer appeals directly to the audience to witness his situation and, in effect, to affirm his solution to his problem. The abrupt change of subject or theme as in "Sweet Sixteen" serves the same purpose. The persona describes his love for a flighty, headstrong young girl who has run away from her home and now wants to "run away from old me, too." The persona is now desperate and the song is really a plea to the woman to do right, love him as he loves her. The third stanza ends with the line, "Seems like everything I do [to try and keep you with me] is in vain."

Then, in a dramatic shift in subject and perspective:

> My brother's in Korea
> My sister's down in New Orleans
> You know I'm having so much trouble, people
> I wonder what in the world's gonna happen to me.

At the level of the love theme, the absence of family ties underscores the persona's loneliness; hence his dependence on this relationship. His scattered family exists within the framework of the ruptured family relationship, caused by the oppressive and repressive system of the country, which characterizes too much of the Afro-American experience. The response to this statement of loneliness is one of complete despair, addressed to "people," the audience whose private pains are set within the same kind of collective experience.

The next stanza is again addressed to the woman and reiterates, at the level of their personal relationship, the persona's realization that he has lost pride, dignity, and a necessary sense of himself as a result of this relationship:

> Treat me mean, baby,
>> but I'll keep on loving you anyway
> But one of these old days, baby,
>> you're gonna give a lot of money to hear someone call my name.

Billie Pierce's version of "Married Man Blues," recorded by Samuel B. Charters in New Orleans in 1954, uses what had become a traditional statement/response description of the problems of loving a married man to place the song within a more universal context. The persona has loved only one man, a married man, in her life. And despite the fact that she "stole him from his wife" she is still in trouble because she has stolen only his affection, not his continued presence. The traditional verse is used to summarize her situation:

> Girls it's awful hard
>> to love another woman's man
> Cause you can't get him when you wanna
>> have to catch catch as catch's can.

The last half-line in the response is Billie's personal variation on the standardized wording, "got to catch him when you can," and the rhythmical variation plays nicely against the established rhythm of the statement. The stanza, in addition, serves as a transition, tying together the fictive first person experiences and the more "real" first person admonitions of the last part of the song.

The second portion of the song opens with an assertion of individuality: "My first name is Billie / and my last name is Pierce." The assertion of individuality and the implied assertion—as action, not mere verbal statement—of self is an important dimension of the blues. Janhienz Jahn (*Neo-African Literature,* 1968) is essentially correct when he describes the blues in terms of this assertion of life-force rather than the usual ones of melancholy and pain. The assertion of self usually comes at the end of the blues song after the description/analysis of the situation or problem and is often the only solution to that problem or situation. In "Married Man Blues," Billie's assertive stance is underscored in successive stanzas which imply some of the values inherent in a good love relationship:

> Aw, you want me to do right there, Little Dee Dee
>> And you ain't doing right yourself
> Well you get yourself another woman
>> And I'll get me somebody else
> Well, at my first time leaving you, baby

>Crying ain't gone make me stay
>Cause the more you cry Dee Dee, baby
>Well the more you gonna drive little Billie away.

The sting of the stanza is balanced by the fact that they are part of the anonymous oral tradition, and Billie Pierce was a master at combining such traditional verses with written songs ("Saint Louis Woman," "Careless Love," for example) to create her own personal versions of these songs. Here, she also underscores the closeness of her musical relationship with her husband, Dee Dee Pierce, who accompanies her on trumpet, by the encouragement spoken throughout this portion of the song to, "Play it nice, play it the way I like it Dee Dee, baby."

This complex interweaving of general and specific, individual and group, finds no direct correspondence to Afro-American literature except in the literary blues. But the evocation of certain first person experiences and the extensive use of multiple voices in Afro-American poetry may be, at least in part, an outgrowth from this characteristic of the blues. Nikki Giovanni's "The Great Pax Whitey" which seems a rather pedestrian and undigested patchwork of folk and personal legend and black nationalist philosophy becomes, when viewed (or better yet, read) as a poem in which a congregation of voices speaks, a brilliant literary approximation of the kind of collective dialogue which has been going on underground in the black community at least since the nineteenth century and of which the blues in its various forms was an important part.

III. TRANSFORMATION

Blues songs are almost always literal, seldom metaphoric or symbolic except in sexual and physical terms. And, while similes are used extensively, much of the verbal strength of the blues resides in the directness with which the songs confront experience and in what Stephen Henderson identifies as "mascon images," Afro-American archetypes which represent a "massive concentration of black experiential energy." Often the mascons are not really images in the literary sense of the word, rather they are verbal expressions which evoke a powerful response in the listener because of their direct relationship to concepts and events in the collective experience. Thus the graveyard and the po' house in "Young Gal's Blues" might be described as universal archetypes or mascons, while the calling of the names in "Sweet Sixteen" is a specifically black one. The latter expression grows directly out of traditional people's belief in the strong relationship between name and personal essence and the corresponding Afro-American preoccupation with titles (Miss, Mr., Mrs. and, with great deliberation and care, Ms.), with the naming of children and the acquisition of nicknames and sobriquets—and who may use them. In such an atmosphere, to call someone out of their name, as the Monkey tells the Lion that the Elephant has done him in the "Signifying Monkey," is punishable, in children, by a beating. And the changing of one's names as most blacks did after emancipation and many more did during the sixties takes on an added significance.

Very often, the meanings of mascons cut across areas of experience usually thought of as separate but which in Afro-American experiences are not mutually exclusive. Thus the term "jelly roll," as Henderson illustrates, moves at a number of different levels, while the expressions centered in the concept of "home" move at both at spiritual and material level, and "The Streets," which has developed into a mascon as a result of the Afro-American urban experience, involves both pleasure and pain. Despite the fact that these expressions are used over and over again by blacks in everyday conversations as well as in more self-conscious verbal events, they escape being cliches because their meanings are deeply rooted in a constantly renewed and thus living reality. They are distinguished from the vernacular vocabulary of black speech in that the vernacular rests on the idea that the standard English version of a word, say "bad" or "dig," has one meaning and the standard black version has another, often contradictory, meaning: excellent and understand. Mascons, on the contrary, concentrate their massive force within the frame of the literal meaning of the standard English word. And it is this literal yet figuratively complex relationship which makes the response in the final stanza of "Sweet Sixteen" such a powerful climax to the song. But one of these old days, the persona tells his woman, you would even get up off some money, just to have back the man I was when I met you, the man that loving you destroyed. Thus mascons are a compression, as well as a concentration, whose power is released through the first person experience.

When Harriet Tubman, in Robery Hayden's "Runagate Runagate Runagate" invites us to "ride my train," it is not merely the thought of the Underground Railroad to which blacks respond. But Harriet's "train" is also the train whose tracks throughout the South were laid by black men who also worked on them as cooks, porters, and red caps and which many blacks rode to the promised land of the North. And despite the fact that trains are no longer a significant part of our day to day reality, they live on in the metaphors of the "Gospel Train" which many plan to ride to glory and the "Soul Trains" which proclaim the black musical presence in the world. It is the stored energy of this mascon which enables Afro-American poets to play so lovingly and meaningful with John Coltrane's name and they capture something of his function as an artist in their use of his nickname, Trane.

Many Afro-American poets have used techniques which approximate or parallel various blues devices and Lucille Clifton, in her first volume of poems, *Good Times,* uses these transformations consistently and successfully. Like the blues, her poems are firmly based in a living black reality which is more concerned with itself than with direct confrontations with white society and its values. There are several poems about whites in the volume, but even here, the impression is of a black person, involved in a conversation with other blacks, who occasionally tosses a comment to the white man she knows is waiting in the wings. His presence does not cause her to bite her tongue, however, and the opening poem "in the inner city," is addressed as much to the white man in the wings as it is to the black audience.

> in the inner city
> or
> like we call it
> home
> we think a lot about uptown
> and the silent nights
> and the houses straight as
> dead men
> and the pastel lights
> and we hang on to our no place
> happy to be alive
> and in the inner city
> or
> like we call it
> home

Clifton's poems are created out of the collective experience which culminates in and is transformed by the inner city. Those experiences in their broader outlines are evoked rather than stated, through vignettes told in the first person; and the individual experience plays against the assumed knowledge of that collective history in much the same way that the communal pattern of statement and response plays against the individual experience expressed in the blues. The inner city of which Clifton speaks is neither that of the "deviants" who inhabit most sociological studies about blacks nor the statistics which politicians manipulate so skillfully for their own gains; it is the community, home. "Inner city" becomes both the literal ghetto and the metaphoric inner landscape of black hearts which has seldom been explored so sensitively and revealingly as in Clifton's *Good Times*.

The spareness of Clifton's poetry depends in part on mascon images. "Pushing," a mascon of enormous contemporary force, is used to climax "For deLawd," Clifton's tribute to the long "line / of black and going on women" from which she comes. Grief for murdered brothers, murdered husbands, murdered sons has kept on pushing them, kept them "for their still alive sons / for their sons coming / for their sons gone / just pushing." And pushing is both the will to struggle on toward a long sought goal, even in the face of enormous odds (as Curtis Mayfield and The Impressions exhort us to do in "Keep on Pushing") and the double consciousness which many would rather not have for it often highlights the futility of trying to "make it" in America (the expression, "I'm so pushed" is used interchangeably with "I'm hipped"). And this reading of "pushing" complements the ironic use of "making it." For it is against the background of the collective experience of "making it through . . . sons" murdered literally and figuratively by the society and the individual prospect of what can happen to her sons that the persona knowingly goes on about her business. The ability to keep on pushing, to keep on keeping on, to go on about one's business is the life-force, the assertion of self amidst collective and individual destruction which comes directly out of the blues tradition. This is what the persona's mother in "Billie's Blues" passes on to her daughter and what makes the closing of that song so delightful:

> Some men call me honey
> Some think that I've got money
> Some men like me cause I'm snappy
> Some because I'm happy
> Some men tell me, Billie
> Baby, you're built for speed
> Now when you put that all together
> It makes me everything a good man need.

The loss of that sense of vitality makes the persona in "Sweet Sixteen" a tragic figure. Clifton expresses this life force again and again, and it provides a continuing frame for and necessary counterpoint to the often fatal despair which also stalks the inner city.

The power of first person experiences is balanced by distancing techniques—shifts in diction, voice, and focus which parallel the ways in which distance is achieved in the blues. After a series of first person poems whose diction hovers marvelously between the standard and the black dialects (and thus embodies both), Clifton will place a poem written from a third person perspective in precise standard diction. The shift in viewpoint immediately makes the subject of the poem its object

> Robert
> was born obedient
> without questions
>
> did a dance called
> picking grapes
> sticking his butt out
> for pennies
>
> married a master
> who whipped his mind
> until he died

until he died
the color of his life
was nigger

"Robert" as both poem and person is such an object and comes after a series of poems in which a female persona talks about members of her immediate and extended family who have lost the battle for psychic survival in the society. The focus within this series of four poems (which begins with "My mamma moved among the days") shifts from the destruction of these others to the survival of the persona, and the series ends with the lines, "I stand up / through your destruction / I stand up." The reference is not only to the destruction of Miss Rosie, who is the subject of this poem, but to the persona's mother, father, and sister who have each appeared in previous poems. Clifton implies that the only thing which makes the destruction of these others somewhat bearable is the persona's ability to stand up, to affirm herself because these others have died that she might live. Robert is an immediate contrast to the lives sketched in these mini-portraits for he begins his existence in defeat and "until he died / the color of his life / was nigger." This poem further enlarges the context in which each poem in the series exists and its impersonal, objective stance returns, at a more abstract level, to the general/collective tone of "in the inner city," the poem which serves as introduction to this sequence and to the volume as a whole. The shift from first to third person perspective provides both an inner and outer view of the inner city and creates an atmosphere which encourages one to enter into and understand the experiences presented in the poems at both an emotional and analytic level. Sequences of poems are used to develop themes beyond the limits of a single poem; and individual poems come, in fact, to function in much the same way that individual classic blues stanzas function within the classic song. The individual expression is always seen within the context of the collective experience.

Lucille Clifton and other poets who work or even attempt to work in a similar mode extend the verbal traditions of the blues in the same way that the Swing of Count Basie and the bebop of Charlie Parker extend the instrumental traditions of the blues, making those traditions "classic" in a recognizably Western sense while remaining true to the black experiences and black perceptions which are their most important sources. But unlike the oral lyrics which, of necessity, preserve their group traditions only in their forms or structures and need a separate history to preserve a concrete sense of the collective life styles, values, and experiences which they represent, poetry, as a written form, carried with it the possibility of functioning simultaneously on both levels. Thus while B. B. King in "Sweet Sixteen" can allude to, even symbolize, collective experiences or internalize the necessary and sustaining relationship between group and individual in the statement/response pattern and structures, Clifton, in her poetry incorporates elements of the older oral traditions, re-asserts the collective at concrete levels even as she deals, through subjective testimony, with individual experiences. And this is the beginning of a new tradition built on a synthesis of black oral traditions and Western literate forms.

Suggested Readings with Similar Theme:

Bell, Bernard W. *The Folk Roots of Contemporary Afro-American Poetry.* Detroit: Broadside Press, 1974.

Benston, Kimberly W. "Late Coltrane: A Re-numbering of Orpheus." *Massachusetts Review* 18 (Winter 1977): 770–81.

Christian, Barbara T. "There It Is: The Poetry of Jayne Cortez." *Callaloo* 9, no. 1 (Winter 1986): 235–39.

Henderson, Stephen. "Worrying the Line: Notes on Black American Poetry." In *The Line in Postmodern Poetry*, edited by Robert Frank and Henry Sayre, 60–62. Urbana: University of Illinois Press, 1988.

HOUSTON A. BAKER JR.

From "Toward a Critical Prospect for the Future" in *The Journey Back: Issues in Black Literature and Criticism* (1980)

Baker urges critics to begin analysis of African American literature by recognizing "the semantic levels of black culture." Explain what is meant by "the semanticity of the word," "the communicative context," and "the lexical and conceptual fields." Why is the scrutiny of language in an African American text important to its meaning? Why are critics encouraged to "hypothesize at the outset of any analysis of black creativity . . . {about} structure . . . beyond the surface of the individual words"? How does Baker echo Neal and Henderson? How does Baker enter discussions of theory with Williams, Smitherman, Snead, and Gates?

. . . If blacks "entered" the English language with values and concepts antithetical to those of the white externality surrounding them, then their vocabulary is less important than the underlying codes, or semantic fields, that governed meaning. What I am suggesting is the possibility that whites—moving exclusively within the boundaries of their own semantic categories—have taken the words of the black work or verbal art at face value, or worse, at a value assigned by their own limiting attitudes and patterns of judgment.

Two brief examples serve to clarify. The first is offered by Charles Chesnutt's *The Conjure Woman*. Published as a volume in 1899, the work seemed guaranteed of success by the white critical acclaim that had earlier greeted one of its stories. "The Goophered Grapevine" had been praised by white readers when it appeared in an 1896 issue of the *Atlantic*. Few readers were aware of Chesnutt's race, and in the heyday of the Plantation School, who could expect a black spokesman to go against the weave of what Oscar Handlin calls the "Linnaean Web." Chesnutt's short story seemed simply another effort in a long line of works dedicated to a portrait of blacks as amiable, childlike creatures devoted to strumming and humming all day on the old plantation. Howells and other white critics lauded the story on this assumption.

There is no absence of linguistic clues to a quite different set of expectations where the collection of stories is concerned, however. In fact, the title of Chesnutt's book reveals his deeper intentions and signals the authentic array

of conditions that govern an appropriate reading of the text. The protagonist—the moving force behind the action of each of *The Conjure Woman*'s stories—is the black conjurer, and as the black historian John Blassingame
writes:

> In addition to these activities [religious and recreational], several other customs
> prevented the slaves from identifying with the ideals of their masters. Because
> of their superstitions and beliefs in fortune tellers, witches, magic and conjur-
> ers, many of the slaves constructed a psychological defense against total depen-
> dence on and submission to their masters. Whatever his power, the master was
> a puny man compared to the supernatural. Often the most powerful and sig-
> nificant individual on the plantation was the conjurer.

Blassingame goes on to point out that by shrewdness and an industrious
countermanding of the slave system the conjurer gained control over blacks
and whites alike.

Such a conclusion, of course, cannot be inferred from the collection's
title alone. It does indicate, however, that white critics unaware of the meaning that the conjurer held for black Americans were ill-prepared to evaluate
Chesnutt's stories. The referents for such critics would have resided totally
outside the lexical and conceptual fields that assured autonomy and a unique
sense of the black self for Chesnutt and for his selected black readers. . . .

If, however, my invocation of Chesnutt seems an example of "justification by
the little-known text," one can turn to a more celebrated work—Richard
Wright's *Native Son*. Having already set forth an analysis of the black folk
concepts and strategies that I feel give semantic force to the novel, I wish to
look for a moment at James Emanuel's analysis of linguistic metaphors in
Wright's text. Insisting that *Native Son* is rooted in a sui generis experience,
Emanuel points out a host of recurrent language structures that mark Bigger
Thomas's fictive development. Images of crucifixion, confinement, claustro-
phobia, heat, and light all speak of the black protagonist's imprisonment by a
white world oblivious to his humanity. The novel's rhetorical structures carry
one, finally, to the folk level of black American culture, to the "forms of
things unknown." Taking the words *furnace, flight, snow, curtain,* and so on at
their face value, however, many white critics have failed to add to our understanding of Wright's creativity.

Thus far in analyzing black American literature and culture I have
talked only of the semanticity of the word. However, while this consideration
is primary, it is but a part of a larger perspective that emphasizes what Professor Elizabeth Traugott designates as "the attitudes fostered by linguistics" in
literary critical investigations. Traugott uses the phrase to specify the governing assumption on the part of literary analysis that the methods and models
of linguistics and the linguistic investigation of texts can yield significant

results when applied to a culture and its verbal art. I have attempted to demonstrate in previous chapters the kinds of concerns that are raised by an attention to the language of black America and its literary works of art. What is ultimately involved, however, is the entire history—the full discourse—that constitutes black American culture.

A final example serves to clarify. A rigorous analysis of the language in chapter eleven of Ellison's *Invisible Man*—the factory hospital episode—reveals a fundamental opposition between two ways of life, two conceptions of human nature. Man at play *(Homo ludens)* stands at one pole, while man at work *(Homo laborans)* stands at the other. The entire chapter (and, indeed, the whole of *Invisible Man*) can be analyzed in terms of this binary relationship.

The chapter begins when a nurse asks the protagonist: "What is your name?" There is a pause, and then the opening triad from Beethoven's Fifth Symphony sounds in the mind of the protagonist. We have a naming ceremony introduced by the opening notes of the most well known, romantic work in the symphonic repertoire. Beethoven shades immediately into the awesome hum of a machine. Rather than counterpart, there is transition: man's epic, romantic spirit is transformed into mechanical energy. For the protagonist, who is bound among the nodes of the machine, the results of this transformation are painful. But when he loses consciousness, Beethoven's and the machine's force fades into an agrarian reverie that is characterized by a "Sunday air" entitled "The Holy City." The song is played by a band which, as the text unfolds, appears increasingly regimented and is finally engulfed by a swarm of white gnats: "the dark trumpeter breathed them in and expelled them through the bell of his golden horn, a live white cloud mixing with tones upon the torpid air." Returning to consciousness, the narrator poses mental questions to his captors:

> Oh, doctor, I thought drowsily, did you ever wade in a brook before breakfast? Ever chew on sugar cane? You know, doc, the same fall day I first saw the hounds chasing black men in stripes and chains my grandmother sat with me and sang with twinkling eyes:
>
> > "Godamighty made a monkey
> > Godamighty made a whale
> > And Godamighty made a 'gator
> > With hickeys all over his tail . . ."

With this brief summary of the episode completed, let me return to the binary relationship postulated above. *Homo laborans*, technological man, seeks the power to organize and control the collective labor needed for industry. Like the rulers of the early irrigation civilizations, he perceives man not as an end in himself, but as a means to an end, a unit of production. The spiritual is subservient to the mechanical for *Homo laborans*—the emotional gives way to

technological rationalism. In chapter eleven, the characters who array themselves around *Homo laborans* are the nurses and doctors, ole Friendly Face
(appearing in the somber garb of a Puritan divine), the scholar, and, preemi-
nently, the Director. The factory is an icon of man as tool-user, as technocrat
or maker.

Man at play, by contrast, is man as a symbolic animal, a "speaking subject." If the ambit of technological man is control and power, the orbit of man
at play is freedom. The most striking representation of *Homo ludens'* opposition to enslaving labor is offered by the black convicts fleeing from the chain
gang. The event is represented as occurring on the same day that the narrator's grandmother sang a folksong whose cosmology—like that of the song
played by the band—begins not with man on earth, but with God in heaven.
The opposition between the secular and the spiritual is profound. *Homo ludens*
is, ultimately, incapable of communicating with those governed by a limiting
conception of man as laborer: "A terrible sense of loneliness came over me;
they seemed to enact a mysterious pantomime. . . . Other faces came up,
their mouths working with *soundless* fury. But we are all human, I thought,
wondering what I meant" (italics mine). What the "I" means, it seems to me,
is that the very nature of the concept "human" is in the process of definition.
Finally, *Homo ludens* is what anthropologists call a "liminal" character, a marginal figure like the shaman, or the active tradition bearers in cultural rites of
reversal. He is representative of what Ellison calls "The mysterious, underground aspect of human personality." The world is upside down—the women
are dressed as men, those at the bottom have assumed control, the royal
household is subject to parody, and the outrageous trickster has won the victory. The narrator reports on his own discovery, "I laughed, deep, deep inside
me, giddy with the delight of self-discovery and the desire to hide it. Somehow I was Buckeye the Rabbit."

The factory hospital designed to make a "new man" of the narrator gives
birth to the playful, ironic, dozens-quipping trickster whose name is "freedom," whose name is "human." There is an air of slow revelation about the
entire chapter, and the words *hidden* and *mystery* recur. *Homo ludens* is hidden
at the margins and is yet to be discovered by the technological "detectives."
The expectation of those who control the society's machinery is characterized
by their refusal to explore the margins. And it is in this region that *Homo
ludens* plays and has his being.

My hypothesis—for this example is obviously abbreviated—is that the
opposition that gives meaning to the factory hospital episode can be viewed
as fundamental for the textual structure of *Invisible Man* as a whole. There is a
suggestion of this in the narrator's questions to the Director. He asks if the
Director knows Messrs. Norton, Emerson, and Bledsoe—all characters
grouped around *Homo laborans*. He further emphasizes his ludic, self-governing
nature when he refuses to accept the bridge as a means of progress at the

end of the chapter. Instead, he plunges into the earth. He takes the subway, the hidden underground. And there he finds, seated across the aisle, a "young platinum blonde" nibbling a delicious apple. The woman who is traditionally invested in America with white, technological, man's morality—the new Eve—is below, awaiting the ironically black and liminal Adam.

Although I suggest that the whole of *Invisible Man* can be understood in terms of the patterning of the factory hospital episode, I do not want to claim there is a single, irreducible formula that "explains" the novel. Surely, there are other oppositions as important as the one discussed here. But since *Invisible Man*'s various chapters take up the same motifs time and again, it seems useful to seek out the generative relationships that give coherence to these motifs. The Battle Royal chapter, the Trueblood encounter, the Liberty Paints episode with Lucius Brockway and the boilers, and the whole of The Brotherhood section can be fruitfully analyzed in terms of the binary relationship that governs the factory hospital chapter. Only a close scrutiny of Ellison's language—almost a reading of the chapter's words as though they were opaque signs of a poetic discourse—enables one to hazard this conclusion.

What one is forced to hypothesize at the outset of an analysis of black creativity is *structure*. One must assume that beyond the surface of the individual words in Ellison's chapter there are complex ordering principles that make possible relationships like the one discussed here. I think one can discover such principles and their dependent structural relations only through an analysis of linguistic textual regularities that are deemed significant within a particular cultural context. The words selected for Ellison's chapter and their various combinations are grounded in a specific cultural history that has seen blacks continuously exploited as laborers and excluded from the ownership or direction of American means (whether land or technology) of production. Given Ellison's monumental brilliance, these basic conditions of the black situation are, not surprisingly, represented in *Invisible Man*.

The search for structural relationships in any literal text, I think, entails a knowledge of the full cultural discourse that provides a context. Man at work and man at play as they appear in *Invisible Man* could hardly constitute a salient opposition in a culture that had never come into contact with an extensive modern technology. Furthermore, if the trickster is not a seminal hero in a culture, one would scarcely expect this folk figure to play the key role assigned to "Buckeye the Rabbit" in the factory hospital episode. Finally, the literary investigator's attention is arrested by words such as *grandmother, folksong,* and *human* only if he or she is aware of black American concerns like the role of the matriarch in black and African cultures, the importance of music as an agency of instruction (and subversion) in black culture, and the omnipresent concern with ontology that has marked black intellectual history.

No analyst can understand the black literary text who is not conscious of the semantic levels of black culture. The journey to this level is by way of the whole discourse comprising black American culture. . . .

Suggested Reading with Similar Theme:

Jones, LeRoi (Amiri Baraka). "expressive language." In *Home: Social Essays,* 166–72. New York: William Morrow, 1966.

From "Rootedness:
The Ancestor as Foundation" (1984)

What is the function of the African American novel? How important is the audience (living and dead) to Morrison? When Morrison writes, "I don't regard Black litera-ture as simply books written by Black people, or simply as literature written about Black people, or simply as literature that uses a certain mode of language in which you just sort of drop g's," how is she echoing Baldwin and Petry and anticipating contempo-rary writers as introduced by Terry McMillian elsewhere in this collection? When Morrison writes that "Song of Solomon" "is indicative of the cosmology, the way in which Black people looked at the world," how is she echoing Henderson, Williams, Baker and others? Morrison enters a conversation with Barbara Smith on a "specific Black feminist model of critical inquiry." Does Morrison agree or disagree with Smith? In specific ways, how does Morrison enter philosophical discussions with James Bald-win and Ann Petry about the creative process and the function of literature? Morrison addresses the Imagination in the creative process. Does her viewpoint differ from those creative writers, starting with Wheatley, who went before her?

The label "novel" is useful in technical terms because I write prose that is longer than a short story. My sense of the novel is that it has always func-tioned for the class or the group that wrote it. The history of the novel as a form began when there was a new class, a middle class, to read it; it was an art form that they needed. The lower classes didn't need novels at that time because they had an art form already: they had songs, and dances, and cere-mony, and gossip, and celebrations. The aristocracy didn't need it because they had the art that they had patronized, they had their own pictures painted, their own houses built, and they made sure their art separated them from the rest of the world. But when the industrial revolution began, there emerged a new class of people who were neither peasants nor aristocrats. In large measure they had no art form to tell them how to behave in this new situation. So they produced an art form: we call it the novel of manners, an art form designed to tell people something they didn't know. That is, how to behave in this new world, how to distinguish between the good guys and the bad guys. How to get married. What a good living was. What would happen if you strayed from the fold. So that early works such as *Pamela*, by Samuel

Richardson, and the Jane Austen material provided social rules and explained behavior, identified outlaws, identified the people, habits, and customs that one should approve of. They were didactic in that sense. That, I think, is probably why the novel was not missed among the so-called peasant cultures. They didn't need it, because they were clear about what their responsibilities were and who and where was evil, and where was good.

But when the peasant class, or lower class, or what have you, confronts the middle class, the city, or the upper classes, they are thrown a little bit into disarray. For a long time, the art form that was healing for Black people was music. That music is no longer exclusively ours; we don't have exclusive rights to it. Other people sing it and play it; it is the mode of contemporary music everywhere. So another form has to take that place, and it seems to me that the novel is needed by African-Americans now in a way that it was not needed before—and it is following along the lines of the function of novels everywhere. We don't live in places where we can hear those stories anymore; parents don't sit around and tell their children those classical, mythological archetypal stories that we heard years ago. But new information has got to get out, and there are several ways to do it. One is the novel. I regard it as a way to accomplish certain very strong functions—one being the one I just described.

It should be beautiful, and powerful, but it should also work. It should have something in it that enlightens; something in it that opens the door and points the way. Something in it that suggests what the conflicts are, what the problems are. But it need not solve those problems because it is not a case study, it is not a recipe. There are things that I try to incorporate into my fiction that are directly and deliberately related to what I regard as the major characteristics of Black art, wherever it is. One of which is the ability to be both print and oral literature: to combine those two aspects so that the stories can be read in silence, of course, but one should be able to hear them as well. It should try deliberately to make you stand up and make you feel something profoundly in the same way that a Black preacher requires his congregation to speak, to join him in the sermon, to behave in a certain way, to stand up and to weep and to cry and to accede or to change and to modify—to expand on the sermon that is being delivered. In the same way that a musician's music is enhanced when there is a response from the audience. Now in a book, which closes, after all—it's of some importance to me to try to make that connection—to try to make that happen also. And, having at my disposal only the letters of the alphabet and some punctuation, I have to provide the places and spaces so that the reader can participate. Because it is the affective and participatory relationship between the artist or the speaker and the audience that is of primary importance, as it is in these other art forms that I have described.

To make the story appear oral, meandering, effortless, spoken—to have the reader feel the narrator without identifying that narrator, or hearing him or her knock about, and to have the reader work with the author in the construction of the book—is what's important. What is left out is as important as what is there. To describe sexual scenes in such a way that they are not clinical, not even explicit—so that the reader brings his own sexuality to the scene and thereby participates in it in a very personal way. And owns it. To construct the dialogue so that it is heard. So that there are no adverbs attached to them: "loudly," "softly," "he said menacingly." The menace should be in the sentence. To use, even formally, a chorus. The real presence of a chorus. Meaning the community or the reader at large, commenting on the action as it goes ahead.

In the books that I have written, the chorus has changed but there has always been a choral note, whether it is the "I" narrator of *Bluest Eye,* or the town functioning as a character in *Sula,* or the neighborhood and the community that responds in the two parts of town in *Solomon.* Or, as extreme as I've gotten, all of nature thinking and feeling and watching and responding to the action going on in *Tar Baby,* so that they are in the story: the trees hurt, fish are afraid, clouds report, and the bees are alarmed. Those are the ways in which I try to incorporate, into that traditional genre the novel, unorthodox novelistic characteristics—so that it is, in my view, Black, because it uses the characteristics of Black art. I am not suggesting that some of these devices have not been used before and elsewhere—only the reason why I do. I employ them as well as I can. And those are just some; I wish there were ways in which such things could be talked about in the criticism. My general disappointment in some of the criticism that my work has received has nothing to do with approval. It has something to do with the vocabulary used in order to describe these things. I don't like to find my books condemned as bad or praised as good, when that condemnation or that praise is based on criteria from other paradigms. I would much prefer that they were dismissed or embraced based on the success of their accomplishment within the culture out of which I write.

I don't regard Black literature as simply books written by Black people, or simply as literature written about Black people, or simply as literature that uses a certain mode of language in which you just sort of drop g's. There is something very special and very identifiable about it and it is my struggle to find that elusive but identifiable style in the books. My joy is when I think that I have approached it; my misery is when I think I can't get there. . . .

I have talked about function in that other question, and I touched a little bit on some of the other characteristics [or distinctive elements of African-American writing], one of which was oral quality, and the participation of the reader and the chorus. The only thing that I would add for this question is the presence of an ancestor; it seems to me interesting to evaluate Black literature on what the writer does with the presence of an ancestor. Which is to say a grandfather as in Ralph Ellison, or a grandmother as in Toni Cade Bambara, or a healer as in Bambara or Henry Dumas. There is always an elder there. And these ancestors are not just parents, they are sort of timeless people whose relationships to the characters are benevolent, instructive, and protective, and they provide a certain kind of wisdom.

How the Black writer responds to that presence interests me. Some of them, such as Richard Wright, had great difficulty with that ancestor. Some of them, like James Baldwin, were confounded and disturbed by the presence or absence of an ancestor. What struck me in looking at some contemporary fiction was that whether the novel took place in the city or in the country, the presence or absence of that figure determined the success or the happiness of the character. It was the absence of an ancestor that was frightening, that was threatening, and it caused huge destruction and disarray in the work itself. That the solace comes, not from the contemplation of serene nature as in a lot of mainstream white literature, nor from the regard in which the city was held as a kind of corrupt place to be. Whether the character was in Harlem or Arkansas, the point was there, this timelessness was there, this person who represented this ancestor. And it seemed to be one of those interesting aspects of the continuum in Black or African-American art, as well as some of the things I mentioned before: the deliberate effort, on the part of the artist, to get a visceral, emotional response as well as an intellectual response as he or she communicates with the audience.

The treatment of artists by the people for whom they speak is also of some interest. That is to say, when the writer is one of them, when the voice is not the separate, isolated ivory tower voice of a very different kind of person but an implied "we" in a narration. This is disturbing to people and critics who view the artist as the supreme individual. It is disturbing because there is a notion that that's what the artist is—always in confrontation with his own society, and you can see the differences in the way in which literature is interpreted. Whether or not Sula is nourished by that village depends on your view of it. I know people who believe that she was destroyed by it. My own special view is that there was no other place where she could live. She would have been destroyed by any other place; she was permitted to "be" only in that context, and no one stoned her or killed her or threw her out. Also it's difficult to see who the winners are if you are not looking at it from that point of view. When the hero returns to the fold—returns to the tribe—it is seen by certain white critics as a defeat, by others as a triumph, and that is a difference in what the aims of the art are.

In *Song of Solomon* Pilate is the ancestor. The difficulty that Hager [youngest of the trio of women in that household] has is how far removed she is from the experience of her ancestor. Pilate had a dozen years of close, nurturing relationships with two males—her father and her brother. And that intimacy and support was in her and made her fierce and loving because she had that experience. Her daughter Reba had less of that and related to men in a very shallow way. Her daughter had even less of an association with men as a child, so that the progression is really a diminishing of their abilities because of the absence of men in a nourishing way in their lives. Pilate is the apogee of all that: of the best of that which is female and the best of that which is male, and that balance is disturbed if it is not nurtured, and if it is not counted on and if it is not reproduced. That is the disability we must be on guard against for the future—the female who reproduces the female who reproduces the female. You know there are a lot of people who talk about the position that men hold as of primary importance, but actually it is if we don't keep in touch with the ancestor that we are, in fact, lost.

The point of the books is that it is our job. When you kill the ancestor you kill yourself. I want to point out the dangers, to show that nice things don't always happen to the totally self-reliant if there is no conscious historical connection. To say, see—this is what will happen.

I don't have much to say about that [the necessity to develop a specific Black feminist model of critical inquiry] except that I think there is more danger in it than fruit, because any model of criticism or evaluation that excludes males from it is as hampered as any model of criticism of Black literature that excludes women from it. For critics, models have some function. They like to talk in terms of models and developments and so on, so maybe it's of some use to them, but I suggest that even for them there is some danger in it.

If anything I do, in the way of writing novels (or whatever I write) isn't about the village or the community or about you, then it is not about anything. I am not interested in indulging myself in some private, closed exercise of my imagination that fulfills only the obligation of my personal dreams— which is to say yes, the work must be political. It must have that as its thrust. That's a pejorative term in critical circles now: if a work of art has any political influence in it, somehow it's tainted. My feeling is just the opposite: if it has none, it is tainted.

The problem comes when you find harangue passing off as art. It seems to me that the best art is political and you ought to be able to make it unquestionably political and irrevocably beautiful at the same time.

Suggested Readings with Similar Theme:

Angelou, Maya. "Shades and Slashes of Light." In *Black Women Writers (1950–1980): A Critical Evaluation,* edited by Mari Evans. Garden City, N.Y.: Anchor/Doubleday, 1984.
Morrison, Toni. *Conversations with Toni Morrison.* Edited by Danielle Taylor Guthrie. Jackson: University Press of Mississippi, 1994.

TONI CADE BAMBARA

Salvation Is the Issue (1984)

What is the role of the African American writer? Bambara responds, "to produce stories that save our lives." How does Bambara define "salvation"? How does Bambara echo Alice Walker? According to Bambara, her creativity is dependent upon language, humor and performance. Referring to Geneva Smitherman, Gale Jackson, and others in this collection, what is the significance of "the power of the word," of performance, of laughter to the African American? When discussing the creative process, how does Bambara enter philosophical discussions with Morrison and Baldwin?

Stories are important. They keep us alive. In the ships, in the camps, in the quarters, fields, prisons, on the road, on the run, underground, under siege, in the throes, on the verge—the storyteller snatches us back from the edge to hear the next chapter. In which we are the subjects. We, the hero of the tales. Our lives preserved. How it was; how it be. Passing it along in the relay. That is what I work to do: to produce stories that save our lives. . . .

Of all the writing forms, I've always been partial to the short story. It suits my temperament. It makes a modest appeal for attention, allowing me to slip up alongside the reader on her/his blind side and grab'm. But the major publishing industry, the academic establishment, reviewers, and critics favor the novel. And the independent press journals can rarely afford to print a ten-page piece. Murder for the genre-deep loyalist who readily admits in interviews that the move to the novel was not occasioned by a recognition of having reached the limits of the genre or the practitioner's disillusion with it, but rather Career. Economics. Critical attention. A major motive behind the production of [*The Salt Eaters*]. . . .

What I enjoy most in my work is the laughter and the outrage and the attention to language. I come from a family of very gifted laughers. I was raised by family and community to be a combatant. Forays to the Apollo with my daddy and hanging tough on Speakers Corner with my mama taught me the power of the word, the importance of the resistance tradition, and the high standards our community has regarding verbal performance. While my heart is a laughing gland and my favorite thing to be doing is laughing so hard I have to lower myself on the wall to keep from falling down, near that chamber is a blast furnace where a rifle pokes from the ribs. The combination makes for a desperado kind of writing some times. Desperado in the Webster sense of outlaw. In the Roget sense of gambler. In the Unamune sense of deep despair joked or high hopes.

I despair at our failure to wrest power from those who have it and abuse it, our reluctance to reclaim our old powers lying dormant with neglect, our hesitancy to create new power in areas where it never before existed and I'm euphoric because everything in our history, our spirit, our daily genius—suggests we do it. . . .

Laughter has its limits, its risks. It can be a screen, a blinder, a way to avoid putting a bold eye on an uncomfortable reality. Just as outrage at oppression can be a dodge, a way of avoiding calling a spade a spade and speaking directly to the issue of personal/collective responsibility and will, or speaking frankly about the fact that we participate wickedly in our ambush every day of our lives. In editing, then, I try to stay mercilessly alert lest I run for cover in a good punch line or hide out in a bogus race pride. Editing with the eye trained on other tasks I assign myself of late—in addition to community exploration, documentation, celebration, critique—too keeps me wary of the laughter-rage syndrome. Laughter frequently glazes over the seams of the casing and cliche rage all but seals the very casing I would split and rip off to get at the inner works, so that underlying design that throws open the path to the new age, the new order in which I envision myself blowing a chorus or two in the language of the birth canal and maybe even of the caul.

What informs my work as I read it—and this is answer to the frequently raised question about how come my "children" stories manage to escape being insufferably coy, charming, and sentimental—are the basic givens from which I proceed. One, we are at war. Two, the natural response to oppression, ignorance, evil, and mystification is wide-awake resistance. Three, the natural response to stress and crisis is not breakdown and capitulation, but transformation and renewal too. The question I raise from "Gorilla" to "Sea Birds" to *Salt* to "Faith of the Bather" is, is it natural (sane, healthy, whole-some, in our interest) to violate the contracts/covenants we have with our ancestors, each other, our children, ourselves, and God?

In *Salt* most particularly, in motive/content/structure design, the question is, do we intend to have a future as sane, whole, governing people? I argue then and in "Faith" as well that immunity to the serpent's sting can be found in our tradition of struggle and our faculty for synthesis. The issue is salvation. I work to produce stories that save our lives.

Suggested Reading with Similar Theme:

Brooks, Gwendolyn. "The Field of the Fever, The Time of the Tall-Walkers." *Report from Part One: An Autobiography.* Chicago: Third World Press, 1972. Reprint, *Black Women Writers (1950–1980): A Critical Evaluation,* edited by Mari Evans. Garden City, N.Y.: Anchor/Doubleday, 1984.

JAMES A. SNEAD

Repetition as a figure of black culture (1984)

Examine Snead's "classification and taxonomy of the dominant tendencies" of Black and European cultures, particularly repetition. Which culture projects a linear model? A cyclical model? What are the strengths of the cyclical model? According to Snead, which major African American writers exemplify in their works some organizing principles of repetition? How does Snead anticipate Bhabha's discussion of "difference"? Define the following terms: repetition, linear, circular, improvisation, polymetry, the cut, call and response, negritude, and difference.

THE SCOPE OF REPETITION IN CULTURE

The world, as force, may not be thought of as unlimited, for it cannot be so thought of; we forbid ourselves the concept of an infinite force as incompatible with the concept "force." Thus—the world also lacks the capacity for eternal novelty.

(Nietzsche, The Will to Power)

After all, people have by now had to make peace with the idea that the world is not inexhaustible in its combinations, nor life in its various guises. How we have come to terms with the discrepancy between our personal growth—the very model of linear development—and the physical plane upon which life unfolds, characterized by general recursiveness and repetition: this must be the concern of culture. "Coming-to-terms" may mean denial or acceptance, repression or highlighting, but in any case *transformation* is culture's response to its own apprehension of repetition.

Apart from revealing or secreting the repetitions of material existence, a third response is possible: to own that repetition has occurred, but that, given a "quality of difference" compared to what has gone before, it has become not a "repetition" but rather a "progression," if positive, or a "regression," if negative. This third response implies that one finds a scale of tendencies from culture to culture. In any case, let us remember that, whenever we encounter repetition in cultural forms, we are indeed not viewing "the same thing" but its transformation, not just a formal ploy but often the willed grafting onto culture of an essentially philosophical insight about the shape of time and his-

206

tory. But even if not in intentional emulation of natural or material cyclicality, repetition would need to manifest itself. Culture as a reservoir of inexhaustible novelty is unthinkable. Therefore, repetition, first of all, would inevitably have to creep into the dimension of culture just as into that of language and signification because of the finite supply of elementary units and the need for recognizability. One may readily classify cultural forms according to whether they tend to admit or cover up the repeating constituents within them.

The important thing about culture is that it should not be dead. Or, if dead, then its transformations must continue to live on in the present. Culture must be both immanent and historical: something *there* and something to be studied in its present form and in its etiology. Our modern notion of "culture" only arises early in this century, after a 500-year period of English usage as a noun of process rather than identification, referring rather to the tending of animals or crops than to types of music, literature, art and temperament by which a group of people is aware of and defines itself for others and for itself. But this initial connotation may still be preserved. "Culture" in its present usage always also means the *culture* of culture: a certain continuance in the nurture of those concepts and experiences that have helped or are helping to lend self-consciousness and awareness to a given group. Culture must not only be immanent now but also give the promise of being *continuously* so. So the second way in which repetition enters the dimension of culture is in the necessity for every culture to maintain a sense of continuity about itself: internal changes notwithstanding, a basic self-identity must not be altered. Strangely enough, however, what recent Western or European culture repeats continuously is precisely the belief that there is no repetition in culture but only a difference, defined as progress and growth.

It was Swift who said that "happiness . . . is a perpetual Possession of being well deceived." We are not far here from a proper definition of culture. At least a type of "happiness" accrues through a perpetual repetition of apparent consensus and convention that provide a sense of security, identification and "rightness." Yet, however fervently culture nurtures this belief, such a sense of security is also a kind of "coverage," both in the comforting sense of "insurance" against accidental and sudden rupturing of a complicated and precious fabric, and in Swift's less favorable sense of a "cover-up," or a hiding of otherwise unpleasant facts from the senses. Like all insurance, this type of *coverage* does not prevent accidents but promises to be able to provide the means to outlive them. Furthermore, this insurance takes full actuarial account of the *most* and *least* likely points of intrusion or corruption to the self-image of the culture, and covers them accordingly.

For example, most cultures seem quite willing to tolerate and often assimilate certain foreign *games*—such as chess, imported to Europe from the Middle East as early as the First or Second Crusade in the twelfth century, or lawn tennis, developed and patented in England in 1874 from an earlier form of tennis. The fate of foreign *words* in language, however, has been frequently less happy, as witnessed in the *coverage* that European national languages institute against diluting "invasions of foreign words," exemplified in England by the sixteenth-century "Cambridge School" (Ascham, Cheke and Wilson), in seventeenth-century France by the purism of Boileau and the Academie Francaise (a linguistic xenophobia which has by no means yet run its course) and by the recurrent attempts to expel foreignisms from the German language beginning with Leibnitz in the seventeenth and Herder in the eighteenth century (most recently seen in the less innocuous censorships of the National Socialists in the current century).

Finally, as in all insurance, you pay a regular premium for *coverage:* culture has a price. Might Swift's phrase "Flaws and Imperfections of Nature" not also include the daunting knowledge that the apparently linear upward-striving course of human endeavor exists within nature's ineluctable circularity, and that birth and life end up in death and decay?

Cultures, then, are virtually all varieties of "long-term" *coverage,* against both external and internal threats—self-dissolution, loss of identity; or repression, assimilation, attachment (in the sense of legal "seizure"); or attack from neighboring or foreign cultures—with all the positive and negative connotations of the "cover-ups" thus produced. In this, black culture is no exception. Cultures differ among one another primarily in the tenacity with which the "cover-up" is maintained and the spacing and regularity of the intervals at which they cease to cover up, granting leeway to those ruptures in the illusion of growth which most often occur in the *deja-vus* of exact repetition.

In certain cases, culture, in projecting an image *for others,* claims a radical difference *from others,* often further defined qualitatively as *superiority.* Already in this insistence on uniqueness and "higher" development we sense a linear, anthropomorphic drive. For centuries (and especially within the last three) Europe has found itself in hot contest internally over this very issue. Culture has been territorialized—and, with it, groups of its diverse adherents. Cultural wars have become territorial wars have become cultural wars again, and indeed into this maelstrom have been sucked concepts of "race," "virtue" and "nation," never to re-emerge. What startles is not so much the content of these cross-cultural feuds as the vehemence and aggression with which groups of people wrangle over where one *coverage* ends and another begins. The incipient desire to define "race" and "culture" in the same breath as "identity" and "nationality" finally coincides with the great upheavals of the seventeenth and eighteenth centuries in Europe—among them, the overturning of the feudal monarchies of central Europe and the discovery and subjugation of black and brown masses across the seas. The word "culture" now gains two fateful senses: "that with which one whole group aggressively defines its superiority *vis-a-vis* another"; and a finer one, "that held at a level above the group or mass, for the benefit of the culture as a whole, by the conscious few (i.e., the distinction between *haute* and *basse culture*)." At the same time as Europeans were defining themselves over against other European nations and even some of them against members of their own nations, they were also busy defining "European culture" as separate from "African culture," the ultimate otherness, the final *mass*. Only having now reached this stage can we make any sense whatever of the notion of "black culture" and what it might oppose.

"Black culture" is a concept first created by Europeans and defined in opposition to "European culture." Hegel, for example, saw "black culture" as the lowest stage of that laudable self-reflection and development shown by European culture, whose natural outcome must be the state or nationhood. In his by no means untypical nineteenth-century view, Hegel said that black culture simply *did not exist* in the same sense as European culture did. Black culture (as one of several non-Western cultures) had no self-expression (i.e. no writing); there was no black *Volksgeist,* as in Europe, and not even particular tribes or groupings of Africans seemed in the least concerned to define themselves on the basis of any particular *Volksgeist.* Hegel (like most of Europe) was confused by the African: where did blacks fit into "the course of *world history?*":

> In this main portion of Africa there can really be no history. There is a succession of *accidents and surprises.*
>
> There is *no goal,* no state there that one can follow, no subjectivity, but only a series of subjects who destroy each other. There has as yet been little comment upon *how strange a form of self-consciousness this represents.*

These remarks give a rather fascinating definition of European culture (at least as Hegel introduces his countrymen in his "we") by inversion:

> We must forget all categories that lay at the bottom of our spiritual life and its subsumption under these forms; the difficulty [in such forgetting when examining Africa] lies in the fact that we repeatedly must bring along that which we have already imagined.

Because Hegel gives the first and still most penetratingly systematic definition by a European of the "African character" (and, consequently, of black culture), albeit in a severely negative tone, it is worth quoting him at length:

> In general it must be said that [African] consciousness has not yet reached the contemplation of a fixed objective, an objectivity. The fixed objectivity is called God, the Eternal, Justice, Nature, natural things. . . . The Africans, however, have not yet reached this *recognition of the General.* . . . What we name Religion, the State, that which exists *in and for itself*—in other words, all that is *valid*—all that is not yet at hand. . . . Thus we find nothing other than man in his immediacy: that is man in Africa. As soon as Man as Man appears, he stands in opposition to Nature; only in this way does he become Man. . . . The Negro represents the Natural Man in all his *wildness and indocility:* if we wish to grasp him, then we must drop all European conceptions.

What we actually understand by "Africa" is that which is without history and resolution, which is still fully caught up in the natural spirit, and which here must be mentioned as being on the threshold of world history.

Hegel's African has an absolute alterity to the European. This fact conveniently enables us to re-read Hegel's criticism as an insightful classification and taxonomy of the dominant tendencies of both cultures. The written text of Hegel is a century and a half old, but it truly still prevails, with regard to the tendencies, in the present-day forms to be discussed later, of the cultures that Hegel describes.

What are the main characteristics that Hegel finds to distinguish black culture from European culture? Interestingly, Hegel begins by implying that black culture is resilient because reticent, or by nature of its very backwardness untouchable: it is totally *other* and incomprehensible to the European, whereas other cultures, such as the native American, have combated the European and have lost:

the subjection of the land has meant its downfall. . . . as far as tribes of men are concerned, there are few of the descendants of the first Americans left, since close to seven million men have been wiped out . . . the entire [native] American world has gone under and been suppressed by the Europeans. . . . They are perishing, so that one sees that they do not have the strength to merge with the North Americans in the Free States. *Such peoples of weak culture lose themselves more and more in contact with people of higher culture and more intensive cultural training.*

Noteworthy here is the persistent connection of physical and territorial suppression, attachment and extermination with cultural inadequacy.

Hegel's definition of black culture is simply negative: ever-developing European culture is the prototype for the fulfillment of culture in the future; black culture is the antitype, ever on the threshold. Black culture, caught in "historylessness" *(Geschichtslosigkeit),* is none the less shielded from attack or assimilation precisely by its aboriginal intangibility (though particular blacks themselves may not be so protected). According to Hegel, the African, radical in his effect upon the European, is a "strange form of self-consciousness" unfixed in orientation towards transcendent goals and terrifyingly close to the cycles and rhythms of nature. The African, first, overturns all European categories of logic. Second, he has no idea of history or progress, but instead allows "accidents and surprises" to take hold of his fate. He is also not aware of being at a lower stage of development and perhaps even has no idea of what development is. Finally, he is "immediate" and intimately tied to nature with all its cyclical, non-progressive data. Having no self-consciousness, he is "immediate"—i.e. *always there*—in any given moment. Here we can see that, being there, the African is also *always already there,* or perhaps *always there before,* whereas the European is *headed* there or, better, *not yet there.*

Hegel was almost entirely correct in his reading of black culture, but what he could not have guessed was that in his very criticism of it he had almost perfectly described the "there" to which European culture was "headed." Like all models that insist on discrete otherness, Hegel's definition implicitly constituted elements of black culture that have only in this century become manifest. Only after Freud, Nietzsche, comparative and structural anthropology and the study of comparative religion could the frantic but ultimately futile coverings of repetition by European culture be seen as dispensable, albeit in limited instances of "uncovering." Moreover, the very aspects of black culture which had seemed to define its nonexistence for the phenomenologist Hegel may now be valued as positive terms, given a revised metaphysics of rupture and opening.

THE TYPES OF REPETITION: THEIR CULTURAL MANIFESTATIONS

They are after themselves. They call it destiny. Progress. We call it Haints.
Haints of their victims rising from the soil of Africa, South America, Asia . . .
(Ishmael Reed, *Mumbo Jumbo*)

Hegel as a prophet of historical development was notorious but not unique. We may accept that his assumptions have long been and still are shared, particularly the view that culture in history occurs only when a group arrives at a state of self-consciousness sufficient to propel it to "their destination of becoming a state":

formal culture on every level of intellectual development can and must emerge, prosper and arrive at a point of high flowering when it forms itself into a state and in this basic form of civilization proceeds to abstract universal reflection and necessarily to universal laws and forms.

The world "state" *(Staat)* is to be defined not as a strict political entity but as any coherent group whose culture progresses from the level of immediacy to self-awareness.

How, then, do European culture and black culture differ in their treatment of the inevitability of repetition, either in annual cycles or in artistic forms? The truly self-conscious culture resists all non-progressive views; it *develops*. Hegel admits the category of change, and even the fact of cyclical repetition in nature, but prefers not to look at it or, if at all, then not from a negative "oriental" but from a positive "occidental" standpoint. In such a view, Hegel states:

Whatever development *{Bildung}* takes place becomes material upon which the Spirit elevates itself to a new level of development, proclaiming its powers in all the directions of its plenitude.

Hence emerges the yet prevailing "third option" mentioned above as a response to repetition: the notion of progress within cycle, "differentiation" within repetition.

So the first category where European culture separates itself from "oriental" and "African" cultures is in its treatment of physical and natural cycles. This separation into "occidental" and "oriental" must seem amusing to anyone familiar with—among other Western texts—Book XI of Ovid's *Metamorphoses,* where the "pessimistic" and "oriental" viewpoint appears in the lips of an "occidental" predecessor of Hegel, Pythagoras:

> Nothing is constant in the whole world. Everything is in a state of flux, and comes into being as a transient appearance . . . don't you see the year passing through a succession of four seasons? . . . In the same way our own bodies are always ceaselessly changing. . . . Time, the devourer, and all the jealous years that pass, destroy all things, and, nibbling them away, consume them gradually in a lingering death. . . . Nor does anything retain its appearance permanently. Ever-inventive nature continually produces one shape from another. . . . Though this thing may pass into that, and that into this, yet the sum of things remains unchanged.

The truth is that cyclical views of history are not "oriental," but were widespread in Europe well before the inception of historicism, which began not with Hegel but long prior to the nineteenth century (and here one might mention as Hegel's precursors Bacon or Descartes in the Enlightenment, the progressive *consummatio* in the eschatology of Joachim of Floris, the Thomist orientation towards teleology, or even go back to the "final" triumph of the Heavenly City of St. Augustine of Hippo). The debate in Western culture over the question of the shape of history, for most of its course, has been pretty evenly waged, with the advantage perhaps initially even somewhat on the side of the cyclical view. Only with the coming of scientific progressivism (as predicted and formulated by Bacon in *The Advancement of Learning* in 1605) was the linear model also to attain pre-eminence, and then not for some 200 years. The now suppressed (but still to be found) recognition of cycles in European culture has always resembled the beliefs that underlie the religious conceptions of black culture, observing periodic regeneration of biological and agricultural systems.

Black culture highlights the observance of such repetition, often in homage to an original generative instance or act. Cosmogony, the origins and stability of things, hence prevails because it recurs, not because the world continues to develop from the archetypal moment. Periodic ceremonies are ways in which black culture comes to terms with its perception of repetition, precisely by highlighting that perception. Dance often accompanies those ritualistic occasions when a seasonal return is celebrated and the "rounds" of the dance (as of the "Ring Shout" or "Circle Dance") recapitulate the "roundings" of natural time: Christmas, New Year, funerals, harvest-time. Weddings especially are a reenactment of the initial act of coupling that created mankind and are therefore particularly well suited as recognitions of recurrence. Conscious cultural observance of natural repetition no longer characterizes European culture. The German wedding festival, for example, the *Hochzeit,* is today fully divested of its original ties to the repeating New Year's festival *Hochgezit,* and the sense of an individual marriage as a small-scale image of a larger renewal and repetition is now gone. Outside of the seasonal markings of farmers' almanacs, the sort of precise celebration of time's passage and return that we see in Spenser's *Shepheards Calendar* or in the cyclical mystery plays has been out of general favor in recent times (or simply consigned to the realm of the demonic as in the Mephistophelean "I've already buried heaps of them! / And always new blood, fresh blood, circulates again. / So it goes on . . .").

Yet the year does still go around: how does European culture deal with perceived cycles? Recurrent national and sacred holidays are still marked, but with every sense of a progression having taken place between them. The "New Year's Resolution" and its frequent unfulfillment precisely recalls the attempt and failure to impose a character of progression and improvement onto an often non-progressing temporal movement. Successive public Christmas celebrations and ornamental displays vie to show increase in size, splendor or brightness from previous ones (although, significantly, the realm of sacred ritual, while immediately coexisting with the commercial culture, still works to bar any inexact repetition of religious liturgy, such as in the Nativity service). Other contemporary cycles, such as the four-year intervals of the Olympic Games and presidential elections, fervently need to justify their obvious recurrence by some standard of material improvement or progress: a new or larger Olympic site or new Olympic records; a new or better political party or personality.

In European culture, financial and production cycles have largely supplanted the conscious sort of natural return in black culture. The financial year is the perfect example of this Hegelian subsumption of development within stasis. For repetition must be exact in all financial accounting, given that, globally, capital ultimately circulates within closed tautological systems (i.e. decrease in an asset is either an increase in another asset or a decrease in a liability, both within a corporate firm and in its relations with other firms). The "annual report" of a business concern, appearing cyclically in yearly or interim rhythm (always on the same "balance-sheet date"), contains ever the same kinds of symbols about the concern's health or decrepitude. It is only the properties of *difference* between year 2 and year 1 (as quantified by numerical changes in the symbols—say, in the cash-flow matrix) which determine how the essentially exact repetitions are to be evaluated and translated into a vocabulary of growth and development. Capital hence will not only necessarily *circulate* but must consequently also *accumulate or diminish,* depending on the state of the firm. Economics and business, in their term "cyclicality," admit the existence and even the necessity of repetition of decline but continually overlay this rupture in the illusion of continuous growth with a rhetoric of "incremental" or "staged" development, which asserts that the repetition of decline in a cycle may occur, but occurs only within an overall upward or spiral tendency.

The discourse used of capital in European economic parlance reveals a more general insight about how this culture differs from black culture in its handling of repetition. In black culture, repetition means that the thing *circulates* (exactly in the manner of any flow, including capital flows) there is an equilibrium. In European culture, repetition must be seen to be not just circulation and flow but accumulation and growth. In black culture, the thing (the ritual, the dance, the beat) is "there for you to pick up when you come back to get it." If there is a goal (Zweck) in such a culture, it is always deferred; it continually "cuts" back to the start, in the musical meaning of "cut" as an abrupt, seemingly unmotivated break (an accidental *da capo*) with a series already in progress and a willed return to a prior series.

A culture based on the idea of the "cut" will always suffer in a society whose dominant idea is material progress—but "cuts" possess their charm! In European culture, the "goal" is always clear: that which always is being worked towards. The goal is thus that which is reached only when culture "plays out" its history. Such a culture is never "immediate" but "mediated" and separated from the present tense by its own future-orientation. Moreover, European culture does not allow "succession of accidents and surprises" but instead maintains the illusions of progression and control at all costs. Black culture, in the "cut," builds "accidents" into its *coverage*, almost as if to control their unpredictability. Itself a kind of cultural *coverage*, this magic of the "cut" attempts to confront accident and rupture not by covering them over but by making room for them inside the system itself.

In one unexpected sphere of European consciousness, however, such an orientation towards the "cut" has survived: on the level of that psychological phenomenon which Freud fully details as the eruption of seemingly unwilled repetitions of the past into the individual's present life—*Wiederholungszwang* or *repetition compulsion*. On the individual psychic level, cultural prohibitions lose their validity. Hence in repetition compulsion, as Freud describes it, repetition—an idiosyncratic and immediate action—has replaced memory, the "normal" access to the past. Instead of a dialogue about a history already past, one has a restaging of the past. Instead of relating what happened in his or her history (Hegel's category of objectivity), the patient re-enacts it with all the precision of ritual. This obsessive acting-out of the repressed past conflict brings the patient back to the original scene of drama. Repetition compulsion is an example of a "cut" or "seemingly fortuitous" (but actually motivated) repetition that appears in explicit contradiction to societal constraints and standards of behavior. Society would censure the act of unwilled repetition as much as or even more than the original trespass: both are against custom

(Sitte), or un-moral *(unsittlich),* but the lack of will in repetition compulsion makes it also uncanny *(unheimlich).* Jacques Lacan's fruitful idea of the *tuché*—the kind of repetition "that occurs *as if by chance"*—seems to complete the identification here of repetition compulsion as one further aspect of non-progressive culture to have been identified within the limits of the European individual consciousness. By virtue of its accidence (or of its accidental way of showing through), the cycle of desire and repression that underlies repetition compulsion belongs together with the notion of the "cut."

Repetition in black culture finds its most characteristic shape in performance: rhythm in music, dance and language. Whether or not one upholds the poet-politician-philosopher Leopold Senghor's attempts to fix the nature of black culture in a concept of *negritude,* it is true that he has well described the role that rhythm plays in it: "The organizing force which makes the black style is rhythm. It is the most perceptible and least material thing." Where material is absent, dialectics is groundless. Repetitive words and rhythms have long been recognized as a focal constituent of African music and its American descendants—slave-songs, blues, spirituals and jazz. African music normally emphasizes dynamic rhythm, organizing melody within juxtaposed lines of beats grouped into differing meters. The fact that repetition in some senses is the principle of organization shows the desire to rely upon 'the thing that is there to pick up.' Progress in the sense of 'avoidance of repetition' would at once sabotage such an effort. Without an organizing principle of repetition, true improvisation would be impossible, since an improviser relies upon the ongoing recurrence of the beat.

Not only improvisation but also the characteristic "call and response" element in black culture (which already, in eliciting the general participation of the group at random, spontaneous "cuts," disallows any possibility of an *haute culture)* requires an assurance of repetition:

> While certain rhythms may establish a background beat, in almost all African music there is a dominant point of repetition developed from a dominant con-versation with a clearly defined alternation, a swinging back and forth from solo to chorus or from solo to an emphatic instrumental reply.

That the beat is there to pick up does not mean that it must have been metronomic, but merely that it must have been at one point begun and that it must be at any point "social"—i.e. amenable to restarting, interruption or entry by a second or third player or to response by an additional musician. The typical polymetry of black music means that there are at least two, and usually more, rhythms going on alongside the listener's own beat. The lis-tener's beat is a kind of *Erwartungshorizont* (to use a term taken from a quite different area) or "horizon of expectations," whereby he or she knows where the constant beat must fall in order properly to make sense of the gaps that the other interacting drummers have let fall. Because one rhythm always defines another in black music, and beat is an entity of relation, any "self-consciousness" or "achievement" in the sense of an individual participant working towards his or her own rhythmic or tonal climax "above the mass" would have disastrous results.

While repetition in black music is almost proverbial, what has not often been recognized in black music is the prominence of the "cut." The "cut" overtly insists on the repetitive nature of the music, by abruptly skipping it back to another beginning which we have already heard. Moreover, the greater the insistence on the pure beauty and value of repetition, the greater the awareness must also be that repetition takes place not on a level of musical development or progression, but on the purest tonal and timbric level.

James Brown is an example of a brilliant American practitioner of the "cut" whose skill is readily admired by African as well as American musicians. The format of the Brown "cut" and repetition is similar to that of African drumming: after the band has been "cookin" in a given key and tempo, a cue, either verbal ("Get down" or "Mayfield"—the sax player's name—or "Watch it now") or musical (a brief series of rapid, percussive drum and horn accents), then directs the music to a new level where it stays with more "cookin"—or perhaps a solo—until a repetition of cues then "cuts" back to the primary tempo. The essential pattern, then, in the typical Brown sequence is recurrent: "ABA" or "ABCBA" or "ABC(B)A" with each new pattern set off (i.e. introduced and interrupted) by the random, brief hiatus of the "cut." The ensuing rupture does not cause dissolution of the rhythm; quite to the contrary, it strengthens it, given that it is already incorporated into the format of that rhythm.

In jazz improvisation, the "cut"—besides uses similar to Brown's—is the unexpectedness with which the soloist will depart from the "head" or theme and from its normal harmonic sequence or the drummer from the tune's accepted and familiar primary beat. One of the most perfect exemplars of this kind of improvisation is John Coltrane, whose mastery of melody and rhythm was so complete that he and Elvin Jones, his drummer, often traded roles, Coltrane making rhythmic as well as melodic statements and "cutting" away from the initial mode of the playing.

Black music sets up expectations and disturbs them at irregular intervals: that it will do this, however, is itself an expectation. This peculiarity of black music—that it draws attention to its own repetitions—extends to the way it does not hide the fact that these repetitions take place on the level of sound only. The extension of "free jazz," starting in the 1960s, into the technical practice of using the "material" qualities of sound—on the horns, for instance, using overtones, harmonics and subtones—became almost mandatory for the serious jazz musician and paralleled a similar movement on the part of European musicians branching out of the classical tradition. But black music has always tended to imitate the human voice, and the tendency to "stretch" the limits of the instrument may have been already there since the wall of the first blues guitar, the whisper of the first muted jazz trumpet or the growl of the first jazz trombonist.

The black church must be placed at the center of the manifestations of repetition in black culture, at the junction of music and language. Various rhetorics come into play here: the spoken black sermon employs a wide variety of strategies, such as particularly *epanalepsis* ("because His power brings you power, and your Lord is still the Lord") or *epistrophe* ("give your life to the Lord; give your faith to the Lord; raise your hands to the Lord"). Emphatic repetition most often takes the form of *anaphora,* where the repetition comes at the beginning of the clause (instead of at the beginning and at the end in the first example above, or at the end in the second case). Such a usage of repetition is not limited to the black church, however, and may even be derived in part from the uses of repetition in the key church text, the Bible, as in the following anaphora from Psalms: "The Lord shall give his people the blessing of peace" (29:10–11).

Both preacher and congregation employ the "cut." The preacher "cuts" his own speaking in interrupting himself with a phrase such as "praise God" (whose weight here cannot be at all termed denotative or imperative but purely sensual and rhythmic—an underlying "social" beat provided for the congregation). The listeners, in responding to the preacher's calls at random intervals, produce each time it "cuts" a slight shift in the texture of the performance. At various intervals a musical instrument such as the organ and often spontaneous dancing accompany the speaker's repetition of the "cut." When the stage of highest intensity comes, gravel-voiced "speaking in tongues" or the "testifying," usually delivered at a single pitch, gives credence to the hypothesis, that, all along, the very texture of the sound and nature of the rhythm—but not the explicit meaning—in the spoken words have been at issue.

Repetition in black literature is too large a subject to be covered here, but one may say briefly that it has learned from these "musical" prototypes in the sense that repetition of words and phrases, rather than being overlooked, is exploited as a structural and rhythmic principle. The sermon on the "Blackness of Blackness" which occurs early in Ralph Ellison's *Invisible Man* lifts the sermonic and musical repetitions (Ellison says he modeled this sequence on his knowledge of repetition in jazz music) directly into view in a literary text—and not just in the repetition of its title. The *ad hoc* nature of much black folklore and poetry, as well as its ultimate destination in song, tends to encourage the repeating refrain, as in this paean to the fighter Jack Johnson:

> Jack Johnson, he de champion of de worl'
> Jack Johnson, he de champion of de worl'
> Jack Johnson, he de champion
> Jack Johnson, he de champion
> Jack Johnson, he de champion of de worl'

The "AABBA" repetitive format of so much black folklore and folk lyric finds its way into the black novel (as it does into the blues) in unaltered form. In Jean Toomer's *Cane*, the mixture of "fiction, songs, and poetry," presented against the theme of black culture in transition, provides a fine opportunity to view some typical (and not so typical) uses of repetition in the black novel. From the poem "Song of the Son" to the very last page, the repetitive forms of black language and rhetoric are prominent until one notices that gradually the entire plot of the novel itself has all along been tending towards the shape of return—the circle:

> O land and soil, red soil and sweet-gum tree,
> So scant of grass, so profligate of pines
> Now just before an epoch's sun declines
> Thy son, in time, I have returned to thee,
> Thy son, I have in time returned to thee.

Toni Morrison continues this use of repetition, particularly in *Song of Solomon*, with Sugarman's song and the final song of "Jake the only son of Solomon." In the latter song, where Morrison describes "the children, inexhaustible in their willingness to repeat a rhythmic, rhyming action game," and the will of black language to "perform the round over and over again," she puts into words the essential component of her own written tradition. Leon Forrest (most notably in *There is a Tree more Ancient than Eden*) and Ishmael Reed are able to tap a long series of predecessors when they include folk-poems and folklore in their narratives, whose non-progressive form they need not feel constrained to justify.

But particularly in the work of Reed (mainly *Mumbo Jumbo*, but also quite noticeably in *The Free-Lance Pallbearers* and *Flight to Canada*) the kinds of repetition we have seen to have been derived from spoken discourse become only an emblem for much wider strategies of circulation and "cutting" in black writing and a model, or supplemental meter, for their future employment. The explicitly parodistic thrust of the title *Mumbo Jumbo* first of all rejects the need for making a definitive statement about the "black situation in America" and already implies, as all parody does, a comparison with, as well as regeneration of, what has come before and the return of a pre-logical past where, instead of words denoting sense, there was "mumbo jumbo." Jes Grew, the main "force" in the novel, besides being disembodied rhythm ("this bongo drumming called Jes Grew") or Senghor's "la chose la plus sensible et la moins materielle," is ironically the essence of anti-growth, the avatar of a time "before this century is out" when, Reed predicts:

> men will turn once more to mystery, to wonderment; they will explore the vast
> reaches of space within instead of more measuring more "progress" more of
> this and more of that.

Jes Grew epidemics appear and reappear *as if by accident:* "So Jes Grew is seeking its words. Its text. For what good is a liturgy without a text?" But there is no text to be found (besides Jes Grew's "rhythmic vocabulary larger than French or English or Spanish"), for the "text" is in fact the compulsion of Jes Grew to recur again and again—the "trace" of one such appearance is *Mumbo Jumbo,* the novel, but at the end of it we are left again with the text of the quest, which is the repetition of the seeking.

Reed elides the "cut" of black culture with the "cutting" used in cinema. Self-consciously filmable, *Mumbo Jumbo* ends with a *"freeze frame"* not only underscoring its filmic nature, but also itself an example of a common cueing device for cinematic "cuts." Reed, also, in the manner of the jazz soloist, "cuts" frequently between the various subtexts in his novel (headlines, photographs, handwritten letters, italicized writing, advertisements) and the text of his main narrative. The linear narrative of the detective story and the feature film (*opening scenes, title, credits, story,* final *freeze frame*) also structures *Mumbo Jumbo,* but there is no progressive enterprise going on here, despite such evidence to the contrary. The central point remains clear right to Reed's very last words: "the 20s were back again. . . . Time is a pendulum. Not a river. More akin to what goes around comes around." The film is in a loop.

THE RETURN OF REPETITION

Repetition is reality and it is the seriousness of life. He who wills repetition is matured in seriousness. . . . Repetition is the new category which has to be brought to light.

(Kierkegaard, *Repetition*)

In almost conscious opposition to Hegel's idea of "progressive" culture, European music and literature, perhaps realizing the limitations of innovation, have recently learned to "foreground" their already present repetitions, "cuts" and cyclical insights. As European music uses rhythm mainly as an aid in the construction of a sense of progression to a harmonic cadence, the repetition has been suppressed in favor of the fulfillment of the goal of harmonic resolution. Despite the clear presence of consistent beat of rhythm in the common classical forms of the ostinato or the figured bass or any other continuo instrument, rhythm was scarcely a goal in itself and repetition seldom pleasurable or beautiful by itself.

Although the key role of "recapitulation" in the "ABA" or "AABBAA" sonata form (often within a movement itself, as in the so frequently ignored "second repeats" in Beethoven's major works) is undisputed in theory, in live performance these repetitions often are left out to avoid the undesirability of having "to be told the same thing twice." Repeating the exposition, as important as it no doubt is for the "classical style," is subsumed within and fulfilled by the general category called "development." By the time the music does return to the home tonic, in the final recapitulation, the sense is clearly one of repetition with a difference. The momentum has elevated the initial material to a new level rather than merely re-presenting it unchanged. Even though the works of Wagner and his followers represent a break from this traditional formal model of development derived from the sonata form, the Wagnerian leitmotiv, for instance, is anything but a celebration of repetition in music. In *The Ring,* Wagner's consummate vehicle for the leitmotivic style of composition, the recurrent musical phrases are in fact a Hegelian progression or extended accumulation and accretion to an ultimate goal or expression that begins somewhere during the early part of the *Gotterdammerung,* or even starting late in *Siegfried*; the leitmotivs are invested in installments throughout *Das Rheingold* and *Die Walkure* and are then repaid with interest by the end of the *Gotterdammerung.*

In the pre-serial era, only Stravinsky took the already present expectations of concealed repetition in the classical tradition and uncovered them by highlighting them. In *Petrushka* (1911) and *Le Sacre du printemps* (1913) particularly, the use of the "cut" and the unconcealed repetition is striking. In the First Tableau of *Petrushka,* an abbreviated fanfare and tattoo from snare drum and tambourine set off the first section (rehearsal numbers 1–29)—itself in ABAACABA form—from the magic trick (30–2), which is the new, much slower tempo after the "cut." The magic trick concludes with a harp glissando and a brief unaccompanied piccolo figure—the next "cut"—leading to the famous "Danse russe" (33–46), overtly repetitive in its ABABA form, which then ends in a snare-drum "cut" (here, in 47, as well as elsewhere—at 62, 69 and 82). In *Le Sacre du printemps* exact repetition within and across sections exceeds anything that had come before it. Moreover, Stravinsky has developed his use of the "cut," varying the cue-giving instrument. Interestingly, both Stravinsky compositions resemble black musical forms not just in their relentless "foregrounding" of rhythmic elements and their use of the "cut" but also in being primarily designed for use in conjunction with dancers.

In European literature, the recovery of repetition in this century is even more striking. Blatant repetitions of the folkloric, traditional or mnemonic sort that had characterized European oral poetry, medieval sagas and other forms of narrative right into late sixteenth-century baroque literature began to be transformed into the pretense of an external reality being depicted, culminating in *literary realism* in the late nineteenth century. The picaresque "cuts" found in the segmented narrative of *Lazarillo de Tormes* (1554) or even *Don Quixote* (1605)—where a quite literal "cut" breaks off the manuscript before chapter 9—were soon becoming a thing of the past, aside from the rare extravagance of Sterne, whose *Tristram Shandy* (1760–7) was an outstanding exception. In a sense, all representational conventions such as literary realism suppress repetition and verbal rhythm in the telling in favor of the illusion of narrative verisimilitude. Thus they would portray an outside world, exhaustible in its manifestations, by the supposedly inexhaustible and ever-renewable resource of writing—hence evading the need for "repeated descriptions" of that world.

Until recently—particularly before the Dadaists, and their "cutting" practices; or the cinema-inspired "montagists," Joyce, Faulkner, Woolf, Yeats and Eliot—this practice had been dominant. Now its dominance has begun to ebb somewhat. With Joyce, most of all, we have realized that the incessant repetition of particular words (such as "pin" or "hat" in the early Bloom chapters of *Ulysses*) are not descriptions of objects seen repeatedly in the external environment and then described, but intentional repetitions of words scattered here and there in a text by its author as if by accident.

Narrative repetition tends to defuse the belief that any other meaning resides in a repeated signifier than the fact that it is being repeated. Among European or American dramatists, Tom Stoppard, in *Travesties,* comes closest to understanding this insight. This play (in which Joyce plays a major role, along with Tristan Tzara and Lenin) not only refuses to cover up its repetitions but makes clear that there must be a definite "cut" between them. The "cut" is explained in the stage directions as a manifestation of the unreliable memory of the main character, Henry Carr:

> One result is that the story (like a toy train perhaps) occasionally jumps the rails and has to be restarted at the point where it goes wild. . . . This scene has several of these "time slips," indicated by the repetitions of the exchange between BENNETT and CARR about the "newspapers and telegrams". . . . It may be desirable to mark these moments more heavily by using an extraneous sound or a light effect, or both. The sound of a cuckoo-clock, artificially amplified, would be appropriate since it alludes to time and to Switzerland.

Underlying this notion of "time" is not just Freud's idea that repetition is a remedy for the failure of memory, but the related and necessary acceptance of rupture: in the smooth forward progress of the play; in the insistently forward motion of "time" on those occasions when history "jumps the rails and has to be restarted at the point where it goes wild."

The cuckoo-clock in *Travesties* (borrowed from the "Nausicaa" chapter of *Ulysses,* where it has a slightly different function) is the perfect signal for "cuts," being itself an emblem of time. When in Act 1 Tzara repeats the world "DADA" thirty-four times in response to Carr's homily "It is the duty of the artist to beautify existence," one begins to think that the word's meaning in the context, or even its etymology (interesting as it might be for "DADA"), are, beside the point. A previous "cut" has made the point more clearly. Tzara (well known in real life for his "cut-ups," or poems stuck together at random), while trying to seduce Gwendolen, cuts up and tosses the words of Shakespeare's eighteenth sonnet (which she has been reciting) into a hat, shakes them up, and pulls the words one by one out of the hat. Instead of the expected random version of the original, a quite lewd poem, using the same words as the former sonnet, emerges:

> Darling, shake thou thy gold buds
> the untrimmed but short fair shade
> shines-
> see, this lovely hot possession growest
> so long
> by nature's course-
> so . . . long-heaven!
> and declines,
> summer changing, more temperate complexion. . . .

What is the point of Stoppard's "travesty" of Shakespeare? The cutting of the sonnet should have produced only "mumbo jumbo," or at best "clever non-sense," as Carr had called Tzara's prior recitation of the word "DADA." But the emergence of the "new" poem is the emergence of the real: instead of poetry, lechery is Tzara's concern. The true message of the sonnet is not tran-scendent (about beauty) but immediate, in that it consists of words on paper that can be cut, but which signify only in the context of speaking, not by virtue of being masterfully arranged. Language—even Shakespeare's—here is shown to be, on the most obvious level, exactly what is there, not what is elsewhere; it is of desire, not of meaning.

The outstanding fact of late twentieth-century European culture is its ongoing reconciliation with black culture. The mystery may be that it took so long to discern the elements of black culture already there in latent form, and to realize that the separation between the cultures was perhaps all along not one of nature, but one of force.

Suggested Reading with Similar Theme:

Gates, Henry Louis, Jr. Introduction to *Figures in Black: Words, Signs, and the Racial Self.* New York: Oxford University Press, 1987.

WILLIAM L. ANDREWS

The First Century of
Afro-American Autobiography:
Theory and Explication (1984)

African American autobiography (the slave narrative) is said to have distinguishable rhetorical aims. Identify these aims. Why is there a need for "rhetorical defense" in the earliest African American autobiography? How do narratives with gaps, literary silences, metaphor as arguments, embedded evaluators, and other coding mechanisms serve the African American writer? Do methods of persuasion (or manipulation) discredit the claim that African American autobiography is purely mimetic? Define the following terms and phrases: mimetic, rhetorical, revisionist, discourse, discursive, and the anthropology of art.

Whatever else it is, autobiography stems more often than not from a need to explain and justify the self. In his seminal article on the "conditions and limits of autobiography," Georges Gusdorf says, "it is precisely in order to do away with misunderstandings, to restore an incomplete or deformed truth, that the autobiographer himself takes up the telling of his story." After all, "no one can better do justice to himself than the interested party." It took "the interested party" of Afro-American autobiography almost fifty years after the initial appearance of the genre in 1760 to begin to prove that no one could do justice to himself better than himself. From these beginnings to the "year of Jubilo" in 1865 when full emancipation was proclaimed, black autobiography evolved into a complex "oratorical" mode best exemplified in the narratives of ex-slaves who had become master rhetoricians on the anti-slavery lecture circuit. In the first one hundred years of its existence, Afro-American autobiography was a genre chiefly distinguished by its rhetorical aims. During the latter half of this century of evolution, Afro-American autobiography addressed itself, directly and indirectly, to the proof of two propositions: 1) that the slave was, as the inscription of a famous anti-slavery medallion put it, "a man and a brother"; and 2) that the black narrator was, despite all prejudice and propaganda, a truth-teller, a reliable transcriber of Southern life and black folk character.

Henry David Thoreau began his account of his experience at Walden Pond by declaring, "I, on my side, require of every writer, first or last, a sim-

223

ple and sincere account of his own life." Thoreau did not bother to explain how one might prove one's sincerity. No doubt Thoreau would not have seen this as a problem, for white autobiographers could assume that their white readership would grant them peer status and would assume their sincerity unless they contradicted themselves or transgressed important moral norms in their narration. Because these conditions—peer relationship between auto-biographer and audience and the assumption of trustworthiness between peers—existed as a matter of course in the white American autobiographical tradition, the white autobiographer's letter to the world has always had a social, cultural, and linguistic sanction, though not always success. When black autobiographers addressed the white world, however, they could assume no such sanction for their self-affirming literary acts. Many undoubt-edly realized that they would have to defend or explain away the same literary egoism that in a white autobiographer might be praised as American pride and self-reliance at its best. Knowing that they could not assume a peer rela-tionship with the average white American reader, many set about writing life stories that would somehow prove that they qualified as the moral, spiritual, or intellectual peers of whites. White America was willing to suspend disbe-lief and assume the sincerity of an autobiographer it identified as a political peer and a racial equal. However, the knowledge that they could not predi-cate their life stories on this racially-based credulity and trust forced black autobiographers to invent devices and strategies that would endow their sto-ries with the appearance of authenticity. This was perhaps the greatest chal-lenge to the imagination of the Afro-American autobiographer. The very reception of his narrative as truth depended on the degree to which his artful-ness could hide his art.

As a class, no American autobiographer has been received with more skepticism and resistance than the ex-slave. Before the rise of the abolition movement, free blacks in the North as well as enslaved blacks in the South were seen as an alien population recognizably "depraved," "vicious," and, for the most part, incorrigible. Abolitionist defenders of the Negro would not deny that the ex-slave had been morally "degraded" by slavery; they insisted, nevertheless, that he could be elevated from his "inferior" condition. But how could readers of slave narratives be assured that this moral rehabilitation had been completed, especially when a leader in the American Anti-Slavery Soci-ety warned the public about the fugitive slave in the North: "Simple-hearted and truthful, as these fugitives appeared to be, you must recollect that they are slaves—and that the slave as a general thing, is a liar, as well as a drunk-ard and a thief." There were those in the abolitionist movement, of course, who cast the matter in a much more sympathetic and potentially clarifying light. As Samuel G. Howe, an interviewer of runaways in Canada put it: "The negro, like other men, naturally desires to live in the light of the truth; but he hides in the shadow of falsehood, more or less deeply, according as his safety or welfare seems to require it. Other things being equal, the freer a people, the more truthful; and only the perfectly free and fearless are perfectly truthful." In this observation, Howe tried to suggest that absolute "perfect" truth, a concept dear to evangelical abolitionism and nineteenth-century America in general, could not be used to measure the value of Afro-American autobiography since the demands of truthfulness and self-preservation were often at odds in the experience of blacks in America. Yet Howe was himself a prisoner of the semantic dichotomies of Victorian moralizing; he could think of no label other than "falsehood" to apply to the words of a black narrator who could not see his way clear to "live in the light of truth." Today our sensitivity to the relativistic truth-value of all autobiography and to the peculiar symbiosis of imperfect freedom and imperfect truth in the American autobiographical tradition makes it easier for us to regard the fictive elements of black autobiography as aspects of rhetorical and aesthetic strategy, not evidence of moral failure. To promote the study of early Afro-American autobiography in this context, rather than in the unrevealing light of Victorian moral and epistemological categories, is one goal of this essay.

Today every historian and analyst of the Afro-American autobiographical enterprise is faced with the problem of what Houston A. Baker Jr., has termed "the anthropology of art," the unearthing (or reconstruction) of the full context in which a genre originated, evolved, and took on cultural significance. In the case of eighteenth- and nineteenth-century black American autobiography, the problem is compounded because of the unprecedented and largely unparalleled situation that black self-writers found themselves in vis-a-vis their white audience. Nevertheless, a partial and instructive analogy to the Afro-American autobiographer's negotiations with his skeptical, if not hostile, white audience does exist. Consider John Henry Newman's relationship to his British audience prior to the creation of the Apologia Pro Vita Sua (1864). Having left the Anglican clergy to become a Roman Catholic priest, Newman found himself under attack in 1864 for having preached, in the words of his accuser, Charles Kingsley, that "truth, for its own sake, had never been a virtue with the Roman clergy," that "it need not, and on the whole ought not to be." A year later Newman published a pamphlet in which he reconstructed the process by which he decided to answer his attacker, via autobiography, rather than by some other mode of rhetorical defense. The priest knew there were many obstacles in the way of his being favorably heard. By virtue of his Catholicism he was regarded as "a member of a most un-English communion," an alien and a subversive "whose great aim [was] considered to be the extinction of Protestantism and the Protestant Church." In pursuit of this mission, a priest's chief weapons were "supposed to be unscrupulous cunning and deceit." The principal charge Kingsley had brought against him was plain and direct, Newman stated: "He called me a liar." Yet "how am I now to be trusted?" Newman wondered, when his greatest foe was not the arguments of Kingsley but "the bias of the court," the court of British public opinion. Newman's analysis of his position in the eyes of this biased court provides an insight into the problems that faced the Afro-American alien, the presumed subversive and guileful deceiver, when he attempted to prove that he was not a liar before the white American court of public opinion. . . .

To "break through this barrier of prejudice" against him, Newman decided that merely arguing Kingsley's charges would have little effect, no matter how well the arguments were made. "What I needed was a corresponding antagonist unity in my defence," the beleaguered priest concluded. "I must, I said, give the true key to my whole life; I must show what I am, that it may be seen what I am not, and that the phantom may be extinguished which gibbers instead of me. I wish to be known as a living man, and not as a scarecrow which is dressed up in my clothes." Though he would answer the specific charges of Kingsley against his veracity and integrity, "such a work shall not be the scope nor the substance of my reply." Instead, the greater theme of his reply would be to "draw out, as far as may be, the history of my mind."

For the Afro-American and his white sponsors, autobiography answered a felt need for a rhetorical mode that would conduct the battle against racism and slavery on grounds other than those already occupied by pro- and anti-slavery polemics. "Argument provokes argument," the editor of the *Boston Chronotype* concluded about the abolitionist controversy in the 1840s; "reason is met by sophistry; but narratives of slaves go right to the hearts of men." Reaching "the hearts of men" was the rhetorical aim of practically all black autobiography in the first century of its existence, whether produced by an ex-slave or not. Afro-American literature of the late eighteenth and early nineteenth centuries is dominated by treatises, pamphlets, addresses, and appeals, all of which employ expostulatory means by which to confront the problem of the black situation in white America. Yet only black autobiography had a mass impact on the conscience of ante-bellum Americans. Did early black narrators realize as clearly as Newman did that this form of witnessing before a skeptical public would earn more converts to the cause than any other mode of address? Certainly experienced abolitionists recognized that first-person narration, with its promise of intimate glimpses into the mind and heart of an actual runaway slave, would be much more compelling to the uncommitted mass of readers than the oratory and polemics of the anti-slavery press. Unlike Newman, however, early black autobiographers left behind very little explicit comment about the strategies and intentions of their narratives. We are left to infer from their autobiographies themselves how much and in what ways these alien and suspect figures felt they had to prove themselves "men" instead of "phantoms" before anything else they said could be received credibly.

Most slave narrators knew that the public did not read their stories primarily to find out what sorts of men these blacks were. Nineteenth-century whites read slave narrative more to get a first-hand look at the institution of slavery than to become acquainted with an individual slave. Many ex-slaves were quite willing to accede to this expectation, especially when told by their abolitionist sponsors that their skeptical public would believe nothing but documentable "facts" in a slave narrative. From the standpoint of the advancement of the cause, abolitionists naturally felt that the most useful black autobiographies would be ones that forced the ugly facts of "the peculiar institution" to the forefront of a reader's attention and kept them there throughout the story. Moreover, American aesthetic standards of the time made a black narrative that exposed the institutional facts of slavery preferable to one that expressed the subjective views of an individual slave. As Emerson had written of all first-person writing in 1840, such literature could be judged according to "whether it leads us to nature, or to the person of the writer. The great always introduce us to facts; small men introduce us always to themselves." Thus the most trustworthy of all slave narrators would be the one who effaced himself behind the universally-applicable "facts" of slavery. The most reliable slave narrative would be one that seemed purely mimetic, one in which the self is on the periphery instead of at the center of attention, looking outside not within, transcribing rather than interpreting a set of objective facts.

Obviously, to follow this agenda was to alienate oneself from one's past and to banish oneself in the most fundamental ways from one's own autobiography. Yet speaking too revealingly of the individual self, particularly if this did not correspond to white notions of "the facts" of black experience or the "nature" of the Negro, risked alienating white sponsors and readers too. Characteristically, the most significant black autobiographers refused this no-win choice between two alienating alternatives. Instead of either conforming to the rules of the literary game or refusing to play at all, they set about changing the rules by which the game was played even as they played along with the game. White American readers believed that the truth about slavery could be revealed through an "objective" recital of facts from an eyewitness, first-person narrator. Slave narratives often illustrate the contradictoriness of this objectivity based on subjectivity. Black narrators' prefaces and public pronouncements generally abide by the proposition that objective facts can be distinguished from subjective perception. However, their actual life stories frequently dispute, sometimes directly but more often covertly, the positivistic epistemology, dualistic morality, and diachronic framework in which antebellum America liked to evaluate autobiography as either history or falsehood. In this way, black autobiographers made their books something like Newman's "antagonist unity." They were "antagonist" works in two senses: 1) in that they function as ripostes against racist charges against black selfhood, and 2) in that they resist the fragmenting nature of "objective" autobiography, which demands that a black narrator achieve credence by objectifying himself and making passive his voice.

The unity of black autobiography in the ante-bellum era is most apparent in the pervasive use of journey or quest motifs. In black spiritual autobiography, the protagonist wishes to escape sinfulness and ignorance in order to achieve righteousness and a knowledge of the saving grace of God. In the slave narrative, the quest is toward freedom from physical bondage and the enlightenment that literacy can offer to the restricted self- and social consciousness of the slave. However, in a number of important black autobiographies of this era, a quest more psychophiterary than literal can be discerned. It is spurred by many motives, perhaps the most important of which is the need of an "other" to declare himself through various linguistic acts, thereby reifying his abstract unreality, his invisibility in the eyes of his readers, so that he can be re-cognized as someone to be reckoned with. Such declarative acts, as we shall see, include the reconstructing of one's past in a meaningful and instructive form, the appropriating of empowering myths and models of the self from any available resource, and the redefining of one's place in the scheme of things by redefining the language used to locate one in that scheme. . . .

Writing autobiography involved Afro-Americans of the late eighteenth and early nineteenth centuries in yet another kind of journey, a search for language through which the unknown within the self and the unspeakable within slavery might be expressed. Many narratives reveal this to have been a frustrating, even anguishing mental and emotional struggle. Rare was the autobiographer who did not apologize for his lack of facility with words and his inability to portray what he experienced in, or how he felt about, slavery. Other blacks lamented the inadequacy of language itself to represent the horrors of slavery or the depth of their feelings as they reflected on their suffering. In some cases black narrators doubted their white readers' ability to translate the words necessary to a full rendering of their experience and feelings. On other occasions narrators questioned whether whites even wanted a thorough account of the truth of slavery. In the aggregate, these statements indicate that, in their attempt to build a community of understanding between whites and blacks, Afro-American autobiographers were sensitive to the weaknesses of each link in the communication chain, from the writer through the linguistic medium to the audience.

Many narrators who said they were unequal to the task that writing put before them became eloquent in the admission of their supposed literary ineptitude. Their modest prefaces and apologetic comments to their readers should not necessarily be taken at face—or, more accurately, at self-effacing—value. A narrator who states that his literary skills are so limited that he must concentrate them on a plain marshalling of the facts of his life may know more about rhetorical art than he gives himself credit for. The very structuring of his experience in story form indicates that he has judged certain facts of his life to be "reportable"; that is, significant beyond their merely factual content, worthy of display in a pattern which inevitably invites the reader's contemplation as well as his belief or disbelief. Even in the least apparently sophisticated first-person narratives, sociolinguists point out, there is enough "embedded evaluation" in various lexical, semantic, and syntactic features of the narrative to indicate the bases on which its narrator judged its reportability. If we can learn to find these "evaluators" in even the barest recitations of biographical facts, we should be able to speak more appreciatively of the coding mechanisms and the art of the "non-literary" black autobiographer. . . .

What could not be reported explicitly in Afro-American experience had to be explored indirectly through metaphor. As Afro-American autobiography evolved, the institution of slavery and the individuality of the slave received increasingly metaphoric treatment as slave narrators realized the necessity of metaphor to their rhetorical mission. Black autobiography was as much a metaphor-making argument as poetry was, in Emerson's view, an argument metrically made. Current theorists of metaphor like Paul Ricocur and Monroe Beardsley say that a metaphor is made when a word undergoes a turn or "twist" in its literal meaning occasioned by some sort of "semantic clash" between itself as the "principal subject" of a statement or expression and another word attributed to it as its "modifier." True metaphors reveal new and infinitely paraphrastic meanings or words in unexpected contexts. They do this by introducing a tension, a "logical absurdity" in Beardsley's terms, between the significations of the "principal subject"—what we have come to call the "tenor" of the metaphor—and its "modifier," or again, more traditionally, its "vehicle." When we encounter an expression that generates a "semantic clash" between subject and modifier, we have the choice of either holding to the familiar significations of the subject and the modifier, in which case we will simply dismiss the expression as absurd. Or, we may jump over the evident contradictoriness of the modifier as attributed to the subject and construe the modifier "indirectly" as significant because it contradicts our presuppositions about what may be attributed to the subject. When the reader discovers the connotations in the modifier that enable it to be construed as a significant attribution of the subject, he also discovers some of the ways in which his presuppositions about the subject were limited. Ideally, then, metaphors do not simply adorn arguments for persuasive purposes. Metaphors are arguments. Their success depends greatly on the capacity of the reader to accept and explore the creative dialectic of the semantic clash until new meanings emerge from the debris of old presuppositions.

There is little challenge to the reader's capacity for intellectual exploration in the "metaphors of self," to use James Olney's phrase, of very early black autobiography. The central metaphor of the black spiritual autobiographer of the late eighteenth and early nineteenth centuries might be summarized as: "I am as Mr. Christian [in *Pilgrim's Progress*] was, a spiritual pilgrim in an unredeemed world." In this case we have what Ricocur calls a metaphor of "simple substitution"; the modifier, Mr. Christian, may be easily substituted for the principal subject of the statement, the black narrator, by simply ignoring the superficial difference of skin color that separates subject and modifier. There is a spiritual identity between Mr. Christian and the narrator as pilgrims that makes it possible to accept the one as an attribute of the other without challenging our presuppositions about either. The "metaphorical twist" here functions as it does in allegory, in which apparent contradictions are reconciled once they are reviewed in an abstract or ideal perspective. . . .

The metaphor-making of the classic slave narrators of the 1840s and '50s participates in the movement toward organic, non-logical literary discourse as espoused by the classic nineteenth-century American Romantics. Eschewing the limitations of logical analogy, black and white narrators of the American Renaissance used metaphors whose "emergent meaning" was not just a function of pre-existent similarities between a subject and a modifier but was an organic outgrowth of the relationship of a subject and a modifier to "the whole which they create by their interaction." What Charles Feidelson Jr., says of the Romantic metaphor in Symbolism and American Literature no less applies to black autobiographers who explored this mode: From their metaphors emerge meanings that could not "fully exist" apart from the whole which only comes into existence itself as a result of the metaphors' having been created. Through this circular logic of the metaphor, the great Afro-American autobiographies of the Romantic era communicate powerfully the paradoxes of black existence in white America.

Afro-American autobiography did not start out offering an image of black selfhood that was either fully unified or notably antagonistic to popular white notions about who (or what) the Negro was. In his study of the Euro-American autobiographical tradition, Karl J. Weintraub finds a basic contrast between writers who identify with "great personality ideals in which their culture tends to embody its values and objectives" and other writers who are convinced "that ultimately no general model can contain the specificity of the true self." The history of Afro-American in its formative century reflects these contrasting views of the self in a creative dialectic. In some respects the image of the Negro evolves from "models" imported from the predominant culture to more individualized self-portraits in which idiosyncrasy and irony are displayed for a variety of reasons. It is also possible to see the genre evolving from what James Olney has termed "autobiography simplex," in which the complex, variegated self instead of a single dominant faculty or motif becomes the focus of attention. Or, one might appropriate from Harold Bloom an idea that suggests another way of understanding the tradition of Afro-American autobiography in the nineteenth century.

The acquisition of literacy, the power to read books and discover one's place in the scheme of things, is treated in many slave narratives as a matter equal in importance to the achievement of physical freedom. In a famous passage in his *Narrative* of 1845, Frederick Douglass spoke of reading as the way he began to define himself via defiance of his master. For the boy Frederick to continue to study reading after being forbidden to do so by his Baltimore master, Hugh Auld, was to initiate a certain kind of "artistic Primal scene," as Bloom might term it, one emanating from an Oedipal "trespass of teaching." Douglass describes his subsequent resistance to this master as more than just intractableness. His behavior is founded on a deliberate "misreading" of everything Auld stands for and believes in. As Douglass put it, "What he most dreaded, that I most desired. What he most loved, that I most hated. That which to him was a great evil, to be carefully shunned, was to me a great good, to be diligently sought." Douglass is rare among black autobiographers in picturing himself as such a radical misreader of the teachings of his master, but he is not alone among black writers of his era who qualify as Bloomian "strong readers," or, as one might just as accurately say, strong "misreaders." David Walker's *Appeal, in Four Articles; Together with a Preamble, to the Coloured Citizens of the World, but in Particular, and Very Expressly, to Those of the United States of America* (1829) represents a signal act of Afro-American "misreading" of a quasi-sacred American text, the U.S. Constitution. Martin R. Delany's novel *Blake; or the Huts of America* (1859–1862) contains "strong misreadings" of Old Testament history and New Testament theory altogether sacred to the predominant culture. The autobiographies of ex-slaves like Douglass and James W. C. Pennington indicate that the writing of their stories could place slave narrators "in the dilemmas of the revisionist," Bloom's term for a reader "who wishes to find his own original relation to truth, whether in texts or in reality . . . but [who] also wishes to open received texts to his own sufferings, or what he wants to call the sufferings of history." The "received texts," the tradition, that Afro-American autobiography "wishes to open" and force the reader "to esteem and estimate differently" (Bloom's emphasis) are the culture-defining scriptures of nineteenth-century America, the Bible and the Declaration of Independence. The "misreading" of these texts in Afro-American autobiography is much more than an act of cultural commentary or moral criticism. It is often a fundamental part of the act of literary and self-creation, of "revisionary replacements" of scriptural ideas of the self with "a word one's own that is also one's act and one's veritable presence." Thus as black autobiography necessarily establishes its relationship to the essential texts of oppressive American culture, it also becomes a revisionistic instrument in the hands of its greatest practitioners. It urges re-vision of the myths and ideals of America's culture-defining scriptures while it demands new sight of white readers to recognize the ways in which autobiography had become a mode of Afro-American scripture.

Regardless of how one speaks of the development of early black autobiography, it is difficult to chronicle the evolution of the genre in patterns of steady "progress." The "tradition" of black autobiography is not layered in strata of groundbreaking predecessors anticipating conscious successors. Some stages of development can be marked in rough outline, but the route of the genre's historical evolution is dotted with detours, dead ends, half-blazed trails, and roads not taken. How, then, can one address what Hayden White has termed "the problem of change in literary history" as it is manifested in the first century of Afro-American autobiography? To do this, one must first posit a working definition of the genre in question, a definition general and inclusive enough to allow the tradition to reveal itself as a dialectic of continuity and change, not as simply a function of the parameters of the definition itself.

In defining autobiography for the purpose of this essay, I do not propose to establish an impregnable theoretical position but only a kind of staging area for further critical operations. Jean Starobinksi states cogently the hesitancy that many critics feel when trying to characterize autobiography in a systematic way. "Autobiography is certainly not a genre with rigorous rules," he points out. "It only requires that certain possible conditions be realized, conditions that are mainly ideological (or cultural): that the personal experience be important, that it offer an opportunity for a sincere relation with someone else." In other words, to write autobiography one must take one's own life (or some major portion of it) seriously enough to find in it a significance that makes reconstructing that life valuable to another. In keeping with both the self- and other-directedness of autobiography, Starobinski's labeling of the genre as "discourse-history" seems to me a helpful kind of general description, though fraught with definitional difficulties which must themselves be faced.

The problem of the historicity of early Afro-American autobiography, and in particular the slave narrative, has been debated for decades. Led by Ulrich B. Phillips, the first historians of American slavery regarded slave narratives as merely an arm of abolitionist propaganda, strong in righteous indignation but weak in factual substance. In the 1960s and '70s, scholars like Eugene Genovese and John W. Blassingame denied that slavery could be fully understood apart from the perspective of it victims. This conviction led to the publication of a number of valuable studies of the institution based on the idea that many slave narratives are reliable historical documents. Today no serious student of slave narrative quarrels with Blassingame's contention that "most of the accounts written by the blacks themselves not only have the ring of truth, but they can usually be verified by independent sources." However, the proven reliability of these narratives as sourcebooks of facts about slavery should not cause us to forget that as historical narratives they are subject to the same "poetic processes" of composition as any other works of that kind. Even the most "objective" and unrhetorical slave narrative is still a "fiction of factual representation," to use Hayden White's apt phrase. Slave narrators and abolitionist editors often tried to write autobiography in the manner of nineteenth-century positivist history, disclaiming fictive techniques of rhetorical aims as hindrances to the understanding of reality rather than as ways of apprehending it. But we must remember that in any slave narrative, no matter how verifiable in its particulars, "the facts do not speak for themselves." It is the narrator, the imputed eye witness historian, who "speaks on their behalf, and fashions the fragments of the past into a whole whose integrity is—in its representation—a purely discursive one."

What, then, does it mean to treat early black autobiography as "discourse" as well as "history"? In one respect, the discursive nature of black autobiography is simply a function of its rhetorical situation. As Lloyd F. Bitzer explains it, all communication is conditioned and structured by its situation. When a complex of persons, events, or relationships presents a problem that can be affected or alleviated by the use of "discourse" to "influence audience thought or action," then a "rhetorical situation" comes into being. Faced with the "exigencies" of slavery and a mass refusal to see blacks as fully human or hear them as truth-tellers, black autobiographers naturally realized that theirs was a rhetorical situation. They could not think of their task as simply the objective reconstruction of an individual's past or as a public demonstration of the qualities of selfhood or as a private meditation on the meaning of a life of struggle. The writing of autobiography became very much an attempt to open an intercourse with the white world. Often the only context or "tradition" that black autobiographers had was their sense of the state of black-white discourse on the questions of slavery, black identity, and the capacity of blacks for reliable discourse in the first place. In some autobiographies we find a covert, often impromptu discourse on what the language of selfhood can mean when addressed to someone who doubts the selfhood of the addresser. At times this kind of reflectiveness and self-consciousness produces what might be called a running metadiscourse on the assumptions, conditions, and conventions necessary to discourse between black narrator and white reader. Regardless of degree of sophistication, however, the early black autobiographer's discursive aims have much to do with the overwhelmingly "oratorical" character of the genre: its didactic intent, its treatment of life as representative or allegorical, its unifying sense of calling and vocation, and its stylistic sensitivity to the arts of persuasion.

It is also useful to keep in mind what Hayden White has posited about all discourse—that is "quintessentially a mediative enterprise." Noting the etymology of the word (discurrere "to run back and forth"), White says that discourse "moves 'to and fro' between received encodations of experience and the clutter of phenomena which refuses incorporation into conventionalized notions of 'reality,' 'truth,' or 'possibility.' " One of my assumptions about Afro-American autobiography is that it is very much a mediative instrument not only between black narrator and white reader but also, in White's more general terms, between alternative ways of encoding reality, some of which are prescribed by "tradition" and others "of which may be idiolects of the author, the authority of which he is seeking to establish." Ultimately, the mode of black autobiographical discourse itself undertakes the task of validating its own reality claims and its author's identity claims. Early black autobiographers seem preoccupied with authenticating their stories and themselves by documenting both according to their fidelity to the "facts" of human nature and experience that white Americans assumed to be true. We shall see, however, that as a discursive instead of a documentary mode, black autobiography is designed to establish the grounds on which one may decide what will count as fact in a narrative and what mode of interpretation is best suited to a full comprehension of that fact. As a rhetorical mode, black autobiography, then, employs various methods of persuading (or manipulating) the reader to make decisions about truth and significance in a narrative consonant with the aim of the autobiographer. Thus Afro-American autobiography mediates between historical, rhetorical, and tropological truth within the discursive framework common to most Western autobiography, a framework of "narrative patterns of the recovered life" and "dramatic patterns of the evolving act of recovery." . . .

Suggested Readings with Similar Theme:

Sekora, John, and Darwin T. Turner, eds. *The Art of Slave Narratives: Original Essays in Criticism and Theory.* Macomb: Western Illinois Press, 1982.

Ferguson, Sally Ann. "Autobiography and Black College Academics." *Auto/Biography Studies* 3, no. 2 (Summer 1987): 34–40.

Braxton, Joanne M. Introduction to *Black Women Writing Autobiography: A Tradition Within a Tradition.* Philadelphia: Temple University Press, 1989.

Rampersad, Arnold. "Biography and Afro American Culture." In *Afro-American Literary Study in the 1990's,* edited by Houston A. Baker Jr. and Patricia Redmond. Berkeley: University of California Press, 1989.

Tate, Claudia. Introduction to *Domestic Allegories of Political Desire: The Black Heroine's Text at the Turn of the Century.* New York: Oxford University Press, 1992.

duCille, Ann. "Introduction: Conventional Criticism and Unconventional Black Literature." In *The Coupling Convention: Sex, Text, and Tradition in Black Women's Fiction.* New York: Oxford University Press, 1993.

JOSEPH HENRY

A MELUS Interview: Ishmael Reed (1984)

How does Reed clarify the statement, "African culture reflects meaning and consciousness as well as experimentation and improvisation"? How does language of the street (slang and colloquialism) function in Reed's writings? Should Reed be categorized as a folk-lorist? As a humorist? As a satirist? Compare Reed's and Smitherman's discussions of African American English. Define the following terms: neo-Hoodooism, necromancer, subversive, Black talk, Voodooism, Vodoun, pluralistic, multidisciplinary, and multi-culturalism.

Interviewer: You once stated that the great restive underground language often referred to as "slang" and "colloquial," rising from American slums and fringe communities, is the real American poetry and prose. In this regard, how has "Black Talk" and what you refer to as the "Neo-Slave Narrative" influenced your essay form?

Reed: The language of the underground, the language of criminals, so-called jargon, changes rapidly—very rapidly—and involves a process that one can associate with inventing poetry or a poetic process. You can pick it up—you know, people in the upper classes feel that it's very hip to know that language of the street. They try to express themselves that way. I think there's poetic genius in this language. I use it a great deal. I was also influenced by slave narratives. I'm always reading slave narratives and using materials from them such as found in *Flight to Canada*. You have Williams Wells Brown who makes an appearance, a cameo appearance—right! There are scenes and inci-dents from the lives of people like Henry Bibb and other slave writers found in *Flight to Canada*. I read a poem yesterday [at the "Ishmael Reed Reading" on October 22, 1982] from *Flight to Canada* where some of the listings were drawn from letters and experiences of fugitive slaves. So, I use that material. I try to exhaust it.

Interviewer: What about the language itself—how do you account for the so-called slang having the kind of creative power that is possesses?

Reed: Well, I'm bicultural. So, my characters speak English as well as other kinds of English. I think my "white" characters are more convincing than say the "Black" characters of Faulkner, Updike, and Fitzgerald.

Interviewer: How do you account for this additional dimension in your characters?

Reed: My work draws upon both Western and Eastern cultural histories. Westerners usually are not aware of the African cultural tradition.

Interviewer: Could you elaborate on the origin and purpose of the aesthetic movement you created back in 1969, referred to as the "New Literary Neo-Hoodooism," taking into account such African components as dance, drums, nommo, magic-religion, and wood sculpture? What impact has it made since 1969 and what is the current state of this art form?

Reed: Okay, the origin of it occurs when the slaves come to this hemisphere, that makes the beginning. The origin comes out of Voodoo. Voodoo is Hoodooism or an American variation of the African vodoun. But I refer to it as the same form practiced by many non-Western cultures also, such as the Native Americans and the Cantonese.

Interviewer: Would it be fair to say that you brought a certain level of consciousness to his new literary aesthetic?

Reed: Oh, certainly, yes. I use it as a process of literature and it is much more respectable now than it was earlier. Henry Louis Gates has a piece out in *Critical Inquiry on Mumbo Jumbo*. So my work has entered the college classrooms. There are a lot of people using the material, Voodooism, and Vodoun—you can't miss it. In a course on Black culture that I'm teaching, I'm using three authors, including Paule Marshall, who draw upon Vodoun. Among other things, it also functions as a literary device. Paule Marshall uses the "Obeah" in her work, which is a neo-African variant in Jamaica and Barbados, Toni Cade Bambara in *The Salt Eaters*, Toni Morrison in *Tar Baby* and John Wideman in *Damballah*. However, I did not create the system of Vodoun. But I was the first one to write it down as Hoodoo, in a conscious attempt to use explanation. These techniques have been around for centuries, which is why I refer to them as "Neo-Hoodooism."

Interviewer: What did you observe about the Afro-American condition which triggered your imagination in this area?

Reed: I was keeping up with the debate that was going on in *Black World* magazine with Larry Neal, my friend. He came up with something referred to as "juju," which he considered to be a part of the Afro-American experience. This particular issue, I recall, had Larry's picture in it and I said to myself—well, the next variation of Vodoun would be Hoodoo—right! Somebody's going to come up with it. I am going to do it! I'm going to come up with Hoodoo as an explanation of statewide variation of neo-African art which is based upon African forms of art containing details which rose in that hemisphere. Thus, I was inspired by Larry Neal. In addition, Neal was one of the best of the Black Nationalist critics. He had a different definition than the rest of them. So Larry Neal served as my first source of information. However, I was also influenced by a painter by the name of Joseph Overstreet. This occurred because I saw some work of his which included vevers [symbolic designs drawn on the ground during Haitian ceremonies]. This experience inspired me to put more study into the art of Vodoun.

Interviewer: So Larry Neal and Joseph Overstreet proved to be aesthetic catalysts in helping you probe the Afro-American condition in a different and perhaps deeper level?

Reed: It was intellectual, but it was also based upon something I heard in the street, something I heard in my family, usually whispered about. And if you're a kid and you hear things whispered about, you become curious about them. You wanted to know what's this stuff being whispered about. So you could say that Larry Neal was the impetus for my "Neo Hoodoo Manifesto," which was published in the *Los Angeles Free Press* in the 1960s.

Interviewer: In this same regard, would you elaborate on the difference you perceive between what you refer to as "the Necromancers" (prophets of a non-Western way of seeing things) and the traditional American Negro leader?

Reed: Well, the Necromancers are more in the tradition of the African Griot, and the Black leaders in this country have been Christianized. As a matter of fact, one could say we have a Christian theocracy, which was selected by the media. The male Anglo media selected these people and demanded that they convert others to Christianity as well as scorn the masses about their pagan ways. In contrast, the Necromancers have their own vision of reality. For their visionaries and prophets, far from being selected by the media, are from the culture of the underground—the conjurer. They are descendents of the conjure people. But you do have conjurers in other cultures also. Getting back to the course on Black culture that I'm teaching, we emphasize that Paule Marshall's *Brown Girl, Brownstones* represents Black hoodoo from the Caribbean or Caribbean Hoodoo. We have Cantonese hoodoo in Louis Chu's *Eat a Bowl of Tea,* where reverence is paid to the Cantonese gods and spirits. We teach John Wideman's books *Hiding Place* and *Dambullah. Dambullah* refers to the serpent god of the sky. Toni Cade Bambara's *Salt Eaters* actually contains rites of possession, exorcism and references to Afro-American gods. I could have called this course "Neo-Hoodooism and Literature." I think that the strongest American antecedent of this art form is not a literary person but a dancer, Katherine Dunham; Zora Hurston too had more of a scholarly approach than an artistic one.

Interviewer: What helped to shape, protect, and preserve the Necromancers from such outside forces as the media?

Reed: This really involves discussing the historical contact between Northern European culture, African culture, and what results from such contact. Ultimately, the Necromancers' view is considered subversive. That this vision survives is a tribute to Black folk culture, which has been kept alive by the masses, although it was scorned by the intellectuals.

Interviewer: Although a close reading of your poetry will reveal that your work falls within the tradition of Dunbar, Toomer, and Tolson, it is a far cry, however, from "policy poetry." This is particularly true of such pieces as "I am a Cowboy in the Boat of Ra," the "Neo-Hoodoo Manifesto," "The Neo-HooDoo Aesthetic" and the "Catechism of a Neoamerican HooDoo Church." Would you describe how the Black movement influenced the shaping of the ideas found therein as well as the architectural process of your form?

Reed: I think you can get some of the rhythms of the Black poetry of Manhattan in my poems. I think I sometimes return to that—a rapping rhythm, as Darwin Turner refers to it. My idea of "Neo Hoodooism," however, is quite different from the Black Nationalist approach because I see West African imagination as capable of being inspired by many different cultures. I think that the Black Nationalists are mono-cultural. The absorptive capacity of "Neo Hoodooism" incorporates European ideas as well as Native American ideas. Some of the notions associated with the Black Movement, that eventually come to reflect its philosophy, were merely Western ideas with a Black facade. These ideas were either given blackness or "blackified."

Interviewer: In the historical scheme of things, would you be willing to view the "Neo-Hoodoo" aesthetic as one ideological strand or level of a diverse Black Movement?

Reed: The "Neo-Hoodoo" aesthetic comes out of my personal experience and represents my need to find something that I could be at home with. It was something that I became devoted to even before I became aware of Black Nationalism. "Neo-Hoodoo" is international. So I don't know whether "Neo Hoodooism" comes out of the Black Movement or not. I don't think it does, because I was personally looking for material that no one had used or tried before. It is possible, though, that the Black Movement may have influenced my need to find a different approach to art and writing, since like it, I was ultimately reaching for a different set of aesthetic values in reaction to Western literary standards. This particular subject surfaces periodically among academics in Afro-American literature.

Interviewer: Your fiction may be described as multidisciplinary and multicultural, drawing upon films, history, comedy, music, and drama—all in a simultaneous present and in an interconnected fashion. This being so, do you really believe that the non-literary individual can achieve an adequate level of reading with one of your texts?

Reed: Sure, even though there may be many crosscurrents, I try to keep things flowing and simple. Examine Paule Marshall's *Brown Girl, Brownstones* where Silla addresses a Barbadian association, which happens to be a property owner's association. At the Youth Division she speaks about her philosophy of life—which reflects the ethics of a dog-eat-dog world. Now, it isn't necessary for the reader to know that this is tantamount to Social Darwinism. The reader does not have to know this term to understand what she's driving at. When the other character, Selina, states that her life is nothing, she doesn't fit in, and that she has no future, we don't have to know that this is an existential cry. It's just a character saying words or expressing a feeling. The reader does not have to know what philosophical systems are behind the characters or the plot. That my fiction incorporates so many different fields reveals the eclectic nature of the "Neo-Hoodoo" aesthetic. So, sure, I think a lot of people read these books because you really do not have to know the hidden system, for example, behind *The Last Days of Louisiana Red* to understand and enjoy it. I think there's something in my work for everyone and I believe that the messages operate on more than the conscious level. I'm always amazed at the diversity of people who read my books. They represent the whole spectrum of life, from different backgrounds and various races. For example, if you study carefully the way Vodoun has been practiced in South America, you will observe the impact of African syncretism in a number of places and among various classes and races of people.

Interviewer: In other words, part of the appeal of your fiction is built into the literary structure of Hoodoo, itself.

Reed: Oh, Yeah! Sure. But you would have to go out of your way to find out that my work is being published. I say this because I do not have a major advertisement campaign or anything. My work is usually sold by word of mouth, a pattern that has remained true for fifteen years now. October 27, 1982, next week, will mark my fifteenth anniversary of the publication of my first novel, *The Free-Lance Pallbearers*. And it's still in print. It has lasted over three generations (three different age groupings), in spite of the fact that I didn't have an eighty thousand dollar or shall I say a big commercial campaign. So, as long as I'm writing, I guess, my "small but vociferous" following will continue to grow. Of course, this includes lay people who like *Yellow Back Radio Broke-Down* and *The Last Days of Louisiana Red*. There's nothing so complex, because we use forms that people are acquainted with and that they know about. We just completed a soap opera film that's being shown around the country to hundreds of thousands of people and they like it. It's a soap opera they can relate to. It has extra soap opera appeal because we bring a high quality of actors, actresses, artists, and intelligent direction. Obviously, the content is something that everybody can understand—domestic conflict. The soap opera form has an available viewing audience, but in order to keep that audience, a lot depends on what the artist does with the form. There are a lot of guys who were writing fugues in Bach's time, but Bach, himself, brought something special to his interpretation. Likewise, we think we're ahead of all the rest of them.

Interviewer: Recently, you have expressed a need for economy in your fiction and the desire to eliminate what you call "verbal silicone" from print. With this representing a new focus for you, how do you maintain immense human mysteriousness and complexity and ward off the possibility of cardboard characterization and weak plot contrivances in your fiction?

Reed: My plots are very intricate and my characterizations are based upon the principles of Afro-American culture, especially folk art. My work is probably more in the tradition of Afro-American folk art—including the art of humor, fantasy, and satire. When people say that I'm just a humorist, or that I just use satire—well, they're simply not aware of the fact that I use a persistent non-Western form of satire. The way the persecuted get back at their exploiters. You see a lot of examples of this in the Afro-American masks, although you won't see it in assimilationist art or novels. That is, you don't see it in existentialist or Marxist literature. But you do see it in Black folklore. So, you see, I'm a folklorist. The reason why I get so much enmity from structuralists and the other guys at Sunday School is because they are not acquainted with it. I went to the Corcoran Gallery in Washington, D.C. and saw a lot of folk work first hand. There was Nellie Mae Rowe who constructed what my mother used to call "what-not" sculpture gardens. I am in that tradition—the tradition of fantasy, humor and satire.

Interviewer: How will you go about shearing the excessive wordage from your writing without diminishing the contribution of Afro-American folklore, a proven source of rich imagery for your fiction?

Reed: I try to use simple elements in my writing. That is, one can express complex ideas in simple ways. That's one of the things wrong with modern culture and universities today; people feel you have to have a lot of jargon and string together a lot of convoluted sentences to say something that an ordinary person would say in a few words. I try to use poetry and common language, even more so now than before. I try to use simple language to express complex ideas. As a matter of fact, I'm now writing and incorporating songs in my work, and I'm more and more beginning to express the Black male point of view, because it's being left out. Black males don't have access to publishing any more. The feminists have taken over publishing and publicity departments now.

Interviewer: Could you elaborate on the extent to which your own work in this instance—*Mumbo Jumbo,* your 'ragtime" novel, draws on the Afro-American heritage and at the same time reflects a dynamic tension as a result of the inclusion of imagery, symbolism, and literary devices drawn from cultures and races world-wide?

Reed: African culture reflects meaning and consciousness as well as experimentation and improvisation. If you look to America, you will find that the cultures are supposed to remain separate; however, if you look at history you'll find that there has always been multi-culturalism. But if you interpret history properly, you will observe the Black presence in Europe and the European presence in Africa. People are mixed all over the world. This is a new idea, where one race or group is segregated over here and another over there. This is ahistorical, because people are always migrating and when they meet up they either fight or make love, and you're not going to stop this. So, my fiction, in part, reflects how I read human history, which is mostly pluralistic. I reject the compartmentalization that people try to impose on history. Other artists have this liberating component in their work also. This would include musicians, painters, and other writers. Black writers tend to go beyond nineteenth century attitudes because of their bicultural heritage. Native Americans tend to be tricultural. Living on the West coast, my work tends to reflect a rather different outlook on things, as opposed to the East, where attitudes tend to be either black or white on issues. However, I'm in a multi-cultural state (California), so I'm in continual contact with many different international cultural trends. The East is black or white.

Suggested Readings with Similar Theme:

Reed, Ishmael. "New-Hoodoo Manifesto." In *Conjure: Selected Poems, 1963–1970*. Amherst: University of Massachusetts Press, 1972.

Fontenot, Chester, Jr. "Ishmael Reed and the Politics of Aesthetics, Or Shake Hands and Come Out Conjuring." *Black American Literature Forum* 12, no. 1 (Spring 1978): 20–23.

Dick, Bruce, and Amritjit Singh, eds. *Conversations with Ishmael Reed*. Jackson: University Press of Mississippi, 1995.

SHAUNEILLE PERRY RYDER

Will the Real Black Theater
Please Stand Up? (1984)

Based on the following statements, how does Ryder summarize the aesthetic and political states of black theater in the 1980s? "We must learn to select our own role models before the media does. . . . It must not be Broadway or die. . . . When the grants go, so goes everything else. . . . Ordinary Black folks were no longer paying to hear their lifestyles scoffed or the language they had left on the corner glorified. . . . Some theater companies are now re-doing black classics that critics consigned to the graveyard; theater groups in different states are exchanging work, and still others have taken the theater into the churches, prisons, bars and streets instead of waiting for the audience to come to them." Discuss how Ryder enters discussions respectively with Larry Neal (Part 3), August Wilson, and Tommy Lott about black theater for the black community; black versus white directors; and the expectations of black audiences.

More than 20 years ago, the Black Theater Movement erupted boldly, changing the complexion and consciousness of "The Great White Way." Today, in the '80s, Broadway still tolerates the presence of a black show every season or so, but its consciousness has changed profoundly.

The showcasing of black performers as brilliant singers and dancers continues, but a look behind the scenes of most of the major commercial productions reveals a complete turnabout from the '60s in the hiring of artistic personnel. Whites are once again writing, producing, directing, choreographing, costuming, managing and composing "black" material; that is, they have reconsolidated the artistic control, and even some of the non-profit theater groups are maintaining backstage staffs that are predominantly white.

At the same time, since today's commercial "hits" no longer need the once-coveted black audience for financial success, there is little concern about what kinds of images of Blacks are put onstage. This is not being compensated for by the non-profit theaters, which *do* need the black audience, but which have not succeeded in building a consistent following. There are a few exceptions across the nation hobbling along on subscriptions and loyal friends but, by and large, everybody—artists and small theater groups alike—is hustling around and trying to make it on everything from grants to concerts to poetry readings to fashion shows. In their desperation, they are assailing

Reaganomics and cut-backs, assailing the black community and corporations and celebrities for non-support, crying the blues, and still engaging in that destructive ritual with the white critics—pretending to hate them, while lusting for their approval at the same time.

The time has come for theater artists to set rhetoric aside and begin to deal, in an honest and constructive way, with the many questions that are outstanding within the artistic community. What, first of all, is "black theater"? The answer seems obvious: Black theater exists wherever Black people engage in the performing ritual before an audience. Yet, conflict over the definition of this phenomenon has plagued black artists for over two decades, and at great cost to unified action. There cannot, nor should there be, an absolute definition, but any matter as divisive as this needs to be examined outside the context of pure emotionalism.

Can a play acted by Blacks, but written, conceived and interpreted by whites, portray the truth of black life or merely reflect white perceptions of the truth—is *Ain't Misbehavin'* the *Porgy and Bess* of the '80s? Maybe instead of "Can a play . . . ," the question ought to be, "Should a play . . . ," etc.

Consider the following: This year marked the 25th anniversary of Lorraine Hansberry's *A Raisin in the Sun.* Hosting one of the major U.S. revivals in Hansberry's home town of Chicago, the Goodman Theater management chose a white director from New York to interpret and stage the work. Being talented and having staged a number of black works in New York over the years, said director is, by this time, probably quite knowledgeable about black life. But it was Hansberry's insistence on a black director, Lloyd Richards, 25 years ago that opened a door on Broadway which has been virtually sealed again. Compounding the irony here is the fact that Richards chose a black director for *his* revival of *Raisin,* even though he heads the Yale Drama School at one of the nation's largest and most prestigious white institutions. In theory, just as white artists often render black works, black artists should be able to have a shot at some new slice of white Americana onstage, but this is simply not happening. There have been some exceptions, of course—Luther James and Israel Hicks have directed "crossover" plays in regional theater; a striking exception is Harold Scott, who headed the Cincinnati Playhouse for a number of years; and Broadway playwright Samm-Art Williams dared to write about white life in *Brass Birds Don't Sing* (his reception, however, was hardly like the one given Michael Bennett for *Dream Girls*). But these departures from the rule are so few as to be mere drops in a bucket.

With alarming persistence, and practically no collective resistance, the numbers of white personnel in our non-profit theaters are continuing to grow. From the artistic to the managerial, control is slowly being monopolized by whites—which throws us back to the thorny matter of defining black theater.

Complicating things further is a division within the black theater community that is as counter-productive as the white invasion. In New York, a never-ending battle rages around the question of whether black theater should be defined by geographical location; i.e., is it black if it's not in Harlem? Last year, at an awards ceremony in support of black theater, speakers and recipients rose one after the other to proclaim themselves residents and/or natives of Harlem. So relentlessly did they beat this drum that others felt compelled to apologize with such statements as "I'm from Harlem too, by way of North Carolina." Historically, New York has reigned as *the* Mecca for the arts; so Blacks, who always reflect in microcosm whatever is going on in the larger society, have their own variety of New York chauvinism. Half of the participants in the Harlem Renaissance were born elsewhere, but the "Apple" gets the credit. This kind of chauvinism works against the forging of links between companies and groups on campuses, in churches, in community centers all over the nation, links that are essential to the advancement of black theater artists and black theater development.

The Black Theatre Alliance attempted to provide a service, but its structure was weak, financial support ceased, and it crumbled. Various other organizations have put forth efforts, but there is no official liaison between them. When the grants go, so goes everything else, and a familiar specter rears its head again: We hate the power structure but we cry crocodile tears when it stops the funding. There are no easy answers, but answers with some degree of viability must be sought. Complaining about our situation and, at the same time, warring among ourselves will accomplish nothing except a diminution of our creativity.

How did we manage to slide from yesterday's euphoria into the dilemma we confront today? Back in the '60s, "Black" was the word onstage and off. Black writers pumped life and vitality back into the anemic American theater, infused it with new sounds, characters, rhythms, energy, language. A few geniuses, most notably Amiri Baraka, were brilliant at finding beauty in the profane and making poetry out of the everyday. If Baraka had his flaws, most of the time he was right on target. Unfortunately, a host of his imitators were not. Eventually, the "liberated" language, along with the romanticized pimp and his women, the brutalized "ho," became the celebrated symbols of black theater. The High Priests of Black vented their rage on panels and in papers that neatly divided the whole of Afro-American culture into two categories: black and Bourgeois. Onstage, "Blacks" were always "street" and "bourgeois" characters who talked with phony English accents and played bridge a lot. The men tended to be idiot savant types or fraudulent clergymen—this, despite the fact that a sizable proportion of the civil rights leaders were ministers.

Black women were, in general, portrayed almost as badly by black writers as they had been traditionally by whites—they were still in the kitchen, still getting beat up, and still praying through it all (some exceptions: Ron Milner, Martie Charles, Charles Fuller, and the forgotten, like Alice Childress, William Branch, and others). For a long time those were the prevalent images. And they were acclaimed. The white critics recognized the vitality and loved it, being at once fascinated, titillated, perplexed, offended and dazzled. The rougher the work, the more they loved it, especially if it attacked them. "Whitey" was the second most frequently heard word, after "mother-fucker." In what must have been an uneasy alliance, black and white critics often found themselves applauding and approving the same things. Mean-while, no one was noticing that those noisy busloads of ordinary Black folks were no longer paying to hear their lifestyle scoffed or the language they had left on the corner glorified.

Tired of being berated and scolded onstage and off, the black commu-nity stopped supporting the theater. Their whispered desires for "some family shows" and "something to make you proud of" fell on arrogant and angry ears. They got labeled as "traitors," so they left. They flocked back in droves to see *Bubbling Brown Sugar* and *The Wiz* and *Eubie* and were especially pleased that these shows were black produced. This hadn't happened since the 1900's—black producers on Broadway. We "serious" folk called these shows "irrelevant" and "not serious" because there Black folks were singing and dancing again, even if, this time, to our own drummer. For an under-standing of what was going on, we could have learned from our history. What was happening had happened before when those gallant pioneers Jesse Shipp, Bob Cole, John Isham, Williams and Walker, J. Rosamond Johnson and oth-ers defied minstrelsy and created what was later to become "the American musical"—they did this with the Lafayette Theatre and, later, with the efforts of Dick Campbell, Abram Hill and the Federal Theatre of the '30s. Each time, we were co-opted and eventually locked out altogether.

In 1983, there was a "new musical" on Broadway. It was called *Amen Corner,* and the program notes indicated, in the *tiniest* of print, that it was "based on the play *Amen Corner*" by James Baldwin! Sure enough, a powerful and moving drama had been turned into a coon show by a white artistic staff, who projected lines like "Jesus don't work for Chase Manhattan, I buy my goods on time" in pseudo-Gospel rhythms. History repeats.

The fact that there is both a commercial and a non-profit theater in this country does not help matters. The stage is a profession for some, a hobby for others, a platform for many, and for a few an outlet for insanity. Every ounce of energy is consumed either working or looking for work. When work comes, it is rewarded either by a vulgar sum or an embarrassing pittance. That work is then subjected to evaluation by real and self-styled critics of all races, who participate in the making and breaking of careers. This situation produces, overall, the most unhealthy narcissism in artists with very little room being left to develop the kind of humanity and commitment that the advancement of Black people in the theater arts demands. No black artist can afford to live within himself alone, any more than he can live on carfare alone.

Is the present rat-race system so firmly entrenched that change is impos-sible? Are there reasonable alternatives? Unless we are reconciled to a theater that serves only as a vehicle for aspiring individuals to move themselves higher on the celebrity scale, we will have to make a change.

There are positive signs. Some theater companies are now re-doing black classics that critics consigned to the graveyard; theater groups in different states are exchanging work, and still others have taken the theater into the churches, prisons, bars and streets instead of waiting for the audience to come to them. Theater-related organizations like AUDELCO are working on developing new audiences—now we must produce and polish the work.

Some celebrities have demonstrated a high degree of consciousness, and we should acknowledge them when they do—we must learn to select our own role models before the media does. Even many theater people do not know about Ira Aldridge or about the pain of Bert Williams. Dick Gregory has always been on the front lines. John Ames and Robert Guillaume have brought dignity to the tube in what could have been age-old stereotypes. Why don't we see Poitier's *Buck and the Preacher* in community centers and churches, along with other film representations of our early history that are aging somewhere on a shelf? What are we waiting for? Lena Horne took a black band and a black female musical director with her to Broadway and gave us a lifetime of history in an evening of singing and dancing.

Each day, new and wonderful black works are being read in places like New York's Frank Silvera workshop, but no real network exists to assure them a long life. It must not be Broadway or die. A compelling example we might learn from lies across the sea in South Africa. The Black people of that troubled land use the stage as their means of cultural expression, as well as political dissent. There are active black theater groups in every major South African city dramatizing the struggles and dreams of the people. It is "serious" theater, and yet, in addition to crying and cursing, it is a theater that laughs and sings and dances. Times are terrible in South Africa, but the theater is at its best.

If the Afro-American tradition in theater is to survive, there must begin to emerge among artists a collective commitment, a will to connect with life outside of ourselves, our neighborhoods, our regions, a will to change the world by becoming a part of it. Otherwise, what we do is show business, not theater. And that is how we will be remembered.

Suggested Reading with Similar Theme:

Shannon, Sandra G. *The Dramatic Vision of August Wilson*. Washington, D.C.: Howard University Press, 1995.

JOANNE V. GABBIN

The Poetry of Sterling A. Brown:
A Study in Form and Meaning (1985)

How is the craft of Sterling Brown influenced by spirituals, work songs, blues and dialect of African American culture? What is the significance of the ballad in Brown's poetry? Define the "blues-ballad" as an art form. Describe Brown as a folk poet. How does Brown exemplify a Black Poetics?

With the same literary perspective used in recreating folk subjects and themes, [Sterling] Brown adopted the language and form of Black folklore. In his poetry the language of Black folk—the dialect, the idioms, the imagery, the style—retains its richness and verve. Likewise, the spirituals, blues, ballads, work songs, tall tales, and aphorisms achieve another level of expressiveness as they are absorbed and integrated. Not once doubting the efficacy of folk speech to express all that the people were, Brown brought the use of dialect in poetry to new respectable heights, despite a debate over its value as a literary medium.

In 1922 James Weldon Johnson, writing in the preface of *The Book of American Negro Poetry,* recognized that Black writers were breaking away from the use of conventionalized Negro dialect. The long association of this kind of dialect with the conventionalized treatment of Black character had convinced Johnson and other writers like Countee Cullen that the poet could not "adequately or artistically" treat a broad spectrum of Black life using this medium. Though Johnson generally applauded the tendency to discard dialect, he feared that Black poets, in an attempt to disassociate themselves from the spurious, often demeaning, traditions of dialect poetry, would lose the "quaint and musical folk speech as a medium of expression." Johnson's indictment, then, was not against dialect, as such, "but against the mold of convention in which Negro dialect in the United States had been set." In his now classic call for originality and authenticity in racial poetry, he anticipated a form of expression that would not limit the poet's emotional and intellectual response to Black American life.

> What the colored poet in the United States needs to do is something like what Synge did for the Irish; he needs to find a form that will express the racial spirit by symbols from within rather than by symbols from without, such as the mere

mutilation of English spelling and pronunciation. He needs a form that is freer and larger than dialect, but which will still hold the racial flavor; a form expressing the imagery, the idioms, the peculiar turns of thought, and the distinctive humor and pathos, too, of the Negro, but which will also be capable of voicing the deepest and highest emotions and aspirations, and allow the widest range of subjects and the widest scope of treatment.

Ten years later Brown, with the publication of *Southern Road,* comes as close to achieving Johnson's ideal of original racial poetry as any Black American poet had before. Appropriately, Johnson had the distinction of introducing Brown's poems to the American reading public.

Mr. Brown's work is not only fine, it is also unique. He began writing just after the Negro poets had generally discarded conventionalized dialect with its minstrel traditions to Negro life (traditions that had but slight relation, often no relation at all, to actual Negro life) with its artificial and false sentiment, its exaggerated geniality and optimism. He infused his poetry with genuine characteristic flavor by adopting as his medium the common, racy, living speech of the Negro in certain phases of real life.

In Brown, Johnson recognized a poet who mined the "unfailing sources" of Black poetry to enrich his own poems. He saw Brown exploring with uncompromising honesty the range of characteristically folk responses—the stoicism in "Memphis Blues," the tragic despair in "Southern Road," the ironical humor of the Slim Greer series, the alienation of "Revelations," and the impulse to keep moving in such poems as "Odyssey of Big Boy" and "Long Gone"—which rang true to Johnson as they would have to the folk themselves.

Brown's exploration of the range of their responses led him to the sacred songs, the spirituals. "As the best expression of the slaves' deepest thoughts and yearnings," the spirituals are emotional, imaginative, and visionary. They reflect, often in rhythms as striking as the melodies are beautiful, the religious nature of Black folk. Their expression of emotions that move to tears and joy, their imaginative interpretation of life and scripture, their fascination with Biblical characters, their preoccupation with sin, evil, and the devil, their personal relationship with "King Jesus" and God, and their visionary treatment of heaven, hell and judgment day are all revealed in these songs.

Many of the essential qualities, themes, and idioms of the spirituals, Brown succeeds in transferring to his own poetry. In "New Steps," an infrequently quoted poem in *Southern Road,* Brown imaginatively handles the themes of saints and sinners competing for the soul of a young man. Here the battle of good and evil is worked out in a rather homely fashion. Sister Annie, overjoyed with the fine "new steps a-climbing to de little Church do'," remains strong in the faith that the church will save her son from ruin. Encouraged that the church is now fine enough to attract her wayward son, she "struts herself down to the sinful Foot." To her disappointment, she sees that the sinners are busy sprucing up the dens of iniquity, "puttin' green paint" on "poolroom den" and "sportin' new lace next the dirty panes." Brown uses a language whose cadence and tone are reminiscent of the spiritual "By an' By," in which the unknown bard sings, "O, by an' by / I'm gwinter lay down my heavy load." He shows Sister Annie continuing the battle against sin in a gesture of one-upmanship though the weight of her armor seems onerous.

> Up de new steps that meeting' night
> Sister Annie drug a heavy an' a weary load.
> New steps a-climbin'—
> O my Lawd
> Lace curtains snow white
> Snow white curtains
> O my Lawd
> Upstairs, downstairs,
> New steps
> O my Lawd. . . .

Though the poet does not reveal who finally wins out, his message is clear and parallels thematically that of the traditional religious song, "Workin' on the Building."

> If I wus a sinner man, I tell you what
>   I'd do,
> I'd lay down all my sinful ways an' work
>   on the building too.
> I'm workin' on the building
>   fer my Lord,
>   Fer my Lord, fer my Lord,
> I'm workin' on the building fer my Lord
>   I'm working on the building, too.

Continuing to work on the building, Sister Annie is a symbol of religious faith and spiritual fortitude.

"New Steps" mirrors the form of spiritual songs and projects the Christian concepts of faith, love, humility, and salvation. Many of the songs retell in capsulized, often dramatic, form significant events and stories recorded in the Old and New Testaments. Some, however, make no direct allusion to Biblical scenes but are inspired by local events, sermons, or the desire for religious social comment. In "New Steps," Brown adopts the dramatic form of many spirituals to spotlight Sister Annie's attempt to bring her boy to salvation. The characters in the story are allegorized (Brother Luck, Miss Joy, Victory). They add to the symbolic richness of the poem in which every element of the setting—"new steps," "the dingy house," "the big white letters," "snow white curtains"—is charged with a metaphorical meaning like that evoked by the chariot, the wheel, and gospel shoes, standard images in the spirituals.

The language in the poem is characterized by economy of statement, and vivid, fresh images: "An the dingy house . . . / Runnin' over wid jazz an' scarlet noise." Brown also punctuates the poem with interjections—"Oh my Lawd"—a typical feature of Black music, and he occasionally, "worries the line" as he has his narrator interject bits of wisdom.

> Good times, seems like, ain't fuh las'—
> Nebber de real good times, dey ain't—

Finally Brown uses an effective incremental style in the chorus to evoke the most powerful image of the poem.

> O my Lawd
> Upstairs, downstairs
> New steps
> O my Lawd. . . .

The themes, the qualities, and the idiom characteristic of the spiritual receive their fullest exploration in another poem appearing in *Southern Road*, "When De Saints Go Ma'ching Home." Using two carefully selected similes and incorporating into his poem a line from the spiritual, he suggests the quiet dignity and solemnity of Big Boy Davis as he tunes up his guitar to play his "mother's favorite."

> Carefully as an old maid over needlework,
> Oh, as some black deacon, over his Bible, lovingly,
> He'd tune up specially for this. There'd be
> No chatter now, no patting of the feet.
> After a few slow chords, knelling and sweet—
> Oh when de saints go ma'chin' home,
> Oh when de sayaints goa ma'chin' home . . .
> He would forget
> The quieted bunch, his dimming cigarette
> Stuck into a splintered edge of the guitar;
> Sorrow deep hidden in his voice, a far
> And soft light in his strange brown eyes;
> Alone with his masterchords, his memories. . . .

As Big Boy sang the saints' triumph song, he would see "a gorgeous procession" of the faithful, those who had held out to the end, marching to the "Beulah Land." There would be Old Deacon Zachary and Sis Joe. Elder Peter Johnson, "steamin' up de grade / Lak Wes' bound No. 9," and "little brown skinned chillen / Wid deir skinny legs a-dancin' would join the heavenly band." However, white folk, as goes his dream, would "have to stay outside."

In keeping with God's promise to take care of his own, those who had shunted him would not be kept behind. Heaven is a place reserved for the righteous, and his folk shall occupy the best place. There would be "another mansion fo' white saints." Ironically, his vision of heaven takes on the pattern of earthly existence; segregation will be preserved.

According to Big Boy's dream, God's judgment was not color blind; it would fall as evenly on the Black folk as the white. Big Boy's buddies—Sportin' Legs and Lucky Sam, Smitty, Hambone, and Hardrock George—would go the way of "guzzlin', cuttin' shines" and bootleggers. Even Sophie, his strappin' brown, could not fit in with the saints of God. One, though, was assured a place. He sees his mother's "wrinkled face, / Her brown eyes, quick to tears—to joy."

> Mammy
> With deep religion defeating the grief
> Life piled so closely about her
> Ise so glad trouble doan last alway,
> And her dogged belief
> That some fine day
> She'd go a-ma'chin'
> When de saints go ma'chin' home.

Part of the effectiveness of the poem lies in Brown's skillful mixture of idiom and his evocation of religious imagery and lyrics in the spiritual. In profiling the saints in the heavenly band, Brown uses folk dialect to clothe the humble and simple faith they brought to their religion. Interspersed with the more formal language, these passages stand in bold relief.

"When De Saints Go Ma'ching Home" is one of the best examples of Brown's effective use of structure. Using the music of this spiritual as his dominant poetic referent, Brown has Big Boy's rendition of this favorite spiritual come alive with the fervor, ecstasy, and drama of Black religious music. Brown uses several of the techniques identified by Stephen Henderson in his important book *Understanding the New Black Poetry*. Brown makes a clear allusion to the song title and adopts it as the title of his poem. The title has the power to evoke the image of a bodacious New Orleans band parading from the cemetery amid the rejoicing of those who are very much alive, or Louis "Satchmo" Armstrong irreligiously belting out the "chant of saints," in one hand his handkerchief which has become a cliche and in the other hand his trumpet which will never be one. Brown forces the reader to incorporate into the structure of the poem his memory of specific passages from the spiritual. Here Big Boy sings the song with solemn, slow chords from his guitar. Brown takes care to write in the inflection and the syncopation.

> Oh when de saints go ma'chin' home
> Oh when de sayaints goa ma'chin' home. . . .

Above all, "When De Saints Go Ma'ching Home" is performance. Brown presents in six dramatic scenes the singer's remarkable vision. Attributing to his singer the skill of the visionary minister who, touched by the Holy Fire, recreates heaven's alabaster gates, the streets of gold, and the manna on celestial tables to coax his reluctant sheep to the fold, the poet imaginatively reenacts the singer's performance. Each section relates a different aspect of the singer's vision, as though the vision were a series of stills that could be viewed separately or run together to produce the moving picture. Kimberly W. Benston, in a brilliant exegesis of the poem, writes that it is "the mode of seeing the hero's songs, the perspectivizing of performance, which constitutes the inner concern" of the poem. In each section the "envisaged saints exist as possibilities not memories, which none is actually present but everyone, under the hero's watchful 'gaze' is immanently represented."

As performance, the poem speaks to the separation between singer and audience, between the self and the community. Benston sees the disjunction between the singer and the audience producing the "deep tension" in the poem and representing its "true subject." This "disjunction" is readily apparent in the structures of the poem. Benston writes, "The poem is framed by acute recognition of this discontinuity: 'He'd play after the bawdy songs and blues . . . he'd go where we / Never could flow'—divorce figured in the distinctions between 'he' and 'we' (self and community) and between the hero and poet (voice/dialect and text/formal diction)." Ultimately, by separating himself from his audience, the singer is capable of a higher vision that has the power to convince his hearers of their own possibility of revision, renewal and re-creation.

In Brown's "Sister Lou," one of the most remarkable monologues in American literature, the speaker—much like the Indian-looking woman Brown met in Coolwell, Virginia—compresses her higher vision of heaven in images as familiar as hearthside implements. Sister Lou at the bedside of an ailing friend bolsters her courage with the familiar images of old dear friends that she will meet "When de man / Calls out de las' train."

Sister Lou has the train, the dominant symbol of escape and separation in folk parlance, serve as the heavenly chariot to take her friend "home." As with the folk, in the imagination of Sister Lou "the scenes of everyday life form continuous allegories" with the material found in the Bible. The woman, when she gets home, would show "Marfa" how to make "greengrape jellies" and bake "a passel of Golden Biscuits" for poor Lazarus, "scald some meal for li'l box plunkin' David and tell the Hebrew children her stories."

> Give a good talkin' to
> To yo' favorite 'postle Peter,
> An' rub the po'head
> Of mixed-up Judas,
> An' joke awhile wid Jonah.

Matching the pantheon of Biblical heroes given in the spirituals, Brown establishes what he believes to be the intimate relationship that exists between Black folk and the heavenly host. Among them, they would be accepted. In heaven, there would be no back doors. "No mo' dataway / Not evah no mo!" There would be pearly gates and their own room, "Openin' on cherry trees an' plum trees / Bloomin' everlastin'." The saints would be compensated for enduring hardship and suffering pain. The folk had faith that their "belief in God enabled them to cling on to life, though poor, miserable, and dying, looking to God and expecting Him, through miraculous and spectacular means, to deliver them from their plight."

Sometimes, however, their faith is shaken. In the poem, "Children of the Mississippi," the victims of the Mississippi flood recall the story of Noah but wonder why they did not receive the sign.

> De Lord tole Norah
> Dat de flood was due,
> Norah listened to de Lord
> An' got his stock on board,
> Wish dat de Lord
> Had tole us too.

In another poem, "Crossing," Brown fuses the doubting of escaping slaves with the spiritual doubting of Christians. As in the spirituals, the freedom from sin gets all mixed up with physical freedom from oppression.

> We do not know
> If any have reached that Canaan
> We have received no word.
> Behind us the belling pack
> Beyond them the hunters
> Before us the dismal swamp.
> We do not know. . . .

It is appropriate that Brown couches their doubts in the poignant language of the sacred songs, for each journey involves uncertainty. Incorporating lines from several traditional songs, Brown effects, as Stephen Henderson suggested in *Understanding the New Black Poetry,* "a particularized response" resulting from the subjective feeling stirred by the reference. Henderson calls this technique the use of "subjective correlative," in contrast to the objective correlative that gained currency in the New Criticism. The following lines illustrates the technique:

> We know only
> That there lies not Canaan
> That this is no River Jordan.

> Still are we motherless children
> Still are we dragging travelers
> Alone, and a long ways from home.
>
> Still with the hard earth for our folding bed
> Still with our head pillowed upon a rock
>
> And still
> With one more river,
> Oh, one wide river to cross.

These lines evoke several spirituals. Dominating the poem is an allusion to the spiritual, "Wasn't Dat a Wide River."

> Oh, Jordan's River is deep and wide
> One mo' river to cross
> I don't know how to get on de other side
> One mo' river to cross.

The "ancient dusky rivers," that Hughes made symbols of the continuity of this people's racial spirit, for Brown become symbols of obstacles that must be bridged. Those who "leapt / From swamp land / Into marshes," those who "grow footsore / and muscle weary" inherit the hardships of their ancestors and stand in need of the encouragement and solace provided by the spirituals. Intrinsic to Brown's language are references to the spiritual lyrics: "Sometime I feel like a motherless child . . . A long ways from home" and "Let us cheer the weary traveler, along the heavenly way." However, his language is formal; departing from the dialect of the sacred song, it reflects a new period of struggle. The "crossing" is not to be considered entirely otherwordly—"This is not Jordan River / There lies not Canaan"—but the crossing represents also the immediate and real crossing over to freedom. . . .

Sterling Brown and his contemporary, Langston Hughes, more than any other New Negro writers, explored the oral tradition and experimented with its forms in the belief that Black folk were creating valuable, original art. They put great stock in the virtuosity of folk expression; they prized its innovation, its freshness of style, and its inclusive quality as artistic exemplars. Of all the forms, the blues received the greatest exploration in their poetry. According to Stephen Henderson, Hughes and Brown "expand and amplify the form without losing its distinctive blues flavor. Poems like Hughes' 'The Weary Blues' and 'Montage of a Dream Deferred' and Brown's 'Memphis Blues' suggest something of their range, even in their respective first volumes of poetry."

Brown's absorption and intensification of the blues form and feeling vary from poem to poem. In "Long Track Blues," Brown, handling the twin blues themes of loving and leaving, departs from the three-line stanza typical of the classic blues but uses the two-line form, the sentiments, the language, and verbal conventions of the standard blues. As folk artists had done before, he makes the railroad "the favored symbol of escape." He renders with fidelity the melancholy of a man who has lost his "lovin' babe."

> Heard a train callin'
> Blowin' long ways down the track;
> Ain't no train due here,
> Baby, what can bring you back?

The familiar ingredients are all here: the distant whistle of the train, the howling dog, the beckoning signal lights, the brakeman's lantern, all of which combine to express the man's lament. A comparison of the stanza from a folk blues and one from Brown's poem shows his close study of the form.

> I went down to de depot, I looked
> upon de board,
> Couldn't see no train, couldn't hear no
> whistle blow.

> Went down to the yards
> To see the signal lights come on;
> Looked down the track
> Where my lovin' babe done gone.

An analysis of these two stanzas shows that Brown approximates the cadence of the blues line with four stresses. He also uses an idiom that captures the sound and sense of railroad lore. However, in this poem the poet runs the risk of being, as George Kent suggests, "too reliant upon a folk form that has, itself, the alliance of the singing voice, instrumental music, facial expression and gesture, to drive itself into our spirit." Yet, to articulate the deeply personal feeling of departure and loss, Brown utilizes symbolism, among other literary conventions, to increase the power of the blues poem, stripped of the oral resources of the blues song. An example is the following stanza:

> Red light in my block,
> Green light down the line;
> Lawdy, let yo' green light
> Shine down on that babe o' mine.

The red light and green light that usually function to keep the rail traffic unsnarled, here have symbolic significance. The red light is a symbol for hard times, bad luck and danger; the green light is a symbol of good times, success, and safety. And on another level the green light represents the presence of spiritual grace and protection. Out there, somewhere down the line is grief, ugly grief,—not to be denied. Hauntingly, the poem suggests the poignancy that comes with preparing to face grief and loss and death.

In another poem, "Rent Day Blues," Brown, using extended dialogue, tells the story of a couple facing rent day without any money. As the man wonders where they will get the rent, his woman turns up with the money from a mysterious source. Though the man is briefly troubled, he finally resolves to let their good fortune stand. In "Rent Day Blues," Brown clearly presents one of the major themes of the blues—poverty and economic uncertainty—within the context of the blues' preoccupation with the love relationship. Here, Brown breaks with the blues tradition by having his blues poem "proceed in a narrative fashion." According to blues critic Charles Keil, the blues lyric rarely proceeds in this fashion but "is designed primarily to illustrate a particular theme or create a general mood." Using dialogue as a narrative technique, Brown is able to add a dramatic dimension and bits of characterization not typical of the blues lyric. For example, in the following stanzas the willingness of the woman to get the rent money any way she can and the man's suspicions and cynicism come through clearly.

> My baby says, "Honey,
> Dontcha worry 'bout the rent,
> Looky here, daddy,
> At de money what de good Lord sent."
>
> Says to my baby,
> "Baby, I been all aroun';
> Never knowed de good Lord
> To send no greenbacks down."

Brown is also experimenting with the rhythm of the blues poem. For example, he infuses a jazz-style offbeat rhythm in the poem. The established pattern appears to be iambic trimeter. However, in the first stanza cited above, the last line breaks from this basic pattern with a syncopated pentameter line. In a solidly aesthetic gesture, Brown is taking on the risk and challenge of the literary rather than the oral poet. . . .

In "Ma Rainey," one of the finest poems in *Southern Road*, Brown skillfully brings together the ballad and blues forms and, demonstrating his inventive genius, creates the blues-ballad. On one level, the poem gives a glimpse of the folk heroine, Ma Rainey. Gertrude "Ma" Rainey, on the vaudeville circuit at the age of fourteen, "heard the blues while trouping up and down her native south land, and started singing them herself to audiences that were spellbound as her deep, husky voice gave them back their songs." In many ways the mother of the blues, she took a youngster named Bessie Smith in her care and lovingly taught her the blues, and the child grew strong in timbre, cadence, and resonance, like her "Ma." Befitting the title Madam "Ma" Rainey, she made her entrance on innumerable stages with a sequined gown hugging her short, stocky frame, an elaborate gold necklace, tasseled earrings, and a brilliant gold-tooth grin crowning it all. Her professionalism was hard won in the Black minstrel shows, medicine shows, traveling road shows, and vaudeville shows where she trained her raspy voice to complement the new instrumental blues stylings.

But even more than being a portrait of the venerated blues singer, the poem serves as an emotional portrait of the people who flocked to hear "Ma do her stuff."

> An' some jokers keeps deir laughs a-going' in de crowded aisles,
> An' some folks sits dere waitin' wid deir aches an' miseries, . . .

Brown celebrates Ma Rainey's charisma that is more than flashy jewelry and sequined gown. He celebrates her skill in the art of improvisation, which Albert Murray says "will enable contemporary man to be at home with his sometimes tolerable but never quite certain condition of not being at home in the world and will also dispose him to regard his obstacles and frustrations as well as his achievements in terms of adventures and romance." Like Larry Neal and Ralph Ellison, Brown also celebrates the power of the blues singer "to reflect the horrible and beautiful realities of life" and to affirm "the value of the group and man's ability to deal with chaos."

In "Ma Rainey," Brown has the blues mode function thematically and structurally to heighten the effect of the poem. In the poem he also uses a technique that is a common practice among several poets. Henderson describes the practice as "forcing the reader to incorporate into the structure of the poem his memory of a specific song or passage of a song, or even of a specific delivery technique." Throughout Brown's poetry there are several examples of this technique. "When De Saints Go Ma'ching Home," "Strong Men," and "Revelations" are among the most notable examples. In the final section of the poem, Brown incorporates Bessie Smith's popular "Backwater Blues." The song, by suggesting the hardships and suffering of the victims of the Mississippi Valley floods, illustrates the dire problems faced by these people and gives, as Charles H. Rowell suggests, an "air of immediacy to the poem."

Brown has also fused the blues form with the ballad to invent the "blues-ballad," which Henderson hails as "a literary phenomenon . . . as distinctive as Wordsworth's lyrical ballad." As structurally effective as it is innovative, the blues-ballad combines the narrative framework of the ballad and the ethos of the blues. The ingenuity of his invention can be best appreciated when one sees how the two traditions come together in a blues-ballad like "Ma Rainey."

Ballads telling of the exploits of Black folk heroes, similar to sixteen-bar or eight-bar ballads of Anglo-Saxon origin, began to appear in America during the second half of the nineteenth century. With the abolition of slavery, Black folk, facing the prospect of freedom, were inspired to compose songs dedicated to the virtues and deeds of their heroes. These ballads bear their names: "John Hardy," "John Henry," "Casey Jones," "Railroad Bill," "Stagolee," and "Frankie and Johnny," among others. Aware of English, Irish, Scottish, and French ballad styles, Black balladeers adopted the classic ballad form which tells a story in a series of stanzas, usually in a progressive, chronologically developed narrative with or without a refrain.

At the close of the century, blues developed as a form out of the hollers of the solitary farmers who worked the rows of Southern fields. Often they sang their hollers, repeating the lines until new lines came to mind that completed the thought and expressed the emotion.

With the introduction of the guitar, capable of producing the moaning, whining, flattened sounds of the human voice, blues took shape. Though the early blues had the eight-bar or sixteen-bar stanzaic structure like the ballads, with the experimentation with the "blues notes" and the African pentatonic scale, the "twelve-bar blues" evolved. The most common but by no means the only structure consisted of three lines of four bars each.

Within this structure, the blues singer improvises his music, and in the act of creation he draws from a stock of favorite verses and familiar rhythmic patterns, and combines them with new lines extemporized out of his melancholy experience. He sings of love and infidelity, poverty and economic uncertainty, lonely travel and dislocation, drinking and drugs, and disasters and death. Unlike the balladeer who extols the virtues of a distant hero, the blues singer is the central character in this song. Therefore, the blues singers themselves become heroes to their hearers. Brownie McGhee, Blind Willie McTell, Huddie "Leadbelly" Ledbetter, Blind Lemon Jefferson, Gertrude "Ma" Rainey, Bessie Smith, Clara Smith, Mamie Smith, Ida Cox—the names are legion—look on their personal calamities and are not destroyed.

Clearly in this cultural tradition, Brown, with a conscious artistry, combines the intensely personal music of the blues singer with the heroic tales and epic scope of the balladeer. The genius of this invention is apparent in "Ma Rainey." Brown takes the explicit, chronological, and narrative elements of the ballad to tell how the people flock in to hear "Ma Rainey do her stuff." And though the ballad form functions well to spotlight this magnificent woman with the "gold-toofed smiles," it cannot accommodate the intimacy, the immediacy, and the emotional intensity that Brown intends for the poem. He needs the blues ethos to suggest the massive concentration of emotion present among the folk in Ma's audience—the work-weary soul, the laughing to keep from crying, the unspeakable sorrow, the needful catharsis. . . .

Suggested Readings with Similar Theme:

Henderson, Stephen E. "The Heavy Blues of Sterling Brown: A Study of Craft and Tradition." *Black American Literature Forum* 14, no. 1 (Spring 1980): 32–49.
Rampersad, Arnold. "Langston Hughes' *Fine Clothes To The Jew.*" *Callaloo* 9, no. 1 (Winter 1986): 144–58.

HENRY LOUIS GATES JR.

Signifyin(g): Definitions [and Theory] (1988)

What makes signifyin(g) "so fundamentally black"? Identify the numerous rhetorical modes of signifyin(g). According to Gates, Smitherman, Henderson, Williams, Andrews, and Hubbard, how is black speech a poetic reference? Define the following terms: encoded vernacular, revision, indirection, double-voiced, intertextuality, embedded trope, free-indirect discourse, trope of Talking Book.

One of the most sustained attempts to define Signifyin(g) is that of Roger D. Abrahams, a well-known and highly regarded literary critic, linguist, and anthropologist. Abrahams published several significant studies of Signifyin(g). To tract Abraham's interpretative evolution helps us to understand the complexities of this rhetorical strategy but is outside the scope of this book.

Abrahams in 1962 brilliantly defines Signifyin(g) in terms that he and other subsequent scholars shall repeat:

> The name "Signifying Monkey" shows [the hero] to be a trickster, "signifying" being the language of trickery, that set of words or gestures which arrives at "direction through indirection."

Signifyin(g), Abrahams argues implicitly, is the black person's use of figurative modes of language use. The word indirection hereafter recurs in the literature with great, if often unacknowledged, frequency. Abrahams explained on this theory of Signifyin(g) in two editions of *Deep Down in the Jungle* (1964, 1970). It is useful to list the signal aspects of his extensive definitions:

1. Signifyin(g) "can mean any number of things."
2. It is a black term and a black rhetorical device.
3. It can mean the "ability to talk with great innuendo."
4. It can mean "to carp, cajole, needle, and lie."
5. It can mean "the propensity to talk around a subject, never quite coming to the point."
6. It can mean "making fun of a person or situation."
7. It can "also denote speaking with the hands and eyes."
8. It is "the language of trickery, that set of words achieving Hamlet's 'direction through indirection.' "
9. The Monkey "is a 'signifier,' and the Lion, therefore, is the signified."

Finally, in his appended glossary of "Unusual Terms and Expressions," Abrahams defines "Signify" as "To imply, goad, beg, boast by indirect verbal or gestural means. A language of implication."

These definitions are exemplary insofar as they emphasize "indirection" and "implication," which we read as synonyms of figurative. Abrahams was the first scholar, to my knowledge, to define Signifyin(g) as a language, by which he means a particular rhetorical strategy. Whereas he writes that the Monkey is a master of this technique, it is even more accurate to write that he is technique, the literariness of language, the ultimate source for black people of the figures of signification. If we think of rhetoric as the "writing" of spoken discourse, then the Monkey's role as the source and encoded keeper of Signifyin(g) helps to reveal his functional equivalency with his Pan-African cousin, Esu-Elegbara, the figure of writing of Ifa. . . .

When a black person speaks of Signifyin(g), he or she means a "style-focused message . . . styling which is foregrounded, of course, is the signified itself, as we have seen in the rhyme scheme of the Monkey tales. The Monkey is called the signifier because he foregrounds the signifier in his use of language. Signifyin(g), in other words, turns on the sheer play of the signifier. It does not refer primarily to the signified; rather, it refers to the style of language, to that which transforms ordinary discourse into literature. Again, one does not Signify some thing; one Signifies in some way. . . .

While several other scholars have discussed the nature and function of Signifyin(g), the theories of Claudia-Mitchell-Kernan and Geneva Smitherman are especially useful for the theory or revision that I am outlining in this chapter. Mitchell-Kernan's theory of Signifyin(g) is among the most thorough and the most subtle in the linguistic literature, while Smitherman's work connects linguistic analysis with the Afro-American literary tradition.

Mitchell-Kernan is quick to demonstrate that Signifyin(g) has received most scholarly attention as "a tactic employed in game activity—verbal dueling—which is engaged in as an end in itself," as if this one aspect of the rhetorical concept amounted to its whole. In fact, however, "Signifying . . . also refers to a way of encoding messages or meanings which involves, in most cases, an element of indirection." This alternative definition amounts to nothing less than a polite critique of the linguistic studies of Signifyin(g), since the subtleties of this rhetorical strategy somehow escaped most other scholars before Mitchell-Kernan. As she expands her definition, "This kind of signifying is not focal to the linguistic interaction in the sense that it does not define the entire speech event."

I cannot stress too much the importance of this definition, for it shows that Signifyin(g) is a pervasive mode of language use rather than merely one specific verbal game, an observation that somehow escaped the notice of every other scholar before Mitchell-Kernan. This definition alone serves as a corrective to what I think of as the tendency among linguists who have fixed their gaze upon the aggressive ritual part and thereby avoided seeing the concept as a whole. What's more, Mitchell-Kernan's definition points to the implicit parallels between Signifyin(g) and the use of language that we broadly define to be figurative, by which I mean in this context an intentional deviation from the ordinary form of syntactical relation of words.

Signifyin(g), in other words, is synonymous with figuration. Mitchell-Kernan's work is so rich because she studied the language behavior of adults as well as adolescents, and of women as well as men. Whereas her colleagues studied lower-class male language use, then generalized from this strictly limited sample, Mitchell-Kernan's data are derived from a sample more representative of the black speech community. Hers is a sample that does not undermine her data because it accounts for the role of age and sex as variables in language use. In addition, Mitchell-Kernan refused to be captivated by the verbal insult rituals, such as sounding, playing the dozens, and Signifyin(g), as ritual speech events, unlike other linguists whose work suffers from an undue attention to the use of words such as motherfucker, to insults that turn on sexual assertions about someone's mama, and to supposed Oedipal complexes that arise in the literature only because the linguist is reading the figurative as a literal statement, like our friend, the Signified Lion.

These scholars, unlike Mitchell-Kernan, have mistaken the language games of adolescents as an end rather than as the drills common to classical rhetorical study as suggested in Lanham's hypothetical synopsis quoted earlier in this chapter. As Mitchell-Kernan concludes, both the sex and the age of the linguist's informants "may slant interpretation, particularly because the insult dimension [of Signifyin(g)] looms large in contexts where verbal dueling is focal." In the neighborhood in which she was raised, she argues, whereas "Sounding and Playing the Dozens categorically involved verbal insult (typically joking behavior); signifying did not." Mitchell-Kernan is declaring, most unobtrusively, that, for whatever reasons, linguists have misunderstood what Signifyin(g) means to black people who practice it. While she admits that one relatively minor aspect of this rhetorical principle involves the ritual of insult, the concept is much more profound than merely this. Indeed, Signifyin(g) alone serves to underscore the uniqueness of the black community's use of language: "the terminological use of signifying to refer to a particular kind of language specialization defines the Black community as a speech community in contrast to non-Black communities." Mitchell-Kernan here both critiques the work of other linguists who have wrestled unsuccessfully with this difficult concept (specifically Abraham and Kochman) and provides an urgently needed corrective by defining Signifyin(g) as a way of figuring language. Mitchell-Kernan's penetrating work enables Signifyin(g) to be even further elaborated upon for use in literary theory.

Because it is difficult to arrive at a consensus of definitions of Signifyin(g), as this chapter already has made clear, Mitchell-Kernan proceeds "by way of analogy to inform the reader of its various meanings as applied in interpretation." This difficulty of definition is a direct result of the fact that Signifyin(g) is the black term for what in classical European rhetoric are called the figures of signification. Because to Signify is to be figurative, to define it in practice is to define it through any number of its embedded tropes. No wonder even Mitchell-Kernan could not arrive at a consensus among her informants—except for what turns out to be the most crucial shared aspects of all figures of speech, an indirect use of words that changes the meaning of a word or words. Or, as Quintilian put it, figuration turns on some sort of "change in signification." While linguists who disagree about what it means to Signify all repeat the role of indirection in this rhetorical strategy, none of them seems to have understood that the ensuing alteration or deviation of meaning makes Signifyin(g) the black trope for all other tropes, the trope of tropes, the figure of figures. Signifyin(g) is troping.

Mitchell-Kernan begins her elaboration of the concept by pointing to the unique usage of the word in black discourse:

> What is unique in Black English usage is the way in which signifying is extended to cover a range of meanings and events which are not covered in its Standard English usage. In the Black community it is possible to say, "He is signifying" and "Stop signifying"—sentences which would be anomalous elsewhere.

Because in standard English signification denotes meaning and in the black tradition it denotes ways of meaning, Mitchell-Kernan argues for discrepancies between meanings of the same term in two distinct discourses:

> The Black concept of signifying incorporates essentially a folk notion that dictionary entries for words are not always sufficient for interpreting meanings or messages, or that meaning goes beyond such interpretations. Complimentary remarks may be delivered in a left-handed fashion. A particular utterance may be an insult in one context and not another. What pretends to be informative may intend to be persuasive. The hearer is thus constrained to attend to all potential meaning carrying symbolic systems in speech events—the total universe of discourse.

Signifyin(g), in other words, is the figurative difference between the literal and the metaphorical, between surface and latent meaning. Mitchell-Kernan calls this feature of discourse an "implicit content or function, which is potentially obscured by the surface content or function." Finally, Signifyin(g) presupposes an "encoded" intention to say one thing but to mean quite another.

Mitchell-Kernan presents several examples of Signifyin(g), as she is defining it. Her first example is a conversation among three women about the meal to be served at dinner. One woman asks the other two to join her for dinner, that is, if they are willing to eat "chit'lins." She ends her invitation with a pointed rhetorical question: "Or are you one of those Negroes who don't eat chit'lins?" The third person, the woman not addressed, responds with a long defense of why she prefers "prime-rib and T-bone" to "chit'lins," ending with a traditional ultimate appeal to special pleading, a call to unity within the ranks to defeat racism. Then she leaves. After she has gone, the initial speaker replies to her original addressee in this fashion: "Well, I wasn't signifying at her, but like I always say, if the shoe fits wear it." Mitchell-Kernan concludes that while the manifest subject of this exchange was dinner, the latent subject was the political orientation of two black people vis-a-vis cultural assimilation or cultural nationalism, since many middle-class blacks refuse to eat this item from the traditional black cuisine. Mitchell-Kernan labels this form of Signifyin(g) "allegory," because "the significance or meaning of the words must be derived from known symbolic values."

This mode of Signifyin(g) is commonly practiced by Afro-American adults. It is functionally equivalent to one of its embedded tropes, often called louding or loud-talking, which as we might expect connotes exactly the opposite of that which it denotes: one successfully loud-talks by speaking to a second person remarks in fact directed to a third person, at a level just audible to the third person. A sign of the success of this practice is an indignant "What?" from the third person, to which the speaker responds, "I wasn't talking to you." Of course, the speaker was, yet simultaneously was not. Loud-talking is related to Mitchell-Kernan's second figure of Signification, which she calls "obscuring the addressee" and which I shall call naming. Her example is one commonly used in the tradition, in which "the remark is, on the surface, directed toward no one in particular":

> I saw a woman the other day in a pair of stretch pants, she must have weighed 300 pounds. If she knew how she looked she would burn those things.

If a member of the speaker's audience is overweight and frequently wears stretch pants, then this message could well be intended for her. If she protests, the speaker is free to maintain that she was speaking about someone else and to ask why her auditor is so paranoid. Alternatively, the speaker can say, "if the shoe fits. . . ." Mitchell-Kernan says that a characteristic of this form of Signifyin(g) is the selection of a subject that is "selectively relevant to the speaker's audience." I once heard a black minister name the illicit behavior of specific members of his congregation by performing a magnificent reading of "The Text of the Dry Bones," which is a reading or gloss upon Ezekiel 37:1–14. Following this sermon, a prayer was offered by Lin Allen. As "Mr. Lin," as we called him, said, "Dear Lord, go with the gambling man . . . not forgetting the gambling woman," the little church's eerie silence was shattered by the loud-talking voice of one of my father's friends (Ben Fisher, rest his soul), whom the congregation "overheard" saying, "Got you that time, Gates, got you that time, Newtsy!" My father and one of our neighbors, Miss Newtsy, had been Signified upon.

Mitchell-Kernan presents several examples of Signifyin(g) that elaborate on its subtypes. Her conclusion is crucial to the place of her research in the literature on Signification. "Signifying," she declares as conclusion, "does not . . . always have negative valuations attached to it; it is clearly thought of as a kind of art—a clever way of conveying messages." A literary critic might call this troping, an interpretation or mis-taking of meaning, to paraphrase Harold Bloom, because, as Mitchell-Kernan maintains, "signifying . . . alludes to and implies things which are never made explicit." Let me cite two brief examples. In the first, "Grace," introduces the exchange by defining its context:

> (After I had my little boy, I swore I was not having any more babies. I thought four kids was a nice-sized family. But it didn't turn out that way. I was a little bit disgusted and didn't tell anybody when I discovered I was pregnant. My sister came over one day and I had started to show by that time.) . . .
> Rochelle: Girl, you sure to need to join the Metrecal for lunch bunch.
> Grace: (non-committally) Yes, I guess I am putting on a little weight.
> Rochelle: Now look here, girl, we both standing here soaking wet and you still trying to tell me it ain't raining/

This form of Signifyin(g) is obviously a long way from the sort usually defined by scholars. One final example of the amusing, troping exchange follows, again cited by Mitchell-Kernan:

> I: Man, when you gon pay me my five dollars?
> II: Soon as I get it.
> I: (to audience) Anybody want to buy a five dollar nigger? I got one to sell.
> II: Man, if I gave you your five dollars, you wouldn't have nothing to signify about.
> I: Nigger, long as you don't change, I'll always have me a subject.

This sort of exchange is common in the black community and represents Signifyin(g) as its more evolved levels than the more obvious examples (characterized by confrontation and insult) discussed by linguists other than Mitchell-Kernan. . . .

II.

The black tradition is double-voiced. The trope of the Talking Book, of double-voiced text that talks to other texts, is the unifying metaphor within this book. Signifyin(g) is the figure of the double-voiced, epitomized by Esu's depictions in sculpture as possessing two mouths. There are four sorts of double-voiced textual relations that I wish to define.

Tropological Revision

By tropological revision I mean the manner in which a specific trope is repeated, with differences, between two or more texts. The revision of specific tropes recurs with surprising frequency in the Afro-American literary tradition. The descent underground, the vertical "ascent" from South to North, myriad figures of the double, and especially double consciousness all come readily to mind. But there are other tropes that would seem to preoccupy the texts of the black tradition. The first trope shared in the black narrative tradition is what I shall call the Talking Book. This compelling trope appears in James Gronniosaw's 1770 slave narrative, and then is revised in at least four other texts published between 1785 and 1815. We might think of this as the ur-trope of the tradition. The form that repetition and difference take among these texts is the first example of Signifyin(g) as repetition and difference in the Anglo-African narrative tradition.

The Speakerly Text

The second mode of Signifyin(g) that I have chosen to represent in this text is exemplified in the peculiar play of "voices" at work in the use of "free indirect discourse" in Zora Neale Hurston's *Their Eyes Were Watching God*. Above all else, Hurston's narrative strategy seems to concern itself with the possibilities of representation of the speaking black voice in writing. Hurston's text, I shall claim, seems to aspire to the status of what she and, later, Ishmael Reed call the Talking Book. It is striking that this figure echoes the first figure repeated and revised in the tradition. Hurston's use is remarkably complex, and accomplished. Free indirect discourse is represented in this canonical text as if it were a dynamic character, with shifts in its level of diction drawn upon to reflect a certain development of self-consciousness in a hybrid character, a character who is neither the novel's protagonist nor the text's disembodied narrator, but a blend of both, an emergent and merging moment of consciousness. The direct discourse of the novel's black speech community and the initial standard English of the narrator come together to form a third term, a truly double-voiced narrative mode. That element of narration that the Russian Formalists called skaz—when a text seems to be aspiring to the status of oral narration—is most clearly the closest analogue of Hurston's rhetorical strategy. The attendant ramifications of this device upon received modes of mimesis and diegesis occupy my attention in this chapter. Finally, I shall use Hurston's own theory of Signifyin(g) to analyze her narrative strategy, including the identification of Signifyin(g) rituals in the body of her text.

Talking Texts

Chapter 5 explores one instance of a black form of intertextuality. Within the limits of the metaphor of the double-voiced that I am tracing from Esu-Elegbara to Alice Walker's novel *The Color Purple,* I have chosen to explicate Reed's novel *Mumbo Jumbo* to show how black texts "talk" to other black texts. Since *Mumbo Jumbo* would seem to be a signal text of revision and critique, cast in a so-called postmodern narrative, the implicit relation among modernism, realism, and postmodernism comes to bear here in the texts of *Invisible Man, Native Son, Black Boy,* and *Mumbo Jumbo.* Again, the relation of mimesis to diegesis shall occupy my attention in *Mumbo Jumbo's* foregrounded double voices.

Rewriting the Speakerly

If Hurston's novel seems to have been designed to declare that, indeed, a text could be written in black dialect, then it seems to me that Walker's *The Color Purple* aims to do just that, as a direct revision of Hurston's explicit and implicit strategies of narration. Walker, whose preoccupation with Hurston as a deeply admired antecedent has been the subject of several of her critical comments, revises and echoes Hurston in a number of ways. Her use of the epistolary form to write a novel in the language seemingly spoken by Hurston's protagonist is perhaps the most stunning instance of revision in the tradition of the black novel. Here, let me introduce a distinction: Reed's use of parody would seem to be fittingly described as motivated Signifyin(g), in which the text Signifies upon other black texts, in the manner of the vernacular ritual of "close reading." Walker's use of pastiche, on the other hand, corresponds to unmotivated Signifyin(g), by which I mean to suggest not the absence of a profound intention but the absence of a negative critique. The relation between parody and pastiche is that between motivated and unmotivated Signifyin(g).

Whereas Reed seems to be about the clearing of a space of narration, Walker seems to be intent on underscoring the relation of her text to Hurston's, in a joyous proclamation of antecedent and descendant texts. The most salient analogue for this unmotivated mode of revision in the broader black cultural tradition might be that between black jazz musicians who perform each other's standards on a joint album, not to critique these but to engage in refiguration as an act of homage. Such an instance, one of hundreds, is the relationship between two jazz greats on the album they made together, Duke Ellington and John Coltrane. This form of the double-voiced implies unity and resemblance rather than critique and difference. The premise of this book is that the literary discourse that is most consistently "black," as read against our tradition's own theory of itself, is the most figurative, and that the modes of interpretation most in accord with the vernacular tradition's theory of criticism are those that direct attention to the manner in which language is used. Black texts Signify upon other black texts in the tradition by engaging in what Ellison has defined as implicit formal critiques of language use, of rhetorical strategy. Literary Signification, then, is similar to parody and pastiche, wherein parody corresponds to what I am calling motivated Signification while pastiche would correspond roughly to unmotivated Signification. By motivation I do not mean to suggest the lack of intention, for parody and pastiche imply intention, ranging from severe critique to acknowledgement and placement within a literary tradition. Pastiche can imply either homage to an antecedent text or futility in the face of a seemingly indomitable mode of representation. Black writers Signify on each other's texts for all of these reasons, and the relations of Signification that obtain between and among black texts serve as a basis for a theory of formal revision in the Afro-American tradition. Literary echoes, or pastiche, as found in Ellison's *Invisible Man,* of signal tropes found in Emerson, Eliot, Joyce, Crane, or Melville (among others) constitute one mode of Signifyin(g).

But so does Ellison's implicit rhetorical critique of the conventions of realism found in Richard Wright's *Native Son, The Man Who Lived Underground,* and *Black Boy.* Reed's parodies of Wright and Ellison constitute a Signification of a profoundly motivated order, especially as found in the text of *Mumbo Jumbo.* Hurston's multileveled use of voice in *Their Eyes Were Watching God* represents a Signification upon the entire tradition of dialect poetry as well as a brilliant and subtle critique of received notions of voice in the realistic novel, amounting to a remarkably novel critique and extension of Henry James's use of point-of-view as point-of-consciousness. Hurston's novel, like Sterling A. Brown's *Southern Road,* amounts to a refutation of critics such as James Welson [*sic*] Johnson who argued just six years before the publication of *Their Eyes* that the passing of dialect as a literary device among black authors was complete. Moreover, by representing her protagonist as a mulatto, who eschews the bourgeois life and marries a dark-complexioned migrant worker, Hurston Signifies upon the female novel of passing, an ironic form of fantasy that she inherited from Nella Larsen and Jessie Fauset. Finally, Walker's decision to place *The Color Purple* in a line of descent that runs directly from *Their Eyes* by engaging in a narrative strategy that tropes Hurston's concept of voice (by shifting it into the form of the epistolary novel and a written rather than a spoken vernacular) both extends dramatically the modes of revision available to writers in the tradition and reveals that acts of formal revision can be loving acts of bonding rather than ritual slayings at Esu's crossroads.

Suggested Reading with Similar Theme:

Mitchell-Kernan, Claudia. "Signifying." In *Mother Wit from the Laughing Barrel: Readings in the Interpretation of Afro-American Folklore, 310–28,* edited by Alan Dundes. Englewood Cliffs, N.J.: Prentice Hall. 1973. Reprint, Jackson: University Press of Mississippi, 1990.

HOMI K. BHABHA

Cultural Diversity and Cultural Differences
(1988)

Postcolonialist critic Homi Bhabha questions whether our focus on cultural diversity does not lead to polarization. He advocates focusing on cultural differences through a third space, a hybridity to define others and ourselves. How significant are the ideological positions of Franz Fanon and Wilson Harris on postcolonialism and colonial imperialism to Bhabha's concept? How does Bhabha enter discussions about differences with Snead? How might Bhabha be read along with Henry Louis Gates Jr. in "Writing 'Race,' and the Difference It Makes"? Define the following terms: hybridity, the Third Space, international culture, difference, diversity.

[The] revision of the history of critical theory rests . . . on the notion of cultural difference, not cultural diversity. Cultural diversity is an epistemological object—culture as an object of empirical knowledge—whereas cultural difference is the process of the enunciation of culture as "knowledgeable," authoritative, adequate to the construction of systems of cultural identification. If cultural diversity is a category of comparative ethics, aesthetics, or ethnology, cultural difference is a process of signification through which statements of culture or on culture differentiate, discriminate, and authorize the production of fields of force, reference, applicability, and capacity. Cultural diversity is the recognition of pre-given cultural "contents" and customs, held in a time-frame of relativism; it gives rise to anodyne liberal notions of multiculturalism, cultural exchange, or the culture of humanity. Cultural diversity is also the representation of a radical rhetoric of the separation of totalized cultures that live unsullied by the intertextuality of their historical locations, safe in the Utopianism of a mythic memory of a unique collective identity. Cultural diversity may even emerge as a system of the articulation and exchange of cultural signs in certain . . . imperialist accounts of anthropology.

Through the concept of cultural difference I want to draw attention to the common ground and lost territory of contemporary critical debates. For they all recognize that the problem of the cultural emerges only at the significatory boundaries of cultures, where meanings and values are misread or signs are misappropriated. . . .

The time of liberation is, as Fanon powerfully evokes, a time of cultural uncertainty, and most crucially, of significatory or representational undecidability:

> But [native intellectuals] forget that the forms of thought and what [they] feed
> . . . on, together with modern techniques of information, language and dress
> have dialectically reorganized the people's intelligences and *the constant principles (of national art)* which acted as safeguards during the colonial period are
> now undergoing extremely radical changes . . .[We] must join the people in
> that fluctuating movement which they are *just* giving a shape to . . . which will
> be the signal for everything to be called into question . . . it is to the zone of
> *occult instability* where the people dwell that we must come.
>
> (My emphasis) (Fanon 1967: 168)

The enunciation of cultural difference problematizes the division of past and present, tradition and modernity, at the level of cultural representation and its authoritative address. It is the problem of how, in signifying the present, something comes to be repeated, relocated, and translated in the name of tradition, in the guise of a pastness that is not necessarily a faithful sign of historical memory but a strategy of representing authority in terms of the artifice of the archaic. That iteration negates our sense of the origins of the struggle. It undermines our sense of the homogenizing effects of cultural symbols and icons, by questioning our sense of the authority of cultural synthesis in general.

This demands that we rethink our perspective on the identity of culture. Here Fanon's passage—somewhat reinterpreted—may be helpful. What is implied by his juxtaposition of the constant national principles with his view of culture-as-political-struggle, which he so enigmatically and beautifully describes as "the zone of occult instability where the people dwell"? These ideas not only help to explain the nature of colonial struggle. They also suggest a possible critique of the positive aesthetic and political values we ascribe to the unity or totality of cultures, especially those that have known long and tyrannical histories of domination and misrecognition. Cultures are never unitary in themselves, nor simply dualistic in relation to Self to Other. This is not because of some humanistic nostrum that beyond individual cultures we all belong to the human culture of mankind; nor is it because of an ethical relativism that suggests that in our cultural capacity to speak of and judge Others we necessarily "place ourselves in their position," in a kind of relativism of distance of which Bernard Williams has written at length (Williams 1985: ch. 9).

The reason a cultural text or system of meaning cannot be sufficient unto itself is that the act of cultural enunciation—the place of utterance—is crossed by the difference of writing or ecriture. This has less to do with what anthropologists might describe as varying attitudes to symbolic systems within different cultures than with the structure of symbolic representation—not the content of the symbol or its "social function," but the structure of symbolization. It is the "difference" in language that is crucial to the production of meaning and ensures, at the same time, that meaning is never simply mimetic and transparent.

The linguistic difference that informs any cultural performance is dramatized in the common semiotic account of the disjuncture between the subject of a proposition (enonce) and the subject of enunciation, which is not represented in the statement but which is the acknowledgment of its discursive embeddedness and address, its cultural positionality, its reference to a present time and a specific space. The pact of interpretation is never simply an act of communication between the I and the You designated in the statement. The production of meaning requires that these two places be mobilized in the passage through a Third Space, which represents both the general conditions of language and the specific implications of the utterance in a performative and institutional strategy of which it cannot "in itself" be conscious. What this unconscious relation introduces is an ambivalence in the act of interpretation. . . .

The intervention of the Third Space, which makes the structure of meaning and reference an ambivalent process, destroys this mirror of representation in which cultural knowledge is continuously revealed as an integrated, open, expanding code. Such an intervention quite properly challenges our sense of the historical identity of culture as a homogenizing, unifying force, authenticated by the originary Past, kept alive in the national tradition of the People. In other words, the disruptive temporality of enunciation displaces the narrative of the Western nation which Benedict Anderson so perceptively describes as being written in homogeneous, serial time (Anderson 1983: ch 2).

It is only when we understand that all cultural statements and systems are constructed in this contradictory and ambivalent space of enunciation, that we begin to understand why hierarchical claims to the inherent originality of "purity" of cultures are untenable, even before we resort to empirical historical instances that demonstrate their hybridity. Fanon's vision of revolutionary cultural and political change as a "fluctuating movement" of occult instability could not be articulated as cultural practice without an acknowledgment of this indeterminate space of the subject(s) of enunciation. It is that Third Space, though unrepresentable in itself, which constitutes the discursive conditions of enunciation that ensure that the meaning and symbols of culture have no primordial unity of fixity; that even the same signs can be appropriated, translated, rehistoricized, and read anew.

Fanon's moving metaphor—when reinterpreted for a theory of cultural signification—enables us to see not only the necessity of theory, but also the restrictive notions of cultural identity with which we burden our visions of political change. For Fanon, the liberatory "people" who initiate the productive instability of revolutionary cultural change are themselves the bearers of a hybrid identity. They are caught in the discontinuous time of translation and negotiation, in the sense in which I have been attempting to recast these works. In the moment of liberatory struggle, the Algerian people destroy the continuities and constancies of the "nationalist" tradition which provided a safeguard against colonial cultural imposition. They are now free to negotiate and translate their cultural identities in a discontinuous intertextual temporality of cultural difference. The native intellectual who identifies the people with the "true national culture" will be disappointed. The people are now the very principle of "dialectical reorganization" and they construct their culture from the national text translated into modern Western forms of information technology, language, dress. The changed political and historical site of enunciation transforms the meanings of the colonial inheritance into the liberatory signs of a free people of the future.

> I have been stressing a certain void or misgiving attending every assimilation of contraries—I have been stressing this in order to expose what seems to me a fantastic mythological congruence of elements . . . And if indeed therefore any real sense is to be made of material change it can only occur with an acceptance of a concurrent void and with a willingness to descend into that void wherein, as it were, one may begin to come into confrontation with a spectre of invocation whose freedom to participate in an alien territory and wilderness has become a necessity for one's reason or salvation.
>
> (Harris 1973a: 60–3)

This mediation by the great Guyanian writer Wilson Harris on the void of misgiving in the textuality of colonial history reveals the cultural and historical dimension of that Third Space of enunciation which I have made the precondition for the articulation of cultural difference. He sees it as accompanying the "assimilation of contraries" and creating that occult instability which presages powerful cultural changes. It is significant that the productive capacities of this Third Space have a colonial or postcolonial provenance. For a willingness to descend into that alien territory—where I have led you—may reveal that the theoretical recognition of the split-space of enunciation may open the way to conceptualizing an international culture, based not on the exoticism or multi-culturalism of the diversity of cultures, but on the inscription and articulation of culture's hybridity. To that end we should remember that it is the "inter"—the cutting edge of translation and negotiation, the in-between, the space of the entree that Derrida has opened up in writing itself—that carries the burden of the meaning of culture. It makes it possible to begin envisaging national, antinationalist, histories of the "people." It is in this space that we will find those words with which we can speak of Ourselves and Others. And by exploring this hybridity, this "Third Space," we may elude the politics of polarity and emerge as the others of our selves.

Suggested Readings with Similar Theme:

Gates, Henry Louis, Jr., ed. *"Race," Writing and Difference.* Chicago: University of Chicago Press, 1985.

Olaniyan, Tejumola. "On 'Post-Colonial Discourse': An Introduction." *Callaloo* 16, no. 4 (Fall 1993): 743–49.

Davies, Carol Boyce. "From 'Post-Coloniality' to Uprising Textualities: Black Women Writing the Critique of Empire." In *Black Women Writing and Identity: Migrations of the Subject*, 80–95. New York: Routledge, 1994.

JOY HARJO

An Interview with June Jordan (1988)

Jordan addresses general problems with the craft of contemporary poetry. How do her comments transcend literary periods? How might the following quotable lines from Jordan lead to dialogue about the function of contemporary poetry and the role of the contemporary poet: "You cannot have any art without form . . . I am consciously and self-consciously both seeking to represent as a poet not only my own experiences . . . but also the experiences of people . . . different . . . from my usual habitat." How does Jordan expand discussions about the role of the African American artist? Define the following terms: vertical poem/poetry, horizontal movement, free verse, and safe place.

Interviewer: Alice Walker has eloquently stated in an interview in the anthology, *The Third Woman,* that we are all working on the same large story. In your first collection of political essays, *Civil Wars,* in an essay written in 1977 addressing how you came to be a poet, you mention the black women poets who were as you say, working on the same poem of a life of perpetual difficult birth. It is now ten years later. What do you feel you have given birth to in your poetry? That's one part of the question. And secondly and perhaps unanswerably, what might that collective poem look like that we are all participating in?

Jordan: First, I think I have been giving birth to myself, progressively, as I have become able to understand and able to tell about what I feel and what I think in every context of my social experience. And I think I have been giving birth to an enlargement of options for other American poets who support the quest on my part for increasing authentic varieties of the American language and our intended multiplying of forms which may qualify as valid poetic form; and third (technical, personal) I believe I have been giving birth to a coherent world view which is passionately determined to include more and more different kinds of people. And because during the last six or seven years I have been privileged to receive more invitations to read my poetry across this country than I can possibly accept, I am able to suppose that these undertakings of my own have perhaps some positive influence and perhaps provide some necessary encouragement of other poets—my peers and younger poets as well. As far as the large collective poem that we are all writing, how would I describe that!

Interviewer: You don't have to answer! I was trying to imagine it.

Jordan: I don't know what the large poem is that all of us have been writing together but separately—but I know that if I shall ever be privileged enough to imagine the content of that poem that I will find myself in the presence of stunning and revolutionary beauty.

Interviewer: Great! In my early years as a poet, I went through a period of revolt against learning or listening to primarily English poets or White American poets especially male, (though now I hold some of that work quite important, precious) because I felt their poetic sense of form must have emerged from patterns of thinking which I admire for ingenuity, but had no respect for, didn't want to perpetuate. Yet I knew that I daily ingested these patterns because of course, I speak English and I write the English language. I searched for other forms of English language and fell in love and learned from Black American poets, Central and South American poets, African poets, any Native American poets I could find which weren't many when I began writing, and especially sought out women's poetry. I hungered for a revolution, or rather a simple acceptance and respect for other voices which I wasn't seeing in the American canon of poetry. Lately I've recognized a current trend by many American poets to return to those established forms of meter, rhyme, shape. It's difficult for me to accept on one hand because I feel that we should be striving for what is truly our own, yet I know I learn more about the inherent power of the particular language, its structure through these forms. But, I know we as writers from our specific communities must have our own forms, that utilize a sense of, say, a uniqueness of Black English, or say, Red English. . . .

Jordan: Well, let me respond to that. First of all, for example, look at the sonnets, sestina and the ballad, these seem to me—these really materialized out of their historical contexts before our century began and that doesn't mean to me that they are no longer viable forms. I view them as options. I think it's a question of attitude—whether you think that because something came from England or from the 19th century that makes it necessarily or even possibly superior to something that say came out of Brooklyn in 1995. We're talking attitude here, so I'll just tell you my attitude is these are available options, but at the same time, for example, yesterday, two days ago rather, in my Poetry Society of America workshop, when students were asking me about speed, how do you acquire or achieve or guarantee speed within a poem: Tempo/momentum to the poem/moving the reader through at a certain pace, I pointed out to them that using the American language we have today, if what you want is speed then you want a vertical movement through the poem rather than a horizontal movement that rests at the end of each line. For example, you cannot use an iambic meter of any sort. OK, now the iambic meter was so popular a couple centuries ago, obviously it must have reflected spoken habits of that time, which, of course, was a much slower time. But, if you think about it, the iambic meter, whether it's tetrameter or pentameter, it doesn't matter—it's da'—da—da'da. To me, the only image I could come up with my students was to say, you know, it's like, if you take one step and then you drag the other one up to where the first foot stops.

Interviewer: That's a useful way to visualize it.
Jordan: That's iambic.

Interviewer: We're doing a faster shuffle here.
Jordan: Obviously, we're not talking about running anywhere with that so it's fine if you want to use an iambic meter for some reason, but be aware that if you do you're not talking fast. That is a way of addressing craft problems from a contemporary perspective, which is what I think obviously anyone in his/her right mind must undertake to do. Right? So, the kinds of metrical stress patterns that we would have to use today for fast movement and also for conformity to our regular spoken habits would mean whatever kinds of words begin on the stress syllable and then move to an unstressed syllable or that begin on a stress syllable and then cluster-stress those syllables together. Like, don't do that! You know, ba, ba, ba. That's fast, that's moving right along. But you have to become aware of that. The next thing that I want to say is that I think that after free verse began flourishing in the 20th century, a lot of people were very confused by that word, free.

Interviewer: They still are.
Jordan: A lot of quite successful poets really don't know anything about craft. There're king of lucking it out as they go along. But because something is free verse doesn't mean that there aren't really structural guidelines, discernible and/or formulable, that would let us understand that we are writing in a form. We are writing in the realm of many forms—let me put it that way—capable of many forms. It is not formless. There are reasons why you should break a line and reasons why you should not break a line. All these reasons are now and forever and will continue to be debatable but they are there. They are reasons formalistic principles that underlie poetry no matter what the designation might be. So, I think that the word free really has had an unfortunate effect, so far, and it's an unnecessarily unfortunate effect. What it should mean to people is that we're now in a space where we can develop many, an infinite number perhaps, of forms dictated by the content and purpose of our poetry. This form or that form but "form." You cannot have any art without form. The other thing I wanted to say is that there are some large genres of contemporary form that so far have not received the kind of critical acknowledgement [sic] they deserve. Just as one example, I mentioned what I call the vertical poem, which originated really in the Black poetry of the 60's and that is poetry which does not depend upon or refer to horizontal metrics at all. It's vertical, rhythmical structure that requires craft,

understanding of the relationship of consonants for example, to tempo or movement through a poem. For example, if a line ends with a word ending in "ed" or "th," that line simply will not flow into the next line. Vertical poetry, as I call it, really emerged in the 60's and it has its own craft requirements which are quite demanding and it's not specific to Black people; it's a form. It's a contemporary form. For example, Susan Griffin, who is a White woman poet, used it very successfully in a poem, she wrote some several years ago to Harriet Tubman and it's a form that I teach to my students in my workshops, whether they are Black or White doesn't matter:—it kind of makes them aware of still another option. . . .

Interviewer: It's quite exciting and hilarious and so on. Your sixth collection of poetry, *Living Room,* emotionally, dramatically moves toward home. The last poem in the collection, "Moving Towards Home," is stunning. It's one of my favorite poems. In that poem you walk through rage and destruction suffered by the Palestinians, which is ultimately suffered by all of us. The poem itself gathers up everyone to take them home. Is there ever any safe place in a poem?
Jordan: Well, substantively I would hope not as far as the poem is concerned, if we're not at risk, I think we're wasting our own and other people's time, but technically, maybe, yeah, I seem to create a safety in the way that I end my work which very often has quite a bit of rhyme. It makes me feel that however agonizing it is, or that whatever it is I happen to be saying or trying to express at the conclusion of the poem, if I can I have da-da'-da-da'-da'-da-da, I feel "whew." Something is still holding firm, do you know what I mean? It's at least the music, most narrowly speaking, holding it firm and—so that kind of safety, yeah, I think remains accessible to us and I know I surely depend upon that kind of technical safety even as I eschew the other kind.

Interviewer: Yes, because I see each poem ultimately if it really works as some kind of risk taking.
Jordan: Yeah, necessarily, yes.

Interviewer: And a poem has to be life-sustaining I believe to be truly useful. And at the end of it, as you have said, find safety in the rhythm, rhyme or whatever can be a harbor.
Jordan: Or both.

Interviewer: When I think of myself as a poet, especially being of a native community in America, I know that the poet, song-maker, town crier, is bound to truth within a particular creative craziness that is farseeing and truthful. The poet's role was/is an active participant in the community and shaped the community, helped direct the community. How do you see yourself as a contemporary poet in the contemporary American community?

Jordan: I see myself, in great part as others see me. I mean, as I go around, I attend to what the apparent expectations are for my visit, for the readings and so on. I also try to think for myself do I feel obliged to meet those expectations and/or do I have other expectations of my own. I guess I am consciously and self-consciously, both, endeavoring to be a verifiably national poet. What I mean by that is that I am consciously and self-consciously both seeking to represent as a poet not only my own experiences, whatever that may mean, but also the experiences of people I may only meet once or twice, let's say in Lincoln, Nebraska, which is very different—a different environment from my usual habitat. For example, as a result of our friendship, I'm very concerned to try and, not to pretend that I am a native American, but rather to focus as best I can upon what I can come to understand and imagine about the Native American experience, both historical experience and the current one. I'm making that effort very consciously.

I have a tremendous amount of good fortune and privilege that's morally incumbent upon me to use in some way that I can hope will prove helpful to people who are not as fortunate as I. I think that as a black human being in America, this is an extremely important task as an artist for me to keep at the center of my work, because it means, among other things, that I'm not accepting other people's imagery about myself. . . .

Suggested Reading with Similar Theme:

A Capsule Course in Black Poetry Writing, edited by Gwendolyn Brooks, Keorapetse Kgositsile, Haki Madhubuti, and Dudley Randall. Detroit: Broadside Press, 1975.
Cavalieri, Grace D. Gaetani. "Rita Dove: An Interview." *The American Poetry Review* (March-April 1995): 11–15.

JERRY W. WARD JR.

From "Alvin Aubert: The Levee, the Blues, the Mighty Mississippi" (1989)

Why have southern writers such as Aubert and Ernest Gaines found it necessary to distance themselves from the South in order to write about it? How important are place, land, and humor to the southern African American writer? How does Aubert echo Henderson and Williams when discussing "saturation"? Is Aubert an ally to contemporary writers who are concerned also "with ordinary life situations, people being born and going to school and graduating and getting married and getting sick and dying and enduring . . . ?" What emerges from a Walker-Aubert discussion about models in the life of the artist? Define the following terms and phrases: thematic cohesiveness, deliberate consistency, up South/down South, nationalism, humanism, and cultural matrix.

Ward: Did you become interested in writing before you were an undergraduate? Which teachers or writers influenced you?
Aubert: I seem to have always been interested in writing, but it took me a long time to get into it. One of the problems, I think, was that I wasn't influenced by anybody, although I was encouraged by Oscar A. Bouise, a professor of English at Xavier at the time, and later helped by the poet Miller Williams, who is now director of the Press at the University of Arkansas. Miller took an interest in my writing when I needed it most. He was teaching at the time across town in Baton Rouge, at LSU. It was Miller who read by first successful poem, "Nat Turner in the Clearing," and suggested that I send it to Motive magazine, in which it was published. It was also Miller Williams who published my first poems to appear in an anthology, *Southern Writing in the Sixties: Poetry* (1967), edited by him and John William Corrington. I really didn't like reading all that much as a teenager. It was a strange combination of motives that led me into writing, quite unusual for a writer, so much so I don't think I can explain it. And now, as a teacher of creative writing, I recall my teenage years when I chide my writing students about not being interested enough in reading. As for literary influences, I think they came from people like John Donne, John Milton, Gerard Manley Hopkins, D. H. Lawrence, and William Butler Yeats—for these are the writers I enjoyed

studying most when I was in graduate school, my formative years, literarily; we didn't read any Black writers then.

By the time I came upon the Black writers, I was already teaching at Southern University, and my literary predilections had already been formed. I wrote my first successful poem in 1962, "Nat Turner in the Clearing," and have been writing poems ever since. That was my break-through poem, and was somewhat miraculously produced. I had just learned of Nat Turner (those of my generation came to Black history late, too) from reading his reprinted "Confessions" in Hoyt Fuller's magazine *Negro Digest,* later to become *Black World.* I was in my office at Southern University, the door shut. I put the magazine down and began writing the poem, which was to be accepted for publication in its first draft form. I never changed a word in it. I refer to the occasion as mystical because it was as though Nat Turner was there in the office with me, dictating the poem.

Ward: There was vision in the creation. The visual, the sensual—these are strong qualities in your work. That the lyric "South Louisiana" (South Louisiana 7). It makes connections between rain and the river, dreams and the "inexhaustible cistern." I supply my reading of that poem with visual memory of cisterns in Convent, the hamlet just up the road from your hometown, and a misty memory of how great a summer I had drinking rainwater. The poem evokes something about a special connection country people must have had with the land, or perhaps a way living with the land, and creativity or imagination. Does the poem symbolize the sense of place in your creative process?

Aubert: Well, the poem is more about the river than about the land. I think we were always more conscious of the river back then, though, as the poem says, "rarely did we drink from it." The rain was our "inexhaustible cistern" during my growing-up days in South Louisiana, our main household water supply, which was caught draining into cypress cisterns from the gutters on the eaves of our houses. A few people had wells, but most of those with wells had cisterns, too, for the ground water level wasn't constant, as I recall. Wells were either high or low, depending also on the rain and the level of the water in the river. I would have to research all that. But ultimately, the poem is more about living with the sky than with the river or the land, I think, and it definitely signifies a sense of place. The land being so level, we had to climb a tree or go to the top of the levee in order to see anything, get a view of the horizon—at least we thought we were seeing the horizon. So it was mostly sky, and the ground directly beneath one's feet. And after that the people on their front porches and in an occasional car or truck that happened to go by. The movie house thus became very important—the vista of the silver screen, a light only the sky could compete with on our leaving the theater on a matinee afternoon. In my writing a sense of place may be less important than a sense of an alternative to the place, or a thirst for otherness. I recall that going on a visit to New Orleans, or leaving home at age 17 for the Army, was almost a transcendental experience; so too was the coming back after an absence, brief or extended, but of course more intense in the case of the latter. The South Louisiana I now write about, I think, is the South Louisiana I might have hoped for in those days rather than one that ever was.

Ward: In a 1972 interview with Charles Rowell, you mentioned that you had to do much thinking about South Louisiana and any connection your growing up there might possibly have with your work as a poet. Can we assume that you have begun to reflect on part of that heritage in the "New Poems (1775–1984)" section of your latest book, *South Louisiana: New and Selected Poems,* and in your short story "Chicken Feathers," which appeared in the final issue of *Obsidian* (Old Series)?
Aubert: When I taped the interview with Charles Rowell, I had moved from Southern University in Baton Rouge to the State University College of New York at Fredonia in the fall of 1970. In 1972 I was just beginning to gain the perspective on South Louisiana I apparently needed in order to write more poems about my life there.

I don't know of many Black writers who have remained in the South, so it is difficult to say whether the generalization I am about to make holds up: Unlike white Southern writers, Black Southern writers seem unable to write about the South—directly out of their Southern experiences—while still living there. Ernest J. Gaines is a classic example. Among the exceptions, of course, would be yourself, Tom Dent, Ahmos Zu Bolton, and Kalamu ya Salaam. Anyway, for myself, at least, I seem to have needed the removal, the distancing from the area of primal experience, so to speak. It may be that Black writers are more subjectively immersed in the Southern experience, with our historical background of slavery and intense post-slavery oppression and all that, and we have thus been inhibited from dealing with our experiences in ways that white Southern writers have not. That may be less so now; I don't know and I may never know, for it's very unlikely that I will take up residence in the South again, except maybe after I retire. But even then, the aesthetic distance I will have acquired over my years of absence from the South may have taken such a hold by then that, if I am still writing eight to ten years from now, as I expect to be, I will still be writing from that distance, even if I should find myself living in South Louisiana again. But I don't want to take that idea too far.

There are of course poems about my particular South Louisiana milieu in my first two collections, *Against the Blues* and *Feeling Through,* but I suppose your question refers more to the very local matter of my African-French-Indian-Creole heritage. The Creole is basic, but it is not the whole of my childhood landscape. To begin with, the Creoles constituted a small minority of the population of my hometown, and one did not venture too far afield in those transportationless days. Thinking of it in terms of religion, which was a particularly important consideration then, the dominant influence was Black Protestant (Baptist). We attended Catholic church, sitting in the three or four pews reserved for "Colored" in the back of the local Catholic chapel—Our Lady of Prompt Succour, it was called—, but it was the more vibrant Black baptist ethos that permeated our lives. See my poem "Baptism" (*Feeling Through* 54–55) on this score, along with "Bessie Smith's Funeral" and "Whispers in a Country Church" (*Against the Blues* 8–9). When we were moved to sing, we didn't sing Catholic hymns like "Mother Dear, Oh Pray for me." We sang, "Precious Lord, Take My Hand" and, on the secular side of it, the blues, of course. Although we never quite dispensed with our private conviction of the religious superiority of our Catholicity, of the sneaking suspicion, encouraged by the teaching of the Church, that when it came to dying and going to heaven, the Baptist people were climbing up the rougher side of the mountain. As for my short story "Chicken Feathers," well, I started out writing that and one outrageous thing led to another. I am not sure I'll write anything quite like it again. Just let me say that I like the middle part of that piece best, Christopher at the river, which is the kind of experience I think I want to get at more in future stories.

Ward: I notice a great deal of humor in your poetry. Does your sense of humor derive from your South Louisiana roots? Do you make a rather fine distinction between what you borrow from folk humor and the humor that comes from a self-consciousness of being in a certain line of Afro-American literary tradition?
Aubert: Well, to begin with, a self-consciousness of being in a peculiar historical, political, social, and cultural situation results from being of African heritage in a racist society. Our predicament, collectively, is so ridiculous it's almost surreal. Add to that the extreme self-consciousness we are forced into, always contemplating ourselves in our predicament as we move about the American landscape, which almost prompts the question "What the hell am I doing here?"—as though there were any alternative, as though there were any place else in the world for us to go. Under such circumstances, the humor is inevitable; it comes with the territory, and a great deal of it is comic relief, providing release from the strictures of a racist ethos. As for the humor in my story "Chicken Feathers," I think I was more after the absurdist effect than anything else. But, in general, in my writings as in my life, I think I just plug into the humor generated by our common predicament on the American scene. As the old blues line goes, "Laughing just to keep from cryin'."

Ward: In the March 1986 portion of our interview you wrote, "Art, for me, is not the absence of social and political consciousness; rather, it is the presence of an aesthetic quality, and that aesthetic quality can come from one's social and political consciousness." Would you clarify what you mean by "aesthetic quality"?

Aubert: As an Afro-American poet I would have to say that the aesthetics of a work of art, of a poem or a story, say, derives from the writer's milieu, his cultural matrix. This has to do with whatever entertaining, instructive, and informing way as well as in a structural sense—realizing that as operational categories these are not necessarily exclusive in a given literary discourse. What I'm talking about here touches on Stephen Henderson's concept of "saturation" (62–66). In reading works of Black American poets you discover a great deal of affective material—material that moves you in various ways because you recognize it as coming from the culture you belong to, as having to do with your life in some way, whether it refers to the kind of music you enjoy—blues, spirituals, jazz, gospel, and so forth—or jokes you have heard told, or the way people talk or tell stories or move about or dance, or the kind of food that's eaten, or a peculiar way of suffering and endurance and so forth. You recognize such cultural encounters, and your spirit responds, "That's good," and you enjoy the poem, smiling to yourself a long time after reading it, entertaining good thoughts about yourself and your people. That is the basis of the Black aesthetic, a basically humanistic, celebratory standard of literary appreciation that comes out of Black life. From the poet's point of view, you recognize in all of this a commitment.

Ward: The committed Black poet?
Aubert: Yes. Most Black artists and writers are committed to such an aesthetic. It's natural for them to be. I think they find it so natural, the exception strikes one as aberrational.

Ward: This notion . . . what you see as innate commitment . . .
Aubert: Something innate, yes that you're born with, branded with. Branded with. We are a beleaguered people, thus our innate commitment to ourselves, to our survival.

Ward: When that is consciously formulated in literary works, we have a signal of nationalism.
Aubert: Which I like to think of as peoplehood, Black humanism. We can never be a nation, but we can become more of a people in the U.S.A., in my way of thinking.

Ward: I throw in the term nationalism because with Kalamu ya Salaam, for instance, we have to talk about it. He definitely declared himself a cultural and political nationalist. I look at Julius Thompson's work and find some kind of nationalism. It is very obvious in certain things Sterling Plumpp has done, especially in his efforts to link African and African-American political experiences. Tom Dent and you are perhaps . . . well, you pick up more options.
Aubert: We walk to the proverbial different drummer. The difference lies, I suppose, in whether or not you want to assume a particular political stance in

your writing. I don't have that kind of systematic ideology—which does not, in my view, reduce my commitment to my people. It's a difference of means, ultimately. . . .

Ward: You lived through several periods in your writing. Do you feel there is a resurgence of past work in the way you are writing now? Are you reworking things from your earlier experiences for the 1980s and 1990s?

Aubert: Well, an ongoing concern of mine is the manner in which Black artists and writers deal with Black life as it goes on every day in the Black community. Black artists have had to concern themselves with the sometimes overwhelming issues of racist oppression—and still do—, but I am also concerned with ordinary life situations, people being born and going to school and graduating and getting married and getting sick and dying and enduring and all of that. I often wonder about these things as they have gone on in my hometown of Lutcher, Louisiana, during the forty or so years of my absence, and in the forty or so years before that. I want to write more about all of that, in novels, stories, and plays.

Ward: You seem to suggest that your current interest is to explore the particular, the specific, as opposed to the general, to the way we as Black writers have gone at history.

Aubert: Yes, but to deal with a different specific, particulars that have not been dealt with all that much, that have fallen through the cracks, the kind of particulars that August Wilson deals with in his plays, that novelists like John Wideman, Toni Morrison, and John McCluskey and poets like Kenneth A. McClane and Thylias Moss deal with in their works, that you, Jerry, deal with in your own poetry and fiction. . . .

Ward: Perhaps we will see more of the up South/down South conflict in your writing.

Aubert: I see up South, in part, as an allusion to how Blacks especially carry our destinies around with us. Because of our high visibility in American society, we carry our common destiny with us wherever we go. The situation calls to mind that perpetual Middle Passage writers talk about, the idea that we are still on that slaveship.

Ward: Like the slaveship in the play we saw recently, *The Colored Museum*, that becomes the jet plane, a modern mode of transportation. . . .

Aubert: Yes, the slaveship as a mental condition we need to get rid of. . . .

Ward: "All Singing in a Pie" is a good opening poem for South Louisiana because it speaks to childhood, childhood memories of blackberry picking and other things that may have happened in and around your hometown of Lutcher in your youth. Childhood is a strong recurring subject or theme in your work. It is not always on the surface. It may appear as an allusion to nursery rhyme or song. The casual reference to childhood may make your work distinct.

Aubert: The concern with childhood is about origins, the need to retrace the route we've come and one's sense of having missed a great deal and thus the need to retrace one's steps. A Black person growing up in South Louisiana in the 1930s and '40s would have missed opportunities people experience universally. You sense a need to go on picking blackberries, to arrive at your final destination with as full a basket as possible.

Ward: So you gather from the past and the present.
Aubert: Yes, but especially from the past.

Ward: We entertain the notion that the past is completed.
Aubert: Well, the Euro-American sense of history encourages that, not the African, in which past, present, and future are coterminous, humanistically so: The ancestors are always with us, as are the living and the yet to be born. The ideal is of continuity rather than completion and of satisfaction in living with people in the present rather than a fretting about the past or a yearning for the future. But I'm not African; I'm African-American and must live and write out of that complexity. . . .

Suggested Reading with Similar Theme:

Lowe, John. "An Interview with Ernest Gaines." In *Conversations with Ernest Gaines,* edited by John Lowe. Jackson: University Press of Mississippi, 1995.

ELEANOR W. TRAYLOR

A Blues View of Life
(Literature and the Blues Vision) (1989)

What is meant by the blues vision? How are language and music used to express African American experience? How do Traylor and Gabbin enter discussions about language and music to express African American experience? Define the following terms and phrases: rootlessness, self-created carrier, mythological carriers of folk traditions, the riffin' method, improvisation, double vision, griot-historian, memory and history, the experience of melody, signs and symbols.

Alex Haley's *Roots* is a rite of voyage; it is a story relating the questor's search for reunion. In such a story, the questor defines himself as the sum of his past and present parts. The quest for achieved totality and fulfillment as he reunited with his source. This is a very old story told by both East and West; it is a very beautiful story; it assures us that we belong to continuity; it suggests that there is order in the universe; it asserts that our job is to find it and be reconciled with it and, therefore, experience the fulfillment that unity achieves.

Significantly, this is not the story that Afro-American Literature has characteristically told nor is it the story told in the oral folklore upon which that literature is, in large part, built. Brer Rabbit, the Signifyin' Monkey, John de Conquer', Stackalee, Shine, the anonymous author of the spirituals, the wandering blues singer, none of these mythological or actual carriers of folk tradition look to the past as object of their quest. To the contrary, we hear them sing: "on my journey now . . ." and "can't nobody turn me around." Neither the folkloric nor the literary traditions deny the value or the desirability of reconcilement with the past. Yet what they emphasize and what they place into language as central experience is not the quest for roots, but the act of shaping rootlessness.

Only one body of world literature, of which I am aware, has offered a character without a navel. Afro-American Literature has offered such a character; that character, called Pilate, appears in the 1977 best selling novel of Toni Morrison, *Song of Solomon*.

Pilate has no navel; yet the navel is the mark of the cord that once tied the child to its parent—its most immediate origin. Once the navel cord is cut, the child breathes for itself, or dies. At birth, then, we are severed from

285

the most immediate past that we come to know. The moment of the severance is crucial and excruciating; at that moment, we live by our ability to improvise, or we die. This story of that living or dying is a serious story; it is a story often told in the signs and symbols of world literature, but no literature that I know of other than Afro-American literature has ventured a character without a navel.

What is the meaning of a character with no navel? The first and most apparent suggestion of such a character is that of a self-created being. How is it possible to create oneself? It is not only possible; it is imperative to create oneself historically if one's history has been denied or cut off and if one would live despite that fact. If one lives despite that fact, one's history must be self-contained; one must be the personal carrier of history. If history is portable, then it lives as long as there is a carrier. The pilot figures of Afro-American folklore—Brer Rabbit, Shine, Stackalee, etc.—are all carriers of antecedents cut-off by a sea voyage so shocking as to appear to kill memory. But memory did not die. What was remembered had to be carried in the individual soul. Pilots appeared in the New World. The Pilate of *Song of Solomon* recalls earlier plots in the folklore and literature of a continuing literary tradition.

The Pilate of *Song of Solomon* does not beg the question of truth like the Pilate of New Testament history. This Pilate, like the pilots which precede her, sees with double-vision which endows eyesight with insight. Such clarity reinvents reality, recreates history, and even forges the possible from the impossible. The image of the self-created carrier, the griot-historian in Afro-American literature, precedes the consummate Pilate of *Song of Solomon* by one hundred and eighty-nine years, lending the navel-less character the textured complexity of tradition. The image of the pilot emerges, for example, in the *Narrative* of Olaudah Equiano or Gustavus Vassa (1789); it appears in the *Narrative* of Frederick Douglass (1845); in the *Conjure Woman* of Charles Chesnutt (1899); in the narrator of Jean Toomer's *Cane* (1923); in *Jonah's Gourd Vine* and *Their Eyes Were Watching God* of Zora Neale Hurston (1934, 1937); in *Uncle Tom's Children* of Richard Wright (1938); in "Sonny" of James Baldwin's "Sonny's Blues" (1958); in Paule Marshall's *Brown Girl, Brownstones* (1959); in Maya Angelou's *I Know Why the Caged Bird Sings* (1971); in *Jubilee* of Margaret Walker (1966); in *Ark of Bones* by Henry Dumas (1970); in the *Mumbo Jumbo* of Ishmael Reed (1972); and in *Train Whistle Guitar* of Albert Murray (1974). The continual image of the pilot conducting a journey through time and space begun by the wrench of rootlessness is a recurring image. Its resonance articulates custom.

A pilot is the necessary navigator of a journey. The journey, continually enacted in Afro-American literature, commences in the Narrative of Olaudah Equiano. The narrator, an imprisoned African boy, tells us that he loses consciousness while he seems buried in the belly of a tall ship, and that, when he regains consciousness upon the deck of the ship, he sees that the shore line of his homeland is gone; all hope of escape and return is lost to him in that moment of awareness. He must choose, whether he will die or whether he will live and claim chaos. He chooses. He endures the horrifying sea-change; he confronts rootlessness. In the process, he improvises upon whatever means are at hand to sustain life and to recreate his all but devastated spirit. His struggle against the overwhelming is the celebration of his Narrative, for he is not overwhelmed.

This narrator's tale of a dreadful rift in experience is told us in a series of riffs—departures—rises and falls—digressions off a central theme. That theme, the "how-I-got-ovah," the "gittin down to git up" theme textured by incremental repetition is as resonant as a melodic line throughout Afro-American narratives from the 1789 *Narrative* of Gustavus Vassa through the 1977 *Song of Solomon* of Toni Morrison. The story of a dreadful rift in experience endured by a pilot or by one who is led by a pilot through chaos of self-determination or re-creation remains the continuous mythic content of Afro-American literary texts. Not only the tale but its method—the riffin' method of the living personal carrier of history—is the tribal mark of the Afro-American teller of tales. What is a riffin' method? The Blues-Jazz musicians, who invented the term, mean by it an improvisation; a departure from the established melodic line or theme of a musical composition. They also mean the manner in which a jam session is performed. At a jam session, a piano, a saxophone, a trumpet, a bass guitar, and drums. Normally when the musicians begin a composition, all instrumentalists play the melodic line together. Usually, all instruments play the melody in harmony; the group may then repeat the melodic line, but this time each instrument assumes its voice or assumes a part: alto, soprano, tenor, and bass. After the melody has, in this way, been established, each instrumentalist takes a solo. The solo becomes his improvisation of the melodic line. The "improv" or riff examines every aspect of the melody that the musician's instrument is capable of, as well as every aspect of the musician's own feeling for the melody. This riff is the musician's personal voice; his or her contribution to the melody that all play together. The riff of each musician develops the experience of the melody in any and every way that the experience of the melody or theme can be heard or perceived. And even saying this much is inadequate to describe the nuances of experience that the blues-jazz musician offers in his riffs.

The Afro-American novelist riffs in this way. Jean Toomer's *Cane,* the beauty of which appears to many readers, has, also, baffled many readers who cannot classify the series of prose vignettes, song-poems, and half-story structures that compose the book. Seen as a blues-jazz composition, the real and deep sense of *Cane* is immediately clear. The narrator of *Cane* identifies himself as "a son" of people whose lives he is describing in his narrative. He says that he is "a son" who has returned "in time" to "carol" (sing of) his people at a certain time in their history before "an epoch dies": he wishes to place their pain and joy, their beauty and horror, their agony and their triumph into rhythmic language which will preserve them as a memorial inspires recollections of greatness. That is the central theme, the melodic line of *Cane*. Like the musician at a jam session, the narrator announces his thematic line, and, then, riffs off that theme with vignettes, song-poems, and half-story/half-play impressions of the individual lives of people whom he wishes us to remember. Like a traveling blues singer, he tells us of his experience among rural and agrarian, among urban and industrial people whose zest and fecundity and love and joy and pain and stupidity and horror and fright and weakness and strength and bitter-sweet glory become his own. Like the blues singer, who tells us of these kinds of experiences and, all the while, invites us to celebrate—for blues music is dance music and dance is a celebration—the narrator also invites us to celebrate. He invites us to celebrate the fact that the ugly, the bone-crushing, the spirit-killing, the brutal and mindless, the arrogant, the blind, mean killers of love, beauty, the humane, and the human have not overwhelmed the people of his narrative.

By the time the tradition of African-American narrators presents the invisible narrator of *Invisible Man,* the greatest celebration of achieving one's name and re-naming oneself has repeated itself for one hundred and sixty-three years. The self-created carrier of history (celebrated in the earliest slave narratives, continues in the fictive narratives which follow, receiving a quintessential recital and new creation in *Invisible Man*) continues through Pilate, the navel-less consummate carrier of history in the *Song of Solomon*.

Thus, the blues-jazz experience of African-American sensibility is not merely an occurrence in music; it is also an occurrence in language. From the perspective of the Blues singer/Blues narrator/Jazz composer then, we may see, with clarity, the shape, the texture, and the encyclical reference of the Blues genius of African American narrative tradition. That genius has wrested the possible from the impossible; it has provided the experience of rootlessness a local habitation and name. It has from chaos forged order: the order of an encompassing new-world literary tradition.

Suggested Reading with Similar Theme:

Wideman, John. "Stomping the Blues—Ritual in Black Music and Speech." *American Poetry Review* (July-August 1978): 43–46.

Baker, Houston A., Jr. Introduction to *Blues Ideology, and Afro-American Literature: A Vernacular Theory*. Chicago: University of Chicago Press, 1984.

Richard J. Powell

The Blues Aesthetic:
Black Culture and Modernism (1989)

As a critique of twentieth century African American and American visual art from a blues perspective, how might Powell's essay be subtitled? How does Powell illustrate Henderson's term "mascon" when critiquing visual art? How would you respond to Powell's question, "Is blues equivalent to modern Afro-American life?" How does Powell echo Bhabha when he calls for the study of the "far-reaching influence" of African American culture?

> Blues is African American
> —Amiri Baraka, *The Music*

When people hear "the blues" they immediately conjure an image of an old black man in the country, playing the guitar (or harmonica) and singing a melancholy ditty about hard times, a lost love, or some other misfortune. Or they flash to Chicago, Memphis, or Harlem in the 1920s and imagine a full-voiced black woman, hands on hips, who sings a more upbeat song of comparable concerns. Or they imagine no one in particular, but equate the music to an emotional state: part euphoria, part doldrums, all heart and guts.

I guess I think about all those things too, when I hear "the blues." But that's not all I think about.

Embedded in the term, contained in those pictures of the old man and full-voiced woman, and woven into the sounds and lyrics and sensations of the music, are certain suppositions about culture and history. We know who the players are in the story of the blues and we know the scenarios that lead up to the creation of the blues. Notions of race, class, social hierarchy, and politics loom over Muddy Waters' licks and Bessie Smith's moans. The history of the blues is part of the history of the United States, and that component is as old and settled as a corroded soda pop sign on a traveler's consciousness. The blues whips up a panorama of extra-musical associations that, whether one chooses to acknowledge them or not, situate it in Afro-American life of this century.

Does this mean the blues is equivalent to modern Afro-American life? In one way of thinking, yes. The fusion of nineteenth century Afro-American work songs and field hollers with the instrumentation and adaptation of

Euro-American traditional ballads brought forth in the late nineteenth century black musical forms that, while not technically considered "the blues," served as the primary ingredients for what it would later become. Most cultural historians place the earliest origins of the blues to this late nineteenth century period, when recently emancipated black Americans began to develop their own communities, travel in wider circles, and enter the economy as free agents. Unfortunately, racial discrimination, stereotypic portrayals of blacks, intimidation, and violence emerged with this cultural expansion of Afro-America. The first inklings of what we now know as the blues are documented from this period, apparently born out of this double-moment of opportunity and denial.

The period immediately following—namely, the twentieth century—needs no point by point description to illustrate how the blues was and is endemic to it. One need only recount the names of a few important blues practitioners—Gertrude "Ma" Rainey, Bessie Smith, Leadbelly, Big Mama Thornton, Muddy Waters, and B. B. King—or the names of a few blues-inspired artists—Duke Ellington, Count Basie, Billie Holiday, Mahalia Jackson, Little Richard, Aretha Franklin, and James Brown—to realize that they and their music are products of the peculiar set of social and cultural circumstances which comprise the twentieth century.

On the other hand, certain aspects of modern Afro-America do not necessarily reflect the sentiments of a blues point-of-view. For many black Americans, assimilation into the white majority came with emancipation and, much later, with a greater involvement in the cultural mainstream of the United States. The outcome were black Americans who were not very different than most white Americans in their taste for music, art, and other cultural offerings. Many Afro-Americans, however, still seem to identify with traditions, folkways, and aesthetic criteria which stand apart from Euro-American models.

It was the understanding that 1) the blues formed a crucial part of modern Afro-America, and 2) modern Afro-America was not necessarily equivalent to the blues, which led me to think about the blues in terms of an aesthetic/an artistic stance/a philosophy. Something that was not just musical, but cultural. A point-of-view that one might inherit, as well as choose to embrace. A particular cultural perspective that grew out of the social condition of black Americans as they entered and dealt with the modern era. A mindset that, given the impact that Afro-Americans have had on modern arts and letters, resonates with many artists today.

To move from the idea of the blues as music to the notion of the blues as cultural ethos is the charge here. Many important theorists in Afro-American culture, such as Ralph Ellison, Amiri Baraka (LeRoi Jones), Stephen Henderson, Larry Neal, Albert Murray, and Houston Baker have acknowledged the far-reaching influence that the blues has had on modern Afro-American culture. Beyond its obvious impact on other Afro-American musical forms (i.e., jazz, gospel, rhythm and blues, etc.), the blues provides much contemporary literature, theatre, dance, and visual arts with the necessary elements for defining these various art forms as intrinsically "Afro-American."

In terms of the visual arts, the blues functions as one of several perspectives which artists encounter in our times. It can either inspire an artist to create a particular work, or it can actually be the model upon which a work is created. To a great extent, if one is knowledgeable about Afro-America—its history, its traditions, its geography, its verbal and visual codes, its heroes, its demons, its ever changing styles, and its spiritual dimensions—then one knows the blues.

So the question arises: why not an "Afro-American" aesthetic as opposed to a "blues" aesthetic? Aren't they one in the same? And I would answer: yes, but the reason for side-stepping the designation "Afro-American" is that it is perceived as both a cultural and racial designation, and while I am comfortable with the cultural part of its meaning, I am not comfortable with the implication that an aesthetic is based solely on race. To put it in simple language: all Afro-Americans do not think about art in the same way. Some Afro-Americans are interested in Afro-American culture, and some Afro-Americans are not.

Along this same line of thinking, some Euro-Americans are interested in Afro-American culture. In fact, more Euro-Americans are interested in Afro-American culture than one might initially assume. And while I would be the first person to say that there is a world of difference between Paul Whiteman and Duke Ellington, between Elvis Presley and Bo Diddley, and between Mike Bloomfield and Jimi Hendrix, I would also say that a significant part of the study of Afro-American culture lies in looking at the far-reaching influence of that culture, regardless of the race or ethnicity of the artists involved.

The concept of a "blues aesthetic" is an attempt to describe selected examples of art in this century, and to delineate several important aspects of this art. Let's be clear: what we are talking about is basic, twentieth century Afro-American culture. The term "blues" is an appropriate designation for this idea because of its associations with one of the most identifiable black American traditions that we know. Perhaps more than any other designation, the idea of a blues aesthetic situates the discourse squarely on: 1) art produced in our time; 2) creative expressions that emanate from artists who are empathetic with Afro-American issues and ideals; 3) work that identifies with grassroots, popular, and/or mass black American culture; 4) art that has an affinity with Afro-U.S.-derived music and/or rhythms; and 5) artists and/or artistic statements whose raison d'etre is humanistic.

Although one could argue that other twentieth century Afro-U.S. musical terms, such as ragtime, jazz, boogie-woogie, gospel, swing, bebop, cool, rhythm and blues, doo-wop, soul, funk, go-go, hip-hop, or rap are just as descriptive as "the blues," what "the blues" has over and above them all is a breadth and mutability that allows it to persist and even thrive through this

Figure 1. George B. Luks, *Cake-Walk,* 1907, monotype on paper, 1907.
Courtesy of the Delaware Art Museum, Gift of Helen Farr Sloan.

century. From the anonymous songsters of the late nineteenth century who sang about hard labor and unattainable love, to contemporary rappers blasting the airwaves with percussive and danceable testimonies, the blues is an affecting, evocative presence, which endures in every artistic overture made towards black American peoples.

> There is nothing about the fellow I work that I don't know. I have studied him, his joy and sorrows. Contrast is vital.
>
> —Black Entertainer
> Bert Williams, from a 1916 interview

> Your problem Langston, my problem, no our problem is to conceive, develop, establish an art era. Not white art painted black. . . . Let's bare our arms and plunge them deep deep through laughter, through pain, through sorrow, through hope, through disappointment, into the very depths of the souls of our people and drag forth material crude, rough, neglected. Then let's sing it, dance it, write it, paint it. Let's do the impossible. Let's create something transcendentally material, mystically objective. Earthy. Spiritually earthy. Dynamic.
>
> —Aaron Douglas
> in a letter to Langston Hughes, ca. 1925

Figure 2. Winold Reiss, *Hot Chocolates,* crayon and pastel on paper, ca. 1929. *Estate of Winold Reiss, courtesy of Shepherd Gallery, New York.*

Two turn-of-the-century works, H. M. Pettit's *Close Competition at the Cake-Walk* and George B. Luks' *Cake-Walk* [figure 1] illustrate how Afro-American culture figures in the modernist visions of two graphic artists. The "Cake-Walk" was a popular dance component, perfected by black vaudevillians, ca. 1900, but thought to have originated in slavery as a kind of choreographed promenade which mocked the manners of well-to-do whites. Pettit's illustration of the Cake-Walk does more than document the dance: it suggests that the most expedient method for capturing the poses, facial expressions, elaborate clothing and dynamism of the Cake-Walk is a photographed, cut-up, reassembled, and touched-up photo-mechanical procedure. George B. Luks' image of the same subject, though fundamentally different because of the monotype's "fine art" distinction, explores comparable modernist ground, as evidenced in the print's animated, blurred, yet decidedly futurist treatment of a high-stepping black couple.

Both works recall not only the broad appeal of an Afro-American performance tradition among various audiences, but the perception of that tradition as part of a new, emerging art in America. Robert Coady, a New York art dealer and publisher of the *Soil,* one of the earliest "avant garde" art maga-

I Needs A Dime For Beer

Down an' Out

If you loves me
Help me when I'm down an' out.
If you loves me
Help me when I'm down an' out.
Cause I'm a po' gal that
Nobody gives a damn about.

'Stalment man's done took ma clothes
An' rent time's most nigh here.
'Stalment man's done took ma clothes,
Rent times most nigh here.
I'd like to buy a straightenin' comb
An' I needs a dime for beer.

Talk about yo' friendly friends.
Bein' kind to you.
Talk about yo' friendly friends
Bein' kind to you:
Just let yo'self git down an' out
An' then see what they'll do.

Langston Hughes.

Figure 3. Aaron Douglas/Langston Hughes Portfolio. *I Needs a Dime for Beer,* offset lithograph, 16 × 11¹/₂ inches. Photo: Manu Sassoonian.
Courtesy of the Schomburg Center for Research in Black Culture, Art & Artifacts Division, The New York Public Library, Astor, Lenox and Tilden Foundations.

zines in this country, mentions the Cake-Walk in a whole litany of American cultural novelties:

> . . . Jack Johnson . . . Bert Williams, Rag-time, the Buck and Wing and the Clog. Syncopation and the Cake Walk. The Crazy Quilt and the Rag Mat. The Minstrels . . .

The *Soil* lasted only five issues, and its plea for new perspective on American art was largely unheard by the majority of American artists, who still worked in reaction to European innovations in art. Nevertheless, a few American moderns understood Coady's Whitmanesque rollcall, especially those parts of the call which saw black performing artists, black music, black dance, black folk arts, and other aspects of black expression as the summation of a particular American "style."

Two of these American moderns, Stuart Davis and Glenn O. Coleman, recorded their encounters with Afro-America in an article for the *New York Sunday Call* in 1915. Their words and sketches, jotted down during an evening excursion to Newark, New Jersey, reveal more than a passing fancy for black culture. For Coleman, a performance by a black pianist in a cabaret had "as much real expression in the music . . . as . . . found in any symphony orchestra." For Davis, black Newark's sounds and scenes were summarized in drawings representing cabaret dancers and bystanders.

Davis, who is described in the article as "SOME player of rag-time," rendered his subjects with a sensitivity for both the cramped dance environment and the dancers. The broadly drawn, gesturing men and women not only situate Stuart Davis within the same school of visual reportage as exemplified by George B. Luks in *Cake-Walk,* but they bear witness to Davis' eventual exploration of the "tempos of jazz" in his later "color-space compositions."

It is important to remember that although the term "blues" does not come into popular usage until the 1920s, these early references to the "Cake-Walk," "rag-time," and other dance and/or musical terms should be interpreted as Afro-American signifiers of the same order. Similarly, these early images by Davis, Luks, and Pettit parallel subsequent images from the 1920s that unequivocally refer to the creators and cultural milieu of "the blues." Some of these works, such as Aaron Douglas' *I Needs A Dime for Beer,* Miguel Covarrubias' *Woman in a Cloche Hat,* and Winold Reiss' *Hot Chocolates,* continue the same folk/performance scenarios as seen in the graphics by Davis and Luks. However, works by Douglas and Reiss surpass the earlier visual forays into Afro-America because these later works confront the thematic and the formal aspects of black culture. In *Hot Chocolates* [figure 2], Reiss depicts the performers of a popular black revue (of the same name) in a fractured, syncopated manner. Responding to the tenets of both the "art deco" style and the blues, Reiss achieves a synthesis in this piece which is analogous to the coming together (ca. 1929) of New York's white elite and the black artists of the "Negro Renaissance."

Aaron Douglas, who was a student of Reiss, also combines modern design principles with Afro-American stylizations. *I Needs a Dime for Beer* [figure 3] was one of several images by Douglas paired with the blues-inspired poetry of Langston Hughes in a portfolio published in *Opportunity* magazine in 1926. Here, the accompanying text, as well as Douglas' sparse silhouettes, perfectly capture the dreamy mood and ironic perspective of many blues performances. Years later, Douglas described his flat and geometric delineation of form as "suggestive of the uniqueness found in the gestures and bodily movements of Negro dance and (in) the sounds and vocal patterns . . . (of) Negro songs . . ."

Though Aaron Douglas is often singled out for his pioneering vision of a new and characteristic Afro-American art idiom during the 1920s, he is paralleled if not slightly surpassed by New Orleans-born Chicago artist Archibald J. Motley, Jr. What distinguished Motley from many of his contemporaries in the 1920s and 1930s was his unprecedented concentration on black subject matter and, more importantly, his conscious manipulation of what he described as the "jazz aspects of the Negro."

After completing his studies at The Art Institute of Chicago in 1918, and after several showings in group exhibitions there, Motley received special mention for his entries in the 1925 Art Institute annual. One of the award-winning works was *Syncopation*, a cabaret scene which was described by one critic as "a vehicle for a free expression of the rhythm of forms and colors . . ." Subsequent works by Motley, which focus on Chicago's street life, cabaret culture, and the Afro-American community in general, are even better examples of the marriage between visual arts and Afro-American culture.

Blues [figure 4] is perhaps one of Motley's more memorable paintings. In spite of its Afro-American theme, *Blues* was actually conceived in a night club in Paris that the artist visited during his stay there on a Guggenheim fellowship. Like many of Motley's paintings, *Blues* presents a stylized and orchestrated study of improvisational patterning under the guise of genre scene. *Blues* begins the visual rhythm with the heads of the profiled trumpeter and trombone player at the extreme left, but breaks the pattern with the heads of the clarinet player on the left and guitarist to his right, whose positions are mirrored by the men dancing on the right side of the canvas. The two couples dancing with each male partner's backs facing outward have generally the same position, but these rhythms, as well, are interrupted. On top of these more obvious design schemes, Motley fragments the composition almost to the point of evoking a quilt or, to a lesser extent, a synthetic cubist painting.

Motley's multiplicity of compositional elements, their interruptions and their reintroductions are not unlike the "riffs" and "stop-time" of a fellow New Orleans-born Chicagoan, jazz legend Louis Armstrong. Working in Chicago around the same time as Motley, Armstrong and his various bands created waves among jazz circles with their unusual approach to timing, soloing, and collective playing. Armstrong's uncanny facility for running the

Figure 4. Painting; ICHi-16135; "Blues", painted in Paris depicts an interracial nightclub of the kind found in both Paris and Chicago; (n.p.); 1929; Creator—Archibald J. Motley.
Collection of Archie Motley and Valerie Gerrard Browne.

musical gamut of notes, and for setting early definitions of "swing" are described by Richard B. Hadlock in his book *Jazz Masters of the 20s:*

> Louis organizes his musical thoughts in a truly remarkable way. His solo (refer-ring to "Potato Head Blues," 1927) is a triumph of subtle syncopation and rhythmic enlightenment; strong beats on weak beats and whole phrases placed against rather than on the pulse create a delightful tension.

The focus on beat accentuation and beat suspension is in the subtleness rather than the explicitness of rhythms. Both Archibald Motley and Louis Armstrong were able to create a sense of rhythmic intrigue through improvis-ing and syncopating against a fairly structured format. For Armstrong, the format is established by the basic melodic scheme and the everpresent beat of his rhythm section, whereas for Motley, his visual departures strut across an implied system of anticipated shapes and recurring intervals. The attenuated, but persistent changes in Motley's Blues have a counterpart in Armstrong's musical virtuosity in that for both artists, the issue at hand concerns "feeling" the beat, rather than seeing or hearing it.

Works by Afro-American artists were not alone in their concern with contemporary black music's formal qualities. For example, paintings like Arthur G. Dove's *Swinging in the Park* (there were colored people there) have the intention of exploring color's relationship to the movements of line and volume: attributes which Dove felt had parallels in particular with jazz music. Dove describes his attitude towards an art of rhythms and improvisatory insight in an exhibition catalogue:

> Just at present, I have come to the conclusion that one must have a flexible form of formation that is governed by some definite rhythmic sense beyond mere geometrical repetition, to express and put in space an idea so that those with sensitive instruments can pick it up, and further that means an expression has to have grown long enough to establish itself as an automatic force.
>
> The play or spread or swing of space can only be felt through this kind of consciousness.

Dove's notion of a rhythmic "flexible form" applies to either visual art or music. The sounds of Duke Ellington, Fletcher Henderson, and other musical luminaries of the 1920s and 1930s address Dove's postulate, with limitless variations and nuances all possible under the aesthetic armature of the blues. Basic characteristics of some blues-formula music—twelve-bar structuring, three-chord progressions, and three-line stanzas—can be reworked according to the artistic demands. Similarly many modern artists, like Dove, found countless ways of expressing themselves while operating through fairly specific, but flexible principles. An expression's improvisational character, or, in Dove's words, its ability to "establish itself as an automatic force," is basic to all Afro-American music and ultimately to all Afro-American art forms.

"Swinging," the key word in the title of Dove's painting worked its way into Depression-era and World War II vocabularies as suggestive of the most popular music of the day. "Swing" bands like Jimmy Lunceford's Orchestra, Cab Calloway's Band, and Benny Moten's Kansas City Orchestra were legendary among audiences because of their commitment to a highly rhythmized, blues-based, dance music.

While some visual artists, like Dove, interpreted this "swinging" style via abstracted form, other artists chose more representational modes to depict the rhythmic "blues" culture of the 1930s and 1940s. Viktor Schreckengost, one of the leading ceramicists during the Depression, created his sculptural grouping of three ecstatic black women, *Glory, Glory* in response to this cultural scene. Simultaneously religious and irreverent, *Glory, Glory* presents conflicting sentiments in a manner akin to the dualities and dichotomies of many blues compositions.

William H. Johnson's *Jitterbugs* also captures the fervor of Afro-American popular culture in the late 1930s and early 1940s. Like George Luks in his 1907 image of the "Cake-Walkers," Johnson interprets the choreographed gymnastics of a black pair of dancers. But in a manner similar to abstractionist Dove, Johnson gives ideographic significance to their animated form. The legs, arms, feet, bodies and even interior space of *Jitterbugs* are rendered in brilliant, quilt-like geometric units. As a product of the "swing" era, *Jitterbugs* vibrates with an energy and rhythmic grace that mirrors the dance, music, and attitude of urban Afro-America ca. 1940.

Other figurative artists utilized more narrative techniques to show their solidarity with a blues aesthetic. Works Progress Administration graphic artist, Fred Becker, gave pictorial life to a standard blues ballad in his John Henry series. In *John Henry's Hand* Becker engraved the often repeated tropes of the black songsters—railroad tracks, cotton plants, serpents, and steel-driving hammers—on the palm of his folk hero.

In Jacob Lawrence's *Rooftops (No. 1 This is Harlem)*, the blues narrative is a panoramic yet highly abstracted scenario, as in the piano blues style known as "boogie-woogie." *Rooftops* communicates a Harlem tale through a steady repetition of form: rectangular buildings, rectangular street signs, rectangular windows, and rectangular fireescapes. Although *Rooftops* sprang from the same muse that inspired Piet Mondrian's legendary *Broadway Boogie-Woogie,* Lawrence's version, with its flat, yet expressionistically-treated geometries, is a more authentic depiction of the blues style.

More problematic than *Broadway Boogie-Woogie* (in terms of identifying an operative blues aesthetic) is the art of Jackson Pollock. Beyond Pollock's exploration of improvisation, it is difficult to suggest anything that would illustrate Pollack's understanding of black artistic sensibilities. However, we do know that blues-based music was the soundtrack for many of Pollock's action-painting sessions and that, according to associates, he listened to jazz in order to "overcome the blockage" that he occasionally faced as a painter.

We also know that the surrealists (for whom Pollock had much admiration in the early 1940s) claimed "jazz" as part of their subconscious heritage. A Pollock drawing from 1943—linear, notational, and vaguely suggestive of animals, human faces, and musical instruments—shows his affinity at that time for such surrealist devices as spontaneous drawing and metamorphic image-making. The drawing also functions as part of a larger corpus of experimental New York culture of the 1940s that, by its very definition, was created with the intention of giving a new twist on earlier artistic models. In this respect, Pollock is much closer to the radical innovations of a Charlie "Yard-bird" Parker or Dizzy Gillespie than one might initially assume. Pollock and especially Parker shared an interest in rethinking "chromatic" relationships: in challenging prevailing approaches to rhythm; in layering their respective artforms with a textual vitality; and in reinvesting themes and /or subject matter in art with a mythic, emotional dimension. Though separated by their chosen media, Jackson Pollock and Charlie Parker are kindred spirits in a period when American society (of which Afro-American culture forms a significant part) was undergoing radical change.

In *Charlie Parker's Favorite Painting* by Gertrude Abercrombie, the surrealist vision is again paired with the spirit of the blues. The painting consists of a landscape, inhabited only by a full moon; an obscure, dark mound in the middle ground; a dead tree; and an odd assortment of objects (a ladder, a wooden box, a lyncher's noose, a scattered pair of pink gloves and one fugitive piece of paper money). Originally entitled *Design for Death (The Noose)*, the painting acquired its present name sometime after 1960. Prior to that, it hung in various Chicago area exhibitions, as well as in Abercrombie's home. According to Abercrombie, the painting was often remarked upon by her friend, Charlie Parker, who along with many other jazz musicians, visited Abercrombie during scheduled stays in Chicago.

The original title suggests a meaning and interpretation for the painting that transcends Charlie Parker proper. But because the various components in the painting seem to have something to do with a lynching, a woman, and/or an exchange of money, many blues-inspired themes, compositions, and performances (i.e., Billie Holiday's "Strange Fruit," Charlie Parker's "How High the Moon," etc.) come to mind. For a surrealist like Gertrude Abercrombie, the confluence of strung-together pictorial elements, a socially-charged theme, a devotee to the paintings as important as Charlie Parker, and a title which changed over the years, made the painting all the more provocative and surreal.

For blues aestheticians like Abercrombie, Dove, and, to a lesser extent, Pollock, the title of a work could potentially communicate messages and intentions over and beyond a work of art's formal qualities. For abstract painter Normal Lewis, a title's ability to signify was most evident in his painting *Harlem Turn White*. Imposed on a brown canvas that is partially covered by small wedges and rubbings of white oil paint, Lewis's title raises countless interpretations. Is the work a comment on changing racial demographics? Is it an allegorical statement on acculturation? Or, is it merely a pun on the process of covering brown canvas with white paint? Given Lewis' unique position in the New York art scene of the 1950s—a connection with both "the New York School" and Harlem-based artists—*Harlem Turn White* is probably all of the above, as well as a perfect synthesis of the artist's personal aesthetics and well-known sense of irony.

Romare Bearden, a friend and associate of Norman Lewis, was also involved in an abstract approach to painting during the 1950s. But unlike Lewis, whose paintings frequently contained veiled, thematic allusions to Afro-America, Bearden's works from this period—large, color abstract paintings—were largely devoid of any references to race or culture.

Sermons: The Walls of Jericho was one of the first works by Bearden that broke away from his earlier involvement in a color field, abstract language. Utilizing cut-up and collaged images from books and magazines, *Sermons* . . . plays on the power of photo-documentary imagery, as well as the then growing interest in Afro-America. The year in which *Sermons* . . . and Bearden's other early collages were conceived—August 1963 through September 1964—was an especially volatile moment in Afro-American history, with almost daily reports of church bombings, student boycotts, race riots, and the murdering of civil rights workers by Southern white segregationists. This was also a period when black American music (especially the music of "Motown," urban Chicago blues, and such jazz legends as John Coltrane and Miles Davis) grew into a definitive cultural statement with a relevance beyond the black community.

The composite impression from Bearden's collage of human and animal parts, African sculpture, and slices of nature, was co-instantaneously fictive and current event-like. In *Sermons* . . . Bearden created a fascinating image of individual artistry and collective sentiment, which challenged viewers to partake of his "truth" through a vehicle that was and is the blues.

As a barometer of black America, blues-based music of the 1960s and 1970s expressed a variety of thoughts, feelings, and opinions. During these years of social upheaval and cultural reassessment, the music became everyone's voice and the musicians became everyone's surrogate self, proclaiming that "People get Ready," demanding a little "Respect," and rhetorically asking "What's Going On."

This call-and-response formula—old as Afro-America itself—is vividly documented in three photographs from this period. Roy Lewis's *Spirit of James and Maceo, Chicago* catches the psychic exchange between "Godfather of Soul" James Brown and his saxophonist Maceo Parker. In Roland Freeman's *Drums in the Park,* a similar moment of artistic communion is captured in the faces and gestures of an impromptu battery and their audience. And in Mikki Ferrill's *Untitled* work, the call-and-response between a performer and his audience on Chicago's Maxwell Street is manifested in ecstatic, religious terms.

While black music has always been held up as a kind of aesthetic ideal among artists of various disciplines, one finds especially in works since 1968 an even greater preoccupation with black music and its creators. Often, this fascination with the music inspired contemporary artists to make their art an homage to the music and its makers.

Archie Rand's *Breakage II-Thurston Harris* is one of several ca. 1971 paintings by the artist that functioned in Rand's own words, as "icons to culture." Thurston Harris, best known for his 1957 hit song "Little Bitty Pretty One," becomes forever etched in our minds via Rand's invocation of his name (along with the names of fifty other jazz, blues, rhythm and blues, and rock n' roll artists). The textured canvas, made so with acrylic resin paint fed through pastry guns and under cake combs, evokes the icing on decorated cakes, as well as the concentric grooves on records. For Rand, the mere utterance of a "blues" name makes one privy to all kinds of cultural "goodies," as this painting implies. The investment of a word/image with so much importance also brings to mind Stephen Henderson's notion of mascon words and constructions in Afro-American literature: words that, when used, "set all kinds of bells ringing, all kinds of synapse-snapping, on all kinds of levels . . ." This mode of "cultural recognition"—whether attempted in the language, in musical phrasings, in visual devices, or in combinations with any of the above—signals the presence of the blues aesthetic.

This exploration of a blues aesthetic has attempted to address itself beyond music and into the whole range of Afro-American data banks and cultural influences. Though it is well documented that many abstract painters were formally attuned to boogie-woogie, swing, and bebop, these musical components are only the most irrefutable examples of a larger pool of blues-idiom resources. The personal dynamics of black urban living can be seen as a vital part of a blues aesthetic and the guiding forces for formal/contextual decision-making in art.

The riffs in art/time that are created by generations of blues aestheticians bring to mind the declaration by Amiri Baraka that "All styles are epochs. They come again and again. What is was, and so forth." One might add to this statement that because styles, like the seasons, are cyclical. They are ultimately revolutionary and redemptive in their presentation. The blues, as the delta of Afro-American cultural reservoirs, spawns inlets of style, that color a vast and graying ocean of western tradition. The aesthetic weight of Afro-American culture bears down benevolently on those who recognize its contribution to modern art.

Suggested Readings with Similar Theme:

hooks, bell. "Aesthetic Inheritances, history worked by hand." In *Yearning: Race, Gender and Cultural Politics*. Boston: South End Press, 1990.

Jones, Gayl. *Liberating Voices: Oral Tradition in African American Literature*. Cambridge: Harvard University Press, 1991.

JOHN EDGAR WIDEMAN

Preface in *Breaking Ice:*
An Anthology of Contemporary
African American Fiction (1990)

In a letter to Terry McMillan, editor of "Breaking Ice," Wideman promotes the concept of "freedom of expression" for the contemporary writer. He cautions contemporary writers, however, not to sacrifice the African American aesthetic tradition—rather, they are encouraged to critique and to extend it. How does Wideman propose critiquing yet extending this aesthetic tradition? What responsibilities are assigned to the audience of contemporary writers? When referring to Imagination, Wideman writes the following: "A Story is a formula . . . Our stories can place us back at the center, at the controls; they can offer alternative realities, access to the sanctuary we carry around inside our skulls . . . {and they can draw} upon a force sustaining both individual talent and tradition." How does he enter discussions with other writers in this collection about the role of the writer, the creative process, and the function of African American literature?

Dear Terry,

Congratulations. It's time we had a new anthology of African-American fiction. I don't know what you've gathered, but I'm sure your sample will be enjoyable and instructive. The notes that follow are wishes, cautions, play with the issues and ideas that could/should, in my view, surface in a collection of contemporary Afro-American writing.

> The African artist allows wide scope to his fantasy in the mask. . . . With colors, feathers, and horns he accomplishes some astonishingly lively effects. In a slow creative process he brings to life a work which constitutes a new unit, a new being. If the sculpture proves to be a success, a helpful medium, the tribe adheres to this form and passes it on from generation to generation. . . . Thus we have a style, a family established formal canon, which may not be lightly discarded. . . . For this reason a style retains its specific character for decades, even centuries. It stands and falls with the faith to which it is linked.
> —*The Art of Black Africa,* Elsy Leuzinger

Since we're seen as marginal politically, economically, and culturally, African-American writers have a special, vexing stake in reforming, revitalizing the American imagination. History is a cage, a conundrum we must escape or resolve before our art can go freely about its business. As has always been the case, in order to break into print we must be prepared to deal with the extra-literary forces that have conspired to keep us silent, or our stories, novels, and poems will continue to be treated as marginally as our lives, unhinged, unat-tached to the everyday reality of "mainstream," majority readers. Magazine editors know that their jobs depend upon purveying images the public recog-nizes and approves, so they seldom include our fictions, and almost never choose those which transcend stereotypes and threaten to expose the fantasies of superiority, the bedrock lies and brute force that sustain the majority's power over the *other.* Framed in foreign, inimical contexts, minority stories appear at best as exotic slices of life and local color, at worst as ghettoized irrelevances.

However, as the assumptions of the mono-culture are challenged, over-run, defrock themselves daily in full view of the shameless media, more and more of the best fiction gravitates toward the category of "minority." The truth that each of us starts out alone, a minority of one, each in a slightly dif-ferent place (no place), resides somewhere in the lower frequencies of our communal consciousness. New worlds, alternative versions of reality are bur-geoning. In spite of enormous, overwhelming societal pressures to conform, to standardize the shape and meaning of individual lives, voices like Ralph Ellison's reach us, impelling us to attend to the *chaos which lives within the pat-tern* of our certainties.

Good stories transport us to these extraordinarily diverse regions where individual lives are enacted. For a few minutes we can climb inside another's skin. Mysteriously, the dissolution of ego also sharpens the sense of self, rein-forces independence and relativity of point of view. People's lives resist a sim-ple telling, cannot be understood safely, reductively from some static still point, some universally acknowledged center around which all other lives orbit. Narrative is a reciprocal process, regressive and progressive, dynamic. When a culture hardens into heliocentricity, fancies itself the star of creation, when otherness is imagined as a great darkness except for what the star illu-minates, it's only a matter of time until the center collapses in upon itself, imploding with sigh and whimper.

Minority writers hold certain peculiar advantage in circumstances of cul-tural breakdown, reorientation, transition. We've accumulated centuries of experience dealing with problems of marginality, problems that are suddenly on center stage for the whole society; inadequacy of language, failure of insti-tutions, a disintegrating metropolitan vision that denies us or swallows us, that attracts and repels, that promises salvation and extinction. We've always been outsiders, orphans, bastard children, hard-pressed to make our claims heard. In order to endure slavery and oppression it's been necessary to culti-vate the double-consciousness of sere, artist, mother. Beaten down by count-less assertions of the inadequacy, the repugnance of our own skin, we've been forced to enter the skins of others, to see, as a condition of survival, the world and ourselves through the eyes of others. Our stories can place us back at the center, at the controls; they can offer alternative realities, access to the sanctuary we carry around inside our skulls. The African American imagination has evolved as discipline, defense, coping mechanism, counterweight to the galling facts of life. We've learned to confer upon ourselves the power of making up our lives, changing them as we go along.

Marginality has also refined our awareness, our proficiency in nonliterary modes of storytelling. Folk culture preserves and expresses an identity, a history, a self-evaluation apart from those destructive, incarcerating images proliferated by the mainline culture. Consciously and unconsciously we've integrated these resources of folk culture into our writing. Our songs, dreams, dances, styles of walk and talk, dressing, cooking, sport, our heroes and heroines provide a record of how a particular group has lived in the world, in it, but not of it. A record so distinctive and abiding that its origins in culture have been misconstrued as rooted in biology. A long-tested view of history is incorporated in the art of African-American people, and our history can be derived from careful study of forms and influences that enter our cultural performances and rituals. In spite of and because of marginal status, a powerful, indigenous vernacular tradition has survived, not unbroken, but unbowed, a magnet, a focused energy, something with its own logic, rules, and integrity connecting current developments to the past. An articulate, syncretizing force our best artists have drawn upon, a force sustaining both individual talent and tradition. Though minstrel shows were popularized as a parody of black life, these musical reviews were also a vehicle for preserving authentic African-derived elements of black American culture. Today rap, for all its excesses and commercialization, reasserts the African core of black music: polyrhythmic dance beat, improvisational spontaneity, incantatory use of the word to name, blame, shame, and summon power, the obligation of ritual to instruct and enthuse. It's no coincidence that rap exploded as the big business of music was luring many black artists into "crossing over." Huge sums were paid to black recording artists; then a kind of lobotomy was performed on their work, homogenizing, commodifying, pacifying it by removing large portions of what made the music think and be. Like angry ancestral spirits, the imperatives of tradition rose up, reanimated themselves, mounted the corner chanters and hip hoppers. As soul diminished to a category on the pop charts, the best from the street said no-no-no, you're too sweet. Try some of this instead. Stomp your feet. Don't admit defeat. Put your hands together. Hit it. Hit. Boom. Crank up the volume. Bare bones percussion and chant holler scream. Our loud selves, our angry selves. Our flying feet and words and raunchy dreams. Instruments not possessed mimicked by our voices. Electronics appropriated. Recording tricknology explored and deconstructed, techniques reversed, foregrounded, parodied. Chaboom. Boom. Sounds of city, of machines of inner space and outer space merge. Boom boxes. Doom boxes. Call the roll of the ancestors. Every god from Jah, Isis, Jehovah, Allah, and Shango to James Brown and the Famous Flames. Say the names. Let them strut the earth again. Get right, children. Rap burst forth precisely where it did, when it did because that's where the long, long night of poverty and discrimination, of violent marginality remained a hunting truth nobody else was telling. That's where the creative energies of a subject people were being choked and channeled into self-destruction.

When an aesthetic tradition remembers its roots, the social conditions (slavery, oppression, marginality) and the expressive resources it employed to cope with these conditions, the counter vision of these conditions it elaborated through art, when it doesn't allow itself to be distracted, that is, keeps telling the truth which brought it into being—the necessity of remaining human, defining human in its own terms, resisting those destructive definitions in the Master's tongue, attitudes and art—then that tradition remains alive, a referent, a repository of value, money we can take to the bank. Afro-American traditions contain the memory of a hard, unclean break. This partially accounts for key postures that are subversive, disruptive, disjunctive. To the brutality that once ripped us away and now tries to rip us apart, we turn a stylized mask of indifference, of malleability, a core of iron, silent refusal. Boom. Chaboom. Boom. While our feet, feet, feet, dance to another beat.

I look for, cherish this in our fiction.

On the other hand—or should I say other face, since the shield I'm raising has two sides and one cannot be lifted without the other—what about the future? Is there any difference between sitting in at an all-white lunch counter and a minority writer composing a story in English? What's the fate of a black story in a white world of white stories? What can we accomplish with our *colors, feathers, and horns,* how can we fruitfully extend our tradition? How do we break out of the circle of majority-controlled publishing houses, distributors, critics, editors, readers? Vernacular language is not enough. Integration is not enough, unless one views mathematical, proportional representation as a goal instead of a step. If what a writer wants is freedom of expression, then somehow that larger goal must be addressed implicitly/explicitly in our fictions. A story should somehow contain clues that align it with tradition and critique tradition, establish the new space it requires, demands, appropriates, hint at how it may bring forth other things like itself, where these others have, will, and are coming from. This does not mean defining criteria for admitting stories into some ideologically sound, privileged category, but seeking conditions, mining territory that maximizes the possibility of free, original expression. We must continue inventing our stories, sustaining, not sacrificing, the double consciousness that is a necessity for any writing with the ambition of forging its own place.

Black music again illuminates glories and pitfalls, the possibility of integrity, how artists nourished by shared cultural roots can prove again and again that, even though they are moving through raindrops, they don't have to get soaked. Their art signifies they are in the storm but not of it. Black music is a movable feast, fluid in time, space, modality, exhibiting in theme and variations multiple relationships with the politically, socially, aesthetically dominant order, the fullest possible range of relationships, including the power and independence to change places, reverse the hierarchy, be the dominant order.

What lessons are transferable to the realm of literature? Is musical language freer, less inscribed with the historical baggage of European hegemony, exploitation, racism? Is it practical within the forms and frequencies of this instrument (written English) to roll back history, those negative accretions, those iron bars and "White Only" signs that steal one's voice, one's breath away?

Are there ways fiction can express the dialectic, the tension, the conversation, the warfare of competing versions of reality English contains? One crucial first step may be recognizing that black/white, either/or perceptions of the tensions within language are woefully inadequate. Start by taking nothing for granted, giving nothing away. Study the language. The way we've begun to comb the past. Rehistoricize. Contest. Contest. Return junk mail to sender. Call into question the language's complacencies about itself. At the level of spelling, grammar, how its taught, but also deeper, its sounds, their mamas, its coded pretensions to legitimacy, gentility, exclusivity, seniority, logic. Unveil chaos within the patterns of certainty. Restate issues and paradigms so they are not simply the old race problem relexified. Whose language is it, anyway?

Martin Bernal in *Black Athena* has traced the link between European theories of race and language. How nineteenth-century theories of language development parallel, buttress, and reinforce hierarchical concepts of race and culture. How social "sciences," the soft core posing as the hard core of academic humanities curricula, were tainted at their inception by racist assumptions and agenda. How romantic linguistic theory was used as a tool to prove the superiority of the West. How uncritical absorption of certain hallowed tenets of Western thought is like participating in your own lynching. Be prepared to critique any call for "back to basics" in light of the research Bernal gathers and summarizes. The great lie that systems of thought are pure, universal, uncontaminated by cultural bias is once more being gussied up for public consumption. Whose Great Books in whose interest must be read? Whose stories should be told? By whom? To what ends?

How does language grow, change? What are the dynamics that allow individual speakers to learn a language, adapt it to the infinite geography of their inner imaginative worlds, the outer social play, the constant intercourse of both? Can the writer love language and also keep it at arm's length as material, a medium, foregrounding its arbitrariness, its treacherousness, never calling it his/her own, never completely identifying with it but making intimate claims by exploring what it can do, what it could do if the writer has patience, luck, skill, and practices, practices, practices?

In it, but not of it. And that stance produces bodies of enabling legislation, a grammar of nuanced tensions, incompatibilities, doors and windows that not only dramatize the stance itself but implicate the medium. A reciprocal unraveling below whose surface is always the unquiet recognition that this language we're using constantly pulls many directions at once and unless we keep alert, keep fighting the undertow, acknowledge the currents going our way and every other damned way, we drown. We are not alone but not separate either; any voice we accomplish is really many voices, and the most powerful voices are always steeped in unutterable silences. A story is a formula for extracting meaning from chaos, a handful of water we scoop up to recall an ocean. Nothing really stands still for this reduction, this abstraction. We need readers who are willing to be coconspirators. It's at this level of primal encounter that we must operate in order to reclaim the language for our expressive purposes. The hidden subject remains: what is our situation with respect to this language? Where does it come from? Where do I come from? Where do we meet and how shall I name this meeting place? What is *food*? What is *eating*? Why do people go to lunch counters? Black music offers a counter integrative model because it poses this species of question about music and fills us with the thrill of knowing yes, yes, the answers, if there are any, and it probably doesn't matter whether there are or not, yay or nay, the answers and the questions are still up for grabs.

Suggested Reading with Similar Theme:

Rowell, Charles. "An Interview with John Edgar Wideman." *Callaloo* 13, no. 1 (Winter 1989): 47–61.

TERRY MCMILLAN

From "Introduction" in *Breaking Ice: An Anthology of Contemporary African American Fiction* (1990)

How does McMillan enter discussions with Hughes, Baldwin, Neal, Bambara, and others about the role of the writer? Who is the New Black Aesthetic (NBA) writer? What is his/her responsibility to himself/herself? To his/her audience? How might the contemporary African American writer respond when asked, "What is the function of African American literature? Is it to instruct? To inform? To entertain? Or more?"

Trey Ellis has coined a phrase which he calls "The New Black Aesthetic," a kind of glasnost. He believes that all contemporary African-American artists now create art where race is not the only source of conflict. We are a new breed, free to write as we please, in part because of our predecessors, and because of the way life has changed. "For the first time in our history we are producing a critical mass of college graduates who are children of college graduates themselves. Like most artistic booms, the NBA is a post-bourgeois movement; driven by a second generation of [the] middle class. Having scraped their way to relative wealth and, too often, crass materialism, our parents have freed (or compelled) us to bite those hands that fed us and sent us to college. We now feel secure enough to attend art school instead of medical school."

Ellis believes, and I support his position, that "new black artists [are no longer] shocked by racism as were those of the Harlem Renaissance, nor are we preoccupied with it as were those of the Black Arts Movement. For us, racism is a hard and little-changing constant that neither surprises nor enrages."

We now comment on ourselves in our work. We can poke fun, laugh at, and pinpoint ourselves as we see fit. Sometimes there is a price for this. From the production of *For Colored Girls Who Have Considered Suicide, When the Rainbow Is Enuf,* by Ntozake Shange, and then Alice Walker's *The Color Purple,* on to Gloria Naylor's *The Women of Brewster Place,* members of the African-American community began criticizing these writers because of their negative depiction of African-American men. "We" had no right to "air our dirty laundry" in front of the white world.

In a recent article appearing in the *Washington Post,* staff writer and *Book World* reviewer, David Nicholson's, "Painting It Black: African American Artists, In Search of a New Aesthetic," states: "True artists often travel lonely roads, but black artists are in the unenviable position of having too much company on their journeys—everybody wants to tell them what to do and how to do it. . . . black literature, film by black filmmakers, black music and black art . . . are expected to carry the weight of politics and sociology. They are subject to the conflicting imperatives—too seldom aesthetic—of various movements and ideologies. They must present a positive image, and they must never, ever reveal unpleasant truths (dissension among blacks, color and caste prejudice) to outside (read "white") eyes.

Most of the literature by African-Americans appearing from the thirties through the early sixties appeared to be aimed at white audiences. We were telling them who we were and what they'd done wrong. Times have changed. We do not feel the need to create and justify our existence anymore. We are here. We are proud. And most of us no longer feel the need to prove anything to white folks. If anything, we're trying to make sense of ourselves to ourselves.

Needless to say, good fiction is not preaching. If a writer is trying hard to convince you of something, then he or she should stick to nonfiction. These days, our work is often as entertaining as it is informative, thought-provoking as it is uplifting. Some of us would like to think that the experiences of our characters are "universal," and yet sometimes a situation could only happen if the color of your character's skin is black. When a writer sits down to tell a story, staring at a blank page, it amazes me how some people are so naive as to believe that when we invent a character, that we've got the entire race of African-Americans in mind; that these characters are supposed to be representative of the whole instead of the character we originally had in mind. Let's face it, there are some trifling men and women that some of us have come across, so much so that we have to write down the effect they had on us. On the other hand, there are also some kind, loving, tender, gentle, successful, and supportive folks in our lives, who also find their way into our work.

But good fiction is filled with conflict, drama, and tension. If we were to spend our time writing lackluster, adult fairy tales, only to please our readers and critics, I know I would be bored to death. I read enough uneventful stories about dull people who live dull lives, and everything that happens to them is dull. As writers, we have a right to choose our own particular focus.

Without a doubt, writing fiction requires passion and compassion. A sense of urgency. Excitement. Intensity. Stillness. For many of us, writing is our reaction to injustices, absurdities, beauty. It's our way of registering our complaints or affirmations. The best are not didactic. They do not scream out "message," nor are they abstractions. Our stories are our personal response. What we want to specify. What we see. What we feel. Our wide angle lens—

our close-up look. And even if the story doesn't quite pinpoint the solution or the answer, it is the exploration itself that is often worth the trip. . . .

Suggested Readings with Similar Theme:

Tate, Greg. "Cult-Nats Meet Freaky-Deke." *Voice Literary Supplement* (December 1986): 5–8.
Ellis, Trey. "The New Black Aesthetic." *Callaloo* 12, no. 1 (Winter 1989): 233–43.

GALE JACKSON

The Way We Do:
A Preliminary Investigation of
the African Roots of African American
Performance (1991)

Define the following terms and phrases: performance, Legba, Yoruba divination, ritual, vodun vere, the idea of created space, memory, reconstruction, diaspora, carnival, neo-African, pan-African, communal text, sacred and secular, Bakongo belief. What are "the steps from African sacred and secular performance through to the oral tradition"? How does Jackson demonstrate Snead's discussion of repetition and a cyclical art form?

> Speak to me so that I may speak to you. By our voices we recognize each other in the darkness. (Ifa divination) Once Spider came to have a calabash filled with all the knowledge in the world. . . . (Ashanti tale)

In the performance of storytelling, we reconstruct and perpetuate the history of a mythic past in order to better understand both that past and our own time in a historic and ritual continuum. In the performance of storytelling, we participate in pure celebration, in ritual, in imparting the moral or the lesson of the story, and in creating the "stage" on which the story can be told.

This storytelling is an attempt to reconstruct a detail of Spider's calabash—its voice, its wisdom, its theater or symbol—in order to illuminate the African philosophical base of African American theater and cultural performance. The black church—its "theater," its pomp, its ceremony—is a signpost on the epic cultural journey of African sacred and secular ritual into the diaspora. This storytelling attempts to reconstruct part of that epic in a juxtaposition of voices and acts, in call and response, along a continuum of African to African American performance—to talk about performance through performance.

> Night falls and we lay our sleeping mats. Day breaks and we roll them up. The one who lays the warp threads must walk back and forth. (Ifa divination)

This is a collage or weaving of story in a preliminary journey towards meaning and recognition. This telling looks to illustrate the steps from

African sacred and secular performance through to the oral traditions, folk-ways, religion, and theatre of the diaspora. This telling is itself an investiga-tive "performance" which attempts to examine the uses of specific symbolic patterns—of actions and words—in the telling and recording of history, in moral instruction, in expressing and coping with a world view which acknowledges duality, in acts of cultural survival, and in the communal cre-ation of the stages on which we are, by all these attributes, regenerated, recre-ated, and transformed.

> If you want to find Jesus,
> Go in the wilderness,
> Go in the wilderness,
> Go in the wilderness. (African American traditional)

This telling begins with, and gathers refrains from, ritual verse from the Yoruba divination text, the *Ifa*. Subsequently I look at other African perfor-mance rituals across the continents. From there I look at our holidays and holy days, at blues and spirituals, at autobiography and folklore, and at the neo-African theaters in which these forms are created and shared as they are performed. The juxtaposition reveals a cultural philosophy rich in symbolic text and act, and with an ordinal, grammatical, and ritual structure of its own. Across the African continent and in the Americas; in old-time religion and Southern burial markers; in carnivals, pinksters, jubilees, susus, and secret orders; in the linguistic "dozens"; and in the religious witness which prefigures black literature in black performance are African symbol systems. And these symbols encode a philosophy of life that is circular, a correlative understanding of divinity and creativity as activated by community, and an understanding of ritual as an ordering and empowering force.

> Orunmilla, carry me in your bag.
> Carry me in your purse so that
> We may go together slowly, so
> That wherever we may be going we
> May go there together. (Ifa divination)

Back and forth along the four winds and into the wilderness, where the pieces of the calabash have fallen, are the routes of migration of African peoples and their cultures, beginning in the "prewritten" history of the Sudanese regions, thousands of years before the forced migrations of the Atlantic slave trade. From this regional and cultural genesis, I draw a working definition of African performance.

In this pan-African context, and perhaps in line with true folk meaning, the term performance refers to a broad spectrum of cultural acts—from reli-gious ritual, to playing mass as carnival, to children's circle games. These cul-tural performance acts are all, at root, a defined series of symbolic gestures,

done in a set manner, having set meanings, and performed with a particular
end in mind (even if the meanings and ends have been lost or forgotten over
time and nothing but the gestures and their ontological "spirit" have survived). These performance acts, in the African context, create a discrete ritually potent and potential moment, a theater, in time.

> Hambone, Hambone where you been?
> All 'round the world and back again.
> Hambone, Hambone what'd you do?
> I got a chance and I fairly flew. (African American folk game/song)

A pan-African poetics of performance is potentially a basis on which
memory and reconstruction happen in the diaspora. William Bascom reminds
us that the Yoruba priests brought the entire text of Yoruba history, mythology, and divination intact in their memories to the "New World." In addition
to the professional performers of music, story, dance, and song, laypersons
also brought with them a distinctively African world view. Consequently, the
Africanness in African American culture is often deeply imbedded in the conceptual framework out of which acts of cultural performance come. My focus
here is on specific shared aspects of these "theaters."

WITNESS AND HISTORY

> Go tell it on the mountain
> Over the hills and everywhere.
> Go tell it on the mountain . . . (African American spiritual)

For the African, the overriding collective truth to be publicly told in the early
history of this country was the story of journey, oppression, slavery, and liberation. In thousands of work songs, blues songs, and spirituals; in thousands of
instances of oral witness and written narratives; in the early publication of
black drama (e.g., William Wells Brown's *The Escape*), African Americans
voiced a communal desire to tell their story and to have it passed on. This
outpouring of witness often used mythological forms which prefigured the
formal religious "witness" of the Afro-Christian church, but are consistent
with its passion, its sense of mission, and its urgency. Over time, and whether
in oral or written narrative, whether in the sanctified church or on a formal
and informal dramatic stage, the meaning and performance of witness would
remain much the same. Sacred or secular, it has been an articulation wrought
from the heart of African American oral performance. As such, it is a wielding
of the power of remembered and performed history. It is the spiritual. It is the
work song. It is the sermon and the narrative which arise from them.

Dis ole hammer
Huh!
Kill John Henry
Huh!
Laid him low, buddy
Huh!
Laid him low. (African American work song)

The African American performance of history charts the actual and the mythic journeys of thousands who tell the same tale in strikingly similar ways. In hundreds of autobiographical recollections of antebellum life, in song and story, African Americans of the early generations wrote a communal text of their own story, imbued with a mission urgent and holy. It is a story of day-to-day, backbreaking labor and how it was expressed in the field holler. It is a story, a historical drama, of how the individual and the community moved to a moment of revelation which swept them into actual and metaphorical wilderness and flight. It is a story of how, against the odds, they escaped the physical and the spiritual clutches of slavery, and of how they survived. And the witness, the telling of that story, is a ritual, a performance which remembers, encodes, and perpetuates the possibility of that survival . . . through the valleys of slavery's inhumanity and despair; across the wilderness, the rivers—the byways of escape which tested both strength and faith in the journey north. Finally, by their witness, that journey is transformed, just as it is transforming. The stark reality of a community's history became, in time, a shared mythological drama.

I know, I know, Lord.
Believer, I know, I know, I know, Lord.
Believer, I know, I know, the road so thorny.
Believer, I know . . . I done cross Jordan.
Believer, I know. (African American religious traditional)

Similarly, in traditional Yoruba society, ritual marks individuals' progress within the community from birth to death. Ritual accompanies us in successfully achieving our predestined journey with fate; it intercedes and negotiates with faith and the ancestors as we go along. A ritual text, the Ifa, is revealed by a system of symbols. That ritual text gives both proverb and proscription, divine performance and divine "writing" to assist in ordering the chaos of incomplete knowledge of the world. Ikin, or palm nuts, are thrown in a ceremony which reveals the symbolic writing of our history and our fate. When we read the palm nuts, we are guided to an Ifa verse, which in turn points our way on the road of life. But before and after the actual ceremony, the priests and petitioner(s) must circle the community, must take a symbolic communal walk. Their "parade" symbolizes both the totality of community involvement in a life and the journey that the individual must take toward faith. The history of the Ifa begins with a story of journey. The history of the Ifa in America begins with the journey imbedded in the remembered text. When, it is reasoned, people see into their own fate, they remember to mark their ancestors in history. When the people were enslaved, Legba, among the gods, shared their slaveship journey.

> O great one, I pay obeisance. The young child does not confront the powerful one. I pay obeisance to Elegba Eshu, who is on the road. (Brazilian cult song to Legba)

THE MORAL LESSON

The narrative act of witness has its parallels and prefigurations in both African and diaspora lore. Here instruction and documentation go hand and hand. Oral history performance is particularly suited to giving social/political/moral instruction, overt or covert. Folk songs and tales, particularly, provide a performance vehicle of extraordinary social possibility and are very useful in the diaspora—small animal tales, for instance. In African societies, and later in the Americas, these tales have passed down the imagination of causality and revolution in nature. In them, small and oppressed animals suffer their oppression (mirroring the condition of races and classes of people) but also use aspects of their oppression to their advantage.

> Didn't my Lord deliver Daniel?
> Deliver Daniel deliver . . . (African American religious traditional)

Sermons and spirituals utilize the same moral methodology and aesthetic play by structuring the performance of witness, with its myth and grandeur, into a complex duet with the parable. Examples abound in African American public performance: The papier-mache dreams of the carnival artists, for instance, resonate with the power, beauty, rhetorical seduction, and righteous witnessing of this duet. Even in strictly sacred "performance," in religious rites across the African American spectrum, the spirit will "move you" and the congregation will "bear you up," since performance and possession are the moral responsibility of those who know. In the telling of this story, sacrifice is not seen solely as tragedy but as an aspect of transformation and, if the truth has survived to be told, as a symbol of actual or potential spiritual power. Here the masks represent not only pathos and bathos but the deep-set duality of Legba: its two-colored face, its two-colored hat.

THE TWO SIDES/THE CIRCLE

> Orunmilla, carry me in your bag.
> Carry me in your purse so that

> We may go together slowly, so
> That wherever we may be going we
> May go there together.

Africans, separated by generations of geographical differentiation, came together under the common oppression of the Atlantic slave trade, consciously and unconsciously forming and reforming a neo-African aesthetic built on African conceptual retentions which were masked. From this shared, subversive, and reconstructed base came a system for reading/improvising or signifying within a theater of communal performance. The masked meanings of African American performance are still very much hidden in their own structures. Africanisms in African American performances are as often hidden as they are evident, and this seems somewhat by design. The conceptual framework, the stage on which dual but non-oppositional systems of symbols or meanings are encoded, by virtue of their masked nature, was built to survive a period underground. Masking, a pervasive element in African performance, has equal weight and meaning in the social history of the diaspora. The masked performances of carnival, jonkonnu, cakewalks, and creole balls play, as do folktales and even slave narratives, between concealment and revelation, between joy and sorrow, between light and dark like a child's circling song. Like them the religious "performance" is both an act of public affirmation and a rite of cloaking, of creating a safe ritual space for believers.

> Sometimes I feel like a motherless child.
> Sometimes I feel like a motherless child.
> Sometimes I feel like a motherless child
> Such a long long way from home. (African American traditional)

> Sometimes I feel like an eagle in de air.
> Some of these mornings bright and fair
> I'm going to lay down my heavy load
> Going to spread my wings and cleave the air. (African American traditional)

The established church standardized the spiritual and took it on the road, where it has been performed as popular theater since the late 1800s. Black and white musical writers put the spiritual and the sermon—something of black song, black dance, and black talk—on the American musical stage, which has, since its inception, been informed, if not by African content, then by the African form. Of course, for African Americans the tension between identity and social constructs has remained (think of Dunbar's "We Wear the Mask," of DuBois's "double-consciousness" and of Washington's conceptual "Veil"). Minstrel theater, for example, parodied observations of black performance in both sacred and secular forums. Subsequently, it brought to the American stage an "original" American form built on a mockery of African performance. When African Americans first began to perform on the mainstream stages of this country, they, in turn, improvised and, in some cases, signified on the black-faced mockery of white minstrel men. As African American theater has developed as an autonomous genre, it has increasingly pulled on the signifying potential of what has become a contemporary enactment of masking. And the festivals of masking remain as well, operating on many public and less public levels—perhaps now driven, in addition, by a new need for catharsis. Beside them, the church has also remained as a stage for a "theater" of revolutionary rhetoric and rebellion, as well as a resource for popular culture.

THE ALTAR/THE STAGE

> The mortar will testify that I see room in which to settle.
> The teteleaf will testify that I see room in which to stretch out.
> The gbebe leaf will testify that I see room in which to dwell. (Ifa divination)

When the Bakongo of Southern Zaire perform a traditional ritual oath, the petitioner stands on a Greek cross drawn into the earth. The vertical line is a line of entrance: a path that crosses into the next world and on which we symbolically gain wisdom and age. The horizontal line is the division between this world and the next. Together, these lines mark a point of intersection between this, the world of the living, and the other, that of the ancestors before and beyond. The Bakongo write this meaning. The cross is in fact understood as given or written by the ancestors, who are our gods. Cuban descendants of the Bakongo call their neo-African cuneiforms la firma "the signature of the spirits." The performance of this ritual is set on a continuum from ancient time. On this point, we sing ritual words (yimbila ye sona), according to tradition. On this point, the petitioner draws a point and sings proscribed words in a meditation. This meditation on the oath on the symbolic crossroads creates the power of god, and brings it—creativity, power, possibility—to the point where we stand. In Bakongo belief, the meditation on the oath on the symbolic crossroads remembers the relationship between the living and the dead, individual and community, communion and continuity. The rite of meditation on the oath retains its power in the diaspora in specific speech acts of witness, in the use of rhyme and repetition (within the very language structures of African Americans), and in the knowledge that what goes around (even if we don't know from where) still comes around.

> Ogbe sprouts firm. It enters into the belly of the forest. Ogun sprouts long and slender. It reaches the road. (Ifa divination)

What stands out in the parallel between African and African American ritual performance is the way in which the performance itself, be it sacred or secular, involves communally creating a moment of potentiality and regenerative possibility—as theater on which to act out existential drama or a stage on which to put potentiality and regenerative possibility into play in both the social and spiritual universe. When stories are told in most of the Francophone Caribbean, the storyteller begins, ends, and punctuates the tale with the call crick or yea crick, to which audience members respond crack or yea crack. Similarly, in most traditional African American churches, the sermon and the service are created by the entire community, participating in a communal performance of worship. Like the African rituals which prefigure them, these African American sacred performances involve the creation of sacred space (or "black space"). In an act of choral movement, shouting, clapping synchronization, and/or call-and-response, which recalls the bond between individual and community, these neo-African performances remain percussive, mythic (or allegorical), circular, improvisational, and double-edged, in the African theatrical mode.

> Wade in the water.
> Wade in the water, children.
> Wade in the water. (African American traditional, Sea Islands)

Bakongo, Ibo, Mendi and Yoruba rituals of community interaction, vodun vere, Bakongo cosmograms—all speak to the idea of created space between the realms of the living and the realms of the dead. It is a ritual space that sings of trouble with a powerful voice and soars toward the sacred with the verve and sensuality of gutbucket blues or sings gutbucket blues with a voice that recalls to the listener his or her higher self. The ritual space is, in the African American case, an alternative stage. In the context of the diaspora experience, it is a needed stage or place for affirming and recreating the drama of existence.

> Eye of secret unseen by evil
> Eye of secret unseen by evil
> The diviner's eyes will not see evil
> The diviner's eyes will not see evil. (Ifa divination)

We stand on a point of infinity. We circle the compound. The party circles the compound in a parade toward the divination ceremony. Carnival circle the parish. The spirit circles the room. The song rises up from the totality. The storyteller rises up out of the communal circle and weaves another circle of enclosure with the tale. The Spider in Ashanti lore spins a web to the heavens to bring to the people all of history in story. Legba takes a journey to the places where he will find the ingredients of prophecy, a journey written before Legba began. Legba learns this from Earth's animals and teaches Orunmilla. Orunmilla carries us in his bag. And we bring Orunmilla to the Americas—

preserving, carrying, concealing, encoding, and protecting ourselves in a journey, neverending, in the rituals of living we perform.

> Members, plumb the line.
> Members, plumb the line.
> Plumb the line.
> If you want to get to Heaven, you got to
> Plumb the line. (African American traditional)

These are performances which move toward the mythological in the recreation of an African universe, performances which are self-consciously ritualistic and which play off the "mainstream" idea of text, performances which increasingly, along this continuum, seek to establish place and order in chaos through symbolic gesture, action, and words. Implicit in all this is the root of oral witness, a statement about the importance of the story of people, about the circle embracing us in an African cosmology of meaning. African performance throughout the diaspora recalls the Yoruba emphasis on becoming gods ourselves, on meeting Legba at the crossroads (in any of his incarnations), of molding the mutability of fate, of becoming, like vodun and santeria practitioners, empowered to "make the gods." These performances of cultural sustenance, survival, and liberation draw on a communal creativity. This cultural community has invested the wilderness, or, more vernacularly, the edge with a potentiality for transformative action. This is place used to generate power. Whether the physical place is the wilderness, the pulpit, or the stage matters little. Here the performer can be mounted by the actual and symbolic power of the ritual itself. It doesn't matter whether the rites are acted, spoken, danced, sung, or written down. The internal rhythm is the same. The intent, the call to power is the same.

> Ogbe closes very generously, was the one who cast Ifa for head, who had knelt and chose his destiny. (Ifa divination)

This is about the way we do culturally—about the drama of dance, about the writing of divination, about the musical telling of tales, about the ordinary and mystical oral conjuring of space, and about the identification marks and road signs to the heavens on hennaed hands.

Suggested Readings with Similar Theme:

Thompson, Robert Farris. *Flash of the Spirit, African and Afro-American Art and Philosophy.* New York: Vintage, 1984.

Dance, Daryl. *Shucklin' and Jivin': Folklore form Contemporary Black Americans.* Bloomington: Indiana University Press, 1987.

Holloway, Joseph. *Africanisms in American Culture.* Bloomington: Indiana University Press, 1990.

Welsh-Asante, Kariamu, ed. *The African Aesthetic: Keeper of the Traditions.* Westport, Conn.: Praeger, 1994.

CHARLES I. NERO

Toward a Black Gay Aesthetic: Signifying in Contemporary Black Gay Literature (1991)

How do African American gay male writers critique and revise the African American literary tradition? How significant is signification to the African American gay writer? What else has Nero revealed about the creative process for many black gay writers? At what levels are aesthetic discussions among black gay writers art or propaganda?

With only a few exceptions, the intellectual writings of black Americans have been dominated by heterosexual ideologies that have resulted in the gay male experience being either excluded, marginalized, or ridiculed. Because of the heterosexism among African American intellectuals and the racism in the white gay community, black gay men have been an invisible population. However, the last five years have seen a movement characterized by political activism and literary production by openly gay black men. Given their invisibility by both black heterosexism and white gay racism, two questions emerge: How have black gay men created a positive identity for themselves and how have they constructed literary texts which would render their lives visible, and therefore valid?

The critical framework that I use is strongly influenced by my reading of Mary Helen Washington's *Invented Lives* and Henry Louis Gates, Jr.'s critical method of signifying. In *Invented Lives,* Washington brilliantly analyzes the narrative strategies ten black women have used between 1860 and 1960 to bring themselves into visibility and power in a world dominated by racism and sexism. Like Washington, Gates's concern is with the paradoxical relationship of African Americans with the printed text, i.e., since Eurocentric writing defines the black as "other," how does the "other" gain authority in the text? To resolve this, Gates proposes a theory of criticism based upon the African American oral tradition of signifying. Signifying is, for Gates, "the black term for what in classical European rhetoric are called the figures of signification," or stated differently, "the indirect use of words that changes the meaning of a word or words." Signifying has numerous figures which include: capping, loud-talking, the dozens, reading, going off, talking smart, sounding, joaning (jonesing), dropping lugs, snapping, woofing, styling out, and calling out of one's name.

As a rhetorical strategy, signifying assumes that there is shared knowledge between communicators and, therefore, that information can be given indirectly. Geneva Smitherman in *Talkin and Testifyin* gives the following examples of signifying:

> Stokely Carmichael, addressing a white audience at the University of California, Berkeley, 1966: "It's a privilege and an honor to be in the white intellectual ghetto of the West."
>
> Malcolm X on Martin Luther King, Jr.'s nonviolent revolution (referring to the common practice of singing "We Shall Overcome" at civil rights protests of the sixties): "In a revolution, you swinging, not singing."
>
> Reverend Jesse Jackson, merging sacred and secular siggin in a Breadbasket Saturday morning sermon: "Pimp, punk, prostitute, preacher, Ph.D.—all the P's—you still in slavery!"
>
> A black middle-class wife to her husband who had just arrived home several hours later than usual: "You sho got home early today for a change."
>
> Effective signifying is, Smitherman states, "to put somebody in check . . . to make them think about and, one hopes, correct their behavior." Because signifying relies on indirection to give information, it requires that participants in any communicative encounter pay attention to, as Claudia Michell-Kernan states, "the total universe of discourse."

Gates's theory of signifying focuses on black forms of talk. I believe that identifying these forms of talk in contemporary black gay literature is important for two reasons. First, the use of signifying by black gay men places their writing squarely within the African American literary tradition. Second, signifying permits black gay men to revise the "Black Experience" in African American literature, and, thereby, to create a space for themselves.

Representing Sexual Desire

Because of the historical and often virulent presence of racism, black literature has frequently had as its goal the elevation of "the race" by presenting the group in its "best light." The race's "best light" often has meant depicting blacks with those values and ways that mirrored white Americans and Europeans. For black writers this has usually meant tremendous anxiety over the representation of sexuality. An excellent example of this anxiety is W. E. B. DuBois's reaction to Claude McKay's 1920 novel *Home to Harlem*. In the novel, McKay, gay and Jamaican, wrote about much of the night life in Harlem, including one of the first descriptions of a gay and lesbian bar in an African American work of fiction. DuBois wrote:

Claude McKay's *Home to Harlem* for the most part nauseates me, and after the dirtier parts of its filth I feel distinctly like taking a bath. . . . McKay has set out to cater for that prurient demand on the part of white folks for a portrayal in Negroes of that utter licentiousness . . . which a certain decadent section of the white world . . . wants to see written out in black and white and saddled on black Harlem. . . . He has used every art and emphasis to paint drunkenness, fighting, lascivious sexual promiscuity and utter absence of restraint in as bold and bright colors as he can. . . . As a picture of Harlem life or of Negro life anywhere, it is, of course, nonsense. Untrue, not so much as on account of its facts, but on account of its emphasis and glaring colors.

The anxiety that DuBois felt was as acute for black women. Mary Helen Washington comments that this anxiety about the representation of sexuality "goes back to the nineteenth century and the prescription for womanly 'virtues' which made slave women automatically immoral and less feminine than white women," as in the case of the slave woman Harriet Jacobs, who considered not publishing her 1860 narrative *Incidents in the Life of a Slave Girl* because she "bore two children as a single woman rather than submit to forced concubinage." The representation of sexuality is even more problematic for black gay men than for heterosexual African Americans because of societal disapproval against impersonal sex, in which gay men frequently engage, and because gay sex is not connected in any way with the means of reproduction.

Revising our Culture's ideas about male-male sexual desire and love is a major concern in Essex Hemphill's collection of poems *Conditions*. In particular, "Conditions XXIV" signifies on heterosexual culture's highly celebrated "rite of passage," the marriage ceremony. Hemphill signifies on the marriage ceremony in an excellent example of "capping," a figure of speech which revises an original statement by adding new terms. Hemphill honors the bonds created from desire by capping on the exchange of wedding bands. In the opening and closing sentences, fingers are not the received place for wedding rings:

> In america
> I place my ring
> on your cock
> where it belongs.

> In america,
> place your ring
> on my cock
> where it belongs.

Vows are also exchanged in the poem, but they do not restrict and confine. Instead, these vows are "What the rose whispers / before blooming. . . ." The vows are:

> I give you my heart,
> a safe house.
> I give you promises other than
> milk, honey, liberty.
> I assume you will always
> be a free man with a dream.

Implicitly, "Conditions XXIV" strips away the public pomp and spectacle of the wedding ceremony to reveal its most fundamental level: desire. By capping on the wedding ceremony, Hemphill places homoerotic desire on an equal plane with heterosexuality.

SIGNIFYING ON THE CHURCH

Historically religion has served as a liberating force in the African American community. Black slaves publicly and politically declared that Christianity and the institution of slavery were incompatible as early as 1774, according to Albert Raboteau in *Slave Religion*. "In that year," Raboteau notes, "the governor of Massachusetts received 'The Petition of a Grate Number of Blacks in the Province who by divine permission are held in a state of slavery within the bowels of a free and Christian Country'." In the petition slaves argued for their freedom by combining the political rhetoric of the Revolution with an appeal to the claims of Christian fellowship. Christian churches were some of the first institutions blacks created and owned in the United States. From 1790 to 1830 ambitious northern free black men like Richard Allen and Absalom Jones circumvented racism by creating new Christian denominations, notably the African Methodist Episcopal and the African Methodist Episcopal Zion churches.

The organized black church, however, has not been free from oppressing its constituents.

In the short story "Cut Off from among Their People," Craig G. Harris does a "heavy sig" on the black family which also signifies on strategies from slave narratives. The story takes place at the funeral of Jeff's lover, who has died of complications from AIDS. Both the family and the church, two major institutions in the heterosexual African American community, are allied against Jeff. The lover's biological family has "diplomatically" excluded Jeff from the decisions about the funeral. At the funeral Jeff is ignored by the family and humiliated by the church. The lover's mother stares at him contemptuously. Jeff is not allowed to sit with the family. The minister chosen by the family only adds to Jeff's humiliation. The minister is asked not to wear his ceremonial robes but instead to wear an ordinary suit.

The "heavy sig" is done by using irony. The minister is exposed as a scoundrel, similar to Levine in *Blackbird* [Duplechan]. At the funeral he delivers a homophobic sermon from the book of Leviticus:

In Leviticus, Chapter 20, the Lord tell (sic) us: If a man lie with mankind as he lieth with a woman, both of them have committed an abomination: they shall surely be put to death; their blood shall be upon them. There's no cause to wonder why medical science could not find a cure for this man's illness. How could medicine cure temptation? What drug can exorcise Satan from a young man's soul? The only cure is to be found in the Lord. The only cure is repentance, for Leviticus clearly tells us, " . . . whoever shall commit any of these abominations, even the souls that commit them shall be cut off from among their people."

After the funeral Jeff is abandoned and left to his own devices to get to the burial site. His humiliation is relieved by a sympathetic undertaker who offers Jeff a ride to the burial site. Ironically, it is the undertaker, the caregiver to the dead—not the minister, who is the caregiver to the living—who offers Jeff the compassion he so desperately needs. Denouncing both the family and the church, the undertaker's remarks to Jeff become the authentic sermon in the story:

I lost my lover to AIDS three months ago. It's been very difficult—living with these memories and secrets and hurt, and with no one to share them. These people won't allow themselves to understand. If it's not preached from a pulpit and kissed up to the Almighty, they don't want to know about it. So, I hold it in, and hold it in, and then I see us passing, one after another—tearless funerals, the widowed treated like nonentities, and these "another faggot burns in hell" sermons. My heart goes out to you brother. You gotta let your love for him keep you strong.

As a result of Harris's use of ironic signifying, one is left to ponder the meaning of the story's title, "Cut Off from among Their People." Who is cut off from their people? The story immediately implies that black gays are oppressed because they are alienated from their families. The opposite, however, is also true: Black families are oppressors, are alienated from their gay children, and thus, suffer. Black families suffer because their oppression robs them of a crucial sign of humaneness: compassion. By their oppression, the family of Jeff's deceased lover has lost the ability to be compassionate.

Harris's strategy—the cost of oppression is the loss of humanity—signifies on slave narratives by authors such as Frederick Douglass. Slave owners' loss of compassion, the sign of humaneness, is a recurring theme in Frederick Douglass's 1845 narrative. Slavery, Douglass contended, placed in the hands of whites "the fatal poison of irresponsible power." Douglass gives numerous grisly examples of his contention: murderous overseers, greedy urban craftsmen, and raping masters. But perhaps none of his examples is meant to be as moving as that of his slave mistress, Mrs. Auld. Originally a woman of independent means, Douglass describes her before "the fatal poison of irresponsible power" took full control of her:

I was utterly astonished at her goodness. I scarcely knew how to behave towards her. She was entirely unlike any other white woman I had ever seen. I could not approach her as I was accustomed to approach other white ladies. My early instruction was all out of place. The crouching servility, usually so acceptable a quality in a slave, did not answer when manifested toward her. Her favor was not gained by it; she seemed to be disturbed by it. She did not deem it imprudent or unmannerly for a slave to look her in the face. The meanest slave was put fully at ease in her presence, and none left without feeling better for having seen her. Her face was made of heavenly smiles, and her voice of tranquil music.

Mrs. Auld even disobeyed the law and taught Douglass some rudiments of spelling. However, Douglass states, "Slavery proved as injurious to her as it did to me. . . . Under its influence, the tender heart became stone, and the lamblike disposition gave way to one of tiger-like fierceness."

"Cut Off from among Their People" is an extraordinary act of "heavy signifying." By using a strategy similar to Frederick Douglass's, Harris equates heterosexism and homophobia with slavery. For upholding heterosexism and homophobia, the church and the black family are oppressors. As rendered by Harris, they are like the Mrs. Auld of Douglass's narrative. They are kind to the black gay man when he is a child, and corrupted by intolerance years later. Their oppression has robbed them of compassion. The black family and their church, thus, have lost the sign of humanity.

GENDER CONFIGURATIONS

The last section of this essay examines gay men and the problem of gender configurations. Specifically, in the black literary tradition gay men have been objects of ridicule for not possessing masculine-appearing behaviors. This ridicule was especially evident in the militant Black Power movement of the 1960s and 1970s. The militancy that characterized that movement placed an enormous emphasis on developing black "manhood." Manhood became a metaphor for the strength and potency necessary to overthrow the oppressive forces of a white racist society. Images of pathetic homosexuals were often used to show what black manhood was not or to what it could degenerate.

One of the oddest works to appear in black gay culture is Billi Gordon's cookbook, *You've Had Worse Things in Your Mouth*. The title itself is an act of signifying. While one may think it odd to include a cookbook here, it is important to keep in mind that that mode of presentation has been used to create social history in two other books by Afro-Americans. National Public Radio commentator and self-styled writing griot Vertamae Smart Grosvenor came to public prominence [with] her 1970 *Vibration Cooking: or the Travel Notes of a Geechee Girl*. The format of the book itself was signifying on the published travel narratives of eighteenth- and nineteenth-century whites such as Frederick Law Olmsted, whose observations on slavery have been treated by some historians as more reliable than artifacts actually left by the slaves. Norma Jean and Carole Darden's 1978 *Spoonbread and Strawberry Wine* was as much a family history of North Carolina middle-class blacks as it was a compendium of recipes.

Like George Wolfe, Gordon signifies repeatedly on racial stereotypes and on middle-class culture. On the cover of his cookbook, Gordon, a three-hundred pound-plus dark-skinned black man, appears in drag. But not just any drag. He is wearing a red kerchief, a red-and-white checkered blouse, and a white apron, calling to mind some combination of Aunt Jemima and Hattie McDaniel in *Gone with the Wind*. As if that were not enough, Gordon signifies in every way imaginable on the American cultural stereotype of mammies as sexless, loyal, no-nonsense creatures. Gordon's character is lusty, vengeful, and flirtatious. Gordon appears in pictures surrounded by adoring muscled, swimsuit-clad white men; she wears bikini swimsuits, tennis outfits, long blond wigs, huge rebellious Afro-wigs, and shocking lame evening wear. As for recipes, one is quite reluctant to try any of them, particularly those from the section called "Revenge Cooking" in which the ingredients include laxatives, seaweed, and entire bottles of Tabasco sauce. Billi Gordon signifies on the American stereotype of the mammy with a sex life is far from loyal, and certainly his character cannot and/or does not want to cook.

CONCLUSION: TOWARD A BLACK GAY AESTHETIC

Restricted by racism and heterosexism, writers such as Samuel Delany, Larry Duplechan, Essex Hemphill, Craig G. Harris, George Wolfe, and Billi Gordon have begun to create a literature that validates our lives as black and as gay. My critical reading of this literature relied upon techniques based in the African American tradition of signifying. The writers discussed in this essay are some of the newest members of the African American literary tradition. Clearly, they also seek to revise the aesthetics of that tradition. Homophobia and heterosexism are oppressive forces which must be eliminated from the social, scientific, critical and imaginative writings within the African American literary tradition.

Suggested Reading with Similar Theme:

Hemphill, Essex. *Brother to Brother: New Writings by Black Gay Men*. Boston: Alyson Publications, 1991.

KARLA F. C. HOLLOWAY

A Figurative Theory:
A Critical Consideration of Voice,
Gender and Culture (1992)

While Holloway disclaims any one theoretical approach to texts by African and African American women, she does proclaim the following when one studies the structure of these texts:

> *a focus on the literary language in terms of patterns; the interaction of language, culture, community and women's voice; the roles of narrative voice and the innervoice; speakerly texts; texts of spoken memory; layering; nurturance of the spoken word within the texts; critical vision; memory recovered through language; vision and act rather than a dominant mode of storytelling.*

Explain how the narrative voice differs in texts by black male writers from that in texts by black women writers. Explain how Holloway's theoretical perspective remains within a Black Poetics. Define the following terms: revision, re/membrance, recursion, oracular text, cyclic, intertextual.

> There were always the prophets—necromancers whose folk
> tales and sermons defied the conventions of plot, conflict,
> causality and motivation
>   Ishmael Reed, "Can a Metronome Know the Thunder or Summon a God?"

In *Sassafrass, Cypress and Indigo,* Ntozake Shange weaves the various textures of words found in recipes, journal entries, narrative streams, poetry, and letters into the pages of her novel in ways that make each one of her carefully chosen words translucent. A consequence of Shange's style is that her text resonates with the sounds from these voices as much as it envisions the collection of her words. Shange's stylistic device clearly designates the importance of the oral origins of her text. In addition, the history within her words and their connection to gendered and cultural sources are as important as emphasis. Indigo is described as a child/woman "with a moon falling from her mouth . . . a consort of the spirits." Her name claims her relationship with darkness and the sky. Indigo embodies the dark colors of blood, the deep colors of the sea, and the depth of the midnight sky. Hers is an ancient fertility—"I've got earth blood, filled up with the Geechees long gone, and the sea." Indigo is, as a child with the "south" in her, left at the end of this book with the creative legacy of her ancestral mentor, a midwife who assures that the community will have the appropriate creative accompaniment of Indigo's ancient talents.

The reclamation of women's voice is the critical accomplishment of contemporary literature by black women writers in America and Africa. Their return to the word as a generative source—a source of textual power that both structures story and absorbs its cultural legacy—is a return to the power of the word itself. It is a recovery of text through the literary and linguistic activity of recursion—a refocusing of meaning back to the semantic and syntactic structures that have assured the unity between meaning and source.

In this critical turn toward language there is a potential to recover a cultural bridge between black women writers of West Africa and America. Certainly, there are important differences in the literary subjects and styles among women of West Africa and African American women writers. This is a given dimension of the contemporary political, cultural, and social differences between them.

There is, however, a compelling historical reason to explore the potential for commonalities among these writers. The cultural history that links black writers in America also calls for an acknowledgment of the West African sources of that history. It is this perspective that allows for an exploration of the intertextual, shared images and patterns among writers with a common cultural history to emerge in the midst of the acknowledged differences between them. The result is an activity that explores how particular manipulations of words and specific ways of arranging meaning call all attention to gender in culture. Attention to the ways that black women writers arrange meaning and specify figures of language circumscribes another way of gathering that cultural community of writers. The gathering makes even more specific the detail of their intimate connection.

Careful and cogent discussions of such thematic issues as class and community, character and nature have invigorated the published criticism of black women's texts. I believe there also has been a more subtle, and sometimes puzzling tendency to avoid an imaginative and theoretical coalescence concerning what we have learned about black women's text—their language, the nature of their literary discourse, and the cultural mythologies that identify them.

A parallel consequence of specifying non-Western cultural metaphors that are a dimension of this literature is the acknowledgment of this as a literature only barely escaped from the hegemony of Western critical ideology. Naming a source outside of this tradition forces the nominative activity to be creative as well as definitive. As an example, consider the epigraphy I have chosen for this chapter. Ishmael Reed specifies "conventionality, causality and motivation" as features likely to be subverted in the "necromancy" of the black text. Reed reminds us of the true history in black letters. It has been consistently nonconventional; its causality has more often than not indicted the ideological base of the West; and its motivation has been to assert the voice and to affirm the humanity that the Western world has conspired to suppress and deny. Interestingly enough, the discussion of this literature within a canon that barely acknowledged its existence and would distract the critical audience away from its complexity (and towards a so-called more "universal" model) has been a process of both affirmation and denial. Most critics of African-American literature, aware of the opposition between the (traditionally black and Third World) subject of the literature under discussion and the (traditionally white and Western) audience for whom that discussion was intended, generally found it safer to affirm the difference of the text without the parallel acknowledgment that the white and Western world was predisposed to undervalue this literature or, even worse, to place it into a sociological frame that would somehow explain to them what they know as the "black man's burden." An essential loss of critical substance occurs in this failed acknowledgment. The dialectic between the critical audience and the text is diminished. A result of this subjective/objective fragmentation is theoretical invisibility or silence.

Traditionally, the differential relationship between a critical theory of literature and its critical audience substantiates a dialectic. However, the perverse consequence of a failed relationship between black literature's critical theory and the canonically chauvinistic Western academy has been the dislocation of the West as the center that frames meanings and inscribes values. In the context of the African-American literary tradition, the displacement has a bi-textual effect. It dissolves the hegemony of Western ideology and affirms the occupation of the necromancers—the creative crafters of the word—within the black literary tradition. Their contemporary and historical work persistently dislocates the superstitions of Western ideologies. The metaphors that identify black traditions of literary theory are those that reach outside of Western history for their source.

This is a selection underscored by Reed's shift from prophet to necromancer in the citation. Spiritual creativity is at the center of the tradition that Reed embraces when he chooses the folktale tellers and sermon deliverers as the tradition's early sources of necromancy. African-American history and African history document that the tellers were women and their stories and songs were the oral archives of their culture.

Revision, the first of three perspectives that organizes this book, represents a gathering of the ways a culture organizes language, the privilege given to particular speakers, and the association between language, voice, and the physical presence of the speaker. Indicative of this gathering are works by black women writers that illustrate what Ishmael Reed calls "an oral . . . talking book" and what Gates calls the "speakerly text." These works revise the parameter of speech and the dimensions of voice in ways that force a critical attention to the intertextual nature of this revision. Reed's purpose is not to characterize the work of black women writers in this instance (indeed, Reed's characterizations of black women writers have often been quite vicious), and Gates cites both Ishmael Reed and Zora Neale Hurston as authors of speakerly texts. I claim revision and the processes of transformation and generation as my theoretical methodology (not only in my citation of Ishmael Reed, but in reference to the language and vocabulary of contemporary critical inquiry) and as the substantive context of the black woman's text. My use of revision as a gender-specific instance foregrounds gendered spheres of knowledge—women's ways of framing and keeping that knowledge in the place of the representation of the "speaking black voice."

The second perspective that organizes this book is (re)membrance. It focuses on the ways that memory is culturally inscribed. Generally, this kind of inscription is assigned to the genre of myth. The mythic dimensions within these works stress the intimacy between myth and cultural memory. In them, the spoken text retains a figurative intimacy to the mythic text. Memory is a tactile path toward cultural recovery. When we complicate this value with the destabilizing activities of traditional historiography, we are forced to acknowledge the distinct versions of memory that myth, as an a priori oral text, recovers. These are works that claim the texts of spoken memory as their source and whose narrative strategy honors the cultural memories within the word. The literary category of myth has traditionally been credited as a source of creative, that is, imaginative activity and a point of genesis of original meanings. An important question to my study is to determine what happens when the connection between creativity and genesis is used as literary method.

The recovery of myth is linked to the emergence of textual complexity. Both myth and memory acknowledge a linguistic/cultural community as the source of the imaginative text of recovered meaning. Attention to the innervision of the word—its approximation of consciousness—is a way of understanding the literary revision of the mythic principle in black women writers' texts. By assuming this perspective, my intention is to stress the use of myth in black women writers' texts as a vehicle for aligning real and imaginative events in both the present and the past and for dissolving the temporal and spatial bridges between them. Within this framework, myth complicates language and imagery. It is a dynamic entity that (re)members community, connects it to the voices from which it has been severed, and forces it out of the silence prescribed by a scriptocentric historicism. Gates's theory that the "two-toned, double-voiced metaphor of the black text's antecedent" is "central to the full explication of the canonical black text" establishes a critical relationship, a mooring, between the spoken texts of myth and the (re)membered consciousness within the literate word.

Recursion is the third perspective that organizes my discussion. Its concerns address the concepts of complexity, layering and the multiplied text.

Black writers' textual voices are layered within the narrative and linguistic structures of both the text itself and the characterization within the text. This layering creates a ritualized, recursive structure that identifies imagery and language particular to the black woman's literary tradition. The ritualistic process of repetition and reflexiveness becomes a linguistic metaphor equal in intent, I believe, to the metaphorical Esu, who, in Gates's critical argument, stands for the critical activity of interpretation and signifyin(g) in the black literary tradition.

WOMEN'S WAYS OF SAYING

Black women writers nurture the spoken word within their texts. The intersections between voice, language, and gender underscore the ways in which black women's writing is different from the feminist text. (My effort to distinguish between them is illustrated in my use of the term "woman-centered" to describe these texts.) The integration of gender and ethnicity is critical to the representation of cultures of West Africa and the diaspora. Western feminists are not likely to see themselves mirrored in the black women's text. Julia Kristeva, for example, argues that symbolic coherence is the achievement of a "mother tongue." This relational vision of maternity and language is not the vision within black women's texts. Although Kristeva's poetic language is expressively chaotic in its gestation, and although this destabilizing and unconscious chaos is an important dimension of the black woman's text, Kristeva's "mother tongue" lacks ownership. This lack of specificity distinguishes the feminist reconstruction from that of the black woman writer for whom possession of the word is a cultural and gendered legacy.

In reference to the English language text, criticism has to acknowledge that literacy, creative and otherwise, has a basic and troubled association with freedom in black America. In colonized Africa, children have been whipped and beaten for using tribal languages in colonial schools. For black people on both continents, the English language has a context of abuse and dehumanization. My point is that when black women writers imaginatively engage this English language in their texts, the sociocultural history in these words requires the processes of revision. Otherwise, the history of these words would be so repressive that any form of creativity with them would be impossible. Ownership of the creative word means making these words work in cultural and gendered ways that undermine the hegemony of the West.

The language of the black woman's text is "acknowledged power" as Barbara Christian suggests in an essay on African women writers. Christian stresses the significance in claiming a linguistic articulation beyond oracy. She writes that "articulation occurs . . . when African women themselves [gained] access to the pen." Christian's discussion shortchanges the relevance of their possession and creation of an oral tradition in framing that literate articulation. Still, its focus on colonialism as a system that contributed to "a prescribed fate of [literary] . . . silence" appropriately identifies the source of their silence as an external construct, foreign to their indigenous cultural behavior. Although it is certainly "access to the pen" that erases this kind of silence, it is spoken language that is metaphorically embraced as the vehicle of this creative power.

Alice Walker's Celie recognizes the survival that language promises as she refuses the silence she is ordered to maintain ("Don't tell nobody" she is warned by Mr.) and chooses to "tell" by writing her soul out of its hiding place. In this novel, Walker signifies upon her subject as her own writing structures the written narrative of Celie's eventual liberation. Celie addresses some of her letters to God—a symbolic address to her spiritual self. However, in a recursive acknowledgment of the voice within and without the text, both Celie and Alice Walker create, tell, and talk back. Celie defies Mr. in the insistence of maintaining her voice. Considering the storm of protest this novel has engendered from a legion of black male critics, it is obvious that Alice Walker has talked back as well. She and Celie both assert their creative rights of gender. Indeed, Walker's deceptively elliptical dedication of this book "To the Spirit / Without whose assistance / Neither this book / Nor I / Would have been / Written" is not an ellipsis at all, but a warning of the linguistic recursion that will frame her story. Because the reader knows, along with Celie and Walker, that this is really a spoken text and that writing is a way to preserve a voice that was threatened, warned, and silenced, *The Color Purple* is actually a long signifying tale.

Motherhood as "membrance," a phrase I use to suggest its physiological and visceral relationship to femaleness, is central to African women writers. It is a theme that not only asserts the ability to create life, but a principle that emerges as central to feminine potential in religion, politics, economics and social spheres. It enlarges the simple biological principle to engage these others. In an essay on this subject in Igbo writers, Carol Boyce Davies calls the African woman writer's interest in motherhood a "preoccupation" that is distinctly "African feminism." Asserting the critical role of motherhood to female identity is an important distinction from Euro-American feminist ideology. It takes the issue of physiological reproduction further than social consequences because it assertively includes this physiology in a woman's sense of self. The preoccupation Davies has noted parallels the linguistic power that also preoccupies Walker's fiction and essays. The complications inherent in motherhood as both a physiological and a metaphysical construct identify a unique bridge between African-American and African women writers.

As an example, consider the significance of the umbilicus between language and creation for Nigerian writer Buchi Emecheta. This emphasis is clear as her character Nnu Ego (*The Joys of Motherhood*) laments, "How will I talk to a woman with no children?" In contrast, works by African-American

women writers often recognize, then sever this symbolic umbilicus, underscoring the tragedy endemic to such separation. Toni Morrison's Pecola *(The
Bluest Eye)* is raped into silence, bears a dead baby, and sacrifices her spirit to
illusion and madness. In her Pulitzer Prize winning novel, Morrison's title
character, Beloved, appears as a spirit daughter, only to become a succubus to
the mother who is victimized by mother-love. Hurston's Janie *(Their Eyes
Were Watching God)* is a "born orator," but her poetry is stifled by her husband
Jody. In consequence, Janie must learn to direct her language inward, eventually recovering her soul. Only at the novel's end is she sufficiently empowered
to call in her soul to see her poetic light and subvert the tragedy silence por-
tends by a birthing of her poetic self.

Davies suggests that several concerns unique to African women and
revealed in their literature may, especially in comparative studies of African
and African-American women writers, reveal "an overall female aesthetic." In
a critical theory that links acts of language to activation of character, the
issues of motherhood and self gain significance as we look at them within the
organization of language.

Textual attention to the devices of language reifies the primary and feminine principle of language. Spiritual rediscovery, loss, and acknowledgment
are structural devices in the arrangement of text and the telling of story in
black women writers' works. Such attentiveness and testimony are evidence
of specific principles of textual organization. It is important not to lose sight
of the cultured and gendered contexts within these fictive encounters because
discovering context may also mean recovering consciousness. This can lead as
well to a critical recovery of cultural organization and patterns of memory
and telling.

MEMORIES WITHIN THE WORD

Myth vitalizes language, giving it a presence outside of the interpretive mode
and forcing its significance to a level where the community's shared meanings
are the basis of its understandings and interactions with both the spiritual
and the physical worlds. Myth is neither one of these worlds; it is both of
them. In its ways of recursive signification, it is the perfect vehicle for
methodology. Signifying is a black trope—a verbal acknowledgment of the
call with a subtle but certain articulation of an implied and responsive thesis.
Similarly, mythologizing is a recognition and an articulation of an implicit,
cultural memory. Gabriel Setiloane notes how, "in their myth about the 'genesis' of things, it is significant that Africans invariably teach that the first
appearance of people was as a group in company . . . it is as a community that
they came." The unity indigenous to such mythology is reflected in a community's emulation of that unity within its own linguistic traditions. Examples

of such unity are explicit in African oral literature, where, as in the folktales of the diaspora, there is obeisance to audience—a linguistic bridge from the metaphorical structures in the story to the collected audience of listeners. Such bridges between the storytellers and the listeners reorganize the (visually) separated subjects and objects back into a metaphorical group that has been collected by words and maintains (even underscores) the community of the storyteller, the listeners, and the story text. Illustrations of these gatherings flourish in contemporary African and African-American oral narratives. The structure of *The Color Purple,* for example, indicates a contemporary vision of this community. In the oral traditions of Hausa, storytelling is both formal and formulaic. There is a consistent structure that introduces story in Hausa, an exchange between the storyteller and the audience. Hurston's records of African-American folktales *(Mules and Men)* set up similar rituals that collect the community of listener, teller, and text. In both the African tradition and the African-American literary (re)membrance of this tradition, the "call" to community meets a "response" from a gathering—a coming together that reflects both to physical and psychological significance of the collective community, linked by story and traditions.

The traditions of myth are also echoed in the literature of the diaspora. Toni Morrison's Shadrack *(Sula)* gathers the community to celebrate the myth of his own making, Suicide Day, the day that at first metaphorically explicates and then literalizes the community's plight. In a similar acknowledgement of a community's involvement in myth. Buchi Emecheta complicates the destruction of the village of Shavi in her novel, *The Rape of Shavi* with the story of a river goddess (Ogene) whom the villagers revere but ignore as they ignore other emblems of their culture. Communal betrayal of myth, memory (tradition), and meaning is intertwined with Emecheta's story of rape. It is significant that the corruption (rape) by Western values in Shavi is layered within the story of a village girl who is raped by one of the Westerners who have invaded her village. The biological legacy of this girl and the cultural legacy of her community are both sacrificial victims in the Emecheta work.

For black women, telling is an activity complicated by a history that in addition to being dominated by a masculine ethic is told in terms that support this ethic. Perhaps it is this reason that makes the tale a black woman writer tells, just in its being voiced, reflect an urge towards a metaphysical definition of one's self. Jean Miller looked for a language to describe women's metaethics as organized around principles of "affiliations and relationships," her point being that even the language of psychology was inappropriate to determine the parameters of women's sense of themselves. Similarly, a critical theory that acknowledges the roles of culture and gender must acknowledge that its thesis is ironically framed by the invisibility of women's writing in traditional theories of literature. Traditional criticisms often work to disable the female and cultural voice rather than to reveal the distinct articulation of those voices.

Mary Poovey proposes that what she terms "materialist feminists" recognize:

> that "woman" is currently both a position within a dominant, binary symbolic order and that that position is arbitrarily [and falsely] unified. On the other hand, we need to remember that there are concrete historical women whose differences reveal the inadequacy of this unified category in the present and the past. The multiple positions real women occupy—the positions dictated by race . . . class . . . or sexual preference—should alert us to the inadequacy of binary logic and unitary selves.

A decentered ethic also shifts the place of logic from one that emphasizes a binary argument (between polar opposites) to one that seems more circular, and more woman-centered. A unitary, individuated self specifically contradicts an idea of the communal self—a presence which I will argue is articulated in the characterizations within black women's writing.

Complexity, multiple presences, and cyclic rather than linear principles are definitive aspects of the works of black women writers. In this sense, telling as a complication of history is also a (re)membrance and a revision of history both in its mythic and its gender-specific dimensions. For example, telling in the form of a goddess's prophecy is an important feature of Flora Nwapa's *Efuru*. Nwapa's title character becomes a priestess of the goddess of the lake, a "symbolic acceptance of self," writes Carol Davies, who claims that such acceptance is a positive not because it includes the realization that her "existence was not totally defined by her motherhood." However, her existence does become enmeshed with a creatrix, and the imagery of the goddess she worships is woven into Efuru's own imagery and the narrative structures of the text. The pronominal reference (marked here with an [*] in a passage Davies also cites) is, I think, deliberately obscured. Because the fertility of both the goddess and Efuru are lamented here, creativity is mythically extended past the physical to metaphysical spirituality—the realm of true creative possibility: "Efuru slept soundly that night. She dreamt of the woman, her beauty, her long hair, and her riches. She had lived for ages at the bottom of the lake. She was as old as the lake itself. . . . She gave women beauty and wealth but she had no child. She [*] had never experienced the joy of motherhood." The recursive nature of the ambiguous "she," that points both to the goddess and Efuru, is an example of the figurative depths of black women's written language. Even if the characters' generative powers fluctuate, are abandoned, raped, or redefined, the language sustains its generative powers.

Later chapters in *Moorings and Metaphors* discuss another important layering that I will note briefly here. The narrative voice within the text is not only the voice of the author and storyteller, but it is intricately woven into the fabric of textual structures. Sometimes, the threads of narrative voice echo a character's soul. In Hurston, narrator and character often exchange tone and poetry. "Certainty of reference" is suspended as the black text speaks both to and of itself—just as Nwapa's Efuru, who is pledged to the goddess, talks both to herself and of her goddess. They are spiritually and linguistically inseparable. In such a speakerly text, the vital, active power of language is not only retained, but is a device of their construction. The communal construction of the black text shares linguistic power—investing itself, its structures, its characters and its events with the same creative power in the process of making itself a reflection of its community. Black women authors' manipulation of that creative power makes such textualizing a specifically female vitalization.

THE ORACULAR TEXT

Oracular, a word that characterizes the contemporary work of black women writers, comes from a classic text of the early twentieth century—Jean Toomer's *Cane*. Toomer's novel foregrounds a narrative voice that chronicles the experiences of women's fracturing experiences within African-American communities. The primary difference between Toomer's work and the text of black women writers is in the presumed role of the narrative voice. The carefully maintained distance between narrative and text distinguishes Toomer's style, and I would argue the style of black male writers, from women's texts. The voice in women's text claims intimate knowledge and ownership of all narrative dimensions. However, I do not find it at all contradictory that the word that specifies a theoretical context for black women's writing introduces one of the most complex works in American literature written by a black male. Toomer's use of "oracular" does promise a text predicated on voices. However, although the density of his text depends on our understanding the exchanges between word and act, it is the terrifying present that dominates Toomer's work—an interpretation borne out in a review of the insistent visual elements within *Cane*. For example, how the smoke appears and curls and caresses the scenes in "Karintha" is described in a language as lingering and as tactile as the scene itself. Appearance and behavior are important thematic emphases achieved through the techniques of language in texts by black male writers.

The organizing principle of *Moorings and Metaphors* is that the oracular texts of black women writers replace an emphasis on appearance with consciousness and on behavior with memory. These are works that reflect an inner speech. The inner voice mediates the critical vision in black women writers' works. Rather than the dominant mode of storytelling, vision and act are proffered as ways toward memory, and memory is recovered through language, Recall, for example, the closing passage referred to earlier from *Their*

Eyes Were Watching God. In the final scene of the novel (which, because it is in a recursive text, is also the first scene of the novel) Janie sits surrounded by her memories of Tea Cake, their days on the muck, and her learning to live as a woman. It is not the visual imagery of sunlight and shadow that crisscrosses the room where she sits that concludes (and also begins) her story; it is her call to her soul to "come in and see" that is the final word of the story. Black women's writing is oracular because it is incantatory. Repetition, recursion, and (re)membrance are its goals because there are activities directed inwards: the oracles we consult are ourselves.

Suggested Readings with Similar Theme:

Foster, Francis Smith. "'In Respect to Females . . .': Differences in the Portrayals of Women by Male and Female Narrators." *Black American Literature Forum* 15, no. 2 (Summer 1981): 66–70.

Tate, Claudia. "ReShuffling the Deck; Or (Re)Reading Race and Gender in Black Women's Writing." *Tulsa Studies in Women's Literature* 7 (1988): 119–32.

Wall, Cheryl. Introduction to *Changing Our Own Words: Essays on Criticism, Theory and Writing by Black Women,* edited by Cheryl Wall. New Brunswick, N.J.: Rutgers University Press, 1989.

Tommy L. Lott

A No-Theory Theory of Contemporary
Black Cinema (1992)

Define black cinema, blaxploitation film, and independent black filmmaker. How have essentialist paradigms for evaluating black cinema and differentiating values of black audiences problematized present African American film criticism? How does Lott enter discussions with Larry Neal and bell hooks? Define Lott's proposed "Third Cinema."

When film scholars are asked to decide which are best among a body of films they identify as "black," what is at stake is something more than merely the aesthetic question of what counts as a good black film. Indeed, they must consider a more fundamental definitional question regarding the nature of *black cinema,* a question that raises deeper issues concerning both the concept of black identity and the concept of cinema itself. I suspect that film criticism has not offered much assistance in clarifying the concept *black cinema* because there exist no uncontested criteria to which an ultimate appeal can be made to resolve these underlying issues. This scholarly morass must be understood in terms of the inherently political context in which the concept of black cinema has been introduced.

The political aspects of the notion of aesthetics in film theory are sometimes shielded by the latent connection between biological essentialism and issues of control in film practice. We can, for example, see a tendency to racialize the political concern with control of the black film image in August Wilson's recent demand for a black director for the movie version of his play *Fences:* "Let's make a rule. Blacks don't direct Italian films. Italians don't direct Jewish films. Jews don't direct black American films. That might account for about 3 percent of the films that are made in this country." Although Wilson's claim might be taken to commit him to accepting any director who lacked the cultural sensibility required for a faithful rendering of his play. But if even a black director could prove unsatisfactory for aesthetic reasons, how do we make political sense of Wilson's demand for a black director, given that there could be some white director who might be more suitable from a cultural standpoint?

I want to advance a theory of contemporary black cinema that accords with the fact that biological criteria are neither necessary nor sufficient for the application of the concept of black cinema. I refer to this theory as a no-theory,

339

because I want to avoid any commitment to an essentialized notion by not giving a definition of black cinema. Rather, the theoretical concern of my no-theory is primarily with the complexity of meanings we presently associate with the political aspirations of black people. Hence, it is a theory that is designed to be discarded when those meanings are no longer applicable.

THE AESTHETIC CRITIQUE OF BLAXPLOITATION

The history of black cinema can be roughly divided into four periods: Early Silent Films (1890–1920), Early Soundies and Race Film (1920–45), Postwar Problem Films (1945–69/70), and Contemporary Films. With regard to the history of black cinema, the so-called blaxploitation period is a relatively recent, and short-lived, phenomenon. Although there has been a siphoning off of black audiences since the early days of race films, nothing approximating the Hollywood onslaught of the early 1970s has occurred at any other time.

The term *blaxploitation* has been used to refer to those black oriented films produced in Hollywood beginning in 1970 and continuing mainly until 1975, but in various ways persisting until the present . However, in addition to its being a historical index, the term is a way of labeling a film that fails in certain ways to represent the aesthetic values of black culture properly. Mark Reid, for instance, expresses this view in his account of the shortcomings of blaxploitation era films:

> Having established the fact that there was a young black audience receptive to thoughts about violence, it should have been possible to create black action films that appealed to this audience while satisfying a black aesthetic. The commercial black action films of the 1970s, however, never reached this ideal because they were not independent productions or because black independent producers relied on major distributors.

Although, as I shall indicate shortly, Reid's criticism rests on a misleading dichotomy between independent and nonindependent films, his remarks inherently acknowledge the role that production and distribution play in shaping the aesthetic characteristics of a film. At a time of financial exigency, some Hollywood studios discovered that there was a large black audience starving for black images on the screen. This situation provided an immediate inducement for them to exploit the box office formula of the black hero [first male, later female] which, subsequently, became the earmark of the blax-ploitation flick.

Although there are many issues raised by blaxploitation era filmmaking that deserve greater attention, I want to focus on the problems of commer-cialism in order to highlight the influence of the market on certain aesthetic characteristics of black movies. First, it needs to be stated, and clarified, that not all blaxploitation era films conformed to the box office formula. Some were not commercially oriented, while others were very worthwhile from a social and political standpoint. To reduce them all to the hero formula, provided somewhat inadvertently by Van Peebles' *Sweet Sweetback's Baadasssss Song,* is to overlook their many differences in style, audience orientation, and political content.

Second, given the history of black cinema, there is a certain logic to the development of the box office formula. The idea of depicting black men as willing to engage in violent acts toward whites was virtually taboo in Hollywood films all the way through the 1960s. But once the news footage of the 1960s rebellions, along with the media construction of the Black Panther Party, began to appear, mainstream films such as *In the Heat of the Night* made an effort to acknowledge [albeit to contain] this "New Negro." Even within these limits, however, what had made Malcolm X appear so radical to mainstream television audiences at that time was the fact that he had *publicly* advocated self-defense.

When *Sweetback* was shown in 1971, it was as immediate success with black audiences because it captured an image of self-defense that gave onscreen legitimation to violent retaliation against racist police brutality. Black heroic violence against white villains rapidly became a Hollywood commodity, and literally dozens of films were produced for black audiences that capitalized on this new formula. It is worth noting here that it was, in many respects, a Hollywood-induced taboo that created a need for such images in the black audience, a need that was then fulfilled by Hollywood. The ultimate irony is that, once these films began to proliferate, there was an organized effort in the black community to demand their cessation.

It is also worth noting that *Sweetback* provoked a critical response that varied among different political factions within the black community, as well as among film critics. Community-based activists who opposed the film's image of black people ranged from cultural nationalists, who wanted a more culturally educational film, to middle-class black protesters, who wanted a film that projected more positive image of the race. As Mark Reid has noted, the film's political orientation, quite interestingly, received both "high praise" from Huey Newton and the Black Panther Party newspaper in Oakland and "denunciation" from a Kuumba Workshop nationalist publication in Chicago. Although Newton was not alone in giving the film critical praise, his allegorical interpretation of the film's sexual imagery was not widely shared among critics, especially feminists concerned with its portrayal of women.

The critical controversy around *Sweetback*'s image of black people is not amenable to resolution on strictly aesthetic grounds, for *Sweetback* clearly represents some version of the black aesthetic. A political debate seems to have transpired between the film's supporters and detractors in an attempt to make the case for either accepting or rejecting the film. Indeed, some critics have argued that *Sweetback* lacks a politicized image, while others have argued that it politicized the image of black people to the point of lapsing into propaganda.

With regard to the role of aesthetics, blaxploitation era films pose a rather peculiar problem for a theory of contemporary black cinema. Can a film count as black cinema when it merely presents a blackface version of white films, or when it merely reproduces stereotypical images of black people?

Commentators have maintained quite different views in answer to this question. James Snead has argued for a very sophisticated notion of recording that requires of black cinema what he calls the "syntagmatic" revision of stereotyped images through the selective use of editing and montage. According to Snead, the syntax of traditional Hollywood cinema must be reworked to recode the black image effectively. However, against the backdrop of Hollywood's pre-blaxploitation era stereotype of black men as sexually castrated buffoons, what rules out the less sophisticated blaxploitation practice of substituting a highly sexualized black male hero who exercises power over white villains as an attempt to record the Hollywood image of black men? Mark Reid asserts, with little hesitation, that "blacks who would find psychological satisfaction in films featuring black heroes have just as much right to have their tastes satisfied as do whites who find pleasure in white heroes such as those in Clint Eastwood and Charles Bronson films." If the creation of black heroic images through role reversals can be considered a recoding technique utilized by blaxploitation filmmakers, then how does this practice compare with other, more avant-garde recording practices of black independent filmmakers?

It can be quite troublesome for a theory of black cinema that relies too strongly on aesthetics to give an account of the influence of blaxploitation films on subsequent black independent films. Given that aesthetic-based theories, such as Snead's want to contrast black independent films with Hollywood produced films about black people, where do blaxploitation films fit into such a juxtaposition? How do we make sense of the charge, brought by a black independent filmmaker, of a fellow black independent filmmaker's having irresponsibly produced a blaxploitation film? The fact that the charge was made suggests that black independent filmmaking is not immune from the aesthetic pitfalls of blaxploitation cinema.

For the present purposes, I am less interested in deciding the question of what films to count as blaxploitation than I am in the implication the appeal to aesthetics, inherent in the accusation, seems to carry for our understanding of the place of aesthetics in a theory of black cinema. To denounce a film such as *Sweetback* as exploitative is to suggest that aesthetic criteria provide the highest ground of appeal for deciding definitional questions regarding black cinematic representation, for the charge presupposes that there is some sense in which to produce a blaxploitation film is to have compromised black aesthetic values. What must be explained, however, is how such films stand in relation to independently made films that were not constrained to violate black aesthetic values in this way. Apparently, the term *independent* does not always mean that a filmmaker has eschewed market concerns. When a blaxploitation film is independently made by a black filmmaker for a black audience, however, to whom has the film's aesthetic orientation been compromised and, further, to what extent do such compromises affect a film's status as a black cinematic work?

Recently there has been a major shift toward independently produced blaxploitation films. This practice makes clear that the biologically essentialist view of black cinema (those films about black people, produced by a black filmmaker, for a black audience) is much too simplistic. One important implication of the aesthetic critique of blaxploitation is that certain aesthetic qualities of a film can sometimes count as much against it being inducted into the canon of black films as the filmmaker's race or the film's intended audience. While the insights derived from the aesthetic critique of black filmmaking practices are undoubtedly healthy signs of sophistication in black film commentary, we must not overlook the fact that these critiques also give rise to many difficulties connected with the problem of how film criticism should relate to a plurality of standards by which black films are evaluated.

One such difficulty that must be faced by aesthetic-based theories of black cinema arises from the fact that, since the mid-1980s, there has been a growing interest in black-oriented cinema, especially black comedy, by white audiences. The success of black television sitcoms, as well as Arsenio Hall's nightly talk show, provides some indication that white audiences are more willing to indulge not so completely assimilated black people than network executives had previously supposed. Spike Lee's humorous social commentary has opened the door for other, similarly inclined, black filmmakers and television producers. All of this comic relief in the television and movie industry has been spearheaded, of course, by the mass appeal of Richard Pryor, Eddie Murphy, and Bill Cosby. Given their influence on the present context for black filmmaking, it seems that a theory of contemporary black cinema cannot postulate the black audience as a necessary ingredient.

A related difficulty that carries greater significance for our understanding of the influence of the crossover audience on the aesthetics of certain films about black people arises from the manner in which Eddie Murphy's attempt to signify on black minstrelsy has simply replaced the old-fashioned minstrel show. Murphy's success in Hollywood was quickly followed by that of his "black pack" cohort Robert Townsend, whose humorous criticism of Hollywood in his very popular film was largely reduced to a shuffle with a critique of itself. As though the hegemony of the Hollywood industry were not enough to contend with, more politically astute filmmakers working in the realm of comedy, such as Spike Lee, are now challenged with finding ways to distinguish themselves from such neo-minstrelsy. Indeed, some filmmakers formerly aligned with the counterhegemonic practices of the post-1960s black independent movement seem to have allowed the white audience for black-oriented humor to so influence their filmmaking that we now have a new generation of blaxploitation cinema. This influence is displayed in the Hudlin brothers' film *House Party,* which seems rigorously to avoid dealing with certain very pressing issues raised in the film (e.g., police brutality) in order not to offend the potential white audience. Unlike Spike Lee's probing satire, which engages in a black-oriented humor that sometimes seems intended to offend white audiences, *House Party* is closer to mindless slapstick.

Although some film commentators have attempted to acknowledge the disparity between the aesthetic values of black audiences and the aesthetic values of filmmakers and critics, film criticism generally tends to adhere to a top-down view of aesthetics, as though audiences have no role to play in the determination of aesthetic values. What the black audience appeal of blaxploitation films (old and new) indicates, against the wishes of many film critics, is that it is misguided to suppose that a filmic work of art, or entertainment, has black audience appeal simply because it aims for a black audience by promoting certain black aesthetic values. In the case of the black independent cinema movement of the 1970s in America, as well as the 1980s black workshop movement in Britain, the attempt to reclaim and reconstruct a black film aesthetics that would somehow counteract the influence of Hollywood's blaxploitation filmmaking has, by and large, not been well received by black audiences, although many of these films have been frequently presented at international festivals, in art museums, and in college courses devoted to film study. How can we best understand the fact that films which aim to present a more authentic black aesthetic are largely ignored by and unknown to black audiences, while being extremely well-received in elite white film circles? Despite their admirable political orientation, such films seem to have achieved the status of art-for-art's sake, with mainly an all-white audience appeal.

This lack-of-a-black audience problem shows the need to resist the tendency of aesthetic-based theories of black cinema to position the aesthetic values of the black artist above those of the black audience. In order for black film commentary to acknowledge more pluralistic criteria by which to assess the artistic value of cinematic works, some weight must be given to the viewpoint of black audiences, inasmuch as it is imprudent at best continually to posit a black aesthetic that very few black audiences share.

Some of these considerations regarding the audience crossover phenomenon in contemporary black cinema argue against the cultural essentialist attempt to define black cinema in terms of aesthetics. As the divisions between independent and Hollywood-produced films about black people begin to dissolve, as a result of the mainstream market for both, it has become extremely difficult to maintain that either a black filmmaker or a black audience is required for a film with a black orientation. To see this, we need only consider the fact that, in addition to his crossover status in the record industry, Prince is virtually neck and neck with Spike Lee as a film-maker, each having four major releases. There is no reason to suppose that, despite a preference among commentators for Spike Lee's version of the black aesthetic, the aesthetic in Prince's movies has any less box office appeal to much of the same audience.

The need for an essentialist theory diminishes, along with the idea of a monolithic black film aesthetic, once we realize that there is no monolithic black audience. There certainly are black-oriented films, some of which are much better than others, but not all of those approved by critics manage to touch base with black audiences (e.g., *To Sleep with Anger*) and many of those condemned by critics have become black audience classics (e.g., *Superfly*). These facts may be difficult to accept, but to advocate a "better" cinema that is significantly different requires a political argument. I will now turn to con-sider the argument I think is presently most viable in a politically confused era dominated by neo-conservative ideology.

BLACK IDENTITY AND BLACK CINEMA

Before I take up the question of how politics and aesthetics can be situated into a theory of black cinema, I would like to insert a word of clarification regarding the prevailing use of the term *cinema* to refer to films as such; for example, movies that were made be shown in theaters. I believe that this restrictive usage is unfortunate, since some fairly good films about black peo-ple have been made for television. The misconception that underlies this nar-row focus on box office movies is exacerbated by the fact that some of the most innovative black filmmaking is presently occurring in music videos. Indeed, the dominant influence of television on black popular culture has some rather interesting implications for black film practices that no theory of black cinema can afford to overlook. Because black urban youth culture has been visually promulgated primarily through television, this segment of the black movie audience has been heavily influenced by black images presented on television. Added to this television orientation is a large black youth mar-ket for blaxploitation films on videocassettes. These influences are displayed quite regularly in what Nelson George refers to as "blaxploitation rap," for example, rap lyrics that have been heavily influenced by blaxploitation films. It is, to say the least, perilous for filmmakers interested in reaching black youth to ignore the single most important medium of visually representing their cultural values.

In Britain, black filmmaking and television are much more structurally connected, since the workshops produce their films for Channel 4 (see Foun-tain; Pines, "Cultural"). Undoubtedly, this structural relation between filmmaking and television will eventually obtain in America once high-definition television is introduced since, with the advent of this new technology, movies as such seem certain to be superseded by television. For all these reasons, I think it wise at this point to expand the concept of cinema to include television.

With regard to politics, there is a very good reason that the biological version of the essentialist definition of black cinema will invariably fall short. Any definition that requires films to be made by black filmmakers in order to be included in the category of black cinema will simply not match the ambivalence engendered by having to place biological over cultural criteria in deciding questions of black identity. This does not mean that, generally speaking, most of us have no idea of what to count as black film. Indeed, the definition of black cinema is a problem by virtue of the fact that, whether it is based on biological or cultural criteria, its viability can easily be called into question.

The DuBoisian worry about the adequacy of Biological criteria as the ultimate ground of appeal when faced with questions of black identity poses the greatest difficulty for the essentialist notion of black cinema. For DuBois, the problem stems from the fact that there is no agreement about how best to define a black person, although there is some sense in which we all operate with some ideas about what constitutes black identity. We need only consider the manner in which we must still grapple with the age-old problem of the "non-black" black person, for example, the person who, though biologically black, does not identify with black culture. Although there can be little doubt that, in the context of the American system of apartheid, the question of whether a particular person counts as black is most often decided by skin color and physical appearance, there are numerous instances in which this honor is withheld strictly on cultural grounds. It is far too common for black people to feel the yoke of oppression at the hands of a white-identified black person. Consequently, as someone perceived to be disloyal to the group, an overly assimilated [Eurocentric] black person can sometimes lose his or her standing in the eyes of other black people. In such cases we can notice how the tension between biological and cultural criteria of black identity is resolved in terms of a political definition of black people. It is for some reason such as this that I am motivated to develop the concept of black cinema within the context of a political theory.

THE CONCEPT OF THIRD CINEMA REVISITED

Without any pretense that I can offer a replacement for the essentialist definition of Black cinema, I want to suggest why I think the Third Cinema movement of the 1960s seems to have been on the right track, although in America certain mainstream co-optational factors have basically derailed it. According to various conflicting reports, the advocates of Third Cinema have come under heavy criticism lately for being, of all things, overly nationalistic. Unfortunately, in an attempt to address this worry, some commentators tend needlessly to equate nationalism with the essentialist view. But the concept of Third Cinema should not be saddled with the myopic vision of essentialists who are constrained by an overemphasis on biological criteria for resolving questions of national identity. What makes Third Cinema third (i.e., a viable alternative to Western cinema) is not exclusively the racial makeup of a film-maker, a film's aesthetic character, or a film's intended audience, but rather a film's political orientation within the hegemonic structures of postcolonial-ism. When a film contributes ideologically to the advancement of Black peo-ple, within a context of systematic denial, the achievement of this political objective ought to count as a criterion of evaluation on a par with any essen-tialist criterion.

The best way to meet the criticism that the concept of Third Cinema is too vague because it allows under its rubric many diverse cultural groups is to recognize that this objection misleadingly imputes an uncontested essentialist paradigm. The Third Cinema movement represents a break with, and resis-tance to, the cultural imperialism fostered by the global expansion of the Hollywood industry. There is an important sense in which it aims to do what Hollywood has done—namely, to reach beyond national boundaries. There is no reason to deny that cultural diversity is a problem among the many ethni-cally distinct black people living together in America, much less a problem among various Third World people from widely different backgrounds in far-away places. But clearly if Europeans, who for centuries have waged war against each other, and are still caught up in their own ethnic rivalries, can construct a concept of themselves as a globally dominant white group, how can it be so much more objectionable for non-white people to construct a global counterconcept by which to defend themselves? The white cultural nationalism of Hollywood's Eurocentric empire requires something like a Third Cinema movement to help non-white people survive the oppressive and self-destructive consciousness that empire seeks to perpetuate.

With regard to black filmmaking practices, the concept of Third Cin-ema provides the rudiments of a theory of black cinema that is most con-ducive to this political function. As a primarily oppositional practice engaged in resistance and affirmation, black cinema need not be presently defined apart from its political function (see Espinosa). I call this a no-theory theory because I see no need to resolve, on aesthetic grounds, the dispute over what counts as blaxploitation. Neither do I see a need to choose between realist and avant-garde film techniques. I am more interested in understanding how any aesthetic strategy can be employed to challenge, disrupt, and redirect the pervasive influence of Hollywood's master narrative. To accomplish this decidedly political objective, black filmmaking practices must continue to be fundamentally concerned with the issues that presently define the political struggle of black people. Hence, I want to advance a theory of black cinema that is in keeping with those filmmaking practices that aim to foster social change, rather than participate in a process of formulating a definition of black cinema that allows certain films to be canonized on aesthetic grounds so as to occupy a place in the history of cinema. The theory we need now is a political theory of black cinema that incorporates a plurality of aesthetic values that are consistent with the fate and destiny of black people as a group engaged in a protracted struggle for social equality.

Suggested Readings with Similar Theme:

Yearwood, Gladstone L. "Towards a Theory of a Black Cinema Aesthetic." In *Black Cinema Aesthetics: Issues in Independent Black Filmmaking,* edited by Gladstone L. Yearwood. Athens: Ohio University, Center for Afro-American Studies, 1982.

Guerrero, Ed. Introduction to *Framing Blackness: The African American Image in Film.* Philadelphia: Temple University Press, 1993.

Smith, Valerie. Introduction to *Representing Blackness: Issues in Film and Video.* New Brunswick, N.J.: Rutgers University Press, 1997.

BELL HOOKS

Introduction:
Revolutionary Attitudes
in *Blacks Looks: Race and Representation* (1992)

Why is hooks urging members of the African American audience to "collectively change the way we look at ourselves"? What is meant by "revolutionary attitudes about race and representation" in the mass media? Why is it necessary for black and white audiences to "think critically about images" of blackness and black people in the mass media? Do images have an ideological intent? Is the real world of image making political? How does hooks enter discussions with Sterling Brown regarding black characters as seen by white writers; with Carolyn Gerald regarding an ideological nature of imagery; and with Tommy Lott regarding marketing of stereotypical images? Define the "context" necessary for transformations of present stereotypical representations of blackness and black people in the mass media. Define the following terms and phrases: other, cultural identity, consumers of images, colonizing image, commodification of blackness, and imperial gaze.

Decolonization . . . continues to be an act of confrontation with a hegemonic system of thought; it is hence a process of considerable historical and cultural liberation. As such, decolonization becomes the contestation of all dominant forms and structures, whether they be linguistic, discursive, or ideological. Moreover, decolonization comes to be understood as an act of exorcism for both the colonized and the colonizer. For both parties it must be a process of liberation: from dependency, in the case of the colonized, and from imperialist, racist perceptions, representations, and institutions which, unfortunately, remain with us to this very day, in the case of the colonizer. . . . Decolonization can only be complete when it is understood as a complex process that involves both the colonizer and the colonized.

If we compare the relative progress African Americans have made in education and employment to the struggle to gain control over how we are represented, particularly in the mass media, we see that there has been little change in the area of representation. Opening a magazine or book, turning on the television set, watching a film, or looking at photographs in public spaces, we are most likely to see images of black people that reinforce and reinscribe white supremacy. Those images may be constructed by white people who have not divested of racism, or by people of color/black people who may see the world through the lens of white supremacy—internalized racism. Clearly, those of us committed to black liberation struggle, the freedom and self-determination of all black people, must face daily the tragic reality that we have collectively made few, if any, revolutionary interventions in the area of race and representation.

There is a direct and abiding connection between the maintenance of white supremacist patriarchy in this society and the institutionalization via mass media of specific images, representations of race, of blackness that support and maintain the oppression, exploitation, and overall domination of all black people. Long before white supremacists ever reached the shores of what we now call the United States, they constructed images of blackness and black people to uphold and affirm their notions of racial superiority, their political imperialism, their will to dominate and enslave. From slavery on, white supremacists have recognized that control over images is central to the maintenance of any system of racial domination. In his essay "Cultural Identity and Diaspora," Stuart Hall emphasizes that we can properly understand the traumatic character of the colonial experience by recognizing the connection between domination and representation:

> The ways in which black people, black experiences, were positioned and subjected in the dominant regimes of representation were the effects of a critical exercise of cultural power and normalization. Not only, in Said's "orientalist" sense, were we constructed as different and other within the categories of knowledge of the West by those regimes. They had the power to make us see the experience ourselves as "Other" . . . It is one thing to position a subject or set of peoples as the Other of a dominant discourse. It is quite another thing to subject them to that "knowledge," not only as a matter of imposed will and domination, but by the power to inner compulsion and subjective conformation to the norm.

That the field of representation remains a place of struggle is most evident when we critically examine contemporary representations of blackness and black people.

For some time now the critical challenge for black folks has been to expand the discussion of race and representation beyond debates about good and bad imagery. Often what is thought to be good is merely a reaction against representations created by white people that were blatantly stereotypical. Currently, however, we are bombarded by black folks creating and marketing similar stereotypical images. It is not an issue of "us" and "them." The issue is really one of standpoint. From what political perspective do we dream, look, create, and take action? For those of us who dare to desire differently, who seek to look away from the conventional ways of seeing blackness and ourselves, the issue of race and representation is not just a question of critiquing the status quo. It is also about transforming the image, creating alternative, asking ourselves questions about what types of images subvert, pose critical alternatives, and transform our worldviews and move us away from dualistic thinking about good and bad. Making a space for the transgressive image, the outlaw rebel vision, is essential to any effort to create a context for transformation. And even then little progress is made if we transform images without shifting paradigms, changing perspectives, ways of looking.

Stuart Hall names this process eloquently in this powerful statement, again from the essay "Cultural Identity and Diaspora":

> Cultural identity . . . is a matter of "becoming" as well as "being." It belongs to the future as much as to the past. It is not something which already exists, transcending place, time, history, and culture. Cultural identities come from somewhere, have histories. But, like everything which is historical, they undergo constant transformation. Far from being eternally fixed in some essentialized past, they are subject to the continuous "play" of history, culture and power. Far from being grounded in a mere "recovery" of the past, which is waiting to be found, and which, when found, will secure our sense of ourselves into eternity, identities are the names we give to the different ways we are positioned by, and position ourselves within, the narratives of the past.

In *Black Looks,* I critically interrogate old narratives, suggesting alternative ways to look at blackness, black subjectivity, and, of necessity, whiteness.

While also exploring literature, music, and television, many of these essays focus on film. The emphasis on film is so central because it, more than any other media experience, determines how blackness and black people are seen and how other groups will respond to us based on their relation to these constructed and consumed images. In the essay "Black Feminism: The Politics of Articulation," filmmaker Pratibha Parmar states, "Images play a crucial role in defining and controlling the political and social power to which both individuals and marginalized groups have access. The deeply ideological nature of imagery determines not only how other people think about us but how we think about ourselves."

Many audiences in the United States resist the idea that images have an ideological intent. This is equally true of black audiences. Fierce critical interrogation is sometimes the only practice that can pierce the wall of denial consumers of images construct so as not to face that the real world of image-making is political—that politics of domination inform the way the vast majority of images we consume are constructed and marketed. Most black folks do not want to think critically about why we can sit in the darkness of theaters and find pleasure in images that cruelly mock and ridicule blackness.

I ask that we consider the perspective from which we look, vigilantly asking ourselves who do we identify with, whose image do we love. And if we, black people, have learned to cherish hateful images of ourselves, then what process of looking allows us to counter the seduction of images that threatens to dehumanize and colonize. Clearly, it is that way of seeing which makes possible an integrity of being that can subvert the power of the colonizing image. It is only as we collectively change the way we look at ourselves and the world that we can change how we are seen. In this process, we seek to create a world where everyone can look at blackness, and black people, with new eyes.

The struggle needs to include non-black allies as well. Images of race and representation have become a contemporary obsession. Commodification of blackness has created a social context where appropriation by non-black people of the black image knows no boundaries. If the many non-black people who produce images or critical narratives about blackness and black people do not interrogate their perspective, then they may simple recreate the imperial gaze—the look that seeks to dominate, subjugate, and colonize.

As a radical intervention we must develop revolutionary attitudes about race and representation. To do this we must be willing to think critically about images.

Suggested Reading with Similar Theme:

Hall, Stuart. "What Is this 'Black' in Black Popular Culture?" In *Black Popular Culture,* edited by Gina Dent. Seattle: Bay Press, 1992.

Jerry W. Ward Jr.

Foreword
in *Black Southern Voices:*
An Anthology (1992)

According to Ward, the "language of {southern} literature is {not} divorced from the language of everyday experiences. . . . The art of {the literature is} maintaining some balance between the forces of history and the forces of personal or collective experience." How does Ward enter philosophical discussions with, among others, Henderson and Smitherman? Discuss Ward's concluding statement: "The visions and voices of black Southern speakers and writers, their perspectives, the history and heritage they make accessible to us serve to clarify, to illuminate, and to persuade us creatively of a truth only now beginning to be universally recognized: like jazz, the literary expressions of the black Southerner constitute America's most genuine gift to the humanistic tradition of literature."

The South, perhaps to a greater extent than is true of other regions of the United States, is considered a place where myth is both lived and created. Visitors to Oxford, Mississippi, might expect to be greeted by the characters who peopled Faulkner's novels; someone exploring southern Georgia is not overmuch surprised to find weathered farmers who would fit perfectly in Erskine Caldwell's sensational stories; the topping for a vacation in New Orleans is to spy at least one Blanche Dubois in the half-shadows of the French Quarter. The stereotype is stronger than the real thing. It is easier, less threatening, to be entertained by the myths of the South than to grapple with the living contradictions, complexities, and tensions that give an authentic shape to the region.

Failure to confront the real is especially noticeable in discussions of Southern literature. Until recently, it had been traditional to pretend that the Southern imagination has been articulated only by white women and men. It was rarely admitted that black women and men had something to say.

This habit of listening to only one set of the voices that give form to the thoughts and emotional responses of Southern culture is treacherous. Listening with half an ear, as it were, one cannot hear the pulsating heart that secures meaning for Southern myth or drama or poetry. This habit is a matter of choice; it is not an accident. In a racist society, people choose not to hear, and thus admit the significance of, the African and then African-American voices that have given uniqueness to the culture and mind of the South since the seventeenth century. If one will not hear the black Southern voices, richly textured and sonorous in the oral traditions and no less eloquent and compelling in the literate traditions, it is impossible to discern fully the beauty and values of Southern literature and imagination.

One of the functions of *Black Southern Voices* is to turn up the volume, to make it possible to hear all the notes—the sorrow songs, the blues and seculars, the dirges and the martial melodies, the jubilees—the full range of sounds representing the history and creativity of a people who were and are cocreators of the South as a literal and figurative realm. The full range of sounds we call literature.

Moreover, *Black Southern Voices* provides an opportunity to reconsider how vision or perspective determines what the voice might say. Perspective is more than the angle from which one looks at something, be the something land and plant life or the people with whom one lives day to day. Perspective concerns the image received by the eye and thoughts the image might evoke. One man looks at a field of cotton, envisions wealth, and sings, as did Henry Timrod in "Ethnogenesis," of King Cotton as

> . . . one among the many ends for which
> God makes us great and rich!

Another man looks at the same field, thinks of the merciless sun and back pains, and sings

> Nobody knows de trouble I see, Lord
> Nobody knows de trouble I see;
> Nobody knows de trouble I see, Lord
> Nobody knows like Jesus.

Here the perspectives are radically different. The difference, in part, is the result of how each man understood his place in the history of the South.

We will never know precisely what the earliest slaves in the South thought and felt. We can be certain, however, they were not mute about what they experienced in their new world. Through oral transmission they passed on their perspectives on slavery. Stolen from their homelands, they felt strongly the loss of what was familiar—freedom, family relationships, a community that shared their languages, values, rituals, and traditions. Slavery necessitated either outright revolt or adjustment to unfamiliar climate and geography, people, language, and customs. How the early Southern slaves responded to slavery can be recovered from the oral literature they created, from their folklore. Many songs deal with the desire to return home; tales that seem at first glance to be quaint, entertaining, are subtle lessons in how lack of power can be used to advantage; spirituals, riddles, folk sermons, work songs, and "how come" and "why" tales reveal much about the slave's daily concerns within the "peculiar institution." The absence of written documents is no evidence that early Southern slaves lacked the ability or desire, in the words of Margaret Walker, to make "a creative and humanistic response to the violent and negative philosophy of white racism."

That we must recover much of the slave's worldview from folklore is important, because we are forced to consider how the denial of access to literacy (or training in reading and writing) played a role in the evolving of black creative expression in the South. On one hand, it forced the slaves to depend very much on memory and invention as they enlarged and transformed the body of folklore. On the other hand, the denial created a great hunger for skill in reading and writing; that skill, as the young Frederick Douglass noted, was indeed "the pathway from slavery to freedom." By diverse means, some slaves did acquire literacy and used it to create, among other forms, the remarkable slave narratives. These narratives themselves embody a considerable amount of folklore.

Such post–Civil War writers as Charles Chesnutt, Sutton Griggs, and Booker T. Washington knew the literary potential of folk materials as did James Weldon Johnson and Zora Neale Hurston and other writers of the New Negro Renaissance. Borrowing from the treasury of folk imagination continues in writing as recent as Brenda Marie Osbey's *Ceremony for Minneconjoux* (1983) and C. Eric Lincoln's *The Avenue, Clayton City* (1988). For black Southern writers, the notion that folk roots are subliterary or wanting in aesthetic integrity is absurd. They have always blended the oral and the written traditions.

Whether we approach them from the angles of history or of literary study, the specialized speech acts of the Southern slave demonstrate their creators, now only nameless presences, were indeed actors rather than objects. Within folklore, as Lawrence Levine discovered in *Black Culture and Black Consciousness: Afro-American Folk Thought from Slavery to Freedom* (1977), lie the contours of the black Southern imagination. From the vantage point of the twentieth century, we can see how the germinal seeds of folklore blossomed into genres. In its many varieties, black Southern literature steadfastly holds to dreams tempered by historical realities. It gives the lie to the idea that the language of literature is divorced from the language of everyday experiences.

The work collected in *Black Southern Voices* focuses mainly on twentieth-century examples of what can be broadly identified as black Southern literature. As has been noted, that literature began with oral creation, evolved from the blending of oral and written traditions, and continues to grow as self-conscious artists adapt or modify their literary heritage to serve contemporary needs. To be sure, there is a dialectic between the spoken and the written within this literature. Richard Wright described these tendencies in "The Literature of the Negro in the United States" (1957) as The Forms of Things Unknown and The Narcissistic Level. Writers who embrace The Forms of

Things Unknown (Henry Dumas is a stellar example) seem most concerned with the features of oral creation, speech and song, the folk. Those who work at The Narcissistic Level may be more concerned with traditional literary forms. Yet, as Stephen E. Henderson cautions in *Understanding the New Black Poetry* (1973), "it is fallacious to think of these two levels as discrete entities, although for the most part the influence has been from the folk to the formal during the periods of greatest power and originality." Henderson's caution is to be taken seriously, for we may find the tendencies or levels crisscrossing in the poetry of Margaret Walker or the fiction of Ernest Gaines or the autobiographical writing of Albert Murray.

By their very nature, anthologies are parts not wholes, and *Black Southern Voices* can only provide an abbreviated historical geography of black Southern literature and thought, a small portion of the immense landscape that has yet to be fully explored and mapped. In that sense, this collection invites us to become familiar with the continuity and change, themes, consciousness and sensibilities, the calls and geometric progressions of response, and the contradictions that are distinguishing features of the terrain.

The very concept of black South as place is based on what Lerone Bennett once called "parahistory," the possibility that Euro-Americans and African-Americans in the South occupied the same space but that their perceptions of time and its significance were fundamentally different. Within this conceptual context, the literature collected here is Southern by virtue of its place of origin and its direct or indirect response to historical circumstances that existed or exist only in the South.

There is, of course, great variety in how the writers respond to Southern experience. Arna Bontemps's *Black Thunder,* a portrayal of the slave insurrection led by Gabriel Prosser, gives us a perspective on plantation economy very different from the one found in Margaret Walker's *Jubilee*. The South we behold in Zora Neale Hurston's *Their Eyes Were Watching God* seems diametrically opposed to the South of Richard Wright's *Uncle Tom's Children.* John Oliver Killens's *'Sippi,* Lance Jeffers's *Witherspoon,* and Alice Walker's *Meridian* can be classified as civil rights novels, but the authors' visions have much more to do with their artistic and political sensibilities than with the Civil Rights Movement as a historical phenomenon. Each black Southern writer brings her or his individual voice and vision to a long history of struggle with the land and the matter of color. As for their white Southern counterparts, the South is both a geography and a state of mind.

In addressing the matter of history as central underpinning for a black Southern literature, Addison Gayle, in his essay "Reclaiming the Southern Experience: The Black Aesthetic 10 Years Later," noted

> an excursion into the cultural past can provide images by which we may measure ourselves as a people; it tells us that we are a people whose history and culture exemplify those values by which men throughout the history of the world

have lived and died, and that these values found their greatest expression in the Western world in the South in the first home away from home for the African-American. It is there, where men and women, having undergone the racial holocaust and survived, that the best examples of a viable Black literary and cultural tradition exist.

Gayle is hinting that history is more than a narrative of events; it is a continuous negotiating with the past and the present, a particular way of sensing the world and valuing the meaning of human existence. Here Gayle is echoing Richard Wright's insistence that literature enable us to make some sense of our struggle beneath the stars. So too black Southern writers embrace the necessity of creating works of art that are grounded in the lived experience of Southern culture. They may share certain formal and thematic similarities with white Southern writers, but they most surely march to the beat of a different parahistorical drummer. That is the only way to make sense of the intensely felt experience of being black and Southern.

This particular way of making sense of experience involves the art of maintaining some balance between the forces of history and the forces of personal or collective experience. Both the matter and the techniques for mastering that balancing art are contained in the oral black folk culture of the South. Touchstone examples are Ernest Gaines's *The Autobiography of Miss Jane Pittman* and John Oliver Killens's *'Sippi*. The poet Tom Dent has commented that Gaines's novel works so well because it dips into "a vast pool of on-going oral literature, retaining and making a small part of it permanent. . . . It [the novel] is built over a long established (possibly African) mode of Afro-American storytelling—elders passing down necessary historical knowledge to younger folk, though the younger person must ritually be tested for acceptability by the elder and his or her agents. The novel is shaped by the form of an older, time-tested oral form; its viability is thus enhanced." In *'Sippi*, as the folklorist William Wiggins has established, oral tradition is crucial to the novel's theme and structure; in addition, Killens used the literary strategies of critical realism to comment on such contemporary concerns as gender, race, and class. Although these novels are but two touchstones among many, they are especially revealing syntheses of the autobiographical, dramatic, and poetic currents that mark black Southern literature: the artistic mastery of specific historical contexts with the complex simplicity that informs the best of world literature, mastery of the mythic impulse.

The visions and voices of black Southern speakers and writers, their perspectives, the history and heritage they make accessible to us serve to clarify, to illuminate, and to persuade us creatively of a truth only now beginning to be universally recognized: like jazz, the literary expressions of the black Southerner constitute America's most genuine gift to the humanistic tradition of literature.

Suggested Readings with Similar Theme:

Toomer, Jean. "The South in Literature." *Call* (1923). James Weldon Johnson Collection. Yale University.

Turner, Darwin T. "The Negro Novelist and the South." *Southern Humanities Review* 1 (1967): 21–29.

Killens, John Oliver. Introduction to *Black Southern Voices: An Anthology of Fiction, Poetry, Drama, Nonfiction and Critical Essays,* edited by John Oliver Killens and Jerry W. Ward Jr., 1–4. New York: Penguin USA, 1992.

From "Walter Mosley (An Interview)" (1993)

Review the mystery writer's comments about the literary models in his life. What is being suggested about models in the life of black writers? Must writers "come out of" another writer who is of the same genre? Or from the same race? Summarize Mosley's position on craft versus politics. What does he say is to be the function of literature, the role of the writer, and the responsibility of the audience? How does Mosley echo Lott, hooks, and Ellison regarding the black audience? How does Mosley echo other contemporary writers, such as McMillan, Eady, and Pate?

TD: Chester Himes, did you ever read him?

WM: Umhum. That's so funny—there're people I like, black male writers, mostly they're poets, it turns out. Somebody like Etheridge Knight makes me so happy I can't stand it. But it's more than just that. I try to think of what lineage is. It seems that so many black writers are always creating who they are in the world, because there isn't the kind of lineage that you have in Eurocentric white male literature, where people actually do come out of each other. You have a great poet who studies under him.

TD: But the critics who write about us are not familiar enough with the tradition to pick some people to say we came out of.

WM: People say Chester Himes about me.

TD: Do they?

WM: They do. But, you see, I don't feel like I came out of Himes. He comes from a very angry, a very disenfranchised place. Life was very hard for him and he needed to get away from it. People didn't pay attention to him. I don't live under the kind of racism that he lived under. And even though I think it made decisions much clearer for him, which in some ways makes things easier, I wouldn't want to trade it. I learned more from [Raymond] Chandler.

TD: Who was the first mystery writer you read?

WM: Ross McDonald. I loved him. I still love him, as flawed as he is.

TD: How do you see yourself fitting in with your contemporaries among black writers?

WM: I was in Philadelphia a couple of years ago. Quincy Troupe was teaching a poetry workshop. I was just sitting in the back listening. It was a black crowd of people. Quincy was saying, "I want everybody to write poetry. I want all black people to be writing poetry and making poetry and living poetry and. . . ." You know how Quincy is, he said that again. He said, "In order to write poetry, you gotta write good poetry, you gotta write real poetry. You can't just be writing something and say it's poetry. Just because you have the right politics, doesn't mean that you're writing poetry." He said, "I hate Bush." He said, "That's right, but it isn't poetry." And it was wonderful. Cause, you know, Quincy is such a powerful guy. Everybody was looking up at him and they were very serious and he was saying the truth. And very often in black art and literature, the mistake is made that the correct political stance makes good art, when indeed the correct political stance has nothing to do with good art. Nothing. The only issue for me is good writing. The job of writing is to hold, somehow, in a crystalline form, the language of the time. When, a hundred years from now, someone reads this, they will know what life was like at the time. They won't need to look at a history book to understand what life was like. They can see it and feel it through the language and description of life in that book. The contract of telling a story is that the reader has to wonder, what's happening next? And then there has to be a subtext, there always has to be a subtext. I think I'm writing good fiction. I mean, I'm not saying I'm the greatest writer in the world.

TD: OK, let me ask you in a different way: Writing mysteries has given you a wide and widely mixed audience. But has the genre restricted you at all? I'm interested in you, but I'm not interested in studying the genre. So, do you feel that there's some other audience out there who has yet to find you?
WM: I'm being slowly, though not so slowly anymore, discovered by a black audience. The mystery audience is almost exclusively a white audience. I pressured my publisher for two years to get me into the various black distributors. They wanted to do it, but it was very hard for them. There was reticence, on behalf of the black distributors, to deal with Norton. They said, "Who else do you publish who's black? He's the only one and you want us to do all this work?" But I think black people are happy that I'm writing.

TD: Yeah, I think so. A funny thing happened. I was watching the news after the inauguration and they said that the new things that are in now that Bill Clinton is president are saxophone pins, and what I would call white soul food, and Walter Mosley. Were you surprised to hear that?
WM: Some people whose bookstore I always read at had given him my books, so I knew he had them. Clinton, not at all a stupid man, wants to reach out for the black community and the Latino community and the gay community and say, "Hey listen, I'm interested." Now, you could look at this with a questioning eye, which, of course, makes sense to do. But at the same

time, I figure this: if he read my books, that means that black language and black life, at least from one point of view, entered his life. Even if it hasn't entered his life, it entered other people's lives who have said, "Let me take a look at this book" and "Wow, this is what he's reading?" So I like it, I'm happy with it, and not idealistically or unrealistically, I think.

TD: Well, it brought you some kind of notoriety. I read an interview with you in "Vanity Fair," where you were asked a lot about being a bi-racial person. Is it a constant subject that people ask you about and therefore annoying?

WM: No, actually, I enjoyed the "Vanity Fair" piece for a variety of reasons. My mother is Jewish, and I was raised among Jews and blacks; my father, obviously, was black. And I'm in a world today where there's all this conflict between Jews and blacks. So, the fact that Christopher Hitchins wanted to concentrate on that, I liked, because it's a dialogue that I don't mind getting at. I was on the Staten Island Ferry once with a guy who I liked a lot, a Muslim, who turned to me and said, "Hitler didn't really kill as many Jews as they said he did, and he really shoudda oughtn't a done it, but the Jews had all the guilder and them Germans just wanted to be free." This is like ten years ago, but I just can't forget it. I don't like anti-Black Jews and I don't like anti-Jewish Blacks. It's not that I don't like them, I just don't like the stance.

TD: But frequently publications treat an interview with a black writer as a situation to talk about race politics, and they'll forget to ask you about your books. There's a point at which any writer would be annoyed at being interviewed at such length without anybody saying, by the way, you write books, don't you? Do you get much of that?

WM: Yeah, that happened, but I wanted to deal with it. I'm kind of easy going. My books came out in England. Yours did too, in fact ours came out at the same time last year.

TD: They interviewed me about the L.A. riot.

WM: But they needed to know, they were asking, "What's wrong with these people?" I didn't feel badly about answering them because I really wanted to get this other point of view.

TD: But, see, no one ever asked me about craft, no one ever asked me questions about how something is made. They really were asking about narrative content and how it compares to reality.

WM: I often change the subject, even when I'm talking to you I do it.

TD: Let me ask you two more things. I take it Easy Rollins is going to be around.

WM: He's going to live a long time. I think I'll keep him alive until maybe 1990, 1991.

TD: You told me you wrote another novel that's not a mystery. What's this other novel?
WM: There've been a few but the book I've finished is called, "R.L.'s Dream." Those are the initials they used to call the musician, Robert Johnson. He was Robert LeRoy until he found out his real name. And that book is a blues novel, not so much about R.L., but about a fictional character who once played with R.L. and is now dying in New York and is trying to come to grips with his life and his history.

TD: You said to me something about wanting to write about the music.
WM: Ah. Now I remember that discussion. The most revolutionary moment of the twentieth century is black American music. I believe that it knocked down the walls of Russia. I believe that it touches and transforms everybody. It certainly starts with the blues. I'm not a musician, but I want to write about what music means. The only way I can write about it. I want to write about a black musical life, Robert Johnson's life. A life that is so hard and painfully and specifically itself that my main character, Soupspoon Wise is his name, says that by leaving the Mississippi Delta, he abandoned the blues, because you couldn't play the blues without a blues audience. You just can't take the blues out of the South. That music belongs there. It belongs on the streets and the roads and the paths. It belongs to the people. He thinks that he abandoned the blues, but this is a realization much later. It's a realization that haunted him. He didn't realize it at the beginning, but he felt it. He felt it from the beginning. His life kind of disintegrated. Now, in his old age, when he's dying, one of the other aspects of the blues. He is trying to come to grips with it.

TD: Did you do anything in this book that you haven't done?
WM: It's written in third person, so there's that. That was very nice because I could deal with my female characters a lot more easily. I'm limited by Easy. Easy, I think, is a very broad big character, maybe bigger than me, in life, but not necessarily in language. In language I have to be careful how Easy talks and what he knows, whereas in third person, it depends on whose shoulder I'm on in that moment. My narrator is closely involved with the other characters, so he takes on the characteristics of whomever we're looking at from that point of view at that moment. So the language can be much more lyrical. I can do a lot more things. The language can reflect the mood. I can get really wild, and I do. I get really wild.

TD: That's good. And what next?

WM: About the near future, I have a four book contract at Norton and that's three mysteries and this book, "R.L.'s Dream." We'll see what happens from here. So, my next four years are spoken for.

Suggested Readings with Similar Theme:

Bailey, Frankie Y. *Out of the Wordpile: Black Characters in Crime and Detective Fiction.* Westport, Conn.: Greenwood Press, 1991.
Tate, Greg. "The Gumshoe Blues." *Village Voice,* 1997, 42, 47.

SANDRA G. SHANNON

Blues, History and Dramaturgy:
An Interview with August Wilson (1994)

According to Wilson, how significant is African American culture, particularly the blues, to African American drama? What is Wilson's position on who should direct black drama? How does Wilson enter discussions with Toni Morrison regarding literary "ancestors"? How does he echo Sterling Brown regarding "black characters as seen by white writers"? What is the playwright's advice to others about writing drama? On portraying characters in drama? According to Wilson, what is the responsibility of the present black playwright? What is the responsibility of writers in general?

Shannon: Early in your career you made a gradual shift from writing poetry to writing plays. How has being a poet affected your success as a playwright?
Wilson: It's the bedrock of my playwriting . . . not so much in the language as in the approach and the thinking. Thinking as a poet, one thinks differently than one thinks as a playwright. The idea of metaphor is a very large idea in my plays and something that I find lacking in most contemporary plays. I think I write the kinds of plays that I do because I have twenty-six years of writing poetry underneath all of that.

Shannon: I'm fascinated by the combination of memory, history, myth-making, and the blues in your work. Do you perceive your role as an historian, as a prophet, as a healer, or perhaps as something else?
Wilson: Well, I just say playwright. Of course, I use history and the historical perspective. For instance, in *The Piano Lesson,* you can see the actor, the character going down a road, and given the benefit of a fifty-year historical perspective, we know how all this turned out. I try to keep all of the elements of the culture alive in my work, and myth is certainly a part of it. Mythology, history, social organizations, economics—all of these things are part of the culture. I make sure that each element is in some way represented—some elements more so than others—in the plays, which I think gives them a fullness and a completeness, creates the impression that this is an entire world.

Shannon: What is your reasoning behind writing a 400-year-old autobiography in ten plays? At what point did you decide upon this strategy?

Wilson: Well, actually, I didn't start out with a grand idea. I wrote a play called *Jitney!,* set in '71, and a play called *Fullerton Street* that I set in '41. Then I wrote *Ma Rainey's Black Bottom,* which I set in '27, and it was after I did that that I thought, "I've written three plays in three different decades, so why don't I just continue to do that?"

Also, everyone assumes that any writer's work—it's not just my work—is autobiographical, that you're writing about yourself. None of the events in the plays are events in my life—none of the characters are modeled after me—because I feel that, if you write your autobiography, you don't have anything else to tell. So I thought when people would ask me that, I'd say, "Well, you know I've got a 400-year autobiography. That's what I'm writing from. There's a whole bunch of material. You never run out of stories."

Shannon: But you're part of the story?

Wilson: Oh, absolutely. I'm definitely a part of the story. I claim all 400 years of it. And I claim the right to tell it in any way I choose because it's, in essence, my autobiography—only it's the story of myself and my ancestors.

Shannon: As you know, I'm in the midst of writing a biocritical study of your work. During my research I've come across quite a few titles and have acquired the scripts of several never-before-published works. For example, you wrote several brief scripts for the Science Museum of Minnesota. The plays that I have read include *An Evening with Margaret Mead, How Coyote Got His Special Powers,* and *Eskimo Song Duel.* Could you talk briefly about that experience?

Wilson: Well, it was a good experience. If nothing else, it was the first time that I was paid for writing, and it was good money, as I recall. There wasn't, though, a whole lot of creativity necessary to document a northwest Indian tale for a group to act out on the anthropology floor. I never could understand why they were willing to pay me so much money to do that. There weren't very many projects assigned because it cost money to get the costumes and to rehearse the actors, to actually put them on the floor. So, once they had two or three things on the floor, they didn't want to have anything else.

To try to make it interesting, I came up with this idea called "Profiles in Science." I was going to write a one-woman or one-man show about various scientific characters, which I did—one on Margaret Mead, William Harvey, Charles Darwin—but none of them was ever performed.

Shannon: You discovered the blues in 1965 with Bessie Smith's "Nobody Can Bake a Sweet Jelly Roll Like Mine." In *Ma Rainey's Black Bottom,* you take up the cause of the blues singer. This also seems to be the case in an earlier play called *The Homecoming.* Could you explain your compassion for the plight of the blues singer?

Wilson: Well, you see, it's the singer, but it's also the music. I think that the music contains a cultural response of black Americans to the world they find themselves in.

Blues is the best literature we have. If you look at the singers, they actually follow a long line all the way back to Africa, and various other parts of the world. They are carriers of the culture, carriers of ideas—like the troubadours in Europe. Except in American society they were not valued, except among the black folks who understood. I've always thought of them as sacred because of the sacred tasks they took upon themselves—to disseminate this information and carry these cultural values of the people. And I found that white Americans would very often abuse them. I don't think that it was without purpose, in the sense that the blues and music have always been at the forefront in the development of the character and consciousness of black America, and people have senselessly destroyed that or stopped that. Then you're taking away from the people their self-definition—in essence, their self-determination. These guys were arrested as vagrants and drunkards and whatever. They were never seen as valuable members of a society by whites. In fact, I'm writing a play which deals specifically with that.

Shannon: Your 1977 play *The Coldest Day of the Year* seems to be about reconciling relationships between African American men and women. What inspired the play? Can you explain the circumstances surrounding its composition?

Wilson: Well, it was undoubtedly inspired by the breakup of my relationship with my girlfriend. It certainly was not written in the language that I write plays in now. I thought that in order to create art out of black life—because I didn't value the way that blacks speak—you had to change it. So you had lines like, "Our lives frozen in deepest heats of spiritual turbulence." Now, if I were going to write it, I guess the guy would just walk up to the woman and say, "How you doing, mama? We're out here in the cold." . . .

Shannon: I think you may have answered this, but which play do you consider to be the beginning of your history cycle—*Fullerton Street* or *Jitney!*? As I have not read *Fullerton Street,* could you give me a synopsis of its plot?

Wilson: *Jitney!* was the first one I wrote. *Fullerton Street* is a play centered in the '40s in which I tried to examine the urban Northerner. What I wanted to do was to show some people who had come north and encountered the cities, and had lost whatever kinds of values they had in the South—almost as if the environment determined that you had to adopt different values in order to survive up here. A husband and wife are living with the husband's parents in their household. It's been six or seven years since they've been up north, and they have become alcoholics, living on and waiting for Welfare checks. In the South they would not have been living like that.

The important action of the play takes place on the night of the Joe Louis-Billy Khan fight, which they listen to around the radio with a group of male characters who are friends of the husband—the young man Moses, who is 25 or 26 years old. After the fight they sit around talking, and they start telling jokes. As the night wears on, one of the jokes degenerates into a vivid description of the lynching of one of Moses's friends, which they had witnessed. I think it was for something for which Moses was the culprit, as opposed to his friend, since white folks can't tell one from the other. So he had a special burden of guilt to carry. It is a very vivid memory, which, from that point in the play, changes his character, and he begins to move closer to at least adopting some new guidelines as he becomes aware of his cowardice. His mother dies—Mozelle—that was the first person I killed off in any of my plays. I remember that, when I wrote the scene of Mozelle dying, I was crying. Tears were falling on the page, and I was trying to write, and the ink was getting all screwed up.

Shannon: You were crying?
Wilson: Oh, yeah! It was like, "Mozelle is dead!" And I had lived with her for so long.

Shannon: There's a lot of death in *Two Trains*. You seem to have gotten good at that.
Wilson: Absolutely. It surprised me. There's death in all of the plays. When I wrote *Joe Turner*, I said, "Hey, good. Nobody died. No death!" Then I started looking back, and there was Mr. Seth's mother, and there's a ghost in *Joe Turner*—Miss Mabel comes back—and there are constant references to death . . . the two babies. I didn't realize it. But death is such an integral part of life; you can't have one without the other.

In *Two Trains,* I wanted to bring in the spectre of death in the persona of West, the undertaker with his black gloves. When I started out, I wanted to have him as a more menacing presence within the play, but he didn't become that menacing character that I originally started to write.

Shannon: Hambone dies, and, of course, Aunt Eater never dies.
Wilson: Hambone dies—the first line in the play is when he talks about the second time that 651 came out. He says, "That was L.D.'s number. If he was still living he'd be in big money." So it starts with L.D. and a reference to the people and Memphis's mother. In a big speech at the end of Act I, Memphis tells about when his mother died. Holloway's grandmother. Bubba Boy's woman dies in the play. West's wife has died.

Shannon: The mule dies.
Wilson: The mule dies. That's kind of appropriate. Memphis is the only one in the community that's making it—he's a rich man.

Shannon: I like that. The play ends on a good note with him getting more than what he expected for the restaurant. What do you think you accomplished in *Jitney!*?

Wilson: I simply wanted to show how the station worked—how these guys created jobs for themselves and how it was organized. There was a head of the station. All of these guys pay their dues $15 a month—and that gives them the right to use that phone. People know the number, then they call up to order a cab. There are certain rules. One is that you can't drink. Otherwise they won't call your number; they'll call somebody else. There was a lot of competition in jitney numbers. There must be a thousand of them. There's a certain one—COURT–1–9802—which has been a jitney number for about forty-five years. If you go to Pittsburgh now and call COURT–1–9802, you'll get a jitney.

Certain stations have different reputations: whether the drivers come on time, are honest, or whatever. But I just wanted to show that these guys could be responsible. They make jobs out of nothing. I think it's very ingenious. Then, of course, I had to get into the lives of the characters. It was an attempt to show what the community was like at the time, to show these five guys working and creating something out of nothing.

Shannon: The Vietnam War is looming, and has a lot to do with the tone of the play. I went back to some lyrics by Marvin Gaye, "What's Going On?" and I find that what he's saying captures the essence of *Jitney!*

Wilson: That's interesting. That was the only song in the '60s. I used to get so mad at popular rhythm & blues of the day. With all the stuff that was going on, Stevie Wonder was singing "My Cheri Amore," and the music wasn't responding to what was happening, except for Marvin Gaye. I remember, when Claude and I were together, I challenged him to go to the juke box and find just one song that had any meaning, and he went over there and found "What's Going On?" And I said, "You're right." James Brown's "Say It Loud: I'm Black and I'm Proud" was also a very important song, which we used in *Two Trains.*

I didn't make the Vietnam Was as large a part of *Jitney!* as I could have. I think it's a personal matter, because even though a tremendous number of blacks were killed, that never, for me . . . there was one person I had known through a friend of his up in the projects. Their son had gotten killed in the war and they had a little wake on the lawn. There was the flag, and you went up and paid your respects. Those were the only marks of the war that ever actually touched me, or my observation of that community. So it was not a large part. If it had been, then I think it would have become a larger part of my work.

Shannon: Like many other nationalists during the 1960s and early '70s, you seem to have been affected by Malcolm X and his unfortunate death. I note that Malcolm X's death looms in the background of *Two Trains Running*. How does his symbolic presence shape the play?

Wilson: Well, it offers an alternative in the sense that, in *Two Trains Running*, there are three ways in which you can change your life. You have Prophet Samuel, Malcolm X, and Aunt Ester. Originally I was going to have someone who was representative of the idea of assimilation—cultural assimilation into American society and adopting the dominant values of the culture. But I couldn't find a character who was willing to take that view. There were people in the community, of course, but not in my play. I couldn't make any of those characters. So that idea became lost. Originally I thought the rally was going to be a more important part of the play than it is—this Malcolm X rally that looms over the play. Somehow it stayed in the background as other stories of the characters moved. So actually Aunt Ester has more impact on the play. Two of the characters do go up to see Aunt Ester. So she has more of an impact than Malcolm. . . .

Shannon: The short piece *The Janitor*, which I read in a recent issue of *Antaeus*, carries a profound message. Can you recall what inspired this work?

Wilson: First of all, I was a member of New Dramatists, and they were having a fundraiser. They asked all the playwrights to write a four-minute play—not a five-minute but a four-minute play. This was rather difficult. How do you write a four-minute play? So I came up with the idea of the janitor, who is someone whom this society ignores yet someone who may have some very valuable information—someone who has a vital contribution to make yet has been relegated to sweeping the floor. He does it for some years, and never once do we think to say, "Hey, do you have anything to say about anything? Do you have any contribution to make other than being a janitor or running an elevator or whatever?" So in that sense we really do not take advantage of all of our human potential. And I look at how the Israelis are absolutely delighted in the fact that they have close to a million Soviet Jews that are coming into the country, and they are looking forward to what those Soviet Jews have to contribute. This is a lot of intellectual power and intellectual potential that is coming in their country, and they're going to use that. And we're sitting over here with 35 million blacks who have a lot of untapped potential—35 million! So there's the idea of not taking advantage of your potential. I thought I'd show this guy here who is sweeping up the floor, and there's this microphone, and he just goes up and starts talking into the microphone.

Shannon: It seems to show that we're caught up in status also—that if you're not of a certain status also, then you don't matter. This is dangerous.

Wilson: Absolutely. They're going to get all of these people with academic backgrounds and status to speak at a conference on youth, and none is going to say as much in all of their days of seminars and conferences as this man says in four minutes. That was my idea in the play.

Shannon: Can you talk about *Black Bart and the Sacred Hills*? What were you trying to achieve? I'm familiar with the story of Black Bart, the cowboy.
Wilson: First of all, it's a musical, and it's kind of zany. It's a satire on American society. I have a character, Black Bart, who is a magician. He used to be a cattle rustler. He broke out of jail, and he created this retreat called the Sacred Hills, and he's making gold out of water. He has an idea he's going to flood the world with so much gold that it's going to be as despised as "cockroaches in a sweet woman's kitchen." Gold is going to be utterly valueless.

Shannon: How do you put together a plot like that? Where do your ideas come from?
Wilson: I'm not sure. I did this from one Sunday to the next. I think it was the idea of satire, and the most brilliant satirist I knew was Ishmael Reed.

Shannon: What was it about Black Bart that made you choose him as a character to build the play around?
Wilson: Well, I think Bart actually has his roots in Bynum and Holloway and all of these kinds of characters—many of their roots are in Bart. Bart started as a series of poems in which this character named Black Bart was a magician, but he was also very philosophical—sort of like Holloway and Bynum.

Claude Purdy heard this series of poems and told me, "You should write a play with that character." I started thinking, and came up with the idea of a multi-cultural satire on American society.

Shannon: I'm curious about the title of *Two Trains Running*. Does the title suggest that black people still have choices?
Wilson: The question we've been wrestling with since the Emancipation Proclamation is, "Do we assimilate into American society and thereby lose our culture, or do we maintain our culture separate from the dominant cultural values and participate in the American society as Africans rather than as blacks who have adopted European values?" On the surface, it seems as though we have adopted the idea that we should assimilate, because one has received more publicity than the other. But if you look at it, you'll find that the majority of black Americans have rejected the idea of giving up who they are—in essence becoming someone else—in order to advance in American society, which may be why we haven't moved anywhere. I see the majority of the people saying, "Naw, I don't want to do that. I'm me." These are the people in the ghetto; these are the people who suffer. You can also look at people who are going well . . . that could be you. They still say, "I don't care. I don't want to do that." They still say no, even though they're suffering for it.

The culture of black America is still very much alive. Black Americans still practice the values that their grandparents had—with some exceptions, of course. For instance, black people . . . we decorate our houses differently.

I've always said that I was going to get together some kind of multi-media presentation that would illustrate all of these things. Because you can take black gospel and white gospel, and put them side by side, and you cannot tell me that these are not different people. And then you take a black person's house and a white person's house . . . both have tables, chairs, and a couch, but our couches have little mirrors on the side.

I'm also collecting and studying business cards. Black folks will generally give you a business card that is very colorful and highly designed and, according to some white folks, looks amateurish. I met a guy last night—Bernie Slain. You may know him. He's got a radio show or a TV show. Anyway, this guy has got a white card with a big yellow star in the center. And he had a black one with big red letters, and it's got its own special symbols up here. He's obviously doing all right, but still he hands out a card that looks like that.

Shannon: You say that there are differences and that black people ought to acknowledge them. It's not suggesting that one person is better than the other.

Wilson: Oh, absolutely not! It's white America that says, "Our way is better than your way. You're not acting right. You're not doing this right. You're not supposed to act like that." I had a line in *Two Trains* that I took out because it was in the wrong place, and I couldn't make it work there in the speech. Holloway was saying, "It's not how you look; it's how you do. You do ugly. If you change the way you do, we'll let you in the game. Otherwise, you stay over there and suffer."

Shannon: Have you followed the Amiri Baraka-Spike Lee controversy over the making of a movie on the life of Malcolm X? What are your thoughts about this issue?

Wilson: We're not talking about something that is going to affect the lives of 35 million black people in America. We're talking about a movie about Malcolm X. I think the real issue should have been made fifteen years ago when Marvin Worth bought the rights to do Malcolm X, and how he sat on the rights for years. He's had five, six different people write scripts for him. He was simply afraid to make the movie. He told me, "You only get one chance." I said, "Yeah, but you got to take that one chance."

I want to know why Quincy Jones and Bill Cosby and all these black people who now say "Malcolm" didn't buy the movie rights and say , "Hey, this is one of our icons. We don't want you to have anything to do with this movie." It should have been in black hands from the beginning. That's what ruined his image. And nobody's talking about that. When Norman Jewison was going to direct the film, I didn't hear one peep from anybody. I didn't hear Baraka then say, "Hey, a white man is directing a film of Malcolm." The only ones that I know that said anything were myself and Spike.

Shannon: Well, it is kind of suspicious now with all of this media frenzy.

Wilson: I think Spike has the right to make whatever kind of movie he wants to make. Ultimately, the people are going to decide. It's the people who will go in there and say, "Yeah, that's Malcolm" or "Naw, that ain't Malcolm." Mao said, "Let a thousand thoughts contend. . . . The strongest idea will always dominate." So, if you don't like the movie, go make your own. Ralph Ellison has said, "The best way to fight a novel is to write another one."

Shannon: You have some very definite ideas on the director's sensibilities in interpreting your work. What is the status of your request that a black director be secured to direct the Paramount release of *Fences*?

Wilson: I said that I wanted a black director from the beginning—I told Eddie Murphy that. Eddie Murphy said, "I don't want to hire anybody just because they're black." Well, neither did I. I mean I wanted somebody who was black and talented. But I have since learned to look behind that phrase "I don't want to hire anybody just because they're black." What, in essence, is being said is that the only qualification that a black person would have is that he or she is black, that the only reason you would have to hire someone would be that person's skin color. All of those black directors in Hollywood and you say, "I want a black director," and they go, "I don't want to hire somebody just because they are black." I say, "Naw, hire them because they are talented."

When they had lined up Barry Levinson, who's a very nice man, to do the film, I met with Barry. Barry wanted to do the film, so I went over to Paramount's office and said, "I don't want Barry to do the film. He doesn't qualify." A qualification was that the director had to be black, that he have some sensibilities to the culture.

This is a drama about the culture. And in these instances, I think you should hire . . . if this were a film about Italian culture, you should hire an Italian director. This is common sense. Now if you have an adventure movie that's not specific to a particular culture, you can hire anybody to direct that. . . .

Shannon: Let me ask you this. How did it feel to have a play on Broadway? What were your emotions?

Wilson: It felt good. But we were in a theater on 48th Street on the left side of Broadway. So you had to go out of your way to get to that theater. There are theaters on both sides of 44th and 45th Streets, but they will not put black plays in some of those theaters. People have to rub elbows during intermission, when they come out and stand on the sidewalk. And at the end of a black play, there's a whole bunch of black folks standing there rubbing elbows. Go up to 48th Street, go up to 47th Street or 46th Street, but you don't get 44th and 45th.

At the time, it was tremendously exciting. It was nice to walk down there . . .

It didn't have my name on the marquee. They said, "Well, you've got to wait. It's your first time and all that." But I think any playwright—first play, last play, or whatever—should have his or her name on the marquee, identifying him as the person who wrote this play. If you have no name value, they don't put your name up on the marquee; they put the actors' names up there in big letters because it's a business, and that's what it's about. It doesn't matter who wrote the play. It doesn't matter whether the play is any good or not. If you can get a star in there to do the role, you're going to have people come to see it. Jason Robards is doing a play right now that has gotten terrible reviews. Here's one of America's premier actors—can't find anything for him to do, nothing worth his talent—so he's in this. I mean, the play got some really bad reviews. But people don't care. They go to the theater to see Jason Robards.

So I had a lot of problems with the way the matter was handled. They didn't put my name on the marquee; we were on the wrong street . . . but it was tremendously exciting to be there.

Shannon: To date all of your plays have featured men occupying center stage. How do you perceive women's roles in your work? Are you concerned that, so far, women have not been the focus of your plays?
Wilson: No, I am not concerned, and I doubt seriously if I would make a woman the focus of my work simply because of the fact that I am a man, because of the ground on which I stand and the viewpoints from which I perceive the world. I can't do that, although I try to be honest in the instances in which I do have women. I try to portray them from their own viewpoint as opposed to my viewpoint. I am to some extent able to step around on the other side of the table, if you will.

Shannon: I see that. That's the basis of the essay that I gave you: The women are strong, and if somebody else perceives them as victims, I think that person doesn't read the plays carefully enough, because these women choose their routes rather than becoming victims of men.
Wilson: I try not to portray any of my characters as victims. There was a line in *Two Trains Running,* when they're tearing down the building and Memphis is talking about what his business used to be and how he used to sell four cases of chicken a week, but now he's down to one case. "But that's all right," he said. "I ain't greedy. I'll take that. Only they don't want me to have that." I took that line "They don't want me to have that" out of the script because it makes him a victim of someone else. They are not doing anything to him personally. It's not like they don't want him to have the business. They're just tearing down the building. . . .

Shannon: I'm interested in that idea of being led by the characters and listening to the characters as opposed to manipulating and creating them. How does that work? How do you allow that to happen?

Wilson: Well, I think the key word is what you just said—allow. You have to allow it to happen. I've learned that if I just write down what I hear the characters say I have a premise: Everything that they say is true. I don't have to use everything that they say, however, to tell the story. But the more I know, the more they talk, the more I learn about the characters. I have the right to censor that, to take parts. I know it's true, but I don't want to use that part. I'm going to use this part. So I just write down whatever they say without thinking.

I started *Two Trains* with the line "When I left out of Jackson, I said I'm gonna buy me a V-8 Ford and drive by Mr. Henry Ford's house and honk the horn. If anybody'd come to the window I was gonna wave. Then I was going out and get me a thirty-odd-six and come on back to Jackson and drive up to Mr. Stovall's house and honk the horn. Only this time I ain't waving." Now when I wrote this, the character did not have a name. I had no idea who he was. But I started, and then it's like, "Who is Stovall? Why does this guy want to get this car and go by Stovall's, etc.?" So I more or less ask the character, "Who is Stovall?" And he says, "Well, I had this old farm down there . . . ," and he starts to explain the whole story about Stovall. Then, he starts talking about Stovall and somehow ends up talking about this woman who left him after nine years, and she wouldn't even shake his hand. Now I have a woman character, and I have to decide whether I am going to go to her and get some dialogue or whether I want her to be a character. I decided that I didn't want her to be a character and that I would just use Risa as a character, and you could see through his relationship with Risa some possibility as to why his wife may have left. Risa has to carry all of the women's stories in the play and somehow make sense of certain things, you know.

I have a couple of short stories with a character named Memphis, who was a farmer—a sharecropper—down in Alabama. I liked that name and decided to use it. It's the name of an Egyptian god. Sterling I decided upon because he's a sterling man. I knew what his name was before I ever wrote a line of dialogue for him, which is unusual. Most of the time I don't know who they are. If I'm writing and I don't know the name, I just put a little dash and keep on going. Say there's this guy who's talking back to Memphis and I don't know who he is. I put a dash.

Holloway's name was originally Brownie, but I had used a Brownie in *Fences.* Troy talks about Brownie. Brownie's kind of an Uncle Tom character, and I didn't want people to think that this was the same Brownie. So I changed his name. I got his name from a blues song.

Shannon: Hambone and Gabriel seem to be similar characters.

Wilson: There is something that I call a "spectacle character." It's part of that. They are both mentally deficient. One has a war wound, which I think is most important. It would make me mad when I read the reviews and they would refer to Gabriel as an idiot or some other kind of description without making reference to the fact that this man had suffered this wound fighting for a country in which his brother could not play baseball. That was the important thing about Gabriel. Gabriel is one of those self-sufficient characters. He gets up and goes to work everyday. He goes out and collects discarded fruit and vegetables, but he's taking care of himself. He doesn't want Troy to take care of him. He moves out of Troy's house and lives down there and pays his rent to the extent that he is able.

There is some correlation between Gabriel and Hambone. But they are very different in the sense that Hambone has a much more important part in *Two Trains*. He has an effect on everybody's life in the play. He starts off as this guy who says, "I want my ham!" But he emerges as most important because of his life and his death. Risa has this relationship with him. Sterling gives him help. Memphis throws him out. Memphis can see himself in Hambone: "Man been 'round here saying the same thing for ten years." Well, Memphis has been around for ten years, too. He has to come to see that.

Hambone's presence and his death affect the whole play. Sterling can resurrect and redeem Hambone's life by taking the ham. This produces the man of action. Without Hambone, you don't have a Sterling. And also it's the demonstration of his willingness to shed blood in order to get the ham. So when he comes back inside, it's very important that there is blood on his face where he cut his face, where he cut his hands. So it's the willingness to bleed, Loomis's willingness to bleed, the willingness to shed blood.

Shannon: "I don't need anybody . . ." What was it?
Wilson: "I don't need anybody to bleed for me. I can bleed for myself." There's also Boy Willie's willingness to engage Sutter in battle. He doesn't say, "Oh, there's a ghost," and run the other way. He goes after the ghost whose presence is made known to him through this force field. He goes toward it as opposed to running from it.

Shannon: Absolutely, Troy's personification of Death through wrestling . . .
Wilson: He's wrestling with Death. In fact, when Troy got shot when he was trying to rob this guy, he fell forward. He says, "When the guy shot me, I jumped at him with my knife." So here's a man who has pulled a knife on somebody who could pull a gun and shoot him. He takes that, but then he comes forward and ends up killing him. So there's always that willingness to shed blood.

Shannon: Are you moved to write plays in the future giving women more voice?
Wilson: I always say whatever the material dictates, that's what I will follow. However, let me tell you about the play that I'm working on now, which was

originally an all-male play. I looked up one day and this woman had come on stage and sat down in a chair. The guys in the play said, "What the hell is she doing here? I thought you told us that this was an all-male play. What's she doing?" Then they started shouting, "Get out of here!" They said, "Get on away from here. Man, what's she doing?" I said, "Hold up a minute. Let's go find out." So I went over and I asked this woman what she was doing, and she said, "I want my own scene." She just sat there, and they're shouting at her. These are crude men who were working. At first when she came in, she said, "Mr. Wilson said that I could come in." That's when they came and got me. And I said, "You want your own scene?" She said, "Yes, I want my own scene." Okay, I closed my tablet up, and I'm thinking about this. In the process of writing this all-male play, this woman emerges into the play. Now I've got to figure out what to do with her—not only that, but she wants her own scene.

Shannon: Could that perhaps be the voice of a critic or two suggesting . . .
Wilson: No, it was the voice of this woman saying, "How are you going to write this play about these guys and not include me in it? I'm a part of it. They didn't get to be who they are without me, etc. You can't ignore me."

Shannon: So this is part of listening to the characters?
Wilson: Yeah, this was unconscious. How could I write a play without a woman in there? That's what I was trying to do. She said, "I got a part in this story. You gonna write a play about blacks in America in the 1940s and ain't going to have no women in it? How ridiculous can you get?" I said, "Well, you're right." So I opened up my pad and said, "Okay, you got your own scene." Then this guy knocks on the door. He has a radio under one arm and a chicken under the other. She knows his name and invites him in, so I close up my tablet.

Now I've got to figure out how I'm going to use this. What's happening is that it is emerging as my man-woman play, which is something that I have, at some point, included in all of the plays, but I have never really focused on black man-black woman relationships. It was a big thing, but it's just not something that I chose. Maybe it's just something that I had been wanting to write for a long time. It's not that I'm crazy: it's just me telling myself, "Okay, you're ready to do this now." I think that I've acquired a certain maturity. So I think that all of that is possible.

Shannon: I've noticed that Pittsburgh locales in two of your plays in particular—*Two Trains Running* and *Jitney!*—are about to be demolished. What does the imminent wrecking ball suggest in these two works? What does the city mean to your plays?
Wilson: I set them in Pittsburgh, I guess, because that is what I know best. I think that a lot of what was going on in Pittsburgh was going on in Detroit,

Cleveland, or anywhere else black Americans were. So the plays actually could be set anywhere there is a black urban community. But there are also some peculiar kinds of things in relation to Pittsburgh. I couldn't set the plays in Cleveland because I don't know Cleveland, but you could transfer them to Cleveland and they would play just as well.

Shannon: In previous interviews, you've noted the influence of the blues, Romare Bearden, Amiri Baraka, and Jorge Luis Borges. What or who influences you most now?

Wilson: I think that they are the same. The blues I would count as my primary influence. I've been more and more influenced by art, whether it is Bearden or any artist. It's the idea of the visual artist and how visual artists think and how they approach a particular subject—what they want to paint. I'm not sure that a writer can use the same approach as a painter. The painter's tools are different—he's working with form and shadow and mass and color and lines—although I think that there are some corresponding things in the tools of the playwright. In some of my characterizations, I use color. So I have become more and more fascinated with painters, and Bearden has become more of an influence from art. Baraka's influence has less to do with the way that he writes and more to do with the ideas that he espoused in the '60s as a black nationalist—ideas that I found value in then and still find value in. I am fascinated with the way Jorge Luis Borges, the Argentine short story writer, tells a story. I've been trying to write a play the way he writes a story. He tells you exactly what is going to happen, even though the outcome may seem improbable. He'll say the gaucho so and so is going to end up with a bullet in his head on the night of such and such. When you meet the guy, he's washing dishes, and you go, "This guy is going to be the leader of an outlaw gang?" You know that he's going to get killed, but how is this going to happen? And he proceeds to tell the story, and it seems like it's never going to happen. And you look up, without even knowing it, and there he is. He's the leader of an outlaw gang.

Shannon: He doesn't spoil the plot by telling it. He sort of initiates suspense.

Wilson: Yes. The suspense is has to do with the how. You know that this guy is going to get shot in the head, but it's so masterfully done that you don't see it coming—even if you stop and say, "Okay, how is he going to get shot?" It just unfolds itself. See, if you write a play like that, the audience will be just intrigued with trying to . . . it's more or less in the play that I'm doing now, which is a murder mystery in which somebody named Floyd Bannister gets killed. There are all kinds of possibilities. Any number of people may have killed Floyd Bannister in the play. And then if you have a scene with Floyd Bannister in it, you go, "Hey, Floyd, you're going to get killed!" You know that about him, so you then have to look at Floyd in whatever relations he is having with anybody in the play. He gets into an argument with someone and you say, "Could that be the guy who kills Floyd?" because you know this. So then you become intrigued just sitting there trying to figure it out. But what most intrigues the audience is that you know he is going to be killed and he doesn't.

Shannon: It sounds challenging to translate that to the stage.
Wilson: Oh, it is. I'm just not sure how to do it. I haven't been sure of how to do anything other than when I started Joe Turner. I started Joe Turner as a short story. On page twelve of the story, I said, "You've got to write another play. Maybe this is the play." I said, "I can't make this story into a play. How am I going to do that?" I wasn't quite sure how to do it, but the fact that I didn't know how to do it was what made it challenging. I say to myself, "If I can do that, it would be quite interesting." I'll try anything. If it doesn't work, I tear it up and start on something else. Writing is free; it doesn't work, I tear it up and start on something else. Writing is free; it doesn't cost you anything. There is nowhere where it says that 500 words cost twenty-five cents or a dollar. They're free. . . .

Shannon: How have the two Pulitzer Prizes affected you?
Wilson: Neither one has affected me. What it does is change the way people look at you, but it doesn't change the way I look at myself. What did I do? I wrote a couple of plays. I've been writing twenty-six years, and I've got a whole bulk of writing. It's what I have chosen to do with my life. Even behind *Ma Rainey,* I didn't just suddenly become a writer and pick up a pen and say, "Oh, I'm going to write a play." I had been wrestling with ideas and forms of writing and trying to say all kinds of things many years before. It's just part of being a writer.

Shannon: Have you seen the sitcom *Roc?* As you know, the whole cast of the Broadway production of *The Piano Lesson* may now be seen every Sunday evening during prime time. What are your thoughts on this transplanted cast and about the show?
Wilson: I like the show. It's a TV sitcom, and I think you have to approach it as that. They're concerned about advertisers; that's where they make their money. They're concerned about the ratings. So we're not going to get world-class drama. I think they did a good job. The only criticism that I have—and it's constructive criticism—is that there is always in the episodes I've seen a moment that I would call a "sharp moment" when the comedy is suspended for a moment.

Shannon: When they deal with serious issues?
Wilson: Sometimes the whole show can deal with serious issues, but even within that . . . one moment was when the father was talking about working

on the railroad and some of the mistreatment everybody got. The fact that you have those kinds of emphases is important.

The criticism that I have is in regard to the character of Roc's brother, Joey, who, as old as he is, is living in his brother's house. His brother has this thing about wanting him to move out anyway. The father I can see living there, but Joey, I think, should be trying to find a way to get out of the house. Joey is a musician, but we have no indication of this; there isn't any interest in his music. We've never seen him engaged with anything. I think the first episode, when he came home, they had a gig, but the band broke up or something. I think he should constantly be trying to put the band back together, and there could be all kinds of humorous reasons that he can't and reasons why he's still there. Then it becomes funny that he can't get out of the house even though he's trying. I think at some point, some episode, something should be seen. Otherwise, he becomes lazy and shiftless like white people seem to think of Joey: "Well, as long as I can live here rent free on my brother and eat his food, I'll do that."

Shannon: That comes through loud and clear, though—that he is a parasite.
Wilson: Joey is always with some woman. If there is a woman sitting at the bar and you go over and talk with her, you should walk over with a certain responsibility. You can't just walk over and think, "You don't mean anything. You're just another woman. There's one over there too, so there ain't no difference in y'all." Yet that's what you get from that kind of portrayal. All Joey has to do is see a woman, and he forgets about everything else. I think this is another white attitude about black men coming through.

Shannon: The writers are basically white.
Wilson: That doesn't matter. If the writers are black, then they're writing what the white man wants them to write. There is always some white person who, having set himself up as a custodian of your experience, will tell you how to do it. The actors go to auditions and have these people tell them, "You're not black enough. You're not buoyant. Can you do it a little more black?"

Shannon: Sounds like *Hollywood Shuffle.*
Wilson: As long as white people maintain those positions, they can say . . . Quincy Jones is not producing the show, as an example; the white guy is. See, it's all filtered through his sensibilities, and they may get some things right, but I think on the whole . . .

Shannon: It's not easy to watch sometimes. Some episodes are troubling.
Wilson: What I absolutely cannot watch is *In Living Color.* And this is done by black folks. "Here we are. We go'n clown. We go'n act up." I haven't watched more than sixty seconds of it. . . .

Shannon: What do you think about the current status of black theater?

Wilson: I think, one, it's not institutionalized. The difference between white theater and black theater is that there are hundreds and hundreds of institutions that support white theater. You can walk into any university, and it has a theater program that supports white theater. You have more than 200 regional theaters in the country with budgets in excess of a million dollars. Only it isn't black. So you really have a lot of institutional support for that I call white theater and nothing for what I call black theater.

At the National Black Theater Conference that they had in Winston-Salem, North Carolina, I was talking with some other people who were pleasantly surprised to find out that everybody did not know everybody that was out there. So that was the first time, in a long while anyway, that everybody became aware of everybody else. Of course, at the conference they talked about the idea of networking. I think, after becoming aware of each other, the next issue is developing an agenda that will carry you forward. I think what I really see a drastic need for is a conference of writers, some serious kind of conference, at which we tackle the problems of writing. I would like to see all writers get together and hash out some ideas. I think it's time for that.

Shannon: Black writers? All writers?

Wilson: Black writers. All writers are important, but I would never try telling anyone what you have to write. You can be a black writer and write whatever you want. I would never tell anyone what to write. You can only write what you feel anyway. I don't want anyone telling me what to write.

That was part of the thing in the '60s. People were talking about the black writer's responsibility. A black writer's responsibility is whatever he assumes that responsibility to be individually. You can't say you're not doing right because you're not writing this kind of material, even though you're black. You may not want to write it. You can't be forced to write it. If they assume that as a responsibility, then you have the basis to sit down and talk about what that responsibility should be—"Did you ever look at it this way?" But you can't force on anyone a responsibility for writing.

The fact is that we have not been writing long. We're relatively new to this. We don't have a large body of literature that has been developed by blacks, because at one time it was a crime to teach blacks how to read and write. Europeans have been writing stuff down for hundreds and hundreds of years. Blacks, coming from an oral tradition, didn't see the necessity to write it down. We just didn't do that. So we're in America—we've been here since the early seventeenth century—and we know that there is a value to writing things down. But still it's something that is relatively new to us.

If writers got together, then we could . . . I'm not talking about coming up with any manifesto. But I think there are some questions of aesthetics and questions of exactly how writers can contribute to the development of the culture that need to be addressed—not contribute to anyone's polemic, to anyone's idea about what we should and should not be doing, but contribute to the thing that remains the basis of our culture. "This is our culture. How can we contribute? How can we develop it?"

Shannon: You're doing just that in your work.

Wilson: I have always consciously been chasing the musicians. Their expression has been so highly developed, and it has been one expression of African American life. It's like our culture is in the music. And the writers are way behind the musicians I see. So I'm trying to close the gap. That is one of the things I like about Bearden's work: He moved art closer to where the musicians were. But they've always been in the forefront. I think writers need consciously to be aware how our expressions as writers achieve the quality of the musician's expression. . . .

Suggested Reading with Similar Theme:

Shannon, Sandra G. *The Dramatic Vision of August Wilson.* Washington, D.C.: Howard University Press, 1995.

Dolan Hubbard

Voices and Visions
in *The Sermon and the African American*
Literary Imagination (1994)

How is the black sermon a ritual form of expression? A rhetorical form of persuasion? Using the grammar of the sermon as a rhetorical form of persuasion, show how the folk preacher and creative writer "regenerate the spirits" of the downtrodden; revise their nature of reality; and call their altered universes to order. Theoretically, how has the "grammar of the sermon" influenced African American writers such as James Baldwin, Ralph Ellison, Toni Morrison, Toni Bambara, and Zora Neale Hurston? How has the "grammar of the sermon" influenced songwriters such as Curtis Mayfield ("New World Order"), R. Kelly ("I Believe I Can Fly"), Stevie Wonder, and Babyface Edmonds?

The triumph of the sermon in the black American literary imagination is a triumph of aesthetics. The sermon and the other black folk forms, though they may have developed, in many cases, from European or American models, were essentially of African derivation, subjected of course to the transformations that American life had brought about. The black folk sermon issued forth out of the ethos of the slave community, a community whose religious experience was colored by "the terror and frustration of day-to-day existence in a society in which the oppressor is identified as Christian."

Furthermore, the black sermon is a testament to black people's powers of conception, a suggestion that their abilities to create, grasp, and use symbols are just as valid as those who oppress and would deny them their humanity. In other words, the black sermon as symbolic language must affirm something. This affirmation finds expression in the community's continual engagement with what it means to be human, which is inseparable from the meaning of reality. Black people continue to grapple with what it means to be black in the West, to engage the twin problems of articulating the self and imagining freedom, and to question the position of blacks in capitalism. In the context of a black American narrative code, black American fiction writers recover the sermon as a repressed formalism.

The grammar of the sermon is a submerged presence in African American discourse. It repeats the rhythms of plot, complication, climax, and resolution. Its end point is, as Spillers reminds us, "cathartic release . . . an instrument of a collective catharsis, binding once again the isolated members of community." The preacher through his ritual form of expression—the sermon—structures the meaning of blackness as he tells the story of a fallen man or woman risen. He regenerates the spirits of his downtrodden community with his meditation on freedom—freedom from sin and freedom to articulate the self.

Within the symbolic universe of the black sermon, the preacher accomplishes a mythic re-vision as well. He recalls the first movement of creation, "In the beginning . . ." Out of primordial chaos God created an orderly world and assigned a preeminent place to man and woman among His creatures. Man and woman were charged with ordering all things in this once pristine world free of racial and gender strife. In their replication of this divine act, black writers, like their preacher counterparts, call "the altered universe of the black diaspora" to order. Through their incorporation of sermonic rhetoric, they echo the call of the black preacher, who steps out of space and time and boldly proclaims, "I'll make me a world."

Black writers are attracted to the sermon because it empowers blackness. It is central to the way in which a black identity is produced and reproduced when the preacher and community in unison engage in the emancipation of the self. These writers employ literary modes all reminiscent of the folk preacher and jazz musician as they draw on all segments of the literary world for their acts of literary production. Like the preacher, the writers extend and revise the nature of reality, which revolves around "the color of sin/the color of skin." The tenor and tone of black American life are shaped by this discourse of difference.

The consciousness of the difference is always existential. Only in the expression of difference does one get back to the African modality that permits us to begin to answer the question: why do Americans of African descent do what they do? The preacher, as well as the bluesman or -woman and jazz virtuoso, is engaged in an enduring search for wholeness. The preacher's cultural productions lead horizontally back to Africa and vertically upward to Heaven as they embody the community's desire to move from race to grace. Much of black American literature is infused with this search for wholeness, which has its roots in the historic black church. . . .

We see evidence of the cultural markings of the sermon in the works of such diverse writers as Frances Ellen Watkins Harper, Jean Toomer, Zora Neale Hurston, Richard Wright, Ishmael Reed, Leon Forrest, Alice Walker, Ernest Gaines, Toni Morrison, Gloria Naylor, Julius Lester, and C. Eric Lincoln. Surveying the emotionally arid landscape of the United States, these novelists use the sermon as the basis for inventing new paradigms of self and society—an impulse engendered by the slave narratives. . . .

Suggested Readings with Similar Theme:

Johnson, James Weldon. Introduction to *God's Trombones: Seven Negro Sermons in Verse.* New York: Penguin Books, 1927.

Long, Charles H. *Significations: Signs, Symbols and Images in the Interpretation of Religion.* Philadelphia: Fortress, 1986.

Hubbard, Dolan. "Call and Response: Intertextuality in the Poetry of Langston Hughes and Margaret Walker." *Langston Hughes Review* 7 (Spring 1988): 22–30.

Blount, Marcellus. "The Preacherly Text: African American Poetry and Vernacular Performance." *PMLA* 107 (May 1992): 582–93.

ROPO SEKONI

Features of Yoruba Trickster Tale Aesthetics (1994)

Sekoni is interested in "describ{ing}, explain{ing}, and evaluat{ing} the sociosemiotic character of the aesthetics of Yoruba trickster tale discourse. . . ." Sekoni promises to focus more on the secular trickster Ijapa (Tortoise) and less on the mythological trickster Esu, but her study focuses on the social communication embedded in the narrative contexts of select mythic and popular trickster tales. Discuss the results of Sekoni's study. Characterize the tricksters in the select narratives. Identify the three components of an aesthetic experience in trickster tales. How do Sekoni, Charles Chesnutt ("The Conjure Woman"), and Cecil Brown ("The Life and Loves of Mr. Jiveass Nigger") demonstrate the philosophical function of the folktale? About the theoretical function of the trickster? Define the following terms: trickster, folktale, polysemous character, moral lesson, rejection, solidarization, affirmation, and negation.

The trickster narrative, or what the Yoruba call alo Ijapa, is an oicotype in relation to other fictive modes within the narratological compass of the Yoruba. On the average, three of every five fictive narratives told in Yoruba homes or gatherings are trickster tales. Tortoise tales constitute a narrative subgenre that appears to be popular, principally among the masses, or the nonhegemonic members of different Yoruba communities. Unlike myths or rituals, performed principally by official historians or ritual priests as spokesman for the culture's hegemonic group, trickster tales are performed in the privacy of homes by grandmothers, elderly aunts, mothers, and sometimes grandfathers, and in recent times by teenagers and adults in urban centers. Such tales are told with a view to examine secular or social conflicts in contradiction to the emphasis in myth and ritual on ontological or primordial conflicts.

A REVIEW OF PREVIOUS THEORIES ON THE TRICKSTER TALE DISCOURSE

One economical way to start the investigation of the aesthetics of the Yoruba trickster tale discourse is to examine briefly some of the ways others have dealt with either the trickster as a character or the tale as a communicational mode in very recent times. The two most related of such studies are Ojo Arewa and G. M. Shreve's work on Zande trickster tales and Robert D. Pelton's study of four West African trickster-figures. These two works also happen to have summarized most of the other contributions considered to be of seminal value to the discussion of African trickster narrative in general.

While Arewa and Shreve, like Propp, Dundes, and Levi-Strauss, focus entirely on the structure of the trickster tale, Pelton focuses exclusively on the characterological aspect of the trickster. In a fairly extensive examination of four trickster-figures: Ananse, Legba, Esu, and Ogo-Yurugu, Pelton attempts to come to grips with the nature and significance of tricksterhood. In an apparent agreement from a characterological perspective with preceding scholars of the trickster, such as Paul Radin and Carl Jung, Pelton draws attention to the liminal and metamorphic potentials of the trickster. He sees the trickster as a means of imaging cosmic crisis and resolving the contradiction ensuing from such crisis by realigning the structure of the cosmos. The source of such realignment and resolution of cosmic conflict, Pelton asserts, is traditionally attributed in "premodern" cultures to the metamorphic power of the trickster, which is motivated by the collision of the ambivalent essence of the trickster. Pelton sees all the tricksters as agents of partial resolution and transformation of cosmic experience characterized by a contradictory structure. He also sees the ambivalent character of the trickster as a useful energy in coping with a situation of recurrent contradiction:

> Thus there is a double doubleness about him: if he parodies sacred mysteries by disguising himself as a bird, by claiming the power to heal, or by fishing with spirits, his parody brings about creation, not destruction; and if he makes a fool of himself in the process, still he reveals himself as wonderful in his power to draw forth the delicate balance of forces that is in the human world. As in his contradiction of the contradictor, he negates negation and thereby gives birth to a dialectic whose aim is not synthesis, but a never-ending juggling of thesis and antithesis.

The present study will benefit from Pelton's insight on both the metamorphic and hermeneutic character of the trickster. But unlike Pelton's work, the emphasis in this study will be on the secular trickster, Ijapa (Tortoise), and not on the mythological, religiously oriented trickster, Esu. While agreeing that Esu and Ijapa (Tortoise) share many things in common, especially their view that everything is alterable, it is important to recognize the aesthetic implications of two similar characters that operate in two different contexts. The "mythic" environment of Esu does not possess as much flexibility as the secular environment of Ijapa. The perpetual juggling of thesis and antithesis that Pelton rightly acknowledges is more evident and purposive in trickster folktales than in trickster mythic tales. A fundamental conceptual difference between our approach is this study and that of Pelton is on the ranking of mythic and folk tales. Pelton dismisses the notion of dichotomy between official and popular views of reality. It is possible that no such distinction exists for the Ashanti, as Pelton has suggested, and this may explain why Ananse serves as mythic and "folktalic" trickster in the Ashanti world. This study will take a position that there is both a popular and an official view in the case of the Yoruba narrative experience and that, more important, this distinction has a significant aesthetic dimension in folktales that may be lacking in mythic narratives. The clear separation between the mythic (official) trickster, Esu, and the folktalic (popular) trickster, Ijapa, in the Yoruba narrative experience will be given more consideration in this study than in Pelton's. It is our view that a recognition by the Yoruba of the semiotic implication of the distinction between a mythic and a social trickster is capable of providing a cue for the understanding of aesthetic communication at the level of the folks.

It is thus our intention in this study to examine the semiotic character of the trickster narrative tradition of the Yoruba from both characterological and narratological perspectives. Moreover, our semiotic analysis of trickster tales will benefit from emic perspectives on the issue of narrative strategies. In other words, we intend to include, as much as possible, indigenous paradigms of aesthetics that have surfaced in the course of the field work during which most of the narratives examined in this study were collected.

THE TRICKSTER AND THE FOLK TALE TRADITION

Unlike the mythic tales studied by Pelton, where Esu is the trickster figure, the trickster in Yoruba folktales is Ijapa (the Tortoise). There are tales that feature other tricksterlike characters, such as the snail, bat, or dog. We shall say more about countertricksters later in this study. Even when the conflict involves extraterrestrial forces such as spirits or some gods, the sources of the conflict never involve the divine trickster. Although there is an etiological tale of linkage between Esu and Ijapa, the conception and resolution of conflicts in which the Tortoise is involved never engage the divine trickster. In fact, a major theme in the etiological tale of Ijapa's connection with Esu is one of apprenticeship and the parting of ways between the two figures. It is remarkable that out of more than five hundred trickster tales collected for this study, only five tales (all of them variants of each other) relate the divine trickster to the secular one. Indeed the tale summarized below is etiological, explaining the origin of the secular antihegemonic trickster.

> In the story of "Esu and Ijapa," Esu was Tortoise's mentor or trainer for many years. A few years after Tortoise's completion of his apprenticeship to Esu, the former was to go on a trip from Ife to Oyo or Benin [some variants say Ondo] and decided to consult Orunmila before traveling. He was advised by Orun-

mila to offer a gift of seven he-goats, seven she-goats, seven gourds of palm oil and seven baskets of Eko to Orunmila. Tortoise protested, drawing the attention of Orunmila to the fact that he had given everything required by convention to Esu at the completion of his training by working for him without pay for two additional years. Orunmila told Tortoise that the choice was his. He, however, made his trip to Benin. He stayed in Benin for about seven months and acquired so much property during the stay that he needed to hire people to bring his things back to Ife. He also came back with a wife, Yannibo. At Idoko, now part of present Ondo town, Tortoise met an old man who asked him to help remove some lice from his head before Tortoise could be allowed to enter the town with Yannibo on a day that women were not allowed to be seen on the streets. The more lice Tortoise removed, the more lice appeared on the old man's head. Most of Tortoise's helpers deserted him. He later, at the insistence of Yannibo, decided to discontinue this interminable assignment. He abandoned his property and along with Yannibo decided to take a detour and thus avoid the town. When Tortoise got to the Ife side of Idoko, he saw this man again, who, laughing at him, told Tortoise that he was Esu, to whom Tortoise had refused to sacrifice but who with Tortoise's abandoned property, got more than he had asked for initially. Tortoise swore not to have anything to do with Esu anymore and resolved to get his things back from other people.

In addition to this story's explanation of Tortoise's final break with Esu, it also demonstrates the former's underdog posture. Tortoise, according to this story, has for long been a victim of relations of domination, which he now openly renounces and avows to invert as he goes to Ife to seek redress of Esu's exploitation of him.

The mythoreligious tales of explaining or rationalizing cosmic arrangements are ordinarily separated from the folktales that are used for examining the social enterprise. The fact that most of the tales told to Yoruba children are about Tortoise and few are about Esu and that every member of the community is a potential narrator of tortoise tales, while Esu tales are usually told by initiates or cult members, draws attention to the separation by the Yoruba of mythic tales from folktales told by the ordinary people about their daily social experience. This separation is also accounted for in the distinction between Itan and Alo. Itan, which includes mythic tales of Esu, are generally accepted by both narrator and narratee as report of what took place in prehistoric time or in metaphysical space. Alo or Iran are on the other hand fictive stories that only share an analogic relation with reality. Unlike Ture in the Azande trickster tradition, which informs John W. Roberts's generalization that African tricksters are part of the continent's mystical and religious forces, the tortoise in Yoruba folklore is as secular in imagination and behavior as John in the realistic African-American trickster tale cycle of John and Old Master.

Tortoise as trickster is rebellious not because of this unknown origin, as Deidre La Pin once implied, but because of his marginalization in a world of hierarchy, size and weight. He is smaller than most of the other characters he outsmarts, and when he is outsmarted himself, all of the countertricksters are usually underdogs to Tortoise. Such countertrickster figures as Snail, Bat, and Squirrel are much smaller than Tortoise. Tortoise's rebellious and metamorphic spirit is thus socially motivated; there is always a need for the underdog to challenge, confront, and even attempt to subvert a system that does not recognize him. Social recognition, acceptance, or elevation of the underdog is not realizable within the existing framework that produces his underdog status in the first place. The triumph of Tortoise over more endowed animals and his occasional defeat by smaller, less endowed animals suggest that tricksterism is a logical reaction to a hierarchical social order by characters that image the underdog. Tortoise's personality conforms with Lawrence Levine's view of African tricksters that "as interested as they might be in material gains, African trickster-figures are more obsessed with manipulating the story and reversing the normal structure of power and prestige."

Some commentators on Yoruba trickster tales have often emphasized the use of such tales for edification of the young ones by drawing attention to the overt didactic statements or moral lesson at the end of the trickster tales or by focusing on the narrational comments of storytellers on the personality of Tortoise as a negative character that children should view as social antitype in their relation to others or events. However, comments from some storytellers and audience members during our field work suggest that the trickster is projected not simply as antitype or a nonexemplary figure but subtly as a hermeneut, or what Pelton also calls a fundamental part of a cultural self-understanding. The notion of the trickster as a metasocial analyst, the image of the surface and hidden dimensions of the social order, is aptly acknowledged in such comments by narrators as "Tortoise draws attention to what children should not do as well as what others, sometimes have to do." Omobomi Osuntuyi, a narrator of more than twenty narratives in the collection on which this study is based, once implied the metasocial status of the trickster when she said to me after a narrative session:

> I enjoy telling my children tortoise tales and I know they enjoy them; I do not know why the children always ask for tortoise tales, but I am excited by Tortoise's many sides, his smartness, courage and resilience. I also think that the children might enjoy the fact that you never know which way a tortoise tale will end.

In trickster tales, the Yoruba do what other societies do in their literature, especially comedy: make social reality problematic by simulating areas of tension in events of social relations enacted by fictive characters. Emic perspectives on trickster tales are almost as varied as the tortoise tale itself, but one common strand in the comments of most narrators and narratees interviewed indicate that a source of aesthetic harmony in Tortoise's tale is the personality of the protagonist as well as the layers of meaning inherent in his action and the tales. The names given by different dialectal Yoruba groups to oral prose fiction reinforce this belief in the multipurpose and polysemous character of trickster tales. Iran and Alo are two common names within the major dialectal Yoruba groups for prose fiction. Iran, common among the Ondo, Ikalae, and Akure, literally means that which is sewn or woven. Alo, the name among the Oyo, Egba, and the Igbomina Yoruba subgroups for fiction, literally means that which is tied together. Alo Ijapa is, as Bola Olalekan, an Ikirun narrator, observes, "the weaving together of strands of action from Ijapa's many sides."

A Semiotic View of Trickster Tale Aesthetics

A semiotic conception of aesthetics is not clearly articulated by practitioners and users of Yoruba fiction, but the possibility of such a notion is implied in some of the comments by storytellers or audience members provided in the preceding discussion. More specifically, the acknowledgment by such culture bearers as Osuntuyi and Olalekan that trickster tales are sources of information or means of social communication between storyteller and audience affirms the epistemic character of trickster tales, and indeed of nontrickster narratives. More important, the notion of prose fiction as the weaving of a well-knit object from strands selected from the many roles of the trickster and its antagonist suggest the recognition on the part of members of the trickster-tale-telling community of the suturing of layers of social meanings in the structure of such tales. The concept of the weaving or joining of layers of meaning raises the need to characterize semiotically the aesthetic transaction that exists in the telling and receiving of trickster tales.

As I have shown elsewhere, the aesthetic transaction evident in Yoruba trickster narrative performance has a semiotic character. Aesthetic experience in trickster tales is made of three inseparable components: captivation of audience, retention of audience attention, and the transfer of cognitive experience to the audience. These three dimensions are, proverbially, three elements of Siamese triplets that can only survive in their jointness. Since trickster narrative performance is, like other performative acts, characterized by an immediate interaction of narrator and audience, the initial contact between both parties instantiates the first effort by the narrator to achieve aesthetic harmony with his audience. Apart from such preliminary formulae as, for example "my story spins and spins and falls on the head of Alabaun {Tortoise]," often used in announcing the shift from the factual world of the narrative community to the fictive experience to be subsequently evoked by the narrator, the initial attraction of the audience to narrative experience depends on three factors that are external to the fictive experience itself.

The first of such factors is the possession of a good and charming voice by the narrator. The other two are the narrator's facility with the language of narration and his ability to use his body—face, trunk, arms, and legs—as materials for the evocation of a fictive experience for his audience and for the structuring of the tale. If a storyteller is to establish a rapport with his audience, he must be consistent in his mastery of the language and should possess an effective voice that can captivate his audience. Since most members of the audience of trickster tales are much younger than the narrator, the storyteller's use of language should be good enough to provide an enviable language-performance model to which members of the audience may aspire in their own use of language. The same condition holds for the narrator's use of paraverbal devices such as gestures, gesticulations, and spatial relations. It is important to note that the verbal aspect constitutes the major code to which other extraverbal devices, such as artifacts and gestures as well as other kinesic and prox-emic codes, are subsidiary and supplementary. The narrator's ability to use his voice and body to convey emotions of characters, to delineate his characters, and to comment on specific actions of such characters are basic materials for the achievement of initial aesthetic harmony with the audience. They serve as devices for diverting the attention of the audience from their private thoughts and preoccupations to the experience of images that are being selected and organized by the narrator with the hope of transferring to the audience ideas about some aspects of the recurrent concern of the social world of the narrator and his audience. After the narrator's use of verbal and paraverbal skills have succeeded in attracting the attention of the audience to the fictive experience, the narrator still needs to retain or hold this attention till the end of the story. Although good verbal and paraverbal skills can help in sustaining audience attention, a more important factor is the organization or structure of the story itself.

The story must be told in a manner that assists the narrator in retaining the intellectual and emotive attention of the audience. Charming voice and good verbal skills become, as the story progresses, secondary sources of aesthetic stimulation. The patterning of images or episodes of the story is the most important single factor in the attainment of the other two elements of aesthetic transaction: emotive and epistemic satisfaction of the audience. These two elements are intricately intertwined such that they can be treated together.

Epistemic satisfaction refers mainly to the ability of the narrator to relate individual images in the trickster's behavior to a specific aspect of human behavior in his community. Unlike Esu's escapades in a metaphysical world, Tortoise's actions, and indeed those of characters involved in conflict with him, must thematize problems faced in the daily praxis of the audience. Images or units of behavior externalized by the trickster and other characters, victims or countertricksters, must, in their combination, be capable of suggesting to the audience the narrator's statement(s) about identifiable concerns in the social experience of the audience. The trickster's actions may smack of the liminal—suspending the structure for purposes of transcending it—as Pelton has acknowledged, but the significance of such actions must be relatable to problems of the daily experience of the narratee. When this happens, as it often does, the hermeneutic or meta-interpretative dimension of the trickster is established for the audience. The notion of the dual function of the trickster tale can thus be grasped by the audience. The primary meaning, or what is otherwise referred to as the moral lesson of trickster tales, may be seen, as often happens, to be in a contradictory relation to the secondary meaning, which is communicated by structural manipulation of the events of the story. Although we hope to address this issue later, it is important to observe now that the primary meaning that is often communicated in the processual aspect of the tale does not account for the entire aesthetic communication between narrator and audience of trickster tales.

Emotive satisfaction, on the other hand, refers to the capacity of the narrator to manipulate the feelings of the audience during the narration in such a manner that the members of the audience will feel encouraged to continue to direct their attention to the narrative experience while it lasts. The retention of audience attention is, however, only attainable through the performer's manipulation of the emotions of the audience. For audience emotion to be successfully manipulated, the storyteller must arrange the images of action in the story in such a way that subsequent images vary audience sensation. More specifically, the storyteller must align the images constituting his story in such a manner that he moves the sensation of his audience back and forth on a spectrum of expectancy that can be characterized on the one extreme by activation, in the middle by stabilization, and at the other extreme by depression. Audience sensation is activated when feeling is aroused or excited by the conception of a conflict requiring a resolution. Sensation is stabilized when a new image that is given to the audience only succeeds in giving an additional but not a conflicting piece of information about an already achieved or depressed sensation. In other words, the sensation of the audience at a particular point during the narrative is stabilized when it remains exactly as it was before the supply of a new image. Finally, audience sensation is depressed when images are given only for the purpose of forestalling or defusing conflict. Thus conflict-producing images activate sensation, while conflict-resolving images depress sensation. Let us illustrate this notion with the analysis of this story "Tortoise and Iroko":

> Once upon a time there was a very serious famine in which trees dried up, leaves dried up, and birds and animals had nothing to eat. The soil also was dry. After a while, both human beings and animals and trees began to die. It was only Iroko tree spirit that was feeling well and remained fresh and green, having acquired many yams as sacrifice from the people. It seemed as if he was using vitality drugs. Tortoise, the trickish person, looked at himself for a while

and asked himself how Iroko spirit was able to look so fresh. He then went to Iroko. When he got there, he greeted Iroko spirit and paid all due respect to him. He introduced his purpose for coming. He said he came to ask how Iroko was able to survive the famine and managed to be fresh as that. He asked Iroko to let him into the secret and promised to pay whatever it would cost him. Iroko then smiled and said that it was not too difficult but asked whether Tortoise would be able to fulfill the only condition he had. Tortoise said he would. He then told Tortoise that he had yams and that he was ready to give Tortoise out of the yams provided Tortoise was able to fulfill the condition to be laid down by him. Tortoise promised that he was ready to fulfill just any condition soon after he was given the yams. Then Iroko laid the condition that if Tortoise was given one yam, he should expect one stroke of club the following morning. Tortoise said that condition even appeared too light for such a gesture and that he was ready to receive the club on any part of his body. Then Iroko gave one yam to Tortoise, and Tortoise left Iroko's house. As he was going, he began to think of how to escape the danger of the stroke of the heavy club. He later arrived at a possible solution. He decided to invite the first animal he met to his house.

In short, as he went further, he saw Goat, then he saw Sheep. They both expressed surprise in their cries. At last Goat approached him and asked where he got the yam he was carrying. . . . Tortoise said it was from his own farm. He said he had plenty of yams in his farm. Goat asked whether she could follow him home and take part of the yam. Tortoise expressed sympathy for the condition of Goat and asked her to follow him. Goat was very happy. She then followed Tortoise home. When they got home they prepared pounded yam with the yam. When they were about to start eating, Tortoise called on Goat and said, "You know what? You cannot just eat the pounded yam like that. You have to do something for me. The job is not tedious to do. It is this: very early in the morning tomorrow at cockcrow, I shall have a visitor, when he comes he will knock at the door. If he calls me, you just answer. Tell him that I am asleep or that I am not at home." Goat replied that that was not difficult to do. He asked that they should start eating. They finished the food at once. They rested a while and went to sleep.

Very early the following morning, Iroko took his club and went to Tortoise's house. Tortoise slept in the inner room but asked the Goat to sleep in the parlor, which is the room closest to the front door. When Iroko came and knocked at the door, Goat answered [the] call and opened the door for Iroko. When Iroko saw her, he immediately gave her a heavy blow. It sent the Goat sprawling on the ground and soon after, she died. When Tortoise saw this, he was very happy. He then took it and dressed it for food. He began to roast it.

In the afternoon of that day Tortoise went to Iroko again and said to Iroko that he did not feel his club at all. If that is the case he would now ask for two yams because one stroke of the club was nothing to him. It was just as though his body was scratched. He asked Iroko to give him two yams and come to give him two strokes of Iroko's cane the following morning. Iroko was annoyed and sternly asked if Tortoise would be able to receive two strokes of his club. Tortoise said that there would be no problem. At once Iroko gave Tortoise two yams, and he began to go to his house.

As he was going, he met Sheep. Sheep expressed surprise at seeing Tortoise with such heavy and fat yams. He offered to follow Tortoise home so as to eat part of the yams. Tortoise asked him to follow. He explained that he got the yams from his own farm. Then Sheep followed Tortoise home. When they got home, they prepared pounded yam with soup from the goat meat. As they were to start eating, Tortoise, holding Sheep's hand said, "Won't we make some agreement on what you would do for me in return for the pounded yam?" Sheep asked what kind of agreement they were to reach. Tortoise said, "It is not difficult. It is simply that I always come out of bed late. I always want to have full rest. My sleep must not be interrupted." He then said that a friend could call on him very early in the morning, and that Sheep should answer him and tell him that Tortoise was not in. He asked Sheep to sleep at the back of the door, so that when his friend knocked at the door, he could open it for him and tell him that he had gone out. Sheep said there would be no problem in that. They then ate and slept.

Very early in the morning, Iroko came again with his club. When he got to Tortoise's house, he knocked at the door as before. Sheep immediately opened the door; before she uttered a word, Iroko had given her two strokes of the heavy club, immediately after which Sheep died. Iroko did not know. He thought it was Tortoise that had appeared to him. He went back to his house. When Tortoise heard what went on between Iroko and Sheep from his bed, he smiled. He felt happy. He had not finished the goat meat of the previous night. Here was the sheep meat [in addition]. He said to himself that that was how he would survive the famine. In the morning he got Sheep dressed as he did the goat the previous day.

He then went to Iroko's house. When he got to Iroko, Iroko was very surprised to see him after the two heavy strokes of the club that morning. He thought it might be Tortoise's ghost. But Tortoise said it was not his ghost. He said his club had no effect on him. He then asked whether there were still yams for him to take. In short, he asked for three yams this time and asked Iroko to come in the following morning to give him three strokes of his club and [said] that maybe he would feel it then. Iroko agreed and gave him three yams. Tortoise took the three yams and began to go home again.

As he was going, he met Boar, who had become very lean because of the famine. When he saw Tortoise, he was surprised and he asked how he got such yams. He approached Tortoise to ask whether he could follow him home to take part of the yams. Tortoise told him that he got the yams from his own farm. He said he had plenty of yams in his farm. He asked Tortoise for a favor and Tortoise granted it. They went together to Tortoise's house. When they got there, they cooked the yam and prepared pounded yam and cooked part of the sheep meat. When they were about to start eating, Tortoise got hold of the hands of Boar as usual. He asked that they should conclude a certain agreement before eating. The wild pig asked what agreement they should reach. Then Tortoise told him that he usually slept late in the bed, but a friend was coming to call him very early in the morning, [and] Boar should open the door for him when he knocked and tell him Tortoise had gone out. The wild pig considered it a very light matter and agreed to do so. After the meal, Tortoise went in to the inner room to sleep, while Boar slept in the parlor at the back of the door.

Very early in the morning Iroko took his club as usual and came to Tortoise's house. When he got to the gate of Tortoise's house, he knocked as usual. Boar heard him and came to open the door. When Iroko saw the figure behind the door he gave him three heavy strokes of the club. Before the third stroke, the pig had fallen dead. Iroko went back. He was sure that he had killed Tortoise this time. Tortoise heard what had happened, and he was very happy again. When he got up, he took the wild pig and dressed it as he did the previous animals.

He then left for Iroko's house. When Iroko saw him, he was sad. He asked himself whether Tortoise would be able to cheat him like this forever. He recounted how he had been giving yams to Tortoise and trying to kill him without success. He became surprised and worried. Tortoise even boasted again that Iroko's club was too weak for him. He even advised that Iroko should order better and stronger clubs. Iroko gave him seven yams and Tortoise went home.

As he was going, he met "Eta" Civet-Cat, a creature unfit for heavy work. He had become lean as a result of the famine. When he saw Tortoise with the yam, he approached him, and Tortoise asked him to follow him to his house. When they got home, Tortoise prepared pounded yams as usual. When they were about to start eating, Tortoise told Civet-Cat that he needed to enter into a certain agreement with him before eating. Tortoise said to Civet-Cat what he had said to the others before him. He asked him to sleep at the back of the door so that when the friend knocked, he could open [it] for him. He agreed and they ate the food. Shortly after going to sleep, a heavy rain started. Civet-Cat was noted for his deep sleep. He slept immediately. The torrent of the rain entered and carried him away. Tortoise did not know this.

Very early in the morning, Iroko, who had been unable to sleep all the night because of anger, came to Tortoise's house and knocked as before. Nobody answered. Tortoise heard his knock and began to call on his guest to open for Iroko as before. When Iroko heard Tortoise's voice, he became much more annoyed. He knocked again with anger. Tortoise continued to call on the cat to open in a low voice. Iroko then kicked open the door and went to Tortoise in the inner room. He met Tortoise and with his might, gave Tortoise [such] heavy blows with his club that Tortoise died immediately. Iroko went back home and began to expect Tortoise to come as usual to boast. He expected Tortoise for about four days. At last he went to Tortoise's house to check him. When he got there he met him dead. That was how Tortoise died.

The initial situation of serious famine and total desiccation in this story supplies the first image of activation of sensation. The extreme situation of mass starvation suggests the need for an urgent or desperate solution of Tortoise. Similarly, activation is suggested in the second image—Tortoise's request for assistance from Iroko—while Iroko's agreement to assist the Tortoise in the third image as long as the latter obeys his injunctions is capable of depressing audience sensation. With Iroko's assistance, the initial conflict is resolved; Tortoise's starvation is temporarily stemmed. However, Tortoise's invitation in the fourth image of Goat to sleep in his anteroom and answer early morning calls by visitors is a sensation-activating unit; it introduces the possibility of another conflict, either between Goat and Iroko or between Tortoise and Iroko. But Goat's response to Iroko, together with the subsequent killing of Goat by Iroko, is a sensation-depressing image. The first conflict between Iroko and Tortoise vis-a-vis food is now apparently resolved. Furthermore, Tortoise's food supply is greatly improved with the protein supply that he now gets from Goat's meat.

Tortoise's second visit to Iroko with the request for more yams and hence more blows reintroduces the activation of sensation with the conception of a new conflict between Iroko and Tortoise. This activated sensation is quickly replaced by depression as Tortoise successfully invites Sheep to come and sleep with him and answer calls for him. The fact that the sheep is a symbol of stupidity among the Yoruba makes its eventual death almost a fait accompli and thus predicts the subsequent killing of Sheep by Iroko. Tortoise's third visit to Iroko again activates sensation in that it renews the conflict between Iroko and Tortoise. Furthermore, Tortoise's invitation of Boar supplies another image of sensation activation. Boar's characteristic unruliness and intractability increase the doubt of the outcome of the Iroko/Boar encounter the following morning. However, with Iroko's killing of Boar, the performer supplies a sensation-depressing image.

Another activation of audience sensation is attempted in Tortoise's further visit to Iroko in that a new and more formidable conflict is conceived with the increase in the number of blows to be given by Iroko. This activated sensation is, however, quickly depressed by Tortoise's invitation of Civet-Cat as his guest. The fact that this is an animal known for its excessive love of sleep suggests easy predictability of the outcome of the Iroko/Civet-Cat meeting the following morning. But surprisingly, sensation is quickly activated by the image of the heavy downpour that washes the cat in its slumber away from the outpost. This activation is then quickly followed by the final depression that accompanies Iroko's killing of Tortoise. This final depression of sensation, reminiscent of poetic justice, shows the final sense of satisfaction and fulfillment of the initial expectation of the audience raised by the series of contracts and their violations between Iroko and Tortoise. We will return to this tale later in the discussion of polysemy and the implication of cultural idealist and materialist views on interpretation and aesthetic response.

This story can be broken into image patterns as follows:

Image Patterns in "Tortoise and Iroko"

Activation Images	Depression Images
Image I: General famine, Iroko's Survival conflicts with Tortoise's starvation—motivation for major conflicts	

Activation Images

Image II: Tortoise's requests for Iroko's assistance—major conflict conceived and further individualized

Image IV: Invitation of Goat into the picture without full knowledge of Iroko—Tortoise deal, potential conflict between Goat and Tortoise or Goat and Iroko

Image VI: Tortoise makes a new deal with Iroko—conflict restored

Image VIII: Sheep is invited to sleep in Tortoise's house—conflict renewed

Image X: Tortoise makes a bigger demand—conflict restored

Image XII: Invitation of Boar—conflict renewed

Image XIV: Tortoise asks for seven yams—conflict restored

Image XVI: Invitation of Civet-Cat—conflict renewed
Image XVII: The rain washes Civet-Cat away, thus allowing a frontal meeting between Iroko and Tortoise—conflict intensified

Depression Images

Image III: Iroko agrees to help Tortoise—partial resolution of conflict

Image V: Goat fulfills obligation for Tortoise and is killed by Iroko—partial resolution

Image VII: Iroko accepts Tortoise's conditions of two yams for two blows—partial resolution

Image IX: Sheep fulfills obligation and is killed by Iroko's blows—partial resolution

Image XI: Iroko accepts Tortoise's request—partial resolution

Image XIII: Boar is killed by Iroko—partial resolution

Image XV: Iroko's acceptance—partial resolution

Image XVIII: Iroko kills Tortoise after several abortive attempts—final resolution of major conflict

The avoidance of satiation is a crucial factor in the narrator's effort at varying audience sensation. While such non-plot-related elements of a story as songs or narratorial comments are means of avoiding satiation, effective and subtle elimination of boredom can only be achieved through the interlarding of different plot-related materials, such as images or episodes that refer directly and those that refer peripherally to the behavior of characters in the story. Narrative images should accordingly be organized into patterns that manipulate audience emotion during narration.

The fluctuation of audience sensation is achievable through the relationship existing between two images that the audience is confronted with as the story progresses. For any narrative act of trickster storytelling to provide full aesthetic fulfillment, the narrator should produce within each narrative experience at least two of the three sensations identified above. Indeed, in all trickster tales, the audience expect and must have their sensation activated and depressed at regular intervals.

LEVELS OF AESTHETICS: INTERACTING PATTERNS OF AUDIENCE IDENTIFICATION WITH THE TRICKSTER

The spectrum of expectable identification with the trickster-protagonist ranges on the one extreme from unconditional rejection to sympathetic identification or solidarization on the other extreme. Unconditional rejection refers to the imposition of the most reprehensible, antisocial and antihuman traits on the trickster. Stories designed to elicit hatred of the trickster from the audience deliberately select images of behavior and action that project Tortoise as ill motivated, maladjusted, insatiable and without scruples. The audience is encouraged, as we will show later in the study, through the manipulation of both processual and paradigmatic aspects of the tale, to laugh at the trickster and condemn him.

Sympathetic identification or solidarization in trickster tales, on the other hand, concerns the portrayal of the protagonist as a "guinea pig," a victim of circumstances that the narrative community would wish to eliminate. Such identification is expected when the protagonist is involved in a protest against the prevailing social authority and, in the process, elicits solidarization from the audience because of his effective or ineffective but courageous attempt at the breaking of what may be acknowledged by the audience as a repressive, obsolete norm.

In terms of the selection and organization of images, the expectable aesthetic response to Yoruba trickster tales can be broken into two: rejection and solidarization. Correspondingly, it can be argued that the trickster tale is capable of two types of aesthetic profile: affirmation and negation. The trickster's current ambivalence, manifested in his Siamese disposition to disruption and reorganization, fits in to the two categories of disorder and order, or norm creation and norm destruction. Storytellers are predisposed by this "ambivalence" to organize their images according to the type of aesthetic response they want to elicit. Images of the trickster as a norm destroyer are often organized into narrative structures meant to encourage norm affirmation on the part of the audience. On the other hand, images of metamorphic adventures capable of resolving community dilemma as well as those that involve willingness by the trickster to endanger himself by challenging, confronting, and breaking questionable or intolerable norms are organized into structures that expose the negative side of existing norms.

Suggested Reading with Similar Theme:

Edwards, Jay. "The Afro-American Trickster Tale: A Structural Analysis." Monograph Series, vol 4. Bloomington: Folklore Institute of the Univeristy of Indiana, 1978.

GENEVA SMITHERMAN

From "Word from the African American Community" in *Black Talk: Words and Phrases from the Hood to the Amen Corner* (1994)

Explain how the Africanized style of speaking the English language is a complex system. Explain Smitherman's statement: "Race is the defining core of the Black Experience; language comes from the same course: the African American experience." How does Smitherman enter discussions with, among others, Henderson, Gates, and Baker? Explain how African American language and culture reflect a "dual heritage." How might words reflect "origin and cultural identity" (and not necessarily social status)? Define the following terms and phrases: Nommo, AAE, Black Talk, oral tradition, Call-Response, two-ness, Hip Hop lingo, coded forms of English, imitation is not considered flattery, and origin and cultural identity.

Black Talk crosses boundaries—of sex, age, region, religion, social class—because the language comes from the same sources: the African American Experience and the Oral Tradition embedded in that Experience. On one level, there is great diversity among African Americans today, but on a deeper level, race continues to be the defining core of the Black Experience. While today's Hip Hop Culture is contributing its own special lingo unrelated to race—phrases such as ALL THAT, IN THE MIX, GIT WIT—it is also reintroducing race-conscious language from previous generations. For example, filmmaker Spike Lee named his production company "FORTY ACRES AND A MULE," a Black expression that goes all the way back to the nineteenth century. His parents' and grandparents' generations put the goal of land for the "Black Nation" on the COMMUNITY's agenda. In the early years of this century, this idea was put forth by various Black Nationalist intellectuals, notably Marcus Garvey. In the 1960s, the concept was worked out in detailed clarity by the Republic of New Africa, embodied in its call for "five states" as reparations for Blacks. Both forty acres and "five states" take us back to the post-Civil War era and the bill passed by Congress in 1866. This legislation was designed to strengthen the Freedman's Bureau (the Federal agency set up to resettle ex-slaves). The most interesting part of the bill, and the most con-

troversial, stipulated that each household of ex-slaves would receive an allot-
ment of forty acres of land (plus some start-up resources, captured in the
expression that has come down to us, forty acres, fifty dollars, and a mule).
This payment for 246 years of free African labor not only would have provided reparations for enslavement but also would have established a base for
self-sufficiency and initiated the economic development of the African American community. President Andrew Johnson, taking over after President
Abraham Lincoln's assassination, vetoed the bill, and Congress was either
unable, or unwilling, to override the veto. The nation's 1866 failure to right
the wrong of enslavement continues to haunt Blacks, particularly in this
period of severe economic crisis and of devastating social effects that result
from an underdeveloped community.

A similar example exists in the concept of COOL, although at first
glance this might not seem to be a race-conscious idea. However, a disem-
powered group daily forced to face the possibility of its destruction can ill
afford to be HOT. With lynch mobs in the old days, police brutality in this
new day—any heat generated by rage and anger could literally be dangerous
to a Black person's health. Hence the value of calmness and maintaining your
cool as a survival strategy. Today's African American youth talk about
CHILLIN, their middle-aged parents still call it being cool, and an eighty-
five-year-old Black man recently referred to the cool coping style as
COPASETIC. . . .

"What Is Africa To Me?"

What is Africa to me
Copper sun or scarlet sea,
Jungle star or jungle track,
Strong bronzed men, or regal black,
Women from whose loins I sprang
When the birds of Eden sang?
One three centuries removed
From the scenes his fathers loved,
Spicy grove, cinnamon tree,
What is Africa to me?
                        —Countee Cullen, "Heritage" (1925)

Down through the years, and especially in the decades since the Civil War,
generations of African Americans have asked themselves the question posed
by Harlem Renaissance writer Countee Cullen. Long since removed from
their native land, many Black Americans feel the same as some Blacks in a
1989 opinion poll I conducted on the name change from "BLACK" to
"AFRICAN AMERICAN": "We are more American than African; we have

been here too long," and "What do they mean about African American? By now we have no African in us." On the other hand, there are also many Black Americans who acknowledge a connection to Africa, what one of the people in the opinion poll called "our origin and cultural identity."

As far as historians, linguists, and other scholars go, during the first half of this century it was widely believed that enslavement had wiped out all traces of African languages and cultures, and that Black "differences" resulted from imperfect and inadequate imitations of EUROPEAN AMERICAN language and culture. George Philip Krapp, writing in the 1920s, is one linguist who held this view about the speech of Africans in America. In the 1960s these opinions came under close scrutiny and were soundly challenged by a number of experts, such as the historian John Blassingame and the linguist J. L. Dillard. Today scholars generally agree that the African heritage was not totally wiped out, and that both African American Language and African American Culture have roots in African patterns. (This view has also been advanced by anthropologist Melville Herskovits and linguist Lorenzo Dow Turner in the 1930s and 1940s, but they were a distinct minority in those days.) Over time, and after prolonged contact with European Americans, Africans in America adopted some Eurocentric patterns, and their African patterns of language and culture were modified—but they were not erased. African American Language and Culture, then, reflects a dual heritage. As Dr. W. E. B. DuBois put it nearly a century ago in *Souls of Black Folk,* "One ever feels his two-ness—an American, a Negro."

The uniqueness of AAE is evident in three areas: (1) patterns of grammar and pronunciation, many of which reflect the patterns that operate in West African languages (for example, many West African languages don't have the English "th" sounds, and in AAE "th" is rendered with the next closest sound, as a "d," a "t," or an "f"); (2) verbal rituals from the Oral Tradition and the continued importance of the Word, as in African cultures; and (3) lexicon, or vocabulary, usually developed by giving special meanings to regular English words, a practice that goes back to enslavement and the need for a system of communication that only those in the enslaved community could understand.

Although here we are concerned only with the words that make up the lexicon, there are correct ways of saying these words, of talking Black, that is, that depend on knowledge of the rules of AAE grammar and pronunciation. Like the popular DJ said to a DUDE who phoned in a request for D. J. Jazzy Jeff & The Fresh Prince's JAM "Summertime": "Okay, man, I'll play it for you, but see, it ain't summertime, it's summahtime." . . .

This Africanized style of speaking the English language is a complicated system, made even more complex by the existence of Euro-American patterns of English within the Africanized English system. Interested readers may consult Lorenzo Dow Turner's *Africanisms in the Gullah Dialect;* Molefi Kete

Asante's "African Elements in African American English" in Joseph Holloway's excellent collection, *Africanisms in American Culture;* J. L. Dillard's *Black English;* Mervyn Alleyne's *Comparative Afro-American;* my own *Talkin and Testifyin;* John Baugh's *Black Street Speech;* Walter Wolfram and Nona H. Clarke's *Black-White Speech Relationships;* Hanni U. Taylor's *Standard English, Black English, and Bidialectalism;* and William Labov's *Language in the Inner city.*

Listed below are only a few of the patterns of AAE grammar and pronunciation. . . .

1. Final and post-vocalic "r." The "r" sound at the end of a word and after a vowel is not heard in AAE. Instead, use of vowel sound, as in "summahtime," as that big-city DJ instructed his caller. The expression "Sure, you're right" becomes SHOW YOU RIGHT. "Torn up" would be TOE UP. Use YO instead of "your." And RAP Music's popular, if controversial, word HO is the AAE pronunciation of "whore." (Not to be confused with "hoe," as the white teacher in the film *House Party* did when she asked her Black male student why he called another Black male student's mother a "garden tool.")

2. Final and medial consonants. Reduce to a vowel sound, or a single consonant sound. Thus, for example, "cold" is COAL in AAE. This can get a bit complicated if a word requires the operation of two rules simultaneously, as for example in the phrase "torn up," where the double consonant "rn" must be reduced, and at the same time, the "r" after the vowel sound deleted. Applying the rules correctly gives you toe, not "ton," as a beginning student of Black lingo produced.

3. Stress on the first syllable. For most words, put the stress, or emphasis, on the first syllable of the word. For example, AAE speakers say PO-leece, not po-LEECE, and DE-troit, not De-TROIT.

4. The vowel sound in words that rhyme with "think" and "ring." In AAE, this vowel is pronounced like the vowel in "thank" and "rang." Thus, "sing" is rendered as sang, "drink" is pronounced drank, etc. This pattern produced the thang of Dr. Dre's "Nuthin' But a 'G' Thang," from his 1992 album *The Chronic.*

5. Indicate tense (time) by context, not with an "s" or "ed." For example, "Mary do anythang she want to" and "They look for him everywhere but never did find him."

6. *"Be"* and *"Bees"* to *indicate continuous action or infrequently recurring activity.* For example, "Every time we see him, he be dressed like that." This is the rule that produced "It bees dat way," which may be shortened to simply BEES.

7. Final "th" sounds become "t" or "f." This pattern gives us DEF, as in "Def Comedy Jam," from the 1970s expression "doin it to death," with the final "th" in "death" pronounced as a "f." This is also where WIT, as in the HIP

HOP phrase GIT WIT you, comes from, with the final "th" in "with" rendered as a "t" sound.

8. "Is" and "Are" in sentences. These words aren't necessary to make full statements; nor are the contracted forms of these words (that is, the "s" for "is" and the "re" for "are"). This is the rule that allows "What up?" for "What's up?"

The African American Oral Tradition is rooted in a belief in the power of the Word. The African concept of *Nommo,* the Word, is believed to be the force of life itself. To speak is to make something come into being; thus senior Black Americans will often use the cautionary statement "Don't speak on it" in the face of some negative possibility GO in DOWN. On the other hand, once something is given the force of speech, it is binding—hence the familiar saying "Yo word is you bond," which in today's Hip Hop Culture has become WORD IS BORN. The Hip Hop expressions WORD, WORD UP, WORD TO THE MOTHER, and similar phrases all stem from the value placed on speech. Creative, highly verbal talkers are valued; RAPpin, LYIN, SIGNI-FYIN, TESTIFYin, PLAYin THE DOZENS, WOOFin—skillful use of these and other verbal rituals from the Oral Tradition is what gets a person PROPS. Which is not at all to say that African Americans DIS the written word. However, like other groups with a surviving Oral Tradition, such as Native Americans, "book learning" and written documents are believed to be limited in what they can convey and teach. CHECK OUT the EDUCATED FOOL.

While it may be an A and B CONVERSATION, Black Talk requires dialogue between "A" and "B" not "A" lecturing to "B." The idea is that constant exchange is necessary for real communication to take place. Scholars refer to this style of talk as "Call-Response." It has been ritualized in the Traditional Black Church, particularly in the back-and-forth exchange between the preacher and the congregation during the sermon. But even outside the Church, whenever African Americans CONVERSATE, Call-Response abounds. Often the verbal responses are punctuated by different kinds of FIVES. The only wrong thing you can do in a Black conversation is not respond at all, because it suggests that you ain't WIT the conversation. BET and WORD are Hip Hop responses that affirm what is being said, as does the older expression, SHOW YOU RIGHT. SCARED OF YOU is a response that acknowledges and celebrates some special achievement or unique action or statement, while SHUT THE NOISE!, as well as the older variation, SHUT UP!, means the exact opposite of what it says, that is "Keep up the noise, Talk on, I'm with that!"

The Black Church has been the single most significant force in nurturing the surviving African language and cultural traditions of African America. Over the centuries, the Church has stood as a rich reservoir of terms and expressions in Black lingo. Straight outa the Church have come expressions like ON TIME, to acknowledge that something occurred at the appropriate psychological moment, and BROTHA/SISTA, as generic terms for any African American; proverbs such as GOD DON'T LIKE UGLY and WHAT GO ROUND COME ROUND; and the ritual of SHOUTin and GITtin THE SPIRIT when moved by the musical "spirit" as SOUL concerts, clubs, cabarets, and other places of entertainment. In the spirit-getting, tongue-speaking, vision-receiving, Amen-saying, sing-song preaching, holy-dancing Traditional Black Church, the Oral Tradition is LIVE! This is so because the Church has not been pressured to take on Eurocentric culture and speech. As the only independent African American institution, the Black Church does not have to answer to white folk!

Paramount in the African American Experience, the Church is a religious as well as a social unit in the community. True enough, the Church adopted Euro-American Christianity, but it Africanized this Christianity. The Church maintained the African concept of the unity of the sacred and secular worlds. That is, all of life is viewed as holy. No wonder, then, that many popular singers came out of the Church and comfortably shift back and forth between the Church and the "world"—DIVA Aretha Franklin comes immediately to mind. Such entertainers incorporate elements of the communication style of the Church into their musical style—James Brown is an excellent example. Today's Hip Hop groups borrow richly from James Brown, which is to say that they are actually reflecting the Africanized communication style of the Church through this borrowing.

What is Africa to the lingo of today's HOODS? It is the source of Nommo and the BLOOD's respect for and celebration of the power of the Word, as can be witnessed today in Rap. It made possible the development of the African American Oral Tradition. It provided the basis for the integrity of Black grammar and the Black Lexicon. Africa is the MOTHERSHIP. And while not all of African American Language and Culture can be traced to African language patterns, a lot of it can. As an ex-enslaved African once said, "Everything I tells you am the truth, but they's plenty I can't tell you." . . .

"THEY DONE TAKEN MY BLUES AND GONE":
BLACK TALK CROSSES OVER

A 16-year-old white Pennsylvanian says his high school is full of "wiggers," whites . . . desperate to adopt black modes of dress and conduct. . . . Call 'em wanna-bes, call 'em rip-offs, call 'em suckers, but they're everywhere—white folks who think they're black. . . . Whites have been riffing off—or ripping off—black cultural forms for more than a century and making a lot more money from them. . . .[Whites] cavalierly adopt . . . the black mantle without

having to experience life-long racism, restricted economic opportunity, or any
of the thousand insults that characterize black American life. . . . It's a curious
spectacle.

—White journalist James Ledbetter
(staff writer for the *Village Voice*),
in "Imitation of Life," Fall 1992, *Vibe* Magazine

In the nineties U.S.A., the "curious spectacle" is everywhere. White males
HOOP on courts in Great Falls, Montana, Oak Park, Illinois, Orange County,
California, and Brownsville, Tennessee, HIGH-FIVIN IT and TALKIN
TRASH, often without the slightest inkling that they are doing a BLACK
THANG. And they think nothing of donning X caps, wearing them side-
ways or backwards as is fashionable in the HOOD. White females sport
TUDES of twenty-first century assertive womanhood as they RAP "Fly Girl"
from Queen Latifah's 1991 album *Nature of {A} Sista*:

> I always hear "Yo, Baby," . . .
> No, my name ain't "Yo,"
> And I ain't got yo "baby."

Coming into their own, white girls issue ultimatums to their WIGGAS,
DROPping SCIENCE from Mary J. Blige's 1991 title cut, "What's the 4 I I?":

> The same ol shit you pulled last week on Kim,
> I'm not havin that. . . .
> So come correct with some respect.

A 1993 article by a European American used the title "A New Way to
TALK THAT TALK" (small capitals added) to describe a new talk show. *The
American Heritage Dictionary,* Third Edition, lists BUG and GRAPEVINE as
just plain old words, with no label indicating "slang" or "Black." Merriam-
Webster's latest (tenth) edition of its Collegiate Dictionary lists BOOM BOX
the same way. A lengthy 1993 article in the *New York Times Magazine,* entitled
"Talking Trash," discussed this ancient Black verbal tradition as the "art of
conversation in the N.B.A." And in his first year in office, the nation's new
"baby boomer" President was taken to task for "terminal HIPness."

The absorption of African American English into Eurocentric culture
masks its true origin and reason for being. It is a language born from a culture of struggle, a way of talking that has taken surviving African language
elements as the base for self-expression in an alien tongue. Through various
processes such as "Semantic Inversion" (taking words and turning them into
their opposites), African Americans stake out claim to the English language,
and at the same time, reflect distinct Black values that are often at odds with
Eurocentric standards. "Fat," spelled *phat* in Hip Hop, refers to a person or
thing that is excellent and desirable, reflecting the traditional African value

that human body weight is a good thing, and implicitly rejecting the Euro-American mainstream, where skinny, not fat, is valued and everybody is on a diet. Senior Blacks convey the same value with the expression, "Don't nobody want no BONE." By the process of giving negative words positive meanings, BAD means "good," STUPID means "excellent," and even the word DOPE becomes positive in Hip Hop, meaning "very good" or "superb."

The blunt, coded language of enslavement SIGged ON Christian slave-holders with the expression, "Everybody talkin bout Heaven ain goin there." Hip Hop language, too, is bold and confrontational. It uses obscenities, graphic depictions of the sex act, oral and otherwise, and it adheres to the pronunciation and grammar of African American English (which the unin-formed deem "poor English"). Thus B-BOYS and B-girls snub their noses at the European American world and the EUROPEAN NEGRO world as well. About the former, European American journalist Upski, writing from the "front lines of the White-Struggle" (in *The Source,* May 1993), says:

> Even lifetime rap fans . . . usually discount a crucial reason rap was invented: white America's economic and psychological terrorism against Black people—reduced in the white mind to "prejudice" and "stereotypes," concepts more within its cultural experience.

About the latter, Armond White, reviewing the 1993 film *CB4* (in *Emerge,* May 1993) writes:

> CB4 offers an unenlightened view of rap. . . . It panders to . . . the black bour-geois fear that only "proper" language and "civilized" attitudes are acceptable means of addressing politics or articulating personal feelings.

But back to the lecture at hand, as Dr. Dre would say—the crossover of African American Language and Culture. Bemoaned by Black writer Langston Hughes ("they done taken my blues and gone"), reflecting on the out-migration of Black Culture during the Harlem Renaissance era of the 1920s when the "Negro was in vogue" . . . analyzed by white writer Norman Mailer in 1957 in his discussion of the "language of Hip" and "white Negroes" . . . resented, even as I write, by BOO-COOS African Americans, like twenty-two-year-old Jamal, in my survey of Black opinion on the WIGGA phenomenon:

> White folk kill me tryin to talk and be like us; they just want the good part. But it don't go like that; you got to take the bitter with the sweet.

Actually, as I said to the BROTHA, there's plenty of bitter to go around. Contrary to popular Black stereotypes, white folks' life is not all sweetness and light. Despite European Americans' higher material circumstances, it really is true that neither man nor woman can live by bread alone. European

Americans live "lives of quiet desperation" too; it's just a different kind of desperation. Which is exactly why Black Talk continues to cross over, doing so today on an unprecedented scale because of the power of post-modern technology.

The dynamism and creativity in African American Language revitalizes and re-energizes bland Euro-talk. There's electricity and excitement in PLAYERS and FLY girls who wear GEAR. The metaphors, images, and poetry in BLACK TALK make the ordinary ALL THAT, AND THEN SOME. African American English is a dramatic, potent counterforce to verbal deadness and emptiness. One is not simply accepted by a group, one is IN LIKE FLIN. Fraternities and sororities don't merely march; they perform a STEP SHOW. And when folk get AMP, they don't fight the feeling, they TESTIFY. For whites, there is a certain magnetism in the African American use of English because it seems to make the impossible possible. I bet you a FAT MAN AGAINST THE HOLE IN A DOUGHNUT. . . .

For WIGGAS and other white folk latching onto Black Talk, that's the good news. The bad news is that there's a reality check in African American English. Its terms and expressions keep you grounded, catch you just as you are taking flight and bring you right back down to the NITTY GRITTY of African American Life. There are rare flights of fancy in this poetry, no chance of getting so carried away that you don't know YO ASS FROM A HOLE IN THE GROUND. Unh-unh. Words like NIGGA reinforce Blackness since, whether used positively, generically, or negatively, the term can refer only to people of African descent. DEVIL, a negative reference to the white man, reminds Blacks to be on the lookout for HYPE. RUN AND TELL THAT, historically referring to Blacks who snitched to white folks, is a cultural caution to those planning Black affairs to be wary of the Judases among them. Such words in the Black Lexicon are constant reminders of race and the Black Struggle. And when you TALK THAT TALK, you must be loyal to Blackness, or as Ice Cube would say, be true to the GAME.

There are words and expressions in Black Talk like TWO-MINUTE BROTHA, describing a man who completes the sex act in a few seconds, and it's all over for the woman. Both in RAP and in everyday talk, the words B (bitch) and HO (whore) are generic references to Black women. GOT HIS/HER NOSE OPEN describes a male or female so deeply in love that he or she is ripe for exploitation. Terms like these in Black Language are continuing reminders that, despite all the talk about Black passion and SOUL, despite all the sixty-minute-man myths, despite all the WOOFIN and TALKIN SHIT, at bottom, the man-woman Thang among African Americans is just as problematic as it is among other groups.

Some African Americans see crossover as positive because of its possibilities for reducing racial tension. Fashion journalist Robin D. Givhan, writing in the *Detroit Free Press* (June 21, 1993), asserts that she is "optimistic about wiggers":

Appreciating someone else's culture is good. An increased level of interest among whites in what makes some African Americans groove can only be helpful to improved race relations.

Yet the reality of race, racism, and personal conflicts, which are often intensified by racism, does make crossover problematic. Whites pay no dues, but reap the psychological, social, and economic benefits of a language and culture born out of struggle and hard times. In his "We Use Words Like 'Mackadocious,' " Upski characterizes the "white rap audience" thus: "When they say they like rap, they usually have in mind a *certain* kind of rap, one that spits back what they already believe or lends an escape from their limited lives." And Ledbetter's "Imitation of Life" yields this conclusion: "By listening to rap and tapping into its extra-musical expressions, then, whites are attempting to bear witness to—even correct—their own often sterile, oppressive culture." Yet it is also the case that not only Rap, but other forms of Black Language and Culture, are attractive because of the dynamism, creativity, and excitement in these forms. However one accounts for the crossover phenomenon, one thing is certain: today we are witnessing a multi-billion-dollar industry based on this Language-Culture while there is continued underdevelopment and deterioration in the HOOD that produces it. In Ralph Wiley's collection of essays *Why Black People Tend to Shout,* which contains his *signifyin* piece, "Why Black People Have No Culture," he states: "Black people have no culture because most of it is out on loan to white people. With no interest."

FROM HOME TO HOMEY

. . . Bridging generations, a good deal of Hip Hop lingo recycles either the same word or a variation of an older term. Words like PAD, IG, FRY, and SALTY appeared in Cab Calloway's 1938 Hepster's Dictionary and are still current today. Would you prefer to BIG-TIME IT (1960s/1970s) or to LIVE LARGE (1990s)? Answer: either, since both refer to SERIOUS material possessions and living the Good life. But neither the sixties nor the nineties generation has anything on seniors who convey the same meaning with their colorful expression LIVIN HIGH OFF THE HOG, that is, living as though you're eating the upper parts of the hog, such as ribs or pork chops, rather than the lower parts, such as pig feet or CHITLINS. The PIMP WALK of the 1960s/1970s, the male strutting style of walking with a slight dip in the stride, is essentially the same as the GANGSTA LIMP of the 1990s; both expressions can be heard today. And though neither is identical to the CAT WALK of earlier years, what is important in all of this is the VIBE, the concept of a style of walking that projects a self-assured, TOGETHA, confident, even cocky man-image. Like walking with ATTITUDE . . . like by your walk conveying the message that you GOT IT GOIN ON.

Basic in Black Talk, then, is the commonality that takes us across boundaries. Regardless of job or social position, most African Americans experience some degree of participation in the life of the COMMUNITY— they get their hair done in African American BEAUTY SHOPS, they worship in Black churches, they attend African American social events, and they generally PAR-TAY with Blacks. This creates in-group crossover lingo that is understood and shared by various social groups within the race—words like KINKY and NAPPY to describe the texture of African American hair; HIGH YELLUH to refer to light-complexioned Blacks; CHITLINS to refer to hog intestines, a popular SOUL food; and a ready understanding of the different meanings of the N-WORD.

As stated, the closest connection between generations in Black Talk, as in today's music, is between Hip Hop and the 1960s/1970s. In addition to the terms given above, other examples of parallel expressions include COOL OUT (1960s/1970s) and CHILL (1990s), meaning, to relax, take it calm and easy; DO in IT TO DEF(1960s/1970s) and DEF (1990s), to describe something that is superb or excellent; RUN IT DOWN (1960s/1970s) and BREAK IT DOWN (1990s), meaning, to explain and simplify something, make it plain; BLOCK BOY (1960s/1970s) and BANJY BOY (1990s), referring to a gay male in FLY culture who dresses like straight males; ALL THE WAY LIVE (1960s/1970s) and LIVE (1990s), to describe an exciting, desirable event, person, place, or experience; and ACE BOON COON (1960s/ 1970s) and ACE KOOL (1990s), to refer to your best friend.

Another feature of Black Talk is the coining of words that capture unique characteristics of individuals. The older term BOGARD (to aggressively take over something) was based on the style of film star Humphrey Bogart, who typically played strong-arm, tough guy roles. Today's generation has contributed OPRAH to the Lexicon, after talk show personality Oprah Winfrey, to refer to the art of getting people to reveal intimate facts about themselves, as Oprah skillfully manages to do on national television.

African American English had its genesis in enslavement, where it was necessary to have a language that would mean one thing to Africans but another to Europeans. Forced to use the English of Ole Massa, Africans in enslavement had to devise a system of talking to each other about Black affairs and about the MAN right in front of his face. Because of continued segregation and racism, this necessity for a coded form of English persisted even after Emancipation, and it underlies the evolution of Black Language. Black Talk's origin in enslavement and the still-unresolved status of Africans in America account for the constant changes in the Lexicon. If and when a term crosses over into the white world, it becomes suspect and is no longer considered DOPE in the Black world. A new term must be generated to take its place. There is a certain irony here because in this cultural circumstance, imitation is not considered flattery. The same lingo generated by the creative juices of the community and considered DEF today can tomorrow become WACK and suitable only for LAMES if it gets picked up by whites. Of course a lot of African American Talk does get picked up by European Americans, especially in this post-modern nineties era, with MTV, BET, "Def Comedy Jam," and the power of the media to spread culture and language rapidly throughout the nation. Nonetheless, the pattern persists: once phrases and terms are adopted by whites, Blacks scramble to come up with something new.

On the other hand, language that does not cross over, regardless of how old it is, continues to be used in the community and to remain HYPE. Examples include most of the vocabulary of the Traditional Black Church and many of the terms referring to male-female relations. For example, "You GOT my NOSE OPEN" is at least half a century old and was used in Big Daddy Kane's 1993 "Very Special" jam. Another example is WHAM BAM, THANK YOU, MAM! (also BIP BAM, THANK YOU, MAM!), used especially by women to refer to a man who completes the sex act in a matter of seconds; this signifyin expression is also at least fifty years old and was used by Mary J. Blige in her 1992 "4 I I" jam. Other terms that don't cross over are words for whites, such as ANN, HONKY, CHARLIE; terms referring to Black hair and other physical features, such as ASHY, LIGHT-SKIN, DARK-SKIN, KITCHEN; and other words that describe Blacks only, such as OREO, COLOR STUCK, TOM.

Though often misunderstood (and even damned) for their NITTY GRITTY language, especially the MUTHAFUCKAS, HO's and NIGGAZ, the Hip Hop generation is coming straight outa the Oral Tradition. In that Tradition, language is double-voiced, common English words are given unique Black meanings, and a muthafucka is never a person with an Oedipus complex. Rather than breaking with the Black past, as some members of the previous generation have tried to do, Hip Hoppers seek to connect with past verbal traditions and to extend the semantic space of Black lingo by adding a 1990s flavor. . . .

Suggested Readings with Similar Theme:

Hurston, Zora Neale. "Characteristics of Negro Expression." In *Negro Anthology*, edited by Nancy Cunard. London: Wishart & Co., 1934. Reprint, *Negro: An Anthology*. New York: F. Ungar Publishing Company, 1970.

Smitherman, Geneva. *Talkin' and Testifyin': The Language of Black America*. Boston: Houghton Mifflin, 1971.

Gòkè-Paríolá, Abíódún. "African American Vernacular English in Colonial and Postcolonial Perspectives: The Linguistic Paradox." *Journal of Commonwealth and Postcolonial Studies* 4 (Fall 1996): 14–23.

Zeigler, Mary Brown. "Introductory Essay: Postcolonial Contexts of African American Vernacular English." *Journal of Commonwealth and Postcolonial Studies* 4 (Fall 1996): 1–13.

MADHU DUBEY

Introduction
in *Black Women Novelists and*
the Nationalist Aesthetic (1994)

Dubey illustrates how in the 1970s " a race-centered aesthetic hindered a just appreci-
ation of the works of black women novelists." Then, she proposes to demonstrate how
novelists Alice Walker, Toni Morrison, and Gayl Jones "reconstruct and supplement the
ideological program of black cultural nationalism." Why do critical approaches to select
literature move from formalism to deconstruction? How have novels by Walker, Morri-
son and Jones "navigat{ed} between two influential contemporary definitions of good
fiction"? Summarize the contributions of the following women critics to the black
women writers literary tradition: Mary Helen Washington, Barbara Christian, Bar-
bara Smith, Deborah McDowell, Valerie Smith, Hortense Spiller, Hazel Carby, Susan
Willis, and Karla Holloway. Define the following terms and phrases: specifying, dia-
logic, experimental nonrealist mode of characterization.

The question of stereotypes versus full characterizations of black women in
fiction forms the central concern of early black feminist critics such as Barbara Christian and Mary Helen Washington. Sketching a developmental
model that is at once normative and descriptive, Christian argues that later
black women novelists "create character rather than type," and "provide
glimpses of reality to revise the distorted black images of the 18th and 19th
centuries." In her similar claim that black women's fiction has historically
progressed from flat stereotypes to three-dimensional depictions of authentic
black womanhood, Washington explicitly identifies black nationalism as the
enabling condition for positive images of black women in fiction: contemporary black women writers are able to portray whole characters imbued with
"complexity, diversity and depth" because of "the political events of the 60s
and the changes resulting from the freedom movement." The struggle
against stereotypes in early black feminist criticism derives its initial impetus
from the war of images waged in Black Aesthetic essays such as Addison
Gayle's "Cultural Strangulation: Black Literature and the White Aesthetic"
and Carolyn Gerald's "The Black Writer and His Role." In Gerald's famous
formulation, the primary function of the black writer is to overturn the "zero

412

image" of blackness projected in white cultural texts. Early black feminist critics resume this necessary work of reversal and revision, regarding the literary stereotype as the most visible site of struggle for cultural control and self-determination.

The more recent black feminist writing on characterization in black women's fiction is also intimately connected to the Black Aesthetic agenda. In her controversial essay "Boundaries: Or Distant Relations and Close Kin," Deborah McDowell overtly places her own deconstructive move against the empowering gesture of reconstruction initiated by Black Aesthetic theorists, and indicates the two elements of the Black Aesthetic discourse on the subject that her own work attempts to challenge and surpass: its imperative that black writers should offer only positive images of black identity, and its construction of identity exclusively around the dynamics of racial difference. As McDowell suggests, the Black Aesthetic emphasis on "a 'positive' black self, always already unified, coherent, stable, and known," although remarkably liberatory when it was first articulated, later operated as a dogmatic stricture on black writers, precluding any exploration of the differences and contradictions that destabilize a monolithic conception of black identity. Further, as McDowell observes, Black Aesthetic discourse constructed race as "the sole determinant of being and identity, subsuming sexual difference."

The contemporary black feminist discourse on identity is motivated by an impulse to displace the prescriptive model of black identity, unified around the sign of race, that was promoted to Black Aesthetic critics. Along with Deborah McDowell, black feminist theorists such as Hortense Spillers and Karla Holloway are insistently foregrounding the "convergences of difference," the "spaces of contradiction," the "polysemic ramifications of fracture," and the persistence of the decentered subject" in black women's fiction. Emphasizing the multiple orders of difference that constitute the black feminine subject, these theorists seek to resist the totalizing moves of other discourses on the subject, such as the definition of "man" in bourgeois humanist ideology, of "woman" in white feminist ideology, and of "black" in black nationalist ideology. In the early black feminist discourse on images of black women in literature, the term black woman tends to congeal into a stable and given category. It is precisely this "critical tendency to homogenize and essentialize black women" that is interrogated in the writing of contemporary black feminist critics such as McDowell, Spillers, and Holloway.

While the current countermove to splinter and decenter the black feminine subject is undoubtedly productive at this particular conjuncture in black literary criticism, we cannot afford to forget the political and affective force of the early black feminist move to construct a unified, essential, and whole self. What this set of moves and countermoves clarifies is the double gesture needed in black feminist theorizations of identity: on the one hand, a continuing appreciation of the cultural history that has produced the black writer's strong investment in the model of a whole, cohesive self, and on the other, a vigilant attention to the differences within the black experience that confound any totalized, unitary definition of black identity.

Recent black feminist revaluations of identity, notably Mae Henderson's "Speaking in Tongues: Dialogics, Dialectics, and the Black Woman Writer's Literary Tradition" and Deborah McDowell's "Boundaries: Or Distant Relations and Close Kin," cited earlier, take Toni Morrison's *Sula* as the exemplary fictional text that can offer, in Henderson's words, "a kind of model for the deconstructive function of black feminist literary criticism." This choice in itself signals a significant departure from earlier images-of-black women criticism, which privileged Alice Walker as the novelist who most successfully achieves complete characterizations of black women. A consideration of *Sula* compels critical attention to the nonrealist modes of characterization explored in the novel, thus displacing the realist assumptions that underwrite the opposition of flat, false stereotype and whole, authentic character. The argument that stereotypes misrepresent black feminine identity presupposes a preexistent real and knowable self that fiction should mirror as accurately as possible. Such an argument unmistakably recalls the realist notion of character as the reflection of a full, coherent self. One problem with installing this model of character as the goal of black women's fiction is that it disables an appreciation of the experimental, nonrealist modes of characterization deployed in so much recent black women's fiction, modes that destabilize the humanist model of identity inscribed in realist fiction.

In an attempt to situate this critical, innovative treatment of character in an indigenous cultural context, critics such as Karla Holloway and Michael Awkward have differentiated the individual self of classic realist fiction from the whole subject posited in some black women's novels, such as Alice Walker's *The Third Life of Grange Copeland* and *Meridian*. Walker's womanist ideology affirms a psychological wholeness that is communally oriented and is explicitly opposed to the self-sufficient individuality of bourgeois humanist ideology. While this distinction works at an abstract, ideological level, it is often difficult to sustain at the level of fictional characterization. Communal intersubjectivity is not easy to represent in fiction, given the novel's lengthy realist legacy of individual characterization. Black women's fiction negotiates this legacy in several different ways and to varying degrees of success; as I argue in my chapter on *The Third Life*, Alice Walker inscribes her oppositional conception of the whole subject through modes of psychological character delineation that inadvertently reinstate the individual self of classic realist fiction.

The novels of Toni Morrison and Gayl Jones, in contrast, consistently employ nonrealist modes of characterization that are unreadable within the terms of images-of-black-women criticism. The realist opposition between flat stereotype and rounded character is rendered inoperative in the fictional worlds created by Morrison and Jones. *The Bluest Eye* and *Eva's Man* draw heavily upon stereotypes of black women, which, according to the evolutionary models proposed by Christian and Washington, should be obsolete by the

1970s. In *Sula* and *Corregidora,* the use of flat, projective modes of characterization serves to denaturalize the "real" and to divest subjectivity of any authentic presence. My discussion of the novels of Morrison and Jones focuses on their parody of realist forms such as the bildungsroman and their selective deployment of grotesque modes of character delineation. These strategies of characterization, even as they construct character around lack, division, and mutilation, always retain the notion of a whole and unified self as an unrepresentable, imaginary ideal. The figuration of black feminine identity in these novels, then, may best be understood as a contradictory interplay between presence and absence, wholeness and fracture.

The black woman novelist's effort to interrupt the realist legacy and to inscribe a black feminine subject other than the discrete individual self is often assisted by her appropriation of black folk cultural forms. As even the titles of so many books and essays on black women novelists indicate, black feminist critics are increasingly turning to metaphors derived from folk culture, such as conjuring, specifying, quilting, and laying on of hands, in order to theorize the distinctive literary and cultural practices of black women. This recent theoretical privileging of folk cultural models may be traced back to Black Aesthetic discourse, which constructed folk forms as the origin of a uniquely black cultural practice. As I argue in the next chapter, folk (and especially oral) forms were valorized by Black Aesthetic critics as the most effective means of representing a unified and essentially black communal consciousness . . .

The Black Aesthetic perception of oral forms—as cultural origins that can withstand the displacement and fragmentation wrought by oppression— reappears in much of the later black feminist writing on the subject. I shall consider at some length Susan Willis's *Specifying: Black Women Writing the American Experience,* which remains one of the most engaging and influential studies of the relation between oral forms and black women's fiction. Willis builds her argument around the verbal ritual of specifying, or name-calling, which she considers to be paradigmatic of the black oral tradition. Specifying, according to Willis, constitutes a "form of narrative integrity" that "speaks for a non-commodified relationship to language, a time when the slippage between words and meaning would not have obtained or been tolerated." Aligning oral culture with the rural South and fiction with the urban North, and conceiving the Northern migration as the single most important development in modern black American history, Willis argues that the urban context produced new cultural forms that were marked by their distance from the oral mode. These new forms, and the novel in particular, depend on metaphorical condensation, which Willis regards as an especially apt mode of figuring historical process, of capturing the historical displacement of black culture from the South to the North.

What is exceptional about Willis's book, and what distinguishes it from so many vernacular studies of black women's fiction, is its historical understanding of the different cultural contexts embedded in oral and fictional forms. Her keen attention to these differences helps Willis to avoid conflating black women's novels with the oral folk materials they strive to recall and appropriate. However, while successfully locating black women's fiction within historical processes, Willis tends to construct oral culture as a prehistorical origin. In particular, her opposition of specifying and metaphor is untenable for several reasons. The first problem is with Willis's choice of specifying as the representative instance that authorizes her generalizations about the "narrative integrity" of all black oral forms. In actuality, black oral forms such as the slave songs, the blues, and the trickster tales exemplify precisely the "slippage between words and meaning," the equivocal quality of the language used by oral artists. The duplicity of oral forms can itself be historically situated; through most of their history in the United States, black artists have had to negotiate the necessity of addressing a double audience. To give only one obvious example, the slave songs encoded two exactly antithetical meanings, one (expressing a religious yearning for heavenly peace) directed at the slavemaster, and the other (voicing their political desire for freedom) intended to inspire the slave community. The linguistic complexities as well as the hidden political intentionalities of black oral culture must necessarily be effaced if it is to operate as a pure cultural origin.

Willis's argument, then, is hampered by its failure to acknowledge that oral culture, too, has a history. Relegating black folk culture to a static rural past, Willis's thesis implies that this culture was simply superseded by the Northern urban migration. However, the new urban conditions spawned new oral forms such as rapping, and modified earlier forms such as the dialect and the blues. As Hazel Carby observes, black writers have had to rethink the very meaning of the category "the folk" in their attempt to represent the new urban folk cultures in literature. Moreover, in privileging the rural South as the foundation of a distinctively black cultural practice, critics tend to canonize Zora Neale Hurston, Alice Walker, and Toni Morrison as exemplary black woman novelists, and to marginalize compelling novelists such as Gayl Jones (whose fiction renders the urban manifestations of oral forms such as the blues) or Nella Larsen, Ann Petry, and Gloria Naylor (who convey the experience of urban dislocation without harking back to a rural Southern origin).

Without investing oral forms with any intrinsic or absolute value, my work focuses on the construction of these forms at a given ideological and literary conjuncture. During the 1960s, black folk culture was assigned a certain ideological value to make it amenable to nationalist intentions. The nationalist assertion that oral forms should authorize a uniquely black literary voice proved to be immensely productive for black women's fiction, which appropriated oral forms to serve the Black Aesthetic function of subverting the authority of white literate culture. However, as I argue in chapter 1, black women novelists were not unreservedly committed to the ideological program of black nationalism; their critical and selective adaptation of oral forms reflects their difference from the Black Aesthetic. In black women's novels of the 1970s, folk culture is subjected to a sharp scrutiny that exposes its often damaging consequences for black women. Some obvious examples of this critique, which I detail in the following chapters, are: the masculine will to power enacted in Soaphead Church's conjuring on Pecola in *The Bluest Eye;* the naturalistic folk philosophy of the Bottom community in *Sula,* which entails a reproductive definition of black femininity; the dialect in *Eva's Man,* with its relentless, derogatory naming of black women as "bitches" and "whores"; and the destructive effects on women and children of the folk figure of the badman, upon whom Brownfield, in *The Third Life of Grange Copeland,* is modeled.

The critical balance (and, at times, ambivalence) with which 1970s black women novelists approach folk forms is even more clearly visible in their representations of community. Many of the celebratory readings of folk material in black women's fiction follow Black Aesthetic theory in suggesting that the use of oral forms enables these novels not only to affirm a communal vision but also to establish a continuous and participatory relationship with their readers. Such readings—for example, Keith Byerman's *Fingering the Jagged Grain* and Michael Awkward's *Inspiriting Influences*—offer an enhanced critical understanding of the ways in which folk cultural models help black women's novels to displace the fictional category of the individual protagonist, as well as the authority conventionally invested in omniscient narration. However, no novel can exactly recreate the reception context of oral forms, nor can oral modes survive intact the process of fictional appropriation. The process transmutes the fundamental attributes of oral forms, such as their assumption of an immediate, interactive relation between the artist and the black community. It is in the charged space of encounter between the oral and fictional modes that black women novelists of the 1970s conduct their explorations of community. The following chapters on the novels of Morrison, Jones, and Walker attempt a detailed formal analysis of the generic modifications, the mutually transformative interchanges produced by the induction of oral modes into this fiction.

What is perhaps most valuable about the proliferating interest in the folk orientations of black women's novels is that it has drawn attention to the remarkable formal achievement of these novels. The increasingly rigorous formal focus of current black feminist criticism supplements earlier thematic studies that sought to clarify the ideological significance of black women's fiction. These studies, such as Gloria Wade-Gayles's *No Crystal Stair* and Carol McAlpine Watson's *Prologue,* argue for the existence of a black feminine fictional tradition predicated on common thematic concerns reflecting the shared historical experience of black women. While such thematic studies supply a wealth of information about the historical contexts of black women's novels, they tend to regard these novels as informative ideological documents that faithfully reproduce historical reality. One problem with applying this reflective model to black literature is that an exclusive focus on themes helps to maintain the form/content split that usually justifies a nonideological analysis of literary texts. Literary criticism has traditionally endorsed a "false dialectic of 'form' and 'content' whereby the artificially imposed terms alternate so that literature is sometimes perceived as content (ideology) and sometimes as form ('real' literature)." Such an opposition between art and ideology is what frequently determines the thematic reading of black literary works as ideological tracts and, conversely, the strictly formal reading of texts that are considered truly literary. Recognizing that form is not the ideology-free domain of pure literature is the first step toward challenging the division between art and ideology. An ideological analysis of form should be particularly useful for black feminist criticism, for it questions the notion of real, nonideological literature that undergirds the formation of dominant literary traditions. These traditions dismiss the works of black writers on the grounds that their ideological nature disqualifies them from the status of true literature.

In order to reverse this long history of exclusion, contemporary black feminist critics are underscoring the need for a simultaneously ideological and formal approach to black literary texts. For example, Cheryl Wall writes:

> Afro-American literature has so often been misread as mimetic representation or sociology. In other words, the verbal text has been treated as if it merely mirrored the social text. To read that way is inanely reductive, but to read black writing as if it has no relation to political reality is to vitiate its power.

As Wall's comments suggest, black critics have strong reasons for investing in the category of the literary, even as they militate against the formalist definition of literature as a category that transcends politics and ideology.

In this respect, again, the theoretical project of contemporary black feminist critics is indebted to Black Aesthetic theory, which attempted to demolish the division between art and ideology. Committed to a radical revaluation of Western aesthetics, Black Aesthetic critics exposed the covert ideological agenda of formalism. Precisely because black literary texts have been historically considered deficient when judged by the aesthetic criterion of universality, some Black Aesthetic critics found it necessary to dispense altogether with the category of the aesthetic. Others, however, preserved a redefined notion of art as a vehicle of ethical and political value. Their desire to assert an intimate and symbiotic connection between art and ideology motivated the Black Aestheticians' conception of literature as a direct reflection of social and cultural experience. Concerned primarily with the thematic content of literary work, Black Aesthetic critics, and especially those who wrote on the novel, regarded form as a transparent medium of ideological meaning. For example, in Addison Gayle's succinct expression, "form is of less importance than the content, or . . . the message. The form is the delivery system while the message is the thing delivered." Successfully challenging a formalist aesthetic at one level, by insisting that all art is ideological, Black Aesthetic theorists, by default, allowed the category of form to remain immune and peripheral to the field of ideological analysis.

Contemporary black feminist literary theory extends the Black Aesthetic gesture of challenging the dichotomy between art and ideology. Without losing sight of the ideological conditionality of all art, black feminist critics are increasingly rejecting the reflective model of Black Aesthetic and early black feminist theory. Hazel Carby, Susan Willis, Valerie Smith, and Karla Holloway, among others, emphasize the mediated status of black women's fiction in an attempt to bring the category of form within the purview of ideological criticism and to reclaim it as a significant component of black literary texts. Such a critical intervention, simultaneously and inextricably formal and ideological, appears especially necessary at present, given the increasing commercial and academic appropriation of black women's fiction. Although more and more black women's novels are being reprinted in glossy new paperback editions and taught in U.S. colleges and universities, these texts are rarely subjected to the intricate formal analysis that is usually reserved for the "masterpieces" of the American literary canon. My work participates in the current black feminist effort to question the critical norms that constitute literature in opposition to ideology, and that thereby, even while admitting black women's fiction into the academy, implicitly deny this fiction the status of "true literature."

My discussion of the ways in which black women's fiction negotiates contemporary ideological discourses draws selectively (and with serious reservations) on Mikhail Bakhtin's "Discourse in the Novel," an essay explicitly intended to "overcome the divorce between an abstract 'formal' approach and an equally abstract 'ideological' approach." Bakhtin's perception of novelistic language as a terrain of ideological struggle displaces the polarities of both formalism and crude Marxism, each of which gives priority either to intrinsic textual properties or to extratextual ideological contexts. In Bakhtin's terms, the novel, in its fictive construction of competing social and ideological discourses, forces the recognition that "language is not a neutral medium that passes freely and easily into the private property of the speaker's intentions; it is populated—overpopulated—with the intentions of others" (p. 294).

Bakhtin's assertion that "language is always half someone else's" (p. 293) may be given special historical resonance in studies of black American narrative. For the earliest slave narrators, the project of writing began as an attempt to appropriate the English language, which was "overpopulated" with the ideological intentions of the dominant white culture. Literacy, which was legally withheld from slaves, was a risky political achievement and, having achieved it, black writers had to articulate themselves in a language that denied the very possibility of black subjectivity. The impossibly ironic position of early black writers who tried to shape the master's language to suit their own intentions, cannot be smugly consigned to ancient history. More than two centuries after the inception of black narrative in America, several black women writers are still engaging the master texts of white American culture, in the form of the Dick and Jane primer in *The Bluest Eye,* the history textbook in *The Third Life,* or the toothpaste advertisement in *Sister X* and the *Victims of Foul Play.* These novels' explorations of black feminine identity gain their ironic edge from a dialogic parody of dominant cultural texts that produce the black woman as a sign of lack. Bakhtin's discussion of the novel's "parodic stylization" (p. 312) of reified literary and social discourses, and its appropriation of popular folk materials, can be immensely suggestive for critical inquiries into the dialogic development of the black novel. Bakhtin's work inflects my discussion of the ways in which black women novelists utilize popular folk forms and styles (such as funk, the blues, quilting, or black speech) to displace the ideological authority of white cultural texts and to refract their own oppositional intentions.

Bakhtin describes the novel's appropriation of different literary and extraliterary languages as a dialogic process, a term that bears a bewildering variety of meanings. Without subscribing to Bakhtin's more generalized definitions of dialogia as an inherent property of all discourse, I draw on his analysis of novelistic dialogia as a "critical interanimation" (p. 296), an "artistically organized" confrontation between unequally powerful social and literary languages (p. 366). In order to theorize the ways in which black women's fiction of the 1970s dialogizes the ideological discourse of black nationalism, I have appropriated and extended two of Bakhtin's more specific usages of the term dialogia to describe the interchanges between two utterances on the same object, and between an utterance and its contexts.

Bakhtin's theory of novelistic dialogia hinges on his assertion that all discourse responds to prior discourses and anticipates possible answering discourses of the future. His discussion of this "internal dialogism of the word" (p. 280) informs my claim that black women's fiction of the 1970s constitutes a highly mediated response to black nationalist utterances on a number of different but interrelated objects, including the black woman, the black community, the question of political change, and the function of art, among others. Black women's novels conduct a subtextual dialogue with black nationalist discourse, adopting the several strategies of directly contradicting, berating, appeasing, beguiling, and dodging an assumed and typical Black Aesthetic reader. The ideological context of black nationalism is thus internalized by these texts, constructed as the hypothetical addressee or interlocutor of their fictional discourse.

The terms text and context are further complicated and stripped of their polarized connotations of inside and outside of Bakhtin's remarks on the "contextualized (dialogizing) framing" of one discourse by another (p. 340).

Arguing that an utterance may be dialogized if it is dislodged from its initial context and framed by another, alien context, Bakhtin refuses a static conception of context as single, fixed, and all-determining. Instead, his dynamic formulation of context as a "system of potentially infinite displacement and substitution" opens the space for strategic misreadings and reaccentuations of a discourse in different contexts. Taking black nationalist discourse as the pretext of black women's novels in the 1970s, I argue that some of these novels dialogize black nationalist discourse by dislocating it from its "original" context and reframing it in an alien fictional context. For example, the black nationalist discourse on reproduction and matriarchy is displaced onto the context of slavery in *Corregidoro*; *Sula* displaces several supposedly radical elements of black nationalist ideology onto the deeply conservative folk vision of its Bottom community; and *The Third Life of Grange Copeland* grafts together, in the character of Grange, the ideologically incongruous figures of the mother and the nationalist. Each of these displacements produces a curious fictional and ideological hybrid that exposes the inconsistencies of black nationalist discourse.

While using some of Bakhtin's concepts to clarify the ways in which black women's novels mediate and critically misread nationalist ideology, I do not hazard any generalizations about the ideologically subversive nature of all black women's fiction. As I demonstrate in the following chapters, if the strategy of displacement used in these novels often illuminates the contradictions of nationalist discourse, it equally marks these novels' capitulation to the terms of this discourse. While much of black women's fiction subverts contemporary ideological discourses on race and gender, it just as frequently submits to the constraints of these discourses. I do not, then, concur with Bakhtin's occasionally essentialist celebration of the authentic novel, which achieves a "liberation" from ideological discourses by the very fact of turning these discourses into fictional objects (p. 348). Bracketing all essentialist definitions of good or true fiction, I seek rather to delineate the ideological construction of the category of good fiction at a specific cultural conjuncture. Through frequent references to contemporary reviews of black women's novels in journals such as *Black World, Freedomways,* and *The Black Scholar* on the one hand, and *The New York Times Book Review, The New Yorker,* and *The Chicago Tribune Book Review* on the other, I show that these works constitute themselves as novels by carefully navigating between two influential contemporary definitions of good fiction. The Black Aesthetic conception of good fiction as didactic and politically useful, and the white literary establishment's promotion of a politically neutral fiction, represent the extreme ideological poles within which black women's fiction of the 1970s was situated. I am reluctant to advance any transhistorical claims about the inherent nature of all black women's fiction, or about the relation between this fiction and contemporary ideological discourses.

Suggested Readings with Similar Theme:

McDowell, Deborah. "New Directions for Black Feminist Criticism." In *Black American Literature Forum,* 1980. Reprint, Elaine Showalter, ed. *The New Feminist Criticism.* New York: Pantheon, 1985.

Willis, Susan. *Specifying: Black Women Writing the American Experience.* Madison: University of Wisconsin Press, 1987.

Christian, Barbara. "The Race for Theory." *Feminist Studies* (Spring 1987): 67–80.

Wallace, Michelle. "Variations on Negation and the Heresy of Black Feminist Creativity." In *Invisibility Blues: From Pop to Theory.* New York: Verso, 1990.

FARAH JASMINE GRIFFIN

Introduction
in "Who set you flowin'?"
The African-American Migration Narrative
(1995)

Define migration narrative in the context of African American literary poetics. Discuss what Griffin calls the "four pivotal moments" of the migration narrative. How does Griffin expand the Johnsonian viewpoint about form in African American literature? How does Griffin enter discussions with Toni Morrison and Karla Holloway about the significance of the ancestor in African American literary narratives? How does Griffin enter discussions with Jerry Ward about the significance of the South in African American literary narratives? Define the following terms: safe space, urban space, migration narrative paradigm, and recursive touchstone.

From the publication of Paul Laurence Dunbar's *Sport of the Gods* in 1902 to Toni Morrison's *Jazz* in 1992, the migration narrative emerges as one of the twentieth century's dominant forms of African-American cultural production. Through migration narratives—musical, visual, and literary—African-American artists and intellectuals attempt to come to terms with the massive dislocation of black peoples following migration. Given the impact of migration and urbanization on African-Americans in particular and American society in general, it is not surprising that this century has witnessed the emergence of this new form.

Most often, migration narratives portray the movement of a major character or the text itself from a provincial (not necessarily rural) Southern or Midwestern site (home of the ancestor) to a more cosmopolitan, metropolitan area. Within the migration narrative the protagonist or a central figure who most influences the protagonist is a migrant. The representation of the migration experience depends on the genre and form of the narrative as well as the historical and political moment of production. Also, each artist's conception of power is directly related to the construction of his or her text.

The narrative is marked by four pivotal moments: (1) an event that propels the action northward, (2) a detailed representation of the initial confrontation with the urban landscape, (3) an illustration of the migrant's

423

attempt to negotiate that landscape and his or her resistance to the negative effects of urbanization, and (4) a vision of the possibilities or limitations of the Northern, Western, or Midwestern city and the South. These moments may occur in any given order within the context of the narrative; in other words, it is not necessary that there be a straightforward linear progression from the South to a vision of the consequences of migration, although this is most often the case.

The migration narrative shares with the slave narrative notions of ascent from the South into a "freer" North. Like the slave narrative and the fiction it inspired, the migration narrative has its own set of narrative conventions. If the slave narrative revolves around the auction block, the whipping, the separation of families, and miscegenation, the migration narrative provides us with lynching scenes, meetings with ancestors, and urban spaces like kitchenettes, dance halls, and street corners. The migration narrative is marked by an exploration of urbanism, an explication of sophisticated modern power, and, in some instances, a return South. Finally, the migration narrative takes shape in a variety of art forms: autobiography, fiction, music, poetry, photography, and painting.

Although literary critics have noted migration as an important theme in African-American fiction, until recently they have been less attentive to the relationship between migration and African-American literary production. The study of twentieth-century black migration has been the province of social scientists, historians, and scholars of African-American music and folklore. Prompted by Robert Stepto's *From Behind the Veil: A Study of Afro-American Narrative* (1979), in the past decade, literary and cultural critics Susan Willis, Hazel Carby, Lawrence Rodgers, and Charles Scruggs have started the important project of situating twentieth-century migration as a major factor in African-American cultural production.

Hazel Carby's work is particularly noteworthy. Carby documents the emergence and development of a black women's blues culture that created "a music that spoke the desires which were released in the dramatic shift in social relations that occurred in a historical moment of crisis and dislocation." For Carby, the 1920s marked a time when established black Northern intellectuals were confronted with large numbers of migrants who challenged earlier notions of sexuality, leadership, and any sense of a monolithic black culture.

Charles Scruggs stresses migration as an important starting point in the study of black literature of the city. Lawrence Rodgers is the first to identify migration with the emergence of a new genre of African-American literature: the Great Migration novel.

This book departs from the foregoing studies in its interdisciplinary focus and in its discussion of a variety of literary, musical, and visual works that were created during the height of the Great Migration and the years that followed it. I have chosen to call these texts migration narratives. The paradigm "migration narrative" provides a conceptual umbrella under which to gather these African-American creative artifacts. In addition to identifying the migration narrative as a dominant form of African-American cultural production in the twentieth century, I have tried to create a way of talking about African-American art that provides comprehensive space for the diversity of gender, class, and sexuality. Through critical readings of migration narratives, I reveal paradigms like "ancestors" and "strangers" that cross class, gender, and genre. This interpretation finds no one static migration narrative; instead these narratives are as diverse as the people and the times that create them.

Most migration narratives offer a catalyst for leaving the South. Although there are different reasons for migrating, in all cases the South is portrayed as an immediate, identifiable, and oppressive power. Southern power is exercised by people known to its victims—bosses, landlords, sheriffs, and, in the case of black women, even family members. To the extent that power is exercised psychically, it relies on the potential victim's fear of the violence that awaits him or her. In fictional texts especially, Southern power is inflicted on black bodies in the form of lynching, beating, and rape. It is dramatized in the spectacle and torture of elaborate lynching and burning rituals. The degree to which Southern power is stressed differs from genre to genre, but there is a consensus that this power is unsophisticated in nature.

Although the narratives tend to represent the South as a site of terror and exploitation, some of them also identify it as a site of the ancestor. The role of the ancestor in the Southern sections of the migration narrative is of great significance to the development of the text. If the ancestor's role is mitigated, then it is likely that throughout the course of the narrative, the South will be portrayed as a site of racial horror and shame. In this instance, the ancestor will be of little use on the Northern landscape. If, on the other hand, the early Southern sections stress the significance of an ancestor, or the blood of any recently deceased black person, then the South becomes a place where black blood earns a black birthright to the land, a locus of history, culture, and possible redemption. If the South is thus established as a place of birthright, then the ancestor will be a significant influence in the migrant's life in the North.

After leaving the South, the next pivotal moment in the migration narrative is the initial confrontation with the urban landscape. This confrontation often shapes the fate of the South (embodied in the migrants themselves, the ancestor, and any retention of the South) in the city. The confrontation with the urban landscape—usually experienced as a change in time, space, and technology as well as a different concept of race relations—results in a profound change in the way that the mechanisms of power work in the city. Here, it seems, power is more subtle and sophisticated. The more sophisticated use of power is not beyond resorting to acts of physical violence on black bodies.

The prevalence of police brutality in urban areas is one example of this. In this instance it is often necessary for migrants to evoke the presence of an ancestor or certain aspects of their Southern folk culture in order to combat the harsh confrontation with the urban landscape.

I have borrowed the concept "ancestor" from Toni Morrison, who argues: "[Ancestors] are sort of timeless people whose relationships to the characters are benevolent, instructive, and protective, and they provide a certain kind of wisdom." I want to extend Morrison's definition of the ancestor to include an understanding of the full ramifications of the term. The ancestor is present in ritual, religion, music, food, and performance. His or her legacy is evident in discursive formations like the oral tradition. The ancestor might be a literal ancestor; he or she also has earthly representatives, whom we might call elders. The ancestor's presence in Southern cultural forms such as song, food, and language sometimes provides the new migrant a cushion with which to soften the impact of urbanization. In *Moorings and Metaphors: Figures of Culture and Gender in Black Women's Literature,* Karla Holloway argues that the ancestor figure "serves as a recursive touchstone" and that "the ancestral presence constitutes a posture of remembrance." (p. 115).

Toni Morrison's Pilate Dead and Julie Dash's Nana Peazant are the quintessential representatives of the ancestor. Pilate is the central female figure of Morrison's *Song of Solomon.* As the daughter of Macon Dead I she is a direct descendant of the flying African. She embodies the history of the Dead clan in her earring and her song. Self-born, possessing no sign of her connection, she is nonetheless the most connected character in the text. She sits on the boundaries, dwells in the borderlands. In her mind she houses not only the songs and stories of the past, but also the remedies, the recipes for nurturance and survival. Pilate is both root and leaf, the transitional space between the ground where the ancestors reside and the sky to which they direct all who revere them. She is both tall and short; both eloquent and illiterate. She speaks freely to the dead, the living, and the unborn.

Similarly, the character Nana Peazant in Julie Dash's film *Daughters of the Dust* possesses the qualities of the ancestor. As family griot, Nana holds her family's history in a box filled with "scraps of memory," her Yoruba-based religious rituals, and her stories. This elder advises her migrating grandchildren: "I'm the one that can give you strength. . . . Take me wherever you go. I'm your strength."

Ancestors are a specific presence in the text. They are found in both its content and its form. Toni Morrison best articulates the role of the migration narrative as repository of the ancestor when she says that her storytelling, like that of the characters in *Song of Solomon,* is an attempt to preserve and pass on the stories and the songs of the African-American past. As far as she is concerned, urbanization and "the press toward upward social mobility would mean to get as far away from that kind of knowledge as possible." According to Morrison, such a fiction "recognizes what the conflicts are, what the problems are. But it need not solve those problems because it is not a case study." In an interview, Morrison even suggested that fiction as ancestor serves as a space for enlightenment, sustenance, and renewal: "There is a confrontation between old values of the tribes and newer urban values. It's confusing. There has to be a mode to do what the music did for blacks, what we used to be able to do with each other in private and in that civilization that existed underneath the white civilization."

While Morrison's fiction seeks to be the repository of the ancestor and eschews becoming a "case study," other migration narratives strive toward a more objective stance. These are dominated by the "stranger." On the pages of the written migration narrative and in the lyrics of many of the musical ones, the migrant often meets a literal stranger who offers (mis)guidance, advice, and a new worldview. The stranger exists in a dialectical relationship with the ancestor. While the ancestor originates in the South and lives in the North, for the most part the stranger is a Northern phenomenon.

My concept of the stranger is greatly influenced, but not circumscribed by, the stranger "who stays" in the work of the German-Jewish sociologist George Simmel. Simmel's stranger is a figure whose membership within a group involves being at once outside and within its boundaries.

Simmel characterizes the stranger who stays as "a potential wanderer . . . [who,] although he has gone no further, has not quite got over the freedom of coming and going. He is fixed within a certain spatial circle—or within a group whose boundaries are analogous to spatial boundaries." Simmel's stranger does not initially belong to the group; instead, he brings qualities into it that are not, and cannot be, indigenous. The stranger is a cosmopolitan figure.

Simmel created his concept of the stranger as a means of understanding the process of migration and urbanization in a European context. In American sociology, "the stranger" evolves into "the marginal man" and is best described in the work of Robert Park. For Park, human migrations produced new personalities, one of which he characterized as the newly emancipated individual, or the marginal man. For this character type, "energies that were formerly controlled by custom and tradition are released. . . . [Such persons] become . . . not merely emancipated, but enlightened." Park continues, "The emancipated individual invariably becomes in a certain sense and to a certain degree a cosmopolitan. He learns to look upon the world in which he was born and bred with something of the detachment of a stranger. He acquires, in short, an intellectual bias." This figure has severed all ties with the ancestor, yet, under Park's definition, this will not inhibit but will further his access to freedom.

In relation to the dominant white society, all migrants are strangers—foreigners driven by persecution to wander in search of a new home. However, within the context of the African-American community, the stranger is that figure who possesses no connections to the community. Migrants who seek to be strangers can never occupy that space fully, but those who come closest "change their discomforts into a base of resistance."

Like Simmel's "stranger," the omniscient narrators of these texts play the role of journalists, streetwise reporters who detach themselves and present the readers with a case for consideration and action. Gwendolyn Brooks has in fact likened herself to a reporter in her attempts to record the daily lives of ordinary black urbanites. Ann Petry used her skills as a newspaper reporter documenting black Harlem of the forties to write her classic novel *The Street,* and with *Native Son* Richard Wright provides us with the novel-as-stranger par excellence. In "Blueprint for Negro Writing," Wright argues that writers are "agents of social change who possess unified personalities, organized emotions [and an] obdurate will to change the world." Wright credited the social sciences for providing him with objective, critical frameworks in which to place his stories.

Richard Wright is an exemplar of the migrant as stranger. In his essay "How Bigger Thomas Was Born," Wright explains how he himself avoided becoming Bigger. Wright's description resembles that of Julia Kristeva's stranger, who, according to Kristeva, "had he stayed home, might have become an outlaw." Wright the protagonist shares with Bigger a sense of disconnection from the stifling folk tradition of the race. The protagonists Bigger and Wright mark the negative and positive consequences of stranger status, respectively. Bigger is devoid of any human connection and does not fill that void with a critical consciousness until he has already become an outlaw. Wright becomes the stranger who possesses the critical consciousness and who occupies the position of cosmopolite.

In terms of form, the texts seem to oscillate between the two encounters with the stranger and the ancestor. In fact, the most sophisticated texts, like Morrison's *Song of Solomon* and Jean Toomer's *Cane,* strive to be sites of the ancestor. Wright's *Native Son* and Petry's *The Street* strive to occupy the space of the stranger, the observer, the social scientist shedding light on a familiar but strange situation. Stevie Wonder's "Living for the City" embodies the conflict between the stranger and the ancestor in both its content and its musical form. The figurations of ancestors and strangers provide useful conceptual tools for understanding the migration narratives; they are both masculine and feminine, male and female, concrete and abstract. In their extremes, ancestors and strangers are polar opposites; in more sophisticated texts they overlap. Sometimes the stranger and the ancestor seem to exist in the same figure. In fact, the most effective ancestors possess qualities of the stranger and the most effective strangers can pass as ancestors. For instance, Pilate glides through the pages of *Song of Solomon* walking a line between the familiar, ancestral mode and that of the "stranger."

The third moment of the migration narrative is the portrayal of the way migrants negotiate the urban landscape. Once situated on the urban landscape, domestic, street, and psychic space are all sites of contestation for migrants and the powers that seek to control them. Again, the ancestor is of great significance in this struggle. These spaces are often sites where the ancestor is invoked; at other times they are sites from which he or she is banished. Often, rejection of the ancestor leads to further alienation, exile, the status of stranger, or sometimes death. The ancestor in turn is a site of negotiation for the construction of a new self. The creation of a new self may be one of the most crucial aspects of resistance to the complexities of the North. However, for many, the sites of the ancestor are stifling and provincial and as such they inhibit the progress and the development of the protagonist.

These spaces are either the locus for producing and maintaining the negative effects of urbanization—fragmentation, dislocation, and material and spiritual impoverishment—or "safe havens" from these negative effects. In the latter instance, they help the migrant to construct an alternate urban subjectivity. (Subject is here used to connote an object of social and historical forces as well as a historical agent.)

I borrow the term "safe spaces" from Patricia Hill Collins, who defines them as places where black women "speak freely" and where domination does not exist as a "hegemonic ideology." She identifies as safe spaces extended families, churches, and African-American community organizations, as well as cultural traditions like the black women's blues and literary traditions. According to Collins these spaces form a site of "resisting objectification as Other." Collins claims such sites "house a culture of resistance."

My use of "safe space" seeks to complicate Collins's definition. First, hegemonic ideology can exist even in spaces of resistance. Second, these sites are more often the locus of sustenance and preservation than of resistance. While sustenance and preservation are necessary components of resistance, I do not believe they are in and of themselves resistant acts. Moreover, safe spaces can be very conservative spaces as well. For my purposes safe spaces provide a way of understanding the possibilities of such sites in the migration narrative. However, the narratives often point out the irony of the term "safe." For instance, in some cases the black church is not necessarily a safe space for black women in light of its gender hierarchy, its stand against birth control and abortion, and its homophobia. In other cases the church is the only site that recognizes and affirms black humanity.

In the migration narrative, safe spaces are available to both male and female characters. At their most progressive, they are spaces of retreat, healing, and resistance; at their most reactionary, they are potentially provincial spaces which do not encourage resistance but instead help to create complacent subjects whose only aim is to exist within the confines of power that oppress them. In many instances these spaces contain both possibilities. In some cases safe spaces are sites where the South is invoked—not just in its horror, terror, and exploitation, but as a place that housed the values and memories that sustained black people. The South emerges as the home of the ancestor, the place where community and history are valued over Northern individualism.

Safe spaces are both material and discursive. Narrative safe spaces are often resistant to traditional narrative form. They appear in song, food, elements of oral culture, the silences around ritual, and in dream sequences. Literal safe spaces in the city are places where rituals can be enacted to invoke the presence of the ancestor in the North: Pilate's kitchen in *Song of Solomon*, Mary's boarding house in *Invisible Man*, the Savoy Ballroom in Harlem, the Jungle Room on Sixty-eighth Street in Manhattan, where new migrants shouted "Let's go home" to band leader James P. Johnson in a call for Southern music. These are all safe spaces where the ancestor is invoked. In this sense, the South is no longer simply a "historical locus" but also a figurative one.

On the other hand, for writers like Richard Wright and James Baldwin, sites like the library provide "safe" space as well as exposure to a world from which their protagonists are excluded. This newfound knowledge can both empower and anger them. In any case, they are aware of the racism of the dominant society as well as the provincial nature of their own communities.

Because safe spaces are created by as well as resistant to sophisticated urban power, they have a tenuous and contradictory existence. A woman's safe space—the home, for instance—might be inhibiting for a man. Similarly, a woman might find the culture of the street, which nurtures an urban black manhood, somewhat dangerous and detrimental to her well-being. Both men and women might find that these spaces are under the control of people and forces that oppress them.

The fourth moment of the migration narrative provides a consideration of the sophistication of modern urban power, an evaluation of the consequences of migration and urbanization, and a vision of future possibilities. For many artists, the North ensures the death and demise of the migrant; for others migration is one step on the road to a cosmopolitan status. Still others, like the rap band Arrested Development, require a return to the South as a means of acquiring racial, historical, and cultural redemption. . . .

The moments described here are constantly revised and challenged. At any given time different interpretations exist side by side. Nevertheless, one interpretation usually emerges as dominant. The major shift in the representation of the migration is prompted by a shift in the understanding of power and the different forms it takes in the North and the South.

During the years following the Harlem Renaissance throughout the Depression to World War II, Richard Wright's version of the migration narrative was the dominant portrayal. For Wright, the South is never a site of possibility for the migrant. Unless he acquires a critical consciousness of the stranger, unless he distances himself from folk culture, he is assured a certain literal or metaphorical "death on the city pavements." Although Zora Neale Hurston provides an alternative to Wright in that her fiction is situated in a racially monolithic South, Wright's is nonetheless the dominant vision. I measure Wright's hegemony not only by the critical attention received by his work, or by the accolades of Book-of-the-Month Club selection and bestseller lists, but also by the degree to which he influenced other African-American writers: Although authors like Chester Himes, William Demby, and Ann Petry differ from Wright in significant ways, they nonetheless have been influenced by him.

The period following the war serves as a kind of transition from Wright's dominance to the emergence of Ralph Ellison. This era is marked by the publication of Ralph Ellison's *Invisible Man* and James Baldwin's *Go Tell It on the Mountain*. Despite both writers' very public disavowals of Wright's influence on their work—indeed neither presents a picture as bleak as that of Wright—they nonetheless share his vision in many ways. Baldwin shares Wright's sense of the stifling nature of black life, yet both he and Ellison appreciate the complexities of African-American life much more than Wright. In so doing, they also suggest the possibilities of the South by privileging the importance of certain elements of black Southern culture to the survival of urban blacks.

Following the Civil Rights and Black Power movements. Toni Morrison's version of the migration emerges as the dominant one. In her work the South becomes not only a site of racial redemption and identity but also the place where Africa is most present. It is not surprising that this emerges as the dominant portrayal of African-American migration following the Civil Rights Movement. If, in fact, the South is a premodern power, it is more susceptible to the forms of social protest that take place there during the Civil Rights Movement. Therefore, it is more likely to be affected by social change. Because of this it can be reconsidered as a burial ground, as a place of cultural origins, home of the ancestors, as a place to be redeemed. The North, however, as a more complex and omniscient power, is not susceptible to the same strategies of the Civil Rights Movement; thus the failure of Martin Luther King in Chicago. Artists who recognize this begin to represent the South in ways only alluded to by their predecessors and to reimagine the possibilities the South holds for African-American people.

Morrison is not the first to have the South reemerge as a site of African-American history and culture; Ralph Ellison, Albert Murray, and Alice Walker precede her. However, Morrison is the first whose texts not only tell the story of the ancestor in the South, but also embody the ancestor. In this way, her significance is not only in the story she tells, but also in the way in which she tells it. I measure Morrison's dominance by the number of scholarly books and articles devoted to her work, the almost automatic appearance of her work on bestseller lists, and her winning of the Pulitzer Prize and the Nobel Prize for Literature.

Although one interpretation of migration may reign at any given moment, it is always challenged by other visions. At times those challenges come from other forms; for instance, film or music may challenge the dominance of a literary artist's interpretation. Oftentimes the challenge comes from within genres; thus one novelist challenges another. Challenges may even come within the work of one artist. As we shall see, Toni Morrison revises and rewrites many of the tropes that she helps to establish. . . .

This study builds upon the foundations of the last twenty years of African-American cultural criticism. It is not a social history, but an attempt to provide historically and theoretically informed close readings of selected migration narratives. In a project of this scope, there are of course many important narratives that have been left out. However, I think that the framework discussed within provides room for the inclusion of a variety of works not discussed in depth: texts of migration from the Caribbean to North American cities like Paule Marshall's *Brown Girl, Brownstones,* texts of migration to the West such as Chester Himes's novel *If He Hollers Let Him Go,* Charles Burnett's films *To Sleep with Anger* and *Killer of Sheep,* and Carrie Mae Weems's photograph series *Family Pictures and Stories* or the plays of August Wilson. The migration narrative is also embedded in the arenas of sport: the integration of baseball, the entrance of blacks into the urban, ethnic game of basketball, and the subsequent stylistic innovations of each game are also possible areas for exploration. It is my hope that this book will encourage further studies of these various forms of the migration narrative.

Suggested Reading with Similar Theme:

hooks, bell. "Homeplace: A Site of Resistance." In *Yearning: Race, Gender, and Cultural Politics.* Boston: South End Press, 1990.

Tuzyline Jita Allan

Introduction:
Decoding Womanist Grammar of Difference
in *Womanist and Feminist Aesthetics,*
A Comparative Review (1995)

Define womanism. How is the concept grounded in culture as well as history? Despite its debatable flaws, how has womanism prompted "active rather than reactive forms of criticism"? How do the following critics help to articulate a literary history of black feminism/womanism: Barbara Smith, Deborah McDowell, Hazel Carby, bell hooks, Patricia Hill Collins, and Cleonora Hudson-Weems. Define the following terms and phrases: oppositional (black and Third World), essentialism, trope of otherness, womanist consciousness, binary opposition, culturally specific differences, history of difference.

Kate Millet's *Sexual Politics* marked a paradigmatic shift in American intellectual life from civil rights to women's rights. The book appeared at a time when black and white women activists, alienated by the male-dominated center of the civil rights movement and the increasingly sexist tone of its revolutionary branch, were beginning to channel their energies into formidable resistance against women's social subordination. *Sexual Politics* is a landmark in more than one sense. Most often acknowledged is the fact that it anticipated the theoretical and critical feminist discourse of the 1970s. Millet argued that the socialization of women into inferior beings had been replicated in the works of D. H. Lawrence, Norman Mailer, Henry Miller, and Jean Genet, an argument that laid the foundation for the two-pronged feminist enterprise of theoretical and critical investigation that has dominated academic inquiry for the past two decades.

As forerunner, *Sexual Politics* also initiated the practice of ethnocentrism within feminist studies. Educated, middle-class white women devised theories about middle-class white women and gave them a universal stamp, thereby erasing or invalidating the experiences of the majority of women, who were excluded from one or both of these categories. Other critics soon challenged these theories and charged their exponents with ethnocentric arrogance and bias. Women's varied cultural, racial, class, and sexual identities, these critics argued, defied homogenization. Besides, what justification was there for

433

positing a middle-class, Eurocentric model of womanhood as the female ideal? Were white feminists appropriating femaleness in the same way that white men had appropriated maleness? And if so, how different then was the feminist enterprise from those male practices of domination it was attempting to expose? Such an interrogation led to the determination that the early theoretical accounts of women's social roles mirrored the self/other dichotomy of phallocentric thought.

Early feminist criticism thus proved just as exclusionary and controversial as the male social structure it decried. The critical project to unearth and reinstate women writers buried beneath age-long patriarchal neglect or scorn seemed to reenact, through its own neglect of nonwhite women, the very process it set out to correct. Critical reappraisals of the literature of Anglo-American women writers omitted or mentioned only cursorily black female writers. In the ensuing backlash, Alice Walker denounced both the practice and the practitioners, citing in her oft-quoted essay, "One's Child of One's Own," a particularly startling example of unbridled ethnocentrism:

> In the prologue to her book, *The Female Imagination,* Patricia Meyer Spacks attempts to explain why her book deals solely with women in the "Anglo-American literary tradition." (She means, of course, white women in the Anglo-American literary tradition.) Speaking of the books she has chosen to study, she writes: "Almost all delineate the lives of white middle-class women. Phyllis Chesler has remarked, 'I have no theory to offer Third World female psychology in America. . . . As a white woman, I'm reluctant and unable to construct theories about experiences I haven't had.' So am I: the books I talk about describe familiar experience, belong to a familiar cultural setting. . . . My bibliography balances works everyone knows *(Jane Eyre, Middlemarch)* with works that should be better known *(The Story of Mary MacLane)*. Still, the question remains: Why only these?"

Spacks's paternalistic tone, universalizing rhetoric, and self-distancing from the Third World female "other" all replicate the masculinist performance of gendered discourse. To realize the full ideological import of her statement, one need simply replace *Jane Eyre, Middlemarch,* and *The Story of Mary MacLane* with, say, *Vanity Fair, The Mayor of Casterbridge,* and *Roderick Random,* respectively. The move reinvokes the hegemonic authority of male-directed canonic critical discourse and simultaneously implicates Spacks in a shared awareness of cultural power.

Barbara Smith referred to the hierarchization of racial gender within the new community of academic feminism as a "barely disguised cultural 'imperialism'," underwritten by resistance to the idea that "Black and female identity . . . coexist." Walker concurred, linking the effort to crystallize white feminism into a normative femininity to white male appropriation of manhood:

It is, apparently, inconvenient, if not downright mind straining, for white women scholars to think of Black women as women, perhaps because "woman" (like "man" among white males) is a name they are claiming for themselves, and themselves alone. Racism decrees that if they are now women. . . . then Black women must, perforce, be something else. (*Gardens,* 376)

Black women's creativity at the beginning of the second wave of twentieth-century feminism also stood in the shadow of what Calvin Hernton would call a "mountain of sexism," a peak as formidable as its racial counterpart. Denounced variously by black feminist critics, "the legacy of male chauvinism in the black literary world" suffered a crushing defeat, ironically, at the hands of a male critic. In the eponymous second chapter of *The Sexual Mountain and Black Women Writers* Hernton launched what Claudia Tate dubbed a "male womanist" attack against what he perceived as "feelings of envy, jealousy, resentment and paranoia on the part of the men" toward black women writers. Hernton stacked up an impressive record of black women's literary production against a pattern of female devaluation within the male-dominated black literary establishment. The catalogue conveyed a sense of unbroken confrontation between black women and men, animated by what Tate called the latter's "phallocentric privilege."

Hernton's essay assumes greater significance beyond marking a radical shift in priorities within the predominant African American critical tradition. It is explicit regarding the range and scope of black feminist insurgency, leaving no doubt as to the promise of vindication embodied in the emergent effort to unearth and reinstate black women's writing. This effort, responding to the concurrent systems of male and white female marginalization already described, began with the need to develop a parallel "historical tradition" located in the nexus of "specific political social and economic experience" unique to black women. The resulting scholarship has been both virtuosic and unrelenting. From Mary Helen Washington's modest but influential trilogy—*Black-Eyed Susan, Midnight Birds,* and *Invented Lives*—to the dazzling architectonics of Henry Louis Gates's Schomburg series, black women's narratives now lend an awesome presence to the American literary landscape, smothering the anxiety of displacement that marked their painful gestation.

The development of black feminist criticism has been slower, though no less dramatic, perhaps because its parallel track bears disproportionately the strains and stresses of the project to rehabilitate black female creativity. The pressure points were evident from the start. Caught between white feminist and black male hegemonies, black feminist critics faced the difficult task of constructing a new identity in both cultures based on a dialectical relationship of cooperation and resistance. Deborah McDowell articulated well the dilemma in her founding essay, "New Directions for Black Feminist Criticism." Inegalitarian productions of femininity and blackness in mainstream feminist and African American discourses, she argued, called for an alternative, competing and un-self-limiting vision from black women. McDowell decried the "decidedly . . . practical" and idealistic tone of early black feminist analysis and challenged its practitioners to move beyond sloganeering and political isolationism to a theoretical level of discourse with ties to black male literature, white feminist criticism and "the critical methodology handed down by white men."

In *Reconstructing Womanhood,* Hazel Carby collapsed the chronological configurations of black feminist criticism—from Barbara Smith's "Toward a Black Feminist Criticism" to Barbara Christian's *Black Feminist Criticism*—in an effort to foreground a historically sound basis for theorizing differences between black and white women. Carby shared McDowell's disdain for the idealistic strain in black feminist criticism but also indicted the whole feminist myth of "a lost [American] sisterhood" on similar grounds. The "boundaries that separate white feminists from all women of color" constitute a "history of difference" that, Carby insisted, cannot be ignored by contemporary feminists. Her reading of this "cultural history" offers a powerful and exciting example of the critical sophistication McDowell advocated. More crucially, in terms of my own objectives in this book, Carby refigured black feminist criticism as "a problem, not a solution, as a sign that should be interrogated, a locus of contradictions."

Standing on a discursive middle ground between McDowell's not-so-sanguine expectations and Carby's hearty historicization, Alice Walker's "womanist" ethos embodies both the frustration and the promise of black feminist criticism. Resolutely idealistic and essentialist, womanism reflects nonetheless a marked acceleration in black feminists' readiness to reframe the sexual debate around culturally specific differences between white women and women of color. Walker spells out her definition of "womanist" in four choral stanzas bearing the following excerpted content, which I have arranged according to thematic importance:

> Womanist: A black feminist or feminist of color. . . .
> Usually referring to outrageous, audacious, courageous
> or willful behavior. Wanting to know more and in greater
> depth than is considered "good" for one. . . .
>
> A woman who loves other women sexually and/or
> nonsexually. Appreciates and prefers women's
> culture, women's emotional flexibility . . . and women's
> strength. . . .
> Committed to survival and wholeness of entire people,
> male and female. Not a separatist. . . .
> Womanist is to feminist as purple is to lavender.
>
> (*Gardens,* xi–xiii)

Even with the filter of metaphor, the last statement fails to conceal the deep lines of division drawn here between black and white feminists. Walker sets up (black) womanism and (white) feminism in a binary opposition from which the former emerges a privileged, original term and the latter, a devalued, pale replica. With this reversal of the existing paradigm of power relations, womanist consciousness becomes the strategic fulcrum of the project of female restoration. Walker intends the major themes of womanist epistemology—audacity, woman-centeredness, and whole(some)ness of vision—to be understood as critical imperatives in the effort to fashion a framework of feminist resistance to patriarchy. These themes will serve as both a structural and a guiding principle of this book, as I examine the merits of Walker's critique of and implicit challenge to white feminist praxis. But first it is helpful to determine the nature of the response to womanism's differentiated presence within feminism.

In the field of contesting attitudes toward womanism, approbation predominates. For many feminists of color, the concept is a rich source of cultural capital in a social economy weighted heavily against them. Consequently, womanism has helped to fortify the long-standing discontent over white feminists' appropriation of womanhood, prompting active rather than reactive forms of criticism. In "Womanism: The Dynamics of the Contemporary Black Female Novel in English," Nigerian-born critic Chikwenye Ogunyemi captures the new critical attitude in her opening sentence:

> What does a black woman novelist go through as she comes in contact with white feminist writing and realizes that Shakespeare's illustrious sisters belong to the second sex, a situation that has turned them into impotent eunuchs without rooms of their own in which to read and write their very own literature, so that they have become madwomen now emerging from the attic, determined to fight for their rights by engaging in the acrimonious politics of sex?

This brilliant conflation of familiar Euro-American feminist themes and texts is a linguistic act that mocks white feminist narratives of victimization, narratives that have themselves, in their exclusivity, victimized nonwhite women. The satiric backdrop helps to illuminate the contrasting image of the womanist writer who "along with her consciousness of sexual issues . . . incorporate[s] racial, cultural, national, economic, and political considerations into her philosophy." The goal of this many-sided vision, Ogunyemi argues, is a gender-free Pan-Africanism ("the unity of blacks everywhere under the enlightened control of men and women"), a far cry from the self-serving idea of a "separatist, idyllic existence away from . . . men's world" that preoccupies the white woman writer.

Barbara Smith had already made the connection between womanism and race, culture, and politics in her introduction to *Home Girls: A Black Fem-*

inist Anthology, published the same year as Walker's *In Search of Our Mothers' Gardens.* "I have always felt," Smith wrote, "that Black women's ability to function with dignity, independence, and imagination in the face of total adversity—that is, in the face of white America—points to an innate feminist potential." Like Walker, Smith locates this quality in the socializing black female ethic embodied in the injunction "Act like you have some sense." The ability to forge a "connection between plain common sense and a readiness to fight for change" bespeaks, for Smith, a culture-specific feminism deserving the distinction conferred by the term "womanist."

What Patricia Hill Collins culls from womanism to assist in her mapping of the epistemological contours of black feminism is a "humanist vision" born out of black women's struggle against multiple oppressions. She posits the womanist idea of "commit[ment] to the survival and wholeness of entire people, male and female" as a recurrent theme among black women intellectuals, from Anna Julia Cooper to June Jordan. These women's "words and actions," according to Collins, "resonate with a strikingly similar theme of the oneness of all human life"—that is, with womanist intensity. Collins thus shares with Ogunyemi and Smith a belief in womanism's culture-specific ability to re(ad)dress the wrongs of white feminist practice.

Africana Womanism: Reclaiming Ourselves, by Clenora Hudson-Weems, offers the first critique of Walker's womanism as it attempts to radically reconfigure the concept. Defined as "an ideology created and designed for all women of African descent," Africana womanism, as Hudson-Weems depicts it, is in full retreat from white feminism, and simultaneously rejects "black feminism, African feminism, [and] Walker's womanism." Hudson-Weems's charge of racism brought up against white feminists is familiar but no less vehement. Indeed, she forecloses all discussion on the subject based on the notion that white women's racist attitudes are immutable. This perspective underlies her critique of black and African feminisms which, she argues, are ideologically doomed by association with white feminism, summed up as "a sort of inverted White patriarchy, with the White feminist now in command and on top." Walker's brand of womanism does not fare any better. Its flaw, according to Hudson-Weems, is in its single-minded focus on "the woman, her sexuality, and her culture," a clear marker of its kinship with white feminism. Africana Womanism, therefore, aims to promote a woman's project on grounds totally unaffiliated with Euro-American feminism and unannexed to black and African feminisms.

Hudson-Weems's womanism may help to explain why prominent black feminist critics have distanced themselves from Walker's womanist theory. Hudson-Weems openly expresses a separatist ideology that Walker only suggests. But, McDowell, Carby, and bell hooks, among others, firmly reject a separatist black feminist enterprise, direct or implicit. These critics are acutely aware of the racist ideologies underlining mainstream feminist praxis and have dueled fiercely with the practitioners. Yet they do not see a sustainable strategy in a separatist or essentialist paradigm of black female subjectivity such as embodied in womanism. Though Carby, for instance, makes no mention of the term in *Reconstructing Womanhood,* it is nonetheless implied in her critique of black feminist critics' "reliance on a common, or shared, experience" for the construction of theory. Similarly, McDowell's warning that a "separatist position" could bring black feminist criticism perilously close to the paralyzing zone of "critical absolutism" both anticipates and undermines the womanist idea. bell hooks's disaffinity with the term, however, is somewhat ambiguous. While she questions its "commitment to struggle and change" and condemns its use as a sundering tool, she puts the blame for its misappropriation not on Walker but on womanist enthusiasts instead: "I hear black women academics laying claim to the term 'womanist' while rejecting 'feminist.' I do not think Alice Walker intended this term to deflect from feminist commitment."

hooks's exoneration of Walker from womanist politics of division reveals a key dilemma "mainstream" black feminist critics face regarding womanism. Refusing on the one hand to indulge its essentialist appetite, they are, on the other, loath to kick up dust around the subject in a way that might offset the healthy respect Walker commands within both black and white feminist circles. In two chapters in *Yearning,* for example, hooks conducts an astute critique of "the constricting notion of blackness" without any mention of womanism. And in a third, she cites the much-rebuked Black Arts Movement as the prototypically essentialist aesthetic in an effort to make her case against being critically "prescriptive"; once again, the more recent example of Walker's womanism is conspicuously absent.

Between the celebratory notes of pro-womanist advocates and the discourse of silence produced by major black feminist critics, then, there is room for a judicious critique capable of evoking at once the formidable and fragile character of womanist theory. Walker's womanism compels analysis if the full import of its cryptic content is to be realized. This content, as I indicated earlier, embodies simultaneously a critique of white (Euro-American) feminist sensibilities and the privileging of an oppositional (black and Third World) womanist consciousness. My objective in this book is to bring the discussion of womanism to a threshold of comparative textual analysis to allow for an expansive view that both supports and challenges the values and assumptions underlying Walker's disagreement with white feminist praxis.

Each of Walker's three core womanist claims—audaciousness, woman- and community-centeredness—finds support in the exigencies of life lived outside the privileged aegis of whiteness and maleness. The first of these—rebellious, audacious behavior—is a rich, self-affirming psychological resource that facilitates survival advantage in the social pecking order. African American women's culture, to cite the example most familiar to Walker, is a highly developed resistance zone infused with womanist directives. Pivotal among these is "womanish" behavior, a gesture of defiance with which the black woman-child responds to the unequal distribution of power in society. As a means of overstepping boundaries in familiar, often familial, settings, womanist audacity becomes in the wider social context an unbidden demolisher of arrogant authority. Paule Marshall's girl-heroine, Selina Boyce, in *Brown Girl, Brownstones,* Toni Morrison's rebel-heroine, Sula, and the consummate heroine, Sojourner Truth, for example, capture this unmistakable quality that runs through black womanhood. Its evocation by Walker within feminism serves to distinguish black feminists' many-sided offensive against patriarchal proscription from their white counterparts' single-minded focus on gender inequality. For Walker, the white feminist bulwark against sexual oppression falls short of the intrepidity that compels the womanist to turn over every stone in the complicated masonry of power relations.

Woman-centeredness, the second key womanist principle, seems at first not only to contravene the unity-seeking ideological position embodied in the third core element of womanism but also to overlook the pro-woman imperatives that constitute white women's prolonged history of sexual politics. It is more likely, however, that Walker brackets a woman-centered unconscious in an effort to direct attention to the construction of black womanhood, a process that configures black female identity as a site of both self-empowerment and affiliation. "Only the BLACK WOMAN can say 'when and where I enter, in the quiet, undisputed dignity of any womanhood . . . then and there the whole Negro race enters with me,' " Anna Julia Cooper agonistically declares in *A Voice from the South.* The idea is reiterated in *Tomorrow's Tomorrow,* even though Joyce Ladner downplays the indomitable image of the black woman: "In many ways the Black woman is the 'carrier of culture' because it has been she who epitomized what it meant to be Black, oppressed and yet given some small opportunity to negotiate the different demands which the society placed upon all Black people." Both statements subsume the distinct cultural space inherent in black women's experience and the sensibilities forged therein. If womanists "prefer women's culture, women's emotional flexibility . . . and women's strength" (*Gardens,* xi), it is because female self-love, like Sojourner Truth's, or Selina's, or Sula's, is a bastion against the cruel fact of hegemonic dominance. Woman-centeredness mirrors to the womanist the fragmented world around her and the need to seek connection.

Thus, the third core womanist tenet posits what I call "whole(some)-ness," a sense of emotional connection between self and Other that reverses the effects of long-term social divisions. The bonding impulse has historically been a powerful determinant in the health of the black body politic. From a painful history of physical and psychic disjuncture has emerged the phenomenon Michael Awkward describes as "Black culture's insistence on unity, even in the face of powerfully divisive opposition." The ideology of black unity throws into necessary relief the incompatible psychic duality memorialized in W. E. B. DuBois's characterization of black identity: "One ever feels his two-ness—an American, a Negro; two souls, two thoughts; two unreconciled strivings, two warring ideals into one dark body, whose dogged strength alone keeps it from being torn asunder." The countervailing pull toward whole(some)ness thus dramatizes the desire to heal a body politic riven by the corrosive forces of history.

Frantz Fanon, in his assessment of racially specific investments, traced the concept of "two-ness" to its colonial roots: "The colonial world is a Manichaen world. It is not enough for the settler to delimit physically . . . the place of the native. As if to show the totalitarian character of colonial exploitation the settler paints the native as a sort of quintessence of evil." To return to "the sphere of psycho-affective equilibrium" involves, for Fanon, an "attach[ment] . . . to a cultural matrix" and, inevitably, the manifest desire for individual and collective wholeness. The return, I believe, is also gendered, paving the way for male-driven nationalistic impulses and female expressions of a broader humanism.

The latter assertion is grounded in the historical facts of black and Third World women's protracted struggle against multiple forms of oppression and barriers to self-growth. "The hearts of Afro-American women," Fannie Barrier Williams declared, "are too warm and too large for race hatred. Long suffering has so chastened them that they are developing a special sense of sympathy for all who suffer and fail of justice." Anna Julia Cooper, another speaker before the World's Congress of Representative Women in 1893, underscored the importance of Williams's statement by exhorting her white female audience to adopt a politics of inclusion: "The cause of freedom is not the cause of race or a sect, a party or a class,—it is the cause of human kind, the very birthright of humanity." And, in an unmistakably critical tone, she warned that woman's cause is not won until her "wrongs are . . . indissolubly linked with all undefended woe." Marie Stewart paved the way both literally and thematically for these nineteenth-century political and literary activists. Recognized as the first black female public speaker, Stewart issued a clarion call for racial unity in anticipation of a multiracial union between her people and the rest of humanity: "I am of a strong opinion, that the day on which we unite, heart and soul . . . that day the hissing and reproach among the nations of the earth against us will cease."

More recently, Bessie Head, artist-guide of southern Africa, lent her deeply spiritual voice to the theme of a common humanity, Walker's third characteristic of womanism. Reflecting on the "attitudes of love and reverence to people" that govern her art, she admitted to appropriating "the word God . . . to deflect people's attention into offering to each other what they offer to an unseen Being in the sky. Where people are holy to each other, war will end, human suffering will end." Visionary, brooding, and alone, Head took refuge in her secular religion of human love.

Clearly, Walker's womanist worldview has a strong grounding in historical and cultural facts which in turn have had a determining effect on black female subjectivity. Less clear, however, is whether womanism can absorb the shocks of an equally strong essentialist undertow. Walker's univocal black/ Third World female subject partakes in the same universalist logic that surfeited its white, Anglo-American counterpart, and if the analogy seems overdrawn, one need only recall the wave of anger over the exclusionary practices of white feminist theorists and critics that crested with the search for alternative visions of womanhood and female creativity. Happily, this search has led to the present state of competing feminisms, thwarting any effort to privilege a particular brand of femininity. Deracializing black feminist thought, however, has proved difficult, probably because pariah memory dies hard. In the peroration to her "talking" book, *The Coupling Convention,* Ann duCille speaks eloquently and unequivocally to the race question in African American literary practice:

> For all our rhetoric about race as socially constructed rather than biologically determined, much of our critical and cultural theory still treats race as natural and transhistorical. To a large extent contemporary tradition building and canon construction are rooted in reified notions of culture as based on race, encapsulated in race. Other imperatives of identity formation, including gender, often become excess baggage not only in the invention of an African American literary tradition but also in the development of a black feminist canon based on the belief in an essential, definitively black female experience and language.

One of my objectives is to identify womanism as a major strand in this essentialist pattern of "identity formation." Walker's race-based womanist theory, I will argue, ignores the fluid and shifting nature of subjectivity, a fact conducive to crossings between such demarcated borders as black/white, male/female, womanism/feminism. Ironically, it is a fact with which Walker is all-too-familiar. In her foreword to Agnes Smedley's novel, *Daughter of Earth,* Walker concedes the fluidity of the female subject when she claims that Smedley, "poor, white, nearly slave-class in the 'free' 'democratic' United States where all whites at least are alleged to have an equal chance at 'making it'—connects herself . . . to all people of her class and vision, regardless of color or sex."

And while Walker has never failed to demonstrate her racial and cultural difference from Virginia Woolf and Flannery O'Connor (two white women writers she holds in high esteem), she is ever conscious of the ties that bind them. Her avowed affinity to Woolf and O'Connor underscores the prescriptive nature of the womanist project. Indeed, it is no coincidence that until *The Color Purple,* as chapter 3 in this study will demonstrate, Walker herself is situated outside the womanist dispensation. Her coming-into-womanism testifies to the fact that black/Third World womanhood is complicated and various, neither the monolithic bogey of early Western feminist discourse nor the coherent subject of womanist construction.

Poststructuralist disdain for essentialism, however, should not blind us to the fact that womanist theory registers a critique of white feminist literary practice and offers a model of resistance against hegemonic domination. Walker's assertion that "womanist is to feminist as purple is to lavender" strikes a theme that disturbs conventional thinking about racial gender and therefore warrants as much scrutiny as her racially essentialist claim. Positing womanism as a problematic, therefore, I intend to simultaneously affirm and interrogate its premises via a close reading of selected texts by white and black feminist writers: *Mrs. Dalloway, The Middle Ground, The Color Purple,* and *The Joys of Motherhood,* respectively. Rather than representing a simple oppositional division between feminist and womanist praxis, these texts offer an opportunity to verify womanist claims and at the same time to reveal their excesses. The first two texts typify, in my view, the kind of bourgeois, liberal feminism which, given its "tendency to overemphasize the importance of individual freedom over that of the common good," not to mention its reification of masculinity, is clearly the target of womanist critique. In Virginia Woolf's *Mrs. Dalloway* I identify a pattern of ambiguous iconoclasm that militates against womanist ideals. My reading of Woolf's sexual, racial, and class politics reveals an ensemble of attitudes symptomatic of the privileged position from which, as womanist critique suggests, the white liberal feminist launches her attack against patriarchy. I note here a complex interplay between Woolf's critique of British patriarchy and her own investment within the dominant ideological economy.

Walker's deep admiration of Woolf provides an incentive for determining whether Woolf was capable of realizing womanism's revolutionary potential. To this end I conduct a womanist reading of *Mrs. Dalloway* that reveals Woolf to be both animated and enervated by the exigencies of her birth, her culture, and her time, an attitude that yielded contradictory messages of resistance and acquiescence.

In chapter 2 the ground shifts from Woolf's modernist disease with the social system to Margaret Drabble's naturalistic portrayal of female victimization in *The Middle Ground.* I identify in this novel a bio-deterministic model of female identity that runs counter to womanism's emancipating ethos. One of the most prolific and successful writers in England today, Drabble bridges the ground between Woolf and Walker, sharing with the former a common cultural and feminist tradition (not to mention the great tradition according to F. R. Leavis) and with the latter the cultural and feminist ferment of these times.

Chapter 3 examines Walker's painful preparation in womanist philosophy, culminating in the epiphanic achievement of *The Color Purple.* The novel, I submit, is a true watershed of the author's (r)evolutionary womanist aesthetic. Its combative call for individual and collective freedom from the constraints of gender, race, class, sexuality, and nationality reverberates with the insistence of an old-time religion. The text's audacity fascinates as much as its message, calling into question, in the preceding texts. This chapter also delineates the cruel ordeal of Walker's womanist awakening, a cathartic experience replete with suggestion for (white) feminist re-vision. The last chapter considers *The Joys of Motherhood* by Buchi Emecheta, a novel that challenges the idea of an intrinsically black womanist identity. Emecheta fits well within the intertextual framework of my argument, given her links and disaffinities with the other authors of this study. Race and culture set her apart from Woolf and Drabble but for over thirty years now England has been home to her, too, a concrete indication of affinity with these writers.

Shared racial, gender, and feminist identities between Walker and Emecheta should make for, according to Walker's hypothesis, a shared womanist sensibility. My reading of Emecheta's novel in chapter 4 points up evidence to the contrary, thereby revealing the essentialist flaw in womanism's central premise. The race-restrictive womanist idea further founders on its own expectations with the revelation of resonant links between and among these writers.

An interpretive method, like mine, that holds white women writers to black/Third World women's standards points to an entirely new zone of critical discourse fraught with possibility for improved relations within feminism. If indeed difference has displaced sisterhood in the grammar of identity politics, then, as Minrose Gwin advises, "it seems important that we as black and white women together not only examine how we read and write biracial female experience, but that we understand how we are read as others in literature, in critical and theoretical conversation, and in life—by other women." Gwin rightly acknowledges that "black women have been doing [this] for centuries," while "white women are just beginning to learn how to do [so]." Enter womanism, its chief virtue being its capacity to mirror to white feminist critics and writers images of the white female subject as Other. The big promise of womanism, therefore, is its function as a trope of otherness, and my reading of difference through womanist eyes is, ultimately, the primary purpose of this book.

Finally, the term aesthetics, as deployed here, denotes the politics of representation rather than the linguistic experimentation generally associated with Stephane Mallarme, Oscar Wilde, or Virginia Woolf.

Suggested Readings with Similar Theme:

Ogunyemi, Chikwenye Okonjo. "Womanism: The Dynamics of the Contemporary Black Female Novel in English." *Signs* 11 (Autumn 1985): 63–80.

Williams, Sherley A. "Some Implications of Womanist Theory." In *Reading Black, Reading Feminist,* edited by Henry Louis Gates Jr. New York: Meridian Books, 1990.

Collins, Patricia Hill. "Defining Black Feminist Thought." In *Black Feminist Thought: Knowledge, Consciousness and the Politics of Empowerment.* New York: Routledge, 1990.

MTUME YA SALAAM

The Aesthetics of Rap (1995)

Music enthusiast Mtume ya Salaam declares his purpose is to provide "a level of under-
standing {about the aesthetics of rap music} usually not available through television
programs or mainstream magazine articles." When defining "good" art, he includes rap
music, calling it, in addition, a distinguishable art form. How does Salaam support his
position? Identify how on the whole "commerce masquerading as art" tactics and "busi-
ness first" attitudes threaten further development of rap music and the quality of its art
form. Salaam writes, "For rap music to develop any further, the artists themselves must
accept the responsibility to create and record with artistic quality as their primary
motivation." What other responsibilities are charged to rap artists? As foreseen by
Salaam, what will be the responsibilities of rap artists in the new millennium? What
will be the function of rap music? How does Salaam enter discussions with Lott about
the pop culture audience and what it has been conditioned to want? Define the follow-
ing terms: lyrics, style, flow, originality, gangsta rap, syncopated chant, and hip-hop
culture.

After reading many articles supposedly concerning rap music—about the
social aspects of rap music, the criminal elements in rap music, the lawsuits
caused by rap music, sampling in rap music, gossip concerning rap musicians,
how other musicians feel about rap music, etc.—I realized that I had yet to
read about the music itself. In other words, I had not read about the "aesthetics" of rap, about the qualities which made particular examples of rap music
good music—not necessarily good rap music, but simply good music.

Good art is distinguished because it possesses at least one—and usually
more than one—attribute such as sincerity, originality, honesty, or creativity.
Good art is usually emotionally involving and/or thought-provoking. These, I
believe, are attributes that almost all "good" art shares. While many rap
records possess these attributes, far more do not. This is true with most art
forms, however. In general, unsuccessful artistic productions far outnumber
successful ones.

To discuss and critique any subject intelligently requires both adequate
knowledge of that subject and the ability to illustrate that knowledge. The
ability to distinguish, qualitatively, between good and bad rap music requires
sufficient knowledge about a variety of rap music, past and present, popular

and less well-known. The majority of articles regarding rap music are written by music critics, or—far too often—social or political personalities who are not knowledgeable enough to be involved in a serious discussion about rap music. Rap music, it seems, is not considered worthy of serious, learned discussion. To those who actually understand the music, though, rap is a true art form—as much so as jazz, classical, rhythm and blues, or rock 'n' roll.

Around 1989, there was a significant and negative change in the artistic direction of rap music. The major record labels began to see the commercial potential for rap music and began signing rapper after rapper without regard to artistic integrity or originality. The music, of course, suffered from this lack of selectivity.

Rap music was first recorded on independent labels, and the independents did not, in general, sign unoriginal or otherwise inferior artists because they had a much smaller margin for error than did the major labels. The indies needed virtually every record they released, if not to become a huge hit, at least to sell well enough not to cost them money. One way the independents could ensure this, in the early days of rap, was simply to sign and record the best rappers they could find. At the time, the audience for rap music was such that quality, hard-core (i.e., non-commercial) material was generally more successful than less artistically inclined material.

The second reason the indies avoided signing inferior rappers was that they depended on the quality of their artists' recordings to establish their overall reputation. Initially, a rap fan could buy any release from such independent rap labels as Sleeping Bag/Fresh, Def Jam, Cold Chilin', Tuff City, Tommy Boy, Next Plateau, or Profile and be assured of hearing a decent, if not always indispensable record. As a generalization, signing too many commercial or just plain bad rappers, by association, would slow the sales of all of that independent's releases, and so the general quality of recorded rap music in the early and mid-'80s remained high.

When the profit-oriented major labels entered the rap scene, however, this fertile breeding ground for good rappers disappeared. Not only did the majors sign many rappers whose skills weren't up to par, the big labels also lured many of the best rappers from the indies with contracts that the indies couldn't match. At the same time, many independents were bought out, either in whole or in part, by the majors. Unlike the smaller companies, the big record companies could afford to release record after record of commercially inclined music without regard to artistic integrity. This practice drastically slowed the artistic development of rap music.

Adhering to the business ethic of most major labels often stunts a musician's artistic—while encouraging his commercial—growth. Big labels see artists who take chances musically as risks, since chance-taking necessarily produces at least as many commercial failures as successes. No major label will knowingly encourage the possibility of commercial failure. Therefore, the majors want little to do with the experimentation necessary to create quality art. Why sign a potential, if not yet accomplished artist, the corporate way of thinking goes, when one can sign an entertainer—a person whose primary goal is monetary rather than artistic success?

This "business first" attitude has contributed to (some would say created) what has become the single biggest threat to the continued development of rap music as an art form—the preoccupation by many rappers with sex and violence. The explosion of sexually and violently explicit lyrics, and the subgenre such lyrics create (i.e., "gangsta" rap), occurred soon after the major labels got into the rap business. The major labels created an environment in which a rapper's main focus became money, not music, and what is the best way for a rapper to make money in a society in which sex and violence sell? To rap about sex and violence.

Not long ago, a rapper's skills and creativity dictated the direction of the music. The music didn't change, the environment changed. As the music grew more popular, it became open to mainstream influences. Other forms of American entertainment exemplify these influences. The number one movie in America is usually either a violent "shoot-em up" or a sex-filled "love" story or thriller. The best-seller list is usually dominated by the same type of material. The majority of rap artists today are simply doing the same thing that mainstream movie stars, popular music stars, and novelists have been doing for years—giving the people what they have been conditioned to "want."

Most rap artists who flourished in the early and mid-'80s (all of whom recorded for independent labels—for example, Run-D.M.C., Mantronix, Ultramagnetic M.C.'s, and , a little later, Eric B. & Rakim) rarely, if ever, depended on sexually explicit or violent lyrics to succeed commercially, although such lyrics sometimes appeared in rap before the advent of the major labels' influence. Artists such as Schoolly-D, Too Short, Ice-T, and N.W.A. all started out on independent labels, and all included sexually or violently explicit lyrics on their recordings. The difference between the above rappers and today's scores of "gangsta" rappers, however, is that the earlier rappers were also original and inventive. There was a level of creativity in the earlier rap music that is lacking in almost all of today's "gangsta" rap recordings. The vast majority of today's "gangsta" rappers are, at the systemic urging of record companies big and small, simply copying copies— repeating and rerepeating the same tired words and themes heard countless times before.

I do not mean to imply that there is anything necessarily bad about art that is sexually or violently explicit. What is bad is commerce masquerading as art. It is unfortunate that in our profit-driven society, entertainers are almost always more visible and influential than artists. Nevertheless, if one is to judge an art form accurately, one must judge the form as created by the artist, not by the all-too-prevalent entertainer.

For rap music to develop any further, the artists themselves must accept the responsibility to create and record with artistic quality as their primary motivation. No amount of outside coercion or legislation can or will "cure" rap music.

That said, I will use the rest of this article to attempt to introduce rap music as an art form. I will not discuss any further, except incidentally, rap music's politics, culture, or preoccupation with violence and misogyny. I think that these issues have been discussed more than enough in the rap forum. I see them as serious and pervasive social problems, not as problems unique to, or predicated by, this particular form of music. I hope that this article provides a level of understanding usually not available through television programs or mainstream magazine articles. I also hope to dispel some myths and clarify some misunderstandings.

Lyrics/Style/Flow/Sound

Because rap music tends to be so unapologetically direct and personal, the great rappers almost without exception write their own lyrics. (This is also the reason very few rappers cover each other's songs.) The word lyrics, when used by rap fans, refers both to the subject matter and the written construction of the song. Critics of rap must consider the same elements commonly found in good poetry—simile, metaphor, and alliteration as well as creative expression, originality, and conveyance of emotion.

Style refers both to the tonal quality in a rapper's vocals and to the level of originality in presentation and delivery. Rakim raps in a near seamless monotone that serves to emphasize his lyrics. Run's style is very dynamic and emotional—his lyrics depend on the intensity of his delivery for their full effect. L. L. Cool J's style is a balance between the two extremes—at times aggressive and unrelenting, emphasizing delivery, and, at other times, measured and deliberate, emphasizing his lyrics. Although styles vary widely among great rappers, all share the common element of originality.

Flow describes a rapper's sense of rhythm and timing. The concept of flow differentiates rap music from other music with spoken lyrics (like, for example, the music of Gil Scott-Heron, The Last Poets, or even Cab Calloway). Rap lyrics are delivered in a rhythmic cadence, not simply recited or melodically half-sung. The quality of the rhythmic delivery is what defines flow. A rapper with good lyrics and style who can't flow is like a singer with a good voice and a well-written song who ignores the melody. When a rapper flows, the lyrics blend into a continuous melodic line like the flow of notes from a jazz soloist's horn. Not surprisingly, this element of rap music is what most inspires frequent comparisons to jazz.

All of the great rappers, like all of the great singers/instrumentalists in other genres, have an intangible sound that distinguishes them from other rappers. Like a fingerprint, this individual sound helps any knowledgeable rap fan identify the better rappers the instant they hear a rapper's vocals. What makes this possible is the concept of "sound"—an artist's non-quantifiable, identifying characteristics.

THE BEGINNING

Rap music, unlike disco or funk, is a new genre unto itself. Disco and funk were variations of an already existing, and therefore familiar, form—rhythm & blues. Rap music, in its purest form, presents an entirely new sound. This is one of the reasons rap music tends to be so misunderstood not only by the general public, but also by "accomplished" music critics—it is completely unfamiliar.

It is important to keep in mind that this phenomenon is by no means unique. Jazz met with an uncannily similar reaction in its infancy. In the early 1900s, jazz was often described as base, vulgar, and devoid of artistic or intellectual relevance. John Coltrane, a man now regarded by many as the preeminent jazz artist of his time, was routinely criticized as being "anti-music." Similarly, early R&B was described as "jungle music"—non-intellectual, discordant noise capable of "corrupting" the masses of unsuspecting American youth. Blues, jazz, and rock 'n' roll were all at one time considered unfit for "polite" or "decent" people.

Rap music is part of a continuum—the latest in a line of new musics created primarily by Black Americans. It has been subject to the same attacks that blues, jazz, and rock 'n' roll have been subject to. Following the same route, rap music has already developed from a regional, underground occurrence to a genre that, while mainstream, is as yet unaccepted by most except for the young and the "hip." By the end of this decade, though, rap will simply be another part of popular American music, neither reviled nor revered. Whether or not this is a good thing for the music, in an artistic sense, remains to be seen.

Rap music, in its essential form, is composed of programmed rhythm and syncopated chant—i.e., drum and voice—beats and rhymes. There is a de-emphasis, often to the point of exclusion, of harmony and melody. To the uninitiated ear, especially one accustomed to the catchy pop songs of mainstream entertainers, this emphasis of rhythm and de-emphasis of melody and harmony can be disconcerting, to say the least. Since most rap music also uses some form of often-difficult-to-decipher vernacular of slang, it is easy to see why the appeal of rap music eludes most listeners who haven't either grown up listening to it or haven't investigated, in a non-prejudicial and informed manner, exactly what this music form has to offer.

In the early and mid-'70s, in New York and most other major American cities, the predominant popular Black musics were funk and disco. However, the younger generation was, consistent with historical precedent, looking for something which reflected their reality more accurately than the pop records of the time.

In many popular records, short bridge-like segments brought the rhythm of the song to the forefront, using the bass and drums while the melodic instruments and the singer(s) sat out. At parties, this "break" was the most affective part of the record—the part of the record the dancers waited and saved their best moves for. Early New York hip-hop D.J.'s began to search funk, soul, disco, and any other records they could get their hands on for the best "breaks." Then, using two turntables and a stereo mixer, the D.J.s would extend and combine the few bars customary on the recordings into new creations that would last as long as the D.J. wanted.

Though none of the existing written accounts of the early years of rap is considered definitive, the men most commonly credited for the earliest developments in rap were Clive "Kool Herc" Campbell, Joseph "Grandmaster Flash" Saddler, and Afrika Bambaataa.

The vocal element was gradually added to these "break beat" creations. Kool Herc, for example, began to use a friend of his, who went by the name of Coke La Rock, as a vocal sideman. Coke would act as the "master of ceremonies," introducing Herc and providing vocals to improve the show and entertain the dancers. Hence, the title M.C. that many rappers still use as part of their stage names.

According to rap legend, Grandmaster Flash was responsible for pushing the vocal aspect further by enlisting a few of his friends to do more complicated vocal rhymes over the break music. He and his rappers—Melle Mel, Cowboy, Kid Creole, Scorpio, and Rahiem—eventually became Grandmaster Flash and The Furious Five, one of the most important of the old-school rap groups.

Soon many others began to concentrate on the vocal, M.C. side of this new form rather than on the instrumental, D.J. side. As the music developed, the M.C.s became more and more influential. The raps became increasingly complex as these artists worked at and developed their craft. What began as simply an extra device to add excitement to the show eventually became the essence of the form.

This artistic exploration and growth went relatively unnoticed by mainstream America, outside of the hipper circles of the New York City club scene, until the release of "Rapper's Delight" (Sugar Hill Records, 1979) by The Sugar Hill Gang—a quickly assembled New Jersey trio of rappers named after their record label. The record was essentially a series of catchy sing-song rhymes delivered over a break from a popular disco song of the period, "Good Times." "Rapper's Delight" was a huge hit but, perhaps not incidentally, considering its huge popularity, did not accurately portray the music that was being created in the Bronx and the other boroughs of New York City at the time.

Most of the underground rappers in New York, while no doubt impressed with the unprecedented commercial success of the New Jersey trio, were unimpressed with the lightweight disco vibe of the record. Though "Rapper's Delight" may not have been a towering success artistically, the record eventually sold over an estimated 2 million copies worldwide and is considered a very important release because it introduced most of the world to rap music.

A second early rap record that achieved great commercial success was "The Message" by Grandmaster Flash and the Furious Five (Sugar Hill Records, 1982). Though this record is generally considered to be better, from an artistic point of view, than "Rapper's Delight," it still did not quite capture the intensity of the existing, non-recorded form of the music. The instrumentation was provided by the Sugar Hill house band and sounded fairly similar to the pop/R&B of the day. Lyrically, the record was a moving narrative which chronicled various tales of urban despair. The record's general tone and phrasing, though, did not differ much from contemporary R&B songs which illustrated the same situations.

Rap music, for myself and many others, started in 1983. Until that point a localized underground of artistic expression and growth—a separate culture called hip-hop—went unrecognized outside of New York. "Hip-hop" culture in the late '70s and early '80s included not only rap music, but graffiti art and break-dancing in equal parts of the whole.

In the early '80s most of hip-hop's lyrics were similar to previous non-hip-hop, spoken/"talk-sung" novelty pop hits. Musically, many of the hip-hop records used breaks from other records rather than unique compositions. (A situation that in recent years has ironically come full circle with sampling.) Some records, like the aforementioned "Rapper's Delight," were simply rapped lyrics over an instrumental version of a popular song of the time. Though there was a strong emphasis on rhythm, recorded hip-hop had not yet evolved into its post-'83 "beats and rhymes" structure. This was the context into which two young men from Hollis, Queens, New York released their debut album; the young men called themselves Run-D.M.C. and their debut changed the face of hip-hop. . . .

THE PERIODS OF RAP'S DEVELOPMENT

There have been at least four distinct periods in the development of rap music so far. The first period—when the early hip-hop D.J.s perfected their craft in parks and house parties—is the hardest to pinpoint, in terms of both exact time period and primary influential forces. The earliest innovators, by definition, were not consciously creating a genre, and a lack of documentation and reference is therefore to be expected. This period lasted from the early '70s to 1979, when The Sugar Hill Gang released "Rapper's Delight."

During the second period, often referred to by rap fans as "The Old School," hip-hop/rap recordings began to be released through independent record labels in and around the New York area. Though the different elements of hip-hop culture—graffiti art, break-dancing, and rap music—would begin to surface in various areas around America, and overseas in various European countries and Japan, the creative forces of hip-hop culture were still coming primarily from its birthplace, New York. This period lasted from 1979 until 1983, when Run-D.M.C. released their debut album *Run-D.M.C.*

The third period, the period that has proved to be the most creative and progressive in rap music so far, lasted from 1983 to approximately 1989. Almost all of the albums that are now considered classics were released during this period. Also during this period, rappers from outside of New York began to gain in popularity and influence, including Schoolly D in Philadelphia, N.W.A. in Los Angeles, and Too Short in Oakland. This was also a time when the music industry and pop music fans in general began to realize not only that rap music was not a fad, but that rap had begun to command considerable influence outside of the genre itself. Run-D.M.C., Eric B. & Rakim, and L. L. Cool J were all at the height of their artistic powers during this era.

The fourth and current period began after 1989, when the major labels' overt commercial concerns and the taste and "morals" (or lack thereof) of the general public began to shape the creative climate of the rap music world. Sales have become the overriding consideration, not an artist's recording solely, or at least primarily, for the sake of creative expression and/or communication. Even those artists who have attempted to remain true to their creative impulses have been routinely faced with artistic compromise in order to succeed commercially.

In 1993 and since then, there has been a noticeable increase in the number of quality rap albums. . . . I hope that this recent increase in quality is not a fluke but a sign that at least some rap artists are becoming more aware of the negative effects commercialization has had on the music. Perhaps we are entering a new and more artistically challenging period for rap music in which the artists will take more responsibility for moving away from exploitative, explicit lyrics and toward more creative and true expression and communication.

Suggested Readings with Similar Theme:

Baker, Houston A., Jr. "Hybridity, the Rap Race, and Pedagogy for the 1990s." *Black Music Research Journal* 11 (Fall 1991): 217–28.

Gladney, Marvin. "The Black Arts Movement and Hip Hop." *African American Review* 29, no. 2 (Summer 1995): 291–301.

An Interview with Cornelius Eady (1995)

Veteran poet Ethelbert Miller asks contemporary poet Cornelius Eady to discuss voice, gender, and vision in his poetry and in the poetry of other contemporary African American writers. According to Eady, what is the significant reason black contemporary poetry should not be regarded as having a single voice? What is the responsibility of the contemporary African American poet to himself? Are there ways that the African American poet might give back to his/her community? Who should judge contemporary African American poetry? How does Eady enter discussions with Terry McMillan, Alexs Pate, and Larry Neal about the African American literary aesthetic? As readers approach a new millennium, how might poets approach the genre in cyberspace?

EM: My first question is taken from the title of one of your poems in *The Gathering of My Name*: why do so few blacks study creative writing?
CE: I don't know if you remember this, Ethelbert, but I lifted the title of that poem from you, or at least from the title of a panel you chaired a few years ago at an AWP conference that was held in Philadelphia. Some of the answers the panel gave were obvious—that writing doesn't make enough money for most students to take a chance on writing as a career, and so on—but your question made me consider other answers. I was teaching at Sarah Lawrence College at the time, and I thought of the feelings of some of the black writing students I had in my workshops. They didn't always feel comfortable writing about certain details of their lives. Very often other students attacked their poems, questioned whether or not it was actually poetic to say what they were trying to say. Very often, as I'm sure you know, when you're in the position of being the only minority faculty member in a department, you find yourself becoming the reality check for the minority students—you know, "is what I'm feeling what I think it is, or am I imagining it?" Sometimes it isn't—and sometimes it is. So the poem arises out of those particulars. It is another way of addressing the issue of cultural ownership of language. You'd be surprised at how many people on both sides of this issue still perceive creative writing as something that is written by and for the white, upper middle class. A lot of black students, fairly or not, take a look at how creative writing is still for the most part taught, printed, and rewarded in this country and conclude it has nothing to do with them, and if they put themselves into that kind of situation, they will hear what they've heard in one form or other for

most of their lives, so why bother? So part of the answer to that question I feel, is that there ought to be a place where writers of color will feel safe to explore certain areas of their lives without the question of whether or not it's "real" poetry. My wife and I are on vacation in Italy with Toi Derricotte and her husband, and we've spent some of our time working out the details of a summer workshop/retreat for black poets, that hopefully, will be held in the second week of July, 1996. We have a working title for the workshop, "Cave Canum" and a possible location in the Hudson Valley in New York State.

EM: In Rebecca Carroll's book *Swing Low* you mentioned the need to expand the definition of "what an African American writer is and what an African American writer can write about." Is there a unique African American voice in literature? How does this voice differ from other black writers around the world?

CE: What I think books like *Swing Low* and *Afrekete* prove is that thinking of African American authors—male and female—as having a single voice is one of the biggest errors you can make. I mean, look at the writers in *Swing Low.* Sixteen black guys bound together by history and culture, but sixteen different ways of writing and thinking about what it means and how to put it on the page. As black writers, we've been aware of this all along, and it's slowly, finally, beginning to seep in to the larger writing and publishing community.

I think that what I was trying to say is that I'm a writer, and though my basic experience is that of an African American male living in the late Twentieth Century, and though that fact will often inform much of what I do, I'm also an American, a New Yorker, a husband, a son, a jazz fan, a musician, a college professor, a friend. Not everything I think or fear or dream is going to be exclusively black, and I reserve the right of bringing these other concerns into my writing when I choose—the same right other writers take as a given. I respect who I am and where I come from, but I think one of the worst things about how racism works, one of the horrible things it does is that it allows other people, black and white, to try and define who you are, how you should think, how you're supposed to talk, how you're supposed to interact with the rest of the world. It can become the right of someone you don't know, and who really doesn't want to know you—and I resist that. I don't think I stop being a black poet or person when I choose to write about a guy dusting off his shoes on a fire escape, or a mouse running across the floor in the Museum of Modern Art. I certainly don't slip from a "black" sensibility to a "white" one in order to write those poems. They simply come from my experience. I argue that these poems are both American and African American—part of our historical legacy, and part of what I think is unique in our writing. Our duality. It's there, so why not acknowledge it, mess with it, use it? While I think we share many similar themes with other black writers in the world, especially the colonial writers, we have the misfortune of being pulled away from knowing our full history, our past, and the mixed blessing of ending up here, where so many others arrived with the notion of trying to reinvent themselves. I would say in general that the main difference between African American writing and other black writing around the world is the difference between the promise in our constitution, and the reality we struggle with daily, both black and white. And when I talk of expanding the definition of African American writing, I suppose I'm talking about pushing that boundary so that it includes areas which haven't been touched, or were left under-explored in that story. I think that's one of the things I was up to in *You Don't Miss Your Water.* My hope was to show my father not as either a villain or an icon, something that I feel is standard operating procedure when writing about black males, but as a complex and contradictory human being. As someone who was the end result of a process.

EM: Do you read a lot of poetry by other black writers? How does the work of these writers influence your own?

CE: Yes, I certainly do read a lot of black poetry. One of the great pleasures I have living in New York is going to the Strand bookstore on E. 12th Street and Broadway and rescuing any volume of black poetry I find there on the shelf. Given the poor distribution most poetry books get in general, and black poetry books in particular, it is sometimes the only way I know that a black author has a new book out, like Michael S. Weaver's *Stations in a Dream* or Alvin Aubert's *If Winter Come.* I also get to meet a lot of younger writers via the Strand, like Darryl Holmes' *Wings Will Not Be Broken,* or Saundra Sharp's *Typing In The Dark.* Right now I'm reading *The Collected Poems of Langston Hughes* for a possible review/essay. Thank God for the Strand! I probably never would have otherwise run into poets like Patricia Smith, or kept up with Tim Seibles. I certainly draw strength from all of their books. I don't think their work influences me as much as it gives me permission to keep doing what I do. No one likes to feel they're writing in a desert, and though New York City isn't exactly a cultural backwater, if I had to depend solely on retail bookstores for my Aframerican poetry books, I'd have died of thirst and hunger a long time ago.

EM: In your poem "Gratitude" you write: "I have lived/in and against my blood." This statement seems to echo W. E. B. DuBois's concept of double consciousness. Could you comment on this point?

EC: I think that line in "Gratitude" is pretty much self-explanatory, especially if you're familiar with DuBois' work. Marilyn Waniek has written an excellent essay on this topic, I think, called "Owning the Masters" that was published in the spring, 1995 issue of *The Gettysburg Review,* if anyone is interested in knowing how it feels to be a black writer pressured by two cultural "traditions."

EM: When did you develop an interest in the blues?

EC: As a listener, in my early teens. Leadbelly was probably the first blues musician I spent any amount of time with, then Bessie Smith when Columbia re-released her work in the early 70's. And of course, there's Son House, the great delta blues singer and slide guitarist who spent his retirement years in my home town of Rochester, New York. I was friends with Michael Fairchild, who now works with the Jimi Hendrix estate. He's the guy who wrote all of the booklets in the CD's of the recent Hendrix re-release series on MCA. Somehow, Michael found out that Son House was still alive, and living only a few blocks away from us. So we all got together and threw him a birthday party. Michael writes about it in one of his booklets. But it wasn't until I was at The University of Alabama at Tuscaloosa, as a Coal/Royalty chair, that I began to think of the blues as literature. I believe it began to hit as I was reading the lyric sheet that came with the CD release of Robert Johnson's complete recording sessions. Take a look at an old English ballad, then read some of Johnson's lyrics. They're both beautiful, spooky, metaphorically rich work about human issues; love, death, betrayal, the after-life, passion, faith, desire. They both use dialects and they scan pretty much the same. So why, I began to wonder, is one considered part of the root of great western thought, and not the other? I believe there's more than one tradition in American poetry, and though the root, the best of the blues is African, its language is filtered partly through the west, and because of that I consider it as much fair game as Matthew Arnold.

EM: Many of your poems celebrate the male blues singer and not the female one. Is that correct? Please elaborate.

CE: Boy, there's a loaded question! That isn't correct. I didn't consciously choose male singers over female. I simply wrote a series of poems on blues singers, male and female, over a period of time, and kept the ones I felt worked. Like any group of poems I write, but since you brought the subject up, if we weren't conducting this interview via the mail, I'd ask you to quick, count all the poems you've read in a published book or literary magazine that celebrate the lives and contributions of African American males in the last ten years that weren't written by a black male? Or how about this: I'm taping a show on Black Entertainment Television that's supposedly a celebration of Black male poets, when the host (a black woman), turns to me and the other guests, and says in effect, "I'm afraid of Black Men. What can we do about this?" And in the awkward silence which followed, every kind, dull, God-fearing dutiful black male I've ever known vanishes. Or how about just before the taping of the show, when I mention the name of Yusef Komunyakaa as a possible guest, and I get a blank stare from the production assistant? You know—Yusef Komunyakaa? the first black American-born male poet to win the Pulitzer? and I wonder how that news could get past him if he works on a TV show about black writers, and he knows about Rita Dove? So could there be a deeper motivation for those poems about black male singers? I do feel that in societal and literary terms we—I mean American black males—are in the process of being reduced to the most dangerous and narrow sort of fictions, of losing what the poet Patricia Spear Jones would call that last bit of control over our lives: the shaping of our own narratives. Which is not what I'm seeing in the recent spate of Black Women's fiction and poetry. I know a lot about how a certain type of black woman character feels and how she views the world, and I'm grateful for that insight, but what do we know about the story of any black male recently that hasn't been shaped by talk shows or local tabloid news programs, or just plain old stupidity? So perhaps subconsciously those poems were a way of trying to keep those guys visible, a reflex against what I perceive as a gathering silence. Or perhaps another way to respond is to say that if we actually live in a time when it can be considered odd, even suspicious for a black male poet to want to write poems about other black males from time to time, then God help us, it really is over, Kaput.

EM: Are some poems (and feelings) beyond the blues? I think of a Jewish writer trying to create in the years following the Holocaust; or today's AIDS victims searching for words and a language that will embrace their condition. **CE:** I'm not sure if I fully understand the point of your question, since I'm not in the business of trying to pit one type of suffering against another. If you're thinking of the narrow, 12-bar, aba structure, that's one thing, but the language within the blues is a nation within a nation. It has great scope, since, to me, it isn't about broadcasting the fact that one feels bad. The blues is more about uttering the things that can't be said about one's life in any other way. It's the how, why, and wherefore of the condition or situation the singer is in, while acknowledging or "signifying" to the listener the larger outside culture. I'm going to tell you a story, but you know it anyway. Like all good literature, the blues appears to be simple but it speaks to complicated, many layered concerns. I mean, let me give you an example by listing at random the titles of a few songs sung by Bessie Smith: "Careless Love Blues," "I Ain't Goin' Play No Second Fiddle," "Them 'Has Been' Blues," "I want Ev'ry Bit of It," "Money Blues," "Lost Your Head Blues." If you put them together, you'll get not only the lyrics, but the fabric and subtext of the world the lyrics come from: what the folks on that block think: their belief systems, (spiritual and worldly), what they eat, how they talk, what they wear, how the men and women get along, all the little stories that you're not going to find in the official record. The telling (and re-telling) of one's story is a shout against silence. So could there be a blues about the world of a Jewish writer, after the holocaust, or AIDS victims trying to describe what's happening to them. Certainly, if the writer chose to use that language, because the signifier that informs Bessie Smith's reality informs both these hypothetical poets. There's a denial of their full existence that gives them a hurt that the world in general doesn't seem to want to hear about. Thinking it out, coming to grips with it, and then letting it out, usually in the presence of those who find themselves in the same boat with you, is why the blues, a lyrical revelation, always works. It is, in the end, a survivor's literature.

EM: In a number of your poems you depict African Americans unable to be accepted . . . race and color is the factor which separates people. Does this happen often to writers in the literary world?

CE: Yes it does, but trying to talk about it in any substantial way is risky, since it's an ugly topic, and nobody likes to think of the literary world as something that operates under the same assumptions as, say, the business world. We'd like to believe that as artists, we deal in the universal, and the one, true measure for any poet is the merit of their work. In theory it's a nice principle, but in reality we tend to overlook who controls the definition of merit. In her essay "Owning the Masters," Marilyn Waniek retells the story of what Wallace Stevens was reported to have said when he heard that Gwendolyn Brooks won the Pulitzer in 1950: "Why did they let the coon in?" You might think it just an unfortunate story from a less enlightened time but some forty years later, in that silly little article on American poetry that ran in the *New York Times* magazine, Carolyn Kizer reports that James Merrill told her when she suggested that Gwendolyn Brooks be considered for the first Tanning Prize from the Academy of American Poets. He said in effect: "She (Brooks) would make an interesting choice. She's a distinguished poet, but we're looking to give the prize to a *master* and Gwendolyn Brooks isn't *quite a master,* don't you think?" (paraphrase and italics mine). What bothers me the most isn't that they finally gave the prize to W. S. Merwin, a fellow chancellor of the Academy, but the unsettling resonance between those two stories about the same poet, four decades apart; not quite a master, not quite real. The similarity between those two stories is chilling, if you dwell on it, if you'd like to believe that we've moved beyond that while no one would deny that something called African American poetry is alive, well and thriving; what those two stories indicate to me is that black American poetry has yet to fully sink in as a legitimate experience. It simply hasn't penetrated the consciousness and marrow of a lot of editors, MFA programs, publishers, book jobbers and review panels who still have a great deal to say about how poetry is considered and disseminated in this country. These things are always tough for me to write about because for all the good intentions and hard work from various quarters, both black and white, these things persist. For example, I would hate to believe that many readers drew pleasure from Fred Chapell being allowed, in the *Georgia Review,* to use the words "lazy" and "slovenly" to describe my line breaks in his review of my book *The Gathering of My Name,* or a reference to prophylactics to describe Yusef Komunykaa's poetic sensibility in *Poetry's* review of his book *Magic City.* I know of a number of black poets who know to keep their poems away from certain "quality" markets the way they know to stay out of certain neighborhoods. While I'm focusing my remarks on Gwendolyn Brooks, I could just as easily have written about you, or Toi Derricotte or any number of Aframerican poets who not only share the difficulties of traversing the page, the same as any writer, but very often find that they have the distraction of explaining and/or defending the results of their vision to all comers. I don't agree that race and color are the only factors which separate people. When it comes to racial issues in America, nobody's hands are clean, but if you want to talk about race as it relates to the literary world, you also have to talk about power and class, and it's hard sometimes to make the observation that the control of ideas and language, the so-called "debate" going on right now about "tradition," is just as political as the control of capital or the issue of redlining neighborhoods. For me, the struggle is less about line breaks and forms than it is about power and status, who gets to wield it, and who gets to keep it. . . .

EM: Are there any great themes American writers should be attempting to write about today?
CE: Well, of course I think one big theme is the issue of race in this country. The argument goes that you can't write poems about this subject without it becoming didactic, but I really believe that's a cop out. We're twenty-five to thirty years past the end of the Black Arts Movement, the boogie man most critics have at the back of their minds when they make those statements, and though we make a great deal of noise about the examined life, it's a place we've had yet to fully explore poetically. To give you an example of what I'm getting at, Toi Derricotte has been struggling for about ten years on a manuscript called "The Black Notebooks," that, when finally completed and published, is going to break a great deal of silence about how we live with race in this country, and what deals we all make to accommodate it. "The Black Notebooks" is a pioneer book, a work that takes us places we haven't touched before in verse. The parts of the manuscript that I've read prove you can take anger, even brutal subject matter, and re-work it into moments so clear and revelatory that we as readers are not only forced to consider who we are and how we operate, but to re-think what's possible in a poem. Toi Derricotte's manuscript suggests that there's a new world to be examined, if one has the guts and the language to go there.

EM: How will the new technology and things such as cyberspace shape the poetry of tomorrow?
CE: Two summers ago, I was a typist. Computers were exotic and suspicious. Now I fax and E-mail with the best of them. A few weeks ago, I tapped into the University of Buffalo's poetry site on the net. There's all sorts of debate going on, as well as a few electronic chapbooks on line. There's a ton of lively talk, writers are meeting writers, information is being traded, and I can't believe that it's bad news for American poetry. On the other hand, I don't feel, even with all the bedazzling potential around us, that things have settled

down enough to see if this is a change in the way we think of audience, if we have reached the point where readers of poetry are ready to let go of the tactile. Poetry, more than any other writing, is an intimate art, and I still think there's something about the proof of a text in one's hands that beats reading it on a lit screen. At least for those of us who didn't grow up in a world where computers were always present.

EM: Can creative writing be taught online?
CE: I don't know, bro' . . . can good interviews be conducted via fax?

Suggested Reading with Similar Theme:

Evans, Mari. "Contemporary Poetry, A Personal Essay." In *African American Literature: Voices in a Tradition,* 643–49. Orlando, Fla.: Harcourt Brace, 1992.

TRUDIER HARRIS

Miss-Trained or Untrained?
Jackleg Critics and
African American Literature
(Or, Some of My Adventures in Academia)
(1995)

According to Harris, what are the prerequisites for anyone who wants to teach or write about African American literature? Why is it necessary for anyone who wishes to critique African American literature to understand the culture out of which the literature emerges? How does Harris define jackleg critics of African American literature? What have been the popular "points of entry" for such critics? How might academic administrators and developers of seminars and workshops help to produce competent teachers, critics, and scholars of African American literature? How has Harris pulled from the philosophers and theorists elsewhere in this book to ground her argument? Define the following terms and phrases: gushers, 1892ers, dabblers, cultural rape, and commodification of and exploitation of African American literature.

The history of education for black people in Alabama in the early twentieth century is a history of training schools. Even into the mid-twentieth century, it was not an unusual find to come across a "Pickens County Training School," a "Tuscaloosa County Training School," or any other county name with the phrase "training school" following it. Training schools were synonymous with "Negro" education; created in keeping with Booker T. Washington's philosophy of education—that is, teaching people to perform useful work—their primary objective was to prepare black people for acceptable jobs in society. Black students were "trained" or "learned" in a variety of practical jobs—farming, sewing, woodworking, and later, auto mechanics, electrical and plumbing repair. I emphasize the word "learned" because, in African American vernacular, it was frequently preferred to the word "taught." A student could say, then, that Dr. Boatright *learned* him how to put soles on shoes, or that Mrs. Johnson *learned* her how to make certain kinds of complicated stitches.

The general philosophy behind the establishment of training schools was that there was a place for black people in the society, and black administrators of sane vision, in the tradition of Dr. Bledsoe in Ralph Ellison's *Invisible Man,* would lead their people into the right paths they should follow. Training schools, therefore, were a double-edged sword. They certainly prepared their pupils for useful work, but they also prepared them to accept their assigned places in the larger society. Nonetheless, training schools were functional, and—in spite of political problems we may have with them—they served useful purposes in the society. They were the first steps to the schools that emphasized classical education (as in literature or fine arts), the preludes to any kind of postsecondary education black people may have received. Even when classical programs were introduced into training schools, they were still referred to as training schools. In my hometown of Tuscaloosa, Alabama, for example, the county training school existed until 1944, well after the principal and many of his faculty had earned masters degrees in various areas of classical education. And training programs in high schools as we know them today existed well into the 1970s and may still be available in some small, out-of-the way places in the South.

I use training schools as the point of departure for this presentation because *basic training* is frequently what I find missing among many so-called scholars of African American literature. **Please note.** This is **NOT** an indictment of non–African Americans studying African American literature, so if that is what you expected from this presentation, you will be sorely disappointed, for there are certainly many of them who have done it and done it well. We have one of those people, Julian Mason, in the room with us today; he has done yeoman work on the poetry of Phillis Wheatley. I think also of Robert Hemenway's biography of Zora Neale Hurston, of Fred Standley's work on James Baldwin, of the many volumes of William L. Andrews, and of the theorizing of Kimberly Benston. Such scholars give honor to the literature and the culture by immersing themselves *substantially* in the materials they need to write sensitively and intelligently about the literature. And since I'm going to talk about SOME of them, I should also emphasize that this is not an indictment of *all* graduate students, for many of them, African American and European American, are seriously, thoroughly engaged in the study of African American literature.

What I am more interested in is the lack of training that I see constantly in blacks, whites, and other folks who profess proficiency in the study of African American literature. This is especially true of a certain group of whites who use African American literary studies as the quick way to fame and fortune—or what they *perceive* to be the quick way to fame and fortune. They therefore locate a few "points of entry" into the literature, identify selected writers and works for focus, and ignore the bulk of the literature and the culture. There is a kind of intellectual dishonesty here, for these folks have little interest in black people and black culture. They are simply appropriating the literature as a means of quick academic capital, in what they perceive to be the going fad. What they do amounts in effect to cultural rape, to the commodification of and exploitation of African American literature—commodification by using it merely to advance their positions, exploitation in the lack of respect for the people, the history, the circumstances out of which the literature was produced. It's fashionable these days to list African American literature as a possible teaching area, and many unprepared academics are going with the fashion.

I lament the trend in which budding scholars and unindustrious senior scholars "discover" an African American work or an author and, like Columbus, announce it to the world. I lament the trend that has spawned a generation of "gushers" (my phrase for them) or "1892ers" (Claudia Tate's phrase for them). With little training and much audacity, these so-called scholars stand before conference audiences and classes spewing forth what they consider gems of wisdom; they are oblivious to the fact that older, less egotistical African American scholars wrote about those same ideas ten or twenty or thirty years ago.

The consequence is that we get a lot of *dabblers* in African American literature. And once the dabbling begins, it continues when these folk go off to teach courses in the area. Not long ago, I was invited to lecture in a college where professors in the English Department had assigned Toni Morrison's *Beloved* and other of her novels. My initial impressive response to that endeavor waned during the question and answer session following my discussion of *Beloved*. I learned that no one in the huge auditorium had ever heard of Margaret Garner, the enslaved black woman who partly inspired Morrison's novel. And I learned that few were familiar with, let alone having read, any of the major critical works or article length discussions of Morrison's work. Indeed, one of the students expressed surprise after the lecture that I had published a book on Morrison. Clearly the professor at least knew my work because I had received the invitation to lecture, so I hope I am correct in blaming the student for that oversight.

But the basic problem remains: these folks don't read. Or they don't read beyond the text or the author that has captured their attention. A woman came up to me recently and excitedly exclaimed about a topic she wanted to pursue in African American literature. She had just observed this pattern, she said, and she wanted to make that her next book project. She expected me to be as excited as she was. What she had not determined at that point—and did not seem particularly interested in determining—was that not only had I written on the topic, but one of my students had completed a masters thesis and subsequently a book project on the subject. Just because this woman had thought of the topic, she considered it original, and that seemed enough for her. In her lack of conducting even preliminary research, this person stood before me in all her 1892, gushing, discovery status, proud that she had come up with an idea that she assumed—in her arrogance, or stupidity, or refusal to read—that no one else had.

I remember an argument with a colleague of mine a few years ago. I had this **same** lament then about gushers and non-readers. There was a lot of

interest in African American literature, I said, but many people who were
interested were using scatter-gun or superficial approaches to the study of it.
They thereby focused on a few strands of hair on the contemporary head of the
tradition instead of looking to see if it had toes, feet, knees, five or six fingers
on each hand, and what kind of shape its trunk took. This colleague maintained that, as far as he was concerned, knowing the tradition wasn't necessary.
If he wanted to focus on Gloria Naylor's *The Women of Brewster Place,* then he
should be able to focus on that work. He didn't need to know about migration
as a theme in African American literature, or about the integral ways in which
black writers use language or music, or about church sisters and preachers, or
the significance of dreams in African American culture as well as in the literature. If he wanted to focus on the borders and boundaries in the novel, then he
need not know very much else about the literature. He could simply present
himself as an "expert" on that particular Naylor novel.

Other so-called scholars of the literature maintain that taking one course
is sufficient for them, so they do that, then ask how they can market themselves as specialists in African American literature, which is one area—at least
according to the October MLA Job List—where opportunities don't seem to
have dried up yet. When I encounter such nonsense, I am reminded—with a
mixture of pain and annoyance—of what a former male colleague of mine
told one of his female graduate students a few years ago. When she asked
about registering for courses in African American literature, he told her that
she might use her course time in better ways and spend her *spare* time reading
African American literature. Indeed, he said, reading African American literature is like reading popular magazines—perhaps *The New Yorker* or *Vanity
Fair.* Even when students express a desire to be trained properly, they thus
sometimes run into institutional obstacles. This professor undoubtedly
intended to imply that other courses were probably more exacting, would
indeed engage the student more intellectually than would those courses in
African American literature. Such students, then, end up taking the one
course and following it by reading—badly—on their own. The result is that
they subsequently go out and embarrass themselves and the institutions from
which they obtain their degrees, because they are ill prepared for the rigors of
scholarly inquiry about African American literature.

Like Deighton Boyce in Paule Marshall's *Brown Girl, Brownstones,* many
of these so-called scholars, ill advised or not, declare that they don't need the
foundational building blocks; they are smart enough to go right to the major
stuff. Deighton thus tells his daughter Selina that he doesn't need the first
manuals in his home study of accounting; he will wait for the later ones with
the good stuff in them. He has the same attitude toward playing the trumpet. Why bother with elementary detail, he exclaims. He says to Selina:

"I almost had it [the song] down, nuh. I tell you, I must have natural talent for
this thing [trumpet]. The book says you must have the scales down pat before

you start playing any song. Even the teacher say so. But I ain worrying with all that. I ain got time to be practicing no scales or learning those foolish little pieces the teacher give me. I looking to play real songs—and fast." (Marshall, *Brown Girl, Brownstones*, 84).

For our contemporary scholars, the "real songs" are the Toni Morrisons and the Alice Walkers; they won't bother with the Anna Julia Coopers or the Marita Bonners, the "scales" of the tradition. They, like their literary counterpart Deighton Boyce, simply end up being embarrassed. At the moment Deighton gathers an audience to hear him "play," he can only produce an ear-splitting noise on the trumpet.

At least Deighton has the decency to be embarrassed. Many of these scholars are not, because in their arrogance, they never surmise that anything is wrong. Consider a recent encounter of mine. I attended a conference at which a graduate student from a prominent research university made a presentation on the Norton critical edition of Jean Toomer's *Cane*, which was edited by Darwin T. Turner. I went to the session because I had focused on *Cane* in my dissertation, had taught it over the years, and wanted to see what an up-and-coming scholar had to say about it. This young white man spent twenty minutes focusing on three footnotes that Turner, or the editors at Norton, had decided to include in the text. Why, he asked, would Turner need a footnote for the word "nigger," say on p. 102, when the word had occurred earlier in the text, perhaps on p. 35, and Turner had not included a footnote there? Why, he further asked, would Turner include a footnote indicating that "mo" was really a shortened form of "more"? He was thoroughly surprised at a scholar of Turner's reputation, this young man went on, for having adhered to what he considered an erratic if not a stupid pattern of footnoting.

Several things struck me about the presentation, but two stand out in particular. If this young man thought focusing on Darwin Turner's footnotes was sufficient substance for scholarly inquiry, then why didn't he check Turner's correspondence with the publisher, or write to the publisher to see who had actually made the decisions about footnoting—that is, IF he considered this a sufficient line of scholarly inquiry (which I didn't)? Such a procedure might have yielded information about the amount of control—or not—that scholars have over volumes they edit, or information about the publisher's perception of the intended reading audience for the book, or what someone had decided that this edition needed in contrast to previous editions of *Cane,* or any number of other things. The young man might therefore have been able to put his own scholarly preparation on display by making a presentation that his listeners would have taken seriously. And the saddest commentary of all is that some of his listeners might not have known that they shouldn't have taken him seriously.

The second thing that struck me about this episode was how this upstart had the gall to beat up on Darwin Turner. If he had engaged Turner's *interpre-*

tations of *Cane* and disagreed with them, I would have found little reason for complaint. Instead, his intent was clearly one-upsmanship against a scholar who had done yeoman work in African American literary scholarship and beside whom this young man was a mere wart on the face of academia. For me, the issue was one of training. If the only thing this young man found worthy of commentary surrounding *Cane* was three footnotes, then he is not the kind of colleague I would like to have in my department. Curious about how he came from the school he did, I called up the one specialist in African American literature in the English department at that institution and asked if she knew this young man. She did not. She had certainly been there long enough for him to have crossed paths with her during the course of his graduate work, yet he had chosen the magazine-reading route in his approach to African American literature, and he had not done a particularly good job of that. His attempt to train himself amounted finally to *un*-training, for there was nothing useful in what he had to say.

In contrast to this focus on Toomer, black women writers usually draw the attention of these so-called scholars. In their solidified positions in the canon, certain African American women writers have particularly attracted the dabblers. For many of these so-called scholars, contemporary black women writers provide relief from the stale and dead or dying traditions to which most undergraduate and graduate students are exposed. When a doctoral or master's student tires of trying to find yet another thesis in Virginia Woolf's *To the Lighthouse,* he or she discovers that Toni Morrison's *Beloved* provides a wonderful area for fresh research. We can only hope that a thesis will move them slightly beyond the dabbling stage. Women's studies majors similarly turn to black women writers to freshen their long papers or projects, whether they focus on topics like the wonderful healing tradition that can be traced through most of these women writers, or whether they focus on the folklore, or the theme of otherworldliness, or something else. White males who haven't published in twenty years can all of a sudden discover Greek mythology in Toni Morrison's *Song of Solomon* and whip out an article on it. Or they can discover scapegoating rituals in Morrison's *The Bluest Eye* or in Alice Walker's *The Color Purple* and whip out a conference paper on that (I have been a listener to such presentations, especially at MLA). Black males who get tired of deaning or other administration can always go to conferences and malign Alice Walker or Gayl Jones for their depictions of black men, or defend themselves against the portraits of them that Gloria Naylor presents (I have similarly heard such presentations, particularly at the College Language Association annual convention).

You will notice that some of the same writers and titles keep popping up because, again, these are the strands of hair on the head of the literature. These are the popular "points of entry" for folks coming to the literature to begin their explorations. Beginning at these points is *not* the problem; *staying there is.*

The double-edged quality of the training school sword that I mentioned earlier could be smoothed out if that concept were applied in this context. Since the natural *place* for scholars of African American literature is indeed *in the academy,* training them to fit into that place would not be contradictory. Thus the political-racial-social conflict that was inherent in traditional training schools for black people would not be a part of contemporary endeavors to train scholars in carrying out their scholarly work in African American literature.

In contrast to the dabblers and the magazine readers, interesting dynamics also develop, as well, for those who do manage the one-course "training" in African American literature. They hit upon a work and a topic in the literature, and they keep going the rounds of conferences making the same or offering a similar presentation (remember the craze with the quilting imagery?). That's where the "jackleg" part of this discussion enters in. "Jackleg" was a name applied to itinerant preachers in African American history who did not have churches of their own; instead, they traveled a particular circuit, making the rounds and delivering sermons that did not have to be altered substantially because their audiences were always new—or so they assumed anyway. And if there was someone in the audience who had heard the sermon before, that person was not likely to offer any public denunciations. So jackleg preachers survived, you might say, mostly on the ignorant of their audiences. Those audiences wanted the sermon, but they could not always judge the freshness or the originality or the accuracy of what they were getting. The word "jackleg" therefore inherently carries connotations of incompetence or minimal competence.

The dabbling or fashionable approach to African American literature is also prevalent in the articles many of us are asked to review for journals. In a couple of cases recently when I was asked to review such articles, I was tempted to write really nasty letters to the editors of those journals. Both articles were barely passable in intellectual content, and they both dealt with ideas that had been long—and well—covered in African American literature; this was particularly the case in one of the instances. The author made her assertions as if no one had ever approached Toni Morrison's *The Bluest Eye* before she came to it. And I blame all of us in the academy for this trend. Many of us professors push graduate students to publish, and some of us are obviously not as diligent as we should be in reading their work carefully before we encourage them to mail it to a journal. And some of these professors are—again—themselves so uninformed about the literature that they have no basis on which to judge the quality of what their students produce.

So, has the time come for us to re-institute the concept of training schools, but expand them to graduate education? Should we resurrect Booker T. Washington here in the 1990s? Well, it is the centennial of his famous—or infamous—1895 Atlanta exposition speech, and he is much on the minds of scholars around the country (there have been many conferences on him, including a couple at Emory). Have we reached the point where we should require students to be trained beyond the catch-all approach that most universities are using nowadays? Should we insist that they study for two or three years under a couple of professors, then, transfer somewhere else and study under another couple of professors? Except for the transfer part, this idea is presumably basic to graduate programs we already have in place. But obviously someone is falling down on the job somewhere, something is going wrong, because the training is not being done adequately.

Perhaps it is time for us to re-institute the process of professional preparation that was prevalent earlier in this country. I remember reading about how Charles W. Chesnutt and other persons wanting to study law in the late 19th century went and figuratively sat at an established lawyer's feet until that person judged them competent enough to go out on their own. They thus "read the law" until they were judged to be competent enough to go out and *practice* the law. Recently I listened to the concert given in part by the Moon Family Band, a traditional music group from Huntsville, Alabama. They are fiddle and banjo players whose reputations extend around the country. The mother of the family recounted how a couple of guys from Oregon knocked on her father's door one night and explained that they had been told to come to Arlin Moon to learn how to make and play banjo. They had been told that he would take them in and teach them. Well, he was amenable to the idea and told them to come on in. The upshot of the story, Mrs. Moon recounted, was that they stayed for *four* years. Her father didn't mind, and when they left, one was a very good banjo player and the other one had learned the art of making banjos. Skills are skills, whether they are the kind we perform with our hands or with our mind. And it takes practice and long-time hard work to execute those skills.

If students are still being told, however, that there is a get-competent-quick scheme for the study of African American literature, we will continue to have the problems we currently have. And perhaps this issue boils down to one of respect—for the literature as well as for the people who devote their lives to carrying out the serious study of the literature. It would be erroneous to assume that, because there are so many job listings in African American literature this year, or any year, that that means a carte blanche acceptance of the work of the budding scholars. Many times, I'm afraid, it simply means that administrations have pacified a certain constituency or that English department chairs can now assert, "Oh well, that's covered. We don't have to think about that anymore." So the dabbling continues because the person isolated in that position of teaching the literature has no one to challenge him or her, no one to encourage them to grow, no one to really care about what they do. They thus go out to conferences and meet the real world and serious scholars of the literature and find themselves in some interpretive space that everyone else in the world has known about for ages.

Perhaps what the dabblers are unconsciously asserting is that they do not have the right, so to speak, to study the literature (their arrogance would suggest otherwise, but just for the sake of argument, let's suppose for a minute that they're saying they don't have the right to study the literature). Or that they lack the background or culture necessary for involved study. Those reasons may be the case, but I seriously doubt and resist them. What I resist is this pervasive notion that black professors and critics have some nebulous gestalt that enables them to understand African American texts infinitely better than their European American and other non-black colleagues. Presumably any of us who went through reputable graduate programs should have some acquaintance with analytical skills, and presumably non-black people in the U.S. have some acquaintance with African American culture. I say presumably because I obviously get surprised on this a lot. Certainly I as an African American professor of literature and folklore have been saturated with those scholarly traditions for almost twenty-five years. And certainly I grew up knowing Brer Rabbit stories that non-blacks may have read only in their adult lives, so that may give me some edge in knowing how those stories function within the culture and in discussion of that culture as manifested in the literature. But, and this is a big BUT, I did not grow up in England being saturated with the tradition of Shakespeare. Nor did I grow up in New England or Maryland being saturated with the traditions that shaped Hawthorne, Melville, and Poe. Yet, as a trained literature professor, I am as competent to discuss those authors and their works as I am to discuss the works of Ralph Ellison, Toni Morrison, and Alice Walker. Why can't non-black scholars, then, who have achieved a book-learning response to Ellison, Morrison, and Walker, become as competent to discuss them as I can become to discuss British and New England writers?

What I willingly face is that the numbers of black faculty who can be hired at any college or university in the United States will always be minimal. Does that mean you cut all courses out of the curriculum that deal with African American culture because European Americans don't have the necessary spiritual gestalt to teach them? Or the necessary desire to learn the tradition fully? If that's the way we feel, then we're in deep, deep trouble. Simple demographics tell us that the numbers of black students going to graduate school is dismal, and those going into the humanities is even more dismal. The majority of the doctoral students I train to do what I do are not black; yet, I want the work of black writers and critics to be discussed in detail in the twenty-first and twenty-second centuries and well beyond that. So I train willing disciples. I train people with good minds to do the work that I do. We never assert that only French people can teach French, or only British folks can teach English literature; in fact, we're still so colonized here in America that most of us teach in departments where a substantial number, if not most, of our requirements for the undergraduate major are in British literature. But we Americans of all stripes and colors happily continue to teach it. And we never assert that only scraggly bearded, linty pants, squinty-eyed, bespectacled, absent-minded people should teach mathematics. We measure such people on the basis of competence. In like fashion, we have to conclude that competent non-black people are going to be treating African American materials in their classrooms for a long time to come.

I mean, let's be serious. Publishers do not go in for money-losing ventures. And a quick check of any *Books in Print* will reveal that the numbers of volumes currently available by and about black people is probably at an all time high. Major publishers are not keeping those books in print because they expect only black professors to use the books. If you put all of us African Americans who teach the literature in the same place, we might fill up a good-sized gymnasium.

It is imperative, therefore, that we try to encourage the ill-prepared and those in the process of becoming prepared to teach and study African American literature to do both competently. No one group *owns* the literature, but African Americans may certainly feel an understandable affinity for the creations of authors within their group. I for one am perfectly willing to encourage people of all races and cultures to study African American literature, but those who would profess to present themselves as researchers and scholars of that tradition must be held accountable for the work they do. To do anything less is not only to embarrass the so-called scholars but to enslave the literature and make it as much captive in the 21st century as African American people were in the 18th century.

Suggested Readings with Similar Theme:

Ford, Nick Aaron. "Black Literature and the Problem of Evaluation." *College Education* 3, no 5 (February 1971): 536–47.

Turner, Darwin T. "The Teaching of Afro-American Literature." In *New Black Voices,* edited with an introduction and biographical notes by Abraham Chapman, 499–503. New York: New American Library, 1972.

McKay, Nellie Y. "Naming the Problem That Led to the Question 'Who Shall Teach African American Literature?' or, Are We Ready to Disband the Wheatley Court?" *PMLA* 113, no 3 (May 1998): 359–69.

JOAN FRY

An Interview with Octavia Butler (1997)

How does Butler define science fiction? What is its function? For whom does Butler write? Butler is the recipient of the prestigious MacArthur Fellowship. By way of what other prestigious awards has the African American science fiction writer been recognized?

How long have you been writing science fiction?

Since 1959, when I was 12, but people only began paying me for it well enough to support me since 1979.

I've heard you talk about the blue-collar jobs you held before you established yourself as a writer. You said that one of the few good things about them was that nobody required you to be pleasant.

Or to smile. That isn't my nature, so it was very nice to be just as grumpy as I felt, because I was getting up early in the morning and writing and then going to work, and the last few hours of the day I was pretty much on automatic. I remember working in a mailing house; I don't even know if those places still exist. They had both machines and people putting together pieces of mail for advertising. It was like an assembly line at a factory, only a little more complicated. You might be doing something with each piece of mail, not just putting them together. You did this over and over and over all day until your shoulders wanted to desert to another body. The only thing I could do to keep myself somewhere near conscious was to sing, very softly, to myself. I don't have the most wonderful singing voice, and the supervisor kept walking by giving me funny looks. Finally she came up and asked, "What are you doing? Talking to yourself?"

She must have thought you were losing it.

People did lose it. That's why I wrote "Crossover" [one of the stories in *Bloodchild*]. I was watching a woman who was clearly going crazy, and there was nothing anybody could do. She had to work at this horrible, boring job, and when she went home, she had to take care of her ailing mother. That was her life. I'm not sure very many people could have held on. "Crossover" is about a woman who works at a factory and is greeted one night by an ex-boyfriend just out of jail—except he's not really there.

What makes the story science fiction?
It's not.

Then what is your definition of science fiction?
Well, it's nice if you use a little science.

So science fiction doesn't necessarily mean space aliens and alternate universes.
It doesn't necessarily mean anything at all except that if you use science, you should use it correctly, and if you use your imagination to extend it beyond what we already know, you should do that intelligently. The reason I've stayed with science fiction to the degree that I have is because you can do almost anything in it. But you have to know about a subject before you can play with it, so I do my research first.

I've noticed that. You're very knowledgeable about a variety of subjects: medicine, biology, zoology. . . .
I'm not, really, but I know how to use the library. And I'm curious about those things anyway, so I'll read idea-producing magazines like *Scientific American* or *Discover* or *Natural History* or *Smithsonian* that tell me things I didn't know before and perhaps direct me to books I wasn't aware of.

Why did you start writing science fiction?
Because of a movie I saw when I was 12 called *Devil Girl From Mars*. I thought, "I can do a better story than that." Of course what I wrote was awful, but I didn't know it. I was having a good time. By the time I was 13 I was bothering editors with my stuff. One thing that contributed to my fascination with the universe in general was the time I spent on my grandmother's chicken ranch between Victorville and Barstow [in California's sparsely-settled high desert], and being able to look up and see the stars and realizing there are parts of the world that human beings don't dominate.

The book of yours most people seem to read first is *Kindred* [Doubleday, 1979]. Why is that?
It's accessible to people who normally don't read science fiction. *Parable of the Sower* [Four Walls Eight Windows, 1993] is another one. *Kindred* is the story of a black woman who unwillingly travels back in time to the antebellum South and has to fight like hell to survive slavery. She's a struggling writer, and before her trips begin, she and her husband are both holding jobs that I had actually held—food processing, clerical, warehouse, factory, cleaning, you name it.

How long did that period of your life last?

Ten years, from 1968 through 1978. After *Patternmaster* came out in 1976, I started working more sporadically, at temporary jobs. I didn't get an awful lot of money for that novel; I've gotten more money for the best of my short stories—but also, things cost a lot less then. The last job I held was in a hospital laundry. In August. Bad. And this was after I had written and sold three novels. When I got the money from the third, I was able to quit and go off to Maryland to research *Kindred*.

Who influenced you as a writer?

My all-time favorite writer is Frank Herbert, who wrote *Dune* [Chilton, 1965]. He wrote a lot of other books, too, and then he wrote a mainstream novel that let me know what to expect if I ever tried it. The jacket copy proclaimed, "His first serious novel." Theodore Sturgeon influenced me—he was a real craftsman. I probably liked *The Synthetic Man* [Pyramid, 1950], which was originally called *The Dreaming Jewels* [in subsequent reprints the book has reverted to its original title], and *More Than Human* [Galaxy, 1953], the best. The writers who influenced me most tended to be those who were the most prolific. John Brunner was very prolific—my favorites are *Polymath* [Ace, 1963], *The Whole Man* [Ballantine, 1964], and *The Long Result* [Faber and Faber, 1965]. Harlan Ellison was a major influence, particularly his short story collection *Dangerous Visions* [Doubleday, 1967]. As a kid, I also read a lot of Felix Sultan. I wasn't allowed to go to the movies, so whenever I heard about one that sounded interesting I would go to the library and check the book out. Sultan tended to write about animals as though they were human—more accurately, as though they were knowingly, although not always willingly, subject to humans. In *Bambi,* for instance, man is always referred to as "He," with a capital letter, as in "God."

And after *Kindred* you wrote *Wild Seed*. That's a book a year for five consecutive years. How did you manage to be so prolific?

I was like a lot of writers. I had all these ideas stored up I had been trying to write for years. Once I was able to actually finish a novel, the flood gates opened and I was able to finish the others, too.

You wrote the Patternist novels first, but you wrote them out of sequence—some are prequels to others, and so on. If someone wanted to read them chronologically, what's the order?

I wrote them completely out of order, yes. Chronologically, *Wild Seed* would be the first, then *Mind of My Mind, Clay's Art* [St. Martin's Press, 1983], *Survivor,* and *Patternmaster*.

What I enjoyed about the Patternist books, *Mind of My Mind* in particular, is what I also enjoyed about *Parable of the Sower* and your story

"Speech Sounds" [winner of the 1983 Hugo Award, one of science fiction's highest honors]; you show a disintegrating urban society—substance abuse, random violence, murder—that really isn't much different from what we see right now.

You're right, it's not that far from some of the problems we have. I tell in the afterword to "Speech Sounds" that we all have some kind of communication deficit that shuts us off from one another. So we wind up not understanding one another, and sometimes envying people who seem to understand each other better.

I was wondering if "Speech Sounds" had anything to do with your dyslexia?

Not at all, because dyslexia hasn't really prevented me from doing anything I've wanted to do, except drive. I can read, for example, but I can't read fast. I never had a problem reading because I was lucky enough to be taught before I got into school by my mother and grandmother.

I've noticed that you give talks and then usually have a question-and-answer period. You don't give readings.

No, I don't because I tend to read things that aren't there. I once volunteered as a reader at the Braille Institute. I felt that I'd been pretty lucky, and I wanted to give something back. So I thought, "At least I can do that." I didn't realize how badly I read aloud until I began reading to these unfortunate blind people who had to listen to me. One of them finally said, "What's the matter? You can see it, why are you doing that?"

Some critics claim you write speculative fiction and others claim you write science fiction. What's the difference?

I would say that speculative fiction is any kind of nonconventional fiction, from Borges to Isaac Asimov. But I don't make any distinction. Labels are something that people just absolutely require, and there's nothing I can do about it. As I've said before, I write about people who do extraordinary things. It just turned out that it was called science fiction.

Are there any other black women writing science fiction? Or do you prefer to be called African-American?

Oh, Lord—labels again! Either one is fine. No, I don't know of any. When Kris Neville was alive, his wife Lil Neville sometimes had a part in his writing—she's black and he was white—but they wrote only under his name.

What was the origin of your Xenogenesis trilogy? [Warner published Dawn in 1987, Adulthood Rites in 1988, and Imago in 1989.]

Well, I got the idea back in the early 1980s . . . from Ronald Reagan.

This I want to hear.

Early on in his administration he used to talk about "winnable nuclear wars" and "limited nuclear wars," and he had this lackey who ran around talking about how if we had a nuclear war you could save yourself if you dug a hole. After you dug the hole you put a door over it and threw dirt on the door and then got down in the hole. After the bombs were finished, you could come out again and again and start up life. I thought, "The American people put these idiots in positions of power—and they're going to kill us! If people actually fall for this crap, there must be something wrong with the people!"

So I set out to figure out what might be wrong with us. I put the problem into the mouths of my alien characters, the Oankali. To them, humans have two characteristics that do not work well together. People are intelligent—no problem, the Oankali were happy to see that—but also we are hierarchical. And since our hierarchical tendencies are older, they tend to focus and drive our intelligence. So I began the books after the end of a horrible nuclear war in which we've one-upped ourselves to death.

In *Dawn,* the first book of the trilogy, your female protagonist awakes to find herself the captive of the Oankali, a group of nonviolent genetic engineers. The woman, who's black, is named Lilith [according to Semitic folklore, Lilith was Adam's first wife] and she's instrumental in starting a new race of human-Oankali beings. I did note the significance of her name, but it made me wonder what other clues I'd missed.

When I write, there are always lots of levels. The first level is, here's an entertaining story; enjoy yourselves. And then there's whatever I put underneath. For instance, there's the young black man Lilith is introduced to by the Oankali. Lilith was an adult when the Oankali got her, but he grew up with the Oankali. Even though he's physically grown, he's never had a chance to learn to be the responsible man he might have become under other circumstances. His situation is, in a way, reminiscent of the survival characteristics that black people developed as a result of slavery, characteristics that were useful in slavery but detrimental later. It's hard to suppress ideas people have in their heads just because they're no longer appropriate, especially when it's a matter of mothers teaching their children. So some of the things that are really hard to talk about in the black community I talked about in *Dawn* and in *Mind of My Mind.* I have no idea who picks up on them and who doesn't. I think some of the academics do, because they expect you to do things like that.

Mind of My Mind is a very violent book—beatings, incest, murder. What exactly are you referring to?

The fact that you have Doro, who has kidnapped a bunch of people and bred them and used them, and after a while, when they're strong enough, they do nasty things to him. But they also do nasty things to everybody else, because they've learned that's how you behave if you want to survive.

Do you think that's another legacy from slavery?

I don't think that black people have made peace with ourselves, and I don't think white America has made any kind of peace with us. I don't think we really know how to make peace at this point.

That's one of the recurring themes in your books. All the humans, with very few exceptions, are capable of betraying one another. Put these individuals into groups and they're even worse.

That's why there's such a problem. And to tell the truth, even if we did know how to get along there would be problems. Even when people are the most absolutely homogeneous group you could think of, we create divisions and fight each other.

In your Xenogenesis books you don't hold out much hope for human civilization as we know it.

We do keep dragging each other back to various and sundry dark ages; we appear to be in the process of doing it again now. And when we're not doing that, we're exploiting our resources to such an extreme degree that they're going to disappear. On National Public Radio there was a woman who spent a number of years studying wolves that had migrated down from Canada into Glacier National Park. At one point she said something like, "If I were a wolf I'd stay in one place until I had used up the resources and then I would move on, but the wolves don't do that." And I thought, "Aha! The wolves have figured something out, at least on a biological level, that we still haven't!" In family bands, when humans lived that way, we didn't stay in one place until there was nothing left. We moved on. Right now it seems that people are being encouraged to see the environment as their enemy. Go out and kill it. If they're really unlucky, they will succeed.

According to the jacket copy on one of your books, your chosen themes are feminism and race.

No. Those are my audiences. My audiences are feminists, blacks, and science fiction readers, with some New Age people as well. There are mainstream readers, too, who don't fit into any of those categories, who read me just because they enjoy my work.

Another motif I've noticed is metamorphosis. In your Patternist books you call it "transition," but some of your Xenogenesis characters undergo similar changes.

We all go through them. I guess the most obvious metamorphosis is adolescence, and after that comes middle age. Adolescence can be an unpleasant metamorphosis. It's the only time I seriously considered suicide.

Another motif you return to is the ability to share another's pain.

In the Patternist books, it's actually being a telepath. People who come through transition are no longer feeling anything they don't want to feel, unless somebody stronger is inflicting it on them. The ones who are struck in transition—maybe they're stuck in a kind of adolescence—are the ones who don't live long because they're wide open, and they're suffering.

One last question about motifs—this one I noticed particularly in the Patternist books—is incest. Where did that come from?

I explain in the afterword to my story "Near of Kin" [one of the stories in *Bloodchild*] that when I was a kid, I was a very strict Baptist. I was raised to read the Bible, really read it, every day. And I noticed that a lot of these Old Testament types were marrying near relatives—Lot's daughters got him drunk and had sex and produced two whole new ethnic groups. I thought, "Wow—instead of getting struck by lightning, they get a reward. They get to be the mothers of whole new people!" I found it very intriguing. In fact I titled a section of *Wild Seed* "Lot's Daughters."

In *Survivor* you're very hard on traditional Christianity.

I wrote the first version of *Survivor* when I was 19 as a result of the rebellion I was feeling, breaking away from my upbringing and all that. The other day I was talking to some high school students, and a young woman with a very severe look on her face said, "Why do you call yourself a former Baptist?" And I thought, "Oh, my. Let's not corrupt the children." So I said, "Well, I belonged to a very strict Baptist sect. Dancing was a sin, going to the movies was a sin, wearing makeup was a sin, wearing your dresses too short was a sin—and 'too short' was definitely a matter of opinion with the ladies of the church. Just about everything that an adolescent would see as fun, especially the social behavior, was a sin. And I'm not talking about sleeping around. I finally reached a point where I really didn't believe I was going to get God mad at me if I danced."

Where do the philosophical ideas in *Parable of the Sower* come from?

From me, really, One nice thing about writing is that it forces you to look at your own beliefs. My character got her *Books of the Living* by my going through a lot of religious books and philosophical writings and stopping whenever I found myself in agreement or violent disagreement. Figuring out what I believed helped me figure out what she believed. And the answers began coming to me in verse. I needed the verses because I was having such trouble with the novel—trouble in the sense that I had problems with my main character being a power seeker, and trouble in the sense that I was slipping into rewriting my old stuff, which is what writers do after a certain point. Either you're a young writer and you're rewriting other people's work, or you're an old writer rewriting your own.

Which of your books has sold the best?

Kindred has been in constant circulation the longest. It was out of print for a while, but it went back into print before any of my others, and it's used in classes more than any other books. [Beacon Press reissued *Kindred* in 1988 as part of its Black Women Writers series; the book has been taught in college-level black history, black literature, women's studies, and science fiction courses.]

Why do you think mystery novels are increasingly being treated as serious literary fiction while science fiction is still relegated to genre status?

I had a friend at Cal State L.A.—I went there for a long time and collected a lot of units in different majors, but I didn't graduate—who would not read science fiction because it was trash. I tried to explain to her that science fiction wasn't all trash—it contained trash like anything else—and I mentioned a book that she liked, George Orwell's *1984*. I said, "That is classified as science fiction." She said, "It can't be science fiction. It was good!" Do you know Sturgeon's Law?

Theodore Sturgeon was a well-known science fiction writer. He's dead now, but supposedly he was on a panel at a science fiction convention once when somebody complained to him, "Ted, 90% of science fiction is shit." And, unfortunately, a lot of people have been trained to believe that science fiction is juvenile, and by the time they're 14 they should be beyond such stuff. Science fiction suffers from its reputation for trashiness and immaturity, which makes it easy for people to judge it by its worst element.

You're clearly concerned with specific social and environmental issues in your work. Is most science fiction escapist, or are there other writers doing what you do?

Oh, goodness, lots of them. Sure. Some write about the problems that I write about, and others write about other problems. Some look for technological solutions and other disparage technological solutions. Some think the world will go to hell and others think it will turn into ice cream. You have the same wide variety in science fiction that you have any place.

Suggested Reading with Similar Theme:

Beal, Frances M. "*Black Scholar* Interview with Octavia Butler: Black Women and the Science Fiction Genre." *Black Scholar* 17 (March/April 1986): 14–18.

DUANE FRANK

"Soul Food" Director Isn't Holding His Breath in *Milwaukee Journal Sentinel* (1997)

What makes the film "Soul Food" African American? What makes it universally appealing? Is Soul Food "a triumph of some greater good"? How does writer-director George Tillman enter discussions with Tommy Lott and bell hooks about images (of African Americans) in the mass media? What is the role of the director/artist? What is the responsibility of the audience? How do Tillman as movie director and August Wilson as stage director echo one another and differ with one another in their philosophical opinions of the African American on the screen and on the stage? Philosophically speaking, is Tillman an NBA writer/director?

Is "Soul Food" the sweet film about black family life by Milwaukee writer-director George Tillman Jr., the little movie that could? Will it change how studios think about black films and affect future releases? Or is it simply a good movie that will have a negligible impact?

The answer to all those questions probably is "yes."

It's tempting to see this modestly budgeted and inordinately successful family film as the triumph of some greater good in Hollywood, where films made for African-American audiences are usually filled with sex and violence.

But "Soul Food" proves two conventional theories: The more specific the tale, the more universal its appeal, and audiences know what they like when they see it.

The story, about a divided family made whole by a strong-willed matriarch and a high-cholesterol diet, cost $7.5 million and earned $20 million after its first two weekends in theaters. "The Peacemaker," with George Clooney, which was released the same day, has earned just over $20 million but cost about $50 million. This bottom-line equation may be the lasting legacy of "Soul Food."

"Hollywood is more concerned with dollars and cents," said Felix Curtis, curator of the Black Filmmakers Hall of Fame in Oakland, Calif. With the success of "Waiting to Exhale," a film that also rejected "stereotypical views of black life, I think they'll take a chance on other films in that genre now," Curtis said. "It's cyclical, but maybe they've turned the corner. Maybe they'll see these films can make money if the budget stays manageable."

Yet, he said, "I don't think it will start a trend. I think the public is still looking for action films."

Tillman is reacting with a similar mix of cautious optimism. Hollywood is paying attention to "Soul Food," he said, but change "will be slow."

"Things didn't change after 'Waiting to Exhale,' " he said of the 1995 film that raised similar expectations for black filmmaking. "But I think that as I continue to make films like that, other new filmmakers" will be allowed to similarly express themselves.

Still, said Tillman, all it takes to start a trend is one successful film. As an example, he cited the way John Singleton's "Boyz N the Hood," which inspired countless if lesser imitators.

Tillman, 27, said he wasn't influenced by Singleton, but by Barry Levinson's "Avalon."

"I showed it to my actors to give them an idea of the film that I wanted to make," Tillman said. "I wanted to do a nostalgic and epic film . . . about the legacy of a family."

Levinson has sent Tillman some scripts. The success of "Soul Food" has resulted in Tillman having discussions about directing a biography of Dorothy Dandridge with Whitney Houston and about directing a film starring Bette Midler.

But he is most interested in directing the life story of the first African-American Navy SEAL. Robert DeNiro and Bruce Willis have expressed interest in playing a role in the film, and Tillman would like to see Mekhi Phifer, who was in "Soul Food," as the lead character.

"I want to continue to do films that are entertaining and story-driven," Tillman said. "But it's got to speak to me. I've got a good sense of what the audience wants to see."

Mark Gramz, vice president of operations for Marcus Theater Corp., which is playing "Soul Food" at a number of theaters, said it was doing "extremely well." Local attendance has been heavier than the national average, he said, and the film could attract big crowds for another six to eight weeks before being eased out of theaters.

The film has attracted some racial crossover, he said.

"The usual audiences at our suburban theaters are predominantly white," Gramz said. However, he estimated that the "Soul Food" audience has been equally divided between black and white.

Tillman said such racial crossover means not only increased box office sales.

"The film speaks to people and leaves something with them at [the] end of the day."

CLAUDIA TATE

Introduction: Race and Psychoanalysis
in *Psychoanalysis and Black Novels,*
Desire and the Protocols of Race (1998)

What are some ways we might read black texts "that engage competing even contradic-
tory needs, demands and desire"? Examine Tate's position on theory/craft vs. politics.
How does the modern black text function like "a racially sensitive psychotherapist"?
Define the following terms and phrases: psychoanalysis, social pathology, biological
determinism, and a racially contextualized model of psychoanalysis.

When I mentioned to one prominent scholar of African American literature
that I was working on a book project that combined black textuality and psychoanalysis, the response was, "Why do you want to do that?" This reply
seemed to be a castigation of my inquiry. Didn't I know that psychoanalysis is
inappropriate and perhaps even detrimental to black agency? I realize that
psychoanalysis offers no clear and immediate path to greater freedom and justice of the sort that at least at one time appeared to be offered by demonstra-
tions, sit-ins, and legal battles. By no means am I suggesting that these
strategies do not work. Rather, I want to turn to literary culture to ask, how
do we read black texts that engage competing, even contradictory needs,
demands, and desire? My investigation suggests that while traditional activist
responses may offer relief from racial oppression, racist attitudes produce
unpredictable, irrational, and complicated effects. Psychoanalysis, I believe,
can help us to not only analyze black textuality but also effectively explain
important aspects of the deep psychological foundations of the destructive
attitudes and behaviors of racism.

But while psychoanalytic theory can help us analyze the social pathology
of racism, its practice has carried a lot of irritating baggage that has made it
virtually an anathema in the black intellectual community. Rather than simply denounce psychoanalysis or regard it as a metadiscourse, I try to understand its own compensatory defenses by questioning the cultural effects of its
Jewish origins in anti-Semitic Austria at the turn of the twentieth century.
Such origins have produced a psychoanalytic practice that silences its own
ideological history by presuming the culturally neutral family as its object of
investigation. This displacement is important because it designates the family

as primarily responsible for the tragic fates of real individuals who, for example, are like Bigger Thomas of Richard Wright's *Native Son* (1940) or Pecola Breedlove of Toni Morrison's *Bluest Eye* (1970).

By isolating the family from society—specifically its economic, political, and technological factors that condition the family—psychoanalytic practice has avoided examining the relationship of social oppression to family dysfunction and the blighted inner worlds of individuals. Instead of regarding individuals and their stories as products of a dialectic of material circumstances and their internalization of them, psychoanalysis, as it generally operates, centers the individual's primary nurturing environment, not the external circumstances that precondition that environment. As a result, psychoanalytic practice relegates the bleak material circumstances of real lives to the background and blames the dysfunction on personal or familial deficiency. No wonder scholars of African American literature and culture shun this model and instead endorse materialist analyses of black novels, for mainstream psychoanalysis effaces racism and recasts its effects as a personality disorder caused by familial rather than social pathology. Hence, there is hardly a leap between shifting the blame from the social trauma of chronic racism to pathologizing the black family, as the infamous Moynihan Report does.

Similar pathologizing was largely the fate of the white women's encounter with Freudian psychology until white feminists took on the project of rewriting Freudian discourse to expose its hidden ideological suppositions about gender. A similar venture on the part of scholars of African American culture can also expose the racialist ideology in psychoanalysis posing as objective findings. In fact, such a venture will reveal that many discourses of scientific "fact," in general, are neither absolute nor truisms but belief structures that reproduce the status quo of white master and black slave as well as male plenitude and female deficiency.

Feminist and gender studies have persistently and effectively undermined the reign of biological determinism in the construction of the Freudian gendered subject. By contrast, though, black critical theory has seldom engaged psychoanalysis, despite the theorists' various undertakings in other areas of structuralism and poststructuralism. With the recent intersection of postcolonial studies and psychoanalysis, though, particularly the revisionist studies of the works of Frantz Fanon, race has reappeared with a vengeance in discussions of psychoanalysis, much like the return of the repressed.

A racially contextualized model of psychoanalysis, I argue, can help us analyze black textuality by identifying the discourse of desire generating the text. Such a model, I suggest, can advance our understandings of racialized behavior in other social settings as well. By referring to psychoanalysis, I am not suggesting that black texts err when contextualizing their narratives with the material circumstances of racial oppression. But I am asking black literary criticism to consider the roles of the narrator and protagonist in constructing various racial dilemmas and also suggesting that we probe such conflicts within and beyond their attribution to race.

I pursue such meaning in this study by considering a black text as a partly self-conscious fantasy. This conceptual framework facilitates our speculating about the author's inscription of pleasure as well as pain in the text. While we cannot gain direct access to the inner world of authors, we can detect and analyze the traces of emotional meaning left behind in print. Ascertaining how this process works in black textuality can, I believe, provide a model for understanding how individuals transform the material circumstances of cultural experience into personal emotional and cognitive meaning. Given the persistence of racial oppression and the demand for black literature to identify and militate against it, the impulse to make the representation of such oppression the primary critical criterion for a black text is understandable. Under these circumstances, black literature evolves so as to prove that racism exists in the real world and is not a figment of the black imagination. As a result, the modern black text functions like a racially sensitive psychotherapist. To borrow the words of one, such works teach black readers to recognize "the parameters of the negative, racist and patriarchal boundaries which traditionally define [black people]" and to dare "to step outside of them" so as "to understand their own individuality, worth and ability [and] to utilize inner strengths in the service of growing and coping." While this type of instruction teaches black readers to project the neurosis and psychosis of racism outside of themselves, unremitting racial trauma demands an unending supply of stories about the black victims of white racism in order to teach new generations of black people how to recognize both gross and subtle racist assault as well as to foster understanding among new generations of whites. For as we might expect, black and white people have very different perspectives about "how prevalent or threatening racism may be." Yet racism is only one type of assault, and it too is complicated by—and hence either mitigated or exacerbated by—other forces of subjectivity.

By repeatedly inscribing the negative effects of racism on black characters, the modernist black text perpetuates fantasies of white power and black victimization that take on lives independent of the material circumstances of real black and white experiences. Consequently, we come to understand social privilege and disadvantage according to racial prescriptions. Other factors are silenced. While things "white" signify entitlement, liberty, and power, things "black" signify penalty, lack, and defect. Such racialized allotments of good and bad are omnipresent. According to another psychotherapist, blackness becomes for many "a focal point for projections of all that we find most unacceptable," while we unconsciously equate whites and whiteness with "safety, goodness and abundance."

What I want to do in this study is to recover from psychoanalysis what is useful for the work it can do to distinguish the workings of desire in black texts that are not direct expressions of racial alienation and to show how desire and race become mutually overdetermined in textual expressions. My objective, then, is not simply to use psychoanalysis to read the five novels; I also want to suggest that the novels can demonstrate how psychoanalysis has repressed race under the mask of gender in the family domain. While I frequently refer to this latter concern throughout this study, I give it the most attention in Chapter 4, on Larsen's *Quicksand.*

By making race and gender a part of the psychoanalytic literary project, I hope to encourage others to formulate new questions about the dialectical relationship between representations of desire and race in black texts, indeed in all kinds of social situations. Such questions will offer us opportunities, to borrow the words of Ralph Ellison, to probe "into the deepest psychological motives of the writer," while also examining the "external sociological factors operating within a given milieu." Such an exploration will suggest factors that not only clarify the creative impulses of writers but also condition the behavior of human subjects.

In an attempt to read the five novels at the center of my study as the products of their authors' interior and external world experiences, each chapter of this study presents a critical model that questions by contextualizing the presumption of the social neutrality of psychoanalysis with the material effects of a historicized black culture. Because these novels reflect the power dynamics of the period of their production, they inscribe complex psychological strategies for adapting to the disturbing effects of social oppression, and they reveal surplus content, as mentioned earlier. Because a black critical perspective has been sensitive only to the effects of racial oppression, the surplus content has generally remained blurred or buried. For this reason, like the five novels, I de-center racial oppression in order to locate this other content. My method does not mean that race is unimportant but simply that it is not the only site of conflict. Race is one important element of an individual's social character and personality. But there are others that are not so easily discerned.

In the chapter on Emma Kelley's *Megda* (1891), I explain why the feminist paradigm of gender inequity (associated with contemporary readings of Louisa May Alcott's *Little Women*) and the racial paradigm of social oppression (associated with Frances Harper's *Iola Leroy*) are inadequate for reading a work that evolves from a perplexing tangle of social positions—a historically black, woman-centered, evangelical cultural context that silences the discourses of race. I use psychoanalytic theory in the context of cultural studies to address weaknesses of both paradigms. In addition, I explain how this novel constructs an imaginary plenitude by using facsimiles of pre-oedipal and oedipal discourses to construct and resolve its narrative conflicts. I refer to these two psychoanalytic discourses because textual conflicts and their resolutions have a striking correspondence to the oedipal and pre-oedipal stages of subjective development.

Chapter 2, on William E. B. DuBois's second novel, *Dark Princess* (1928), also combines cultural criticism and Freudian/Lacanian psychoanalytic theories to call attention to this novel's implicit but nevertheless comprehensive plot about the lost mother that forms the novel's enigma. This plot energizes the novel's eroticism and propagandistic mission. Desire and propaganda not only organize *Dark Princess*; they also form persistent themes in DuBois's other writings, especially, I will explain, in his "Criteria of Negro Art" in the *Crisis* and his *Quest of the Silver Fleece*. The overdetermined relationship of desire and propaganda prompts me to ask under what conditions a personal fantasy can sustain a successful work of propaganda and indeed inspire the social activism that characterized DuBois's life and works.

In Chapter 3, on Richard Wright's *Savage Holiday,* I refer to object-relations theory to uncover a basic plot line of material betrayal and character splitting that appears throughout Wright's work, particularly *Black Boy* and *Native Son*. But in these more celebrated works this plot and this character technique are masked under the compulsive plots of interracial violence. I argue that *Savage Holiday* gratifies the unspeakable desire of matricide that Wright's other major works conceal. Disclosing the centrality of the matricidal desire in Wright's fictions also helps to clarify his narrative logic, which repeatedly produces rapid and often confusing transitions between heterosexual tension and racial hostility.

Chapter 4 examines the relationship between desire and death in Nella Larsen's *Quicksand*. Here I reread the protagonist's fate as not simply the demand of black bourgeois sexual repression but as the overdetermination of female fetishization, self-alienation, racism, and abandonment. Because *Quicksand,* like the other novels in this study, has been the object of traditional racialized and/or gendered readings that have routinely disregarded enigmatic content in the novel, it exemplifies the mediation of two often conflicting domains of meaning: the mimetic representation of social protest and the rhetorical performance of unconscious desire.

In Chapter 5, I argue that *Seraph on the Suwanee,* by Zora Neale Hurston, critiques the sadomasochistic tendencies of romantic love and the essentialized constructions of race by encoding these issues in a story about female self-discovery and romantic fulfillment. Seraph employs the mask of white privilege to depict these critiques and to explore stories of class and gender oppression that are denied to the black female protagonists Isis of *Jonah's Gourd Vine* and Janie of *Their Eyes Were Watching God*.

While it is my hope that these chapters provide provocative readings of the five novels and related canonical works, my engagement of psychoanalytic theory and African American literature is meant to demonstrate how black cultural studies and psychoanalytic criticism can help us to appreciate the covert and often latent content inscribed in writing (and other forms of expression) and thus to obtain a more thorough understanding of the role of desire in the creation of meaning.

Suggested Readings with Similar Theme:

Rampersad, Arnold. "Psychology and Afro American Biography." *Yale Review* 78 (August 1989): 1–18.

Tate, Claudia. "Desire and Death in *Quicksand* by Nella Larsen." *American Literary History* 7 (1995): 234–60.

———. "Freud and His 'Negro': Psychoanalysis as Ally and Enemy of African Americans." *Journal for the Psychoanalysis of Culture and Society* 1, no. 1 (Spring 1996): 53–62.

ALEXS PATE

Making Home in the New Millennium:
Reflections (1999)

How does Pate define the contemporary writer in the new millennium? According to the novelist, what is the function of contemporary African American literature? How does Pate's aesthetic position echo the positions of Wideman and McMillan? To whom must the contemporary writer be true—to his/her literary ancestors? To himself/herself? To his/her contemporary audience? What is truth? Does Pate's definition of truth differ from W. E. B Dubois's? From Langston Hughes's? From Petry's? From Neal's? From Morrison's? From Baldwin's? Discuss Pate's definition of individuality. In the writer's definition, how does he echo Locke and others (art for people's sake)? Or, does he espouse literature for art's sake? Or, literature for some new purpose?

I am in the process of constructing a home for myself. It is the thing I most need. Indeed whenever I sit down to write I engage the forces that exist within me that seek to locate, to affix myself, organically, holistically to some sense of home. That place where I am understood. Where my goodness is manifest. Where my rage is assuaged. But it has been a difficult journey. I am at peace so little of my waking life. Lately I have wondered whether perhaps I am somehow the culprit. Maybe I cause my own discomfort. I fear I am too enamored with struggle. Too ready and willing to fight some amorphous, all knowing power. The struggle. The struggle for which there is no end. And for me, no sense of security that I would associate as home.

I was taught to be this way as an African American man. As a black writer, I had to make my work about the convoluted struggle of black people to define themselves. Even a cursory review of African American literature presents this challenge. This is what it means to be a black writer.

Literature has always been a significant and essential component in the culture of African Americans. From the beginning, even during slavery, the act of writing, the creation of literature, has been one of political necessity. To tell the stories of the people. To build identity and strength. To forge community and fellowship. But perhaps one of the most important qualities of this expression is that the act of writing established our humanity. In a time when many people in this country really believed that black people were not human beings, the writings of early African Americans, Lucy Terry and Phillis Wheatley for example, offered "proof" that we could think and write. That we could create. Any discussion of black writing, even a discussion of craft must—to be historically valid—involve at least a tangential digression into ideas and politics.

I've been a writer for a lot of years. A lifetime of years. Through intense fears. Occasional tears. I started writing in earnest while in the Navy. But I was doing it even before then. In high school I wrote poetry. Heady soulless stuff. Driven only by my desire to impress. With words. I have always wanted people to look up and realize I had something to say. I have felt, since I began writing in earnest, that I was a part of a new breed of black writers. We cared about culture and community, but we were also trying to locate ourselves in this era of the new millennium. A context that is post-million man march. Connected to, perhaps created by Jean Toomer, Zora Neale Hurston, Toni Morrison, Alice Walker, James Baldwin, Richard Wright, John A. Williams, Ishmael Reed and so many others and yet something different. Post Post. Not necessarily better, but different; an extension.

African American literature must be in constant motion. It is like the blood of our culture. It must reach for possibilities not yet seen. It is the proof of our growth and our best hope for the future. This should be one of the functions of any "aesthetic." It must be capable of keeping the culture moving. But even as I absorbed that notion of the black aesthetic advanced during the seventies I found myself searching for a more fundamental rationalization for my work. A more personal kind of truth. A kind of truth that reflected my own particular struggle which is not above or significantly different from that of black folks in general. But it is not always found in the voices of those who speak of the responsibilities of black artists. They are often more concerned—perhaps understandably—with the external demands and consequences of white racism than personal, individual growth.

Thinking of this subject reminds me of an experience. I live in the newurban centerslice of Minneapolis/St. Paul, Minnesota. There are a surprising number of emerging African American artists here of all levels and genres. Still, to a black visitor from Chicago or New York, I occasionally detect a kind of superiority of knowledge based on the fact that they live in more densely black communities. As if everybody who lives in Minnesota was born there and never traveled anywhere. In fact, I grew up in North Philadelphia as my first two novels make clear. Recently I was asked to introduce a well-known poet and writer at a local function. I agreed because it was a tremendous opportunity to pay my respects to someone who has been such a pivotal force in the development of African American literature. I composed what I thought (hoped) was an unmitigated gush. We must pay our respects to people who blaze trails. Fight battles. Fall. Struggle. Who show us how its done. This is the job of each succeeding wave of artists. We must insure that the people who made it possible for us are properly remembered. Honored. It is one of the things that I feel passionate about.

I should mention that before I launched into my celebratory introduction, I myself was honored by a local literary organization for my service and in the process it was mentioned that I was currently enjoying "success" for having written *Amistad: The Novel* which was based on the screenplay of Michael Franzoni for the Debby Allen, Steven Spielberg film. At the time, my book was on the *New York Times's* bestseller's list. It was at the bottom of the list, but it was there and I was pretty happy. Despite the issues surrounding the film, I felt I had, within the constraints, provided a perspective that was needed to balance the film.

And then I proceeded to pay my deep and heartfelt respects to this significant cultural and literary icon. And what did he do? Well, from my perspective, the brother got up and totally dissed me. In my own town. He said, "Thank you brother Alexs for those remarks. And enjoy your success. It won't last long." I knew what he was saying. Past signifying. Gone long past that. He was saying that I could not be successful working for white people. But he had obviously never read *Losing Absalom* or *Finding Makeba.* He didn't know that publishing *Losing Absalom* made me feel successful. And nobody made a dime on that book. But it will always be my biggest success. Or reading at the Harlem Public Library. I felt very successful that day. Or any reading in which my mother and sister and brother are present. That's success. The rest is America. The rest is trying to be something to the outside world. He didn't know a damned thing about me. Certainly not enough to know what my literary urges were or what I really stood for.

And that is the point. Just when you think you've found home, you realize that you don't quite fit. I expected an open-armed welcome. What I got was chastisement, which is what the "movement" was best at.

It is time for the folks who stand guard before the doors of the black literary canon to recognize and appreciate the increased diversity that will be evident among the new black writers. Yet, we must guard against this momentary instinct of defining contemporary African American literature by its lowest common denominator. We'll all be dancing to Prince's "1999" at the dawn of the new millennium. And no matter how righteous, we must accept that there is more than one movement going on.

The fact of the matter is that the Black Arts Movement did not make us free. I think I understand why. But we struggle now in a way that many people in the 1960s would have had a hard time imagining. Or perhaps they did imagine it. Maybe that's why it settles on the landscape of history as a necessarily desperate movement. Albeit an unrequited one. The manifestations of our racist and race obsessed society has our community in absolute turmoil. In the 1970s the Black Arts Movement wanted to bring black folks together. Believed it could. But the 1980s cured that delusion. We are a fractured community now, our identities refracted through the myriad cuts in the glass. But perhaps even more frightening is the despair that is ambient around us. We have labored in the field of race matters for so long that many of us only know how to talk to white people (and when we do its usually a scream). Or we attack our own people for not being righteous enough.

The New Black Aesthetic must understand that racism is out there, that we live in the belly of the beast, but turn instead to the challenge of healing and making ourselves whole. We must tend to our own souls. Tell the truths about our selves for ourselves. This might be the responsibility of the black artist now or at least a major component of any black aesthetic in the new millennium. We must define and reveal ourselves as individuals who are part of a collective. Come from behind the masks we wear for white people. Remove the veil of the outlaw, the assimilated corporate manager, the dedicated administrator and reveal ourselves. To our children. Tell them who we really are. Talk to them about our dreams deferred. About our tears. And to make that manifest in an aesthetic metaphor I return to the notion of home. Or more precisely homes.

I am a builder of homes. Of people. Of moments. A novel is a house with many rooms. The architect is the poet, is the novelist. It is a noble profession, perhaps even sanctified. When I think of James Baldwin, Richard Wright, John Edgar Wideman, Langston Hughes, Zora Neale Hurston, Amiri Baraka, Charles Johnson, Lucille Clifton, Toni Morrison, Gloria Naylor, or Haki Madhubuti, I think of sanctified people. Called by the swirling energy of life itself to construct realities which breathe even after their time has passed. To read *Their Eyes Were Watching God* now, in 1999, is to be enshrouded in a vision and flow of life long gone from the marrow of my bones. And yet I somehow smell the sweet cane sugared air of Hurston's world. Or the grimy streets of Chester Himes's Harlem.

These writers and many many more shape the dreams of those who read them. The first thing any African American who wants to be a writer must understand is that you must be able to imagine your own success. Practice at it. Because quiet as it's kept, some of us have a terrible time with success. We know how to deal with defeat and pain. We've been there. Done that. Besides when it comes to art, black artists have always been suspicious of other black artists who are successful. The question looms, "How exactly did you manage that?" But success is something that we should embrace. It is, after all, our world. And yet, to experience that success, a developing writer will experience failures, barriers.

When I tell young writers that they have to be prepared for rejection and people ignoring you and long years of hard work and getting nothing in return (except the unexplainable joy of expression) I realize there is no way to adequately prepare for the challenge of becoming a novelist. But here are some ideas: A good novel has a fire burning in the hearth. You can always find warmth within it. Consequently, for my tastes, even a harsh satire like the one I am currently in the midst of, must have at least one fireplace (which the reader might never see or even know it exists). Every story must have heat. And windows so that the reader can see inside enough to know they would like to visit. And windows so that once inside there is always light. We must build sturdy walls so that the roof will be secure and we will be dry. And beautiful floors to walk on. The floor should creak a bit. And there should be both natural and artificial light. A wondrous kitchen is almost always necessary. For feasts and fights. The kitchen is the place we find ourselves. And a place for books. Even within a story other books have a place. Every board, every brick, every nail must be carefully, lovingly set. A good story must not come apart. And once written it should try to stand forever. Try to stand the onslaught of mindless critics who spend so much time earning a salary for major newspapers that they don't get a chance to write novels themselves and so resent anyone else who does in a way that is different from what they'd do. But of course they don't. This is quite a force to survive. But a good story will.

As the builder you must understand that every story is held together not by love and cooperation, but by strife and conflict. Every story is about trouble. No story can be successful without it. Every town is River City. And in every house, every family, every relationship is riddled with contradictions and secrets. If somehow these are exposed (which any good writer must do), they will result in conflict. Which means your story has a chance to engage us. Your house must be interesting enough to make us gasp. Laugh. Groan. The details once we look at it carefully might make us cry.

You must build what you know is the truth. And you must expect your readers to know the truth when they read it. Anything else will fall, no matter how much conflict or love exists within it. And, for my tastes, it should try to mean something. It should try to be more than confection. Something rich, respectful of the traditions which have given birth to it.

I am in the process of constructing a home for myself. It is the thing I most need.

African American Literary Criticism in Context

1773–1894   **Nature vs. Nurture**

1773   Rush, Benjamin. *An Address to the Inhabitants of the British Settlement in America, Upon Slave-Keeping*, 4. Philadelphia: John Dunlop.

————. *A Vindication of the Address: To the Inhabitants of the British Settlements, On the Slavery of the Negroes in America, In Answer to a Pamphlet entitled "Slavery Not Forbidden by Scripture; Or, a Defense of the West Indian Planters from the Aspersions thrown against them by the author of the Address By a Pennsylvanian*, 3. Philadelphia: John Dunlop.

Wheatley, Phillis. "On Imagination." In *The Collected Works of Phillis Wheatley*. Reprint, edited with an essay by John C. Shields, New York: Oxford University Press, 1988.

————. "To Mæcenas." In *The Collected Works of Phillis Wheatley*. Reprint, edited with an essay by John C. Shields, New York: Oxford University Press, 1988.

————. "To the Publick." In *Poems on Various Subjects, Religious and Moral*. London. Reprint, viii. Philadelphia: J. Crukshank, 1786.

1764   Kant, Immanuel. *Observations on the Feeling of the Beautiful and Sublime*, trans. John T. Goldthwait. Berkeley: University of California, 1960.

1782   Sancho, Ignatius. "Letter LVII." In *Letters of the Late Ignatius Sancho*. London: Nichols Red Lion.

1787   Jefferson, Thomas. *Notes on the State of Virginia*, Book II. London: Stockdale.

1845   Lanusso, Armand. Introduction to *Les Cenelles: A Collection of Poems by Creole Writers of the Early Nineteenth Century*. New Orleans.

1854   Forten, Charlotte. Journal of Charlotte Forten (July 28, 1854).

1859   Published. *Weekly Anglo African Magazine* (1859–1865).

Wilson, Harriet. Preface to *Our Nig; Or, Sketches from the Life of a Free Black. In a Two Story White House, North, Showing That Slavery's Shadows Fall Even There*. Reprint, New York: Vintage, 1983.

1865   Horton, George Moses. *Naked Genius*. Raleigh, N.C. Reprint, *Naked Genius: The Poetry of George Moses Horton*. Edited by William Carroll. Chapel Hill: The University of North Carolina Press, 1977.

1873   Harper, Frances Ellen Watkins. *Fancy Etchings* (April 24, 1873). Reprint, *Christian Recorder*. Reprint, *A Brighter Coming Day: A Frances*

Ellen Watkins Harper Reader, edited by Frances Smith Foster. New York: The Feminist Press, 1980.

1880   Chesnutt, Charles W. Second Journal (May 29, 1880). Reprint, *The Journals of Charles W. Chesnutt,* edited by Richard H. Brodhead. Durham: Duke University Press, 1983.

1884   Published. *A.M.E. Church Review* (1884–1909).
Wheatley, Phillis. "An Hymn to the Morning." In *The Collected Works of Phillis Wheatley.* Reprint, edited with an essay by John C. Shields. New York: Oxford University Press, 1988.

1892   Cooper, Anna Julia. *A Voice from the South.* Reprint, *Publication of the Schomburg Library,* edited by Henry Louis Gates Jr. with an introduction by Mary Helen Washington. New York: Oxford University Press, 1988.

1895–1954 Art or Propaganda?

1895   Founded. The American Negro Academy (an intellectual think group).
Matthews, Victoria Earle. "The Value of Race Literature: An Address Delivered at the First Congress of Colored Women of the United States." Reprint, Shirley Wilson Logan, ed. *With Pen and Voice, A Critical Anthology of Nineteenth-Century African American Women.* Carbondale: Southern Illinois University Press, 1995.

1898   Mossell, N. F. (Mrs). "Life and Literature." *A.M.E. Church Review* 14 (January): 318–26.

1899   Chesnutt, Charles W. *The Conjure Woman.* Cambridge: Riverside Press.

1900   Published. *Colored American Magazine* (1900–1909).
Hopkins, Pauline. Preface to *Contending Forces: A Romance Illustrative of Negro Life North and South.* Boston: The Colored Co-Operative Publishing Co. Reprint, New York: AMS, 1971.

1901   Chesnutt, Charles W. "Superstitions and Folk-lore of the South." *Modern Culture* 13 (May): 231–32, 235.

1903   DuBois, W. E. B. "Of Our Spiritual Strivings." In *The Souls of Black Folk.* Chicago: A. C. McClurg.

1904   Published. *Voice of the Negro* (1904–1907).

1910   Published. *Crisis* (the official organ of the National Association for the Advancement of Colored People).

1911   DuBois, W. E. B. "Writers." *Crisis* 1 (April): 20–21.

1913   DuBois, W. E. B. "The Negro in Literature and Art." *Annals of the American Academy of Political and Social Science* (1913): 233–37.

1914   Dunbar Nelson, Alice. "A Poet and His Song." *A.M.E. Church Review* (October): 121–35.

1917–1935   The Harlem Renaissance literary movement.

1919   Conference. The Second International Pan-African Congress.

1921   DuBois, W. E. B. "Negro Art." *Crisis* (July): 55–56.

Johnson, James Weldon. Preface to *The Book of American Negro Poetry Chosen and Edited with an Essay on the Negro's Creative Genius.* New York: Harcourt Brace & Company.

1923   Published. *Opportunity: A Journal of Negro Life.*

Toomer, Jean. "The South in Literature." *Call* (1923). James Weldon Johnson Collection. Yale University.

1924   Braithwaite, William Stanley. "The Negro in Literature." *Crisis* 28 (September 1924): 204–10.

DuBois, W. E. B. *The Gift of Black Folk: Negroes in the Making of America.* Boston: Stratford Co. Reprint, with new introduction by Herbert Aptheker, Millwood, N.Y.: Kraus-Thomson Organization, Ltd., 1975.

Thurman, Wallace. "Art and Propaganda." *Messenger* 6 (April): 111.

1925   Published. *Survey Graphic.*

Locke, Alain, ed. *The New Negro.* New York: Atheneum.

1926   Published. *Fire!! Devoted to Younger Negro Artist Magazine* (one issue).

Chesnutt, Charles W. "The Negro in Art: How Shall He Be Portrayed?" *Crisis* 33, no. 1 (November): 28–29.

DuBois, W. E. B. "Criteria of Negro Art." *Crisis* 32: 290–97.

Hughes, Langston. "The Negro Artist and the Racial Mountain." *Nation* 122 (1926): 692–94.

Schuyler, George S. "The Negro Art Hokum." *Nation* 121: 662–63.

1927   Johnson, James Weldon. Introduction to *God's Trombones: Seven Negro Sermons in Verse.* New York: Penguin Books.

Thurman, Wallace. "Negro Artists and the Negro" *New Republic* 52 (August 31): 37–39.

1928   Published. *Harlem* (1928).

Published. *News-Bulletin* (an official organ of the Association of Teachers of English in Negro Colleges [later to become *CLA Journal* and the College Language Association]).

Fauset, Jessie. "Introduction." In *The Chinaberry Tree.* New York: Boni & Liveright.

Johnson, James Weldon. "The Dilemma of the Negro Author" *American Mercury* 15 (1928): 477–81.

Locke, Alain. "Art or Propaganda?" In *The Critical Temper of Alain Locke: A Selection of His Essays on Art and Culture,* edited by Jeffrey C. Stewart. New York: Garland Publishing.

Thurman, Wallace. "High, Low, Past and Present." *Harlem* 1, no. 1 (November): 31–32, 35.

1929   Conference. The Durham-Fact-Finding. April 17–19, Durham, N.C.

Calverton, V. F., ed. *An Anthology of American Negro Literature.* New York: Modern Library.

1930   Brown, Sterling A. "Our Literary Audience." *Opportunity* 8 (February): 42–46, 61.

1931   Chesnutt, Charles W. "Post-Bellum, Pre-Harlem." *Crisis* (June): 193–94.

1932   Published. *Le'gi'time De'fense* (Paris, France).

Brown, Sterling A. "A Literary Parallel." *Opportunity* (May): 152–53.

Thurman, Wallace. *Infants of the Spring*. New York: MaCaulay.

1933   Published. *L'etudiant noir* (organ of the Negritude literary movement, Paris, France).

Brown, Sterling A. "Negro Characters as Seen by White Authors." *Journal of Negro Education* (April): 179–203.

1934   Published. *Challenge* (1934–1937).

Brawley, Benjamin. "The Promise of Negro Literature." *Journal of Negro History* (1934): 53–59.

Hurston, Zora Neale. "Characteristics of Negro Expression." In *Negro Anthology,* edited by Nancy Cunard. London: Wishart & Co. Reprint, *Negro: An Anthology*. New York: F. Ungar Publishing Company, 1970.

Johnson, James Weldon. Foreword to *Challenge* 1, no. 1 (March): 1.

1935–1953   The Chicago Renaissance literary movement.

1935   Hurston, Zora Neale. *Mules and Men*. Philadelphia: Lippincott.

Kerlin, Robert T. *Negro Poets and Their Poems*. Washington, D.C.: Associated Publishers.

1936   Published. *New Challenge* (1936–1937).

Ford, Nick A. *The Contemporary Negro Novel*. Boston: Meador.

1937–1960   The Negritude literary movement, Paris, France.

1937   Conference. Second National Negro Congress. October 15–17, Washington, D.C.

Brown, Sterling A. *The Negro in American Fiction*. Washington, D.C.: Association in Negro Folk Education. Reprint, New York: Atheneum, 1969.

West, Dorothy. *New Challenge* 2, no. 2 (Fall): 4.

Wright, Richard. "Between Laughter and Tears." *New Masses* 5 (October): 22, 25.

———. "Blueprint for Negro Writing." *New Challenge* (1937): 53–65.

1938   Miller, Loren. "Hollywood's New Negro Films." *Crisis* 45 (1938): 8–9.

1940   Published. *Negro Digest.*

Published. *Phylon: Race and Culture.*

Hughes, Langston. *The Big Sea, An Autobiography*. New York: Knopf.

Wright, Richard. "How 'Bigger' Was Born." In *Native Son*. New York: Harper and Row.

1941   Davis, Arthur P., Sterling A. Brown, and Ullysses Lee, eds. *The Negro Caravan*. New York: Arno.

Hughes, Langston. "The Need for Heroes." *Crisis* (June): 184–85, 206.

1942   Published. *Negro Digest* (1942–1951; 1961–1970).

Hurston, Zora Neale. *Dust Tracks on a Road*. Philadelphia: Lippincott.

1944   Published. *Negro Story* (1944–1946).

Watkins, Sylvester C., ed. *Anthology of American Negro Literature*. New York: Random House.

1945   Brown, Sterling A. "Spirituals, Blues and Jazz: The Negro in the Lively Arts." *Tricolor* 3 (April): 62–70.

Conrad, Earl. "American Viewpoint: Blues School of Literature." *Chicago Defender,* December 22, 11.

Ellison, Ralph. "Richard Wright's Blues." *Antioch Review* 5 (Summer): 198–211.

Johnson, Fenton. "Editor's Mailbox." *Negro Story* (May/June): 5.

1947   Published. *Pre'sence Africaine (Leopold Senghor, Aime' Ce'Saire, and Le'on Damas).*

Bontemps, Arna. "The Harlem Renaissance." *Saturday Review of Literature* (March): 12–13, 44.

1948   Gloster, Hugh M. *Negro Voices in American Fiction.* Chapel Hill: University of North Carolina Press.

1949   Baldwin, James. "Everybody's Protest Novel." *Partisan Review* 16 (June): 578–723. Reprint, *Notes of a Native Son.* Boston: Beacon Press, 1955.

Wilkerson, Doxey A. "Negro Culture: Heritage and Weapon." *Masses and Mainstream* (1949): 3–24.

1950   Pulitzer Prize awarded to poet Gwendolyn Brooks for *Annie Allen.*

Ford, Nick Aaron. "A Blueprint for Negro Authors." *Phylon* 11: 384–87.

Hurston, Zora Neale. "What White Publishers Won't Print." *Negro Digest* 8 (April): 85–89.

Petry, Ann. "The Novel as Social Criticism." In *The Writer's Book,* edited by Helen Hull. New York: Harper and Brothers.

Phylon 11 (Special Issue).

1951   Baldwin, James. "Many Thousand Gone." *Partisan Review* 18 (November-December): 665–68. Reprint, *Notes of a Native Son.* Boston: Beacon Press, 1955.

Brown, Lloyd W. "Which Way for the Negro Writer." *Masses and Mainstream* 4 (1951): 53–57.

1952   Fanon, Frantz. *Black Skin, White Mask.* Translated by Charles Lam Markmann. New York: Grove Press, 1967.

1953   National Book Award for *Invisible Man* by Ralph Ellison.

Ellison, Ralph. "Twentieth-Century Fiction and the Black Mask of Humanity." *Confluence* (December): 3–21. Reprint, *Shadow and Act.* New York: Random House, 1964.

1954–1964   The Civil Rights movement.

1955–1975 Cultural Autonomy and Understanding the Art of Black Poetry, Drama, Fiction, and Criticism

1955   Chester, Alfred, and Velma Howard. "The Art of Fiction: An Interview [with Ralph Ellison]." *Paris Review* 2 (Spring): 55–71. Reprint, *Shadow and Act,* 169–83. New York: Random House, 1964.

Logan, Rayford W., Eugene C. Holmes, and G. Franklin Edwards, eds. *The New Negro Thirty Years Afterward.* Washington, D.C.: Howard University Press.

1956 Conference. The Conference of Negro-African Writers and Artists. September 19, Paris, France.

Butcher, Margaret. *The Negro in American Culture.* New York: Knopf.

Davis, Arthur P. "Integration and Race Literature." *Phylon* 17, no. 2 (1956): 141–46. Reprint, *The American Negro Writer and His Roots,* 34–40. New York: The American Society of African Culture, 1959.

Ivey, James. "First Negro Congress of Writers and Artists." *Crisis* 63 (1956): 593–600.

Jahn, Janheinz. "World Congress of Black Writers." *Black Orpheus: A Journal of African and Afro American Literature* (September): 39–46.

1957 Published. *Black Orpheus* (1957–1976).

Published. *College Language Association Journal (CLA Journal),* formerly *News-Bulletin* (an official organ of the College Language Association).

Wright, Richard. "The Psychological Reactions of Oppressed People." In *White Man, Listen!* Reprint, with an introduction by Cedric Robinson, 1–43. New York: Harper Perennial, 1995.

1958 Bone, Robert. *The Negro Novel in America.* New Haven: Yale University Press.

Ellison, Ralph. "Change the Joke and Slip the Yoke." Reprint, *Shadow and Act.* New York: Random House, 1964.

Hughes, Langston, and Arna Bontemps, eds. Introduction to *The Book of Negro Folklore.* New York: Dodd, Mead and Company.

1959 Conference. The Conference of Negro Writers. New York, N.Y.

Founded. The American Society of African Culture.

Published. *Freedomways* (1961–1976).

Published. *Liberator* (1961–1971).

The American Negro Writer and His Roots. New York: The American Society of African Culture.

Fontaine, William T. "Toward a Philosophy of the American Negro Literature." *Pre'sence Africaine* nos. 24–25 (February-May): 165–76.

Hansberry, Lorraine. *A Raisin in the Sun* (on Broadway).

Jackson, Blyden. "A Golden Mean for the Negro Novel." *CLA Journal* (December): 81–87.

Killens, John Oliver. "Opportunities for Development of Negro Talent." In *The American Negro Writer and His Roots,* 64–70. New York: The American Society of African Culture.

Redding, J. Saunders. *To Make A Poet Black.* Chapel Hill: University of North Carolina Press.

1961 Ellison, Ralph. "That Same Pain. That Same Pleasure: An Interview." R. G. Stern. December 3 (Winter): 30–32, 37–46. Reprint, *Shadow and Act.* New York: Random House, 1964.

Fanon, Frantz. *The Wretched of the Earth*. Translated by Constance Far-rington. New York: Grove Press, 1963.

1962   Baker, James K. "An American Writer in Africa" (interview with J. Saunders Redding). *Negro Digest* 12, no. 2 (December): 41–48.

Baldwin, James. "The Creative Process." In *The Price of the Ticket*. New York: St. Martin's/Marek, 1995.

Roach, Max. "Jazz." *Freedomways* (Spring): 173–76.

1963   Founded. Dasein Poet Workshop (Washington, D.C.).

Founded. Free Lance Poet Workshop (Cleveland, Ohio).

Founded. Umbra Poets Workshop (Lower East Side Manhattan).

Published. *Dasein* (1961–1969).

Published. *Umbra Magazine* (1963–1975).

Berger, Art. "Negroes with Pens." *Mainstream* 16 (1963): 1–6.

Ellison, Ralph. "The World and the Jug." *New Leader* 46 (December): 22–26. Reprint, *Shadow and Act*. New York: Random House, 1964.

Herndon, Calvin. "Umbra Poets." *Mainstream* 16 (1963): 7–13.

Hill, Herbert, ed. *Soon, One Morning: New Writing by American Negroes, 1940–1962*. New York: Knopf.

Jones, LeRoi (Amiri Baraka). *Blues People: Negro Music in White America*. New York: William Morrow and Company.

———. "The Myth of a 'Negro Literature'."*Saturday Review*, 20 April, 20–21. Reprint, *Home: Social Essays*, 105–15. New York: William Morrow, 1966.

1964   Founded. California Bay Area Writers (San Francisco, Calif.).

Founded. Free Southern Theatre (Jackson, Miss.).

Founded. Uptown Writers Movement (with LeRoi Jones, Larry Neal, and others in Harlem).

Published. *Soulbook* (1964–1976).

Ellison, Ralph. *Shadow and Act*. New York: Random House.

Ford, Clebert. "Black Nationalism and the Arts." *Liberator* (February): 14–16.

1965–1976   The Black Power movement.

1965   Symposium. The Task of the Negro Writer.

Founded. Black Arts Repertory Theatre/School (BARTS) by LeRoi Jones.

Founded. Broadside Press by Dudley Randall (Detroit, Mich.).

Founded. Harlem Writers Guild (with John O. Killens, Maya Angelou, and others).

Davis, Ossie. "The Significance of Lorraine Hansberry." *Freedomways* (Summer): 397–402.

"The First World Festival of Negro Art." *Negro Digest* (August): 62–68.

Fuller, Hoyt W. "The Task of the Negro Writer as Artist." *Negro Digest* (January): 10–48, 81–89.

Record, C. Wilson. "The Negro as Creative Artist." *Crisis* (1965): 153–58, 193.

Redding, J. Saunders. "The Problems of the Negro Writer." *Massachusetts Review* (Autumn-Winter): 57–70.

Turner, Darwin T. "A Primer for Critics." *CLA Journal* 8, no. 3 (March): 217–23.

1966   Published. *Journal of Black Poetry* (1966–1973).

Bontemps, Arna. "The Negro Renaissance: Jean Toomer and the Harlem Writers of the 1920s." In *Anger and Beyond: The Negro Writer in the United States,* edited by Herbert Hill, 20–36. New York: Harper and Row.

Cayton, Horace R. "Ideological Forces in the Work of Negro Writers." In *Anger and Beyond: The Negro Writer in the United States,* edited by Herbert Hill, 37–50. New York: Harper and Row.

Childress, Alice. "A Woman Playwright Speaks Her Mind." *Freedomways* (1966): 75–80.

Gross, Seymour, and John Edward Hardy, eds. *Images of the Negro in American Literature.* Chicago: University of Chicago Press.

Hill, Herbert, ed. *Anger and Beyond: The Negro Writer in the United States.* New York: Harper and Row.

Jones, LeRoi (Amiri Baraka). "expressive language." In *Home: Social Essays,* 166–72. New York: William Morrow.

———. "The Myth of a 'Negro Literature'." In *Home: Social Essays,* 105–15. New York: William Morrow.

Llorens, David. "Writers Converge at Fisk University." *Negro Digest* (June): 54–68.

Mason, Julian. Introduction to *The Poems of Phillis Wheatley,* xxii–xxvi. Chapel Hill: University of North Carolina Press.

Neal, Larry. "The Black Writer's Role." *Liberator* (June): 6–9.

———. "Toward a Relevant Black Theatre." *Black Theatre* (1966): 14–15.

Redding, J. Saunders. "Since Richard Wright." *African Forum* (September): 21–31.

Turner, Darwin T. "The Negro Novel in America: In Rebuttal." *CLA Journal* (1966): 123–34.

1967   Conference. The Fisk University Second Black Writers' Conference.

Founded. Third World Press by Haki Madhubuti.

Published. *Negro American Literature Forum,* changed to *Black American Literature Forum,* and then *African American Review.*

Berrian, Albert H., and Richard A. Long, eds. *Negritude: Essays and Studies.* Hampton, Va.: Hampton Institute Press.

Cruse, Harold. *The Crisis of the Negro Intellectual.* New York: William Morrow.

Dent, Tom. "The Free Southern Theater." *Negro Digest* (April): 40–44.

Fuller, C. H., Jr. "Black Art and Fanon's Third Phase." *Liberator* (July): 14–15.

Jones, LeRoi (Amiri Baraka). "What the Arts Need Now." *Negro Digest* (April): 33–34.

King, Woodie, Jr.. "Black Theatre: Weapon for Change." *Negro Digest* (April): 35–39.

Majors, Clarence. "A Black Criterion." *Journal of Black Poetry* (Spring): 15–16.

Patterson, Lindsay, ed. *Anthology of the American Negro in the Theatre.* New York: Publishers Company.

Turner, Darwin T. "The Negro Novelist and the South." *Southern Humanities Review* 1 (1967): 21–29.

Ward, Douglas Turner. "Needed: A Theater for Black Themes." *Negro Digest* (December): 34–49.

1968   Brown, Sterling A. *The Negro in American Fiction: Negro Poetry and Drama.* New York: Arno Press and *The New York Times.*

Chapman, Abraham. *Black Voices: An Anthology of Afro-American Literature.* New York: New American Library.

Dixon, Melvin. "Black Theater: The Aesthetics." *Negro Digest* (July): 41–44.

Dodson, Owen. "Playwrights in Dark Glasses." *Negro Digest* (April): 30–36.

Drama Review 12, no. 4 (Summer) (A Special Issue on Black Theatre).

Ellison, Ralph. "A Dialogue with his Audience." *Barat Review* (1968): 51–53.

Emanuel, James A., and Theodore Gross. *Dark Symphony: Negro Literature in America.* New York: Free Press.

Fuller, Hoyt W. "The Critic Will Learn. *Negro Digest* 18, no. 1 (November): 53.

———. "A Survey: Black Writers' Views on Literary Lions and Values." *Negro Digest* (January): 10–48, 81–89.

———. "Towards a Black Aesthetic." *Critic* 26, no. 5.Reprint, *The Black Aesthetic,* edited by Addison Gayle Jr. Garden City, N.Y.: Doubleday, 1971.

Hill, Herbert. "The Negro Writer and the Creative Imagination." *Art in Society* (1968): 244–55.

Jones, LeRoi (Amiri Baraka), and Larry Neal, eds. *Black Fire: An Anthology of Afro-American Writing.* New York: William Morrow.

Karenga, Ron. "Black Nationalist Cultural Organization." *Pre'sence Africaine* 66 (2nd Quarter): 197–98.

Knight, Etheridge. "Statement on Poetics." In *The New Black Poetry,* edited by Clarence Major. New York: International Publishers.

Neal, Larry. "The Black Arts Movement." *Drama Review* (Summer): 27–39.

———. "Cultural Nationalism and Black Theatre." *Black Theatre* (1968): 8–10.

————. "A Survey: Black Writers' Views on Literary Lions and Values." *Negro Digest* 17, no. 3 (January): 35.

1969 Founded. The Black Academy of Arts and Letters (with C. Eric Lincoln as its first president).

Founded. BLKARTSOUTH, formerly Free Southern Theater.

Published. *Nommo* (1964–1972).

Baraka, Imamu Amiri (LeRoi Jones). "The Black Aesthetic." *Negro Digest* (September): 5–6.

Bigsby, C. W. E., ed. *The Black American Writer.* 2 vols. Baltimore, Md.: Penguin Books.

Brown, Cecil. *The Life and Loves of Mr. Jiveass Nigger.* New York: Ecco Press.

Bullin, Ed, ed. *New Plays from the Black Theatre.* New York: Bantam.

Cook, Mercer, and Stephen E. Henderson. *The Militant Black Writer.* Madison: University of Wisconsin Press.

Fuller, Hoyt W. "Black Images and White Critics." *Negro Digest* (November): 49–50.

Gayle, Addison, Jr., "Black Literature and the White Aesthetic." *Negro Digest* (July): 32–39.

————, ed. *Black Expression.* New York: Weybright & Talley.

Gerald, Carolyn F. "The Black Writer and His Role." *Black World* 18 (1969): 42–48. Reprint, Addison Gayle Jr., ed. *The Black Aesthetic.* Garden City, N.Y.: Doubleday, 1971.

Johnson, Helen Armstead. "Playwrights, Audiences and Critics." *Negro Digest* (April): 17–24.

Majors, Clarence. *The New Black Poetry.* New York: International Publishers.

Neal, Larry. "Any Day Now: Black Art and Black Liberation." *Ebony* (August): 54–58, 62.

Rodgers, Carolyn. "Black Poetry Where Its At." *Black World* 18, no. 11 (September): 7–16.

Turner, Darwin T., ed. *Black American Literature: Essays, Poetry, Fiction, Drama.* Columbus, Ohio: Merrill.

1970 Pulitzer Prize awarded to playwright Charles Gordon for *No Place to Be Somebody.*

Published. *Black Creation* (1970–1975).

Published. *Black World,* formerly *Negro Digest* (1970–1976).

Brown, Lloyd W. "Ralph Ellison's Exhorters: The Role of Rhetoric in *Invisible Man.*" *CLA Journal* (March): 289–303.

Cade, Toni (Bambara) *The Black Woman, An Anthology.* New York: New American Library.

Chapman, Abraham, ed. *New Black Voices.* New York: New American Library.

Evans, Mari. "Contemporary Black Literature." *Black World* (June): 4, 94–98.

Gayle, Addison, Jr. *Black Situation.* New York: Horizon Press.

Gibson, Donald B., ed. *Five Black Writers: Essays on Wright, Ellison, Baldwin, Hughes, LeRoi Jones.* New York: New York University Press.

Gilman, Richard. "White Standards and Negro Writing." *Negro American Literature Forum* 3 (Winter): 111–16.

Lee, Don (Haki Madhubuti). "Voices of the Seventies, Black Critics." *Black World* 19, no. 11 (September): 24–30.

Neal, Larry, et. al "A Symposium on 'We Righteous Bombers.' " *Black Theatre* 4: 16–25.

Rainwater, Lee, ed. *Black Experience: Soul.* New Brunswick, N.J.: Trans-action Books.

Rodgers, Carolyn. "The Literature of Black." *Black World* (June): 5–11.

Seale, Bobby. "October 1966, Black Panther Party Platform and Program." In *Seize the Time, The Story of the Black Panther Party and Huey P. Newton. New York: Random House.*

Taylor, Jeanne A. "On Being Black and Writing for Television." *Negro American Literature Forum* (1970): 79–82.

Turner, Darwin T. "Afro-American Literary Critics: An Introduction." *Black World* 19, no. 9 (July): 54–67. Reprint, *The Black Aesthetic,* edited by Addison Gayle Jr. Garden City, N.Y.: Doubleday, 1971.

Walker, Margaret. "The Humanistic Tradition of Afro-American Literature." *American Libraries* 1 (October): 849–54.

Williams, John A. "My Man Himes: An Interview with Chester Himes." *Amistad I, Writings of Black History and Culture.* New York: Random House.

1971   Founded. Arts and Humanities Institute by Stephen E. Henderson (Howard University, Washington, D.C.).

Bennett, Lerone, Jr., "The Challenge of Blackness." *Black World* (February): 20–26.

Davis, Arthur P., and Saunders J. Redding, eds. *Cavalcade: Negro American Writing from 1760 to the Present.* Boston: Houghton.

Ford, Nick Aaron. "Black Literature and the Problem of Evaluation." *College Education* 3, no. 5 (February): 536–47.

———. "Confessions of a Black Critic." *Black World* (June): 30–43.

Gayle, Addison, Jr., *The Black Aesthetic.* Garden City, N.Y.: Doubleday.

———, ed. *Bondage, Freedom and Beyond: The Prose of Black Americans.* New York: Doubleday.

Gerald, Carolyn F. "The Black Writer and His Role." In *The Black Aesthetic,* edited by Addison Gayle Jr. Garden City, N.Y.: Doubleday.

Hayden, Robert, David J. Burrows, and Frederick R. Lapides, eds. *Afro-American Literature: An Introduction.* New York: Harcourt Brace Jovanovich.

Henderson, Stephen E. "Blues, Soul and Black Identity: The Forms of Things Unknown," Black Books Bulletin (Fall): 1–15, 36–38.

Huggins, Nathan I. *Harlem Renaissance.* New York: Oxford University Press.

Jeffers, Lance. "Afro-American Literature, the Conscience of Man." *Black Scholar* 2, no. 5 (January): 47–53.

Jones, LeRoi (Amiri Baraka). "Black (Art) Drama Is the Same as Black Life." *Ebony* (February): 74–76, 78, 80, 82.

Karenga, Ron. "Black Cultural Nationalism."In *The Black Aesthetic,* edited by Addison Gayle Jr., 33. Garden City, N.Y.: Doubleday.

King, Woodie, Jr., and Ron Milner, eds. *Black Drama Anthology.* New York: New American Library.

Lee, Don (Haki Madhubuti). "Black Critic." In *Dynamite Voices: Black Poets of the 1960s.* Detroit: Broadside.

Rodgers, Carolyn M. "Un Nat'chal Thang—The Whole Truth—Us." *Black World* (September): 4–14.

Smitherman, Geneva. *Talkin' and Testifyin': The Language of Black America.* Boston: Houghton Mifflin.

Walker, Alice. "The Unglamorous But Worthwhile Duties of the Black Revolutionary Artist, or . . ." *Black Collegian,* September/October, 5, 43, 46.

1972   Barksdale, Richard, and Keneth Kinnamon, eds. *Black Writers of America.* New York: Macmillan.

Brooks, Gwendolyn. "The Field of the Fever, The Time of the Tall-Walkers." In *Report from Part One: An Autobiography.* Chicago: Third World Press. Reprint, *Black Women Writers (1950–1980): A Critical Evaluation,* edited by Mari Evans. Garden City, N.Y.: Anchor/Doubleday, 1984.

Brown, Lloyd W. "The Expatriate Consciousness in Black American Literature." *Studies in Black Literature* 3, no. 2 (Summer): 9–12.

Harrison, Paul Carter. "Black Theater and the African Continuum." *Black World* (August): 42–48.

———. *The Drama of Nommo.* New York: Grove Press.

Kent, George. "Introduction." In *Blackness and the Adventure of Western Culture.* Chicago: Third World Press.

Long, Richard, and Eugenia Collier, eds. *Afro-American Writing.* New York: New York University Press.

Ogban, P. Mego. "Reflections on Language, Vision and the Black Writer." *Black World* 22, no. 2 (December): 40–47.

Randall, Dudley, ed. *The Black Poets.* New York: Bantam Books.

Reed, Ishmael. "The Neo-Hoodoo Aesthetic." In *Conjure: Selected Poems, 1963–1970.* Amherst: University of Massachusetts Press.

———. "New-Hoodoo Manifest." In *Conjure: Selected Poems, 1963–1970,* 20–25. Amherst: University of Massachusetts Press.

Riley, Clayton. "The Creative Black Man—Artists Stuggle to Overcome Limiting Concepts of Art." *Ebony* (August): 134–39.

Turner, Darwin T. "The Teaching of Afro-American Literature." In *New Black Voices,* edited with an introduction and biographical notes by Abraham Chapman, 499–503. New York: New American Library.

Williams, Sherley A. *Give Birth to Brightness: A Thematic Study of Neo-Black Literature.* New York: Dial.

1973 The Phillis Wheatley Poetry Festival. November 5–6, Jackson State College, Jackson, Miss.

Founded. Congo Square Writers Union by Thomas C. Dent (New Orleans).

Baker, Houston, Jr. "Report on a Celebration: Dunbar's One-Hundredth Year." *Black World* 22, no. 4 (February): 81–85.

Cosgrove, William. "Modern Black Writers: The Divided Self." *Negro American Literature Forum* (Winter): 120–22.

Fabre, Michel. *The Unfinished Quest of Richard Wright.* New York: William Morrow.

Gibson, Donald B. *Modern Black Poets: A Collection of Critical Essays.* Englewood Cliffs, N.J.: Prentice Hall.

Henderson, Stephen E. "The Forms of Things Unknown." In *Understanding the New Black Poetry: Black Music and Black Speech as Poetic References.* New York: William Morrow.

Hudson, Theodore. *From LeRoi Jones to Amiri Baraka: The Literary Works.* Durham: Duke University Press.

Mitchell-Kernan, Claudia. "Signifying." In *Mother Wit from the Laughing Barrel: Readings in the Interpretation of Afro-American Folklore,* 310–28 edited by Alan Dundes. Englewood Cliffs, N.J.: Prentice Hall, 1973. Reprint, Jackson: University Press of Mississippi. 1990.

Molette, Carlton W., II. "Afro American Ritual Drama." *Black World* (April): 4–12.

O'Brien, John, ed. *Interviews with Black Writers.* New York: Liveright.

Patterson, Lindsay. Introduction to *Black Theater,* ix–xii. New York: New American Library.

"Reports on Black Theater, USA." *Black World* 22, no. 6 (April): 14–37, 83–95.

Review of *Understanding the New Black Poetry: Black Music and Black Speech as Poetic References,* by Stephen E. Henderson. *Black Creation* (Fall): 43–44.

Schatt, Stanley. "You Must Go Home Again: Today's Afro-American Expatriate Writers." *Negro American Literature Forum* 7, no. 3 (Fall): 80–82.

Wagner, Jean. *Black Poets of the United States from Paul Laurence Dunbar to Langston Hughes.* Translated by Kenneth Douglas. Urbana: University of Illinois Press.

1974   Founded. The Combahee River Collective (a black feminist group, Boston, Mass.).

Bell, Bernard W. *The Folk Roots of Contemporary Afro-American Poetry.* Detroit: Broadside Press.

Brown, Lloyd W. "The Black Aesthetic and Comparative Criticism." *Counsel on National Literature Report* (January): 5–8.

Coro, Jacqueline. *The Blinking Eye: Ralph Ellison and His American, French, German, and Italian Critics, 1952–1971.* Metuchen, N.J.: Scarecrow Press.

Davis, Arthur P. *From the Dark Tower.* Washington, D.C.: Howard University Press.

Exum, Pat Crutchfield, ed. *Keeping the Faith: Writings by Contemporary Black American Women.* Greenwich, Conn.: Fawcett.

Govan, Sandra. "The Poetry of the Black Experience as Counterpoint to the Poetry of the Black Aesthetic." *Negro American Literature Forum* 8, no. 4 (Winter): 288–92.

Jordan, June. "On Richard Wright and Zora Neale Hurston: Notes Toward a Balancing of Love and Hatred." *Black World* (August): 4–8.

Richmond, M. A. *Bid the Vassal Soar: Interpretive Essays on the Life and Poetry of Phillis Wheatley and George Moses Horton.* Washington, D.C.: Howard University Press.

Sherman, Joan. *Invisible Poets: Afro Americans of the Nineteenth Century.* Urbana: University of Illinois Press.

Skeeter, Sharyn J. "Black Women Writers: Levels of Identity." *Essence,* May, 58–59, 76, 89.

Washington, Mary Helen. "Black Women Image Makers." *Black World* (August): 10–18.

1975   Published. *Obsidian: Black Literature in Review,* later became *Obsidian II.*

Barksdale, Richard. "White Triangles, Black Circles." *CLA Journal* (June): 465–76.

Bell, Bernard W. "Folk Art and the Harlem Renaissance." *Phylon* 36, no. 2 (June): 155–63.

Bogle, Donald. "Black Humor—Full Circle from slave quarters to Richard Pryor." *Ebony* (August): 123–26, 128.

A Capsule Course in Black Poetry Writing, edited by Gwendolyn Brooks, Keorapetse Kgositsile, Haki Madhubuti, and Dudley Randall. Detroit: Broadside Press.

Cargos, Harry James. "The Black Writer: A White Perspective." *Negro American Literature Forum* (Fall): 100–102.

Everett, Chestyn. "Tradition in Afro-American Literature." *Black World* 25, no. 2 (December): 20–35.

Gayle, Addison, Jr. *The Way of the New World and the Black Novel in America*. Garden City, N.Y.: Anchor/Doubleday.

Henderson, Stephen E. "Saturation: Progress Report on a Theory of Black Poetry." *Black World* 24, no. 8 (June): 4–17.

Parks, Carole A. "First National Conference of Afro-American Writers." *Black World* 24, no. 3 (January): 86–92.

Randall, Dudley. "Black Publishers, Black Writers: An Answer." *Black World* 24, no. 5 (March): 32–35.

Shange, Ntozake. *For colored girls who have considered suicide when the rainbow is enuf.* New York: Macmillan.

"Symposium on Black Criticism." *Black World* 24, no. 9 (July): 64, 65, 97.

Taylor, Clyde. "The Poet's Work—Henry Dumas: Legacy of a Long Breath Singer." *Black World* 24, no. 11 (September): 4–16.

Thompson, Larry. "The Black Image in Early American Drama." *Black World* 24, no. 6 (April): 54–69.

Washington, Mary Helen. Introduction to *Black-eyed Susans*, 9–32. Garden City, N.Y.: Doubleday/Anchor.

1976–2000 Aesthetic Values, Reconstructions of Blackness and Boundaries, and Postmodernism

1976   Summer seminar. Afro-American Literature: From Critical Approach to Course Design. June 6–17, sponsored by The Modern Language Association and the Afro-American Studies Department at Yale University (purpose was to move scholars away from sociological and ideological criticism and toward structuralist and comparative modes of analysis).

Published. *Callaloo, A Black South Journal*, later called *a Journal of African American and African Arts and Letters*.

Published. *First World, An Intellectual Journal Published by and for Black People* (Atlanta, Ga.).

Alexander, Margaret Walker. "Some Aspects of the Black Aesthetic." *Freedomways* 11 (1976): 95–102.

Baker, Houston A., Jr., ed. *Reading Black: Essays in the Criticism of African, Caribbean and Black American Literature*. Ithaca, N.Y.: Africana Studies and Research Center, Cornell University, Monograph Series, No. 4.

Billingsley, R. G. "Innocence and Freedom: The Image of White America in Black Literature." *First World* (September): 51–55.

Jackson, Blyden. *The Waiting Years: Essays on American Negro Literature*. Baton Rouge: Louisiana State University Press.

Long, Richard A. "Renaissance Personality: An Interview with George Schuyler." *Black World* 25, no. 4 (February): 68–78.

Murray, Albert. *Stomping the Blues.* New York: McGraw Hill Book Company.

Neal, Larry. "The Writer as Activist—1960 and After." In *The Black American Reference Book,* edited by Mabel H. Smythe. Englewood Cliffs, N.J.: Prentice Hall.

Rampersad, Arnold. *The Art and Imagination of W. E. B. DuBois.* Cambridge, Mass.: Harvard University Press.

Redding, J. Saunders. "Afro-American Culture and the Black Aesthetic: Notes Toward a Re-Evaluation." In *Reading Black: Essays in the Criticism of African, Caribbean, and Black American Literature,* edited by Houston A. Baker Jr. Ithaca, N.Y.: Africana Studies and Research Center, Cornell University, Monograph Series, No. 4.

Redmond, Eugene B. *Drumvoices: The Mission of Afro-American Poetry.* Garden City: N.Y.: Doubleday.

Rowell, Charles H. "Diamonds in a Sawdust Pile: Notes to Black South Writers." *Callaloo* 1 (December): 3–9.

Stepto, Robert B., and Dexter Fisher, eds. *Afro-American Literature: The Reconstruction of Instruction.* New York: Modern Language Association.

Thompson, Robert Farris. *Black Gods and Kings.* Bloomington: Indiana University Press.

Walker, Alice. "Saving the Life That Is Your Own: The Importance of Models in the Artist's Life." In *In Search of Our Mothers' Gardens.* Orlando, Fla.: Harcourt Brace.

Ward, Jerry W., Jr. "Dreams and Promises: The Southern Black Cultural Alliance." *Callaloo* 1 (December): 51–53.

1977 Benston, Kimberly W. "Late Coltrane: A Re-numbering of Orpheus." *Massachusetts Review* 18 (Winter): 770–81.

Dixon, Melvin. "Toward a World Black Literature and Community." *Massachusetts Review* 18, no. 4 (Winter): 750–67.

Ellison, Ralph. "The Little Man at Chehaw Station: The American Artist and His Audience." *American Scholar* (Winter): 25–48.

Fontenot, Chester, Jr. "Alice Walker: Diary of an African Nun and DuBois Double-Consciousness." *Journal of Afro-American Issues.* Reprint, Roseann P. Bell, et. al, eds. *Sturdy Black Bridges,* 150–56. New York: Doubleday, 1979.

Gayle, Addison, Jr., "A Blueprint for Black Criticism." *First World* (January-February): 41–45.

Hemenway, Robert E. *Zora Neale Hurston.* Urbana: University of Illinois Press.

Henderson, Stephen E. "The Question of Form and Judgement [*sic*] in Contemporary Black American Poetry." In *A Dark and Sudden Beauty: Two Essays in Black American Poetry,* edited by Houston A. Baker Jr. Philadelphia: University of Pennsylvania.

Lehman, Paul. "The Development of a Black Psyche: An Interview with John Oliver Killens." *Black American Literature Forum* 11, no. 3 (Fall): 83–89.

Levine, Lawrence W. *Black Culture and Black Consciousness: Afro-American Folk Thought from Slavery to Freedom.* New York: Oxford University Press.

Miller, Jean Marie A. "Images of Black Women in Plays by Black Playwrights." *CLA Journal* (June): 494–507.

Smith, Barbara. "Towards a Black Feminist Criticism." *Conditions: Two* 1, no. 2 (1977): 25–44. Reprint, Gloria T. Hull, Patricia Bell Scott, and Barbara Smith, eds. *But Some of Us Are Brave.* New York: Feminist Press, 1982.

West, Cornel. "Philosophy and the Afro-American Experience." *Philosophical Forum* 9, nos. 2–3: 117–487.

Wideman, John Edgar. "Defining the Black Voice in Fiction." *Black American Literature Forum* 11, no. 3 (Fall): 79–82.

1978   Pulitzer Prize awarded to fiction writer James Alan McPherson for *Elbow Room.*

Founded. Black Classic Press (Baltimore, Md.).

Davis, Arthur P. "Novels of the New Black Renaissance (1960–1977): A Thematic Survey." *CLA Journal* (June): 457–87.

Edwards, Jay. "The Afro-American Trickster Tale: A Structural Analysis." Monograph Series, vol 4. Bloomington: Folklore Institute of the University of Indiana.

Fontenot, Chester, Jr. "Black Fiction: Apollo or Dionysus." *Twentieth Century Literature* (Fall): 73–84.

———. "Black Fiction: From Tragedy to Romance." *Cornell Review* 3 (Spring): 115–23.

———. "Ishmael Reed and the Politics of Aesthetics, Or Shake Hands and Come Out Conjuring." *Black American Literature Forum* 12, no. 1 (Spring): 20–23.

Gates, Henry Louis, Jr. "Preface to Blackness: Text and Pretext." In *Afro-American Literature: The Reconstruction of Instruction,* edited by Dexter Fisher and Robert B. Stepto, 44–69. New York: Modern Language Association.

Gover, Robert. "An Interview with Ishmael Reed." *Black American Literature Forum* 12, no. 1 (Spring): 12–19.

Madhubuti, Haki R. "Black Writers and Critics: Developing a Critical Process Without Readers." *Black Scholar* 10, no. 4 (November/December): 35–38, 39–40.

McCullough, Ken. "Reflections on Film, Philosophy, and Fiction: An Interview with Charles Johnson." *Callaloo* 1, no. 4 (October): 118–28.

Reed, Ishmael. *Shrovetide in New Orleans.* New York: Doubleday.

Thomas, Lorenza. "The Shadow World: New York's Umbra Workshop and Origins of the Black Arts Movement." *Callaloo* 1, no. 4 (October): 53–72.

Traylor, Eleanor W. "Two Afro American Contributions to Dramatic Form." In *Indigene: An Anthology of Future Black Arts*, 29–39. Philadelphia: Black History Museum Committee.

Turner, Darwin T. "Introductory Remarks about the Black Literary Tradition in the United States of America." *Black American Literature Forum* 12, no. 4 (Winter): 140–47.

Wideman, John. "Stomping the Blues—Ritual in Black Music and Speech."*American Poetry Review* (July-August): 43–46.

1979   Bell, Roseann, Bettye J. Parker, and Beverly Guy-Sheftall. *Sturdy Black Bridges.* New York: Anchor.

Johnson, Abby Arthur, and Ronald Maberry Johnson. *Propaganda and Aesthetics: The Literary Politics of African-American Magazines in the Twentieth Century.* Amherst: University of Massachusetts Press.

Lott, Eric. *Love and Theft. Blackface Minstrelsy and the American Working Class.* New York: Oxford University Press.

Martin, Sharon Stockard. "The Invisible Reflections: Images and Self-Images of Black Women on Stage and Screen." *Black Collegian,* May/June, 74–81.

Stepto, Robert. *From Behind the Veil: A Study of Afro-American Narrative.* Urbana: University of Illinois Press.

Williams, Sherley A. "The Blues Roots of Contemporary Afro-American Poetry." In *Chants and Saints,* edited by Robert B. Stepto and Michael Harper. Urbana: University of Illinois Press.

1980   Founded. Middle Atlantic Writers Association (MAWA) (Baltimore, Md.).

Baker, Houston A., Jr. "Anthropology of Art." *Black American Literature Forum* 14, no. 1 (Spring): 30–31.

———. "Toward a Critical Prospect for the Future" In *The Journey Back: Issues in Black Literature and Criticism.* Chicago: University of Chicago Press.

Christian, Barbara. *Black Women Novelists: The Development of a Tradition, 1892–1976.* Westport, Conn.: Greenwood Press.

Fowler, Carolyn (Carolyn F. Gerald). Preface to *Black Arts and Black Aesthetics: A Bibliography,* v–xxxi. Atlanta: First World Foundation.

Henderson, Stephen E. "The Heavy Blues of Sterling Brown: A Study of Craft and Tradition." *Black American Literature Forum* 14, no. 1 (Spring): 32–44.

McDowell, Deborah. "New Directions for Black Feminist Criticism." In *Black American Literature Forum* 14, no. 4 (Winter): 153–54.

Reprint, Elaine Showalter, ed. *The New Feminist Criticism.* New York: Pantheon, 1985.

O'Meally, Robert G. *The Craft of Ralph Ellison.* Cambridge: Harvard University Press.

Skerret, Joseph T. "The Wright Intepretation: Ralph Ellison and the Anxiety of Influence." *Massachusetts Review* 21 (Spring): 196–212.

Thelwell, Mike. "As a Sounding Brass and a Tinking Cymbal—Modernist Fallacies and the Responsibility of the Black Writer." In *The Next Decade: Theoretical and Research Issues in Africana Studies,* edited by James E. Turner. Ithaca, N.Y.: Africana Studies and Research Center, Cornell University Press.

1981   Pulitzer Prize awarded to fiction writer Alice Walker for *The Color Purple.*

Pulitzer Prize awarded to playwright Charles H. Fuller for *A Soldier's Play.*

Founded. Kitchen Table: Women of Color Press.

Founded. The Langston Hughes Society (Baltimore, Md.).

Published. *Langston Hughes Review.*

Published. *MAWA Review.*

Baker, Houston A., Jr. "Generational Shifts and the Recent Criticism of Afro-American Literature." *Black American Literature Forum* 15, no. 1 (Spring): 3–21.

Foster, Frances Smith. "'In Respect to Females . . .': Differences in the Portrayals of Women by Male and Female Narrators." *Black American Literature Forum* 15, no. 2 (Summer): 66–70.

Gibson, Donald B. "Introduction: Preface to a Social Theory of Literature." In *The Politics of Literary Expression: A Study of Major Black Writers.* Westport, Conn.: Greenwood Press.

Harris, Trudier. "Three Black Women Writers and Humanism: A Folk Perspective." In *Black American Literature and Humanism,* edited by R. Baxter Miller, 50–74. Lexington: University Press of Kentucky.

Irele, Abiole. *The African Experience in Literature and Ideology* London: Heinneman.

Jaye, Michael C., and Amy Chalmers Watts, eds. *Literature and the Urban Experience: Essays on the City and Literature.* New Brunswick, N.J.: Rutgers University Press.

Lewis, David Levering. *When Harlem Was in Vogue.* New York: Oxford University Press.

Miller, R. Baxter. " 'Does Man Love Art?' The Humanistic Aesthetic of Gwendolyn Brooks." In *Black American Literature and Humanism,* edited by R. Baxter Miller. Lexington: University Press of Kentucky.

Morrison, Toni. "City Limits Village Values: Concepts of the Neighborhood in Black Fiction." In *Literature and the Urban Experience:*

Essays on the City and Literature, edited by Michael C. Jaye and Amy Chalmers Watts. New Brunswick, N.J.: Rutgers University Press.

Render, Sylvia Lyons. Introduction: Chestnutt—the Writer. In The Short Fiction of Charles W. Chesnutt, 11–15. Washington, D.C.: Howard University Press.

1982   Hakatuni, Yoshinobu. *Critical Essays on Richard Wright.* New York: G. K. Hall.

Hull, Gloria, Patricia Bell Scott, and Barbara Smith, eds. *All the Women are White, All the Blacks are Men, But Some of Us Are Brave.* New York: The Feminist Press.

Kennedy, Adrienne, and Margaret B. Wilkerson. "Adrienne Kennedy: Reflections." *City Arts Monthly* (February): 34.

Scarupa, Harriet Jackson. "E. Ethelbert Miller: Partisan of Literature." *New Directions* (July): 24–29.

Sekora, John, and Darwin T. Turner, eds. *The Art of Slave Narratives: Original Essays in Criticism and Theory.* Macomb: Western Illinois Press.

Special Issue on Sterling Brown. *Callaloo* 5, no. 14–15 (February-May).

Willis, Susan. "Eruptions of Funk: Historicizing Toni Morrison." *Black American Literature Forum* 16, no. 1 (Spring): 34–47.

Yearwood, Gladstone L. "Towards a Theory of a Black Cinema Aesthetic." In *Black Cinema Aesthetics: Issues in Independent Black Filmmaking,* edited by Gladstone L. Yearwood. Athens: Ohio University, Center for Afro-American Studies.

1983   Published. *Sage* (Atlanta, Ga.).

Giovanni, Nikki, and Margaret Walker. "Content and Intent: Some Thoughts on Writing, Criticism and Film." In *A Poetic Equation: Conversations between Nikki Giovanni and Margaret Walker.* Washington, D.C.: Howard University Press.

Mason, Ernest. "Black Art and the Configuration of Experience: The Philosophy of the Black Aesthetic." *CLA Journal* (1983): 1–17.

Shacocia, Bob. "Interview with James Alan McPherson." *Iowa Journal of Literary Studies* (1983): 6–33.

Smith, Barbara, ed. Introduction to *Home Girls: A Black Feminist Anthology.* New York: Kitchen Table.

Tate, Claudia. *Black Women Writers at Work.* New York: Continuum.

1984   Founded. The Zora Neale Hurston Society (Baltimore, Md.).

Andrews, William L. "The First Century of Afro-American Autobiography: Theory and Explication." In *Studies in Black American Literature.* Vol. 1, edited by Joe Weixlmann and Chester Fontenot Jr. Greenwood, Fla.: Penkevill.

Angelou, Maya. "Shades and Slashes of Light." In *Black Women Writers (1950–1980): A Critical Evaluation,* edited by Mari Evans. Garden City, N.Y.: Anchor/Doubleday.

Baker, Houston A., Jr. Introduction to *Blues Ideology, and Afro-American Literature: A Vernacular Theory.* Chicago: University of Chicago Press.

Bambara, Toni Cade. "Salvation Is the Issue." In *Black Women Writers (1950–1980): A Critical Evaluation,* edited by Mari Evans. Garden City, N.Y.: Anchor/Doubleday.

Evans, Mari. "My Father's Passage." In *Black Women Writers (1950–1980): A Critical Evaluation.* Garden City, N.Y.: Anchor/Doubleday.

Fontenot, Chester, Jr. "Visionaries, Mystics, and Revolutionaries: Narrative Postures in Black Fiction." In *Studies in Black American Literature.* Vol. 1, edited by Joe Weixlmann and Chester Fontenot Jr. Greenwood, Fla.: Penkevill.

Gates, Henry Louis, Jr. "The Blackness of Blackness: A Critique of the Sign and the Signifying Monkey." In *Black Literature and Literary Theory,* edited by Henry Louis Gates Jr., 285–321. New York: Methuen.

Henry, Joseph. "A MELUS Interview: Ishmael Reed." *MELUS* 11, no. 1 (Spring): 81–93.

Hurston, Zora Neale. "My People! My People!" In *Dust Tracks on a Road: An Autobiography,* edited and with an introduction by Robert E. Hemenway. Urbana: University of Illinois Press.

Johnson, Barbara. "Metaphor, Metonymy and Voice in 'Their Eyes Were Watching God'." In *Black Literature and Literary Theory,* edited by Henry Louis Gates Jr. New York: Methuen.

Lorde, Audre. "The Master's Tools Will Never Dismantle the Master's House." In *Sister Outsider.* New York: Crossing Press.

Morrison, Toni. "Rootedness: The Ancestor as Foundation." In *The Black Women Writers (1950–1980): A Critical Evaluation,* edited by Mari Evans. Garden City, N.Y.: Anchor/Doubleday.

Ryder, Shauneille Perry. "Will the Real Black Theater Please Stand Up?" *Freedomways* 24, no. 1 (First Quarter): 23–27.

Salaam, Kalamu ya. "Lorraine Hansberry: Unhonored as a Prophet." *Black Collegian* (March/April): 45–46, 48.

Sanchez, Sonia. "Ruminations/Reflections." In *Black Women Writers (1950–1980): A Critical Evaluation,* edited by Mari Evans. Garden City, N.Y.: Anchor/Doubleday.

Snead, James A. "Repetition as a figure of black culture." In *Black Literature and Literary Theory,* edited by Henry Louis Gates Jr. New York: Methuen.

Thompson, Robert Farris. *Flash of the Spirit, African and Afro-American Art and Philosophy.* New York: Vintage.

Walker, Alice. *In Search of Our Mothers' Gardens.* New York: Harcourt Brace Jovanovich.

Washington, Mary Helen. "I Sign My Mother's Name: Alice Walker, Dorothy West, and Paule Marshall." In *Mothering and Mind: Twelve Studies of Writers and Their Silent Partners,* edited by Ruth Perry and Martime Watson Broronley, 143–63. New York: Holmes and Meier.

1985   Published. *The Dictionary of Literary Biography.* Edited by Trudier Harris and Thadeous Davis.

Beyerman, Keith E. *Fingering the Jagged Grain: Tradition and Form in Recent Black Fiction.* Athens: University of Georgia Press.

Christian, Barbara. *Black Feminist Criticism.* New York: Pergamon Press.

Baker, Houston, Jr. "Critical Change and Blues Continuity: An Essay on the Criticism of Laryy Neal." *Callaloo* 8, no. 1 (Winter): 70–84.

Davis, Charles T. *Black Is the Color of the Cosmos: Essays on Afro-American Literature and Culture, 1942–1981,* edited by Henry Louis Gates Jr. New York: Garland Publishing.

Gabbin, Joanne V. "The Poetry of Sterling A. Brown: A Study in Form and Meaning." In *Sterling A. Brown: Building the Black Aesthetic Tradition.* Charlottesville: University Press of Virginia.

Harris, Trudier. *Black Women in the Fiction of James Baldwin.* Knoxville: University of Tennessee Press.

Hernton, Calvin. "The Sexual Mountain and Black Women Writers." *Black Scholar* 16, no. 4 (July/August): 2–11.

Ogunyemi, Chikwenye Okonjo. "Womanism: The Dynamics of the Contemporary Black Female Novel in English." *Signs* 11 (Autumn): 63–80.

Pryse, Marjorie, and Hortense Spillers. *Conjuring: Black Women, Fiction, and Literary Tradition.* Bloomington: Indiana University Press.

Taylor, Clyde. "Decolonizing the Image: New U.S. Black Cinema." In *Jump Cut, Hollywood, Politics and Counter-Cinema,* edited by Peter Steven. Toronto: Between the Lines.

1986   Andrews, William. *To Tell a Free Story: The First Century of Afro-American Autobiography.* Urbana: University of Illinois Press.

Baker, Houston A., Jr. "Belief, Theory and Blues: Notes from a Post-Structuralist Criticism of Afro-American Literature." In *Belief vs Theory in Black American Literary Criticism.* Vol. 2, edited by Joe Weixlmann and Chester Fontenot Jr. Greenwood, Fla.: Penkevill.

Beal, Frances M. "*Black Scholar* Interview with Octavia Butler: The Women and the Science Fiction Genre." *Black Scholar* 17, no. 2 (March/April): 14–18.

Bone, Robert. "Richard Wright and the Chicago Renaissance." *Callaloo* 9, no. 3 (Summer): 446–68 (Special Issue on Richard Wright).

Callaloo 9, no. 3 (Summer). "Richard Wright: A Special Issue."

Christian, Barbara T. "There It Is: The Poetry of Jayne Cortez." *Callaloo* 9, no. 1 (Winter): 235–39.

Ellison, Ralph. *Going to the Territory.* New York: Random House.

Jordan, Jennifer. "Cultural Nationalism in the 1960s: Politics and Poetry." In *Race, Politics and Culture: Critical Essays on Radicalism of the 1960s,* edited by Adolph Reed Jr., 29–60. New York: Greenwood Press.

Jordan, June. "The Difficult Miracle of Black Poetry in America; or Something like a Sonnet for Phillis Wheatley." *Massachusetts Review* 27: 252–62.

Long, Charles H. *Signification: Signs, Symbols and Images in the Interpretation of Religion.* Philadelphia: Fortress.

McDowell, Deborah E. Introduction to *Quicksand and Passing,* by Nella Larsen, ix–xxxi. Boston: Beacon Press.

Miller, R. Baxter. *Black American Poets Between Worlds.* Knoxville: University of Tennessee Press.

Rampersad, Arnold. "Langston Hughes' *Fine Clothes To The Jew.*" *Callaloo* 9, no. 1 (Winter): 144–57.

———. *The Life of Langston Hughes.* 2 vols. New York: Oxford University Press.

Tate, Greg. "Cult-Nats Meet Freaky Deke." *Voice Literary Supplement* (December): 5–8.

1987   Pulitzer Prize awarded to playwright August Wilson for *Fences.*

Pulitzer Prize awarded to poet Rita Dove for *Thomas and Beulah.*

Conference. The Study of Afro-American Literature: An Agenda for the 1990s. April 9–11, hosted by the University of Pennsylvania.

Founded. The Dark Room Collective (a creative writing workshop, Cambridge, Mass.).

Asante, Molefi Kete. *The Afrocentric Idea.* Philadelphia: Temple University Press.

Baker, Houston A., Jr. "In Dubious Battle." *New Literary History* 18 (Winter): 363–70.

———. *Modernism and the Harlem Renaissance.* Chicago: University of Chicago Press.

Bell, Bernard W. Introduction to *The Afro-American Novel and Its Tradition.* Amherst: University of Massachusetts.

Benston, Kimberly W., ed. *Speaking for You: The Vision of Ralph Ellison.* Washington D.C.: Howard University Press.

Carby, Hazel V. Introduction to *Iola LeRoy,* by Frances Ellen Watkins Harper, ix–xxvi. Boston: Beacon.

Carby, Hazel V. *Reconstructing Womanhood: The Emergence of the Afro American Woman Novelist.* New York: Oxford University Press.

Christian, Barbara. "The Race for Theory." *Feminist Studies* (Spring): 67–80.

Dance, Daryl. *Shucklin' and Jivin': Folklore from Contemporary Black Americans*. Bloomington: Indiana University Press.

Dixon, Melvin. *Ride Out the Wilderness: Geography and Identity in Afro American Literature*. Urbana: University of Illinois Press.

Ferguson, Sally Ann. "Autobiography and Black College Academics." *Auto/Biography* 3, no. 2 (Summer): 34–40.

Gates, Henry Louis, Jr. Introduction to *Figures in Black: Words, Signs, and the Racial Self.* New York: Oxford University Press.

———. "What's Love Got to Do With It?: Critical Theory, Integrity and the Black Idiom." *New Literary History* (Winter): 345–62.

———. *Writing "Race" and the Difference It Makes*. Chicago: University of Chicago Press.

Hernton, Calvin C. *The Sexual Mountain and Black Women Writers, Adventures in Sex, Literature, and Real Life*. New York: Anchor.

Johnson, Charles. *Being and Race: Black Writing Since 1970*. Bloomington: Indiana University Press.

Joyce, Joyce Ann. "The Black Canon: Reconstructing Black American Literary Criticism: New Literary History." *New Literary History* (Winter): 335–44.

———. " 'Who the Cap Fit': Unconsciousness and Unconscionableness in the Criticism of Houston A. Baker Jr. and Henry Louis Gates Jr." *New Literary History* (Winter): 371–84.

McDowell, Deborah. "The Changing Same: Generational Connections and Black Women Novelists." *New Literary History* 18 (Winter): 281–302.

Mooty, Maria K., and Gary Smith, eds. *A Life Distilled: Critical Essays on Gwendolyn Brooks*. Urbana: University of Illinois Press.

Morrison, Toni. "The Site of Memory." In *Inventing the Truth: The Art and Craft of Memoir*, edited by William Zinsser, 103–24. Boston: Houghton.

Smith, Valerie. *Self Discovery and Authority in Afro-American Narrative*. Cambridge: Harvard University Press.

Washington, Mary Helen. "The Darkened Eye Restored: Notes Toward a Literary History of Black Women." In *Invented Lives: Narratives of Black Women 1860–1960*. Garden City, N.Y.: Doubleday.

West, Cornel. "Minority Discourse and the Pitfalls of Canon Formation." *Yale Journal of Criticism* 1 (Fall): 193–201.

Willis, Susan. *Specifying: Black Women Writing the American Experience*. Madison: University of Wisconsin Press.

1988   American Book Award for *Mama* by Terry McMillan.

Pulitzer Prize awarded to fiction writer Toni Morrison for *Beloved*.

Founded. Eugene B. Redmond Writers' Group (St. Louis, Mo.).

Founded. National Black Arts Festival (Atlanta, Ga.).

Awkward, Michael. "Race, Gender and the Politics of Reading." *Black American Literature Forum* 22, no. 1 (1988): 5–27.

Baker, Houston, Jr. *Afro-American Poetics, Revisions of Harlem and the Black Aesthetics*. Madison: University of Wisconsin Press.

Bhabha, Homi K. "Cultural Diversity and Cultural Differences." *New Formations* 5: 5–23.

Callahan, John F. *In the African American Grain: The Pursuit of Voice in Twentieth-Century Black Fiction*. Urbana: University of Illinois Press.

Foster, Frances Smith. Introduction to *Iola LeRoy*, by Frances Ellen Watkins Harper, xxvii–xxxix. New York: Oxford University Press, 1988.

Gates, Henry Louis, Jr. "Signifyin(g): Definition [and Theory]." *The Signifying Monkey, A Theory of Afro-American Literary Criticism*. New York: Oxford University Press.

————, ed. *The Schomburg Library of Nineteenth-Century Black Women Writers*. New York: Oxford University Press.

Harjo, Joy. "An Interview with June Jordan." *High Plains Literary Review* (Fall): 60–76.

Henderson, Stephen. "Worrying the Line: Notes on Black American Poetry." In *The Line in Postmodern Poetry*, edited by Robert Frank and Henry Sayre, Urbana: University of Illinois Press.

Hubbard, Dolan. "Call and Response: Intertextuality in the Poetry of Langston Hughes and Margaret Walker." *Langston Hughes Review* 7 (Spring): 22–30.

Leitch, Vincent B. "Black Aesthetics." *American Literary Criticism from the 1930s to the 1980s*. New York: Columbia University Press.

Martin, Reginald. "Hoodoo as Literary Method: Ishmael Reed's True Afro-American Aesthetic." *Ishmael Reed and the New Black Aesthetic*. New York: St. Martin's Press.

Mason, Theodore O., Jr. "Between the Populist and the Scientist: Ideology and Power in Recent African American Literary Criticism, or The Dozens as Scholarship." *Callaloo* (Summer): 606–15.

Shields, John C., ed. *The Collected Works of Phillis Wheatley*. New York: Oxford University Press.

Smith, Valerie. "Gender and Afro-Americanist Literary Theory and Criticism." In *Speaking Gender,* edited by Elaine Showalter. New York: Routledge.

Stevenson, Brenda. *The Journals of Charlotte Forten Grimké*. New York: Oxford University Press.

Tate, Claudia. "ReShuffling the Deck; Or (Re)Reading Race and Gender in Black Women's Writing." *Tulsa Studies in Women's Literature* 7 (1988): 119–32.

Weixlmann, Joe, and Houston Baker, eds. *Black Feminist Criticism and Critical Theory*. Vol. 3. Greenwood, Fla.: Penkeville Publishing Co.

1989 Conference. Looking Back With Pleasure: A Celebration. Salt Lake City, Utah.

Founded. Roots & Wings, A Cultural Bookplace (Montgomery, Ala.).

Andrews, Dwight D. "From Black to Blues: Toward a Blues Aesthetic." In *The Blues Aesthetic: Black Culture and Modernism,* edited by Richard J. Powell, 37–39. Washington, D.C.: Washington Project for the Arts.

Ashcroft, Gareth Griffiths, and Helen Tifflin, eds. *The Empire Writes Back: Theory and Practice in Post-Colonial Literature.* London: Routledge.

Awkward, Michael. *Inspiriting Influences: Tradition, Revision and Afro-American Women's Novels.* New York: Columbia University Press.

Baker, Houston A., Jr., and Patricia Redmond. *Afro-American Literary Study in the 1990s.* Chicago: University of Chicago Press.

Baldwin, James. *Conversations with James Baldwin.* Edited by Fred L. Standley and Louis H. Pratt. Jackson: University Press of Mississippi.

Braxton, Joanne M. "A Tradition Within a Tradition." In *Black Women Writing Autobiography: A Tradition Within a Tradition.* Philadelphia: Temple University Press.

———, and Andree Nicola, eds. *Wild Women in the Whirlwind: Afra-American Culture and the Contemporary Literary Renaissance.* New Brunswick, N.J.: Rutgers University Press.

Butler-Evans, Elliott. *Race, Gender, and Desire, Narrative Strategies in the Fiction of Toni Cade Bambara, Toni Morrison and Alice Walker.* Philadelphia: Temple University Press.

Cephas, John. "The Blues." In *The Blues Aesthetic: Black Culture and Modernism,* edited by Richard J. Powell, 15–17. Washington, D.C.: Washington Project for the Arts.

Ellis, Trey. "The New Black Aesthetic." *Callaloo* 12, no. 1 (Winter): 233–43.

Harris, Leonard. Introduction to *The Philosophy of Alain Locke, Harlem Renaissance and Beyond.* Philadelphia: Temple University Press.

Lee, Spike. "Spike Lee Replies: 'Say It Ain't So Joe'." *New York,* 17 July, 6.

Lubiano, Wahneema H. "Constructing and Reconstructing Afro-American Texts: A Consideration of the Critic as Ambassador and Referee." *American Literary History* (Summer): 442–47.

Majors, Clarence. "Necessary Distance: Afterthoughts on Becoming a Writer." *Black American Literature Forum* 23, no. 2 (Summer): 197–212.

Morrison, Toni. "Unspeakable Things Unspoken: The Afro-American Presence in American Literature." *Michigan Quarterly* (Winter): 1–34.

Murray, Albert. "Regional Particulars and Universal Statement in Southern Writing." *Callaloo* 12, no. 1 (Winter): 3–6.

Neal, Larry. *Visions of a Liberated Future: Black Arts Movement Writings.* New York: Thunder's Mouth.

Powell, Richard J., "The Blues Aesthetic: Black Culture and Modernism." In *The Blues Aesthetic: Black Culture and Modernism,* edited by Richard J. Powell, 19–35.. Washington, D.C: Washington Project for the Arts.

Rampersad, Arnold. "Psychology and Afro-American Biography." *Yale Review* 78 (Autumn): 1–18.

Rowell, Charles H. "An Interview with John Edgar Wideman." *Callaloo* 13, no. 1 (Winter): 47–61.

Traylor, Eleanor W. "A Blues View of Life (Literature and the Blues Vision)." In *The Blues Aesthetic: Black Culture and Modernism,* edited by Richard J. Powell, 43–44. Washington, D.C.: Washington Project for the Arts.

Wall, Cheryl, ed. *Changing Our Own Words: Essays on Criticism, Theory and Writing by Black Women.* New Brunswick, N.J.: Rutgers University Press.

Ward, Jerry W., Jr. "Alvin Aubert: The Levee, the Blues, the Mighty Mississippi." *African American Review* 23, no. 3 (Fall): 415–40.

Washington, Mary Helen. Foreword to *Their Eyes Were Watching God,* by Zora Neale Hurston. New York: Harper and Row Publishers.

1990   National Book Award for *Middle Passage* by Charles Johnson.

Pulitzer Prize awarded to playwright August Wilson for *The Piano Lesson.*

Founded. The Richard Wright Circle (Boston, Mass.).

Published. *Negro Periodicals in the U.S.* (series) by Negro University Press.

Benston, Kimberly W. "Facing Tradition: Revisionary Scenes in African American Literature." *PMLA* (January): 98–109.

Collins, Patricia Hill. "Defining Black Feminist Thought." In *Black Feminist Thought: Knowledge, Consciousness and the Politics of Empowerment.* New York: Routledge.

Dundes, Alan, ed. *Mother Wit from the Laughing Barrel: Readings in the Interpretation of Afro-American Folklore.* Englewood Cliifs, N.J.: Prentice Hall, 1973. Reprint, Jackson: University Press of Mississippi.

Foster, Frances Smith. Introduction (II) to *A Brighter Coming Day: A Frances Ellen Watkins Harper Reader,* edited by Frances Smith Foster. New York: Feminist Press at the City University of New York.

Gates, Henry Louis, Jr. "Authority, (White) Power, and the (Black) Critic: It's All Greek to Me." In *The Nature and Context of Minority Discourse,* edited by Abdul R. JanMohamed and David Lloyd. New York: Oxford University Press.

———, ed. *Reading Black, Reading Feminist: A Critical Anthology.* New York: Meridian Books.

Gotera, Vicente F. "Lines of Tempered Steel: An Interview with Yusef Komunyakaa." *Callaloo* 13, no. 2 (Spring): 213–29.

Holloway, Joseph. *Africanisms in American Culture.* Bloomington: Indiana University Press.

Holloway, Karla F. C. "Revision and (Re)membrance: A Theory of Literary Structure in Literature by African American Women Writers." *African American Review* 24, no. 4 (Winter): 617–31.

hooks, bell. "An Aesthetic of Blackness: Strange and Oppositional." In *Yearning: Race, Gender, and Cultural Politics.* Boston: South End Press.

————. "Homeplace: A Site of Resistance." In *Yearning: Race, Gender, and Cultural Politics.* Boston: South End Press.

Langston Hughes Review 9, nos. 1–2 and 10, nos. 1–2 (1990–91). "Special Issue on George H. Bass."

McMillan, Terry. Introduction to *Breaking Ice: An Anthology of Contemporary African-American Fiction,* xx–xxii. New York: Penguin USA.

Pearlman, Mickey. "An Interview with Gloria Naylor." *High Plains Literary Review* 5, no. 1 (1980): 99–107.

Wallace, Michelle. "Variations on Negation and the Heresy of Black Feminist Creativity." In *Invisibility Blues: From Pop to Theory.* New York: Verso.

Wideman, John Edgar. Preface to *Breaking Ice: An Anthology of African American Contemporary Short Fiction,* v–x. New York: Penguin USA.

Williams, Sherley A. "Some Implications of Womanist Theory." In *Reading Black, Reading Feminist,* edited by Henry Louis Gates Jr. New York: Meridian Books.

1991   Published. *Richard Wright Newsletter* (Boston, Mass.).

Published. *Transitions* (Durham, N.C.).

Bailey, Frankie Y. *Out of the Woodpile: Black Characters in Crime and Detective Fiction.* Westport, Conn.: Greenwood Press.

Baker, Houston A., Jr. "Hybridity, the Rap Race, and Pedagogy for the 1990s." *Black Music Research Journal* 11 (Fall): 217–28.

————. *Workings of the Spirit: The Poetics of Afro-American Women's Writing.* Chicago: University of Chicago Press.

Black American Literature Forum, Special Issue on Film.

Davis, Arthur P., J. Saunders Redding, and Joyce Ann Joyce. *The Negro Cavalcade: African American Writing from 1760 to the Present.* Washington, D.C.: Howard University Press.

DiGaetani, John L. "Ed Bullins." In *A Search for a Postmodern Theater: Interviews with Contemporary Playwrights,* edited by John L. DiGaetani. New York: Greenwood Press.

Fabre, Michel, ed. *From Harlem to Paris: Black American Writers in France, 1840–1980.* Urbana: University of Illinois Press.

Gibson-Hudson, Gloria J. "African American Literary Criticism as a Model for the Analysis of Films by African American Women." *Wide Angle* 13, no. 3-4 (July-October): 45–55.

Harris, Trudier. *Fiction and Folklore: The Novels of Toni Morrison.* Knoxville: University of Tennessee Press.

Hemphill, Essex, ed. *Brother to Brother: New Writings by Black Gay Men.* Boston: Alyson Publications.

Jackson, Gale. "The Way We Do: A Preliminary Investigation of the African Roots of African American Performance." *African American Review* 25, no. 1 (Spring): 11–22.

Jones, Gayl. *Liberating Voices: Oral Tradition in African American Literature.* Cambridge: Harvard University Press.

Mobley, Marilyn Sanders. *Folk Roots and Mythic Wings in Sarah Orne Jewett and Toni Morrison: The Cultural Function of Narrative.* Baton Rouge: Louisiana State University Press.

Nero, Charles I. "Toward a Black Gay Aesthetic: Signifying in Contemporary Black Gay Literature." In *Brother to Brother: New Writings by Black Gay Men*, edited by Essex Hemphill. Boston: Alyson Publications.

Smith, Lionel David. "The Black Arts Movement and Its Critics." *American Literary History* (Spring): 93–110.

Troupe, Quincy. "A Conversation with Terry McMillan." *Emerge* (October): 51–56.

Wallace, Michele. *Invisibility Blues From Pop to Theory.* New York: Verso.

1992 Nobel Prize for Literature awarded to Derek Walcott.

Founded. African American Literature and Culture Society (Baltimore, Md.).

Founded. Carolina African American Writers' Collective by Lenard Moore (Raleigh, N.C.).

Appiah, Kwame Anthony. *In My Father's House, Africa in the Philosophy of Culture.* New York: Oxford University Press.

Blount, Marcellus. "The Preacherly Text: African American Poetry and Vernacular Performance." *PMLA* 107 (May): 582–92.

Dash, Julie. "Dialogue Between bell hooks and Julie Dash." In *Daughters of the Dust: The Making of an African American Woman's Film*, 27–67. New York: New Press.

Evans, Mari. "Contemporary Poetry, A Personal Essay." In *African American Literature: Voices in a Tradition*, 643–49. Orlando, Fla.: Harcourt Brace.

Giovanni, Nikki. *Conversations with Nikki Giovanni.* Edited by Virginia C. Fowler. Jackson: University Press of Mississippi.

Hall, Stuart. "Cultural Studies and Its Theoretical Legacies." In *Cultural Studies*, edited by Lawrence Grossberg, Cary Nelson, and Paula Treicher, 277–94. New York: Routledge.

———. "What Is this 'Black' in Black Popular Culture?" In *Black Popular Culture*, edited by Gina Dent. Seattle: Bay Press.

Holloway, Karla F. C. "A Figurative Theory: A Critical Consideration of Voice, Gender, and Culture." In *Moorings and Metaphors: Figures of Culture and Gender in Black Women's Literature*, 19–38. New Brunswick, N.J.:Rutgers University Press.

hooks, bell. "Revolutionary Attitudes." In *Black Looks: Race and Representation*. Boston: South End Press.

Jones, Kirkland G. "Folk Idiom in the Literary Expression of Two African American Authors: Rita Dove and Yusef Komunyakaa." In *Language and Literature in the African American Imagination*, edited by Carol Aisha Blackshire Belay. Westport, Conn.: Greenwood Press.

Killens, John Oliver, and Jerry W. Ward Jr., eds. *Black Southern Voices: An Anthology of Fiction, Poetry, Drama, Nonfiction and Critical Essays.* New York: Penguin USA.

Lott, Tommy L. "A No-Theory Theory of Contemporary Black Cinema." *African American Review* 25, no. 2: 221–36.

Morrison, Toni. *Playing in the Dark: Whiteness and the Literary Imagination.* Cambridge: Harvard University Press.

Olaniyan, Tejumola. "African American Critical Discourse and the Invention of Cultural Identities." *African American Review* 26, no. 4 (Winter): 533–45.

Powell, Kevin, and Ras Baraka. *In the Tradition: An Anthology of Young Black Writers.* New York: Published for Harlem River Press by Writers and Readers Publishing.

Sale, Maggie. "Call and Response as Critical Method: African-American Oral Traditions and *Beloved.*" *African American Review* 26 (1992): 41–50.

Samuels, Wilford D. "Soothsayer and Interpreter: Darwin T. Turner and African American Literary Criticism." *Langston Hughes Review* 11, no. 2 (Fall 1992): 15–27.

Tate, Claudia. Introduction to *Domestic Allegories of Political Desire: The Black Heroine's Text at the Turn of the Century.* New York: Oxford University Press.

Ward, Jerry W., Jr. Foreword to *Black Southern Voices: An Anthology.* New York: Penguin USA.

1993   Ernest J. Gaines is awarded The Southern Book Award and the John D. and Catherine T. MacArthur Foundation Fellowship.

Nobel Prize for Literature awarded to Toni Morrison.

Pulitzer Prize awarded to poet Yusef Komunyakaa for *Neon Vernacular.*

Rita Dove is appointed Poet Laureate of the United States.

Founded. The PreScholars in the Humanities Society by Hazel Arnett Ervin (Raleigh, N.C.).

Founded. The Toni Morrison Society (Baltimore, Md.).

Andrews, William L., ed. *African American Autobiography: A Collection of Critical Essays.* Englewood Cliffs, N.J.: Prentice Hall.

Davis, Thulani, "Walter Mosley (An Interview)." *Bomb* 44 (Summer): 52–57.

duCille, Ann. *The Coupling Convention, Sex, Text, and Tradition in Black Women's Fiction.* New York: Oxford University Press.

Dyson, Michael Eric. *Reflecting Black: African American Cultural Criticism.* Minneapolis: University of Minnesota.

Gates, Henry Louis, Jr., and K. A. Appiah, eds. *Alice Walker: Critical Perspectives Past and Present.* New York: Amistad.

Guerrero, Ed. Introduction to *Framing Blackness: The African American Image in Film.* Philadelphia: Temple University Press.

Harper, Phillip Brian. "Nationalism and Social Division in Black Arts Poetry of the 1960s." *Critical Inquiry* (Winter): 234–55.

Langston Hughes Review 12 (Spring) "Special Issue on Langston Hughes."

Mitchell, Angelyn. *Within the Circle.* Durham, N.C.: Duke University Press.

Morrison, Toni. Interview. "Toni Morrison: The Art of Fiction CXXXIV." *Paris Review* 128 (1993): 83–125.

Mullane, Deirdre, ed. *Crossing the Danger Water: Three Hundred Years of African American Writing.* New York: Anchor.

Olaniyan, Tejumola. "On 'Post-Colonial Discourse': An Introduction." *Callaloo* 16, no. 4 (Fall): 743–49.

Shannon, Sandra G. "Blues, History and Dramaturgy: An Interview with August Wilson." In *African American Review* 27, no. 4 (Winter): 539–59. Reprint, Sandra G. Shannon, ed. *The Dramatic Vision of August Wilson.* Washington, D.C.: Howard University Press, 1995.

Sundquist, Eric J. *To Wake the Nations.* Cambridge, Mass.: Harvard University Press.

Wright, Richard. *Conversations with Richard Wright,* edited by Keneth Kinnamon and Michel Fabre. Jackson: University Press of Mississippi.

1994   Gwendolyn Brooks awarded the Jefferson Lectures by NEH.

Symposium. Black Women in the Academy: Defending Our Name, 1894–1994. January 13–15, sponsored by Massachusetts Institute of Technology, Wellesley College, and Radcliff College.

Conference. Furious Flower: A Revolution in African American Poetry. September 29–October 1, sponsored by James Madison University.

Founded. Alain Locke Society (Boston, Mass.).

Adell, Sandra. *Double-Consciousness/Double Bind: Theoretical Issues in Twentieth-Century Black Literature.* Urbana: University of Illinois Press.

Davies, Carol Boyce. "From 'Post Coloniality' to Uprising Textualities: Black Women Writing the Critique of Empire." In *Black Women, Writing and Identity: Migrations of the Subject,* 80–95. New York: Routledge.

Dubey, Madhu. "Introduction: Black Feminist Criticism." In *Black Women Novelists and the Nationalist Aesthetic*. Bloomington: Indiana University Press.

Fabre, Genevieve, and Robert O'Meally. *History and Memory in African American Culture*. New York: Oxford University Press.

Gates, Henry Louis, Jr., ed. *African American Women Writers, 1910–1940*. New York: G. K. Hall.

Greene, J. Lee. *Blacks in Eden: The African American Novel: First Century*. Charlottsville: The University Press of Virginia.

Harper, Brian Phillip. *Framing the Margins, The Social Logic of Postmodern Culture*. New York: Oxford University Press.

Harper, Michael, and Anthony Walton. *Every Shut Eye Ain't Sleep*. Boston: Little Brown.

Hubbard, Dolan. "Voices and Visions." In *The Sermon and the African American Literary Imagination*. Columbia: University of Missouri.

Joyce, Joyce Ann. *Warriors, Conjurers and Priests. Defining African-Centered Literary Criticism*. Chicago: Third World Press.

Lewis, David Levering, ed. *The Portable Harlem Renaissance Reader*. New York: Penguin USA.

Lowe, John. *Jump at de Sun: Zora Neale Hurston's Cosmic Comedy*. Urbana: University of Illinois Press.

Majors, Clarence. "Necessary Distance: Afterthoughts on Becoming a Writer." *African American Review* 28: 37–47.

Miller, E. Ethelbert. *In Search of Color Everywhere: A Collection of African American Poetry*. New York: Steward, Tabori & Chang.

Morrison, Toni. *Conversations with Toni Morrison*. Edited by Danielle Taylor Guthrie. Jackson: University Press of Mississippi.

North, Michael. *The Dialect of Modernism, Race, Language and Twentieth-Century Literature*. New York: Oxford University Press.

Reilly, Charlie. *Conversations with Amiri Baraka*. Jackson: University Press of Mississippi.

Sekoni, Ropo. "Features of Yoruba Trickster Tale Aesthetics." In *A Sociosemiotic Study of Yoruba Trickster Tales*, 1–26. Westport, Conn.: Greenwood Press.

Smith, Theophus H. *Conjuring Culture: Biblical Formations of Black America*. New York: Oxford University Press.

Smitherman, Geneva. "Word from the African American Community." In *Black Talk: Words and Phrases From the Hood to the Amen Corner*. Boston: Houghton Mifflin.

Welsh-Asante, Kariamu, ed. *The African Aesthetic: Keeper of the Traditions*. Westport, Conn.: Praeger.

1995   Allan, Tuzyline Jita. "Decoding Womanist Grammar of Difference." In *Womanist and Feminist Aesthetics*. Athens: Ohio University Press.

Bobo, Jacqueline. *Black Women as Cultural Readers.* Irvington, N.Y.: Columbia University Press.

Boyd, Herb, and Robert L. Allen. *Brotherman: The Odyssey of Black Men in America.* New York: Ballantine Books.

Cavalieri, Grace D. Gaetani. "Rita Dove: An Interview." *The American Poetry Review* (March-April): 11–15.

Dick, Bruce and Amritjit Singh, eds. *Conversations with Ishmael Reed.* Jackson: University Press of Mississippi.

Ellison, Ralph. *Conversations with Ralph Ellison.* Edited by Maryemme Graham and Amrijit Singh. Jackson: University Press of Mississippi.

Fikes, Robert, Jr. "Escaping the Literary Ghetto: African American Authors of White Life Novels, 1946–1994." *Western Journal of Black Studies* 19, no. 2: 105–12.

Franklin, V. P. *Living Our Stories, Telling Our Truths, Autobiography and the Making of the African American Intellectual Tradition.* New York: Oxford University Press.

Gaines, Ernest. *Conversations with Ernest Gaines.* Edited by John Lowe. Jackson: University Press of Mississippi.

Gladney, Marvin. "The Black Arts Movement and Hip Hop." *African American Review* 29, no. 2 (Summer): 291–301.

Griffin, Farah Jasmine. Introduction to *"Who set you flowin'?" The African-American Migration Narrative.* New York: Oxford University Press.

Guy-Sheftall, Beverly. "Introduction: The Evolution of Feminist Consciousness Among African American Women." In *Words of Fire.* New York: Free Press.

Harris, Trudier. "Miss-Trained or Untrained? Jackleg Critics and African American Literature (Or, Some of My Adventures in Academia)."

Long, Worth. "The Wisdom of the Blues—Defining Blues as the True Facts of Life: An Interview with Willie Dixon." *African American Review* 29, no. 2 (Summer): 207–12.

Marable, Manning, ed. "Blueprint for Black Studies." In *Beyond Black and White: Transforming African American Politics.* New York: Verso.

McDowell, Deborah. *"The Changing Same," Black Women's Literature, Criticism and Theory.* Bloomington: Indiana University Press.

Miller, E. Ethelbert. "An Interview with Cornelius Eady." *Crab Orchard Review* 2, no. 2 (Spring/Summer): 83–93.

Mullen, Bill, ed. *Revolutionary Tales, African-American Women's Short Stories From the First Story to the Present.* New York: Dell.

Olaniyan, Tejumola. *Scars of Conquest/Masks of Resistance: The Invention of Cultural Identities in African, African American and Caribbean Drama.* New York: Oxford University Press.

Pettis, Joyce Owens. *Toward Wholeness in Paula Marshall's Fiction.* Charlottesville: University Press of Virginia.

Plant, Deborah G. *Every Tub Must Sit on Its Own Bottom: The Philosophy and Politics of Zora Neale Hurston.* Urbana: University of Illinois Press.

Reed, Ishmael. *Conversations with Ishmael Reed.* Jackson: University Press of Mississippi.

Salaam, Mtume ya. "The Aesthetics of Rap." *African American Review* 29, no. 2 (Summer): 303–15.

Shannon, Sandra G. *The Dramatic Vision of August Wilson.* Washington, D.C.: Howard University Press.

Sundquist, Eric J. *Cultural Contexts for Ralph Ellison's "Invisible Man."* Boston: Bedford Books.

Tate, Claudia. "Desire and Death in *Quicksand* by Nella Larsen." *American Literary History* 7 (1995): 234–60.

1996 Symposium. Body Politics and Black Woman. November, sponsored by Duke University.

Founded. African American Literature Book Club Web Site <www.aalbc.com/kalamu.htm>.

Founded. Cave Canem (retreat/workshop for black poets at Mt. St. Alphonsus Monastery on the Hudson River, Esopus, N.Y.).

Founded. Runagate Press by Kalamu ya Salaam and Kysha N. Brown (New Orleans).

Published. *Black Renaissance NOIRE.*

Published. Zora Neale Hurston Newsletter.

Christian, Barbara, ed. *Introduction to Everyday Use,* by Alice Walker. New Brunswick, N.J.: Rutgers University Press.

Donaldson, Melvin, ed. *Cornerstone: An Anthology of African American Literature.* New York: St. Martin's Press.

Gòkè-Paríolá, Abíódún. "African American Vernacular English in Colonial and Postcolonial Perspectives: The Linguistic Paradox." *Journal of Commonwealth and Postcolonial Studies* 4 (Fall): 14–23.

Hernton, Calvin. Foreword to *The Collected Stories of Chester Himes,* ix–xii. New York: Thunder's Mouth Press.

Majors, Clarence. *The Garden Thrives: An Anthology of Contemporary African American Poetry.* New York: Harper Perennial.

Mishkin, Tracy. "Theorizing Literary Influence and African American Writers." In *Literary Influence and African American Writers.* New York: Garland Publishing.

Tate, Claudia. "Freud and His 'Negro': Psychoanalysis as Ally and Enemy of African Americans." Journal for the Psychoanalysis of Culture and Society 1, no. 1 (Spring): 53–62.

Wall, Cheryl A., ed. *Introduction to Sweat,* by Zora Neale Hurston. New Brunswick, N.J.: Rutgers University Press.

Wintz, Cary D., ed. *The Harlem Renaissance 1920–1940, Interpretation of an African American Literary Movement.* Hamden, Conn.: Garland Publishing Co.

Zeigler, Mary Brown. "Introductory Essay: Postcolonial Contexts of African American Vernacular English." *Journal of Commonwealth and Postcolonial Studies* 4 (Fall): 1–13.

1997 Symposium. Myth, Memory, and Migration: The Black and White South in the Cultural Imagination. October 2–4, sponsored by the University of Alabama at Tuscaloosa.

Conference. Yari Yari: Black Women Writers and the Future Organization of Women Writers of Africa and the New York University's Africana Studies Program. October 15–18.

Symposium. Creative Women During the Chicago Renaissance. November 6–8, sponsored by Agnes Scott College, Decatur, Ga.

Founded. Afro American List Web Site <afroam-1@columbia.edu>.

Founded. The Charles Chesnutt Society (Atlanta,Ga.).

Founded. The George Moses Horton Society (Chapel Hill, N.C.).

Unveiling of Commemorative U.S. Stamps for African American Literary Writers and Critics: Maya Angelou, Mari Evans, June Jordan, Stephen E. Henderson, and Henry Louis Gates Jr. (Smithsonian Institute, Washington, D.C.).

Andrews, William L., Frances Smith Foster, and Trudier Harris, eds. *The Oxford Companion to African American Literature.* New York: Oxford University Press.

Dorris, Ronald. *Race: Jean Toomer's Swan Song.* New Orleans: Xavier Review Press.

Ferguson, Sally Ann. "Unmaking Blackness: The Excoloured Men of Charles W. Chesnutt and James Weldon Johnson." In *Critical Essays on James Weldon Johnson,* edited by Kenneth Price and Lawrence Rence. New York: G. K. Hall.

Frank, Duane. "Soul Food" Director Isn't Holding His Breath. *Milwaukee Journal Sentinel,* 11 October.

Fry, Joan. "An Interview with Octavia Butler." *Poets and Writers, Inc.* (March/April): 58–69.

Gates, Henry Louis Jr. "The Welcome Table [James Baldwin]." In *Thirteen Ways of Looking at a Black Man.* New York: Vintage.

————, and Nellie Y. McKay, eds. *The Norton Anthology of African American Literature.* New York: W. W. Norton.

Houston, Helen R., and Frances Smith Foster. *Teaching with "The Norton Anthology of African American Literature": A Guide for Instructors.* New York: W. W. Norton.

McKay, Nellie Y., and Kathryn Earle, eds. *Approaches to Teaching the Novels of Toni Morrison.* New York: Modern Language Association.

Miller, James A. *Approaches to Teaching Richard Wright.* New York: Modern Language Association.

Price, Kenneth, and Lawrence Rence. *Critical Essays of James Weldon Johnson.* New York: G. K. Hall.

Rodgers, Lawrence R. *Canaan Bound: The African-American Great Migration Novel.* Urbana: University of Illinois Press.

Shannon, Sandra G. "In Their Respective Corners: A Post-Debate Interview with August Wilson."

Smith, Valerie. *Representing Blackness: Issues in Film and Video.* New Brunswick, N.J.: Rutgers University Press.

Tate, Greg. "The Gumshoe Blues." *Village Voice,* 42, 47.

Ward, Jerry W., Jr., ed. *Trouble the Waters, 250 Years of African American Poetry.* New York: Mentor.

1998   Conference. Black Women Writers and the "High Art" of Afro-American Letters. May 15–17, University of California, San Diego.

Summit. The National Black Theatre Summit I. July 12–15, Atlanta, Ga.

Conference. "The Ground Together," An Interdisciplinary Conference Assessing the Cultural Ground on Which We Stand. October 10, Howard University, Washington, D.C.

Founded. The African Grove Institute for the Arts (Hanover, N.H.).

Published. *Furious Flower: A Video Anthology of African American Poetry 1960–95* by Joanne Gabbin. Website: <www.newsreel.org>.

Andrews, William L., and Nellie Y. McKay, eds. *Toni Morrison's "Beloved."* New York: Oxford University Press.

Graham, Maryemma, Sharon Pineault-Burke, and Marianna White Davis. *Teaching African American Literature: Theory and Practice.* New York: Routledge.

Gwaltney, John Langston. *DryLongso: A Self Portrait of Black America.* New York: The New Press.

Hill, Patricia Liggin, Bernard W. Bell, Trudier Harris, R. Baxter Miller, Sondra A. O'Neale, and William J. Harris, eds., with Horace C. Porter. *Call and Response: The Riverside Anthology of the African American Literary Tradition.* Boston: Houghton Mifflin.

McKay, Nellie Y. "Naming the Problem That Led to the Question 'Who Shall Teach African American Literature?'; or, Are We Ready to Disband the Wheatley Court?" *PMLA* 113, no. 3 (May): 359–69.

Roediger, David. *Black on White: Black Writers on What It Means to Be White.* New York: Schocken Books.

Tate, Claudia. "Introduction: Race and Psychoanalysis." In *Psychoanalysis and Black Novels, Desire and the Protocols of Race.* New York: Oxford University Press.

1999   Conference. Race and Representation: A Millennial Affair. April 9–10, Duke University.

Published. Black Issues Book Review, <bibookreview@cmabiccw.com>.

Published. *Souls, A Critical Journal of Black Politics, Culture and Society.*

Website. <afam-lit@listserv.uic.edu> (for the discussion of African American literature/criticism).

Clark, Keith. "Black Male Subjectivity Deferred?: The Quest for Voice and Authority in Lorraine Hansberry's *A Raisin in the Sun*." In *Black Woman Playwrights: Visions of American Stage*, edited by Carol Marsh Lockett, 87–111. New York: Garland.

Diedrich, Maria, Henry Louis Gates Jr., and Carl Pedersen, eds. *Black Imagination and the Middle Passage*. New York: Oxford University Press.

Lee, Robert A. *Designs of Blackness, Mappings in the Literature and Culture of Afro-America*. Sterling, Va.: Pluto Press.

Pate, Alexs. "Making Home in the New Millennium: Reflections."

Plasa, Carl, ed. *Toni Morrison: "Beloved."* Irvington, N.Y.: Columbia University Press.

2000 Conference. Looking Back with Pleasure II: A Celebration. Salt Lake City, Utah.

Index

The Editor

♦

Hazel Arnett Ervin is an associate professor in the Department of English and Linguistics at Morehouse College, where she teaches African American literature. She is the editor of *Ann Petry: A Bio-Bibliography* (G. K. Hall) and contributed articles on Petry to the *Oxford Companion to African American Literature*. Her work appears in *Callaloo, CLA Journal,* and the *Langston Hughes Review*. Forthcoming works include a short history of African American literary criticism and critical collections of essays on Ann Petry and Stephen Henderson.